KW-010-168

The Law Applied

Peri Bearman is Associate Director of the Islamic Legal Studies Program (ILSP) at Harvard Law School.

Wolfhart Heinrichs is James Richard Jewett Professor of Arabic in the Department of Near Eastern Languages and Civilizations at Harvard University.

Bernard G. Weiss is Professor of Arabic and Islamic Studies at the University of Utah.

THE LAW APPLIED

Contextualizing the Islamic Shariʿa

A Volume in Honor of Frank E. Vogel

Edited by

Peri Bearman
Wolfhart Heinrichs
Bernard G. Weiss

I.B. TAURIS
LONDON · NEW YORK

Published in 2008 by I.B.Tauris & Co Ltd
6 Salem Road, London W2 4BU
175 Fifth Avenue, New York, NY 10010
www.ibtauris.com

In the United States of America and Canada distributed by Palgrave Macmillan
a division of St. Martin's Press, 175 Fifth Avenue, New York, NY 10010

Copyright © Peri Bearman, Wolfhart Heinrichs, Bernard G. Weiss, 2008

The right of Peri Bearman, Wolfhart Heinrichs, Bernard G. Weiss to be identified as the author of this work has been asserted by the author in accordance with the Copyright, Designs and Patent Act 1988.

All rights reserved. Except for brief quotations in a review, this book, or any part thereof, may not be reproduced, stored in or introduced into a retrieval system, or transmitted, in any form or by any means, electronic, mechanical, photocopying, recording or otherwise, without the prior written permission of the publisher.

ISBN 978 1 84511 736 8

A full CIP record for this book is available from the British Library
A full CIP record for this book is available from the Library of Congress

Library of Congress Catalog Card Number: available

Printed and bound in Great Britain by TJ International Ltd, Padstow, Cornwall

CONTENTS

PREFACE

I am privileged and pleased to have been given the opportunity to participate in this volume honoring Frank Vogel, inspite of the fact that I am not a scholar of Islamic law meriting inclusion in the illustrious roster of individuals whose essays fill this collection. I am, however, a colleague and good friend of Frank's, as well as a fellow comparative law scholar, and from those vantage points can attest to Frank's signal contribution not only to the intellectual life of Harvard University but also to the fostering of dialogue within the Islamic world and between it and the international community more generally.

Frank deserves enormous credit and gratitude for having envisioned, established, and then directed with great success Harvard's Islamic Legal Studies Program. The Program, under Frank's direction (and with very able assistance from Peri Bearman) has sought to provide an objective and open forum in which scholars and practitioners from both within and outside the Muslim world might come together to challenge and learn from each other. Through a range of activity, from courses it has put on to conferences it has hosted to scholarship it has published to the superb library collection it has helped build, the Program has more than amply fulfilled this admirable vision. Over the years, the Program has hosted visitors with a broad range of perspectives, imaginatively finding ways to encourage individuals with very different approaches to work together fruitfully. The same ecumenical spirit is to be found in the topics of conferences—which have ranged from Islamic finance to marriage contracts to the law of *waqf*—and in the Program's monograph series, which has published works on Muslims and Islamic law from medieval Granada to contemporary Indonesia. Indeed, it is a part of the genius of the Program's conception that it has endeavored to address Islam from its birth in the Middle East to the United States today.

The Program's breadth and generosity of spirit very much mirrors its founding director. Frank Vogel is someone whose scholarship and teaching have ranged from issues of the interpretation of traditional Islamic texts to the ways in which Islamic banks have adapted to the dictates of international finance to the challenges posed by the Muslim world's engagement with contemporary notions of human rights. That work has always been performed with high intelligence, broad learning and much integrity. It is no wonder that Frank's peers, many of whom are represented in this volume, have seen fit to elect him as the first president of the International Society for Islamic Legal Studies. And yet, notwithstanding these important scholarly and associated pre-occupations, Frank is someone who always found time for students—especially so in the aftermath of 9/11 in view of the many challenges those events posed for Muslims.

I will miss Frank as a colleague as he takes retirement and yet the Program he established remains an enduring symbol of his talent, dedication, and humanity—as does his scholarly writing, his promotion of the field, and his nurturing of generations of students. And so, again, it is a privilege and pleasure to be a part (however small) of this volume of tribute to my friend, Frank Vogel.

Bill Alford
Henry L. Stimson Professor of Law
Vice Dean for the Graduate Program and International Legal Studies
Director of East Asian Legal Studies
Harvard Law School

FOREWORD

Upon the imminent retirement of Frank Vogel from Harvard Law School, a number of his friends and colleagues joined forces to present him with a volume, to show not only their great appreciation for his work and collegiality but also for the strides he personally made in accelerating the growth of Islamic law as an academic discipline. Frank has been a tireless advocate of the study and teaching of Islamic law as a living, breathing legal system, and nowhere is this most visible, outside of his own writings, than in the research program he founded at Harvard Law School, where students and scholars of the law could delve into their more arcane interests with the knowledge that in this oasis they would be respected and listened to, regardless of their viewpoint. Tolerated at best, ignored at worst, by the larger field of law, it would take a calamitous act in 2001 to propel Islamic law into the mainstream legal consciousness; at this moment, an increasingly greater number of American law schools offer a course in Islamic law, but when Frank peddled his dream of situating Islamic law within the family of laws, back in the late 1980s, it was almost unheard of. The academy has much to thank Frank for in terms of foresight and abilities, and this volume is but a small token of its gratitude and admiration.

It was no easy task to decide on a list of participants for the volume at hand. An original list was drawn up, but three hefty volumes seemed on second thought perhaps a bit much. The editors were compelled to perform the thankless task of winnowing and deleting, as if there were rhyme or reason as to who, among Frank's many personal and professional friends, would be asked to contribute. The contributors who make up this volume were invited ultimately with an eye not only to variety in their disciplinary approaches and backgrounds, but also to their presumed capacity to withstand a battery of nagging from one of the editors, who shall remain nameless. For agreeing with such enthusiasm, for submitting their papers more or less on time, and in general for remaining very good-natured during the entire process, the contributors have earned our most heartfelt gratitude.

The title "The Law Applied" plays a double role: it captures Frank's insistence that Islamic law cannot be studied properly if one ignores the law in practice, while also encapsulating the overarching theme of the contributions, whether they are dealing with Islamic law as such or Islamic law from a comparative perspective or law proper as it interacts with religion or the state. Each contributor was asked to frame, insofar possible, his or her work in light of Frank's interests in law and religion and law and governance and the result is a microcosm of the extensive research and thought that characterizes the field today. In their reach from early Islam through the Mamluks and the Ottomans to the modern period, and their coverage of a wide range of analysis—from position papers by foremost Muslim intellectuals to tiny gems of case studies to far-reaching meditations on the moral and social forces of law—the twenty contributions also reflect the challenge and breadth of the field.

We begin the volume with the one essay that does not deal with Islamic law, but raises core issues that dominate the rest of the volume, namely, that by Charles Donahue, Paul A. Freund Professor of Law at Harvard Law School. Donahue focuses on specific examples of the kind of reform that was implemented through the use of law: the change in the nature of charity (from direct individual pious giving to the poor—"the poor ye always have with you"—to more institutionalized forms of charity designed to build infrastructures that will eradicate or at least reduce poverty on a permanent basis), the change in the method of prosecution of prostitutes in such manner as would curtail prostitution in London rather than merely demanding payment of fines, the change in the nature of marriage litigation (from civil suit to criminal prosecution), the change from a hands-off attitude to lewd behavior in public places to a more vigorous criminal prosecution of such behavior (remarkably like the *ḥisba*). These are all sixteenth-century changes contemporaneous to the Reformation but not necessarily the consequence of the Reformation since one can trace roots of such reform back as far as the twelfth century (the time of the Cluniac reforms). Reform through law, as Donahue writes, reflects "a willingness on the part of the community to proceed against such offenses in the name of the community. [...] to enforce conformity to a set of norms and behaviors that corresponded to prevailing moral and religious notions of proper behavior." Donahue emphasizes the role of the courts, religious and secular, in the implementation of reforms, through which European society built a strong sense of public space and public life within that space. The theme of "law applied" is very prominent in Donahue's account; and although there is only a whisper of Islam, there is much in Donahue that is instructive, and that reminds us that the themes found in the bulk of the volume are not unique to Islam but manifest themselves in the European experience as well.

Commonalities between the Islamic legal experience and the Western one also underlie John Makdisi's essay on twelfth-century reform in English property law, for which he hypothesizes an antecedent in an Islamic legal notion. Reform in its Islamic legal context is mirrored in the papers that discuss legal realism: those of Halper (reconciling Islamic legal doctrine with social justice in the Islamic Republic of Iran), Stilt (reconciling Islamic legal doctrine with socio-economically driven political priorities in early Mamluk Egypt), Peters (reconciling Islamic legal doctrine with the customary practice of sharecropping in Ottoman Egypt), and Cammack/Feener (reconciling Islamic legal doctrine with the customary understanding of joint marital property in Indonesia). That the law is not just what is found in rules or texts or books, but is in the final analysis always how it plays out in practice—that is, what the judge or the state says it is—also resounds in Masud, Layish, Sonbol, and Messick (whose personal account of past Yemeni sojourns offers an intimate encounter with law on the ground). The authority of the state and its capacity to reform—even when that reform is a re-turn, as Halper has phrased it—figure prominently in Mallat and Lau, the latter also sharing with Gleave, Johansen, Lindsey/Kingsley, and An-Naʿim a discussion of governance by divine law and its perceived idea of morality. From An-Naʿim, who cogently argues that the divine should be separated from the state because "any Shariʿa principle that is enforced through the coercive authority of the state ceases to be part of the normative system of Islam," the theme segues to Freamon who proposes returning the religion to the believer with a new Qurʾanic hermeneutic that takes into account the contemporary milieu—"the circumstances, foreknowledge, and perspective"—of twenty-first-century Muslims, making the religious law again applicable in the personal realm. Interpretation, and how one reads, and uses, text is the primary concern of Hurvitz and Weiss, whose interest in this was sparked by the theories of non-Muslim legal thinkers, Robert Cover and Hans-Georg Gadamer, respectively. Finally, Zysow examines, in his unparalleled way, the Muslim theological debate on wherefore the obligation to obey God, a debate that is not alien to Western theological and political theorist discourse as obedience informs the very existence of law and authority. With this final chapter highlighting the morality embedded in and embodied by law, the volume comes full circle back to the legal and moral reforms introduced by Donahue.

The Harvard Law School, and its Islamic Legal Studies Program, will be a bleaker place without Frank Vogel, without his vision, his dedication to his students and to the field he chose—or perhaps, that chose him—and his intellectual prowess. We wish him the best in everything, and hope to engage him, and be engaged by him, in conversation—academic and mundane, but always riveting—for a long time to come.

June 22, 2007 Peri Bearman, Wolfhart Heinrichs, and Bernie Weiss

1

REFORM, RENEWAL, RELIGION, AND SOCIAL DISCIPLINE

Reflections of a Medievalist

Charles Donahue, Jr.

I was recently asked to give a paper at a conference on religion and social discipline in the early modern period, to speak from the point of view of a medievalist to a group of people who are not medievalists.[1] I approached the topic with some trepidation. I wanted to say something about the relationship to law of the religious reform movement of the eleventh century, sometimes called the Gregorian Reform, and that of the sixteenth century, sometimes called The Reformation. That, in itself, was a scary proposition for someone who cannot claim any special expertise in the eleventh-century reform and none at all in that of the sixteenth. To make matters worse, making a comparison or drawing a connection between moments in the history of Christianity in the West seemed to call for some attempt to relate the two to the history of reform movements in other religions, a topic where my knowledge descends to the point of nothingness.

I turned to the library.[2] Surely, there must be a large and sophisticated literature in the area of comparative religion that would at least give us tools to talk about the phenomenon, that would tell us what to look for, if not what the answers might be? There are, of course, many fine studies of particular reform movements, renewal movements, revival movements, in Christianity, Judaism, Islam, Hinduism, and Buddhism and on what seem to be similar phenomena among non-literate peoples. The literature generalizing about these phenomena, however, does not seem to be very large. (Whether it is sophisticated is not for me to decide.) Perhaps more to the point, none of the general literature that I found takes into account the eleventh-century reform, and relatively little of it takes into account that of the sixteenth century. We hear of cargo cults and millenarianism, Reform Judaism and Wahhabism, modern Islamic fundamentalism and Hare Krishna. Some effort has been made to relate these phenomena to certain relatively recent movements in Protestantism: the two Great Awakenings in the United States, the broader Evangelical and Pentecostal movements. But I looked in vain—perhaps I did not look far enough—for an attempt to relate these phenomena to what I regard—and I do not think that I am alone—as the two most important movements in the history of Christianity in the West, the reform movement of the eleventh century and that of the sixteenth.

Let us begin with some particulars about the fifteenth and sixteenth centuries. Some years ago Wilbur K. Jordan published a series of monographs on charitable giving in England, principally in wills and testaments, over the very long sixteenth century (1480–1660).[3] His main findings were two: (1) there was a huge increase in such giving over the course of the century, and (2) the objects of charity changed: Medieval Englishmen gave to have masses said for their souls and to distribute food to the poor; early modern Englishmen gave to social infrastructure: schools, hospitals, work houses, even roads and bridges. Jordan saw both phenomena as being related to the English Reformation. Economic history was not Jordan's long suit, and his first finding pretty much collapsed when reviewers pointed out that he had failed to discount his numbers for the massive inflation that had occurred over the course of the sixteenth century. The second finding did not collapse, and his works are still occasionally cited for it. The statute of superstitious uses, a decidedly Protestant statute, certainly reflects, if it did not produce, a decline in enthusiasm for gifts to have masses said for the deceased.[4] The shift, however, from gifts for the immediate relief of poverty to the support of infrastructure to relieve poverty on a more permanent basis is not connected with Protestantism in the direct way that the decline in gifts for masses is. Indeed, this longer-range approach to the problem of poverty has been found in many places in Europe, including areas that were staunchly Catholic.[5] It seems to correlate with urbanism rather than with confession.

Some years after Jordan, Richard Wunderli published a monograph in which he pointed out that there was a shift in the way that prostitutes were dealt with by the legal system in London.[6] In the fifteenth century, they appeared before the ecclesiastical courts. The professionals among them hired compurgators who supported the prostitutes' oaths that they were innocent of the charges. The court charged them a relatively stiff fee for court costs, and they went back to their business. In the late fifteenth and early sixteenth centuries, before the Reformation was in the wind, the secular authorities in London began to prosecute these women in the secular courts. Compurgation, or its secular equivalent, oath-helping, was not allowed, and, needless to say, the London juries returned convictions pretty regularly. Shannon McSheffrey's recent work would seem to confirm Wunderli's findings and argues for extensive secular regulation of marriage, the family, and sexuality in late medieval London.[7]

Obviously, there is much that separates the relief of poverty from the suppression of prostitution. The two moves, however, have this in common. Both involve making use of law to make a change in what is deemed to be an undesirable social phenomenon. In the first case, the legal device of the testament and the charitable trust is used to create institutions that will address the problem of poverty over a long period of time. (A number of the schools and hospitals founded by sixteenth-century testators are still in existence today.) In the second case, the mechanism of enforcement of the penal law is changed in the hopes of discouraging the undesirable activity by obtaining more convictions and imposing harsher penalties.

I have recently completed a large comparative study of litigation about marriage in the later Middle Ages.[8] One of my findings is that in the fifteenth century marriage litigation, particularly in the area that might be described as Franco-Belgian (the north of France and the area covered by modern Belgium), increasingly took the form of criminal prosecutions rather than civil suits between the parties. If a couple made a contract to marry and then did not have it solemnized, they were prosecuted. In the fourteenth century, such litigation was more often in the form of a civil suit between the person who wanted the contract performed and the one who did not. But the sentence book that survives from Brussels from the mid-fifteenth century has very few civil actions in marriage matters, except for separation cases. The sentence registers from nearby Cambrai have some civil actions for marriage contracts, but there are more criminal cases of this type. There are also a number of separation cases brought in the criminal mode. One of the couple is charged with adultery or both are charged with not living together. Perhaps as important as this shift to the criminal mode is the rhetoric of the sentences. In rather marked contrast to the situation in the fourteenth century, at least in England, the heightened rhetoric of the sentences from Cambrai and Brussels, particularly the latter, suggests that the judges thought that the whole institution of marriage in the diocese was spinning out of control.

Marjorie McIntosh has recently published a remarkable study of the prosecution in local courts in England of a series of offenses, none of which can be regarded as particularly serious, but all of which can, in certain social contexts, be annoying: scolding, eavesdropping and nightwalking, sexual offenses (particularly prostitution), disorderly alehouses, the maddeningly vague "bad governance," hedgebreaking, vagabondage and living idly, giving lodging to strangers (known as "subtenants"), and gaming.[9] Prosecutions for these offenses can be found all the way back to the late fourteenth century. Such prosecutions increase markedly in the fifteenth century, particularly in market towns. They become very common in the sixteenth century. McIntosh sees some connection between the increase in such prosecutions and the Puritan movement, but she is reluctant—as she must be granted her data—to attribute all of the increase to that movement. Puritanism, as we understand the term, did not exist in fourteenth- or fifteenth-century England.

Once more, there is much that separates litigation about marriage and prosecution of the type of behavior that was, in many cases and until quite recently, the mainstay of police courts. What these two phenomena have in common is that they evince a willingness on the part of the community to proceed against such offenses in the name of the community. We should be careful not to exaggerate this difference. Prosecutions have to come from somewhere, and if the offense has a victim, it is very difficult to prosecute without the victim's cooperation. But in some of these cases, there is no victim, at least in the traditional sense. "Social control" is the usual descriptive term for what seems to be going on here, although the term used by the organizers of the conference, "social discipline," seems preferable.

The phenomena described here go far enough back that we should be reluctant to make any direct connection with Protestantism in general, or various forms of Calvinism, in particular. An increase in incidence comes during the period of Protestantism, so we might be tempted to see these phenomena as having been reinforced by Protestantism, or the reform movement of the sixteenth century generally. Their origins, however, clearly antedate the Reformation, and one has to wonder to what extent their increase is the product of increasing wealth, increasing population, and greater social organization rather than a change in sentiment brought about by the Reformation. To the extent that this is correct, we would argue that the men and women of the twelfth and thirteenth centuries would have done the same thing if they could have, but they did not have the capacity.

This last argument should not be carried too far. Investment in social infrastructure did increase markedly over the course of the sixteenth century. Since we now have reason to believe that the total amount of charitable giving in real pounds sterling did not increase much in that century, that increase in investment came at the expense of masses, candles, and distributions of bread to the poor. The ecclesiastical system of prosecuting prostitution in mid-fifteenth century London was more of a licensing system than anything designed to eradicate the trade. That was changed in the late fifteenth and early sixteenth centuries to a system that had the latter end in mind, however ineffective it ultimately proved to be. The shift from civil to criminal litigation about marriage was gradual, but we see it happening in the mid-fifteenth century. One of the most interesting findings that emerges from McIntosh's massive longitudinal study of lower-level courts is that many courts did not prosecute such offenses in the earlier periods. Some did, but an increasing proportion did so over the course of the period from 1370 to 1600.

So we have a puzzle. We do have a change, and the change is not simply that society was able to address problems that it was incapable of addressing before. In the case of three of our four examples there were methods of dealing with these problems in the fourteenth century; the methods changed in the fifteenth. In the case of the fourth example, we are poorly informed of the ways in which communities who did not prosecute dealt with these problems, but the institutions that ultimately came to deal with these problems were in existence, at least in the fourteenth century, and in many cases earlier. The changes do, however, correlate with the beginnings of increasing economic activity, the beginnings of a rising population, and greater urbanization with its attendant social organization.[10] They do not correlate particularly well with the Reformation, though the Reformation almost certainly enhanced the trend. The puzzle is that we have a change in attitude that seems to antedate the religious phenomenon that is thought to have caused it. The change in practice correlates nicely with increasing capacity to engage in the practice, but the practice is not so noticeable before, even in places that had the capacity to engage in it.

I am not sure that I have a satisfactory solution to this problem. What I am going to offer, however, will attempt to relate these fifteenth-century developments to the reform movement of the eleventh century.

* * *

Let me begin with an account and an argument with which I only partially agree. R. I. Moore has argued that the years 950–1250 see the emergence of what he calls a "persecuting society."[11] The argument is powerfully constructed. In this period Europeans began systematically to prosecute heretics, to exclude lepers from the society, and to persecute Jews. To these three examples, on which Moore did original research, he adds two others based on the work of others, the persecution or prosecution of male homosexuals and the persecution or prosecution of witchcraft. All of this, he tells us, is new. None of these things had happened in the earlier Middle Ages. He then constructs an elaborate argument for explaining the phenomenon. The major social change in these years, as he sees it, was the movement from a segmentary society to a society in which transactions were based on money. The loss of the old certainties of the face-to-face society produced a powerful feeling of loss of purity and a sense that out there there were powerful and dangerous forces conspiring to undermine society. Hence the search for scapegoats. And scapegoats were easy to find. Jews, heretics, lepers, gays, and witches abounded and could be seen as forming a vast conspiracy that had to be stopped. The movements for repression began, in Moore's view, with the elites. The church proved to be a powerful force to harness reason in support of the repressive move. The end result was the Albigensian crusade, systematic construction of houses for lepers (*leprosaria*), pogroms against the Jews, and their expulsion from various areas and their confinement to ghettos in others.

What are we to make of this argument? As with any historical argument, if the historian has done his or her job well, there probably is something to it. There is no question that, as part of the reform movement of the eleventh century, there seems to be increasing concern about heresy, that this concern comes to focus in the twelfth century on the Cathars of southern France and similar groups in northern Italy, and that this concern resulted in the Albigensian crusade of the first half of the thirteenth century. There is no question that there was a great increase in the construction of *leprosaria* in the twelfth and thirteenth centuries. There is no question that anti-Semitism increases in the twelfth and thirteenth centuries, that various popular legends about, for example, Jews murdering Christian children and using their bodies for ritual purposes seem to originate in the twelfth century. Whether the persecution and prosecution of gays is a characteristic of the twelfth century is a matter of more doubt. There does seem to have been some of it in the thirteenth century.[12] So far as witchcraft is concerned, prosecution or persecution is at best an isolated phenomenon until the great European witch craze, which cannot be firmly dated until much before the beginning of the sixteenth century.[13]

My main problem with Moore's argument, however, lies not in my doubts about two of his five examples. My main problem has to do with the eleventh century and with his claim that something new happened in that century, or at least, something that was new for the Middle Ages. Moore's evidence for the eleventh century rests largely on isolated instances, some of which are not well documented. In 1022, 14, or maybe it was 16, accused heretics were burned at Orléans. Moore asserts that they were the first heretics to be executed in Western Europe since Priscillan of Avila in 383. There are two problems with that statement: First, what Moore should have said is that they were the first heretics that we know about. To say that there is much that we do not know, particularly about the law that was actually enforced, in the early Middle Ages is perhaps to overstate the extent of our knowledge. Second, even Moore admits that accusation of heresy, even conviction for heresy, and execution for heresy are two different things. The church remained ambivalent for some time about the wisdom of cooperating with secular authorities in the extirpation of heresy, particularly when it might lead to execution, and without at least some cooperation of the church, prosecution of heresy could not take place.

The story about leprosy and lepers is even more complicated. Much is still not known about Hansen's disease and its incidence. It is debated whether there was a substantial increase in the disease in the twelfth and thirteenth centuries. That lepers should be excluded from the community is an ancient principle found in the book of Leviticus (13:45–6), and repeated in legal sources throughout the early Middle Ages. Leprosy throughout the Middle Ages was regarded as a great misfortune, and the leper an object of charity. In this regard there is a marked contrast with attitudes toward heretics and Jews, and probably toward gays and witches. The evidence would seem to suggest that there was a substantial increase in *leprosaria* in the twelfth and thirteenth centuries. There was also a substantial increase in the number of enclosed privies and in the number of establishments in which the cows lived in a separate building from the family. I'm not sure that we are seeing anything more here than the effects of greater wealth and greater control over the environment. I suspect that most lepers, if given the choice of living in a *leprosarium* or begging on the streets, would have opted for the former.

So far as Jews are concerned, the evidence is similar to that with regard to heretics. Isolated instances of anti-Semitism appear in the eleventh century. That they do not appear in the tenth tells us much about the poverty of our sources for that century. Moore, who is normally quite careful about mentioning the origins of his phenomena in the ancient world, fails to mention that a remarkably virulent collection of anti-Semitic laws may be found in the Visigothic Code of the seventh century, and the *Usatges de Barcelona* of the twelfth century illustrate a remarkable continuity with the past in this instance as in many others.

The key, then, to understanding Moore and to coming to grips with this phenomenon, if it exists, is the twelfth century. Once we have decided that a phenomenon exists in the twelfth century, we will probably be able to find its origins in the eleventh, and we will probably not be able to find it in the tenth, granted how little we know about the tenth. The question then is whether Moore is right that the twelfth century sees the emergence of a persecuting society. A great deal has been written about the achievements of the twelfth century. No society is without its dark side, and the emergence of particularly virulent forms of anti-Semitism may be one of the dark sides of the twelfth century. Even here, however, I think we must be cautious. The Talmud was burned in the thirteenth century not in the twelfth, and in the twelfth century the Biblical scholars in Paris learned Hebrew from the rabbis, admittedly in order to refute the rabbis' interpretation of the text. How we are to treat the increasing concern with heresy, which certainly is a product of the twelfth century and which was to lead to the inquisition and the Albigensian crusade in the thirteenth century, is another question. Much depends on something that we can probably never know: the extent to which the Cathars were an organized religion set up in deliberate opposition to orthodox Christianity—in which case they were a genuine threat, however one thinks they ought to have been treated—or, alternatively, to what extent the organization of the Cathars was solely in the minds of the persecutors.

Let us then tell the story in a somewhat different way, putting these phenomena in a somewhat different context from Moore's.[14] In the eleventh century churchmen looked around them, and they did not like what they saw. In the preceding centuries, the church had been called upon more and more to support the defense of the realms in which it found itself and to use its lands to support knights. The Carolingian view of kingship was theocratic and sacral. Coronation was a kind of orders giving the king, and particularly the emperor, a sacred character. By the eleventh century the military role of ecclesiastical land and the religious role of the king had combined to turn bishops and abbots into great feudal barons. They were appointed by the king. They received the *regalia* of their office, including the ring and staff—symbols of their spiritual authority—from the king or emperor. They did homage to him; they led their knights into battle. This feudalization (a term of which we have learned to be very careful) of the church was accompanied, perhaps inevitably, by serious abuses. Simony (the sale of ecclesiastical offices) was rampant. The ideal of clerical celibacy was hardly even preached much less observed. Religious observance in monasteries was lax or worse. At the parish level, at least in some places, religious observance hardly existed. Also at the parish level, feudalization of a different sort had taken place. The local lord owned the church, and the parish priest was the lord's man.

The first wave of the reform movement goes back into the tenth century with the reform of the monasteries under the leadership of the great Burgundian abbey of Cluny. In this reform the emperor participated. The emperor Henry II (973–1024) of Germany led an essentially monastic reform movement. He and his empress Kunigunde were both canonized as saints. The second wave of reform comes in the mid-eleventh century with Pope Leo IX and is firmly associated with Pope Gregory VII. The Gregorian program of reform is an interesting one: (1) an end to simony, which in turn leads to an end to lay investiture, and to an end to lay ownership of churches; (2) enforcement of clerical celibacy; and (3) general moral reform. To achieve all these things the reformers sought recognition of the primacy of spiritual power over temporal, of the power of the pope over that of any lay magnate, and—perhaps this is the most important feature for subsequent history—a radical separation of the clergy from the laity.[15]

Hence, the eleventh century was a period of reform and that reform movement continued into the twelfth century and beyond. At first the effort was one of persuasion. Bishops should not buy their offices; priests should not be married. Much had to be done to define what the rules were or ought to be. Over the course of the twelfth century the effort shifted from one of law-finding and dispute resolution to one of law enforcement. Whether one wants to call that a persecuting society is, perhaps, a matter of taste. But perhaps it is not just a matter of taste. Persecution has a decidedly pejorative connotation, prosecution normally does not. The first example of inquisitorial process that we have was a case brought against the abbot of Pomposa who was not accused of heresy but of simony and mismanagement of monastic funds.[16] He seems to have been the late twelfth-century equivalent of the late Ken Ley. What Moore regards as persecution when it comes to heretics would, for most people, be regarded as effective prosecution when it comes to the behavior of the abbot of Pomposa.

In my view the tools for either persecution or prosecution really were not in place until the beginning of the thirteenth century. How one reforms society and extirpates crime without trampling on individuals and engaging in pogroms is a genuine issue, and one with which the West was to struggle from the thirteenth century to this very day. It is not an issue much before that century because the capacity to prosecute on a large scale was not there. Lawyers had a great deal to do with providing that capacity, both in building institutions and in developing the ideas that the institutions were to use. Economic growth provided the resources. Whether the lawyers could also control what they had unleashed is an issue with which we are still living.

Behind the lawyers of the twelfth century was the reform movement of the eleventh. Those of us who worry about such things argue among ourselves as to how direct the connection was.[17] Most of us would now agree that the power struggle between the holy Roman emperor and the pope, which occupied both for a considerable portion of the two centuries from the mid-eleventh to the mid-thirteenth, cannot be directly connected to the founding of the faculties of Roman and canon law at Bologna, events that we are coming increasingly to date in the mid-twelfth century. At least, they were not connected in the sense that the emperor founded one and the pope the other in order to provide arguments for each side of the controversy. At the same time there was an efflorence of canonistic activity in both Italy and France from the mid-eleventh through the early twelfth century, and the connection between this activity and the reform movement is pretty obvious. Gratian of Bologna's *Concordance of Discordant Canons*, written, in my view, probably in the 1120s or the early 1130s, became the textbook for the canon lawyers of Bologna. His great work is clearly the work of a reformer, but, interestingly enough, of a reformer who was not particularly interested in the high politics of the reform movement.[18] His work is chiefly devoted to an elaboration of the hierarchical structure of the church, with little about the relationship of that structure with secular authority, and to a whole series of hot-button topics that concerned the reformers of his day: among them, simony, church property, procedure, and marriage. His book could be, and was, used to create a panoply of ecclesiastical institutions, most notably a hierarchical structure of courts. These courts could be, and were, used to implement the principles of the reform in the thirteenth century.

For the thirteenth century we are better informed about the structure and jurisdiction of these courts than we are about their functioning. Some records have survived, however, and they reveal sophisticated institutions dealing for the most part with civil cases.[19] The jurisdiction of these courts varied from region to region. Jurisdiction over marriage, church property and offices, and testaments was quite common. In some areas we find jurisdiction over defamation, assault (particularly if a member of the clergy was involved), and contractual obligations. There are also hints, which become better documented in the fourteenth century, of a lower-level, largely criminal, jurisdiction that dealt predominantly with sexual offenses, mostly fornication and adultery, but also discipline of the lower clergy, minor cases of blasphemy, sabbath-breaking, and so on.

The changes that we outlined at the beginning of the essay and which we dated, as a general matter, to the mid-fifteenth century occurred in institutions that had been in existence since the mid-thirteenth century, perhaps before that in some places, and they probably represented changes in practices that had been in existence since the mid-thirteenth century if not before. Viewed against this background, it is perhaps important to emphasize what these changes were not. They do not represent a sudden willingness on the part of the society to attempt to enforce conformity to a set of norms and behaviors that corresponded to prevailing moral and religious notions of proper behavior. That willingness had existed since the twelfth century, and institutions capable of enforcement had existed since the thirteenth. (The willingness had probably existed before that: the institutions probably had not, at least not in a form that we can see.) The changes of the later Middle Ages do represent some shift in where that enforcement would take place. In London, ecclesiastical institutions seem to have been found wanting and a shift was made to secular institutions; similar shifts may have occurred elsewhere as well. The central royal courts in England began to replace the ecclesiastical courts in entertaining actions for defamation in the early years of the sixteenth century, again before the Reformation.[20] More subtle is the shift from reliance on action by the parties to reliance on prosecution. That seems to have been happening in the same period, however, at least with regard to marriage, perhaps more on the Continent than in England. Most subtle of all is the shift in the nature of charitable giving. Much of the shift cannot be dated before the Reformation. The statutory prohibition on the enforcement of gifts for masses and the dissolution of the monasteries, both of which are clearly connected with the shifts in charitable giving, are emphatically products of the Reformation. And yet, new ideas about poor relief appear in urban circles, both Catholic and Protestant, in the sixteenth century and do not seem to be connected in any direct way with the Reformation. And, of course, the foundation of hospitals and schools was not new in the sixteenth century.

Therefore we return to our puzzle with, perhaps, a better understanding of what lies in back of it. A religious reform movement of the eleventh century produced a flurry of intellectual activity in the twelfth century, with some creation of institutions of enforcement. Those institutions were solidified in the thirteenth century. The fourteenth century, at least in England, also sees a reform movement insofar as the law is concerned, but that movement is not normally connected with trends in religious thought in that century. The creation of the justices of the peace and a substantial increase in the jurisdictional reach of the central royal courts in that century is normally associated with the disruptions caused by the French wars and the Black Death.

There was, however, a religious reform movement in England in the fourteenth century, one that we associate with the name of John Wycliffe (ca. 1325–84). The movement ultimately became the heretical movement known as Lollardry. On the Continent there were a number of developments that Georges de Lagarde gathered under the name of "The Birth of the Lay Spirit at the Decline of the Middle Ages."[21] Be that as it may, we see in the fourteenth century, particularly in its second half, numerous manifestations of lay personal piety. The organized church no longer seemed able to contain spirituality.

Now when we get to the fifteenth century, this lay spirituality certainly did not decline. It may even have gotten stronger. The invention of moveable type led to the production of large numbers of devotional books for the laity. The pre-Reformation religious culture of England has been nicely described in Eamon Duffy's *The Stripping of the Altars*.[22] From a modern point of view it is a rather gloomy kind of spirituality, focusing as it does on the passion of Christ, sin and penance, preparation for death, and personal mortification, but its intensity cannot be denied.

* * *

Does this have anything to do with the changes in the nature and intensity of law enforcement that we noticed in the same period? This may be a question that can only be asked and not answered. The changes that we noted are deliberate enough, but the reasons for them are not articulated. They are not articulated because, by and large, they take place within the context of existing institutions. No one needed to justify the creation of a new institution to deal with a new problem. An existing institution could be made to serve a somewhat different function. Further, the changes that both McIntosh and I have noted are incremental, the kind of thing that one notices only when one starts coding cases and adding them up, and they take place, as it were, off the radar screen. A society that had a substantial problem with violent crime and jury corruption is unlikely to raise to the conscious level a steady increase in the prosecution of neighborhood scolds.

For evidence that there is some connection between the religious reform movement of the fourteenth century and what happens with regard to law enforcement in the fifteenth, I turn not to a layman, but to a priest, John Lydford, who was a practicing canon lawyer all his life, and who died as canon of Exeter and archdeacon of Totnes around the age of 70 in 1407. Lydford's personal *Notebook* has survived.[23] Practical forms for courts ranging in importance from that of the chancellor of Oxford to the Roman *curia* fill much of its pages. The emphasis on episcopal authority is strong. The proper conduct of visitation and discipline of the clergy, both regular and secular, with perhaps some emphasis on disciplining the former, are much in evidence. For Lydford, heresy, in which he had a considerable interest, was a legal problem, not a theological one. His experience with the endowment of New College, Oxford, for Bishop William Wykeham seems to have led to a broader interest in endowment generally. Today, we might find him as a lawyer for a non-profit or a charity. That Lydford was unsympathetic with the Lollards does not mean that he was unsympathetic with reform. By and large, however, it was a reform that focused on abuses that were clear violations of the law and could be dealt with by enforcement of the law: the prior of Newark would be deprived for maladministration of funds (nos. 185–7, 190–1); Ralph Tregrisiou must resign the rectory of Quethiock if he becomes dean of Exeter, but only when he obtains firm possession of the latter benefice (no. 246). Lydford will not question the whole system of papal provision to benefices. That he was capable, however, of thinking about what we call the broader policy implications of something that was clearly lawful is suggested by his inclusion in the *Notebook* of a dialogue among theologians and lawyers, probably developed in an academic context: "Whether it is a meritorious thing to appropriate parish churches to corporate bodies" (no. 282).[24]

Lydford's testament gives us some sense of the man. He gives legacies to five chaplains, the preferment of at least one of whom, the *Notebook* suggests, he was instrumental in securing. He gives a legacy of £10 for studies to his clerk James Carslegh. The latter obtained a BCivL at Oxford after Lydford's death and ended his career as official of Exeter.[25] Carslegh's preservation of the *Notebook*, with his own subsequent additions, was an act of *pietas* that ensured that the book has come down to us. Of Lydford's law books we hear nothing in the testament, but his executors gave books to Exeter College, Oxford. Lydford's copy of the *Decretals* may have been in the hands of his kinsman, John Lydford, Jr., for the flyleaf of the book has survived indicating the loan. What we do hear of in the testament is Lydford's beautiful, large, noted breviary, his new *Legenda sanctorum et temporalis*, and his fair Bible. These are the books of a man who could have appeared in choir and who had the reference materials for composing sermons. He was not an ascetic; the testament also mentions a black maple cup out of which he had drunk much good wine.[26]

The major gift to an ecclesiastical institution in Lydford's testament is £20 to the dean and chapter of Exeter with minute instructions as to how they are to celebrate his anniversary for twenty years. The next largest gifts are the £10 to his clerk for his studies and £10 for the roads and bridges of Exeter. The residue of his estate is to be distributed by his executors among the poor (with careful instructions as to how the executors are to determine that the poor really are poor).

The standard first "legacy" in testaments in this period, used in a large number of medieval testaments, and appearing in such documents into the sixteenth century is: "In the first place, I legate my soul to God, and to the Blessed Virgin and all his saints, and my body to be buried in the parish church of X." Lydford's is unusual: "I commend my soul to God, my maker and saviour, beseeching him who bought my soul and the souls of all the faithful with his precious blood, to deal with it according to his mercy, when it should have passed from this vale of misery, of his exceeding great kindness and goodness ineffable."[27] This is a theological statement of the kind that we normally associate with the Reformation and the Counter-Reformation. When we couple this with the elaborate instructions designed to insure that the money that he left behind be used for the good for which he intended it and with his equally elaborate insistence that not much be spent on his funeral, we begin to wonder if Lydford, the prosecutor of Lollards, had not caught some of the spirit of the Lollard reform.

* * *

Let us return to R. I. Moore's explanation for what he calls the formation of a persecuting society in the twelfth century. He argued that a major social change occurred in these years. A segmentary society changed to one in which transactions were based on money. The loss of the old certainties of a face-to-face society produced a powerful feeling of loss of purity and an imagining of powerful and dangerous forces conspiring to undermine society. There is no question that there was a great increase in economic activity in the twelfth century. It is hard to put numbers on it, but the percentage increase in gross domestic product may have been as great or greater than in any century before the nineteenth. (Recall, however, that one can produce dramatic percentage increases in gross domestic product if one starts from a low base.) Whether that increase involved a change from a segmentary society to one based on money is much more controversial. I am reminded of M. M. Postan's famous essay "The Rise of a Money Economy," in which he argued that the concept was meaningless because the process was so gradual.[28] One does find conspiracy theories about Jews and heretics in the twelfth century, more about the latter than the former. Conspiracy theories about gays and witches are later, much later in the case of witches. Evidence of conspiracy theories about lepers is thin in all periods.

If Moore's explanation does not seem quite to explain, perhaps we should go back to the articulated concerns of the reform movement. There is no question that many in the movement had a profound sense that society was somehow corrupt. The sources of the corruption were money and sex. The sacred was being bought and sold, priests were living with concubines, lay people were committing incest. We have to pull up our socks, or we will all go to hell, quite literally. The result, though it took quite a while to achieve it, included a fairly radical separation of the clerical from the lay segments of the society, the creation of a legal system designed to enforce the rules, and considerable elaboration and alteration of the rules (including a substantial reduction in the range of the incest prohibition).

There is no question that the economic revival of the twelfth century made all of this, or a great deal of it, possible, just as it made possible the building of great Romanesque and Gothic cathedrals, but did it have anything to do with the reform movement itself? Profound social changes are, in some instances, related to religious movements. Many anthropologists connect the cargo cults of the Pacific with the social changes and anxieties brought about by the arrival of Westerners, and we can take that for our purposes as plausible. The question is whether this particular religious reform movement can be seen as a product of social change. As historians we are committed to the notion that things change, and if we look hard enough, we can almost always find social change. The particular social change, however, that Moore posits may not have been quite so dramatic as he makes it out to be, and, perhaps more important, to the extent that it occurred, it occurred in the twelfth century not the eleventh. But the reform movement is emphatically a product of the eleventh century.

If we move to the fifteenth century, there can be little question that this century saw a substantial economic revival. The great economic surge of the sixteenth century and its accompanying inflation were built on it. The revival was spotty. Some areas, including the northeast of England, declined, but the overall trends in both gross domestic product and population seem to have been up. The economic revival probably produced an increase in vertical distance in the society. It also produced some social movement. All of these phenomena probably increased in the sixteenth century. There is, I would suggest, more evidence to link the increased amount of law enforcement in the fifteenth and sixteenth centuries to economic and social factors than there is in the case of the twelfth and thirteenth centuries.[29]

Just as there is more evidence to attribute the increased amount of law enforcement to social and economic factors in the fifteenth century than there is in the twelfth, so too there is less evidence to attribute it to religious factors. We have argued that there was a kind of religious revival among lay people in the fifteenth century, though it is not often noted. It was certainly not of the scale and significance of that of the eleventh century, and it had nothing like the impact of that of the sixteenth century. Certainly there was nothing like the religious conflict that there was in the sixteenth century, conflict that seems to have produced the most dramatic instance of legal scapegoating that the West had ever seen, the hunting of witches.

And yet—and this will be my last point and my most dangerous of a series of dangerous generalizations—the religious revival of the fifteenth century, if such it was, does seem to fit in with something that is found quite often in religious reform movements, but is not characteristic of all religious reform movements: a tendency to turn to law. Reform, renewal, and revival seem to be almost constants in religious history. The Christian doctrine of the fall of man offers an explanation for why it is necessary, but such movements are also found in religions that do not have such an explicit doctrine of the human tendency to sin. Perhaps this is because, as one wag is alleged to have said, the doctrine of the fall of man is the one doctrine of the faith for which there is ample empirical evidence. But many religious reform movements do not explicitly appeal to law. Reform Judaism is almost the opposite. Many reform movements appeal to the individual conscience and urge the believer to reform himself, frequently with the aid of the reformer but without much, or even any, emphasis on law. Luther read the Letter to the Romans as antinomian, though he became more open to law at the end of his career. He never, however, abandoned his notion that justification comes by faith in Christ alone and that that faith comes only through the gift of God's grace. Other Christian reform groups have been committedly antinomian; the Society of Friends (Quakers) is a notable example.[30]

The eleventh-century reform was not like that. It turned early and often to law. The Calvinist reform did the same. Modern Islamic reformers frequently urge return to the Shariʿa. The eighteenth-century Islamic reform movement known as Wahhabism did the same. In all cases, of course, there were, and are, arguments about the law. Reformers who make use of law have a tendency to appeal to an earlier and, in their view, uncorrupted version of the law, but their use of law is undeniable.

There is no obvious explanation for why some religious reform movements make use of law and some do not. The amount of religious law, of course, varies substantially from religion to religion, but the use of law by reformers does not correlate very well with the amount of religious law. Some Jewish reform movements have made use of the Jewish legal tradition, some have not. Christianity, in comparison with Judaism, has less law, but both the eleventh-century reform and that of Calvin made considerable use of law, while that of Luther and of the Quakers did not.

I think there is at least a partial explanation for why the legal reform movements focus on particular topics. Simony was of large concern in the twelfth century. It was of less concern in the sixteenth.[31] Witchcraft was of great concern in the sixteenth century. It was not of particular concern in the twelfth. In the case of simony, there is evidence that the twelfth-century reformers, though they exaggerated, were concerned about a real problem. The ecclesiastical arrangements of the day made the corruption that they called simony almost inevitable. Witchcraft is more complicated, because so much of the talk of it was the product of heightened imagination and conspiracy theories. When we look, however, at the confessions that were not the product of torture or irresistible social pressure, there does seem to have been a core group of people in that century (perhaps they existed earlier as well) who were messing around with magic. At least some scholarly accounts of Muḥammad Ibn ʿAbd al-Wahhāb suggest that his concern with possibly idolatrous or polytheistic devotion to shrines, tombsites, and Sufi saints was not misplaced. In short, what I am suggesting is that reform movements, at least those that get off the ground, tend to focus on something that really exists, indeed, something that ought to have made the adherents of the religion uncomfortable.

Perhaps we can put this suggestion together with the problem that we posed in the previous paragraph: why some religious reform movements turn to law and some do not. We need to exclude here reforms, renewals, and revivals that depend on a direct revelation to the leader, one that leads, in essence, to the founding of a new religion. My suggestion here cannot account for Bahaʾism and the Church of Jesus Christ of the Latter Day Saints (Mormons), or, indeed, for what happened in Christianity in the first or early second century. Reform movements, renewals, and revivals that purport to remain true to the traditions of the religion in which they arise (even if they ultimately are declared heretical) are faced with choices; the longer and more complicated the tradition of the religion, the more complicated the choice. If there is, however, within that tradition a legal tradition that can be used to achieve the goals of the reformers, they will use it. The perception of what is wrong and needs reform comes first; recourse to the legal tradition, if it exists, is instrumental. Obviously, if what is perceived of as in need of reform is the whole legal tradition, then recourse will not be had to it. Reform Judaism, the young Luther, and the Second Vatican Council of the Roman Catholic Church, in different ways, provide examples. Early Christianity, though this is far from clear, may be another. Examples, however, of recourse to the legal tradition to implement the reform are quite easy to find. Many, if not all, of the prophets of the Hebrew Bible, the Christian reform movement of the eleventh century, and many, though not all, of the reform movements in Islam provide examples.

Looking at these examples from the distance that one must take in order to make generalizations like these, the examples of reforms that move away from the law ("antinomian" is too strong a word, though each of these reform movements had antinomian strands) all had something in common: The religion that they sought to reform had in its contemporary unreformed state a strong legal tradition that was being enforced. The examples of law-based reforms, by contrast, sought to reform a religion that had, in the view of the reformers, moved away from its legal tradition. There are, of course, complexities. The prophets of the Hebrew Bible issue blanket condemnations of those who have moved away from the law entirely by worshipping pagan gods, but they also condemn those who focus on the minutiae of ritual law and ignore their obligations to the poor, the widow, the orphan, and the stranger.

The movement that I find hard to fit into this pattern is Calvinism. One might begin an explanation with the fact that Calvin himself was trained as a lawyer. He was predisposed to find the famous "third way," a use for law in a religious system that was firmly committed to predestination. Some of his followers became antinomians, though my understanding is that this term was always a pejorative among mainstream Calvinists. Perhaps a chronological explanation will help, though I must confess that the chronology is tight. One does not normally find reactions in religious movements coming so quickly. If we are right that fifteenth-century western Christianity was firmly committed to religious law and its enforcement, the antinomian strand in the young Luther fits our pattern quite nicely. Calvin comes about a generation later. By Calvin's time the perverse consequences of Luther's antinomian streak were all too obvious. Anabaptism was not something that Calvin wanted to encourage, much less peasant revolts. The move to law in Calvinism may thus have been a reaction to the antinomian strands in earlier Protestant movements. When Calvinism moved into areas that had not adopted Lutheranism, much less Anabaptism (France, England, the Low Countries), its use of law was not a reaction to what had been happening previously but a powerful reinforcer of it. This would account for what we see in England and probably for what we see in what is now Belgium (though the complexities there are substantial). Beyond that we should not go; so far as I am aware, the comparative work has simply not been done.

It will be noted that all of my examples are taken from monotheistic religions that profess a belief in a personal god. Indeed, they all come from religions that recognize, though in different ways, the authority of the Hebrew Bible. Part of the reason for this is that I know even less about other religions than I do about the ones that I have discussed with far more confidence than my knowledge warrants. There is, however, I think, a reason why reform movements in the "religions of the book" should sometimes turn to law and sometimes not. Belief in a single, personal God encourages anthropomorphism. The tendency is resisted in all three traditions, but it is there. Believers ask the question, sometimes quite naïvely, what does God think of me? And the analogies that they think of are those of a social superior or a parent. Reformers will appeal to this instinct (I am not saying that what they do is consciously manipulative), and like the Hebrew prophets they can say one of two things, "God is angry at you because you have done X," or "God loves you; do Y." Like the Hebrew prophets, they will, of course, say both; but the emphasis of reform movements tends to be in one direction or the other. Law can be harnessed either to discourage certain behaviors or to encourage certain behaviors, but in the West it is more often used, and perhaps more successfully used, for the former than for the latter purpose. Law can be used to assuage the anger of others or of a divine being; it is much more difficult to use it to promote the love of others or of a divine being. Hence, if the emphasis of the reform movement is on the sins of the people and the divine wrath that has followed or will follow, law is more likely to be used than it is if the focus is on the failure of the people to respond lovingly to God's call. All of my examples, including Calvinism, fit this pattern, but one: This time it is the Lutheran reform that is hard to explain. Here the best that I can do is to say that even at his most antinomian, Luther had some use for law. It would not lead the believer to justification; only a response in faith to God's grace could do that, but it could show the person who was struggling how much he or she was in need of God's grace, and it could serve to restrain those who remained outside the realm of grace.

We have come a long way without coming to many firm conclusions. Three conclusions stand out: (1) There is nothing particularly Protestant or Calvinist about the concern for social discipline that emerges in the sixteenth century; indeed, it does not seem to emerge in the sixteenth century but in the fifteenth. (2) In the fifteenth century this concern seems to have roots that go back to the religious reform movement of the eleventh century. That movement had substantial ramifications in the twelfth and thirteenth centuries; it may have lost its moorings in the fourteenth century, to be revived in the fifteenth. (3) Religious reform movements do not necessarily have legal ramifications, but some do. There may be an explanation for why some do and some do not, but it is not apparent in the literature, and the general suggestions that I have made about this phenomenon must be regarded as tentative in the extreme.

NOTES

[1] "Law, Religion, and Social Discipline in the Early Modern Atlantic World" (Newberry Library, Chicago, Friday, October 6, 2006). The paper benefited greatly from comments by Philip Gorski, author of *The Disciplinary Revolution: Calvinism and the Rise of the State in Early Modern Europe* (Chicago: University of Chicago Press, 2003), who clearly was not convinced by my account of the fifteenth century, but was generous enough to suggest that there might be something to my argument about the eleventh. The version of the paper printed here is close to the original talk, including some informality of language and notes that are more "suggestions for further reading" than full documentation. I have also used the notes to try to come to grips with some of Gorski's comments.

[2] I began with Joseph L. Blau, "Reform," in *The Encyclopedia of Religion*, 2d ed., 11:7651–56, and Kenelm Burridge, "Revival and Renewal," in idem, 7784–90, and pursued the bibliographies given there.

[3] W. K. (Wilbur Kitchener) Jordan, *Philanthropy in England, 1480–1660. A Study of the Changing Pattern of English Social Aspirations* (London: G. Allen & Unwin, [1959]); idem, *The Charities of London, 1480–1660. The Aspirations and the Achievements of the Urban Society* (London: Allen & Unwin [1960]); idem, *The Charities of Rural England, 1480–1660. The Aspirations and the Achievements of the Rural Society* (London: Allen & Unwin [1961]).

[4] 1 Edw. 6, c. 14 (1547) (S.R., iv, 24).

[5] See Carl R. Steinbicker, *Poor-Relief in the Sixteenth Century* (S.T.D. dissertation, Catholic University of America, 1937) (a tendentious work and out-of-date, but it does establish the point that the type of poor relief with which Jordan is concerned is not peculiarly Protestant).

[6] Richard M. Wunderli, *London Church Courts and Society on the Eve of the Reformation* (Cambridge: Medieval Academy of America, 1981).

[7] *Marriage, Sex, and Civic Culture in Late Medieval London* (Philadelphia: University of Pennsylvania Press, 2006).

[8] Charles Donahue, *Law, Marriage, and Society in the Later Middle Ages: Arguments about Marriage in Four Courts* (forthcoming, Cambridge University Press).

[9] Marjorie Keniston McIntosh, *Controlling Misbehavior in England, 1370–1600* (Cambridge: Cambridge University Press, 1998).

[10] Philip Gorski in his comments at the conference questioned whether these factors played much of a role, granted the fact that two of the areas that see the most extensive use of social discipline, at least in the seventeenth century, Scotland and New England, are not areas noted for either economic development or urbanization. Perhaps I was overly influenced by the work of Gorski's fellow sociologist, Donald Black, *The Behavior of Law* (New York: Academic Press, 1976), though the correlation between increased economic activity and increased litigation has been noted by many authors. The point that needs to be emphasized here, however, is that a certain level of social organization and economic capacity is probably necessary, though it is certainly not a sufficient condition, for the kind of disciplining with which we are concerned. To say that Scotland and New England had, at least by the seventeenth century, achieved those minimal levels approaches, of course, the tautological.

[11] R. I. Moore, *The Formation of a Persecuting Society: Power and Deviance in Western Europe, 950–1250* (Oxford: B. Blackwell, 1987).

[12] See John Boswell, *Christianity, Social Tolerance, and Homosexuality: Gay People in Western Europe from the Beginning of the Christian Era to the Fourteenth Century* (Chicago: University of Chicago Press, 1980).

[13] The literature is vast, but there seems to be a consensus about the chronology. E.g., H. R. Trevor-Roper, *The European Witch-Craze of the 16th and 17th Centuries* (Harmondsworth: Penguin, 1978); Brian P. Levack, *The Witch-Hunt in Early Modern Europe* (Harlow: Pearson Longman, [3]2006).

[14] This account is derived from Charles Donahue, "A Crisis of Law? Reflections on the Church and the Law over the Centuries," *The Jurist* 65 (2005), 1–30. See

Uta-Renate Blumenthal, *The Investiture Controversy: Church and Monarchy from the Ninth to the Twelfth Century* (Philadelphia: University of Pennsylvania Press, 1988); Brian Tierney, *The Crisis of Church and State, 1050–1300* (Englewood Cliffs: Prentice-Hall, 1964); Gerd Tellenbach, *Church, State, and Christian Society at the Time of the Investiture Contest*, trans. Ralph Francis Bennett (Toronto: University of Toronto Press, 1991).

[15] Professor Blumenthal (private communication) suggests that not all the reformers espoused what a later age would see as clericalism. Gregory VII, for example, tried to engage the laity in his reform movement (and was criticized for doing so).

[16] *Licet Heli*, X 5.3.31 (Innocent III, 1198), in Emil Friedberg (ed.), *Corpus iuris canonici* (Leipzig: B. Tauchnitz, 1879–81; repr. Graz: Akademische Druck, 1955), 2:760–61.

[17] Part of the reason for our puzzlement is that the work of Anders Winroth (*The Making of Gratian's Decretum* [Cambridge: Cambridge University Press, 2000]) has forced us to redate much of what happened at Bologna. My own view is that Winroth is not radical enough about the date of the "first recension" of Gratian's work. I also think that he is a bit too radical about the non-existence of Roman-law studies at Bologna in Gratian's time, but I agree with him that we cannot be sure about this period, and we certainly do not have anything like a "faculty" of Roman law until the 1140s.

[18] Stanley Chodorow, *Christian Political Theory and Church Politics in the Mid-Twelfth Century: The Ecclesiology of Gratian's Decretum* (Berkeley: University of California Press, 1972).

[19] E.g., *Select Cases from the Ecclesiastical Courts of the Province of Canterbury, c. 1200–1301*, ed. Norma Adams and Charles Donahue, Publications of the Selden Society 95 (London: Selden Society, 1981).

[20] *Select Cases on Defamation to 1600*, ed. R. H. Helmholz, Publications of the Selden Society 101 (London: Selden Society, 1985), lxviii–lxix, lxxiii–lxxv. In Helmholz's view the rise of this action was necessitated by the fact that the central royal courts were at the same time, indeed from some years before, preventing the church courts from entertaining defamation actions that involved the imputation of a secular crime.

[21] Georges de Lagarde, *La naissance de l'esprit laïque au déclin du moyen age* (Louvain: E. Nauwelaerts, 1956–1970).

[22] New Haven: Yale University Press, [2]2005.

[23] *John Lydford's Book*, ed. Dorothy M. Owen (London: HMSO, 1974).

[24] *num quid sit merito in appropriare collegiis ecclesias parochiales.*

[25] A. B. Emden, *A Biographical Register of the University of Oxford to A.D. 1500*, 3 vols. (Oxford: Clarendon Press, 1957–59), 1:363.

[26] *The Register of Edmund Stafford (A.D. 1395–1419)*, ed. F. C. Hingeston-Randolph, The Episcopal Registers of the Diocese of Exeter (London: G. Bell & Sons, 1886), 389–90. This is an abstract in English rather than the Latin text.

[27] I have taken the liberty of converting Hingeston-Randolph's abstract into a quotation. I may have a word or two wrong, but the abstract at this point has all the hallmarks of a quite literal translation.

[28] *Economic History Review* 24 (1944), 123–34, in idem, *Essays on Medieval Agriculture and General Problems of the Medieval Economy* (Cambridge: Cambridge University Press, 1973), 28–40.

[29] For Philip Gorski's criticism of this point, see above, n. 10. Here, I need more of an answer, because pretty clearly much of European society in the fourteenth century had the minimum level of social and economic capacity to engage in the kind of social disciplining that we see more of in the fifteenth century. The best that I can do is to suggest, as I did previously, that in many areas other concerns, wars and the Black Death, overwhelmed the will to engage extensively in such activity in the fourteenth century. Clearly, the social and economic variables will not, by themselves, allow us to predict the quantity of such disciplining that will occur in one society as compared to another, as Gorski's examples of Scotland and New England show. Changes in these variables may, however, be correlated with increases in such activity within a given society. However low the level of economic activity was in Scotland in the sixteenth and seventeenth centuries when compared to England, it was clearly much higher in those centuries than it had been in the previous two centuries.

[30] As the generalizations get broader and broader, the bibliography, of course, gets larger and larger. My account of the western developments has been strongly influenced by James M. Gustafson, *Protestant and Roman Catholic Ethics: Prospects for Rapprochement* (Chicago: University of Chicago Press, 1978), and John Mahoney, *The Making of Moral Theology: A Study of the Roman Catholic Tradition* (Oxford: Clarendon Press, 1987). Frank Vogel first introduced me to Ibn ʿAbd al-Wahhāb and Wahhabism, and what little that I know about it that is not derived from conversations with Frank and from his works is derived from *The Encyclopaedia of Islam*. Peri Bearman put me on to a wonderful book by Michael Cook, *Commanding Right and Forbidding Wrong in Islamic Thought* (Cambridge: Cambridge University Press, 2000), which I was able to read only in the "*Readers' Digest*" version: *Forbidding Wrong in Islam: An Introduction* (Cambridge: Cambridge University Press, 2003).

[31] Philip Gorski reminds me that some Protestant authors saw the whole medieval system of benefices as simoniacal. *Disciplinary Revolution*, 148–50. And, of course, the sale of indulgences provoked considerable reformist concern.

2

THE KINDRED CONCEPTS OF SEISIN AND *ḤAWZ* IN ENGLISH AND ISLAMIC LAW

John Makdisi

The concept of seisin lies at the core of the transformation of English law into the common law we know today. In the twelfth century it provided a means by which land could be recovered more quickly and safely than the long and dangerous process of the writ of right. Under the writ of right a person whose property had been usurped had to prove ownership to regain it. The process was long because several delays were permitted. The proof was difficult since there was no comprehensive recording system to provide the proper evidence of ownership. When insufficient proof was provided, the action on the writ of right turned to God to determine which party was right. Each party was called to do combat or provide a champion who would do combat on the faith that God would make the true owner the victor—in a battle that could easily mean the death of one of the combatants.[1] Seisin provided a solution to this problem.

In the second half of the twelfth century King Henry II instituted a new action called the assize of novel disseisin.[2] Proof of property right in this action did not depend on one's ownership of property but rather on the nature of one's possession. If a person possessed property in a certain way called seisin, then he could depend on the assize of novel disseisin to put him quickly back in possession of it if he were disseised.[3] Furthermore, the assize introduced a new method of proof. A body of twelve people from the community was called on to "view" the property and determine an answer to the factual question of seisin. This body based itself on factual evidence that required neither an appeal to the supernatural nor the danger of mortal combat. It was not long before the assize of novel disseisin became the preferred action for recovering one's property, and the writ of right fell into disuse.

There is no doubt that the concept of seisin is fundamental to an understanding of the transformation that took place in English law in the twelfth century. It is therefore somewhat surprising that a clear understanding of this concept has remained rather elusive. In 1886 and 1888 Frederic William Maitland published two short but very influential articles entitled

"The Mystery of Seisin"[4] and "The Beatitude of Seisin."[5] In them he described the concept of seisin in the twelfth and thirteenth centuries as he interpreted it from the extant sources, especially Bracton's monumental 13th-century work, *Tractatus de Legibus et Consuetudinibus Angliae*.[6] In 1973 Donald Sutherland agreed with Maitland's conclusions in his scholarly work *The Assize of Novel Disseisin*,[7] but his study of the cases suggested that the concept of seisin as interpreted by Maitland from Bracton was never implemented in point of actual fact. Unfortunately, the cases are rather short on explanation. Glanvill wrote a treatise[8] in the late twelfth century but it also is short on explanation. Bracton's work, while it stands out for its comprehensive analysis of seisin, is still not very clear on some crucial points. Unfortunately, today, we continue to maintain a shaky understanding of the concept.

A few years ago I wrote an article on the Islamic origins of the common law[9] and explored institutional, structural, and geographical reasons for looking to Sicily as the melting pot for Norman and Islamic ideas of government that eventually found their way to England. In the course of its analysis the article briefly examined the relationship between the Islamic[10] and English concepts of ownership and possession. I was impressed by the fundamental similarity of ideas between the two legal systems in this area of the law. It accorded with the several other parallels I had noted in other areas. Yet, if the English action on the assize of novel disseisin really had an antecedent in the Islamic action of the *istiḥqāq*, I was puzzled that the English law of seisin seemed to deviate in some unexplained ways from the Islamic law of possession. I have taken this opportunity on the occasion of a tribute for my longtime friend and colleague, Frank Vogel, to reexamine this issue and come to new conclusions. This paper takes a fresh look at Bracton, confirms the legitimacy of Sutherland's dispute with Bracton as interpreted by Maitland, but suggests a new interpretation of the concept of seisin that differs from that of Maitland and reconciles Bracton with the cases analyzed by Sutherland. It then compares this new interpretation of the concept of seisin with the Maliki concept of *ḥawz* in their constitutive elements, their legal effects, and the procedures by which they are proved in court. The comparison demonstrates a much closer fit between the two concepts than I originally thought existed. It gives added support to my theory that the uniqueness of the common law, as distinguished from the Roman-based civil law system, is derived primarily from Islamic law.

Bracton's Concept of Seisin

Bracton starts his chapter on civil actions with a description of "the barest minimum of possession," that is, naked intrusion on another's property.[11] The intrusion occurs upon a vacant possession,[12] and it is called naked "because unprotected by any vestment."[13] The intruder has "no spark of right," and the possession remains naked "until a vestment is acquired through time and peaceful possession."[14] How much time? Bracton states that "[i]f the intruder is ejected quickly, *within a year* according to some, before he has time [in possession], long and peaceful, he will not recover by the assise of novel disseisin."[15] It is clear from this passage that the intruder is not considered to be vested in possession until a year has passed. After a year, the vestment that is acquired through time and peaceful possession gives the possessor a right to possession that is protected by the assize of novel disseisin against anyone who tries to eject him. In other words, naked possession has ripened into seisin, the level of possession protected against disseisin by the assize.

Bracton is clear that an intruder's possession may take as long as a year to ripen into seisin, but a few pages later Bracton states that in certain circumstances the intruder's possession immediately ripens into seisin. If an intruder takes possession and is immediately ejected by "one having no right," the intruder has a "tenuous seisin" that permits him to bring an action on the assize and recover his possession.[16] The difference between the seisin that takes a year to obtain and the seisin that is gained immediately is clarified by an earlier passage in Bracton's work. As against those

> who have no right they at once begin to have a free tenement and right and begin to possess. And when there has been long, continuous and peaceful possession they begin to possess as against all, and to have a free tenement, so that they cannot be ejected without writ and judgment.[17]

Seisin is gained immediately against one having no right, but it must wait a year before it is gained against those having a right to the property. How one gains seisin against another person is determined by the nature of one's relationship with that other person.

Once an intruder gains the status of seisin through possession for one year, he gains protection by the assize of novel disseisin even against the true owner. What is this protection? The true owner cannot eject the intruder without writ and judgment. He cannot use self-help to remove the intruder but rather must bring an action on the assize or on the writ of right to have him removed. If the true owner violates this proviso and uses self-help to reinstate himself in his property, the intruder can bring an action on the assize to have the true owner removed from the property. At this point the assize is no longer available to the true owner, and he is compelled to bring an action only on the writ of right if he wants his property back.[18] The protection of seisin does not prevent the true owner from getting his property back; it merely prohibits him from using self-help to get it back.

From these passages Bracton clarifies the function of the assize of novel disseisin as it relates to intruders. The assize protects every intruder against a subsequent dispossessor who has no right to the property. It protects every intruder against a subsequent dispossessor who is the true owner if the intruder has enjoyed one year of continuous undisputed possession. It does not protect the intruder at any time if the true owner brings the assize against the intruder to have him removed from the property.

These rules pertain to an intruder, one who enters upon a vacant possession that is possessed neither *corpore* nor *animo*.[19] The rules pertaining to a disseisor of one who is already possessing the property with seisin appear to be different. Bracton states that a disseisor gains seisin against the possessor after four days:

> If [the possessor] is present at the time of the disseisin, let him then re-eject the disseisor at once, on the same day if he can.... [If not,] let him on the next day, the third or the fourth (or later with proper extension), do what ought to be done on the first, because if he could not expel him on the first day, he may nevertheless, on the next day and the next, gather his strength, collect arms, and call upon the aid of his friends; if he waits for a longer time, he will be taken to have condoned the *injuria* and to have extinguished it completely.[20]

The possessor who has been ejected keeps his seisin *animo*, though not *corpore*, after the dispossession, but after four days the failure on the part of the disseissee to regain his possession through self-help causes it to be lost, both *animo* and *corpore*, "by acquiescence, dissimulation, negligence, weakness, despair, or negligent impetration," and the disseisor acquires seisin.[21] At this point the disseisor cannot be disseised through self-help and will be reinstated in the property if self-help is used.[22] The true lord who has been disseised must rather bring an action on the assize himself in order to regain his property.[23]

The four-day rule for acquisition of seisin by a disseisor appears at odds with the one-year rule for acquisition of seisin by an intruder. In the next section we shall see that Maitland points this out in his article "The Beatitude of Seisin" and attempts to interpret and explain it, even though he is surprised that a disseisor should have only four days to wait before he obtains seisin while an intruder must wait so much longer. Sutherland adopts and approves Maitland's interpretation of Bracton but sheds light on the existing state of the law at the time. He points out that the existing cases on the assize of novel disseisin show no four-day rule being applied to give seisin to disseisors who seek protection of the assize. While he believes the rule is what Maitland interprets it to be, it did not exist in reality.

Sutherland's Dispute with Bracton as Interpreted by Maitland

Maitland explains the spirit of the assize of novel disseisin in Bracton's day by the following example:

> *A* is the true owner, or very tenant in fee simple, of land and is seised of it; he lives on it and cultivates it himself; there comes one *B* who has no right whatever; he casts *A* out and keeps him out, by force and arms. When, we must ask, does *A* cease to be seised and when does *B* begin to be seised?...*A* must turn *B* out within four days; otherwise *B* will have a seisin protected by the assize. Such is the case if *A* was actually on the land and was himself cast out.[24]

Maitland applauds the four-day rule over a no-time rule as "very natural, especially if there is to be a possessorium so strict that it will protect even a vicious possession [a possession obtained by the use of force] against self-help of the owner."[25] It would not be fair to allow a person who has disseised an owner—especially where the disseisor has achieved his objective by force—to remain in possession without giving the owner a chance to throw him back off the land. But Maitland is somewhat surprised that the owner has only four days to achieve the ejectment of his disseisor and remarks:

> This extreme rigour is so remarkable and yet has so seldom been remarked, that were not Bracton's text very clear I should doubt whether I had understood it; but I think that if others will read the whole book on the Novel Disseisin they will come to the conclusion that has here been stated.[26]

Maitland remarks on the discrepancy of the four-day rule when compared with the one-year rule for gaining seisin in the case of the intruder.[27] Maitland's

> explanation for this seeming favour shown to a disseisor as contrasted with an intruder, is that (albeit a disseisin is a much more serious injury than an intrusion) the person who is really entitled to be in possession is much more likely to get speedy notice of a disseisin than of an intrusion; he may well not know that a right to enter has accrued to him until the intruder has been upon the land for some months.[28]

Thus Maitland interprets Bracton to give only a four-day window of opportunity to the owner to eject a disseisor who has no right whatever to his land:

> [T]he main point which needs attention is this, that when once the short period of four days (or it may be a little longer) has elapsed, the disseisor has acquired a seisin which is protected against all men. If ejected even by the rightful owner, he will have the assize and he will be reinstated in his possession.[29]

Sutherland accepts Maitland's interpretation of Bracton's four-day rule, and repeats Maitland's observation that it created "a surprisingly tight limitation of the owner's right to self-help."[30] He then proceeds to demonstrate from an analysis of assize cases in the thirteenth century that there was no four-day rule but rather a much more permissive rule that allowed self-help over a longer period of time. As one example, he gives a case in which the presiding justice was Henry of Bracton himself:

> 1250. Robert sold his land to Walter and later sold the same land to Richard. Richard ejected Walter. Six months later, Walter returned and disseised Richard, who brought the assize. Ruled, that he may not recover.[31]

Other cases allowed a true heir to eject her disseisor after a period of two weeks, and a first purchaser from an owner to eject her disseisor who was the second purchaser from the owner without inquiry into how long she took to disseise him.[32]

On the other hand, it was possible to leave the disseisor in occupation of the land for too long, thus losing the right to disseise the disseisor. For example:

> In 1223 several freeholders were disseised of rights of common pasture when the owner of the soil ploughed and planted it. They waited until the crop sprang up and then claimed their common rights by putting their animals in to graze on the shoots. It was ruled that this was illegal.[33]
>
> In 1281 it was judged that where a tenant had allowed his neighbour to put up a bank that constituted a nuisance, and allowed the bank to stand undisturbed for a whole year, he might not thereafter throw it down on his own authority....[34]

Sutherland concludes that

> when we find that the rule was never used in litigation but that many cases were decided without reference to it, and when we consider how hesitantly and ambiguously Bracton puts it on the one occasion

> when he explains it directly, then surely his statement of it loses its power to govern the other passages in his treatise....[35]

Sutherland considers the four-day rule a product of Bracton's private speculation. There may well have been a four-day rule that no disseisor who gained his disseisin in the face of opposition was protected by the assize until he occupied the property for four days, but the corollary that every disseisor was thereafter protected no matter how bad his title "did not in fact follow, either in good logic or in English law."[36] In other words, Sutherland allows for the fact that some cases might have followed the four-day rule, but certainly not all the cases, as is demonstrated by his research.

A New Interpretation of the Concept of Seisin

The four-day rule certainly creates a puzzling situation in light of the fact that Bracton was not only a scholarly treatise writer but, in fact, a justice who presided over cases brought on the assize of novel disseisin.[37] How could he mistake so obviously a rule that he himself was in a situation to apply and appears to have actually ignored in those cases over which he presided where it was applicable? An answer to this enigma starts to suggest itself when reading the summary of a case provided by Sutherland concerning disseisins by heirs. The case is all the more interesting due to the fact that it also was heard by Bracton:

> 1250. John enfeoffed William of land and died four days later. William held for three weeks; then John's heir came and disseised him. Henry of Bracton, who heard the case, ruled that his three weeks' seisin was not sufficient in itself to get William a recovery by the assize; he had to prove that the feoffment had been complete, effective, and valid.[38]

William remains in possession for more than four days before John's heir dispossesses him, yet he loses the action on the assize for failure to prove his own better right through a valid feoffment. Under Maitland's interpretation of Bracton, he should win on the assize because three weeks should be enough to give him seisin. This is a good example by Sutherland to show that the cases vary from Maitland's interpretation of Bracton. But this case has an added element. If William had been able to prove a valid feoffment from John, he would have prevailed. In other words, three weeks' possession was not enough to give seisin to William if he could not prove the valid feoffment, but he would have had seisin if he could have proved it. The key to explaining Bracton's four-day rule may lie in the proof of a better right to ownership as between the two parties.

Sutherland focusses on the fact that "[t]he rule that the courts really used was that the *owner* could disseise a usurper provided that he acted without undue delay,"[39] which is seen in several cases to extend as much as several months. But how long did a *nonowner*, who could claim a better right than the usurper to the property only by prior possession, have to dispossess a usurper? Could it be that a nonowner (or at least one who could not prove his better right to ownership of the property in the action on the assize) could disseise a usurper only if he acted within the four-day period? We have already seen that a prior possessor can remove a usurper from his possession if the prior possessor brings an action on the assize. Prior possession is superior in right to subsequent possession, and the prior possessor gains seisin immediately against one having no right. The issue here, however, is how long a prior possessor has in order to exercise self-help to regain his possession. A careful reading of Bracton suggests that Bracton does in fact state a four-day rule for nonowner prior possessors to regain their property from a usurper, while owner prior possessors have one year. Maitland did not see this distinction because Bracton was exceedingly unclear in his discussion of the issue.

First, Bracton discusses the case of intrusion in which he gives the owner of the property a full year to recover the land through self-help.[40] At this point he does not discuss the case of a disseisin because he is still in the chapter on civil actions and saves the discussion of disseisins for the next chapter on the assize of novel disseisin. However, the result is to leave this case of intrusion as a seeming anomaly in light of his subsequent statements concerning the four-day rule for disseisins. It would have been helpful for Bracton to indicate at this point that the one-year period also applied to disseisins so as to allow an owner of the property a full year to recover the land through self-help.

Later when Bracton discusses the four-day rule, he begins by referring to *ille qui ita disseisitus est* (him who was so disseised), then to the *disseisitus* (disseised), then to the *possessor* (possessor).[41] But then Bracton begins to use the term *verus dominus* (true lord/true owner) to describe the disseisee.[42] This is unfortunate because it immediately gives the impression that the true lord is subject to the four-day rule. In fact, Bracton uses the term true lord in this context to indicate that even a true lord would be subject to defeat under the assize "[i]f he disdains the assise and presumes to usurp his possession by force rather than judgment."[43] The idea is not that a true lord would be subject to the four-day rule, but that the true lord must not be negligent by allowing his disseisor to gain seisin before he has exercised his self-help. The time lapse that must occur before the true lord is considered negligent in not pursuing self-help is not discussed at this point in Bracton's text.

Then Bracton states that "one who has a wrongful seisin, *by disseisin or intrusion*, and is disseised by one having no right" has sufficient seisin to prevail in an action on the assize as a prior possessor against the one having no right.[44] On the other hand, he may not prevail on the assize against a true lord and "may be ejected with impunity by the true lord if time sufficient for title has not passed."[45] It is uncertain from this text what passage of time must occur before possession ripens into the "title" of seisin. Bracton merely states that "if the [disseisor or intruder] holds peacefully for a time, he cannot be ejected by the true lord without writ and judgment, provided the time is such as may suffice for title."[46] It would have been helpful if Bracton had stated at this point that the passage of time is about a year.

So much for the confusion that Bracton's text engenders. What does Bracton state that demonstrates his distinction between the four-day rule and the one-year rule for dispossessors depending on whether they can prove their true ownership? In the passage on the intruder, Bracton specifies one year (according to some) as the period of time that must pass before a true heir is prevented from ejecting an intruder.[47] In an earlier passage on acquiring possession, he had stated that title by seisin can be gained "where one has put himself into vacant seisin by intrusion" by "long, continuous and peaceful possession."[48] Therefore, long, continuous, and peaceful possession can be equated to the one-year period mentioned in the passage on the intruder. Further inspection of the passage on acquiring possession then reveals that in the same context that the intruder gains seisin after long, continuous, and peaceful possession, so also does a disseisor after a disseisin.[49] It is apparent in this passage that the disseisor gains title by seisin only after the year is over.

Also, Bracton speaks of the intruder and disseisor together in a later passage concerning those who are protected by the assize.[50] Both are protected by the assize if they are disseised by one having no right. The feoffees of both are protected by the assize if they are disseised by a true owner without writ or judgment, as long as they have held "peacefully for a time" that is "such as may suffice for title." Both "may be ejected with impunity by the true lord if time sufficient for title has not passed." Bracton also states: "Similarly, remedy and restitution by the assise lies for him who is in seisin wholly without any title, by disseisin or intrusion, and is disseised without judgment, against all, whether they have right or not, provided he has the time that suffices for title." By speaking of the intruder and the disseisor together in this way, Bracton's reference to "time that suffices for title" is strongly suggestive that the time is the same for both. Since it is one year for the intruder who is dispossessed by a true owner, then it follows that it would be one year for the disseisor who is dispossessed by a true owner.

While the one-year rule can be derived implicitly from Bracton's work for the case of the disseisor who is dispossessed by the true owner, Bracton states the four-day rule explicitly. A disseisor gains seisin four days after his disseisin, and the disseisee who retakes the land after four days violates the assize of novel disseisin.[51] This passage starts from the premise that there are two self-help ejections. It does not mention that either party is the true owner but speaks about disseisor and disseisee. The only evidence of better right in this case is the prior possession of the first possessor. When read in light of the passages analyzed above for the one-year rule, Bracton appears to be saying that a prior possessor who cannot prove that he is a true owner is given four days to regain his possession through self-help, but if he can prove he is a true owner, then he is given one year.

This new interpretation of Bracton accords with the cases that Sutherland uses to reject an absolute four-day rule. In Bracton's 1250 case where John's heir disputes the possession of land with William, William claims he was enfeoffed by John.[52] William takes the land under claim of right as the enfeoffee of John. His dispossessor takes the land from him three weeks later under claim of right as John's heir. There does not appear to be any question that the dispossessor is John's true heir. The heir has apparently satisfied his burden to prove that he is. At this point the burden of proof shifts to William to prove that he is John's feoffee: "he had to prove that the feoffment had been complete, effective, and valid."[53] If he satisfies his burden of proof, then he wins the action on the assize because he is the true lord. If he does not satisfy his burden (and he does not), then he loses on the action because John's heir is considered the true lord and his pursuit of the remedy of self-help ejectment within one year, namely three weeks, is valid.

Maitland's interpretation of Bracton misses the point when he uses the example of a true owner ejected by one who has no right whatever and states that the true owner has only four days to eject his disseisor through self-help.[54] The true owner who can prove as much in the action on the assize has one year, not only according to the cases as pointed out by Sutherland, but also according to Bracton when Bracton is properly interpreted. The four-day rule applies only to the dispossessed prior possessor who cannot prove ownership relative to his dispossessor. If the prior possessor cannot eject his dispossessor within four days, then his remedy is to bring an action on the assize to get his possession back. The assize is available upon disseisin not only to the true owner but also to this prior possessor. It is also available to one who has been disseised by a true owner if the true owner has abused the system and used self-help to reinstate himself upon the land after the passage of one year. The assize is available in the latter case to the non-owner not for being wrongfully disseised but rather for being disseised without judgment.[55] At this point the only remedy the true owner will have left is an action on the writ of right.[56]

Having clarified the concept of seisin as it was protected in the action on the assize of novel disseisin, we turn now to its comparison with the concept of *ḥawz* in Islamic law. Both seisin and *ḥawz* indicate a level of possession that receives protection beyond naked possession (known as *yad* in Islamic law). As we will see, these two concepts are remarkably similar in their constitutive elements, their legal effects, and the procedures by which they are proved in court.

The Constitutive Elements of Seisin and *Ḥawz*

As noted above, the conditions for obtaining seisin as against a true owner in English law are stated by Bracton to be "long, continuous and peaceful possession."[57] He states that the length of time is "left to rightly exercised discretion,"[58] but he indicates in his passage on the intruder that it is one year according to some.[59] The time must also be continuous. It is not continuous if the true lord makes even an unsuccessful effort to eject the possessor or brings an action and diligently pursues it to remove the possessor. The time must also be peaceful, that is, without dispute by a rightful claimant. Bracton states that if such a possession satisfying these three elements is obtained, then possessors gain "a free tenement, so that they cannot be ejected without writ and judgment."[60] But there is also a fourth element. Bracton states that

> possession and a free tenement is acquired through time, without title and livery, by the acquiescence and negligence of the true lord,... unless it is by license, which can be revoked at any time; and so if it is of grace, for grace is a matter of will and such are revoked by a contrary will; and so where it is by stealth, as where [it is enjoyed] by night or granted by bailiffs in the absence of their lords; and so if it is for an uncertain payment, changed and altered each year or each time.[61]

The qualification that a possession by license or grace cannot ripen into seisin establishes a further condition that the possessor must hold the land as his own and not in the name of another person.

The conditions for obtaining *ḥawz* in Islamic law are quite similar: (1) manucaption of the thing (*waḍʿ al-yad ʿalā l-shayʾ*), (2) enjoyment of ownership (*taṣarruf al-milk*) coupled with the open claim of ownership (*daʿwā l-milk*), (3) by the possessor claiming it for himself (*iḍāfatuhu ilā nafsihi*), (4) passage of a long duration of time (*ṭūl al-zamān*), i.e., ten months or one year, during which time the land does not leave the possessor's patrimony, and (5) absence of contestant (*ʿadam al-munāziʿ*).[62] Furthermore, the taking of possession must not be by grace, i.e., a taking by the will of the grantor, or by usurpation (*ghaṣb*), i.e., a taking unjustly the good of another by violence.[63]

The Legal Effects of Seisin and *Ḥawz*

The legal effect of obtaining the status of seisin is to protect against disseisin through self-help by any other person, including the true owner. Seisin is gained immediately against a person who has no right and dispossesses a prior possessor; the prior possessor can use self-help to regain his possession within four days or he can bring an action on the assize to regain his possession. Suppose, however, that a prior possessor is dispossessed by a person having no right but does not bring an action on the assize until the second possessor has enjoyed a "long, continuous and peaceful possession" of one year? In other words, let us assume that A, having no right whatsoever in Blackacre (land that is owned by O), enters and possesses it, following which B, having no right whatsoever in Blackacre, enters it, ejects A, and possesses it for one year in continuous and peaceful possession. Can the prior possessor still regain his possession by bringing an action on the assize? Or does this change the status of B towards A so that now B can withstand not only an attempt by A at self-help repossession but also an attempt to regain possession through an action on the assize?

Bracton states that as between two possessors having no right to the property, the first possessor wins on the assize "since neither of them has right, neither fee nor free tenement."[64] This remark suggests that if one were to have a free tenement there would be some right to possession that does not otherwise exist. A free tenement is gained by an intruder through the "long, continuous and peaceful possession" of one year. Could it not also be obtained in this time period by a second possessor against his prior possessor, and, if so, could it not also give him sufficient title through seisin to withstand the prior possessor's action on the assize? Bracton does not give us this rule in so many words, but it makes sense. It would also follow that if the prior possessor could establish seisin of long, continuous, and peaceful duration preceding that of the subsequent possessor, then the prior possessor would win. In other words, as between two possessors with no right in the property other than their possession, the one having seisin of "long, continuous and peaceful possession" of one year will prevail on the assize, and if both have such seisin, the one who is prior will prevail.

Islamic law espouses this very principle in its concept of *ḥawz*. Where one does not know to whom the origin of property belongs (*mā juhila aṣl al-milk li-man huwa*) as in the example above of A and B, A would win if A had *ḥawz*, regardless of whether B had *ḥawz* or not, but A would lose to B if A did not have *ḥawz* and B had.[65] *Ḥawz* is a seisin of long, continuous, and peaceful duration, and if the interpretation of Bracton is correct in the preceding paragraph, then *ḥawz* accomplishes in Islamic law the same legal effect as this concept of seisin accomplishes in the common law.

The Procedures by which Seisin and *Ḥawz* are Proved

The procedures by which seisin and *ḥawz* are proved in court differ on some details but on the whole are very similar. In an action on the assize of novel disseisin, the English plaintiff makes his plaint to a court that has jurisdiction to order execution of judgment.[66] The court then sends a writ to the sheriff containing the names of the plaintiff and the defendant and directing him to ensure that the property is secure against usurpation or transfer, to take pledges for prosecuting from the plaintiff, to "cause twelve free and lawful men of that neighborhood to view the tenement and cause their names to be written down," and to summon them to the recognition and ensure by gage and safe pledges that the defendant is there as well.[67] The defendant can then challenge the propriety of the complaint for procedural defects, such as the manner in which he was brought into court, and, if this does not work, can then give a direct denial or a justification of his circumstances to which the plaintiff has then to respond.[68] The process of claim and counterclaim back and forth between the parties helps to narrow the issue to a specific question that can then be put to the assize for resolution.

The assize is a group of people designated to determine who has the better case on the basis of evidence reviewed. It is composed of a body of twelve sworn people drawn from the neighborhood to give an answer unanimously about a matter each of them has seen or heard, which is binding on the judge, to settle the truth concerning facts in a case between ordinary people, which case is submitted to the assize upon a judicial writ obtained as of right by the plaintiff.[69] Since the truth is important, hearsay beyond reliable reports is not allowed.[70] No longer is the determination of truth in such a case left to divine intervention as it had been originally in the writ of right when proof was achieved through a duel. The assize is charged with investigating and determining truth by each person's own knowledge, and this task makes it important for the parties to get their case clearly before it.[71] As Milsom puts it, "[t]he court, no longer just presiding over the ritual formulation of a question to be put to an oracle beyond the need of human guidance, but now in some way responsible for the answer, may be inclined to let the defendant depart from the ancient general denial, and to specify his own facts."[72] The process of pleading has now become "an uncomfortable necessity imposed by the jury, whose fallibility ha[s] broken up the comfortable old pattern of a general question to be put to an infallible test."[73]

In the action for recovery of property (*istiḥqāq*) in Maliki Islamic law, the plaintiff who claims to be owner of the land files a complaint (*maqāl*) claiming that the defendant has taken his land without right. The judge (*qāḍī*) then invites the defendant to recognize the facts alleged by the plaintiff or to deny them. Of course, if the defendant recognizes the facts by an acknowledgment, the case is over, but if he does not, he gives a general denial with a claim of ownership ("it is my property and my possession") without being required to indicate how he owns the property. Since the defendant is presumed to own the property from the fact of his possession (*yad*) of it, it is the plaintiff who has the burden of proof of his ownership either by testimonial proof (*mulkiyya*) or proof that he has acquired the land from the defendant. It is not until this proof is provided that the defendant is required to challenge the propriety of the complaint on procedural grounds or to give a justification for his denial of the substance of the complaint.[74]

The plaintiff is allowed some delays during which to provide his proof until the judge sets a final delay (*talawwum*) of three days. If the proof is not forthcoming, the judge nonsuits him, the defendant wins on the basis of his possession, and the matter becomes res judicata (*ḥakama ʿalayhi bi-qaṭʿ ḥujjatihi*). In this way the mere possession (*yad*) of the land becomes the presumption of ownership (*milk*). If the Islamic plaintiff provides testimonial proof (*mulkiyya*), he produces an evidentiary document (*bayyina*), which states that the claimant is the owner of the land. This document is attested by two honorable witnesses (*ʿudūl*, who are qualified by the process of *tazkiya* to testify) or by twelve good witnesses (*lafīf*, who are men of good life and customs but who have not undergone the process of *tazkiya*).[75]

The *lafīf* is a body of twelve sworn people drawn from the neighborhood to give an answer unanimously about a matter they have seen or heard, which is binding on the judge, to settle the truth concerning facts in a case between ordinary people, which case is submitted to the jury as of right by the plaintiff.[76] When the testimony of the witnesses is taken for the purpose of documenting it, it is generally agreed that each witness must expressly indicate the existence of each one of the conditions unless the witness is learned. In addition, the witness must indicate the basis of his knowledge (*mustanad*), such as frequentation (*mukhālaṭa*) of the land, neighborly relations (*mujāwara*), direct view of the facts (*muʿāyana*), and personal examination of the facts (*al-iṭṭilāʿ ʿalā l-aḥwāl*). Direct affirmative testimony (*shahādat al-batt*) is the usual form of such testimony, but testimony by common report or of public notoriety (*shahādat al-istifāda*) is also permitted; testimony by hearsay (*shahādat al-samaʿ*), what the witness hears some other unnamed person say, is not permitted.[77]

Once the evidence (*bayyina*) is produced by the plaintiff, the judge interpellates (by a procedure called *iʿdhār*) the defendant on it and invites him to submit (*taslīm*) to it or to defend against it. The defendant is first permitted to raise exceptions to the testimonial proof, such as the fact that the witnesses are incompetent by reason of enmity (*ʿadāwa*) towards him or complacence (*mulāṭafa*) toward the plaintiff, or the witnesses have retracted (*rujūʿ*) their testimony, or the testimony is improbable (*istibʿād*) or suspicious (*istirāba*) or lacks a legal basis (*mustanad*), or there are contradictions (*tanāquḍ*) between the terms of the complaint and the testimonial proof, or one of the conditions for establishing the proof of ownership is missing in the *bayyina*. If the defendant raises an exception, the judge then has to interpellate the plaintiff on it and, if the exceptions raised by the defendant prove to be good, the case can be won by the defendant on this basis. If not, then the burden of proof shifts to the defendant who is permitted to defend his own ownership by stating the basis of his claim and proving it.[78]

If the defendant agrees with the plaintiff's proof he can defend by countering with proof that he acquired the land from the plaintiff. This proof is usually accomplished by producing a document of purchase or gift notarized with the testimony of two *ʿudūl* witnesses (or possibly by twelve *lafīf* witnesses) at the time of the acquisition. It is not sufficient to prove that the land has been acquired from a third party because the mere possession of the property by the third party at the time of transfer does not prove ownership by the third party. If proof of acquisition from the plaintiff is produced by the defendant, the judge then interpellates the plaintiff by the *iʿdhār* procedure, much the same way as for testimonial proof. If the plaintiff cannot win by way of an exception to the validity of the defendant's proof, the plaintiff is then nonsuited because it is not possible for him to use witnesses to affirm the fact that the land never left his patrimony.[79]

On the other hand, the defendant can produce proof by introducing his own evidence of ownership (*mulkiyya*). If this proof is not reconcilable with the plaintiff's, then there is a conflict of *mulkiyya*s between the parties. The judge then interpellates (*iʿdhār*) the plaintiff on the defendant's proof and invites him to submit (*taslīm*) to it or to defend against it. The plaintiff is first permitted to raise exceptions to the testimonial proof, and if he does so, the judge then has to interpellate the defendant on it to the end that if the exception proves good, the plaintiff can win his case. If not, then the judge has to determine which of the two proofs is to receive preference (*tarjīḥ*). He gives the preference to the proof that indicates ownership extending further back in time (on the principle that there is a presumption of continuity (*istiṣḥāb*) in favor of the older proof). If the two proofs are of equal value and neither is preferred, then they are annulled reciprocally (*tasāqaṭa*). The possessor wins the case by virtue of his possession. If both parties have possession of the property, then it is partitioned between them.[80]

The comparison of seisin with *ḥawz* demonstrates the remarkable similarities that exist between the two concepts—similarities that support my thesis concerning the Islamic origins of the common law. Although historiographical problems in determining the precise nature of seisin have obstructed our view in this area, it is hoped that this article has helped to clarify the obscurities and focus attention on the kindred nature of seisin and *ḥawz* in their constitutive elements, their legal effects, and the procedures by which each of these concepts were used to provide protection for possession as proof of ownership.

NOTES

[1] Proof by battle was founded on the belief that God would intervene. The plaintiff proposed battle by a complaint witness, and the defendant met this challenge with a champion of his own. The case was decided for the victor whom God was considered to have favored. This form of proof was introduced to England by the Normans in the eleventh century and it persisted until it was abolished by statute in 1819. Other actions also used forms of proof primarily founded on the belief that God would intervene with a sign of the truth or would induce fear that would generate the truth. In the proof by ordeal, a person carried a red-hot iron or was lowered into a pool of water. If the hand did not burn or the body did not sink, the person was pronounced innocent. Proof by compurgation relied on the fear that the oath-taker would have of incurring God's punishment if he took a false oath. The defendant swore to his denial of the plaintiff's claim and a designated number of compurgators supported his denial by their own oaths that he was telling the truth. James Thayer, *A Preliminary Treatise on Evidence at the Common Law* (New York 1969), 25, 35 n. 1, 39, 43, 45; Austin Lane Poole, *From Domesday Book to Magna Carta 1087–1216* (Oxford [2]1955), 402; William Holdsworth, *A History of English Law* (Methuen [5]1942), 1:305, 310.

[2] The assize of novel disseisin is thought to have been instituted in the middle of the 1160s. Maitland states that "a definitely possessory remedy does not seem native to the law of our own race; that when it appears in England..., it bears witness to the influence of alien jurisprudence." Frederic W. Maitland, "The Beatitude of Seisin I," *L. Quarterly Rev.* 4 (1888), 26 [hereinafter Maitland, "Beatitude"]. Maitland thought that this alien jurisprudence was Roman law, possibly working through the medium of Canon law, but he noted that there was not an exact correlation. See Maitland, "Beatitude," 26–7. My own work suggests that the action originated from the action of *istiḥqāq* in Islamic law. See John Makdisi, "The Islamic Origins of the Common Law," *N. Car. L. Rev.* 77 (1999), 1681–85 [hereinafter Makdisi, "Islamic Origins"].

[3] Seisin is described by Maitland as *assize-possession*. See Frederic W. Maitland, "The Mystery of Seisin," *L. Quarterly Rev.* 2 (1886), 493 n. 1. This is an appropriate synonym because the possessory right called seisin that was protected by the assize of novel disseisin was not given to every possessor, but rather only to certain people in certain situations. The action on the assize thus caused the concept of seisin to become quite unique as a hybrid between possession and ownership. Maitland also emphasized in a later article how summary this action was: "To begin with, 'personal service' (to use a modern term) was unnecessary; to attach the defendant's bailiff was enough; there could be no essoin; there could be no vouching to warranty of any one not named in the writ; the assize could be taken by default, no pleading to issue was necessary; the question for the recognitors was defined in the writ." Maitland, "Beatitude," 28.

[4] Frederic W. Maitland, "The Mystery of Seisin," *L. Quarterly Rev.* 2 (1886), 481.

[5] Frederic W. Maitland, "The Beatitude of Seisin," *L. Quarterly Rev.* 4 (1888), 24 (part I), 286 (part II).

[6] *Bracton on the Laws and Customs of England,* transl. Samuel E. Thorne (Cambridge, Mass.: Harvard University Press, 1977) [hereinafter Bracton].

[7] Donald Sutherland, *The Assize of Novel Disseisin* (Oxford: Clarendon Press, 1973) [hereinafter Sutherland].

[8] *The Treatise on the Laws and Customs of the Realm of England Commonly Called Glanvill,* ed. G. D. G. Hall and M. T. Clanchy (Oxford: Clarendon Press, 1993).

[9] John Makdisi, "The Islamic Origins of the Common Law," *N. Car. L. Rev.* 77 (1999), 1635.

[10] "Islamic" in this study refers to the Maliki school of legal thought that existed in North Africa and Sicily in the eleventh and twelfth centuries when the Normans invaded Sicily. Maliki law was used by the Normans in their governance of Sicily and, through the many contacts that existed between England and Sicily at this time, was known by the Normans who governed England. Makdisi, "Islamic Origins," 1717–30.

[11] Bracton, 3:13.

[12] A vacant possession is one that is "possessed neither *corpore* nor *animo*," such as property where the owner has died and the heir has not yet entered upon the property. Bracton, 3:14; also Bracton, 2:157. Seisin may be acquired *corpore* and *animo* in a number of ways, such as by receiving land as a gift and farming it. If the person leaves the property on a journey and leaves no one in possession, he still has seisin *animo* but not *corpore* until he returns. If the person dies on his property, he has seisin *corpore* but not *animo* until his body is taken from the property. Seisin is not lost until it is lost both *corpore* and *animo*. Bracton, 2:130–34, 154–56; Bracton, 3:270; Frederick Pollock and Frederic William Maitland, *The History of English Law before the Time of Edward I* (Cambridge [2]1898), 2:34.

[13] Bracton, 3:13.

[14] Ibid., 3:13–14.

[15] Ibid., 3:15–16 (emphasis added).

[16] Ibid., 3:27.

[17] Ibid., 2:157.

[18] Ibid., 3:23–4.

[19] See n. 12, supra.

[20] Bracton, 3:22. A possessor who is absent from the property has more time in which to use self-help to regain his property before the disseisor gains seisin. The amount of extra time is determined by how far away he is at the time, when he could have found out about the disseisin, and the reason for his absence. For example, if he were out of the country on a pilgrimage to St. James, he would have a little over 59 days to use self-help. See ibid., 3:22–3.

[21] Ibid., 3:22–3.

[22] Ibid., 3:23–4. As in the case of the intruder, the possessor using self-help, once he has been removed from the property by the action on the assize, will be barred from use of the assize thereafter. The true owner must seek his remedy through the writ of right.

[23] Ibid., 3:23.

[24] Maitland, "Beatitude," 28–9.

25 Ibid., 32.
26 Ibid., 33–4.
27 This discrepancy was noticed in another treatise written in the thirteenth century called *Britton*. *Britton* was based on Bracton's treatise and was popular for centuries, but its authorship remains uncertain. Theodore F. T. Plucknett, *A Concise History of the Common Law* (Boston [5]1956), 265–66. Maitland states that *Britton* "objects, 'because it seemeth to me that an intruder should not be in a worse condition than a disseisor would be;' a remark which shows once more that, in his opinion, a disseisor would gain protection in less than a year." Maitland, "Beatitude," 34 (footnote omitted).
28 Maitland, "Beatitude," 34.
29 Ibid., 33.
30 Sutherland, 98, 102.
31 Ibid., 99.
32 Ibid., 98, 100.
33 Ibid., 100.
34 Ibid., 101.
35 Ibid., 102.
36 Ibid., 103.
37 Bracton's *Tractatus de Legibus et Consuetudinibus Angliae* was completed before the end of 1256. Samuel E. Thorne, "Translator's Introduction" to Bracton, 1: vii, xlii. Bracton was a justice in the court *coram rege* from October 1247 till about July 1251, and from June 1253 till about July 1257. From his first recorded assize commission in February 1248 until October 1257, the close and patent rolls show that Bracton received 355 assize commissions, and even a few more after that time. C. A. F. Meekings, "Henry de Bracton, Canon of Wells," *Studies in 13th Century Justice and Administration* 7 (1981), 141–43.
38 Sutherland, 107.
39 Ibid., 103 (emphasis added).
40 Bracton, 3:15–16.
41 Ibid., 3:21–2.
42 Ibid., 3:23–4.
43 Ibid., 3:23.
44 Ibid., 3:27 (emphasis added).
45 Ibid., 3:27.
46 Ibid., 3:27.
47 Ibid., 3:15–16.
48 Ibid., 2:157.
49 Ibid., 2:157.
50 Ibid., 3:27.
51 Ibid., 3:22.
52 Sutherland, 107. See text at n. 38, supra.
53 Idem, 107.
54 See text at n. 24, supra.
55 Bracton, 3:23. Bracton confirms this point further on when he states that the "remedy and restitution by the assise lies for him who is in seisin wholly without any title, by disseisin or intrusion, and is disseised without judgment, against all,

whether they have right or not, provided he has the time that suffices for title. Ibid., 3:27. The time that suffices for title in this case would apparently be that which gives him a free tenement, i.e., one year.

[56] Ibid., 3:23–4.

[57] Ibid., 2:156.

[58] Ibid.

[59] Ibid., 3:15.

[60] Ibid., 2:157.

[61] Ibid.

[62] J. Lappanne-Joinville, *Recueil de jurisprudence chérifienne* (Paris 1952), 4:173 [hereinafter Lappanne-Joinville]. The claiming of the land for oneself is also known as attribution (*nisba*). Ibid., 192.

[63] Ibid., 219, 221–22.

[64] Bracton, 3:27.

[65] Lappanne-Joinville, 175.

[66] Bracton, 3:46.

[67] Ibid., 3:57–8.

[68] Robert C. Palmer, *The County Courts of Medieval England: 1150–1350* (Princeton 1982), 90.

[69] Makdisi, "Islamic Origins," 1681–85. A typical writ that was given to one who was disseised of his free tenement unjustly and without judgment is provided in Book 32, Chapter 33 of Glanvill, *supra* n. 8, at 167–68:

> The king to the sheriff, greeting. N. has complained to me that R. unjustly and without a judgment has disseised him of his free tenement in such-and-such a vill since my last voyage to Normandy. Therefore, I command you that, if N. gives you security for prosecuting his claim, you are to see that the chattels which were taken from the tenement are restored to it, and that the tenement and the chattels remain in peace until the Sunday after Easter. And meanwhile you are to see that the tenement is viewed by twelve free and lawful men of the neighbourhood, and their names endorsed on this writ. And summon them by good summoners to be before me or my justices on the Sunday after Easter, ready to make the recognition. And summon R., or his bailiff if he himself cannot be found, on the security of the gage and reliable sureties to be there then to hear the recognition. And have there the summoners, and this writ and the names of the sureties. Witness, etc.

[70] See Melville Madison Bigelow, *History of Procedure in England from the Norman Conquest* (Rothman Reprints, 1972, [1]1880), 335 (emphasizing that the jurors have to be "sufficiently acquainted with the facts by personal knowledge or by reliable report ('de visu et auditu,' in the language of the time)"); C. T. Flower, *Introduction to the Curia Regis Rolls, 1199–1230 A.D.* (London 1944), 444–45 (reporting a case where a report "by many and by those who best ought to know the truth of the matter" is considered acceptable).

[71] See Thayer, supra n. 1, at 114 (discussing the situation of a jury that has to decide a special pleading). The terms *assize* and *jury* are closely related but do serve to distinguish two different functions that were performed by each respective body of twelve neighbors:

> Such a body called in, not by the original writ, but in the course of the action, to determine a question of fact raised by the pleadings, gets the name

> of a jury (*jurata*) as contrasted with an assize (*assisa*); the *assisa* is summoned by the 'original' writ issued out of the chancery before there has been any pleading; the *jurata* is summoned by a 'judicial' writ issuing out of the court before which the action is proceeding, and it comes to answer a question raised by the pleadings. Any considerable development of this principle, however, lies in the future; in Glanvill's book we see no more than this, that the practice of referring a disputed question to a body of 'recognitors' is beginning to extend itself outside the limits of the assizes.

F. W. Maitland, *The Form of Action at Common Law: A Course of Lectures*, ed. A. H. Chaytor and W. J. Whittaker (Cambridge 1909, 1936), 28–9.

[72] S. F. C. Milsom, *Historical Foundations of the Common Law* (^{2}1981), 42.

[73] Ibid., 59.

[74] Lapanne-Joinville, 170–71.

[75] Ibid., 171–72. A description of the *ʿudūl* and the *lafīf* can be found in Louis Milliot, *Introduction a l'étude du droit musulman* (Paris 1953), 737–38, and Louis Milliot, *Recueil de jurisprudence chérifienne* (Paris 1920), 1:116–24, both of which are translated in Makdisi, "Islamic Origins," 1732–39.

[76] Makdisi, "Islamic Origins," 1695.

[77] Lapanne-Joinville, 174–75.

[78] Ibid., 178.

[79] Ibid., 180, 188–89.

[80] Ibid., 180–82, 184–85.

3

"LEGAL REALISM" IN TEHRAN
Gender Law and the Transformative State

Louise Halper

In Iran, where what Robin Wright calls "the last great revolution" took place a quarter-century ago,[1] political transformation was intended, at least according to the Islamist groups that succeeded in taking power, to effect divine governance. In the construction of the post-revolutionary state, there was no discovery of a new legal system, no jurisprudential search for law that matched the times, of the sort that led to the Code Napoléon or the Soviet legal code. Instead, the aim of the new leaders of Iran was to govern by divine law, as expressed in revelation, in traditions of the Prophet and his Imamic descendants, and in the practices of interpretation by religious scholars. The law the state would apply predated the state that was to apply it; indeed, the application of that law was the whole purpose of the state.

Governance by divine law (*siyāsa sharʿiyya*) was hardly new. Other states and state-like entities had for centuries been successfully governed in that manner, with space allowed for custom, the practical needs of governance, and the exigencies of administration. But in the years since Western colonialism and imperialism penetrated the Muslim world, religious law had been to a large extent cut off from the quotidian practices of the state, as civil codes in fields considered central to the projects of modernization and/or Westernization replaced the Islamic juristic tools of analogy, comparison, and non-precedential, but persuasive, scholarly opinion. Codified fields included commercial law, and hence, to a large extent, the law of contract; the law of injury (whether public criminal law or the private law of delict/tort); and the administration of law.

From the mid-nineteenth-century Ottoman *Mecelle* onward, the history of law in the Muslim world is in large part a history of displacement, replacement, and substitution of the body of the law. While juristic religious scholarship remained central only to the law of marriage, family, and succession, and was constrained even there, in the colonial situation, legal constraints on marriage were direct. Indirect in the formally non-colonial state, they nonetheless reflected the control even that state had, in its processes for registering marriage and divorce, over what had once been simply a private contract, which like most other contracts, was enforced privately by religious law.

The Iranian revolution of 1979 produced the first reversal of the movement away from religious law. A civil code containing both public and private law, and constraining, though not replacing, the Islamic law of marriage and family, was eliminated, and *siyāsa shar'iyya* was established. In the West, that turn was largely understood as a re-turn: religious fundamentalists were attempting to recreate a medieval world, figuratively turning their backs on the turn to modernity and to the West that the Shah had represented.[2]

Re-turn was perhaps the *tropos* of some. Yet it was certainly clear at that moment, though it seems to have become much less so in the ensuing years, that the mobilization of Iranian society against the Pahlavi dynasty was broad enough to encompass virtually every ideology that existed in the Iran of that day: secularists, left, liberal and conservative; Islamists from reddest red to greenest green; atheists and agnostics; Communists, nationalists, tribalists; feminists and anti-feminists; workers, blue-collar and white-; peasants and bureaucrats; bazaaris and intellectuals—the anti-Shah movement was as inclusive a coalition as imaginable.

Inevitably, differences that had melted in the heat of revolution crystallized again when the question was no longer ousting the monarchy, but replacing it. The prestige of Ayatollah Khomeini as both leader and symbol of opposition carried over to popular support for the constitution of an Islamic Republic, but even he could not alone determine how Iran was to be governed. The politics of the immediate post-revolutionary moment required of Khomeini an effort to keep a grip on the coalition that had overthrown the Shah.

He was challenged by events and circumstances, both internal and external. First, each substantial part of the coalition had its own aims. The aims of some could be realized within an Islamic state, to which the strong left secular forces were wholly or somewhat opposed. Second and not unrelated to the first, the United States, as sponsor of the Shah, would be immediately antagonistic to any form of government that did not assume a position like that of the Shah vis-à-vis the United States in the Cold War. While Khomeini was anti-Communist, he had had leftist allies in the revolution; and, at the same time, he was anti-American as well. Third, the revolution had itself awakened ideas or created demands among constituencies that had hitherto not been directly salient in politics.

It is of the third point that I want to speak and in particular, of women. The "Woman Question," the issue of women's rights, and in particular, of their suffrage, had certainly been in politics in the period before the revolution, but women themselves were not, by and large, political actors. In the early sixties, as opposition to the Pahlavi dynasty became fiercer, and Shah Mohammad Reza looked for new sectors of support to balance the ever-larger opposition forces, he had tried to mobilize women into his so-called "White Revolution."[3] But it was precisely on the issue of votes for women that Khomeini (at least ostensibly) first emerged into public opposition in 1963.[4] In fact, it was not the Shah, but the anti-Shah coalition, that succeeded in mobilizing women, including women from the working class and the peasantry who hitherto had no political voice or presence in the public sphere.

Women of the popular classes were for the most part devout and their anti-Shah sentiment was overwhelmingly with Khomeini, who urged their participation in the revolutionary opposition. Indeed, his opposition to female suffrage did not survive the demise of the Shah. In the struggle over power that immediately replaced the successful anti-Shah struggle with competition among the anti-Shah forces, women's support was both crucial and available to the supporters of the Islamic Republic and its constitution of Shariʿa.

Thus, the birth of the Islamic Republic of Iran (IRI) took place in a social context at odds with that figured in the tradition of *siyāsa sharʿiyya*. Women, and in particular, women of the popular classes, had been solicited as active participants in the public space and they were for the first time in a position to exert their agency politically. Moreover, this had happened in a transformative context, where the claim of many of those whose religion coincided with their politics was that the divine message was one of equality and social justice. Social justice had never existed since the days of the Prophetic and Imamic leadership,[5] but under the divine law, it could return. That promise would be hard to redeem, but it was harder still to revoke.

But the new power relations of the post-revolutionary moment made re-turn to divine law problematic, for the divine law itself was problematized, in the sense that its meanings had to be rethought and the law itself recontextualized. While that process is in theory never alien to Shariʿa, in practice such a large-scale recontextualization as that demanded by the creation of an Islamic republic was unfamiliar.

As I have noted above, the most temporally proximate examples of recasting Shariʿa were, in their essence, retreats. In the period of colonialism and neocolonialism, the question had been what parts of divine law could survive the penetration of a dominating external force and what could be held in abeyance or modified or preserved for the future. But the Iranian revolution presented the opposite question: how could divine law be resuscitated as the constitution of a new Islamic state that understood itself as wholly committed to the just purposes of the divine for humanity?

In regard to women, revolutionary success posed the most interesting question: what did the social justice and equality commitments of divine law mean for a group that had previously been voiceless, but whose voice had been summoned precisely in response to the appeal to those commitments? Such a question rarely arises; when it does, law is necessarily transformed.

While a simplistic view of Islamic law would claim its divine origin makes it fixed and unchangeable, the millennium of expansion of the Muslim world between the Qur'anic revelation and the Western penetration would hardly have been possible were that the case. Shariʿa is considered law for all times and all places and thus must suit each time and place.[6] Its principles remain unchanging, but the social situations in which those principles apply are both different from each other and always in the process of changing internally. Hence, *fiqh*, the jurisprudential application of Shariʿa, varies from society to society and from time to time. The jurist cannot understand the legal principle applicable to decision, without knowing the context of its application.[7] Indeed, the jurist may be required to defer to others more knowledgeable for explication of that context.[8]

From the first days of the IRI, the application of Shariʿa to women could not be constrained within the forms it had assumed in a society where women had yet to claim a place in public life. Certainly such constraint was contemplated in the declaration that the existing civil law of marriage and divorce was void and would be replaced by religious law; in the attempt to lessen women's economic participation in the workforce; in the removal of women from certain positions of authority, including the judiciary; in the closing of some areas of work and study to women; in sexual segregation of public spaces; in reinstatement of a criminal code that assigned different penalties for violence against men and women; and, most notoriously in the West, in the requirement of the *ḥijāb*, the covering for women, in public. Yet, each of these constraining attempts came under attack, most failed to be fully instituted, and some have disappeared entirely.[9]

Immediately after the revolution, an imperative of unity operated not only on those supporters of the new republic who might not have chosen its Islamic character, but also on those who might have liked to have a little less republicanism in their Islamic state. That is to say, the continued assent of significant portions of the revolutionary coalition to Khomeini's leadership required a variety of political moves on his part including, most pertinently for this paper, the continuation of the political mobilization of women encouraged by the whole revolutionary coalition, not excepting its religious component. In the most dangerous days leading up to the revolution, Khomeini had made clear his position in that regard. "Women have the right to intervene in politics. It is their duty."[10] Women at every level of society, including the popular classes, had been urged to participate and come out on the streets alongside men, in a moment new to the country's history.[11]

Not only did women's participation have a profound effect on the politics of the era, it had an even deeper effect on these women themselves. Their participation, sanctioned, indeed insisted upon, by undisputed religious authority, changed the traditional view of the place of women, in the minds of women, of men, and of their families.[12] That women had a place—were *obliged* to take a place—in the public sphere was no longer the order of the Shah and his westernizing and corrupting forces, but the wisdom of those whose responsibility it was to understand, to interpret, and to command obedience with divine law. The result was the "altered... consciousness of many women, particularly among the poor, the working class and lower-middle class women, about their political potential."[13]

After the success of their efforts, these women supported Khomeini. This was critical, given the political situation immediately after the revolution, when the Islamists, despite the important role they played in the revolution, did not go unchallenged for the post-revolutionary leadership of Iran. Thus, despite Khomeini's earlier opposition to the Shah's plans for female suffrage, after the fall of the monarchy he did not act to disenfranchise women because he needed their support to consolidate the leading position of Islamist forces in the post-revolutionary situation.

Instead, Khomeini asked women to come out to vote, first for the constitution of the Islamic Republic approved in December 1979, and then in March 1980 for the election of candidates who backed him. Indeed, he went further: for women, voting was a "religious, Islamic and divine duty."[14] Thus, women's political participation was encouraged at the highest level; their mobilization sanctioned as divine. But mobilizing women is not like tuning a radio; it cannot be turned on and off as needed. Mobilizing women also meant giving them a space to voice their concerns and, more importantly, it meant their concerns had to be addressed. This was particularly the case in regard to state regulation of marriage, divorce, and the family. It is in respect to that law that I would like to examine two processes of legal change I referred to before, that is, the identification of the aims of the law and the contextualization of its application.

The Law of Marriage and Divorce in Iran

Among the earliest steps taken by Khomeini upon his return to Iran in February 1979 after fifteen years of exile was to denounce as "un-Islamic" the civil code of marriage and divorce promulgated by the Shah's government in 1967 and amended in 1975. Under the Shah's Family Protection Law (FPL), initiation of divorce had become available to women as well as to men and divorce had to be registered by the state, rather than simply taking place in the form of *ṭalāq*, the husband's threefold oral renunciation of the wife. The husband's polygamy rights were limited and made dependent upon the first wife's consent and the court's permission.[15] A 1975 amendment gave the courts discretion to diverge from traditional religious practice in granting custody to the divorced mother or support to the ex-wife.[16]

While the FPL had been denounced as un-Islamic and dangerous to women, even women who supported the IRI did not see it that way. They were shocked to learn that, with Shariʿa the new law of the state, they could be divorced without cause and without further entitlement to support or to the custody of their children. Women's unhappiness with the new legal regime's lack of congruence with their domestic lives, their complaints, and resistance, led to amelioration of the law's consequence through procedural modifications. These procedural modifications in practice led to a relatively swift return to the FPL.[17] And by the early 1990s, the letter of the law was itself changed to duplicate, or indeed to better, the discarded FPL in text as well as in practice.

While the FPL had been denounced as un-Islamic, it was not officially repealed, although new religious courts were soon created to hear divorce cases.[18] Throughout the decade of the eighties, comprehensive legislation regulating marriage and divorce remained elusive, with the FPL, administrative regulations, and appellate decisions acting as gap-fillers for procedural questions not addressed by Shariʿa,[19] while the Majles, or parliament, the ulama, or religious establishment, and the women's press argued publicly and privately over what was to be done about "the crisis of marriage."[20] Not until the Divorce Reform Law of 1989 were the sources of law applying to marriage and divorce agreed upon, and legislation passed to rationalize them with existing rules and opinions.[21]

In 1992, that law was further amended, resulting in the creation of a new family code, which, while similar to the FPL, actually went farther in protecting women in respect to divorce and custody.[22] Among other changes, a right to a post-marriage monetary settlement for the divorced wife was added in a fair wage (*ujrat al-mithl*) being awarded her as compensation for housework and childcare undertaken during the course of the marriage.[23] In 1996, a second similar compensatory provision was added: the divorced wife's right to her *mahr*, the marriage gift that serves as dower, in current dollars, taking into account the rate of inflation since her marriage. It is the legal framing of these two new rights of compensation that I wish to discuss.

Compensatory Reforms

In classical marriage law, the divorced wife has no right to further financial support if the marriage ends on account of the husband's exercise of *ṭalāq*, his right to unilateral divorce.[24] The marriage contract does not require anything of the wife save obedience and sexual services; it is in return for this pledge that she is entitled to *nafaqa*, or ongoing maintenance during the course of the marriage, and the *mahr*, a gifted capital sum similar to dower in the common law, guaranteeing her maintenance in case of his death or her repudiation. The *mahr* is due immediately upon marriage, but its payment is usually deferred at her pleasure. The wife has no right to any post-divorce support other than this marriage gift.[25]

At divorce, the *mahr* gives the wife some protection against inequities in the gendered contract she has entered. Because the *mahr* is meant to be a capital sum, one capable of generating income for the support of the divorced or widowed wife, its payment can be onerous for the husband.[26] If the husband wants a unilateral divorce, she is entitled to her *mahr*; this can dissuade him from the divorce or push him to make arrangements for her post-divorce support. Alternatively, she can waive the *mahr* to get custody of the children, for whose support he remains responsible, or to get him to agree to a divorce, should she want one.

But if the *mahr* is no longer a capital sum, its utility to the wife is lost, either as a source of support or as a bargaining chip. With the enormous inflation that has plagued Iran almost since the first days of the revolution, the value of older dower gifts has diminished tremendously. In the words of Marzīyah Ṣiddīqī, a woman member of the Majles, "Many past dowries won't even cover taxi fare to court."[27]

The Majles made several attempts to deal with this issue. In 1982, at Khomeini's wish, it included in the form marriage contract a provision that if the husband exercised his unilateral power of divorce, he had to split up to half of the proceeds of the marriage with his ex-wife.[28] This could provide protection for women married after the new contract went into effect, but not for those married under an old form of contract. Indeed, the longer a woman had been married, the more debilitating was adherence to a fixed *mahr* amount. Hence, another tack was tried.

As noted, the essence of the marriage bargain is the trade of the wife's obedience for her maintenance by the husband. While it may be assumed that the wife will also maintain the home and care for the children, the contract itself does not make this explicit. The woman who does these things is not paid for her labor on an ongoing basis.[29] This became a peg for the novel, but not irreligious, notion that divorced women were owed wages for the housework and childcare they had performed during the marriage.

Payment of wages for housework is not explicitly required, but neither is it barred, since it is a principle of *muʿāmalāt*, or the religious account of human relationships, that labor should be compensated.[30] By requiring wages for housework, assessed by a court at the time of divorce, the Majles was in effect creating a right to payment for the wife that was a supplement to the *mahr*. That wage payment would come due in current dollars if the husband exercised his right of unilateral divorce.

Nonetheless, there were some problematic aspects to the new law. The Majles did require that the form contract include the provision that the wife would be due her wages in case of divorce,[31] but once again that left the woman who had married before the contract revision uncovered. And the assessment was available only if the court decided that the divorce was not her fault.[32] Also, if a court ruled that her contribution had been voluntary, or that the custom of her community was to expect such labor be uncompensated, he would not be charged to pay for it.[33]

In the end, in 1996, the Majles bit the bullet and explicitly required that the *mahr* be inflation-indexed to the price of gold as reported by the Central Bank of Iran, thus providing the wife secure access to post-marriage support.[34]

These changes in the law originally passed the Majles, but not the Council of Guardians, the non-elected body of clerical jurists constitutionally mandated to review all legislation for its compatibility with Islam. Instead it was referred to the Expediency Council, which saw the wisdom of allowing the passage of the law, regardless of the stance of the Guardian Council. In other words, a series of attempts to create a more equitable framework for divorce was approved not only by elected representatives, but by religious leaders as well.[35] The pressure for such changes in the divorce law was not only widely felt but was strong enough to prevail.

Social Justice

The revolutionary and post-revolutionary mobilization of women's agency and the partly-consequent, partly-causative problematization of the religious view of gender had made inevitable changes in the understanding of divine law. But how could the position of women in a marriage contract that was understood to be a contract between parties with unequal power to contract be improved without violating either the substance or the spirit of that law? The substance of the law could not be violated by a facial change in Shari'a, e.g., annulling men's unilateral power of divorce, nor could its spirit be violated by introducing an alien conception like natural right into an obligation-based theory.

The solution was to imply a term into the marriage contract,[36] a fairly standard procedure wherever a legal regime of contract is recognized. The parties to a contract may fail to foresee events that impact on their expectations of the contract or they may have naturalized some foundational element of contract, failing to recognize its temporal limitations. When unexpected events occur or when conditions change, a judge may find it necessary to read an extra term into the agreement. She may do this by assuming that the parties omitted to make explicit shared understandings that were nonetheless implicit, and which may be discovered by analogical, deductive or inductive reasoning from other contract terms or the contract as a whole. On the other hand, she may decide that the parties, whatever their private understandings or beliefs might have been, can be rightly held to a social or customary account of the missing term because such an outcome is efficient, fair, certain or conserving of judicial resources.

In my view, it is the latter course that was chosen in respect to these new terms in the marriage contract—wages for work and the inflation-indexed *mahr*. That is because the contract itself, originally understood as private, later came to be viewed as a bargain to which the state was at least implicitly a party. And it was precisely because the state was dedicated to divine justice that it was open to the demand, voiced by women through the women's press in a campaign unifying a broad array of political viewpoints, that it step in to right a balance that had been disrupted by the previous understanding that divorce was completely under the control of the husband. The purpose of the contract was family harmony, also a purpose of the state, as reflected in its constitution that regards the family as a foundational social institution.[37] Hence, there is a public interest in this contract, equal to the interests of its makers.

This can be seen in legislative debates on the issue. Thus, among the reasons such terms could be added to the contract, proponents of change argued that it would be "socially unjust" not to imply them,[38] that such terms could be implied because time and place are meaningful in Islamic jurisprudence,[39] that today religion is not understood to leave management of a divorce entirely in the hands of the male spouse,[40] and that such provisions protect the family, rather than diminish it.[41] Each of these arguments refers to a social outcome and implies a social setting within which justice is not only that which is fair to the participants but also that which serves society. Legal change is possible and in fact necessary in that situation.

The attack on traditional understandings of the law of marriage and divorce was thus in the form of two related legal arguments, neither unfamiliar to American jurisprudence. In American legal history, we might, for comparison, think of moments when the law comes to be seen in a new light. Before the Civil War, when the one-time slave Frederick Douglass claimed that the Constitution was anti-slavery, he was opposed even by abolitionists. They thought, and rightly in some historical sense, that the text of that document reflected fatal compromises with slavery. But Douglass' argument was meta-historical: whatever the literal text of the Constitution said and whatever devil's bargains it reflected, the document itself was a moment in human progress and hence deeply anti-slavery. After the Civil War, Douglass was proved correct. What some have called the Second Constitution, with the Thirteenth, Fourteenth, and Fifteenth Amendments and the subsequent history of a century of struggle for a jurisprudence of federalized freedom, instantiated as common belief Douglass's conception of the first.

The rise of Legal Realism is such a moment as well. I will not step into the debate about the chronology of legal realism, but there is no doubt that common-law American jurisprudence had its own revolutionary moment. Between the end of the nineteenth century and the success of the New Deal, a great change in jurisprudence occurred. A formalist entity known as the law, capable of yielding determinate answers to questions posed by those trained in its scholarship, was replaced by a more pragmatic or positivist view of law as social product. The corollary was that its creation could be consciously undertaken by an elected legislature, informed by social knowledge and subject to the approval or disapproval of those who sent them to legislate. In the latter view, law was not discovered, but made; and if it was to be made, it should be made socially and consciously.

Here I want to focus on just one part of what I have said about Legal Realism, namely, that the making of law can/should be informed by social knowledge. Some of the Realists were of the view that social knowledge was also scientific and thus determinate; that there was indeed an answer to social problems, both definite and value-free. Lawmaking is, in this view, an abstracted version of administration. It is in this sense that I think one might speak of legal realism in post-revolutionary Iran: that is, there is a visible attempt to make law that is responsive to social needs. Because of the commitment to Shariʿa, this law is not being "made" in the legislative sense, yet its interpretation is taking place within a legislative forum and the consequence of this legislative reinterpretation is a substantial shift in its application.

The first form of reinterpretation is the one I have cited in reference to Frederick Douglass's argument regarding the constitution, namely, that its teleology actually excludes its current interpretation. The parallel argument made in respect to the women's situation in Iran was that the very purpose of divine law is the equality of humanity in its ability to recognize and follow the ends of God. Nor is it the case that in that pursuit, one gender is considered more apt than another; rather, both have equal status before God. I hasten to add that the argument does not necessarily imply the equivalence of men and women, nor a rights-based jurisprudence.[42] Nonetheless, the argument implies that any exception to equal treatment requires a justification as to why the intent of the Framer (so to speak) is not aligned with equal treatment in this case.

That justification must necessarily relate to innate difference, even if not inequality, and the argument as to innate difference necessarily assumes a different form in modern society. There both the state of scientific knowledge and the *Zeitgeist* limit the acceptable extent of innate gender differences, since science and common understanding agree that men and women in fact have more differences among them than between them. One is left with reproductive biology and not a lot more. Hence the area of equality of treatment grows, while the area of difference, even difference that does not imply inequality, of necessity shrinks.

The second argument is related, but has to do not with the nature of divine law itself, but the means by which it can be applied to the human, the non-divine. In that context, it is recognized that changing conditions require the law to respond; law need not attempt to prevent change, but should adapt to it. It is indeed the fact of changing conditions that led in the United States to the Realist turn. The tremendous economic transformations of the post-Civil War era created a new reality and new questions that the deductive and analogical modes of reasoning of formalist legal thought could not resolve, at least to the satisfaction of the majority of the society. The response was the recognition that law could not ignore society and that society could indeed change law, though it had hitherto been conceived of as existing metaphysically and producing determinate answers to queries posed by those fitted by intellect and training to the science of law-knowing.[43]

Divine law, of course, *is* unchangeable. But, like any other law, it must be applied. *Fiqh* is the science of its application, by which answers are found for particular questions. In deriving these answers, the jurist must take into consideration whether the conditions of life—the time and place within which Shariʿa is being applied—have changed since similar questions arose earlier. If conditions have changed, a *fiqh* ruling made on the basis of previously-existing conditions must of necessity be reconsidered to see whether the changes are relevant and material to the existing rule. Nor is legislation exempt from this process. There has always been room in Muslim societies for customary and administrative law to facilitate the application of Shariʿa within the society. Hence legislation is neither barred nor discouraged so long as it is not inconsistent with Shariʿa. Obviously that consistency too is a question of time and place. The move to contextualization frees legal interpretation from the closed circle of past juristic practices and has indeed given rise to an intellectual current that attempts to assimilate feminism to divine law. It is perhaps more sociological jurisprudence than Legal Realism, but it is certainly a move in the direction of legal realism.

To conclude, I understand that the term "Legal Realism" which I have used in my title is a peculiar one to describe legislative changes in a republic governed by divine law. And I do not want to be thought of as doing much more than speaking metaphorically. But I think that metaphor allows us to talk broadly about mechanisms of change in gender-relevant law and the relationship law, any law—law as revelation or law as constitution—bears to its society. And when talking of society, I quite explicitly mean to include power relations and not simply collective culture. It is particularly important to make this clear in respect to law that today inevitably works within a state, whether or not its originary is understood to precede the state. State power is perhaps the most direct means by which society directs law; as sociologist Radhika Chopra writes, "The state is a social process with the juridical legislative power to effect change."[44] Hence, the control of state power is central to how law is understood. Here where the state was transformed and the central legal act of transformation was reversion to an unchangeable divine law, it was nonetheless the case that the understanding of divine law of the constituency that supported the transformation of the state inevitably infused the state's understanding as well.

NOTES

[1] Robin Wright, *The Last Great Revolution: Turmoil and Transformation in Iran* (New York 2000).

[2] By the light the present casts on the past, we see the natal moment of the trope of the "Islamic fundamentalist" who is today so powerfully figured in Western discourse.

[3] Parvin Paidar, *Women and the Political Process in Twentieth-Century Iran* (Cambridge 1995), 271.

[4] Ibid.

[5] Twelver Shiʿis, who are by far the largest religious community in Iran, believe that the Twelfth Imam, the last descendant of the Prophet to serve as the present religious leader of the community, lives hidden from the world of action to which he will one day return to make himself publicly known and establish divine justice. Hamid Dabashi, *Authority in Islam. From the Rise of Muhammad to the Establishment of the Umayyads* (New Brunswick, NJ 1989), 120. The potential of this chiliastic tradition was mobilized in the course of the Iranian revolution.

On a trip to Iran in Fall of 2002, I happened to arrive on the birthday of the Hidden Imam; that is the day many people think is marked out for his return. Shops and homes were decorated with flowers and lights, while welcome signs were at every street corner we passed in Tehran that evening.

[6] This is reflected in the existence of multiple schools of Islamic law, each of which reflects a different substantive and procedural approach to decisional application of the sources of law. See generally, *The Islamic School of Law*, ed. Peri Bearman, Rudolph Peters and Frank E. Vogel (Cambridge, Mass. 2005).

[7] This understanding has been particularly important for Shiʿi schools of law, for Shiʿi jurists rely less upon consensus than their Sunni counterparts and their determinations are understood to be binding upon their followers. Ashk P. Dahlen, *Islamic Law, Epistemology and Modernity: Legal Philosophy in Contemporary Iran* (New York 2003), 52.

[8] Abdulaziz Sachedina, "The Ideal and Real in Islamic Law," in *Perspectives on Islamic Law, Justice, and Society*, ed. R. S. Khare (Lanham, MD 1999), 22.

[9] Interestingly, it is in respect to *ḥijāb* that there has been most success in imposing an historically-approved condition upon women, no doubt because many women already wore *ḥijāb* and also because of the peculiar political and social history of covering during the Pahlavi dynasty.

Ḥijāb was banned by Reza Shah in 1936; women who appeared in public in chador risked public uncovering by police and even arrest. Paidar, supra n. 3, at 105. Men who wanted jobs in the modernized economy and state bureaucracy Reza Shah was attempting to build were required to demonstrate their allegiance by requiring European dress for their wives and daughters. Houchang Chahabi, "Dress Codes for Men in Turkey and Iran," in *Men of Order: Authoritarian Modernization under Atatürk and Reza Shah*, ed. Touraj Atabaki and Erik-Jan Zürcher (London 2004), 215.

The unveiling policy was revoked in 1941 after Reza Shah was forced by the Allied powers to abdicate; the revocation was an attempt to create popular support for his son, Mohammed Reza Shah, who assumed the throne. Nikki Keddie, *Roots of Revolution: An Interpretive History of Iran* (New Haven 1981), 113.

[10] Azadeh Kian-Thiébaut, *The Secularization of Iran: A Doomed Failure? The New Middle Class and the Making of Modern Iran* (Paris 1998), 222 (quoting Ayatollah Khomeini, September 16, 1979).

[11] See generally, Mary E. Hegland, "Aliabad Women: Revolution as Religious Activity," in *Women and Revolution in Iran*, ed. Guity-Nashat (Boulder, Colo. 1983).

[12] Interview with Dr. Abdolkarim Souroush, Visiting Professor, Princeton University, in Princeton, NJ (May 7, 2003).

[13] Nikki R. Keddie, "Women in Iran Since 1979," *Social Research* 67 (2000), 413.

[14] Nesta Ramazani, quoting Ayatollah Khomeini, in "Women in Iran: The Revolutionary Ebb and Flow," *Middle East Journal* 47 (1993), 411.

[15] Behnaz Pakizegi, "Legal and Social Position of Iranian Women," in *Women in the Muslim World*, ed. Lois Beck and Nikki Keddie (Cambridge, Mass. 1978), 221.

[16] Ibid., 219.

[17] Ziba Mir-Hosseini, "Women and Politics in Post-Khomeini Iran: Divorce, Veiling and Emerging Feminist Voices," in *Women and Politics in the Third World*, ed. Haleh Afshar (London 1996), 145 [hereinafter, "Divorce, Veiling"].

[18] Maryam Poya, *Women, Work and Islamism: Ideology and Resistance in Iran* (London 1999), xvi.

[19] Paidar, supra n. 3, at 276–77.

[20] Ibid., 284.

[21] Ibid., 276. These included the Civil Code of 1931, the FPL, the 1979 law creating the Special Civil Courts, as well as other pieces of legislation. Poya, supra n. 18, at xvi.

[22] "Divorce, Veiling," 144.

[23] Ibid.

[24] In respect to this right, the parties to the marriage contract do not have equal capacity to contract, for unilateral divorce is a gendered prerogative of the husband. In this sense, the marriage is understood to be the "property" of the husband, not of the wife. Baber Johansen, *Contingency in a Sacred Law: Legal and Ethical Norms in the Muslim Fiqh* (Leiden 1999), 204. Her property in the marriage is her right to *mahr* and *nafaqa*. She is otherwise competent to enter into contracts as an equal: her capacity to contract is not affected by her marital status, either before or after the marriage.

[25] However, the husband remains responsible for supporting his children, and for support of his ex-wife for the period of three menstrual periods (*ʿidda*) after he pronounces the *ṭalāq*, to determine that she is not pregnant with his child.

[26] Ziba Mir-Hosseini, "Tamkin: Stories from a Family Court in Iran," in *Everyday Life in the Muslim Middle East*, ed. Donna Lee Bowen and Evelyn A. Early (Bloomington, Ind. ²2002), 148.

[27] *Zan-e Rūz* (Iran), December 21, 1996. (All translations from *Zan-e Rūz* are by Ali Korangy, newly minted Ph.D. in Near Eastern Languages and Civilizations, Harvard University, and are on file with the author.)

[28] Ziba Mir-Hosseini, *Marriage on Trial: Islamic Family Law in Iran and Morocco* (London [2]2000), 57. Mir-Hosseini says that in her attendance at the divorce court in Tehran in 1988, she came across no cases in which the claim to proceeds of the marriage was raised. Ibid., 58.

[29] The social failure to compensate women's domestic labor is also problematized by American feminists in the divorce context. See, e.g., Joan Chalmers Williams, review of Zillah R. Eisenstein, "Feminism and Post-Structuralism: The Female Body and the Law," *Mich L. Rev.* 8 (1990), 1776 ("just as [housework/childcare] is invisible inside marriage, it is invisible upon divorce. So when judges make support or property awards, they often ignore completely or seriously undervalue the economic worth of those services.... [S]ociety demands work from women and then refuses to acknowledge that women are doing it, or even that it is 'work' at all," ibid., 1788–89).

[30] Shariʿa regulates both acts relative to the divine and acts relative to other humans, the former *ʿibādāt*, the latter *muʿāmalāt*. Ziba Mir-Hosseini, "The Construction of Gender in Islamic Legal Thought and Strategies for Reform," *Hawwa* 1 (2003), 11.

[31] "The Question of Wages for Work is Worthy of Presentation to the World Stage," *Zan-e Rūz* (Iran), December 4, 1993 (interview with Ali-Akbar Nateq-Nuri) [hereinafter, Nateq-Nuri].

[32] It is unclear why uncompensated labor should be tolerated in that case. Interview with Dr. Safai, *Zan-e Rūz* (Iran) December 18, 1993 [hereinafter, Safai]. Safai, a well-known lawyer, said he was "of the opinion that a woman should also be able to request a determination of wages even if she is at fault in a divorce. If a woman has this right, then why shouldn't it exist regardless of the reason for divorce?"

[33] Ibid.

[34] *Zan-e Rūz* (Iran), December 28, 1996.

[35] It is worth noting that each of these efforts came to fruition *before* the election of Mohammad Khatami to the presidency in 1997. This suggests the extent to which reform was not a product of Khatami's election, but its cause, suggesting as well that the outcome of the most recent election which created a more conservative Majles is not likely to reverse the advancement of women, as some have predicted.

[36] It was Khomeini who introduced this solution to the Iranian context, by reviving the notion extant in some schools of Islamic law that a woman could insist on contract conditions that improved on her marital status, such as the husband's delegation to her of a proxy to utilize his power of *ṭalāq* to divorce herself under certain conditions, such as his entrance into a second marriage.

[37] *Qānūn-i Asāsī-yi Jumhūrī-yi Islāmi-yi Īrān* [The Constitution of the Islamic Republic of Iran], art. 12 [1980], available at http://www.iranonline.com/iran/iran-info/Government/constitution-1.html.

[38] *Zan-e Rūz* (Iran), December 28, 1996 (citing the arguments of supporters).

[39] Ibid. (citing remarks of Majid Ansari, a member of the Majles).

[40] *Zan-e Rūz* (Iran), December 21, 1996 (interview with Ayatollah Makarim Shirazi).

[41] Nateq-Nouri, supra n. 31. Both Nateq-Nouri and Makarim were considered conservatives in Iranian politics of the 1990s.

[42] See, e.g., Ayatollah Morteza Motahhari, *Woman and Her Rights* (1974), available at http://www.al-islam.org/WomanRights (last visited Nov. 9, 2006). His book, written before the Islamic Revolution, has become the "official discourse of the Islamic Republic on gender." Ziba Mir-Hosseini, *Islam and Gender: The Religious Debate in Contemporary Iran* (London 2000), 23.

[43] Morton Horwitz, *The Transformation of American Law, 1870–1960: The Crisis of Legal Orthodoxy* (Oxford 1992).

[44] Radhika Chopra, review of Rajeshwari Sunder Rajan. *The Scandal of the State: Women, Law, and Citizenship in Postcolonial India* (Durham, NC 2003). http://www.hnet.org/reviews/showrev.cgi?path=254891094819802

4

PRICE SETTING AND HOARDING IN MAMLUK EGYPT

The Lessons of Legal Realism for Islamic Legal Studies

Kristen Stilt

One of the main purposes of Frank Vogel's book, *Islamic Law and Legal System: Studies of Saudi Arabia*, is "to contribute to the understanding of Islamic law by studying it in the process of its application."[1] This purpose derives from Vogel's assessment that "Our lack of knowledge of the systems by which Islamic law is and has been applied has greatly hindered our understanding of this law."[2] Further, he noted, "Continued ignorance of the law in practice weakens our understanding of Islamic religion, Islamic history, and Muslim societies past and present. But most of all, it undermines our understanding of Islamic legal doctrine and theory."[3]

Vogel's concerns remain pressing, and his own work serves as needed guidance to scholars of Islamic law today. Many studies that aim to advance the knowledge of Islamic laws or legal systems are formalistic and provide little insight into the ways the legal system worked and the many different factors that influenced legal actors and their actions. This formalism is generally exhibited in one of two ways. In the first, an author adopts the classic formalist tenet that rules and logic alone are what decide cases before a judge or other decision-maker. The goal then becomes a dissection of the legal decision, which might be a court decision or fatwa, in order to discern the Islamic (or other) law that produced it. In this type of formalism, the legal rules and doctrine that are deduced from the decisions are enshrined as the sole explanation for the decision. There is no room in this approach to seek to identify social, cultural or political factors that may explain in whole or in part the decision.

The second type of formalistic study in Islamic law is doctrinal. While useful in many ways, these studies should be explicit that they are an attempt to reconstruct the legal rules accepted as authoritative by a particular school of law, or particular scholar, at a particular moment in time. The doctrine itself cannot tell us if and how the rules were applied, by whom and to whom, and the consequences. It may be the case that the legal rules as determined in this kind of scholarship were accepted as authoritative by decision makers and that they strove to apply them. The rules may have had little effect in practice and thus such a synthesis of rules is better described as intellectual history.

The area of Islamic legal studies is not the first with a need to address the challenge of legal formalism. A movement called legal realism developed and gained strength at the beginning of the twentieth century in American legal studies in response to the prevailing formalism of that time. The realists challenged the idea that solely legal rules determined the outcome of a legal question, and that the legal rules necessarily produced one "correct" answer. Their concern was with understanding adjudicated results, and they believed that exclusive focus on the legal rules was misguided because judges tend to respond to the facts of the case and what they think is fair given the social context, rather than confine themselves to narrowly applying rules of law.[4]

Legal realism transformed legal studies. As Brian Leiter writes:

> By emphasizing the indeterminacy of law and legal reasoning, and the importance of nonlegal considerations in judicial decisions, the realists cleared the way for judges and lawyers to talk openly about the political and economic considerations that in fact affect many decisions. This is manifest in the frequent discussions—by courts, by lawyers, and by law teachers—of the 'policy' implications of deciding one way rather than another.[5]

The legal realists convinced the legal academy that the study of law must include not only the laws themselves but also an understanding of the other factors that influence the legal decision-making process.[6]

The field of Islamic legal studies unfortunately has been slow to appreciate the relevance and usefulness of legal realism to the long-standing dispute in Islamic legal studies over the level of formalism in the application of Islamic law. As is the case in legal systems generally, there is an intellectual step between the law on the books and the law in action, and much room for discretion, consciously or not, on the part of the implementer of the law—whether judge or other—in this step. Beginning with these premises, a study of Islamic law in a particular time and place should ask questions such as: How did the legal system function? How was the relevant law determined in any given case? How was the law applied, by whom, and to whom? What were the factors influencing those officials who applied the law? What was the relationship between the legal text and the context of daily life?

Recognizing the relevance of such factors does not conflict with the religious provenance of the law. However, denying the relevance of social circumstances to the application of the law does a great disservice to the study of Islamic law by turning it into an abstraction. Further, failure to consider the applicability to Islamic law of methods from other fields of legal studies leads to the unsupportable notion that Islamic law is exceptional and cannot be studied in a comparative manner.

This article draws upon the lessons of the legal realists and follows in the line of Vogel's work and his call for more attention to law's application. My case study is the application of law by the *muḥtasib* in early Mamluk Cairo and Fustat (648–802/1250–1400). The *muḥtasib*, best described as an inspector of the markets and public spaces in general, was a legal official charged with "commanding right and forbidding wrong," and was tasked with patrolling public streets, especially in the marketplaces, and enforcing laws as he understood them whenever he encountered a violation.[7] The realists dealt with judicial decisions, and specifically appellate decisions. The *muḥtasib* is not a judge, of course, but was an applier of the law and resembled a judge in that regard. Even without a perfect correlation to the legal actors with whom the realists were concerned, it is very useful to suggest that the lessons of the realists are relevant to the position of the *muḥtasib* and to any other Islamic legal actor.

This article will examine instances of the *muḥtasib*'s decision-making in areas related to food availability and pricing. This implicates the legal rules on price setting and hoarding. The goal is to assess the factors that went into the application process and to show that viewing the particular factual situation alongside doctrine and the general context allows a much fuller explanation of decision-making by the *muḥtasib*s. By including as much traditionally non-legal information as possible for each case, we can see that the *muḥtasib*'s actions resulted from a combination of social, economic, and political factors; the potentially applicable laws; and the particular personality of the *muḥtasib*. These results show that a formalist approach to these cases would have resulted in a narrow and skewed perspective of the application of law.

There are many examples in the historical chronicles of the *muḥtasib*'s actions in matters of food availability and pricing in Mamluk Cairo and Fustat, making this topic ideal for this study because of the comparisons and contrasts among cases that it allows. The general population also associated the *muḥtasib* with availability and cost of food. The vast majority of price issues involved the fundamental food stuffs of wheat, barley, and the like, and the final product, bread. For example, in the middle of the year 782/1380, the Nile's rise was not sufficient, and prices of crops rose. People tried to acquire and store food, and general anxiety increased. The people then sought to improve the situation by calling for the dismissal of the *muḥtasib* of Cairo, Shams al-Dīn al-Damīrī, and asked for the return of the previous *muḥtasib*, Jamāl al-Dīn al-ʿAjamī. And indeed al-ʿAjamī was reinstated, and the people celebrated and rejoiced. The reason for their enthusiasm was that "bread had been difficult to find in the market, and for a few days unavailable. They thought that the arrival of al-ʿAjamī would be a blessing, and it was as they thought. On that day a number of ships laden with crops arrived and the prices decreased."[8]

This report reveals that the *muḥtasib* was linked in the minds of the people with prices and availability of food. Even without a tangible causal link between the new *muḥtasib* and the arrival of goods (for they most likely had left their point of origin before al-ʿAjamī was reinstated), he gets the credit for the new food and decreasing prices.[9] As will be seen in the cases that follow, when prices rose and food was unavailable, the people often held the *muḥtasib* responsible, as did the Sultan.[10]

A significant characteristic of the grain market was that the Sultan and the amirs controlled large amounts of grain and other agricultural products, which had a substantial effect on the market. Part of the taxes collected in kind by the central government was "assigned to emirs, Mamlūks, and other officials of the state as direct payments of salaries and compensation for expenses incurred in the fulfillment of their duties."[11] Such assignments (*iqṭāʿ*s) "remained the largest claim on the grain produce of Egypt in the Mamlūk period."[12] These grain owners depended on the market to acquire income to purchase other items they needed.[13]

Price setting and hoarding of food are standard topics in texts of Islamic jurisprudence (*fiqh*). The jurists agree on the general rule that price setting is prohibited.[14] The proof for this is the widely-cited *ḥadīth*:

> The prices were high in Medina at the time of the Prophet, and the people said to him: Messenger of God, the prices are high, so set prices for our sake. The Messenger of God said that God is the establisher of prices, the one who contracts and expands the market, and the one who provides subsistence. I want to meet God free from any claims against me that I oppressed any one of you in terms of person or property.[15]

There were exceptions to this general rule, and the Maliki school was the most permissive overall in allowing the ruler to set prices when serving the public interest required it.[16]

While price setting is usually discussed in contexts of high prices, scholars treated the issue of raising prices in the same manner as lowering prices. According to the Malikis, the price prevailing in the market is to be respected, such that if one or a few sellers reduce their prices to lower levels, they are ordered to either return to the prevailing rate or leave the market. The proof text for this rule is a *ḥadīth* according to which ʿUmar b. al-Khaṭṭāb passed a man selling raisins in the market, and he told him: "Either raise the price, or leave our market."[17]

The other Sunni scholars rely upon a longer version of this same *ḥadīth* as proof that price setting of any kind is impermissible. According to this version, when ʿUmar returned home from the encounter in the market with the raisin seller, he reconsidered the situation and then summoned the merchant and said to him: "What I said to you today is neither a decision nor a ruling from me, but only something that I wanted in the interest of the people of the town. Sell wherever and however you want."[18]

A related legal topic is the hoarding of goods and the penalty imposed upon the hoarder. There was disagreement among the Sunni schools of law about virtually every aspect of the laws of hoarding, such as what goods were protected by these laws, and what penalty was to be imposed on the hoarder. In general, though, scholars agreed that essential food, such as wheat and bread, was covered by the rules prohibiting hoarding.[19] Scholars who took a less aggressive approach to the remedy would simply require that the hoarder sell, and if the hoarder refused, they would demand punishment of the hoarder such as through imprisonment. Scholars following this approach would not advocate a seizure of the goods and sale of them at the set price, on grounds that this would be a taking of property. Scholars with a more forceful approach to remedies for hoarding prescribed forcible sale of the hoarders' goods, and a return of the proceeds to the hoarder.

Case Study 1: Price Setting and Hoarding at the Fustat Granaries

A significant case of grain prices that involved the *muḥtasib* in the period studied occurred in 736/1336, during the third reign of Sultan al-Nāṣir Muḥammad (709–41/1310–41). The reports of this episode are full of details about the role of the *muḥtasib*, his jurisdiction, his relation to the Sultan and amirs, and the way that those in power applied the law.

Events began with reports of rising wheat prices, from fifteen dirhams per *irdabb*[20] to twenty and then to thirty in a short period of time, such that people's daily lives were greatly affected. The price continued to rise, to forty dirhams per *irdabb*; the amirs and others with grain stocks then refrained from selling, expecting a continuing rise in price. The Sultan feared the consequences of this, and so when wheat reached fifty dirhams per *irdabb* he called for Najm al-Dīn, the *muḥtasib* of Cairo, and criticized him. Najm al-Dīn served as *muḥtasib* from 720/1320–21 till his death in 737/1336, and we may conclude that by this time, just shortly before his death, he was not as energetic and able as the Sultan would have wanted him to be. The Sultan did not replace him, though, but supplemented his work by empowering the governor (*wālī*) of Cairo, ʿAlāʾ al-Dīn al-Marwānī, to act alongside the *muḥtasib*.[21]

And the governor did indeed take action. He beat a number of millers and bread bakers with whips, but the situation just worsened. Shops in Cairo and Fustat closed, and bread could only be bought with great hardship. People crowded around each bakery in such force that the governor had to station guards to keep order.[22] The Sultan ordered that grain be brought from Gaza, Karak, Shawbak, and Damascus, and it was announced in Cairo and Fustat that wheat was not to be sold for more than thirty dirhams per *irdabb*, and whoever sold for more than that would have his property confiscated (perhaps referring to the profit, the sale amount or all of his grain). The Sultan ordered the amirs not to violate this order. But the amirs and brokers of grain merchants refrained from selling at all, and the situation deteriorated. Brokers secretly sold for sixty and seventy dirhams per *irdabb*, and amirs took grain from their storehouses on the grounds that it was to supply the daily needs of their households, but they were probably selling it on the side at a higher price.[23]

The Sultan was distressed by the people's suffering, and knew that the amirs controlled most of the grain. He summoned Ḍiyāʾ al-Dīn, whose abilities in the service of the state were well known, and appointed him *muḥtasib* of Fustat, after he had initially refused the position.[24] Ḍiyāʾ al-Dīn went with the notoriously brutal amir Sayf al-Dīn Alakuz[25] to Fustat, and the first thing Ḍiyāʾ al-Dīn did was record how many *irdabb*s were in the storehouse of each amir and how much that amir would need to provide for his household and animals until the time of the arrival of new crops. Then he sealed all of the storehouses of the amirs and summoned the brokers, guards, and grain measurers and made them swear that they would not open the storehouses except with the *muḥtasib*'s permission.[26]

Every day Ḍiyāʾ al-Dīn would go to the storehouses and take out grain, and began by providing it to the millers at thirty dirhams per *irdabb*, which was the maximum price for all grain sales per the Sultan's earlier order. But brokers of the amirs Bashtāk and Qawṣūn were violating these rules and selling for more than thirty, and so the amir Alakuz was called to Fustat whereupon he flogged the brokers with whips and exposed them to public disgrace. When the Sultan was informed of their transgression, he too punished them severely. After that, no amir dared to open his storehouse without the *muḥtasib*'s permission.[27]

At the same time, the Sultan, who was making efforts to bring more grain into the city, ordered the governors of the regions to bring all grain available to Fustat to be purchased at thirty dirhams per *irdabb*. Despite all these measures, however, the Sultan learned that some amirs were still hoarding their grain from the market and selling outside of the established regime. But the neighbors of these storehouses helped out, either by raiding their supplies or by turning them in to the governor, who took what they had and distributed it to the millers.[28] A witness was sent to each oven to monitor the amount of wheat brought to it, and efforts were made to ensure equal distribution of bread around the city. The people's agitation from the difficulty in finding bread decreased, as did the floggings of millers and bakers. The arrival of shipments of grain from Damascus and then Upper Egypt brought the crisis to an end.[29]

This event involved both price setting and hoarding. At first, the Sultan announced that grain could only be sold for thirty dirhams, which is a price-setting order. If the scholars who permitted price setting when the public interest dictated it had been asked to give an opinion on this action, it is likely that they would have authorized the Sultan's action given the terrible state of affairs reported by the chroniclers. Even at that time, the reports convey a sense that merchants were not selling their wares, yet the case was not treated as one of hoarding at this early stage. The price had risen from fifteen to fifty dirhams, grain owners were refraining from selling, and the people were greatly affected. The price-setting announcement did not come from the *muḥtasib*, however. This was a large-scale crisis, encompassing both major cities and requiring grain to be brought from other parts of the sultanate, so it is not surprising that the price setting came down from the highest level. In case of smaller problems, as will be seen below, it was more than likely the *muḥtasib* who announced the price.[30]

The Sultan ordered the amirs and grain brokers to obey this order, but in response they refrained completely from selling—the situation then became fully a problem of hoarding. The hoarding could have been addressed earlier. Indeed, when appointing the new *muḥtasib*, the Sultan knew that the amirs controlled the grain and that they wielded enough power that they might simply refuse to sell. Nevertheless, it appears that the Sultan was not prepared to, or did not yet think it necessary to, directly confront the amirs and instruct them to actually sell. The Sultan called in Ḍiyāʾ al-Dīn to command hoarders to sell, and he required that the sale price be thirty dirhams, the same as the Sultan's price-setting order.

The prominent role of Fustat and its *muḥtasib* in this event is noteworthy. The *muḥtasib* of Cairo was not replaced, but was reinforced by the governor of Cairo, who for all practical purposes superseded him.[31] As a result, the position of the *muḥtasib* of Fustat now took on critical importance in the matter, and the Sultan convinced an individual who was known for his capabilities to take the position. Correspondingly, the storehouses of Fustat were where the real action took place, and they were needed to supply both Cairo and Fustat. The Cairo grain market seemed irrelevant (although, of course, not Cairo's bread market and the needs of Cairenes). Perhaps Cairo's storehouses were depleted before those of Fustat.[32]

Fustat's significance in the event was due to its port and grain storehouses, with al-Maqrīzī reporting that grain arrived at the docks of Fustat, not of Cairo.[33] Between the time of the decline of Maqs as Cairo's port and the development of Bulaq, Fustat was a significant port for grain arriving from Upper Egypt, and its granaries were located near to its banks.[34] These were the granaries at issue in the event, and so the Sultan needed a *muḥtasib* in Fustat to deal with them. It would not be efficient to divert the *muḥtasib* of Cairo to the task, and leave Cairo without this important regulator at a time of food crisis.

Another important aspect of this event is the relationship between Cairo's *muḥtasib* and governor and the relationship between Fustat's *muḥtasib* and the amir Alakuz. Neither *muḥtasib* carried out the heavy punishments, but had their tough man for that task. It was not at all unusual for a *muḥtasib* to take care of light punishments, but then turn over the offender to someone else, such as the Sultan, an amir, governor or judge, for more significant discipline. This practice may have been due to the *muḥtasib*'s preference not to get too involved in the dirty details of the punishment.

This event could be boiled down to a case of price setting due to public necessity and an aggressive approach to hoarders who refused to sell. And indeed *fiqh* texts could be used to argue that the actions of the Sultan and *muḥtasib* are attributable entirely, and even solely, to the legal rules themselves. Such a formalistic reading is possible but imprecise. Many other factors came into play alongside legal rules to produce the effects. The Sultan played a prominent role in the controversy, and announced the set price himself. The Sultan backed fully his newly appointed *muḥtasib*. This is the only case studied of a successful response to hoarding. The success can be explained by the fact that the Sultan and *muḥtasib* were strong enough to together confront the amirs. The Sultan could have claimed that hoarding was occurring much earlier in this event and attempted to take action, but other examples of failed attempts to force hoarders to sell suggest that the Sultan was prudent to wait until he had his strong *muḥtasib* in place. The event is explained more by the personalities involved than by the rules of hoarding.

Case Study 2: An "Agreement" on Wheat Prices to Please the Political Powers

In 738/1337, the price of agricultural produce decreased to the point that an *irdabb* of wheat from Upper Egypt was sold for ten dirhams, an *irdabb* of wheat from Lower Egypt for eight dirhams, and beans and barley for six dirhams per *irdabb*. Even at these prices, sales were stagnant. The affairs of the troops (*jund*) came to a halt as a result of the low prices since troops were paid in wheat and had to sell it on the market to acquire other products they needed. In an effort to earn a little more money, the brother of al-Nashw, the supervisor of the fisc, along with an accomplice, forced (*ṭarḥ*) merchants to buy their wheat for an extra two dirhams per *irdabb*.

Separately, al-Nashw complained about Ḍiyāʾ al-Dīn, *muḥtasib* of Cairo, because the price of flour and bread was high in comparison to the price of wheat.[35] The millers were the ones benefiting from the situation, it seemed, because they were buying cheap wheat but then selling flour at a disproportionately high price. The price of bread, then, reflected the price of the flour. There did not seem to have been complaints by consumers about bread prices. But the powerful al-Nashw was displeased by the low wheat prices and the effect it was having on the military troops. Al-Nashw then ordered the governor of Cairo to summon the *muḥtasib* and the millers and work out an average price of wheat, so that there was not such a difference in price between wheat and bread.[36]

Al-Nashw's brother's tactic was employed by later amirs and even sultans when they wanted to sell their grain at high prices, but it was not yet widely used at this time. Instead of simply dictating higher prices to the millers and requiring them to buy at that price, the *muḥtasib* was ordered to work with the millers to come to a new price. This kind of price agreement strongly suggests that the *muḥtasib* negotiated with the grain merchants and millers to come to a fair or just amount for the sale of wheat and every subsequent by-product to the bread sold to consumers. Unfortunately for consumers, they seem to have received no benefit from low wheat prices.

*Muḥtasib*s, even strong ones, sometimes gave in to pressures from amirs, and this example demonstrates how law was at times caught in the middle of power politics. But al-Nashw was something of a special case, and by this time, he had an ample reputation for oppression.[37] Shortly after this event, he was able to secure this *muḥtasib*'s dismissal. This is the first indication of an amir interfering so directly in the appointment or dismissal process for the position of *muḥtasib*.[38] In light of al-Nashw's particular power, his interference with pricing here is more easily explained and understood.

Some jurists who permit price setting state that the price should be determined through negotiations between the producers and the *muḥtasib* or political leader. The producers should not be denied some profit, they argue, or they will have no incentive to produce in the future. Others do not require such a consultative process. One way to understand these events is to argue that al-Nashw wanted the *muḥtasib* to discuss prices with the millers in order to follow the consultative line of thought about price setting. A formal look at the events could produce that explanation. But knowing the background and personality of al-Nashw, it is difficult to interpret his decision in any way other than that he was seeking the best possible outcome for himself and the troops. Had he known what price of wheat would produce that outcome, he might have instructed the *muḥtasib* to require the millers to buy at that price. Without an understanding of market dynamic, he had to order the *muḥtasib* to consult with the millers in order to determine the ideal price from his own perspective. The millers were apparently willing to enter into these discussions due to al-Nashw's political power.

Case Study 3: Price Setting in Order to Raise Bread Prices

A few months after Ibn al-Uṭrūsh was appointed *muḥtasib* of Cairo in 748/1348, he was greeted by a hail of stones from the people. The reason was that at a time when the price of bread increased and one dirham purchased only six to seven *raṭl*s of bread, some of the bakers sold eight *raṭl*s for one dirham, that is, slightly cheaper. Ibn al-Uṭrūsh summoned these discount bakers and beat them. The people were angry with the *muḥtasib* and they threw stones at his door until the governor came and beat them away.[39]

This case highlights the complex network of prices, although the chroniclers recorded very little information about the details. We do not know why prices were six to seven *raṭl*s per dirham, but given the *muḥtasib*'s reaction to the lower prices by a few bakers and the reaction of the people against efforts to keep prices higher, we may presume that there had been instability in the prices of bread prior to this event and that everyone was worried about maintaining a stable rate that was reasonable from their individual perspectives. The rate must have still been unstable, since the *muḥtasib* perceived one or a small number of under-sellers to be a threat.

Another possibility is that the *muḥtasib* was concerned primarily about the prices of grain on behalf of the amirs and other grain owners. Falling bread prices would eventually affect grain sales and would cut into the profits shared by grain owners and their brokers, along with millers and bakers. This possibility seems plausible since this *muḥtasib* was more attached to the ruling elite than most others of this period. His professional career began in Damascus, where in 744/1343 he was appointed its *muḥtasib*. He gained that position, however, with the assistance of an amir, and the people there were upset with his appointment due to his ignorance of Islamic law.[40] While serving as *muḥtasib* of Cairo, in 749 he was appointed military judge in the Hanafi school and held that position until his death.[41] His appointment and long service as military judge is also a good indicator that he was well connected to the Mamluk regime.

The schools of law disagreed about how the person who sells below the prevailing market price is to be treated. According to the Malikis, the school that was the most permissive on the ability of the leader to set prices, the price prevailing in the market is to be respected. If one or a few sellers sell under it, they are ordered to either return to the prevailing rate or leave the market.

In this case of the bakers selling eight *raṭl*s of bread for a dirham when the going rate was six to seven *raṭl*s for a dirham, the *muḥtasib* Ibn al-Uṭrūsh physically punished the under-sellers to prevent them from conducting their transactions at this rate. A more sophisticated *muḥtasib* might have followed ʿUmar's example and warned that if they did not raise their prices, they would have to leave the market. This strategy would only be effective if the merchants respected, or feared, the *muḥtasib* and would fear the consequences of disobeying him. An ignored verbal order would have been an embarrassment to the *muḥtasib*. Perhaps knowing what would happen if he simply issued a command, Ibn al-Uṭrūsh went straight to the level of physical punishment without trying a verbal admonishment first. Not surprisingly, the bread-consuming public became angry, saw the *muḥtasib* as working against their interests, and threw stones at his door.

This case highlights the way in which the demands of various interest groups related to one another. If the price of bread dropped, it would eventually affect the price of grain, which was owned by the amirs. Ibn al-Uṭrūsh had built his career not through scholarship or even by being a solid bureaucrat, but rather by currying favor with the amirs in power. In this light, it is not surprising that as *muḥtasib*, he was less worried about the people's access to affordable bread than about his own status with his patrons.

A formal view of these events could demonstrate that the *muḥtasib* was trying to keep the market for bread and its raw materials stable. In doing so, he could not allow merchants to sell bread at costs above the market rate or perhaps even the rate the *muḥtasib* had set himself earlier. He set prices either of his own accord or due to an order of the Sultans or powerful amirs, and since at least the Malikis might have allowed this, we could conclude that the *muḥtasib* was simply applying the law most applicable to the situation. But such an interpretation ignores the many different factors that seem to have caused the reported result. In particular, the personality of the *muḥtasib* is significant. Had the *muḥtasib* been someone whose fortunes were not too intimately linked to the amirs, perhaps this event never would have happened.

Case Study 4: The Consequences of Lowering Bread Prices

Shams al-Dīn al-Damīrī's appointment as *muḥtasib* of Cairo in 776/1374 came at a time of increasing prices due to concern over the inadequacy of the Nile's rise. The prices of wheat (100 dirhams per *irdabb*), barley (60), and beans (50) were troublesome to the people. A few days after Shams al-Dīn's appointment, he dispatched a number of carriers with loads of bread, and they traversed Cairo up to the citadel accompanied by drums and cymbals. It was announced that two and 3/4 *raṭl*s of bread would now cost one dirham, whereas the price had been two and 1/3 *raṭl*s for a dirham. With this parade of bread, Shams al-Dīn was clearly trying to show to the people that as *muḥtasib* he would take charge of bread prices and make this basic product affordable. And the people were happy—except that bread could not be found in the markets for five days, and people crowded around the ovens in search of it.[42]

With the people in despair, it was ordered that more bread be made and sold without a set price. The prices of foodstuffs rose, and by the beginning of the next month wheat reached 110 dirhams per *irdabb*. Within two weeks, al-Maqrīzī was reporting the beginnings of an epidemic, and deaths of the poor from hunger were numerous.[43] The cause or the nature of the epidemic is not given, but al-Maqrīzī's use of the term indicates that it was more than a case of some deaths due to lack of food. Inadequate diets probably allowed an illness to find easy victims among undernourished people and thus spread quickly. By the month of Ramadan, the disease had spread to the wealthy as well, and the prices of luxury goods, like chickens and melons, also increased. Hunger and death were rampant.[44]

Two months later, though, new supplies of wheat arrived and prices decreased, with bread being sold at four *raṭl*s per dirham.[45] When the situation began to improve, or at least the rate of death slowed, Shams al-Dīn, who had remained in the position of *muḥtasib* throughout the crisis, declared the price of bread to be eight *raṭl*s per dirham, up from five and 1/3 *raṭl*s per dirham. The millers then refused to purchase wheat for more than eighteen dirhams per *irdabb*. Because of the low price of bread, the bakers would only be willing to pay so much for flour, which meant that the millers could not pay more than eighteen dirhams for an *irdabb* of wheat and still supply the bakers without a loss. The importers refused to sell for such a low price, and they returned in their boats with their goods to the places from which they came. The absence of wheat in the market caused the price to reach 34 dirhams per *irdabb*. Then bread could not be found for a few days and when it was available, it was sold for less than six *raṭl*s per dirham.[46] With a brief mention that the epidemic then abated, al-Maqrīzī ended this long narrative on rising prices and the spread of disease.[47]

The *muḥtasib*'s actions were not very effective in this case. He focused on the part of the problem most visible to the people—the price of bread—and neglected to acknowledge that the price of bread is related to the price of flour, which is connected to the price of wheat. He also unilaterally set prices when there were difficulties in the market but no signs of a crisis, which is the classic price setting prohibited by law. If there were any domestic wheat supplies being hoarded, the *muḥtasib* did not try to regulate the price and their availability so that it was possible to sell bread for the amount he specified.

In any case, the price of wheat was a much more difficult issue, since the amirs controlled so much of the market. Most likely, it would have required a firm order from the Sultan to deal with the grain prices on a macro level, either by aggressively searching for new supplies or giving his backing to forcing amirs to sell what supplies of grain they had. At this time, however, the young Ashraf Shaʿbān was Sultan, and his authority was under growing threat from Barqūq, who would ultimately seize the sultanate for himself. The ability of Sultan Ashraf Shaʿbān's state to take control of the situation may have been limited by his own tentative status. Furthermore, the implementation of such an order would require a strong *muḥtasib*, and people probably lost confidence in al-Damīrī after he could not deliver on his first attempt to control bread prices.

In the second wave of the crisis, we get a valuable piece of information about the importers of wheat. Importers arrived with much-needed wheat, but they would not sell for the low price the local millers were offering. Significantly, there is no mention of the *muḥtasib* trying to force the importers to sell their wheat at a price the local millers could afford to pay. There was recognition that importers were outside of the regulatory framework, and that they had the right to turn around and sail away, in search of a better market. The Sunni schools of law agreed that the importers played a special role and that they were not subject to any price controls in effect in the market. They had the right to decide if they wanted to sell in the particular market. If they were forced to comply with local rules, then they would not return to that market for fear of being forced to sell, or forced to sell at a specific price. Even the Maliki *muḥtasib* Shams al-Dīn al-Damīrī, who set bread prices on other occasions, did not attempt to control the importers sitting at the port and deciding whether they wanted to sell to the Cairo merchants.

This complex report could be reduced to the legal explanation that the *muḥtasib* simply set prices when he had no legal justification for doing so, since even for the Maliki school there has to be a public interest at stake in order to set prices. At the beginning of the report the situation seems like one of rising prices but not a crisis. This conclusion would lend support to the idea that a liberal use of price setting is not only illegal but also bad from the perspective of the outcome, since in this case the result was a worse situation for the consumers. In examining this event, a narrow reading would leave out the important detail that the *muḥtasib* focused on bread, and not its component ingredients, to regulate. His misunderstanding of the market, more than any ignorance of the law, explains this event.

Case Study 5: A *Muḥtasib*'s Struggle to Retain Authority

The case discussed here is preceded by the suggestion that Sultan Barqūq was imposing grain sales to acquire funds for an expedition to Damascus.[48] Then at the end of 796/1394, the Nile failed to reach its expected level, and prices rose in anticipation of shortages to come, with wheat increasing to 40 dirhams per *irdabb*. The people shouted at the *muḥtasib* Ibn al-Burjī, complained about him to the Vice-Sultan (*nāʾib*) Sūdūn (Barqūq being in Syria by this time), and, according to one report, even wanted to stone the *muḥtasib*. So the Vice-Sultan ordered the governor of Cairo, amir ʿAlāʾ al-Dīn al-Ṭablāwī, to take charge of the matter of prices.[49]

The governor ordered the storehouses to open and sell at "God's price." He threatened those who did not open their storehouses and sell within three days with seizure of their goods, presumably to be sold. The agents of the amirs obeyed, and the price came down a little,[50] but they soon slowed down their selling, and the fear of famine increased.[51]

This case is difficult to describe as one of drought or serious shortage in the city's food supply. While the rising prices were inconvenient and some people were not selling, it was not the same level of crisis as seen in other examples, and in particular there was no evidence that people were suffering because of the failure of merchants to sell. Instead of working through the office of the *muḥtasib* and supporting the *muḥtasib*'s authority to manage or at least monitor the situation, the Vice-Sultan threw up his hands and told the governor to deal with the problem.

But governors did not typically handle these kinds of matters, and the governor probably had little awareness of the details of market practices, policies or rules. So it is not surprising that, in broad sweeping measures, he ordered the opening of storehouses and sale at "God's price." This was the easiest order the governor could give, because it had little content. "God's price" is a reference to the well-known statement by the Prophet that "God is the price setter" and thus the Prophet would not set prices himself.[52] So the governor commanded that the merchants sell but he would not specify the price. The result was not a major success, for although the merchants did sell some grain, prices only decreased slightly. This exposes the limitations of requiring sales without announcing the price. On the one hand, it does not force grain holders to sell at a price so low that they will employ all kinds of tricks to avoid selling, but on the other, it does not cause a major change in the market to make goods more affordable and available to the people.

The *muḥtasib* was clearly bypassed in this matter, with the Vice-Sultan directly ordering the governor to assume responsibility for the matter of prices.[53] Perhaps the Vice-Sultan lost confidence in Ibn al-Burjī when the people complained about him, yet he did not replace the *muḥtasib* or ask the governor to work with him (as in the case of the Fustat granaries) but rather treated him as irrelevant.

Ibn al-Furāt provided an insightful postscript to the affair: The judge Saʿd al-Dīn al-Baqrī found fault with the governor for his order to open the warehouses and sell at "God's price" and for getting involved in what is related to the *muḥtasib*'s affair. The judge threatened to inform the Sultan of the governor's actions, whereupon the governor ceased his involvement after the prices decreased a little and the people were reassured by the decrease.[54]

With this information, we are able to enter the domain of competing jurisdictions and professional rivalry. This governor of Cairo was ambitious, and Ibn al-Burjī ceded his authority very easily. The judge's complaint shows that in the Mamluk bureaucracy, there was a conception of the *muḥtasib*'s sphere of authority and that an incursion into it was unacceptable to some, or at least the results of it were unacceptable. Was this judge standing up for the *muḥtasib*'s jurisdiction and what that meant for closer adherence to the law? This problem of high prices did not fully resolve itself with the governor's actions, and throughout the year 797/1395 there were reports of high prices and a slow economy, leading to the next event.

This case could be described as one in which someone finally understood the law. The order to sell at God's price indeed comes from the *ḥadīth* in which the Prophet refused to set prices. Rather than impose a price, the governor basically told everyone to sell at the price of their choosing. It would be easy to conclude that this case shows that leaders in the Mamluk Sultanate knew that the law viewed God as the price setter, and thus humans were to refrain from acting in this area. This interpretation would ignore the individuals involved, as well as the fact that the governor probably did not know what price to impose in order to be effective. Enough ineffective price-setting events had occurred by this time that it must have been known that unless all of the right factors line up, the price-setting effort will fail.

Case Study 6: A *Muḥtasib* Challenges the Political Powers

At the beginning of 798/1395, the price of wheat came down to 60 dirhams per *irdabb* and the people were happy.[55] But then due to forced sales, the price rose to 110.[56] The chronicler Ibn al-Furāt explained that there was a dispute between a powerful amir and al-Bakrī, *muḥtasib* of Fustat, over the forced sale of wheat at a high price "in excess of the limit" (*al-zā'id ʿan al-ḥadd*).[57] Al-Bakrī resigned from the position of *muḥtasib* of Fustat and, in what must have been a daring move, sat in the mosque of ʿAmr b. al-ʿĀs, and told the people: A powerful amir "summoned me on account of the forced sale of wheat. They had imposed it at the price of 80 dirhams per *irdabb*, then 90, and the people were sad because of that. And he ṭold me to impose it at 110 dirhams, and I resigned."[58]

This indicates that the *muḥtasib* had been taking part in forcing sales. The Sultan heard of this affair while he was in the Cairo suburb of Siryāqus, summoned al-Bakrī, and reinstated him to the position of *muḥtasib* of Fustat. He also decreed to give to al-Bakrī and to the *muḥtasib* of Cairo 10,000 *irdabb*s of wheat to be imposed on the millers at the price of 100 dirhams per *irdabb*.[59]

The situation of food prices and availability did not improve, and the Sultan undertook to provide large amounts of bread to the poor.[60] A major problem was the lack of additional food coming into the market. In Cairo and Fustat, prices were high due to shortages of goods and for seven days bread could not be found in the shops. Wheat was sold for 175 dirhams per *irdabb* and flour for 200. Bread, when found, was sold for one-half dirham for one *raṭl* of bread.[61]

And then the event that all had been waiting for happened—ships filled with produce arrived at the docks of Cairo and Fustat.[62] With the abundance of imports, prices decreased, to the point that wheat was sold for 50 dirhams per *irdabb* and four *raṭl*s of bread for a dirham.[63] Ibn al-Furāt added that if it were not for forced sales, the price would have decreased even further.[64] This statement must indicate that while the new arrival of goods would have allowed for a fall in prices as demands were met, wheat belonging to the Sultan or amirs was being imposed on some merchants at a price higher than what might have occurred naturally, and this was keeping average prices up. The merchants were forced to absorb the "cost" to the Sultan and amirs of the low grain prices.

Low prices created another problem—the grain importers were displeased and realized that at these falling prices they would not be able to recover their capital investment and the expenses of their travel. They refused to sell in Cairo and Fustat and went off to Alexandria, in search of higher prices. Seeing that the supply of grain was slowing, the millers and bakers produced less bread, and the people, seeing this, rushed to try to buy bread and suffered from these efforts.[65]

The people went to the Sultan and complained about the lack of food, at which point the Sultan ordered the amir al-Ṭablāwī to take control of the matter.[66] Ibn al-Furāt added that Barqūq specified that al-Ṭablāwī should punish millers and brokers and that the *muḥtasib* al-Damāmīnī (who had been appointed four months earlier) should beat four of the biggest millers and sellers of bread with whips and sticks and order them to increase production of bread. But these millers and sellers did not heed the *muḥtasib*, and the matter worsened.[67] Then it was ordered that a loaf of bread should be sold for one-fourth dirham, and the people desperately sought and fought with each other for it.[68]

The *muḥtasib* of Cairo, al-Damāmīnī, noted the rise in prices, the lack of goods, and how the city was reacting to the situation. He hid at home for three days out of fear that the people would attack him. Al-Ṭablāwī had to rescue him from his home and protect him from a near stoning by the people.[69] The Sultan dismissed al-Damāmīnī and appointed Shams al-Dīn al-Makhānasī,[70] with the mediation of al-Ṭablāwī. There were two significant aspects to this appointment. First, as al-Maqrīzī reported, it was without the payment of money, which by that time had been a common condition imposed for appointment to public office.[71] Secondly, according to Ibn al-Furāt, al-Makhānasī actually stipulated as a condition of his appointment that he would not be required to impose forced sales.[72] The people celebrated his appointment, although the situation took some time to improve.

Three aspects of his appointment are very significant. First, the Sultan must have been desperate enough for an effective *muḥtasib* that he was willing to forego a payment to the Sultan from the new *muḥtasib* that by this time had become fairly typical. Secondly, the new *muḥtasib* saw that his predecessor had nearly been killed by the people and attributed the problems in the food pricing and supply system in large part to the forced sales that the *muḥtasib* had in the past been responsible for carrying out. Third, the previous *muḥtasib* had played a role in forced sales, at least for some time. He participated under pressure, it seems, but he was pushed to his limits by the Sultan and finally refused to go further. This new appointee had enough bargaining power—although we are not told why—in order to secure that, at least in theory, he would not be required to do this.[73]

We do not know if the previous *muḥtasib* objected to the forced sales for pragmatic reasons or because he thought they were illegal. The jurisprudence on hoarding and price setting does not discuss a political leader forcing sales of his own goods on merchants at inflated prices as a way of raising revenue for the leader or his officials, such as the amirs. In a way, these forced sales (*ṭarḥ* or *rimāya*) are a tax on the merchants, because they purchase the goods from the Sultan or amirs at a rate that is above market, then sell those goods to the public, usually for less than they paid. The difference is for the benefit of the Sultan at the merchant's expense. This can be distinguished from setting prices or forcing a hoarder to sell, because there are no proof texts that offer justification for *ṭarḥ* or *rimāya*, and extra (and illegal) taxes have been condemned in the law books and manuals.

This case could be seen as a triumph of the law over political power, and perhaps in this one case it is a fair characterization. By this point in time, however, sultans and amirs commonly used the tactic of forcing sales at inflated prices upon merchants. This is the only recorded case in which a *muḥtasib* resisted involvement in this illegal practice. As the Mamluk Sultanate declined in power throughout the 1400s and the corruption of the sultans and amirs increased, the position of the *muḥtasib* also declined. This study ends in 1400, but it is well documented that the *muḥtasib*s of the Mamluk Sultanate in the fifteenth century were almost without exception linked to the amirs; indeed, amirs even held the position of *muḥtasib*.

Conclusions

We can imagine ways in which these case studies could have been examined only with legal rules as stated in *fiqh* texts. Lengthy and contorted interpretations could have been developed in an attempt to explain how the *muḥtasib* applied the law to the particular case without any mention of the social, political or economic background factors, or any discussion of the identity of the *muḥtasib*. I could have constructed an elaborate jurisprudence that tried to bring all of the idiosyncrasies of the situations somehow under the formal heading of the law. But such a study would have resulted in the concoction of a jurisprudence that is unpersuasive and, if brought to bear on another case of the *muḥtasib* and food pricing and availability, would have no explanatory power.

Alternatively, we can conceive of the conclusion that the *muḥtasib*s simply knew nothing about the laws they were supposed to be applying. The chroniclers did not describe the *muḥtasib*s pondering over *fiqh* books, and in the absence of this information we have to assume that their decisions were arbitrary. Any hint that the laws were known and relevant was a mere coincidence. Under this approach, the Mamluk Sultans were following their own interests only, and the *muḥtasib*s, who sometimes did come from the class of religious scholars, in turn just carried out the Sultans' orders. Since Islamic law is a religious law that should have been formally applied without room for human intervention, according to this line of formalist thought, if it was not applied in an ideal way, then it must not have been applied at all.

Neither of these approaches is meaningful, and both avoid the social context of the law and its application. We do not have evidence that the *muḥtasib*s were consciously and painstakingly applying what they thought was relevant law, but we also do not have evidence of widespread neglect of the law. A prudent conclusion from these case studies is that the actions taken by the *muḥtasib*s and others in power in these cases are explained by extra-legal factors and legal factors. The scope of analysis must be broad, as I have shown, and must include a far bigger picture than just the *muḥtasib*, the particular facts of the case, and the works of *fiqh*. Searching deep and wide for relevant information in each case allows us to see that in addition to the law, other causal factors included the willingness of the Sultan to lend the enforcement power of the state to the problem; the cleverness, popularity, and respect of the *muḥtasib*; and the overall availability of grain in the cities (albeit hoarded) and in the Sultanate.

This article also concludes that scholars of Islamic law can and should make productive use of the lessons of the legal realists. It also strongly encourages Islamic law scholars to place themselves in the context of the larger field of legal studies, and to consider the applicability of developments in other areas of legal studies to Islamic law scholarship. Legal systems involving Islamic law have unique attributes, but they are still legal systems and must be recognized as such. This article has shown that an approach born in twentieth-century American legal studies greatly assists us in understanding an instance of the application of medieval Islamic law.

NOTES

1 Vogel, *Islamic Law and Legal System*, xi.
2 Ibid.
3 Ibid., xii.
4 Leiter, "Legal Realism," 720–25.
5 Leiter, 723.
6 Ibid.

[7] Michael Cook thoroughly examined the Qur'anic injunction to command right and forbid wrong as it is incumbent upon every Muslim in his *Commanding Right and Forbidding Wrong in Islamic Thought*. He dealt with the individual obligation, though, and not how it operates when the specific official of the *muḥtasib* is charged with undertaking it.

[8] *Sulūk*, 3:395.

[9] They also could, of course, have been hovering a short distance away from the docks.

[10] This was not always the case—there are numerous reports in the historical chronicles of food shortages and high prices, albeit in less significant cases, without any mention of the *muḥtasib*. The explanation may be that the *muḥtasib*s were more likely to be involved in serious cases or those with unusual circumstances, and the chroniclers were keen to report such cases. Another possibility is that for the less serious cases, chronicle reports were shorter and less likely to include full details.

[11] Lapidus, "The Grain Economy of Mamlūk Egypt," 3–4.

[12] Ibid.

[13] Ibid., 2; Shoshan, "Grain Riots and the 'Moral Economy'," 463.

[14] *Fiqh Encyclopedia*, "Taʿsīr."

[15] Transmitted by Anas b. Mālik. *Sunan Ibn Mājah*, 2191; *Sunan al-Tirmidhī*, 1235; *Sunan Abī Dāwūd*, 2994 (all *ḥadīth* citations refer to *Mawsūʿat al-ḥadīth al-sharīf*).

[16] *Fiqh Encyclopedia*, "Taʿsīr."

[17] *al-Muwaṭṭaʾ*, 1164.

[18] al-Ḥimyarī, ʿAbd al-Razzāq, *al-Muṣannaf*, 14906.

[19] *Fiqh Encyclopedia*, "Iḥtikār."

[20] A unit of dry measure.

[21] *Sulūk*, 2:394. Al-Maqrīzī described this *wālī* as an oppressive tyrant.

[22] al-Maqrīzī, *Ighātha*, 33–4.

[23] *Sulūk*, 2:394.

[24] Lapidus states that the Sultan "appoint[ed] a new market inspector with full powers." Lapidus, *Muslim Cities in the Later Middle Ages*, 54. Sabra states that the Sultan appointed a new *muḥtasib* "with wide powers." Sabra, 145. There is no evidence, however, that Ḍiyāʾ al-Dīn was granted any special powers with his appointment. Rather, he was known for his abilities in public office; apparently it was because of these abilities that he was a good candidate for *muḥtasib* of Fustat at time of crisis. He was not given wider powers than other *muḥtasib*s, but was able to accomplish more in the position.

[25] The amir Alakuz was "the torture officer for al-Nāṣir Muḥammad" and "admit[ted] being a *ghutmī* [a "disparaging term—to describe those Mamluks who failed to learn proper Arabic"] to emphasize his rudeness." Rabbat, "Representing the Mamluks," 70–1 and n. 34.

[26] *Sulūk*, 2:394–95.

[27] Ibid., 2:395.

[28] Ibid., 2:395–96.

[29] Ibid., 2:396.

[30] The Sultan at this point in his reign also was better placed than some Sultans discussed below to take tough comprehensive measures.

[31] In addition to the apparently lesser role of Cairo in this crisis, the identity of the *muḥtasib* of Cairo could have had something to do with his holding on to his position. He was the cousin of the two preceding *muḥtasib*s of Cairo, which is unusual for this period, in which *muḥtasib*s were generally not related to one another; the position clearly was not an inherited one.

[32] See Lapidus, "The Grain Economy," 6.

[33] *Sulūk*, 2:396.

[34] Nelly Hanna, *An Urban History of Bulaq in the Mamluk and Ottoman Periods*. As Hanna explains, the port at Fustat remained significant until around 780/1378, when the Red Sea trade route began to bypass Qus for taxation purposes and entered land at Suez or Tur. Goods then traveled overland to the Delta, and arrived in Cairo on boats coming from the north of the city. Hanna, 15–16. According to Hanna, "the new itinerary excluded Miṣr and passed via Būlāq instead, hence the decline of one and the rise of the other." Ibid., 16.

[35] Ḍiyāʾ al-Dīn was replaced in Fustat six months after his appointment in Cairo.

[36] *Sulūk*, 2:438.

[37] When he was arrested the next year, the people celebrated for three days near the citadel. *Sulūk*, 2:479–80.

[38] Al-Nashw's ability to force him from office may have been related to the return of chief judge Jalāl al-Dīn to Syria in 738/1337, because he had been a patron and protector of Ḍiyāʾ al-Dīn.

[39] *Sulūk*, 2:758.

[40] Ibid., 2:653.

[41] Ibid., 2:772. Al-Maqrīzī reported that prior to that time there had only been a *qāḍī ʿaskar* for the Shafiʿi school.

[42] *Sulūk*, 3:232–33.

[43] Ibid., 3:233.

[44] Ibid., 3:233–37.

[45] Ibid.

[46] Ibid., 3:239.

[47] Ibid.

[48] *Sulūk*, 3:799; Ibn al-Furāt, 9:366.

[49] *Sulūk* 3:818; Ibn al-Furāt, 9:387.

[50] *Sulūk*, 3:818.

[51] Ibid.

[52] al-Tirmidhī, 1235; Abū Dāwūd, 2974.

[53] Petry discusses the biography of al-Ṭablāwī but states that he was actually appointed *muḥtasib*. Petry, 215. I believe that Ibn al-Burjī remained *muḥtasib* until 797/1395. *Sulūk*, 3:773, 839.

[54] Ibn al-Furāt, 9:387.

[55] Ibid., 9:427.

[56] *Inbāʾ al-ghumr*, 1:507.

[57] Ibn al-Furāt, 9:427.

[58] Ibn al-Furāt, 9:427–28. Note that the *muḥtasib* of Cairo resigned in 798/1395 but the Sultan also reinstated him less than a month later. Perhaps both *muḥtasib*s were protesting forced sales.

[59] Ibid., 9:428.
[60] Ibid., 9:432; *Sulūk*, 3:853–54. This included instructing the same amir al-Ṭablāwī to provide bread to the poor in Cairo and Fustat. Ibid., 9:433–34.
[61] Ibn al-Furāt, 9:434–35.
[62] Ibid., 9:435. The port of Bulaq is specifically mentioned—contrast this with the case of the Fustat granaries in which only the Fustat port was involved.
[63] Ibn al-Furāt, 9:439; *Sulūk*, 3:859.
[64] Ibn al-Furāt, 9:439.
[65] *Sulūk*, 3:859; Ibn al-Furāt, 9:439.
[66] *Sulūk*, 3:859; *Nuzhat al-nufūs*, 1:430, even specifies and says take control of the matter of "*ḥisba*," but it is still clear that he was not appointed *muḥtasib*.
[67] Ibn al-Furāt, 9:439.
[68] *Sulūk*, 3:860; Ibn al-Furāt, 9:439.
[69] *Sulūk*, 3:860; Ibn al-Furāt, 9:439–40.
[70] There are several variations of the spelling of his name, but this seems the most common.
[71] *Sulūk*, 3:859–60.
[72] Ibn al-Furāt, 9:440.
[73] *Sulūk*, 3:996.

BIBLIOGRAPHY

Cook, Michael, *Commanding Right and Forbidding Wrong in Islamic Thought* (Cambridge: Cambridge University Press, 2002).

[*Fiqh Encyclopedia*] *Wizārat al-awqāf wa l-shu'ūn al-islāmiyya. Al-Mawsūʿa al-fiqhiyya*, 41 vols. to date (Kuwait 1983–).

Hanna, Nelly, *An Urban History of Bulaq in the Mamluk and Ottoman Periods* (Cairo: IFAO, 1983).

al-Ḥimyarī, ʿAbd al-Razzāq b. Hammām, *al-Muṣannaf* (Markaz al-Turāth al-Jāmiʿ al-Kabīr, CD-ROM).

Ibn al-Furāt, Muḥammad b. ʿAbd al-Raḥīm, *Tārīkh Ibn al-Furāt*, vols. 7–9, ed. Qusṭanṭīn Zurayq (Beirut 1936–42).

Ibn al-Ṣayrafī, *Nuzhat al-nufūs wa l-abdān fī tawārīkh al-zamān* (Cairo, 1970–94).

Lapidus, Ira M., *Muslim Cities in the Later Middle Ages* (Cambridge: Cambridge University Press, 1984).

——. "The Grain Economy of Mamluk Egypt," *Journal of the Economic and Social History of the Orient* 12 (1969), 1–15.

Leiter, Brian, "Legal Realism," in *The Philosophy of Law: An Encyclopedia*, ed. C. B. Gray, 2:720–25 (New York: Garland Publishing, 1999).

al-Maqrīzī, see *Sulūk*.

——. *Ighāthat al-umma bi-kashf al-ghumma*, ed. Yāsir Sayyid Ṣāliḥīn (Cairo, 1999).

Mawsūʿat al-ḥadīth al-sharīf (CD-ROM version, 2.1).

Petry, Carl, *The Civilian Elite of Cairo in the Later Middle Ages* (Princeton: Princeton University Press, 1981).

Rabbat, Nassar, "Representing the Mamluks in Mamluk Historical Writing," in *The Historiography of Islamic Egypt (c. 959–1800)*, ed. Hugh Kennedy (Leiden: Brill, 2001), 69–75.

Sabra, Adam, *Poverty and Charity in Medieval Islam* (Cambridge University Press, 2000).

Shoshan, Boaz, "Grain Riots and the 'Moral Economy': Cairo, 1350–1517," *Journal of Interdisciplinary History* 10/3 (Winter 1980), 459–78.
[*Sulūk*]. al-Maqrīzī, *Kitāb al-Sulūk li-maʿrifat duwal al-mulūk*, 4 vols., eds. Saʿīd ʿAbd al-Fattāḥ and Muḥammad Muṣṭafā Ziyāda (Cairo, 1956–73).
Vogel, Frank E., *Islamic Law and Legal System: Studies of Saudi Arabia* (Leiden: Brill, 2000).

5

SHARECROPPING IN THE DAKHLA OASIS

Shariʿa and Customary Law in Ottoman Egypt

Rudolph Peters

In this essay[1] I will present and analyse two documents from a family archive found in the town of al-Qaṣr (henceforth, al-Qasr) in the Dakhla Oasis. They contain arrangements regarding a sharecropping contract and I will show that these must be regarded as attempts to reconcile legal doctrine with customary practice. The documents were found during clearance activities in connection with the restoration of an early eighteenth-century mud brick house, carried out by the Qasr Dakhleh Project (QDP) under the aegis of the Dakhleh Oasis Project. In the rubble of the ruined house a considerable number of objects and written pieces of paper were found.[2] According to local informants, the house was already abandoned before 1940, probably due to its sudden collapse. The pieces of paper are the remains of a family archive belonging to a branch of the Qurashī family. Their study may shed light on the pre-modern history of this little Islamic town. Although much of the paper material consists of scraps or small fragments of documents, there are also many complete or nearly complete documents. These include religious texts, personal letters, magical texts, amulets, and about 170 legal documents or documents regarding financial transactions, dating from 1579 (987 AH) to 1929. The documents have been numbered and placed between glass plates for conservation, and are now stored in the storerooms of the Egyptian Antiquities Organization Inspectorate of Dakhla. My colleague Fred Leemhuis of the University of Groningen, who is in charge of the QDP, asked me to examine and eventually publish the legal material.

Family archives are important for historical research. Their special value is that they give a great deal of information on a specific family and are, therefore, a rich source for social history. Such information cannot easily be culled from public archives, unless these are completely digitized and searchable. But even then, family archives have an added value because they usually contain many documents of minor importance (receipts, IOUs, lists of creditors, etc.) not found in the state archives. The documents found in al-Qasr are for these reasons of great significance. In fact, they are unique, since very little is known of the Ottoman history (nor of any other period) of the town. There are rumours that there exists a privately held manuscript chronicle of the town. However, I have not seen it and cannot judge its value as a source. The holdings of the Egyptian state archives must undoubtedly contain documents relative to al-Qasr. However, since in the main archive, Dār al-Wathāʾiq al-Qawmiyya (DWQ), only about 10% of the material has been catalogued, it will be difficult to conduct a specific search. Moreover, the main holdings of this archive, i.e., the documents of the Egyptian government, do not go back further than 1822, when a fire destroyed the then existing records. Shariʿa court records exist from earlier periods. Those of the provincial courts are now available either in the DWQ (where they were housed in recent times) or in the Dār al-Maḥfūẓāt, an archive belonging to the Ministry of Finance. These archives may offer better prospects, but at the moment it is still unclear whether or not the records of the al-Qasr court are preserved, and if so, where they are located.

The legal documents found in al-Qasr consist mainly of contracts, often notarized in court, of receipts of payment of taxes, appointment of proxies, and notes regarding debts or expenses. In addition I have found a few charitable endowment deeds (*waqfiyya*), judicial sentences, and fatwas. The documents that I have studied so far clearly point to the fact that the Qurashī family, or at least that part of it that lived in this house, was mainly involved in agriculture. More than half of the documents are related to agricultural activities: lease or sale of land or of water rights, sharecropping, or the payment of taxes on land or springs and wells. In addition there are some documents regarding the maintenance of a spring and lists made by individual farmers of those from whom they leased water rights. I have found no documents indicating that the family was engaged in cattle breeding, trade, or artisanal production, nor documents related to the sale of the date harvest. The family seems to have belonged to the notables of the town: Among them, there were several judges and administrative sheikhs.

Al-Qasr used to be the main town of the Dakhla Oasis. It is situated about 350 km west of Luxor, halfway between the Nile and the present-day Libyan border. Nowadays the town of Mut has taken over its function as administrative centre. The town of al-Qasr goes back to Roman times, as evidenced by the remains of a Roman wall that were recently discovered and dated. An important source of livelihood was agriculture, made possible by the abundance of springs and wells, located mainly to the south and east of the town. These wells were in private hands, often owned collectively by tens of persons. A substantial part of the documents deals with titles to water, evidently just as important as titles to land.

The inhabitants of al-Qasr followed the Shafiʿi school of jurisprudence and the Shariʿa court of the town was also Shafiʿi. Nearly all of the deeds that were registered in court bear the name of a Shafiʿi qadi, whose main task, like that of other qadis, was notarizing contracts and depositions. From the titles used in the documents it is clear that the local qadis felt themselves to be part of the Ottoman judiciary. They referred to themselves as the deputies (*nāʾib*, *khalīfa*) of the Ottoman qadi of the Western Oases (*qāḍī l-Wāḥāt*, or *al-nāẓir fī l-aḥkām al-sharʿiyya fī kāmil aqālīm al-Wāḥāt*). This is consistent with the legal practice in Ottoman Egypt before the nineteenth century. The Hanafi qadis appointed to various cities in Egypt would have deputies belonging to the other schools, adjudicating disputes and registering documents according to their own school, but under the supervision of the Hanafi qadi.

The two documents presented here were written with an interval of sixteen years, each on one side of an undamaged piece of paper measuring 15 by 39 cm.[3] The first document is an unofficial copy of a notarized contract. The last sentences mention that it has been notarized (*ṭalab al-ḥukm bihi*) by a qadi. Since there is no heading with the name and the seal of the judge, as we find in other documents, I assume it was an unofficial copy of the original one. It is signed by four witnesses. The second document, written overleaf, is not notarized and is signed by two witnesses. One of the parties is Ṣāliḥ Muḥammad Ṣāliḥ al-Qurashī, whose papers are part of the al-Qurashī collection. He was a farmer and appears between 1771 and 1801 in eight documents of the collection, all of them contracts with regard to land, palm trees, or water rights, and without exception concluded with relatives. According to these documents, he cultivated plots south and west of the town.

The documents are not only of interest for social history, they are also relevant for legal history, or rather for the history of the application of the Shariʿa. They show how local jurists tried to reconcile customary practices with the legal doctrines of Islamic jurisprudence. In Islamic law, according to most schools of jurisprudence, there is no general theory of contract because the law regards as valid and binding only those contracts that are expressly mentioned and permitted in the law. If parties conclude contracts not recognized by the law, such contracts are void and cannot be enforced in a court of law. Thus, classifying customary agreements in accordance with the Shariʿa is important. Since the community of al-Qasr was in the habit of concluding certain sharecropping contracts that were not regarded as valid under Shafiʿi law, the jurists sought creative solutions by characterizing these contracts differently. However, these new classifications posed new legal problems. Realizing this, the jurists of al-Qasr also invoked the authority of custom, in the event the binding character of the contract would not be recognized.

The first document runs as follows:

Glory to God alone.

This is a *ja'āla*[4] regarding cultivation (*iṣlāḥ*) and a written document regarding customary practice (*iṣṭilāḥ*), whose purport will be specified and whose implications will be explained, [namely], that the honourable Shaykh al-ʿArab Muḥammad Abū Khalīfa al-Muḥājī (?)[5] al-ʿAmrānī (?) has requested that his following statement be witnessed (*ishhād*). He has offered a *ja'āla* undertaking and has agreed with both al-Zaynī Ṣāliḥ, son of the late Muḥammad Ṣāliḥ al-Qurashī, and Muḥassib, son of the late Riḍā, with regard to a parcel (*qiṭ'a*) of land on which there are here and there some old palm trees, in the region of the al-Najābīn spring, south of the town of al-Qasr, and known as the Farmers' Patch (*buq'at al-fallāḥīn*), confined by four boundaries: to the south on the western side [a plot] owned by the heirs of ʿAlī ʿAṭiyya and on the eastern side [a plot] owned by ʿUbayd ʿAbd al-Ghafūr (?), to the north the road (*al-ṭarīq*), to the east [a plot] owned by his aunt Fāṭima, and to the west the pond, as well as with regard to a piece (*khaṭṭ*) of land near the aforementioned spring close to the alleyway (*zuqāq*), confined by four boundaries: to the south the road, to the north [a plot] owned by the heirs of Abū Khāṭir, to the east [a plot owned by] Sulaymān Majīd, and to the west the rest of the piece of land owned by Muḥammad ʿAlī and his co-owners, exactly as here delimited, inherited by the aforementioned Muḥammad from his mother Umbāraka, daughter of the late Muḥammad Fāyid al-Muḥājī, to the effect that the aforementioned persons al-Zaynī Ṣāliḥ and Muḥassib, plant that part of the land that lies fallow with various kinds of crops in accordance with their ability and desire and look after the land by guarding, inundating, and fertilizing it [with manure] and by trimming [the plants], and that in consideration of what they have planted, they will be entitled to one third, eight *qīrāṭ*,[6] to be divided among them in three parts, one third for the aforementioned Ṣāliḥ, one third for the aforementioned Muḥassib, and one third for Muḥammad, the landlord (*al-mujā'il*), on account of the [already existing] plants, and moreover, Muḥammad will also be entitled to two thirds, sixteen *qīrāṭ*, on account of the land and the irrigation (*al-riḍā'*). Whatever God—Who is to be praised and Who is exalted—causes to grow, regardless of whether or not it has been planted, will be divided along the lines of the aforementioned *ja'āla* in accordance with the fact that they have agreed upon it (*tawāfaqū*) and consented (*raḍū*) to it in conformity with the Shariʿa. Now, consent has legal effect (*al-riḍā ḥukm*). [Moreover], this is the custom (*'urf*) of the people of the region and the practice (*iṣṭilāḥ*) of the people of the oasis. It has been enjoined that custom must be followed, at least to the extent that it is regarded as valid. That is the case according to the honourable scholars (*al-sāda al-'ulamā'*) on the basis of any of the four legal schools because of the words of God—Who is exalted—in his clear Book, addressing the Lord of Messengers: "Keep to forgiveness (O Muḥammad), and enjoin kindness (*ʿurf*) and turn away from the ignorant." [Q 7:199] [The *jaʿāla* has been concluded] in a valid and legal manner, in a pleasant spirit and a joyful mind (*ʿan ṭīb qalb wa-sharḥ ṣadr*), and was provided with an authorization regarding its being witnessed (*thubūtuhu*), with the request for a legal ruling (*ṭalab al-ḥukm bihi*) and with a behest for the witnessing of the latter. It was [then] witnessed and that took place and was recorded on the blessed Friday, the last day of excellent month of Ṣafar in the year 1206, twelve hundred and six [28 October, 1791].

Witnesses
ʿAbd al-Laṭīf Yūsuf al-Muḥājī
Ibrāhīm ʿAbd Allāh Muṣṭafā
Muḥammad ʿUthmān
Masʿūd Muḥammad al-Muḥājī

The other document reads as follows:

Glory to God alone

A division and an agreement took place between Muḥammad Khalīfa, mentioned overleaf, Ṣāliḥ Muḥammad, mentioned overleaf, and Muḥassib Riḍā, mentioned overleaf, as to all of the shares mentioned overleaf with regard to the third of the plants mentioned overleaf, since one third of the plants were to be divided among those mentioned overleaf in three thirds. Now the [part] to which Ṣāliḥ, mentioned overleaf, is entitled is two young Ṣaʿīdī palm trees (*wudāya*),[7] a palm sapling (*ʿuzb*) in the middle of the field, and also a pomegranate tree with wood at the south end [of the plot]. [The division took place] in a valid and legal way as the aforementioned persons divided the aforementioned plants before they began to bear fruit. Then Muḥammad Khalīfa undertook to irrigate the aforementioned palm trees (*wudy*) until they bear fruit, [from which moment] every one, pursuant to the stipulations of the *jaʿāla*, shall irrigate in proportion to his share. He [Muḥammad Khalīfa] requested that this accordingly be witnessed (*ishhād*). That took place and was recorded in the month of Rabīʿ al-ākhar, one of the months of the year 1222, twelve hundred twenty two [i.e., between 8 June and 7 July 1807].

As witness thereof
Ibrāhīm Muṣṭafā
As witness thereof
Al-Qurashī ʿAbd al-Ghafūr Ḥusayn [?]

In the first document, the owner of two plots of land, on one of which some palm trees were already growing, promises two other men, on condition that they plant and cultivate trees, a share of 1/9 each in what they have planted on the fallow parts of the plots. The landowner takes 7/9 of the trees, i.e., his customary share of two thirds increased with one ninth, apparently in consideration of the fact that one plot had already some palm trees on it belonging to him. Part of the arrangement was a stipulation that the landlord will irrigate the plants until the moment they start to bear fruit and that after that moment all parties to the contract shall water the plants in proportion to their shares. Almost all other *jaʿāla* documents in the collection include this clause, which was apparently part of the customary law governing this arrangement. That this clause was omitted here must be due to an oversight of the scribe and cannot have been deliberate since in the second document it is referred to as part of the contract.

In the second document, dated sixteen years later, Ṣāliḥ's share is defined and transferred to him. It consists of two young palm trees, one sapling, and a pomegranate tree. The division took place at a time when the palm trees Ṣāliḥ had planted had not yet borne fruit, since, in accordance with customary law, Muḥammad undertakes to continue to water them until that moment. Ṣāliḥ had this contract written on the back of his copy of the original contract. If Muḥassib also had a specific share assigned to him, it must have been recorded on the back of his own copy.

I found eight *jaʿāla* documents in the collection. One of them, written in 1866 CE,[8] is a contract in which more than fifty persons, who together own a spring, contract two persons to repair the spring for a share in the property rights. A judge's note in the margin, dated about a year and a half after the contract was concluded, indicates that there were some problems with its implementation: it states that the remuneration is only due after the completion of the tasks and that the person who undertook the task can only claim it from the other parties if he can prove that they are owners of the well. The other *jaʿāla* documents,[9] dated between 1773 and 1823 CE, deal with sharecropping of planted trees and are practically identical to the first document presented here, except that most of them include the stipulation about the irrigation.

According to the terms mentioned in the document, it is a typical *mughārasa* contract, that is, a sharecropping contract whereby a landowner agrees with a person (the sharecropper) that the latter plants trees on his land and cultivates them in exchange for a share in them (or, in addition, a share in the land), to be transferred to him after they bear fruit.[10] The question then arises why this contract is called *jaʿāla* and not *mughārasa*. In order to answer this we must consider what the different legal schools say about these contracts.

Let us first consider the position of the schools on sharecropping (*muzāraʿa, musāqāt, mughārasa*).[11] It is a contract that can be construed as either hire of labour or lease of land, both called *ijāra* in the works of jurisprudence. The crucial problem, however, is that it is a contract in which one of the performances, i.e., the wages or the rent, is uncertain, because it involves the future transfer of ownership of objects that do not exist at the time of the contract and whose quantity and value are not precisely determined. This constitutes a form of risk (*gharar*) which vitiates the contract. Therefore, it cannot be a valid lease of land or hire of labour. The Malikis construe it as a form of partnership (*sharika*), but this also brings about legal constraints. However, there exists a Prophetic tradition (*ḥadīth*) that is regarded by most schools as legitimizing an exception to the principle that the performances in a contract must be precisely specified. The *ḥadīth* relates that, after the conquest of Khaybar, the Prophet Muḥammad concluded a contract with the Jews who were living there, stipulating that they could remain on the land and cultivate the palm orchards, but had to pay one half of the crop to the Prophet.[12] The law schools, however, differ on the legal implications of this *ḥadīth*. Most schools allow on the strength of the *ḥadīth* some form of lease of land against a part of the crop. Only Abū Ḥanīfa maintained that such contracts were forbidden. His argument was that the *ḥadīth* is unclear on a number of legal points, and therefore may not be regarded as introducing an exception to a general principle of the law of contracts. For instance, the Jews might have been slaves (who cannot have ownership rights) or the obligation to pay half of the date harvest may have been imposed on them not by contract but by the state as taxation for non-Muslims (*kharāj*). However, Abū Ḥanīfa's students Abū Yūsuf and al-Shaybānī regarded the contract as valid and their opinion became the prevailing one in their school because it was customary practice.[13]

The Hanbalis allow sharecropping contracts (both *muzāraʿa* and *musāqāt*) with hardly any restrictions. The Malikis make a distinction between *muzāraʿa* and *musāqāt*. The former is valid, according to them, but only under certain conditions and by virtue of a rather complicated legal construction. They view it as a composite of three separate contracts: lease, rent, and partnership. The parties must agree on a fixed rent of the land and fixed wages of the labour in order to circumvent the problem of uncertainty of the wages or rent. The rent and wages may be balanced so that neither party is in debt to the other. On that basis they conclude a contract of partnership and share the profit (the harvest, which can be of all types: fruits, cereals, cotton) in equal proportions. On the other hand, a *musāqāt* contract is held to be valid by them without fixing the rent and the wages and for unequal shares between landowner and labourer. However, such a contract may only be concluded with regard to fruit trees.[14] The Shafiʿis do not allow *muzāraʿa* at all but, like the Malikis, regard *musāqāt* contracts as valid, but only with regard to grapes and dates. Al-Shāfiʿī's argument is that the legitimacy of *musāqāt* is a permission by way of exception (*rukhṣa*) based on the *ḥadīth* (there is also a similar one regarding grapes) and that exceptions to rules may not be extended by analogy. Another controversy is the remuneration of the person who contributes his labour: should that only be a share in the crop (as in the contracts of *muzāraʿa* and *musāqāt*) or is the labourer allowed to receive part of the trees that he has planted (as in the *mughārasa* contract)? Malikis and Hanbalis regard the latter contract as valid; the Shafiʿis and the Hanafis do not allow it.

The jurists of al-Qasr were obviously well aware of this position of the Shafiʿi school. They therefore tried to cast the contract in another mould, that of *jaʿāla*. The idea of constructing this form of sharecropping in this way must have come from jurists familiar with Maliki jurisprudence. For Maliki jurists point out that the *mughārasa* contract, which they regard as valid, is like *jaʿāla*:

> As to *mughārasa*, that is a contract whereby a man hands over his land to another who will plant trees on it. There are three modes of it: (1) hire (*ijāra*), whereby a person plants for the owner for fixed wages; (2) *juʿl* (a synomym of *jaʿāla*, RP), whereby a person plants trees for the owner on condition that he acquire a share of what grows out of it [the saplings]; (3) something between hire and *juʿl*, whereby a person plants for the owner on condition that he acquire both a share of that [planting] and of the land.[15]

It is doubtful, however, that such a legal construction is valid according to the Shafiʿi doctrine.[16] The Shafiʿi jurists define *jaʿāla* as "the undertaking to give a specific remuneration (*juʿl*) for work, regardless of whether it[s amount] is defined and known or unknown and difficult to define precisely" (*iltizām ʿiwaḍ maʿlūm ʿalā ʿamal maʿlūm aw majhūl yaʿsur ḍabṭuhu*). *Jaʿāla* is therefore a legal act that can be used to contract labour for producing a result if the amount of labour required for it cannot be determined. This result may be to restore something, such as the finding and returning of stray cattle or lost objects, or to produce something new, such as the digging of a well until the water appears, or teaching a skill to someone. It differs from hiring labour (*ijāra*) in that for *ijāra* to be valid and binding the amount of work must be specified. The *jaʿāla* contract, therefore, is an exception to the strict rule that in synallagmatic contracts the performances must be known and well defined. The textual basis for the exception is Q 12:72: "They said: We have lost the king's cup, and he who bringeth it shall have a camel-load, and I (said Joseph) am answerable for it."[17] In addition there is a tradition according to which the Prophet approved of an arrangement whereby a person who was bitten by a snake undertook to pay thirty sheep to a person who would recite the Qurʾan in order to heal him, in the event he succeeded.[18] The remuneration is only due if and when the desired result has been produced. Jurists stress that *jaʿāla* is not a contract but a unilateral legal act of the person who promises the remuneration. He is entitled to revoke his promise at any time until the result has been achieved and the reward is due. However, in order to prevent unfair advantage, he must pay standard wages (*ujrat al-mithl*) if the labour accomplished until that moment is beneficial to him, for instance if the object of the *jaʿāla* is the digging of a well until it reaches the water table and the *jaʿāla* is revoked before water is reached. According to the Shafiʿi doctrine, it is essential for the *jaʿāla* that the remuneration is well defined; otherwise the conditions are the same as for the rent or wages in a contract of lease or employment. And here, I think, lies the crux in the application of the *jaʿāla* contract to sharecropping, for the remuneration does not exist at the time of the *jaʿāla* and is not well defined.

The document shows that the person who drafted it was familiar with the unilateral character of the *jaʿāla*. In conformity with standard practice, the documents in our collection record synallagmatic contracts as declarations of both parties, such as: A has bought from B and B has sold to A. In this document we find only that the landlord requests that witnesses hear that he undertakes (*jāʿala*) to pay a remuneration on certain conditions. Only at the end of the document is it mentioned that the other parties agreed to the arrangement. Moreover, I believe that the lawyer who wrote the document was well aware of the problematic character of the way the sharecropping contract was framed. For this reason he also invoked custom (*ʿurf*) as a ground for regarding the contract as valid and binding. At the end of the first document there is the following statement about the validity of customary law (also found in some other *jaʿāla* documents)[19]:

> Now, consent has legal effects (*al-riḍā ḥukm*) and that is the custom of the people of this region and the customary practice (*iṣṭilāḥ*) of the people of the oasis. It has been ordered that custom must be followed, at least to the extent that it is regarded as valid. That is the case according to the honourable scholars (*al-sāda al-ʿulamāʾ*) on the basis of any of the four legal schools because of the words of God—Who is exalted—in his clear Book, addressing the Lord of Messengers: "Keep to forgiveness (O Muḥammad), and enjoin kindness (*ʿurf*)[20] and turn away from the ignorant." [Q 7:199]

It seems as if the lawyer who drafted the document is saying here: "Yes, I know that the way this contract is constructed is not entirely in conformity with Shafiʿi doctrine. However, this is the way we always do it here in the oasis; moreover, it is the will of the parties and therefore it must be regarded as valid and binding." But even this argument would not pass the scrutiny of strict Shafiʿi jurists. Under Shafiʿi law, custom cannot override provisions of the Shariʿa. Shafiʿi doctrine is rigorous in this respect, as illustrated, for instance, by the fact that, unlike the other schools, it regards the contract of *istiṣnāʿ* (a contract whereby a person pays another to manufacture something for him, which is a transaction about objects that do not exist at the time of the contract) as not valid despite the fact that it is a customary transaction.[21] We do not know whether the validity of the contracts recorded in these documents were ever tested in a court of law. However, it seems that this did not bother the inhabitants of al-Qasr very much.

The documents examined in this essay, as well as most others found in al-Qasr, show that its inhabitants were committed to their Shafiʿi *madhhab*. Otherwise they could have had recourse to the Maliki school. *Madhhab* shopping was common practice in Ottoman Egypt. In most major towns, there were, in addition to the Hanafi supreme qadi appointed by the Porte, deputy qadis of the three other schools of jurisprudence. As shown by the court records from that period, people would go to the qadi who could formulate contracts or draft endowment deeds as they wanted it. People knew that in order to found a religious endowment (*waqf*) with certain specific clauses you had to go to the Hanbali qadi, for instance, or to another for a specific type of lease.[22] There are no indications at all that this practice was considered to be blameworthy. Therefore, it is striking that the inhabitants of al-Qasr stuck to the Shafiʿi doctrine, although sharecropping in the form they practised it was valid under Maliki and not under Shafiʿi law. It is not clear why they did not ask a Maliki qadi (and there are one or two documents signed by a Maliki qadi in al-Qasr)[23] to draw up a *mughārasa* contract. Instead the drafter of the document invoked two general principles as a justification of the binding force of the contract: the fact that it was sanctioned by custom and the fact that is was based on mutual agreement. However, neither would have carried any weight in a Shafiʿi court of law.

NOTES

[1] This is a revised version of a paper presented at the Customary Law in the Middle East Workshop, Dept. of Near Eastern Studies, Princeton University (May 13–14, 2006) with the title "Shariʿa and Customary Law in al-Qasr (Dakhla Oasis, Egypt) in the Eighteenth Century."

[2] For more information on the project, see http://weekly.ahram.org.eg/2006/787/heritage.htm.

[3] Document D.04.291 recto and verso.

[4] *Jaʿāla* (also pronounced *jiʿāla* and *juʿāla*) is a legal arrangement whereby one person undertakes to pay a remuneration to another person after the latter has completed a task. See below for the legal discussion concerning this contract.

[5] The question marks indicate that the original Arabic text was not entirely clear.

[6] *Qīrāṭ* in this context is not a square measure, but is used for a share of 1/24.

[7] I am grateful to several inhabitants of al-Qasr for explaining to me the agricultural terms in the documents during my stay there in February and March 2006.

[8] D.05.063 from 1283 H.

[9] D.05.045 recto, dated 1217; D.05.045 verso, dated 1217; D.05.049 recto, dated 1198; D.04.166, dated 1187; D.04.277, dated 1239; D.04.228r, dated 1220.

[10] *Mughārasa* is one instance of a group of sharecropping contracts, to which also belong *musāqāh* and *muzāraʿa*, i.e., agreements whereby a person undertakes to cultivate another person's land for one or more years in exchange for a share in the crop.

[11] Unless otherwise indicated, this part relies on Ibn Rushd, *Bidāyat al-mujtahid*, 2 vols. (Cairo: Muṣṭafā al-Bābī al-Ḥalabī, 1960) 2:244–51 (*kitāb al-musāqāh*), and William J. Donaldson, *Sharecropping in the Yemen: A Study in Islamic Theory, Custom and Pragmatism* (Leiden: Brill, 2000), chs. 3 and 4.

[12] al-ʿAsqalānī, *Bulūgh al-marām fī adillat al-aḥkām* (Cairo: Dār al-Kitāb al-ʿArabī, n.d.), no. 765, where the variants are also listed.

[13] Shaykhzāde, *Majmaʿ al-anhur fī sharḥ Multaqā al-abḥur*, 2 vols. (Istanbul, 1301 H.), 2:393–94.

[14] ʿAbd al-Raḥmān al-Jazīrī, *Kitāb al-Fiqh ʿalā al-madhāhib al-arbaʿa*, vol. 3: *al-Muʿāmalāt* (5th impr., Cairo: al-Maktaba al-Tijāriyya al-Kubrā, n.d.), 4, 21–5.

[15] Ibn Juzayy, *al-Qawānīn al-fiqhiyya* (N.p.: n.d.), 212 (kitāb 4, bāb 3: Fī al-muzāraʿa wa l-mughārasa).

[16] See al-Ramlī, *Nihāyat al-muḥtāj fī sharḥ al-Minhāj* (Cairo: Dār al-Fikr, 1969), 5:465–81.

[17] It is an episode from the Yūsuf story. After he had hidden his precious cup in Binyamīn's luggage and the brothers were leaving the town, it was announced that this cup was missing and that the person who found it would get a camel load of goods as a reward.

[18] al-Bukhārī, *Ṣaḥīḥ* (*kitāb al-ṭibb*).

[19] See, e.g., D.04.166 and D.05.045 verso.

[20] Most Qurʾan exegetes explain the word *ʿurf* in this context as fear of God and observance of His commands, or as *maʿrūf*, i.e., fair and equitable, and not as custom. However, some jurists, especially the Malikis, regard this text as a command to take custom into account. See Mohammad Hashim Kamali, *Principles of Islamic Jurisprudence* (Cambridge: Islamic Texts Society, 1991), 284, 292.

[21] See, e.g., Jalāl al-Dīn ʿAbd al-Raḥmān al-Suyūṭī, *al-Ashbāh wa l-naẓāʾir fī qawāʿid wa-furūʿ fiqh al-shāfiʿiyya* (Beirut: Dār al-Kutub al-ʿIlmiyya, 1990), 99.

[22] R. Peters, "What Does It Mean to Be an Official Madhhab? Hanafism and the Ottoman Empire," in *The Islamic School of Law: Evolution, Devolution, and Progress*, ed. P. Bearman, R. Peters, and F. Vogel (Cambridge, Mass.: ILSP/Harvard University Press, 2005), 147–58.

[23] E.g., a divorce on grounds of abandonment (which is a ground for divorce under Maliki but not under Shafiʿi law) pronounced by a Maliki qadi, authorized by the regular Shafiʿi qadi. D.05.050, dated 1116 H.

APPENDIX ONE

D.04.291 recto

الحمد لله وحده|
هذه جعالة على الاصلاح ووثيقة محررة على الاصطلاح يعرف مضمونها|
ويوضح مكنونها اشهد على نفسه المحترم شيخ العرب محمد ابو خليفة المحاجي [؟] العمراني [؟] انه|
جاعل ووافق كل من الزيني صالح بن المرحوم محمد صالح القرشي ومحسب بن|
المرحوم رضا على جميع قطعة ارض مخللة بالنخيل الكبير (وتعرف[1]) بعين|
النجابين الكاينة قبلي مدينة القصر وتعرف ببقعة الفلاحين ويحصرها|
حدود اربعة القبلي بعضه من غربي بيد ورثة علي عطية وبعضه من شرقي |
بيد عيد عبد الغفور[؟] والبحري الطريق والشرقي بيد خالته فاطمة والغربي|
البركة وجميع خط ارض بالعين المذكورة بجوار الزقاق ويحصره|
حدود اربعة القبلي الطريق والبحري بيد ورثة ابو خاطر والشرقي سليمان|
مجيد والغربي بقية الخط بيد محمد علي وشركايه بحد ذلك وحدوده الايل|
الى محمد المذكور اعلاه من والدته امباركة ابنة[2] المرحوم محمد ابو[3] فايد[؟] المحاجي [؟]|
على ان الزيني صالح المذكور ومحسب المذكور يغرسوا خلو الارض |
من انواع الغراسات على حسب طاقتهم وارادتهم ويباشروا الارض|
المذكورة بالصيانة والغراق والتزبيل والتقليم ويكون لهم في نظير غرسهم|
الثلث ثمانية قراريط يقسم بينهم اثلاثا ما هو لصالح المذكور الثلث|
ومحسب الثلث ومحمد المجاعل الثلث بحق الغرس ولمحمد ايضا الثلثان[4]|
ستة عشر قيراطا بحق الارض والرضاع ومهما اطلع الله سبحانه وتعالى|
بغراس وغير غراس يكون على اسوة الجعالة المذكورة حسبما توافقوا ورضوا|
على ذلك الرضى الشرعي والرضى حكم وذلك عرف اهل البلاد واصطلاح اهل الواحه|
والعرف مامور به وذلك على ما يرى صحته ذلك عند السادة العلما على قاعدة مذهب من المذاهب الاربعة[5]
لقوله تعالى في كتابه المبين خطابا لسيد المرسلين خذ العفو وامر بالعرف واعرض عن الجاهلين[6] جعالة[7]
صحيحة شرعية وهما|
عن طيب قلب وشرح صدر مشمولا (؟) بالتوكيل في ثبوته |
وطلب الحكم به وسوال الاشهاد فيه وبه شهد وجرى ذلك|
وحرر في يوم الجمعة المبارك ختام شهر صفر الخير الذي هو |
من شهور سنة 1206 ستة ومايتان والف|

شهوده
عبد اللطيف يوسف حجاج عفي عنه
شهوده
ابرهيم عبد الله مصطفى عفي عنه
شهد
محمد عثمان [؟]

شهد على المجاعل المذكور
الحاج مسعود محمد

D.04.291 verso

الحمد لله وحده
وقعت القسمة والمراضاة ما بين محمد خليفة المذكور باطنه|
وما بين محمد صالح المذكور باطنه وما بين محسب رضا المذكور باطنه في كامل|
الحصص المذكورة باطنه في الثلث الغرس المذكور باطنه لكون ان ثلث|
الغرس يقسم بين المذكورين اثلاثا فكان الذي استحق لصالح ودايا اثنتان|
صعيديتين وعزب بوسط الغيط وايضا شجرة وعود رمان قبلي|
قسمة صحيحة شرعية لكون ان المذكورين قسموا الغراس المذكور قبل ان|
يثمر حينئذ الزم نفسه محمد خليفة المذكور بسقي الودي المذكور الى حين|
يثمر على شرط الجعالة كل احد[8] يسقي على قدر حصته حسبما اشهد|
على نفسه يذلك جرى ذلك وحرر في شهر ربيع الاخر الذي هو من شهور سنة 1222 |
اثنين وعشرون ومايتان والف|

شهد بذلك ابراهيم مصطفى
شهد بذلك القرشي [...؟] حسين

NOTES

[1] To be deleted, scribal error.
[2] ابوا
[3] ابنت
[4] ابوا
[5] الثلثشاي(؟)
[6] الابع
[7] القرآن 7:199
[8] Parallel text in D.04.166:

والرضا حكم وعرف بلا دهم والعرف مامور به على قاعدة مذهب من المذاهب الاربع على ما يرى صحته ذلك عند الساده العلما رضي الله عنهم اجمعين [لقوله تعالى في كتابه المبين] خطابا لسيد المرسلين خذ العفو وامر بالعرف واعرض عن الجاهلين

[9] احدا

6

JOINT MARITAL PROPERTY IN INDONESIAN CUSTOMARY, ISLAMIC, AND NATIONAL LAW

Mark E. Cammack and R. Michael Feener

This essay is a preliminary investigation into the various ways in which conceptions of marital property have been elaborated in idioms of customary law, Islamic jurisprudence, state legislation, and case decisions in Indonesia. Given constraints of space for contributions to this volume and the still developing state of the field, the material presented here should by no means be taken as exhaustive, but rather as a working outline and an attempt at charting the course of developments that aims to stimulate further discussion of the topic in international scholarship.[1] It is hoped that this initial exploration will not only provoke specialist critiques on points of detail and suggestions of additional material for consideration, but that it will also invite further comparative reflection on the complex dynamics of social values, Islamic jurisprudence (*fiqh*), and positive law in modern Muslim societies.

The Concept of Joint Marital Property in Indonesian Custom

The doctrine of joint marital property (Ind. *harta bersama*) is recognized in the Indonesian National Marriage Law enacted in 1974, and is currently applied by both the Islamic courts (*Pengadilan Agama*), which have jurisdiction over the marriages of Indonesian Muslims, and the general courts (*Pengadilan Negeri*), which administer the law of marriage for all other citizens.[2] The roots of the doctrine have their source in patterns of Southeast Asian customary practice, which have over the course of the Islamization of the Indonesian Archipelago come to be known as *adat*.

Indonesia is home to dozens of different ethnic groups, each of which possesses its own distinct language and sense of cultural identity. In the late nineteenth and early twentieth centuries, Dutch scholars participated in an extensive project of surveying and cataloguing customary practice, or *adat*, throughout their colonial territories with the aim of formulating authoritative statements of traditional law (in Dutch *adatrecht*). On the basis of this research the Dutch-controlled areas of the archipelago were divided into nineteen distinct *adat* groups. Although this reflected the existence of considerable regional differences in customary practice, the system also identified some customs that were believed to be shared by all or nearly all of the various *adat* groups. One custom that was found to be nearly universal was the approach to the treatment of property within marriage. In his influential survey of *adat* law in the Dutch East Indies, B. ter Haar remarked on the wide distribution of nearly analogous conceptions of joint marital property known under a diverse range of regional names, including *harta suarang* (West Sumatra), *barang perpantangan* (Kalimantan), *chakkara* (South Sulawesi), *druwe gabro* (Bali), *guna kaya* (Sunda-West Java), and *ghuna ghana* (Madura).[3] This concept is also well documented in Aceh where it is referred to as *hareuta, atra* or *laba sihareukat* as well as *atra* or *laba meucharikat*. However, it is most often referred to using the Javanese term *gono-gini*, and more recently in Bahasa Indonesia as *harta bersama*.

The basic Indonesian customary principle of marital property is the recognition of a marital estate or community of jointly owned property. This joint property is distinguished from the separate property that belongs to the individual husband or wife. The definitions of joint and separate property and the formula for division of the property upon termination of the marriage differ from one ethnic group to the next. The largest and politically dominant ethnic group in Indonesia is the Javanese, who occupy the eastern two-thirds of the island of Java. The Javanese term *gono-gini* refers to property acquired by the couple during the marriage through the efforts of either of the spouses. The personal property that each spouse brings into the marriage or acquires by personal gift or inheritance while married is referred to as *harta gawan*. Each party has the right to manage his or her individual property as *harta gawan*. However, control over marital property is shared by both, as neither spouse can sell or encumber marital property without the consent of the other.

Although marital property is widely considered to be owned jointly by the spouses during the marriage, various *adat* communities hold differing views on how the property is to be divided when the marriage ends by death or divorce. If the marriage is terminated by divorce, each party receives a share of any property that was owned jointly during the marriage. The actual division of the shares, however, can follow any number of established local practices. Javanese custom generally divides marital property according to the formula of two parts for the husband and one part for the wife. This rule and its underlying rationale were expressed in a widely known adage that describes the different manner in which Javanese men and women traditionally carried burdens. Men typically attached a basket to each end of a pole (*pikul*) that was then balanced on the shoulder, while women generally carried a single basket on the back (*gendong*). The Javanese *adat* formula "*sepikul segendong*" reflects the view that since men conventionally carry twice as much weight as a woman, it is deemed appropriate that their entitlement to marital property is twice as large. Other manners of the division of joint marital property in case of divorce are documented for different *adat* groups across the archipelago, including practices of distributing equal shares to both husband and wife, as well as local mechanisms for contextualized, situational arrangements that attempt to account for differential contributions of the respective spouses over the course of the marriage. Nevertheless, Ter Haar, in a body of work that has been of considerable influence upon subsequent generations of Indonesian jurists, determined the 2:1 division to be "the Indonesian standard."[4]

Students of Islamic law may recognize in this a reflection of the gendered differentiation of inheritance shares. However, the actual roots of this formulation in Indonesian contexts are more difficult to determine precisely. *Adat* law scholars have duly noted that tripartite allocations of marital property are also evidenced in areas of the archipelago with historically little or no tradition of Islamic influence. Furthermore, in texts from Muslim societies of the region in which the impact of selective *fiqh* norms are clearly apparent, there is evidence of earlier customary practices of analogous 2:1 divisions between husband and wife, even where this may contravene other established Shariʿa norms. One example of this phenomenon may be seen in the pre-modern Malay legal digest *Undang-undang Melaka*, which stipulated, for example, that upon the death of a debtor husband his creditor cannot burden the deceased's wife and children with the whole sum that is owed. Rather, the debt must be divided such that the dependents are held responsible for one-third the total amount only, with the remaining two-thirds comprising a loss to the creditor.[5]

In later Muslim societies of the archipelago, such as that of late nineteenth-century Aceh surveyed in the two-volume ethnography of Snouck Hurgronje, the established *fiqh* practice of deducting all debts from the determined value of the estate before its division and distribution to heirs was followed. In such cases, too, customary considerations of joint marital property were inserted into the process as a further phase of deductions from the estate before the division of the remainder as reckoned according to the system of shares stipulated by Islamic inheritance law. Snouck remarked on this by noting that the practice observed in various districts of Aceh of deducting joint marital property (Ac. *atra sihareukat*) from the estate and allocating it to the surviving spouse did not in any way compromise the survivor's entitlement to also receive her or his lawful share of heritable property as determined by Shariʿa stipulations.[6]

The customary basis for the surviving spouse's claim to marital property in such cases is the recognition that the marital relationship involved an element of economic partnership. In some areas of Aceh, as well as in other parts of the Indonesian archipelago, these partnerships were characterized by the participation of the wife as well as the husband in working their fields. However, even in cases where the couple's earnings were clearly the fruits of one party's labor, well-established practices of dividing joint property were upheld, often through the employment of traditionally-sanctioned legal fictions that established the joint participation of both parties in the productive partnership. Snouck details one telling example of this in the case of an Acehnese husband from the highlands who leaves his wife behind in order to work on a coastal pepper plantation. In such a case tradition maintained that the wife's provision of a bundle of fish, rice, and betel nut (Ac. *bu kulah*) to the husband when he set out on his journey to the plantation be considered the initial "capital" in the venture, thus entailing a form of partnership.[7] However, articulating the concept of marital property in the idiom of *fiqh* as a form of partnership presented its own problems. This was especially the case for Indonesian legal scholars because of restrictions on the characteristics of a legally valid partnership established within the Shafiʿi school of law, which has historically been dominant among Indonesian Muslims.

The Rationalization of Joint Marital Property as Islamic Law

Adat conceptions of joint marital property have long been rationalized in terms of the categories of Islamic jurisprudence. These arguments are predicated on the classification of marriage as a form of partnership (Ar. *sharika*) and marital property as gains from that partnership. In assimilating marriage and marital property to *fiqh* categories regarding economic partnerships, Indonesian legal scholars have had to confront the fact that the Shafiʿi school of Islamic law takes a more restrictive position on partnership than does any of the other established Sunni schools.[8] In particular, Shafiʿi authorities generally do not recognize the types of partnerships that most closely match the economic arrangements typically found in Southeast Asian marriages. In fact, in his oft-translated reference handbook of Shafiʿi law, the Dutch scholar Th.W. Juynboll made a special point of mentioning that a considerable exception to the general rule against the recognition of the type of partnership characteristic of joint marital property arrangements in that school is to be found in various *adat*-sanctioned practices of Indonesian Muslims.[9]

The earliest articulation of the doctrine of joint marital property in terms of *fiqh* concepts is commonly attributed to an eighteenth-century scholar hailing from Kalimantan (Borneo) by the name of Muḥammad Arshad b. ʿAbd Allāh al-Banjārī (d. 1812). This author is most widely known for his *Sabīl al-muhtadīn*, which was commissioned by the local sultan in 1779 as a request to produce a Malay text of Shafiʿi law. However, the *Sabīl al-muhtadīn* is a work focused on the regulation of religious practice (*fiqh al-ʿibādāt*) and thus does not speak to issues relevant to discussions of joint marital property. When asked where one can find Banjārī's writings on the issue, Indonesian scholars and jurists refer one to his work entitled *al-Farā'iḍ*. Nevertheless, while it appears that the title of this work is almost universally known, knowledge of its actual content is considerably more restricted. There appears to be no published edition of the text currently available in print, and—despite repeated queries at bookshops in various Indonesian cities, as well as to colleagues in Europe, North America, Australia, and within Indonesia itself—we were unable to locate a copy. Thus we have not yet had a chance to examine this purportedly most authoritative text, and we are left to conclude that although contemporary *fiqh* justifications of the validity of joint marital property often make a point of referencing this early Malay work, it is in fact read by very few, if any, and actual knowledge about the issue in contemporary Indonesia derives from more historically proximate discussions.

The earliest local treatments of the issue in terms of Shafiʿi jurisprudence that are still generally available in Indonesian bookshops appear to be those produced by the Batavia-based Hadrami scholar Sayyid ʿUthmān b. ʿAbd Allāh b. ʿAqīl b. Yaḥyā al-ʿAlawī (d. 1914).[10] Sayyid ʿUthmān's discussions of the subject are notably published in *jawi*-script Malay, rather than Arabic, and can be found presented briefly in his *Kitāb Qawānīn al-sharʿiyya*. This work has been of considerable influence on the development of Islamic law as administered by the state in Indonesia, as it was widely disseminated for use as a manual by colonial-era Shariʿa court judges, and remains in limited commercial circulation to this day.[11] In section (*faṣl*) 16 of this text, Sayyid ʿUthmān opens his discussion with reference to the Sundanese and Javanese terms *seguna sekaya* and *gono-gini*, making it clear that such treatments of marital property "have already become established as *adat*" although they are not recognized by [Shafiʿi] Islamic law.[12] Recognizing that the actual distribution of the property upon termination of the marriage is governed by various local practices, he argues that the fairest way to divide such property in case of divorce would be according to the respective degrees of effort put into its earning by each spouse. In cases where the joint marital property was accumulated using capital belonging to one of the spouses, rather than solely on their joint labor, his view was that the original capital and a reasonable return of profit must be restored to the party who supplied it.[13] In his brief discussion of the topic, Sayyid ʿUthmān conspicuously avoids complicated jurisprudential issues such as the classification of marriage as a partnership in a way that facilitates an apparently seamless incorporation of this Indonesian *adat* institution into the administrative practice of the Islamic religious court system.[14]

Later generations of Muslim authorities in Indonesia, particularly those associated with Muslim reformist movements in the early twentieth century, were perhaps even more willing to bypass such technical problematics and chose not to engage with the details of established *madhhab* rules as a matter of principle, rather than simply out of expedience. One of the most influential voices of this kind, A. Hassan (d. 1958), did just that in an oft-reprinted fatwa on marital property (Mal. *harta sepencaharian*) included in the popular collection of early twentieth-century responsa entitled *Soal-Jawab*.[15] In answering a question on whether or not the children of a deceased wife have a claim on her portion of the marital property, Hassan initiates a discussion of marriage as a partnership of labor (*sharikat al-ʿabdān*) without feeling any need to even mention the fact that this is a category of partnership that is not recognized by traditional Shafiʿi jurists. This frees him up to deal directly with the issue of whether or not there was an agreement (*perjanjian*) to form a partnership, arguing that just because there is no explicit contract this does not mean that the property has no clear owner, and that it is common sense that property of this kind should be treated as if it was co-owned by both spouses in equal shares.[16] This fatwa is thus notable not only because of its studied avoidance of *madhhab*-oriented restrictions, but also because of the way in which it posits the universal application of a 1:1 division of the marital property, rather than it simply being a local, ethnically-specific exemption to the 2:1 "Indonesian standard" upheld by many authorities discussing the issue both before and since Hassan's day.[17]

The most developed, and most frequently referenced, discussion of *adat* conceptions of joint marital property in relation to Islamic law in modern Indonesia is that of the Acehnese jurist Ismail Muhammad Syah (d. 1995), who is popularly known by the abbreviated name Ismuha.[18] Ismuha wrote his thesis on joint marital property at Yogyakarta in 1960.[19] Over the years that followed he continued to develop his thoughts on the issue while engaged with new developments in Indonesian law. Following the landmark changes of the 1974 Marriage Act, Ismuha published a revised and expanded edition of his thesis, which has since come to be seen by many Muslim jurists in Indonesia as the definitive statement on the subject.[20]

After an introductory discussion of the differential legal status of various ethnic groups throughout the history of the Indonesian Republic, Ismuha frames his approach to the issue of joint marital property with reference to Indonesian national law (including the landmark 1974 Marriage Act) and the established foundations of the doctrine in *adat* law. However, in his treatment of the subject Ismuha makes clear that what is most important to him is not custom per se, but rather a reading of the legal validity of this particular *adat* institution in light of its commensurability with Islamic law.[21] Thus the bulk of the book is taken up with issues that arise in evaluating the status of joint marital property from the perspective of Islamic jurisprudence, the central problematic of which is the extent to which marriage can be regarded as a type of partnership (Ind. *perkongsian*). The task of his investigation is then set at both identifying exactly what technical category of partnership (Ar. *sharika*) is constituted by *harta bersama*-type *adat* arrangements, and then determining whether such a mode of partnership is authorized by the Shariʿa. Analogous work, as has already been shown, had been undertaken in an abbreviated form by earlier authors such as A. Hassan. The difference here is that Ismuha chose to engage directly with the particularity (and diversity) of established positions among the classical schools of Islamic law, rather than simply avoiding the complications of *madhhab* restrictions altogether.[22]

With regard to the first of these exercises, Ismuha examined aspects of Indonesian conceptions of joint marital property with regard to such matters as the respective contributions in labor, capital, or any combination thereof from both partners (spouses), the division of partnership profits, and the rights of the respective parties with respect to partnership assets. Through these means he determined that the type of partnership engendered by *harta bersama* understandings of marital property is best classified as both *sharikat al-ʿabdān* and *sharikat al-mufāwaḍa* in the sense that according to dominant Indonesian understandings, marriage comprises both a "partnership of labor" (*al-ʿabdān*)[23] and a form of "unlimited partnership" (*mufāwaḍa*).[24] These categories, however, are not universally valid among scholars of the four Sunni schools of law and the strongest rulings against such arrangements happen to be found within the Shafiʿi school.

Through his survey of the rulings of Shafiʿi scholars alongside those of scholars representing other schools, Ismuha points to the fact that such partnership arrangements are regarded as permissible (*mubāḥ*) by the other three established Sunni schools. He then works both to contextualize, and in the process considerably restrict, al-Shāfiʿī's own condemnation of *mufāwaḍa* partnerships, as well as to highlight what he sees to be the "rationality" and other benefits of the allowance of such arrangements by jurists of the Hanbali, Hanafi, and (to a lesser extent) Maliki schools.[25] These moves then facilitate his overall argument that there is no impediment to Indonesian Muslims following the rulings of a school other than that of al-Shāfiʿī if doing so allows them to thereby accommodate a well-established and socially beneficial customary practice. Ismuha emphasizes that this is permissible because traditional Shafiʿi rulings on the matter are not based upon any clear scriptural proof text (*naṣṣ*). He also observes that the very nature of a marriage partnership inhibits the kind of dishonest dealing that was of concern to those scholars who disapprove of those forms of partnership outside the marriage context. However, the main points upon which Ismuha's arguments in favor of recognizing joint marital property clearly rest are his invocation of the concept of public benefit (*maṣlaḥa*) and the *fiqh* maxim "Custom has the weight of law" (*al-ʿāda muḥakkama*). In fact, the penultimate chapter of his book, entitled "Islamic Shariʿa for All Places and Times" vaunts the flexibility and adaptability of Islamic law by emphasizing the fact that the Qurʾan is concerned with general statements of principle, rather than detailed rulings, and by highlighting the benefits of broad jurisprudential principles (*qaidah-qaidah kulliyah*) emphasizing the Shari'a's concerns with preventing harm and promoting benefit to individuals and society, as well as its in-principle openness to accepting established customary practice in Muslim communities.[26]

The justifications for recognizing customary conceptions of marital property as legitimate in terms of both Islamic and Indonesian national law worked out by Ismuha met the needs of many jurists over the years that followed. Among the most prominent later advocates of these positions has been Sayuti Thalib, who held the chair in Islamic law at the University of Indonesia, and authored a primary teaching text on Muslim family law. In that work's chapter covering wealth held by husband and wife (*harta kekayaan suami isteri*), Thalib draws heavily on Ismuha for his survey of comparative school rulings, as well as on A. Hassan's work in classifying marital property as a *sharika al-ʿabdān* partnership. However, Thalib goes further than either of these two earlier authorities in detailing the means by which such a partnership comes into being, stipulating that such an arrangement can be confirmed by state legislation or even by a prevailing sense of customary acceptance of the practice by the community, as well as by an explicit written or oral agreement between the spouses. He also adds an important note on what he sees to be the modern social benefits deriving from the customary practice of joint marital property, particularly its perceived influence on discouraging both divorce and polygamy.[27]

Incorporation of Marital Property in Indonesian Legislation

The goal of replacing Dutch-era marriage laws with national legislation was an announced priority in Indonesia from the early days of the Republic, and efforts to enact marriage legislation began shortly after independence. Although a number of marriage law proposals were debated in the 1950s and the 1960s, none of these proposals was enacted. The principal point of contention related to whether to enact a single set of marriage and divorce rules applicable to all Indonesians (the position generally favored by secular nationalists) or to provide different marriage laws for different religious/cultural communities (favored by Muslim advocates for state enforcement of Islamic law). One common element in all of these proposals, nevertheless, was the recognition of marital property. The marital property provisions were generally similar in the "secular" and "Muslim" marriage law proposals, with their most consistent point of variance being that partnership principles play a noticeably greater role in the proposals intended specifically for Indonesian Muslims.

The first marriage law proposal following independence was prepared under the direction of the Ministry of Religious Affairs in 1954. The committee charged with drafting the legislation had initially intended to produce a single set of rules for the entire population. That plan was abandoned because of pressure brought to bear on the committee by Muslim organizations, and the draft that was eventually submitted was intended to apply to Muslims only. This document included four short articles on property rights within marriage. The first two articles sought to establish that each spouse retains his or her separate property after marriage, and that the husband may not use the property of the wife for the support of the household. The third article provided for joint marital property, defined as "wealth resulting from the joint efforts of the spouses during the marriage." Upon dissolution of the marriage, the marital property is to be divided based on the size of each partner's contribution. The final section authorized the parties to make alternative arrangements regarding property during marriage by agreement prior to the marriage.

The Ministry of Religious Affairs' bill, however, was never introduced in the legislature. Instead another marriage law proposal was presented to parliament in 1958. This law had been drafted by a group of women members of the legislature under the direction of Mrs. Soemari. The marital property provisions of the Soemari draft were generally similar to those of the Muslim marriage law. However, the marital property provisions in the Soemari draft were not as clearly based on the partnership rationale. Rather, the article on division of the marital estate upon dissolution of the marriage prescribed a "just" or "fair" division of the property. The article also authorized an award of a share of the marital property to the couple's children.

Two further unsuccessful attempts to enact marriage legislation were made in the late 1960s after the replacement of the Sukarno government by the New Order regime of President Suharto. One of the proposals was intended to apply generally, while the second was for the Muslim population only. Both proposals included the doctrine of marital property, and both defined joint property in similar terms as property acquired during the marriage through the efforts of either of the spouses. The proposals nevertheless differed with respect to division of the property. The proposal intended for general application would have divided marital property equally between the spouses, whereas the Muslim marriage law proposal more ambiguously prescribed a "just" division of marital property, leaving open the possibility of appealing to alternative systems for dividing joint property in case of divorce.

A national marriage act was finally passed in 1974. One of the major reasons this proposal succeeded when earlier efforts had failed was because the Suharto government, which by this time had accumulated considerable power, placed its full support behind the law. The legislation that was enacted was not, however, the same bill that the government had originally proposed. The original proposal was for an essentially secular marriage law that allowed almost no room for application of Islamic law.

That proposal drew harsh criticism from certain segments of the Muslim community, and the bill that was ultimately enacted has been embraced by Indonesian Muslims as giving legislative recognition to Islamic law.[28]

The 1974 Marriage Act, like all previous marriage law proposals, incorporates the doctrine of marital property, with the subject being treated in three short articles. Property acquired during the marriage is declared to constitute marital property, while property owned prior to the marriage or acquired during the marriage by gift or inheritance is separate property (Article 35). The provision regarding division of marital property states that when the marriage ends as a result of divorce "marital property shall be divided according to the law of the parties" (Article 37). The official elucidation to this article explains that what is meant by the law of the parties is "religious law, *adat*, or other law." The corresponding provision of the original draft mandated an "equal division between husband and wife." Although the official reasons for this revision have never been made clear, the change was almost certainly made in response to demands by Muslim political interests involved in negotiations over the Marriage Act in the legislature.

The doctrine of marital property receives the fullest legislative treatment in the Indonesian Compilation of Islamic Law. The Compilation is an Indonesian language code of marriage, inheritance, and trust (*waqf*) rules that was drafted by representatives of the Ministry of Religion and the Supreme Court and promulgated in 1991 through a presidential instruction. As the title suggests, the Compilation purports to represent a restatement of existing Indonesian Islamic legal principles.[29] The stated purpose of the Compilation is to provide a uniform and accessible body of rules for use by judges in deciding the cases that come before Indonesia's Islamic courts.

The substance of the doctrine of marital property in the Compilation does not differ fundamentally from prior formulations. Unlike the Marriage Act, however, some of the terminology used in the document reflects *fiqh* conceptions of "partnership" (Ind. *syirkah*) as discussed above. The Compilation defines marital property as property acquired during the marriage by the husband or wife either individually or together, regardless of which spouse formally holds title to the property (Article 1(f)). Each spouse retains ownership over his or her separate property after marriage (Article 86). Unless the parties specify otherwise, property acquired during the marriage as a result of inheritance or gift is the separate property of the recipient (Article 87). Marital property includes tangible and intangible property, personal and real property, and rights and obligations (Article 91). Neither the husband nor the wife may sell or transfer marital property without the consent of the other spouse (Article 92). The Compilation gives the parties broad power to enter into agreements regarding rights over property in marriage. Such agreements, however, must be in writing and authenticated by the state marriage registrar (Article 47). The spouses can agree to combine their separate property or to segregate marital property provided the agreement "is not inconsistent with Islamic law" (Article 47).

The Treatment of Marital Property in Indonesian Courts

The concept of marital property has long been justified in terms of both *adat* and Islamic jurisprudential principles, and the two concepts of marital property have been applied by different court systems in both the colonial and post-independence periods. Under a regulation promulgated by the Dutch in 1882, Islamic tribunals were granted jurisdiction over the marriage and inheritance of Indonesian Muslims. This jurisdiction was subject to an important limitation, however. The Islamic courts had the authority to decide questions regarding the validity of Muslim marriages and to hear divorce cases filed by Muslim women, but had no authority to decide matters involving rights to property. Jurisdiction over matrimonial causes involving property claims lay in the general courts. In the 1930s the Dutch further restricted the powers of the Islamic courts in Java and South Kalimantan by transferring jurisdiction over Muslim inheritance to the general courts. The law applied by the general courts in matrimonial and inheritance matters was *adat*. This was true even if both the parties involved were Muslim.

The Dutch Royal Decree of 1882 remained the primary legal basis for Indonesian Islamic courts for more than forty years after independence. In 1989 the century-old Dutch statute was finally superceded with the enactment by the Indonesian legislature of a Law on Religious Courts (Law No. 7/1989).[30] The Religious Courts Act expanded the jurisdiction of the Islamic courts and placed the Islamic judiciary on an equal footing with the general courts. Under the Act, the Islamic courts have full authority to apply the Marriage Law for Indonesian Muslims, including deciding questions regarding marital property, and have a non-compulsory jurisdiction over Muslim inheritance. Despite the fact that earlier Islamic courts lacked formal jurisdiction over marital property and inheritance, they nevertheless routinely heard disputes regarding matrimonial property and inheritance based on the parties' agreement to have the case decided according to Islamic law. In principle, however, the marital property of Indonesian Muslims was formally governed by *adat* principles applied by the general courts.

Information on the implementation of Islamic law in Indonesia prior to independence is very limited. We have, however, located a handful of decisions by colonial-era Islamic courts (*Raad Agama*) on the island of Java from the first decades of the twentieth century that apply the doctrine of joint marital property. While practice probably differed significantly across the archipelago, these decisions provide some insight into the treatment of marital property in Islamic tribunals organized under Dutch colonial auspices prior to the establishment of the Indonesian state. From this material it appears that the *Raad Agama* applied the doctrine of joint marital property primarily in two contexts. The first type of case involved suits by divorced wives against their former husbands to recover their share of the marital assets. Although Indonesian practice recognized several grounds by which a wife could obtain a judicial order of divorce, all the marital property cases we examined were based on divorce by repudiation by the husband (*talāq*). In such cases, the wife's entitlement to a share of the marital estate seemed to be generally assumed. The only disputed issue in any of the cases was the determination of which property should be classified as joint marital property, and what assets remained the individual property of the respective spouses. In one case, for example, the husband argued that one item claimed as marital property was in fact given to him as a gift from his parents, and thus fell outside of established definitions of joint marital property (*gono-gini*). Once the sum of joint marital property was duly established, the courts generally divided it based on the ratio of two parts to the husband and one part to the wife.

The second type of case applying the doctrine of joint marital property involved inheritance matters within Muslim families. The question of marital property rights did not arise in all inheritance cases. When it did arise, however, the court first determined and distributed the marital property to the surviving spouse before proceeding to divide the remainder of the estate according to established inheritance shares. The surviving spouse thus received both a share of the marital property as well as his or her share of the estate.

The legal basis for the marital property doctrine in these cases was often left ambiguous. In referring to marital property the courts used both *adat* terminology (*gono-gini; guna kaya*) and also local derivations of the Arabic technical term *sharika*. In one case the court was requested to divide the marital property (*gono-gini*) according to the "religious law" (*hukum agama*).[31] The decisions were usually very short, and reasoned justification for the result were virtually non-existent. The decisions consist primarily of a recital of the parties' claims, a description of the property, and a summary of the testimony of witnesses. The court typically announced its decision without any citation of authority or legal argument. In some published cases, however, there were informal citations of sources informing the decision, including for example references to Sayyid ʿUthmān's *Kitāb Qawānīn al-sharʿiyya*.[32]

The partnership theory occasionally receives tacit acknowledgement in the written decisions, but the courts show no interest in resolving disagreements between the parties concerning their relative contributions to the household economy, and in none of the cases we looked at did the contribution of the spouses to the couple's earnings affect either entitlement or the size of the share. In the case of *Padmi v. Kartasaribun*,[33] for example, the plaintiff-wife (Padmi) presented a detailed statement of the tasks that both she and her husband performed in planting and harvesting rice. The defendant husband disputed his wife's claims, but the court made no apparent effort to resolve the issue, and there is no indication that the court's decision was predicated on a finding that the property claimed by the wife was produced through her efforts. In summarizing the testimony of the witnesses the court noted that each witness testified that the property claimed by Padmi was acquired after the couple was married. The question that engaged the parties concerning the nature and extent of their efforts in generating household wealth was apparently not addressed by the witnesses and did not enter in the decision. Without citing any authority or giving any reasons, the court divided the property two parts for Kartasaribun and one part for Padmi.

Today Indonesia's Islamic courts (*Pengadilan Agama*) apply rulings more self-consciously elaborated in terms of Islamic marital property principles, whereas the separate system of general courts apply certain *adat* formulations in deciding questions of marital property. While these factors would appear to be conducive to the independent development of the two doctrines—one emphasizing local tradition and the other conceptualizations of joint marital property in the formal idiom of partnership—the latter has actually played only a minor role in the elaboration and application of rulings on marital property, and thus in practice the "Islamic doctrine" as applied by the religious courts is hardly distinguishable from the *adat* rule.[34]

During the first two decades after independence the Indonesian Supreme Court used its jurisdiction over appeals from both the civil and the Islamic courts to introduce important changes to the doctrine of marital property. Although the Supreme Court's decisions were based on *adat* rather than Islam, the Court's *adat* jurisprudence has been influential in the development of Islamic marital property doctrine in Indonesia. The most important development in *adat* marital property doctrine concerns the size of the parties' shares. The Supreme Court first addressed this issue in 1959 in an appeal from an inheritance decision by the civil court for the District of Bojonegoro (East Java). The lower courts had decided the case in line with the predominant view within Javanese *adat* that a surviving husband is entitled to a two-thirds share of the marital property. The Supreme Court reversed, ruling that the spouses were entitled to an equal share of the marital property. The Court wrote,

> In Central Javanese Society the feeling has long begun to grow that because of the equal participation of women in the national struggle, it is just that a widow receive half of the marital property, so that this has become the *adat* of Central Java.[35]

The 1959 decision dealt exclusively with the marital property law for the Javanese. Under the law as it existed at the time, the archipelago was divided into nineteen separate *adat* regions, each with its own distinctive body of doctrine. Changes to Javanese *adat* did not affect the law for other groups. But the decision declaring an equal division of marital property under Javanese *adat* was not so much reflective of the Court's view of Javanese custom as it was of the Court's commitment to a set of substantive values associated with Indonesian nationalism. The nationalist movement in Indonesia was conceived in terms of liberation (*merdeka*) from the "feudalistic" and hierarchal bonds of tradition, and the values of freedom and social equality informed much of the Court's early jurisprudence.

Although the Court's appeal to the nationalist struggle had broad resonance, declaring new *adat* is a delicate matter. This is especially true should the Court in Jakarta presume to announce new *adat* for regions outside of Java. Indonesian politics has always been characterized by various degrees of "Outer Island" resentment of Javanese political and cultural domination, and the Indonesian Supreme Court proceeded cautiously in announcing changes to marital property doctrines for the country's other *adat* communities. But the Court gradually extended the rule that marital property is to be divided equally between husband and wife to other groups.[36] More fundamentally, through its decisions on marital property and inheritance, the Court redefined the concept of *adat* itself by imagining it within a national framework.[37] As used by the Supreme Court, *adat* came to be understood as embodying the values and practices of the Indonesian people as a whole, rather than the immemorial practice of local communities. Once this step had been taken it was but a natural progression to extend the doctrine of marital property even to *adat* communities that had not previously recognized it.[38]

During this same period the Court also issued pronouncements on other aspects of the law of marital property that re-evaluated certain established *adat* positions. Thus, in a 1956 case the Supreme Court rejected the contention that a wife is not entitled to a share of the marital property if she does not contribute actively to its creation. Under the Court's new reading of "customary law," "all property that is acquired during the marriage is included in the *gono-gini*, even though the result of the husband's efforts alone."[39] In the same case the Court rejected the argument that a wife loses her rights to marital property if she deserts her husband.

The number of cases involving marital property decided by the Islamic courts has grown steadily since the passage of the Religious Courts Act in 1989, but marital property cases still comprise only a very small percentage of the courts' caseload. In 1990 the courts across the country reported a total of only 73 cases raising claims for marital property. By 1999 that number had risen to 301, and by 2002 the total number of marital property cases had reached 353. These figures probably understate the number of decisions involving marital property, since they may not include all of the cases in which a claim for joint marital property is made in connection with the suit for divorce. Even so, it is clear that marital property decisions comprised only a small part of the total cases decided by the courts.

Islamic courts are more frequently called upon to apply marital property doctrines in deciding inheritance cases. The number of inheritance cases processed by the Islamic courts each year is larger than the number of marital property cases, but inheritance filings nevertheless comprise only a small part of the courts' docket. Although the numbers fluctuate, Islamic courts typically decide fewer than 1,000 inheritance cases each year, which is less than one percent of the courts' annual caseload of more than 150,000 filings.

Although the decisions of Indonesian courts are not routinely published, both the Ministry of Religion and the Supreme Court publish collections of select Islamic court decisions for distribution to judges. Based on our review of these sources, we have found several dozen decisions that touch on the doctrine of *harta bersama*. Because our sample is not necessarily representative, the marital property decisions available to us may present an imperfect picture of the courts' treatment of the doctrine. The decisions nevertheless illustrate the types of issues raised in marital property suits and the general approach taken by the courts in addressing those issues.

Most of the decisions we have reviewed apply the doctrine in a straightforward fashion with little dispute or discussion. Property acquired during the marriage is classified as marital property, and property owned prior to the marriage or acquired by gift or inheritance during the marriage remains the separate property of the respective spouses. Although no court has addressed the issue directly, the courts have not been receptive to the argument that property acquired during the marriage through the efforts of one of the spouses only should be categorized as the separate property of that spouse.[40] With a small number of exceptions, marital property has been divided equally between the spouses in accordance with the guidelines stipulated in the 1991 Compilation of Islamic Law.

The most common subject of contention in marital property suits concerns the classification of the property as either joint or separate. The underlying dispute in most of these cases concerns purely factual issues, e.g., was the property acquired before or after the marriage, was it purchased with funds that constitute separate property, or was it given as a gift to one of the spouses? Typical of such cases is the 1999 decision by the Islamic court for Jayapura, West Irian in the case of *Tabi bin Rua v. Supinah binti Sutikno*[41] in which the court rejected the argument of the defendant wife that a truck acquired during the marriage and claimed by the plaintiff as marital property should actually be considered to be separate property because it was purchased with investment funds from the wife's family.

We have found a small number of cases that raise more basic questions concerning the characterization of property as either joint or separate. One important issue that has received attention both by the courts and in academic discussions concerns the status of pension and other rights accruing to civil servants and members of the Indonesian armed forces. In a meeting of Islamic High Court judges held in 1995 it was agreed that savings and insurance benefits for civil servants (*Tabungan dan Asuransi Pegawai Negeri*/TASPEN) constitute marital property because the premium for the benefit is deducted from the employees monthly salary.[42] Another related question concerns the status of Workers Social Security (*Jaminan Sosial Tenaga Kerja*/JAMSOSTEK) benefits. This includes compensation paid to replace lost earnings resulting from work related accidents or death, illness, pregnancy, or childbirth. The courts have reached conflicting decisions on whether these payments qualify as marital property. At the 1995 meeting of Islamic High Court judges it was agreed that Workers Social Security payments should be classified as marital property because they are obtained as a result of a household workers partnership.[43]

Another issue raised in a number of cases we reviewed concerns the effect of infidelity or other marital transgressions on rights to marital property. According to *adat* in Java, Sunda, South Sulawesi, and perhaps other regions, a wife lost her right to a share of the marital property if she committed adultery. This rule was reflected in expressions found in local languages for being "thrown out of the house empty handed"—*metu pinjungan* (Java), *balik taranjang* (Sunda) *solari bainenna* (Makassar).[44] In the 1950s, however, the Indonesian Supreme Court expressed its opposition to the principle that fault bars a spouse's entitlement to marital property. The defendant-husband in the case argued that his wife lost her right to marital property because she had deserted him.[45] In rejecting the defendant's claim, the Court stated categorically that the *adat* principle relied upon does not exist. The general courts applying *adat* principles have also rejected the argument that a wife loses her entitlement to a share of the marital estate if she is "disobedient" under the Islamic doctrine of *nusyuz* (Ar. *nushūz*).[46]

The Compilation of Islamic Law addresses the subject of disobedience by wives, but the doctrine is not linked to rights to marital property. A wife is deemed *nusyuz* under the Compilation if she fails "to devote herself both physically and spiritually to her husband within the limits established by Islamic law" (Article 84). A finding of *nusyuz* results in loss of the right to financial support, but marital property rights are apparently not affected. An earlier draft of the Compilation did state that the apostasy of either spouse resulted in a loss of her or his right to marital property rights (Article 105), but that provision was not included in the final approved version of the Compilation.

Despite the lack of legal support for the argument, men continue to raise misbehavior by their wives as a bar to the latter's claims on marital property.[47] These recent claims appear to have fared no better than those made in the past; in all of the cases we have examined the husband's argument that his wife should be denied marital property because of her wrongdoing was denied. The continuing assertion of spousal disobedience in marital property cases is apparently a result of popular opinion among some Muslims that a wife who is *nusyuz* is not entitled to marital property. Yahya Harahap, who surveyed Muslim opinion on this issue during the preparation of the Compilation of Islamic Law, has written that the opinion persists within some Muslim circles that acts of disobedience by the wife can be the basis for the loss of marital property rights.[48]

Both the Marriage Act and the Compilation of Islamic Law include provisions permitting the marriage partners to enter into agreements either before or during the marriage altering the treatment of their property. Although marital property agreements are probably rare, the use of modified marriage contracts is well known among Indonesian Muslims. It has long been customary for Muslim men to pronounce a conditional repudiation (Ind. *taklik talak*) at the time of the marriage declaring that a repudiation would automatically occur if the husband were to commit certain named actions. The use of the conditional repudiation became so common in Indonesia that a standard version of the contract was printed on the back of official Indonesian marriage certificates.[49]

Agreements regarding the treatment of property within marriage figure in two of the cases we reviewed. In *Elvianis Syam v. Thabrani Rab*[50] the agreement was concluded at the time of a remarriage following a divorce. The couple married in 1979, divorced in 1986, and then remarried in 1987. At the time of the 1987 remarriage the couple entered into a detailed agreement that set forth various rights and obligations during the marriage and specified the parties' respective rights in their considerable assets. In 1991 the wife filed a claim seeking an order of divorce and division of all property acquired during the course of the marriage. The validity of the agreement was not addressed in the decision, and the terms of the agreement were incorporated in the court's order.

In another case that included a marital property agreement, the agreement was declared invalid. The case of *Kamaluddin v. Cik Tamah*[51] involved the marriage of a previously unmarried man to an older, divorced woman. The wife brought a modest estate to the marriage, including a house, the surrounding land, and approximately two hectares of farmland. Prior to the marriage the couple had entered into an agreement which, as described in the subsequent divorce suit, gave the husband the right to use and enjoy the couple's property during the marriage but granted him no claim to ownership should the marriage end in divorce.[52] The suit for divorce was initiated by the husband, who claimed that the failure of the marriage was due to his wife's incessant ridicule of his inferior social status. The defendant urged the court to reject the plaintiff's claim for a share of the marital property on the grounds of the earlier agreement. Although the validity of the agreement was apparently not raised in the complaint, the court declared it invalid on the basis that it was "inconsistent with Islamic law." In support of this conclusion the court quoted a Prophetic report stating that "Muslims are bound by their agreements, except for those that permit that which is forbidden or forbid that which is permitted."

The court in the case of *Kamaluddin v. Cik Tamah* did not explain in what respect the agreement was improper. In its decision the court emphasized that "marriage is a contract or partnership (*perkongsian*)," and that property acquired during the marriage must be divided according to the law of partnership and the law of Islam. Assuming these principles underlie the invalidation of the couple's property agreement, this would seem to suggest that any agreement that completely deprives one of the spouses of property acquired during the marriage will not be enforced.

One last issue involving court disputes over joint marital property concerns the application of the *harta bersama* principle in situations where a man is married to more than one woman. The Supreme Court first set forth the approach to be used in such cases in a 1958 decision under *adat* principles. The case arose as a result of a gift of rice land made by the deceased husband to the daughter of his second wife. The children of the first wife sued, claiming that the rice land was part of the marital estate of the first marriage and for that reason could not be given away. The Supreme Court stated that the rule to be applied in such situations is that,

> When there is more than one marital estate as a result of the marriage of a man to more than one woman, it is appropriate to regard and treat each estate individually, each standing separate from the other. Thus, there exists a distinct marital estate for each family, and upon the death of the husband the first wife and her children are only entitled to marital property earned as a result of her marriage, and likewise with the second wife and her children.[53]

The rule that each marriage gives rise to a separate marital estate is incorporated in both the 1974 Marriage Act (Article 65) and the 1991 Compilation (Article 94). This principle applies both to polygamous marriages and to cases in which a man remarries following the death or divorce of his first wife.

The rule that a separate marital estate exists for each marriage has the virtue of conceptual elegance. Allocating property among multiple marriages presents obvious problems of proof, however. In cases of successive marriages that do not overlap, the courts generally focus on the date the property was acquired, and assign the property to the marriage that existed at the time the property was obtained.[54] Sometimes, however, the date of acquisition is not easily determined. In one case, for example, the deceased husband obtained the title to a plot of farm land as a result of having worked the land over a twenty-year period. Because the plaintiff was married to the deceased for twelve of those twenty years, the court awarded her 12/20 of one-half of the property as her share of the marital estate.[55] The difficulty of allocating property among multiple marriages is, of course, greater in the case of polygamous marriages, since it is often impossible to say whether a plot of land or a motorcycle purchased while a man was married to two women derived from the efforts of one of the marriages or both.

The allocation of marital property rights in polygamous marriages is addressed in one of the cases we reviewed.[56] The plaintiff in this case sued her husband of 37 years for an order of divorce and her share of the marital estate. Thirteen years after the marriage of the plaintiff to the defendant, the defendant had taken a second wife without the plaintiff's knowledge or consent. In ruling on the plaintiff's claim for marital property, the court distinguished between assets acquired before the defendant's second marriage and those acquired afterwards. The court ruled that property acquired before the defendant's second marriage constituted marital property of the plaintiff and the defendant, and divided the property equally between the parties. The property acquired during the period the defendant had two wives was divided in three equal parts: one-third was awarded to the plaintiff, and the remaining two-thirds was declared to constitute marital property belonging to the defendant and his second wife. The Supreme Court later upheld the lower court's ruling without comment.[57]

Conclusion

The doctrine of joint marital property justified in terms of Islamic partnership principles is to our knowledge a uniquely Southeast Asian phenomenon. The development of an Islamic law of marital property is also to some extent indicative of more general features found within Southeast Asian Islam, particularly in its accommodation of the role of women in a predominantly agricultural economy. This chapter has examined the process by which a principle of customary law has been locally "Islamicized" through its creative integration into an idiom of *fiqh* norms, as well as the legislative and judicial application of that reconceptualized principle to resolve various concrete problems of positive law. The material here is specific to modern Indonesia, and the way in which both its colonial history and its post-independence governmental system have dealt with *adat* and Islam as sources of law. Nevertheless, beyond its interest to Indonesia country specialists, the development of *harta bersama* examined here provides a study in the processes of legal change that can shed some comparative light on the complex and dynamic interactions of religious, customary, and modern positive law in other Muslim societies.

NOTES

[1] We have been unable to include here, for example, any discussion of fatwas on the subject produced for Muslims from the Indonesian Archipelago by muftis based in the Hijaz, Hadramawt, and elsewhere in the Middle East. The focus of this chapter then is on the evolution of the interpretation and application of this aspect of Muslim family law within Dutch colonial and Indonesian national contexts. This breakdown of source bases is to a considerable extent an arbitrary and artificial one, but one that nevertheless had to be made. There is material of potential importance in sources that we have not been able to discuss here, and we hope to see this explored further in future studies.

[2] It also continues to be upheld in the autonomous region of Aceh even after the province was granted the authority to formally implement its own Shariʿa legislation (Ind. *qanun*) in 2001. For more on the implementation of Islamic law in contemporary Aceh, see, Moch. Nur Ichwan, "The Politics of Shariʿatization: Central Governmental and Regional Discourses of Shariʿa Implementation in Aceh," and Tim Lindsey, M. B. Hooker, Ross Clarke, and Jeremy Kingsley, "Shariʿa Revival in Aceh," both in *Islamic Law in Contemporary Indonesia: Ideas and Institutions*, ed. R. Michael Feener and Mark E. Cammack (Cambridge, Mass.: ILSP/Harvard University Press, 2007).

[3] This work is available in an English translation as: B. ter Haar, *Adat Law in Indonesia*, trans. A. Arthur Schiller and E. Adamson Hoebel (Jakarta: Bhratara, 1962), 209–13.

[4] This despite the fact that as far back as 1900 Snouck Hurgronje, in his official capacity as special advisor to the colonial government, called attention to the diverse and constantly evolving nature of the *adat* regulation of joint marital property in the archipelago and even noted then contemporary trends for interpreting established local practice in light of Islamic law. See, for example, C. Adriaanse and E. Gobée (eds.), *Ambtelijke Adviezen van C. Snouck Hurgronje: 1889–1936*, 3 vols. (The Hague: Martinus Nijhoff, 1957), 1001–02 [XVII(5)–38].

[5] Liaw Yock Fang (ed.), *Undang-Undang Melaka: The Laws of Melaka* (The Hague: Martinus Nijhoff, 1976), 168.

[6] C. Snouck Hurgronje, *The Achehnese*, 2 vols., trans. A. W. S. O'Sullivan (Leiden: E. J. Brill, 1906), 1:438.

[7] Ibid., 1:365–66.

[8] For a concise statement of established Shafiʿi views on valid and invalid categories of partnership that inform these discussions, see Aḥmad ibn Naqīb al-Miṣrī's *'Umdat al-sālik*, which is available in the bilingual ed. *Reliance of the Traveller: A Classic Manual of Islamic Sacred Law*, trans. Nuh Ha Mim Keller (Beltsville, Md.: Amana Publications, 1994), 417–18.

[9] Th. W. Juynboll, *Handleiding tot de kennis van de Mohammedaansche wet volgens de leer der Sjâfiʿitische school* (Leiden: E. J. Brill, 1930), 203.

[10] For more on the life and legal writings of Sayyid ʿUthmān, see Nico Kaptein, "Sayyid ʿUthmān on the Legal Validity of Documentary Evidence," *Bijdragen tot de Taal-, Land- en Volkenkunde* 153–1 (1997), 85–102.

[11] Snouck Hurgronje's appreciative comments on this handbook for colonial Shariʿa court judges, composed by his primary Arab collaborator in the Indies, can be found in "Sajjid Oethman's gids voor de priesterraden," in idem, *Verspreide Gescrhiften—Gesammelte Schriften* (Bonn: Kurt Schroeder Verlag, 1923), IV.1:283–303.

[12] ʿUthmān b. ʿAbd Allāh b. ʿAqīl b. Yaḥyā al-ʿAlawī, *Kitāb Qawānīn al-sharʿiyya li-ahl al-majālis al-ḥukūmiyya wa l-iftāʾiyya* (Bogor: Maktaba ʿArafāt, 1313H), 82.

[13] Ibid., 82–3.

[14] Somewhat more detailed discussions of the topic by Sayyid ʿUthmān, referenced to a concise compendium of proof texts, are found in one of his lesser known works: ʿUthmān b. ʿAbd Allāh b. ʿAqīl b. Yaḥyā al-ʿAlawī, *Masāʾil daʿwā harta antara dua laki isteri atau antara ahli-ahli warith satu sama lain* (Batavia: n.p., 1298H/1881).

[15] For more on A. Hassan and his broader body of work on issues of Islamic law, see R. Michael Feener, *Muslim Legal Thought in Modern Indonesia* (Cambridge: Cambridge University Press, 2007), Chapter 2.

[16] A. Hassan, *Soal-Jawab Masalah Agama*, 2 vols. (Bangil: Penerbit PERSIS, 1996), 1:413–14 (no. 199).

[17] In his treatise on Islamic inheritance law, Hassan also considers *gono-gini* and analogous *adat* conceptions of joint marital property to be forms of a *sharikat al-ʿabdān* partnership. However, there he appears to remain open to a range of divisions of the property upon the death of one spouse beyond a simple 1:1 bifurcation. A. Hassan, *al-Farāʾiḍ* (Jakarta: Tintamas, 1964), 127.

[18] For an overview of his life and work, see Luthfi Aunie, Misri A. Muchsin, and Sehat Ihsan Shadiqin (eds.), *Ensiklopedi Pemikiran Ulama Aceh* (Banda Aceh: Ar-Raniry Press, 2004), 437–63.

[19] This work was first published as *Adat Gono-Gini Ditinjau dari Sudut Hukum Islam* (Jakarta: Bulan Bintang, 1965).

[20] *Pencaharian Bersama Suami Isteri Ditinjau dari Sudut Undang-undang Perkawinan Tahun 1974 dan Hukum Islam* (Jakarta: Bulan Bintang, 1986).

[21] Ismuha, *Pencaharian Bersama*, 19.

[22] Attention to issues of cross-school comparison is a major theme across nearly all of his published work, and is something that he evidently regarded as a necessary element of preparing Indonesian jurists for dealing with the interpretation of Islamic law in the modern world. In fact, Ismuha was also responsible for the Indonesian language translation of one of the major modern works of comparative Muslim jurisprudence, Maḥmūd Shaltūt and Muḥammad ʿAlī al-Sayis, *Muqāranat al-madhāhib fī l-fiqh* (*Perbandingan Mazhab dalam Masalah Fiqih*, Jakarta: Bulan Bintang, 1973), the text of which was intended specifically for use by students in the law and education faculties of the IAIN State Institutes for Islamic Studies in Indonesia.

[23] However, the situation can become more complicated if one or more partners contribute capital in addition to labor. See, for example, Ismuha, *Pencaharian Bersama*, 62–3.

[24] That is, a form of partnership based on *fiqh* standards of agency (*wakāla*) and surety (*kafāla*) and requiring full commitment from both partners to maintain equality in the balance of labor and/or capital contributions, as well as in liability and legal capacity.

[25] Ismuha, *Pencaharian Bersama*, 74–7.

[26] Ibid., 84–100.

[27] Sayuti Thalib, *Hukum Kekeluargaan Indonesia Berlaku bagi Umat Islam* (Jakarta: Penerbitan Universitas Indonesia, 1986), 79–92.

[28] The Act does not explicitly incorporate Islamic law, and there is little or nothing in the Act that is recognizably "Islamic." But Article 2 of the Act that specifies the requirements for a valid marriage defines a marriage as valid when performed according to the "religious law" of the parties. This language has been interpreted as essentially incorporating Islamic marriage doctrines for Muslims.

[29] For a discussion of the background to the promulgation of the Compilation, see Ahmad Imam Mawardi, "The Political Backdrop of the Enactment of the Compilation of Islamic Laws in Indonesia," in *Sharīʿa and Politics in Modern Indonesia*, ed. Arskal Salim and Azyumardi Azra (Singapore: Institute of Southeast Asian Studies, 2003), 125–47.

[30] Mark Cammack, "Indonesia's 1989 Religious Judicature Act: Islamization of Indonesia or Indonesianization of Islam?" *Indonesia* 63 (1997), 143–68.

[31] Decision of the *Raad Agama* for Kraksaan dated December 8, 1907 (23/1907).

[32] Decision of the *Raad Agama* for Jember dated July 21, 1935 (241/1935).

[33] Decision of the *Raad Agama* for Jepara dated April 7, 1935 (No. 1/1935).

[34] The existence of a difference in principle but not in fact between Islamic and *adat* marital property rules is reflected in an early decision of the Indonesian Supreme Court (*Mahkamah Agung*) dated April 14, 1956 (Reg. No. 24 K/Sip 1953). The case involved a suit by a widowed wife against one of her sons to recover property controlled by her son following the death of her husband. The *Raad Agama* for Praya in Central Lombok had determined that the surviving wife was entitled to one-third of the "*harta perkongsian*" and a one-eighth share of the remaining two-thirds as heir to his property. The defendant challenged the decision in the Supreme Court on the ground that the governing law is *adat* rather than Islamic. The Supreme Court agreed. The Court solicited advice on local *adat* from the District Court in Lombok regarding "the division of partnership property" and "whether a wife who has received a share of the partnership between herself and her husband is still entitled to receive a portion of the estate of her deceased husband." The District Court obtained the testimony of local *adat* experts, and supplied the following response: First, "the concept of partnership, which has connotations of trade, is not recognized in local *adat* concerning the relations between husband and wife, but *adat* does recognize the joint efforts of husband and wife during marriage under the term *gono-gini* with a 2:1 division between husband and wife." Second, so long as the widow does not remarry after the death of her husband, even though she is not entitled to inherit a share of the *gono-gini*, she may be granted a share of from one-eighth to a maximum of one-third for her efforts in maintaining the estate.

[35] Supreme Court decision dated February 11, 1959 (No. 387 K/Sip/1958).

[36] Supreme Court decision dated April 4, 1960 (No. 120 K/Sip/1960); Supreme Court decision dated November 14, 1962 (No. 290 K/Sip/1962); Supreme Court decision dated April 19, 1961 (No. 64 K/Sip/1961).

[37] Daniel S. Lev, "The Supreme Court and *Adat* Inheritance Law in Indonesia," *The American Journal of Comparative Law* 11/2 (1962), 205–24.

[38] In 1971 the High Court for Medan upheld a wife's claim for *harta bersama*, even though the couple were from South Tapanuli—an area that did not recognize a doctrine of marital property. In its decision the court stated that in accordance with the legal development in Indonesia it is considered to be just that property acquired during marriage is partnership property (*harta syarikat*) that must be divided equally upon divorce. Decision of High Court for Medan dated December 30, 1971 (No. 389/1971). This decision was later approved by the Supreme Court: Supreme Court decision dated May 23, 1973 (K/Sip/1972).

[39] Supreme Court decision dated November 7, 1956 (No. 51 K/Sip/1956).

[40] E.g., in the decision of the Islamic court for Pekanbaru dated September 19, 1991 (No. 153/1991), ruling that a store constituted marital property because it was acquired during the marriage despite the argument of the wife that the store was acquired through her efforts alone.

[41] Decision of Islamic court for Jayapura dated February 15, 1999 (No. 112/1999).

[42] Abdul Manan, "Beberapa Masala Hukum Tentang Harta Bersama," *Mimbar Hukum* 33 (1997), 56–73. The question of the status of civil service benefits came before the Islamic court for Malang in a slightly different context in 1991. The plaintiff in that case sued her former husband for a share of a house that the couple had occupied during the marriage under a rental/purchase contract with the government. The contract, which was offered to the husband in his capacity as a civil servant, provided for a series of installment payments resulting in the eventual acquisition of title to the property. According to undisputed evidence presented at the hearing, the market value of the house was more than twenty times the purchase price. The court rejected the defendant's arguments that the house did not qualify as marital property. Because the husband acquired the right to the house during his marriage to the plaintiff, the plaintiff also acquired both a right to the house and an obligation to make payments by virtue of the fact that she was his wife. But while the court ruled against the defendant on the question of the character of the property, the court did not completely reject his arguments. The court acknowledged that the Compilation prescribes an equal division of marital property between the spouses, but found that the defendant's acquisition of the right to the contract in his position as a civil servant entitled him to a two-thirds share of the value of the property, and ordered the defendant to deliver one-third of the value of the house to the plaintiff after the contract had been paid in full.

[43] Ibid.

[44] Ter Haar, *Adat Law*, 181.

[45] Supreme Court decision dated November 7, 1956 (No. 51 K/Sip/1956).

[46] High Court for Banda Aceh Decision dated October 26, 1981 (No. 195/1981).

[47] In the Supreme Court the husband argued that his wife was not entitled to marital property because she had destroyed the family by committing adultery

with her boyfriend. The Court did not address the merits of this argument, but stated that it involved evaluation of the evidence and therefore could not be raised on cassation. Decision of Supreme Court dated January 30, 1993 (No. 97 K/AG/1992).

[48] Yahya Harahap, *Kedudukan, Kewenangan, dan Acara Peradilan Agama* (Jakarta: Sinar Grafika, 2001), 278. All of the cases in our sample in which entitlement to marital property is linked to sexual indiscretion involve claims by husbands alleging misbehavior by their wives. We have found no case in which infidelity by the husband is made the basis for an argument that he should be denied his share of the marital property.

[49] Daniel S. Lev, *Islamic Courts in Indonesia: A Study in the Political Bases of Legal Institutions* (Berkeley: University of California Press, 1972), 163; Hisako Nakamura, *Conditional Divorce in Indonesia*, Occasional Publications 7 (July 2006), published by the Islamic Legal Studies Program, Harvard Law School (available in print or at www.law.harvard.edu/programs/ilsp/publications/occasional.php).

[50] Decision of the Islamic Court for Pekanbaru decided January 13, 1991 (No. 159/1991).

[51] Decision of the Islamic Court for Kotabumi dated August 7, 1986 (No. 64/1986).

[52] The agreement may have been an attempt to reproduce the result prescribed by custom. The *adat* in Sunda (West Java) and perhaps other regions did not recognize marital property in marriages between rich women and poor men. In Sunda such marriages are called *nyalindung kagelung*, which, roughly translated, means "hiding behind [a woman's] hair bun." See Bushar Muhammad, *Pokok Pokok Hukum Adat* (PT Pradnya Paramita, Jakarta, 1975), 19.

[53] Supreme Court decision dated September 10, 1958 (No. 248 K/Sip/1958).

[54] E.g., in the Supreme Court decision dated March 1, 1990 (No. 2563 K/Pdt/1988) in which the courts rejected a claim made by the daughter of the deceased's first wife to property acquired while the deceased was married to his third wife.

[55] Decision of the Islamic court for Nganjuk dated October 4, 1990 (No. 696/1990).

[56] Decision of the Islamic court for Batusangkar dated July 27, 1995 (No. 251/1994).

[57] Decision of the Supreme Court dated January 8, 1998 (No. 243 K/Ag/1996).

7

A STUDY OF WAKĪʿ'S (d. 306/917) *AKHBĀR AL-QUḌĀT*

Muhammad Khalid Masud

Introduction

A history of Islamic law of the pre-modern Muslim world is still to be written. What we have is a history of Muslim jurists (*fuqahāʾ*), and of the development of their doctrines as schools. Some, often scanty, information about the laws introduced by Muslim rulers, judgments of qadis (judges), and judicial procedure is available, but existing histories of Islamic law do not take them into account. Consequently our knowledge about the relationship between law and state is influenced greatly by Muslim jurists' vision of law and state.

The judgments of the qadis are rarely available before the sixteenth century; some fairly early judgments are reported in collections of juristic opinions (fatwas) such as that of al-Wansharīsī (d. 1508).[1] Information about the laws introduced by rulers may be culled from the annals of history, especially in local histories. Such information is also available in the biographies of judges, early examples of which are Wakīʿ's (d. 917) *Akhbār al-quḍāt*, al-Kindī's (d. 961) *Taʾrīkh al-wulāt wa l-quḍāt fī Miṣr*, and al-Khushanī's (d. 971) *Taʾrīkh al-quḍāt fī l-Andalus*.

This essay explores the state of judicial organization, the relationship between qadis and the state, and the role of jurists under the Umayyad and the early Abbasid caliphs, the formative period when the state was attempting to systematize the administration of justice, with special reference to Wakīʿ's *Akhbār al-quḍāt*. To my knowledge this work has not yet been studied from this perspective.

In his 1930 lectures on the early development of Islamic law, Joseph Schacht placed great emphasis on the importance of judicial practice and remarked about Wakīʿ's *Akhbār al-quḍāt* that "[t]his book tells us about another phenomenon of legal activity, that is development of law in judicial practice."[2] He recommended this book as a main source for the study of judicial activity in this period. Schacht observed that the role of judges in law-making in this period was so eminent that John of Damascus (d. 749) refers to them as the "lawgivers" of Islam.[3] In these lectures, Schacht referred to *Akhbār al-quḍāt*, along with Mālik's *al-Muwaṭṭaʾ* and al-Ṭabarī's *Ikhtilāf al-fuqahāʾ* as three important sources for this formative period.

It is not possible within the limits of this paper to present a full and critical study of the book. I shall focus on the nature of judgeship and the administration of justice. Before proceeding to an analytical study of this treatise, let me briefly introduce Wakīʿ, his period, and his work.

Wakīʿ and His Period

Wakīʿ flourished in a period of extreme political instability under the early Abbasids. The period is marked by several revolts (e.g., by the Zanj and Saffarids) and the struggle for power between the caliphs and their Turkic army commanders. Six caliphs succeeded each other within nine years (247–256/861–870). Culturally and intellectually, however, the period was richly productive. Most of the seminal works on the Qurʾan, *ḥadīth* and *fiqh* were written in this period. The great collections of *ḥadīth* and the influence of the *ḥadīth* movement, which propounded the centrality of the Prophet's practice (*sunna*), stimulated debates over the role that should be assigned to the Prophetic reports in matters of law, and this in turn sparked interest in jurisprudence and questions concerning the sources of Islamic law. The *ḥadīth* movement also impacted theology (*kalām*), especially in displacing reason (*ʿaql*) as a source of knowledge. Intellectually it was a period of the systemization of various sciences. Wakīʿ's work *Akhbār al-quḍāt* may be seen in this general context.

Life[4]

Wakīʿ's full name is Abū Bakr Muḥammad b. Khalaf b. Ḥayyān b. Ṣadaqa al-Ḍabbī.[5] He is, however, better known by the name of Wakīʿ, an added name which literally means sturdy, strong, and established. It is also used to refer to the leader of a herd of sheep. Almost every chronicle in the Abbasid period mentions Wakīʿ's death among the events of the hijri year 360, but gives no further details about his life. We do not know much about him other than that he began his career as a secretary to the judge Abū ʿUmar Muḥammad b. Yūsuf b. Yaʿqūb, who served in Baghdad during the years 284–296/879–908.[6] Among his writings, the following ten are known:

Ghurar al-akhbār fī akhbār al-quḍāt wa-taʾrīkhihim wa-aḥkāmihim
Kitāb al-Anwāʾ
Kitāb al-Baḥth
Kitāb al-Taṣarruf wa l-naqd wa l-sikka
Kitāb al-Ramy wa l-niḍāl
Kitāb al-Sharīf
Kitāb al-Ṭarīq

Kitāb ʿAdad āyāt al-Qurʾān wa l-ikhtilāf fīhi
Kitāb al-Musāfir
Kitāb al-Makāyīl wa l-mawāzīn

To my knowledge, only the first, the subject of analysis in the present essay, has been published. Ibn al-Nadīm (d. 995) notices the versatility of interests in Wakīʿ's works. Others also refer to this diversity.[7] *Al-Sharīf* is an encyclopedic work written on the pattern of Ibn Qutayba's (d. 889) *al-Maʿārif*, and is one of al-Masʿūdī's (d. 956) sources for his *Murūj al-dhahab*.[8] *Al-Ṭarīq* is about the history of countries and roads. Other works deal with weights and measures, weapons, mints, coins, and seasons. This versatility in literature and various sciences suggests that Wakīʿ was a man of letters (*adīb, kātib*), not particularly a specialist in Islamic law. Despite biographers mentioning *fiqh* as a subject of his particular interest, only two of his works are connected, though indirectly, with Islamic law: *Akhbār al-quḍāt*, and *ʿAdad āyāt al-Qurʾān*. Abū Bakr Ibn Mujāhid calls the latter a definitive work on the subject.[9]

Abū ʿUmar, the qadi with whom Wakīʿ worked, was greatly interested in *ḥadīth*, and a voluminous *Musnad* is attributed to him.[10] Wakīʿ's own interest in *ḥadīth* is evident in his passion for collecting those transmitted by judges. For the qadis, the *ḥadīths* of interest were either a statement of law or a judgment handed down by the Prophet Muḥammad. Scholars are divided, however, on the quality of Wakīʿ's scholarship on *ḥadīth*. Ibn al-Qifṭī (d. 1248), Ibn al-Jawzī (d. 1257), Ibn Kathīr (d. 1372), and al-Jazarī (d. 1429) do not question the quality of his scholarship, while al-Baghdādī (d. 1071), Ṣalāḥ al-Dīn al-Ṣafadī (d. 1362), Ibn Ḥajar al-ʿAsqalānī (d. 1448), and Ibn al-ʿImād al-Ḥanbalī (d. 1671) are very critical of his work in historiography and *ḥadīth* studies. Al-Ṣafadī dismisses him as a narrator of popular stories of the past (*ayyām*), an uncritical teller of tales (*akhbārī*),[11] and Abū l-Ḥusayn al-Munādī claims that his scholarship was not sound.[12] One may attribute this criticism to differences in criteria used among scholars, especially after the formative period, to determine the soundness of *ḥadīth*. Their claims about Wakīʿ are not truly tenable as most historians and biographers did rely on Wakīʿ's works.[13]

Wakīʿ's biographers do not indicate whether he belonged to any school of law. This fact suggests that either being affiliated with a school of law was not required for a qadi in this period, or the schools (*madhhabs*) were still in formation.

The *Akhbār al-quḍāt*

ʿAbd al-ʿAzīz Muṣṭafā al-Marāghī (d. 1945) edited Wakīʿ's *Ghurar al-akhbār fī akhbār al-quḍāt wa-taʾrīkhihim wa-aḥkāmihim*. It was published in 1947 in three volumes under the short title *Akhbār al-quḍāt* with extensive notes by the editor. Also included is an index of cases mentioned in the book.

Several reprints of this edition have appeared since, but a critical edition is still needed. As it stands now, the edition suffers from several flaws. For instance, some notices and a list of judges appearing at the end of the printed edition belong to a period after Wakīʿ's death. Apparently, these lists and notices were added by the copyists to bring their work up to date. The editor also provides subtitles which often do not reflect what follows.

Wakīʿ's *Akhbār al-quḍāt* stands out among other contemporary books of this nature by virtue of its coverage of all the territories under the caliphate; the others are largely limited to the accounts of a particular city or area. Examples of the latter are Abū ʿUbayda al-Baṣrī's (d. 209/824) *Akhbār quḍāt al-Baṣra*, limited to Basra, and al-Kindī's *Akhbār quḍāt Miṣr*, limited to Egypt.

The work begins with an introduction, in which Wakīʿ explains the purpose of his book and justifies its scope as a history of judges of all cities from the period of the Messenger of God up to the author's time, reporting their biographies, judgments, opinions, and genealogies. Wakīʿ's introduction deals with the following subjects: a definition of the idea of judgment and justice; difficulties entailed in the profession of judgeship; condemnable types of judgment, i.e., those reflective of personal predilection and oppression; praiseworthy types of judgment, i.e., those based on the revealed book; bribery; intercession; the qualifications of a judge; and the duties of a judge.

The history of the judges in this work is divided geographically. Wakīʿ begins with Medina, and then proceeds to Mecca and al-Taʾif. Basra and Kufa take up more space than Damascus, Palestine, Ifriqiya (Tunisia), Spain, Harran, Mawsil, Egypt, Baghdad, Madaʾin, Khurasan, Wasit, and Ahwaz. Wakīʿ reviews the judicial history of each of these cities chronologically, starting from Prophet Muḥammad's time to his day. He gives the names of the judges and those of the governors and caliphs who appointed them. He records brief biographies of the judges, their dates of appointment, and their judgments. His notices are styled on the pattern of *ḥadīth*s. First he mentions in chronological order the individuals from or through whom the information came to him, in the shape of a chain of authorities (*isnād*), and then he provides the text of the information. It is also significant that Wakīʿ is interested in the literary activity of judges in addition to their judicial achievements. Apparently, like other state officials, judges in this period tended to be men of letters.

Wakīʿ clarifies that the purpose of his work is not to repeat existing information but to fill in the gaps. He has therefore given more space to those judges whose contributions were not widely known at his time. In my view this claim is particularly noteworthy. It indicates that the compilers of *ḥadīth* had neglected or were uninformed of some *ḥadīth*s that were known among these judges. The point invites further investigation into the question of whether this means that the *ḥadīth* compilers and these judges employed different criteria of authenticity. About the judgments he says: "I narrated whatever came to my knowledge about judges whose legal opinions and judgments remained less reported, while they were current during the days of their appointment" (Wakīʿ 1947, 1:5).[14] Wakīʿ mentions here the names of Shurayḥ and Ibn Shubruma among those whose opinions and judgments were less known in his days, which verifies the fact that Shurayḥ was not the legend he would later become, as claimed by Tyan and Schacht.[15] The judges whom Wakīʿ treats at considerable length include Iyās b. Muʿāwiya (2:212–374), Shurayḥ (2:189–398), and Ibn Shubruma (3:36–129).

Administration of Justice

Wakīʿ describes for us in the most basic terms the actual legal system of Islam and the administration of justice. I have selected several statements and reports from the *Akhbār al-quḍāt* that disagree with later writings, especially the manuals written for qadis. These excerpts will highlight the differences between Wakīʿ and other jurists who wrote on the subject.

The Position of Qadi

Wakīʿ gives a list of qadis in the early period of the Prophet Muḥammad and the first four Caliphs, but most of those who are listed as qadis in this period served also as governors and administrators. In several passages he states that there were no qadis in this period, and that it was the Umayyad caliph Muʿāwiya (r. 661–680) who began appointing qadis (1:105, 1:110).[16] This statement appears to contradict other statements he makes here and there. In one passage he says that in the early days of Islam a qadi functioned as an expert on doctrine (*muftī*) (1:288). Wakīʿ's statement could mean that there were no qadis acting as judges in the capital Medina, and that it was Muʿāwiya who first appointed them there. This would have been so because the Prophet and the early caliphs acted as qadis in Medina. The qadis were appointed in other cities but they performed these duties together with other functions as representatives of the centre. Wakīʿ's statement about Muʿāwiya clarifies that qadis in the Umayyad period were officials who settled disputes on the authority of the caliph. They were no longer solely experts to be consulted or arbiters (*ḥakam*) chosen by the parties to the dispute.

Since the close of the Umayyad period, a qadi was clearly an appointee and representative of the caliph from whom the qadi derived his authority. Qadi ʿAbd al-ʿAzīz b. al-Muṭṭalib's (d. 141/757) statement "I am his judge and my judgment is his judgment" (1:204) reveals the basis of his authority. Regarding the qadis in the Abbasid period, Wakīʿ states repeatedly that "it was the governors who appointed qadis" (1:184). Qadi Saʿīd b. Salmān al-Musāḥiqī's notice in Wakīʿ (1:238) shows that Caliph al-Mahdī (r. 775–785) made these appointments in writing. Letters were written in the name of the caliph and issued by the governors. Wakīʿ reports several incidents in which qadis were appointed and dismissed summarily by these governors (1:190). Stories are also reported about conflicts between qadis and governors (1:297) and between qadis and caliphs (1:266). In these cases the qadi's judgment was often overruled. There are also stories reported about the supervision of judges in the districts by higher judges who reviewed their judgments (1:270).

According to Wakīʿ, the judiciary was misused by Caliphs al-Muʿtaṣim (r. 833–842), al-Wāthiq (r. 842–847), and al-Mutawakkil (r. 847–861) to impose state doctrines. Their chief qadi Aḥmad b. Abī Duʾād carried out inquisitions targeting the beliefs of people regarding whether the Qurʾan was created or not (3:294). Wakīʿ contends that "the caliphs corrupted the schools of law in this period" (3:294), which comment probably refers to either the misuse of legal interpretation by the state authorities or the caliphs restricting qadis to apply the doctrines of a specific school of law. In fact, after the inquisition period, the Abbasid caliph al-Qādir bi-llāh patronized a "juridical theology" that developed under the influence of the Hanbali *ḥadīth* movement, the Shafiʿi school of law, and Ashʿari theology.[17]

Composition of the Court

Although the Shariʿa court is ordinarily constituted of a single qadi, Wakīʿ notes some important instances where the court consisted of more than one qadi. In 137/754 two qadis—ʿUmar b. Āmir al-Sulamī and Sawwār b. ʿAbd Allāh—sat together in Basra (2:35). However, when there was a conflict between them in a case, the governor dismissed one of the judges, or his judgment. Wakīʿ also notes instances where others sat together with the qadi. He refers to a case before judge Shurayḥ when several elders were present (2:213). It is not clear whether they functioned as a jury or as a traditional council of justice.

Another noteworthy instance is that of judge Abū l-Bakhtarī (d. 192/807) who was given a list of twenty-seven jurisconsults to assist him when he was appointed. He confirmed only seven of them (1:247). The judges are usually advised to consult scholars and jurists, but Wakīʿ notes an instance where Qadi ʿAbd al-ʿAzīz b. al-Muṭṭalib refused to do so (1:26).

Wakīʿ mentions the following as court officials and assistants to the qadi: a guard (*ḥaras*, 1:132, 1:145, 1:203); a policeman, assistant, or secretary (*jilwāz*, 2:215); a prison warden (*sajjān*, 1:132); and a secretary, clerk (*amīn*, 2:58).

There are also reports indicating the practice of maintaining judicial records. Sawwār (d. 143/760) was the first to systematize the office of the judge and begin maintaining registers (*sijillāt*) for cases (2:58). Wakīʿ mentions a specific court building in Ahwaz where copies of judgments were preserved (3:320). Khālid b. Ṭalīq (Caliph al-Mahdī's qadi) made two copies of every decree, each attested by witnesses. One copy was preserved in the records office (2:125).

Qualifications of a Qadi

Wakīʿ suggests three essential characteristics of a qadi: a qadi does not accept bribes, cannot be humiliated, and cannot be tempted (1:7). He also recommends that qadis be appointed from well-off and noble families (1:76). Compared with the requirements prescribed by the jurists this list seems minimal. Caliph ʿUmar b. ʿAbd al-ʿAzīz required a qadi to be strong, blameless, chaste, gentle, and knowledgeable about preceding judgments and practices (*sunan*) (1:77). The caliph dismissed a weak qadi, ʿAbd al-Raḥmān b. Yazīd b. Ḥāritha, for settling a dispute by paying the disputed money to the claimant from his own pocket (1:134).

Wakīʿ does not accept reports of the dismissal of qadis at face value. Al-Zuhrī (d. 143/760) is reported to have been dismissed after being accused of praying without making ablutions. He was punished and imprisoned for being remiss. Wakīʿ refutes this story, saying that al-Zuhrī belonged to a noble family of Banū ʿAwf who had served as qadis in Medina since early Islam, and that, in fact, al-Zuhrī was disgraced because there was some personal enmity between him and some people in Medina (1:213). Wakīʿ also notes the independence of judges in their personal habits. Two qadis, Shurayḥ and Sharīk (d. 177/793), used to drink *ṭilāʾ* (2:212) and *nabīdh* (3:162), respectively, both of which were drinks whose lawfulness was controversial among the jurists.

Wakīʿ remarks that the training of a judge differed from that of a jurist (1:350): a judge received his training as an apprentice working with a judge. Judges belonging to well-off families did not receive salaries for a judgeship (1:229, 2:11, 2:125, and 3:7).

Court Premises

According to Wakīʿ, most of the judges used mosques as courts for judgment (1:145, 1:162, 2:125, 2:428, 3:135). The qadi Saʿīd b. Ibrāhīm even executed punishment in the mosques (1:162). This practice militates against the sacredness of the mosque, on account of which the jurists disallowed the use of mosque premises as courts.[18] Early qadis also held courts in their own houses (1:275), in the marketplace (1:399, 3:206), and even on the roadside (1:333).

Qadis and Other Offices

The offices of judge, police chief, and market inspector (*muḥtasib*) were compatible. For instance, a police chief in Medina was also appointed a qadi (1:227). Ibn Shubruma twice refused appointment as overseer of the police (3:118), while Saʿīd b. Ibrāhīm held the posts of qadi and *muḥtasib* at the same time (1:174).

Procedure

Judicial practice differed considerably from the juristic doctrines (*fiqh*) on evidence, witnessing, and oath-taking. The jurists do not accept a written document without testimony. However, qadis al-Ḥasan al-Baṣrī (2:11) and al-Shaʿbī (2:416) accepted documents written between qadis without asking for witnesses. According to Wakīʿ, Ibn Abī Laylā was the first judge to ask witnesses for a letter written to him by another qadi.

Normally cases were decided by demanding a witness from the plaintiff and an oath by the defendant. The judges' criteria of acceptable witnesses, however, differed from those of jurists. Qadis Zurāra (1:293), Ibn Abī Laylā (3:117), Ibn Shubruma (3:117), and Iyās b. Muʿāwiya (1:331) decided cases on the basis of only one witness, while the jurists required two witnesses. Abū Bakr Ibn Ḥazm allowed a son to testify in favour of his mother (1:146), and Shurayḥ allowed it in favour of the father (2:276).

Regarding the criteria for refusing a witness, judges differed with each other. Shurayḥ did not allow the testimony of a person prosecuted for wrongfully accusing another of adultery in a court (2:284), while Abū Bakr Ibn Ḥazm did allow it (1:146). The jurists regard such testimony as invalid. ʿAbd al-Malik b. Yaʿlā rejected the testimony of a person who missed Friday prayers for three consecutive weeks without any excuse (2:17). Sulaymān b. ʿUlātha rejected the witnesses who did not pray in the mosque and who did not perform the pilgrimage despite capacity (3:217). Sawwār rejected a witness who drank *nabīdh* (2:83).

It appears that the social standing of witnesses carried more weight in the assessment of evidence than did the juristic formal criteria. The crucial question for a qadi was whether a witness was called to verify the facts of a case or to support the claim of the plaintiff. In the latter case a witness must be reliable to the satisfaction of the judge.

Islamic Law Between Jurist and Judge

In his introduction Wakīʿ invokes an attribute of God which one hears rarely: The One Who judges by what is right (*al-qāḍī bi l-ḥaqq*). This attribute implies that judging is an attribute of God and, therefore, a judge must be accountable only to God. Quoting the Qurʾanic verse commanding Muḥammad to judge by "that which God has made to appear reasonable to you (*arāka*)" (Q 4:105), he comments that God did not even delegate His powers of dispensing justice to the Prophet Muḥammad. The majority of the scholars in early Islam claimed that the Qurʾanic verses calling for judgment in accordance with what God revealed (Q 5:44–7) referred to the people of pre-Qurʾanic scriptures. Wakīʿ dismisses these claims, arguing that these verses, in fact, refuted judgments based on arbitrary and discretionary powers of judges or kings (1:34).

Wakīʿ only mentions the Qurʾan and *ḥadīth* as sources of law, beyond which a judge is free to use his own reasoning (*ijtihād*). In their judgments in the cases reported in *Akhbār al-quḍāt*, the qadis rely mostly on common sense and local custom, including the drawing of lots (1:91). Several stories about Iyās b. Muʿāwiya refer to his using common-sensical tricks to expose the falsehood of claims in his court (1:331). Out of a total of 59 cases in the early period, in only one case does the qadi refer to a *ḥadīth*.

We find the qadis divided on two questions. In the event of a conflict between a *ḥadīth* and a personal opinion, Ibn Sīrīn and al-Ḥasan al-Baṣrī preferred *ḥadīth*, even when it reported the opinion of a Companion of the Prophet over the opinion of a jurist. Qadi Iyās b. Muʿāwiya disagreed with al-Ḥasan al-Baṣrī, saying, "We know more about judgeship than you do" (1:337). Caliph ʿUmar b. ʿAbd al-ʿAzīz supported al-Ḥasan al-Baṣrī and dismissed Iyās.

In a recent study, I have analyzed several divorce cases reported in the *Akhbār al-quḍāt*, which are applicable here.[19] I will briefly report on my findings. The Qurʾan prescribes, "For divorced women is a parting gift (*matāʿ*). This is a duty upon the righteous (2:241)" and "There is no blame on you if ye divorce women before consummation or the fixation of their dower; but bestow on them a parting gift. The wealthy according to his means, and the poor according to his means;—a gift of a reasonable amount is a duty (*ḥaqqan*) upon those who wish to do the right thing. And if ye divorce them before consummation, but after the fixation of a dower for them, then half of the dower (is due to them), unless they remit it" (Q 2:236, 237). The payment of a parting gift[20] appears to have been a Qurʾanic innovation designed to reform the pre-Islamic practice of divorce and turn it into a graceful separation (*taṣrīḥun bi-iḥsān*, 2:229). The jurists found these verses about a parting gift and dower (*mahr*) to be in conflict with each other. They made Qurʾan 2:237 the principal verse, which qualifies the other general verses. The qadis, on the other hand, mostly regarded the parting gift as obligatory in all divorces.

In the *Akhbār al-quḍāt*, all of the Umayyad qadis treated the payment of *matāʿ* as an obligation incumbent upon the man upon the act of divorce, upholding its payment in all the divorce cases. Later jurists, on the other hand, generally treated it as a right arising from marriage and made its payment subject to the conditions of the marriage contract. (Of the four Sunni schools of law, only the Shafiʿis consider *matāʿ* a right that arises from divorce, but even they do not regard it as an obligation upon the husband if the wife initiates the divorce.)

The qadis of Iraq and Egypt were frequently faced with having to decide whether a parting gift was a voluntary payment or an obligation. As is reported in al-Kindī:

> A husband and wife brought a legal action to the court of Qadi Tawba b. Nimr [d. ca. 120/738] in Egypt. In the middle of the hearing, the husband divorced his wife. The qadi then ruled that the husband

should pay a parting gift to his wife. Although the husband refused, the qadi did not press him because, in his opinion, the payment was not compulsory. Subsequently, when the same man appeared before the same qadi in another dispute, the qadi refused to accept him as a witness because, by refusing to pay a parting gift to his divorced wife, he had acknowledged that he was not a pious and God-fearing person, thereby disqualifying himself as a witness.[21]

Wakīʿ narrates a similar report from the court of Shurayḥ, in which Shurayḥ rebukes the husband, asking whether he is not God-fearing and kind. Among the qadis, it is only Shurayḥ who raised questions about the consummation of the marriage and payment of the remainder of the dower in relation to the parting gift. Quite possibly, the legal implications of the parting gift were already being debated among Shurayḥ's contemporaries, and Shurayḥ was the first qadi to begin to apply it in practice.

Concluding Remarks

The analysis of the *Akhbār al-quḍāt* undertaken in the preceding pages has led us to some important information about early judicial practice. Along with the details related to the administration of justice, this study has also yielded significant information about the origin and growth of judicial organization. According to Wakīʿ, the institution of judgeship did not formally exist before the Umayyads and that institution grew out of muftiship.

We have also found that on several points judicial practice differed from juristic doctrine. In the *matāʿ* cases, for example, qadis judged on the basis of the Qurʾanic rulings, whereas the jurists developed a complex set of doctrines that were not in principle beneficial to the divorced wife. It is almost as if the jurists constructed laws in order to preserve the status quo, while the judges followed the reformative spirit of the Qurʾan in order to transform divorce into a graceful separation.

Emile Tyan cautioned against writing the history of Islamic law—and especially the history of the administration of justice—while relying only on *fiqh* texts and manuals for qadis authored by the jurists. He urged that greater attention be given to works on the history and biography of the qadis. The present study reiterates this cautionary note, recommending the same alternative approach—we must pay more attention to those who settle disputes by relying on the Qurʾan and *ḥadīth* as precedent in combination with local judicial practice.

NOTES

1 See David S. Powers, *Law, Society, and Culture in the Maghrib, 1300–1500* (Cambridge: Cambridge University Press, 2002).

[2] Joseph Schacht, "Thalāth muḥāḍarāt fī ta'rīkh al-fiqh al-islāmī," in Ṣalāḥ al-Dīn al-Munajjid (ed.), *al-Muntaqā min dirāsāt al-mustashriqīn* (Cairo: Lajnat al-Ta'līf wa l-Tarjama wa l-Nashr, 1955), 97.

[3] Joseph Schacht, *An Introduction to Islamic Law* (Oxford: Clarendon Press, 1964), 25.

[4] al-Khaṭīb al-Baghdādī's (d. 1071) biographical notice seems to be the main source of information about Wakīʿ's life. Most of the later biographical works rely on this information. See al-Khaṭīb al-Baghdādī, *Ta'rīkh Baghdād* (Cairo: Maṭbaʿat al-Saʿāda, 1931), 5:234–37.

[5] Brockelmann's error in identifying Wakīʿ's name and date of death (*Geschichte der Arabischen Litteratur*, S I, 225) has been corrected by F. Sezgin (*Geschichte des Arabischen Schrifttums*, I, 376).

[6] Ibn al-Nadīm, *al-Fihrist* (Cairo: al-Maktaba al-Tijāriyya, n.d.), 166.

[7] al-Baghdādī 1931, 5:236; Ibn al-Jawzī, *al-Muntaẓam fī ta'rīkh al-umam wa l-mulūk* (Beirut: Dār al-Kutub, 1992), 13:186; Jamāl al-Dīn al-Qifṭī, *Anbā' al-ruwāt ʿalā anbā' al-nuḥāt* (Cairo: Dār al-Kutub al-Miṣriyya, 1955), 3:124; Abū l-Fidā' Ibn Kathīr, *al-Bidāya wa l-nihāya* (Beirut: Dār Iḥyā' al-Turāth, 1988), 11:148; Shams al-Dīn al-Jazarī, *Ghāyat al-nihāya fī ṭabaqāt al-qurrā'* (Maṭbaʿat al-Saʿāda, 1933), 2:137.

[8] al-Masʿūdī, Abū l-Ḥasan, *Murūj al-dhahab* (Beirut: Dār al-Andalus, 1965), 1:23.

[9] al-Baghdādī, *Ta'rīkh Baghdād*, 5:235.

[10] al-Ziriklī, Khayr al-Dīn, *al-Aʿlām* (Beirut: Dār al-ʿIlm li l-Malāyīn, 1980), 7:148.

[11] al-Ṣafadī, Ṣalāḥ al-Dīn, *al-Wāfī bi l-Wafayāt* (Damascus: Maṭbaʿa Hāshimiyya, 1953), 3:43.

[12] al-Baghdādī, *Ta'rīkh Baghdād*, 5:236; Ibn Ḥajar al-ʿAsqalānī, *Līsān al-mīzān* (Hayderabad: ʿUthmāniyya, 1912), 5:156; Ibn al-ʿImād al-Ḥanbalī, *Shadharāt al-dhahab fī akhbār man dhahab* (Cairo: Maktabat al-Qudsī, 1931), 2:249.

[13] Franz Rosenthal, *A History of Muslim Historiography* (Leiden: E. J. Brill, 1952), 340.

[14] From this point onward, references to Wakīʿ's text, by volume and page, will be inserted into the text.

[15] Emile Tyan, *Histoire de l'organisation judiciare en pays d'Islam* (Leiden: E. J. Brill, 1960), 1:75–6; Joseph Schacht, *The Origins of Muhammadan Jurisprudence* (Oxford: Clarendon Press, 1959), 229.

[16] See Khalid Masud, "Procedural Law Between Traditionists, Jurists and Judges, the Question of Yamīn maʿ al-Shahīd," *Al-Qanṭara* 20 (1999), 389–416.

[17] George Makdisi, *Religion, Law, and Learning in Classical Islam* (Ashgate: Variorum, 1991), ch. II, 5–47.

[18] Ḥasan Ibrāhīm Ḥasan, *Ta'rīkh al-Islām al-siyāsī wa l-dīnī wa l-thaqāfī wa l-ijtimāʿī* (Beirut: Dār Iḥyā' al-Turāth al-ʿArabī, 1965), 3:309 writes that Caliph al-Muʿtaḍid forbade qadis from sitting in mosques.

[19] See my "The Award of Matāʿ in the Early Muslim Courts," in *Dispensing Justice in Islam*, ed. Muhammad Khalid Masud, Rudolph Peters, and David S. Powers (Leiden: Brill, 2005), 349–81.

[20] Schacht, *The Origins of Muhammadan Jurisprudence*, 101, Muhammad Asad, *The Message of the Qur'ān* (Gibraltar: Dār al-Andalus, 1980), 54, and ʿAbdullāh Yūsuf

ʿAlī, *Qur'ān, English translation* (Medina: Ministry of Ḥajj and Endowments, 1992), 107 translate the term "parting gift" respectively as "obligatory gift," "alimony," and "suitable gift."

[21] al-Kindī, Abū ʿUmar Muḥammad b. Yūsuf, *Kitāb al-Wulāt wa-kitāb al-quḍāt*, ed. Rhuvon Guest as *The Governors and Judges of Egypt* (Leiden: E. J. Brill, 1912), 344.

8

THE HERITAGE OF OTTOMAN RULE IN THE ISRAELI LEGAL SYSTEM

The Concept of *Umma* and *Millet*

Aharon Layish

Introduction

This essay[1] presents an anomaly in the Israeli legal system created by changing political circumstances. At the core of the anomaly are the concepts *umma*, the Muslim political entity, and *millet*, a communal framework regulating the status and organization of the tolerated religious communities (Christians and Jews) in the Ottoman Empire. Being a residue from the reality of a sovereign Islamic state, these concepts, once dissociated by historical circumstance from the legal and cultural framework in which they arose, required adjustment to the alien juridical environment of a non-Muslim country with its Western political and socio-cultural orientation. Oddly, the substance (though not the terminology) of these concepts, with some indispensable changes, have survived into the present during a period of almost ninety years after the collapse of the Ottoman Empire. The issue under study represents a highly instructive example of what sociologists and anthropologists designate as "legal pluralism"[2]—in this specific case—transmitted from the multi-religious and communal structure characterizing the Ottoman Empire.

In the Qur'an, the term *umma* signifies a religious community corresponding to that of *milla*. Beginning with the chapters, or suras, of the Medinan period, the term acquired the narrower connotation of an autonomous Muslim entity coupled with political authority and religious and social components.[3] The term *milla* had a variety of denotations throughout Muslim history; thus, for instance, in sixteenth-century Jerusalem, it designated the Muslims rather than the tolerated religious communities.[4] Towards the end of the Ottoman Empire, as *millet* it signified both "a religious community" and a national entity.[5]

The *millet* system is based on the concept of protection (*dhimma*) granted by means of a contract between the Muslim sovereign and the protected subjects: the first party undertakes to ensure the rights of the second party to manage its own communal and religious affairs, and to provide safety and immunity against arbitrary acts; the second party responds by professing loyalty to the first party. The protection reflects a tolerated status, a citizenship of secondary degree. A series of signs were designated to identify the protected subjects (*dhimmīs*) from the Muslims.[6]

In a Muslim state, the *umma*, the Muslim political entity, is the sovereign; hence there is no need to define its legal status. Islamic law (Shariʿa) regulates also the status of the non-Muslims in the state. Broadly speaking, the Shariʿa courts were state courts and their jurisdiction comprised also non-Muslims. In the second half of the nineteenth century, civil courts designated to apply the new codes, including the Mejelle, the Ottoman civil code, were constituted beside the Shariʿa courts.

Benjamin Braude has found that, contrary to conceptions firmly rooted in Western literature on the Ottoman Empire, the *millet* system was not a unified, organized, and institutionalized system, but rather "a set of arrangements, largely local, with considerable variation over time and place" obtained with each of the older communities—the Greeks (embracing all the orthodox Christian subjects of the sultan), the Armenians, and the Jews—and within which framework a measure of legal autonomy was granted to each community.[7]

The first cracks in the *millet* system, with signs of a reshuffling of the relations between the Muslim *umma* and the *millets*, appeared in the nineteenth century. On the theoretical level (though not necessarily in practice) the *Hatt-ı Hümayun* decree of 1856 proclaiming equality between Muslims and non-Muslim subjects of the Empire[8] was in glaring contradiction to the very nature of the *millet* concept. Moreover, the protection that European powers granted to members of various *millets* by means of extra rights (*berāt*), anchored in the Capitulations agreements (whose scope increased progressively from the sixteenth century onwards), transformed them from the status of dhimmis under the protection of Islam to something approaching the status of resident foreigners or foreign nationals, that is, subjects of the Domain of War (*dār al-ḥarb*), whose duties and rights were defined by the West rather than by Islam.[9] Broadly speaking, in spite of these events, the *millet* system as an organizational framework survived until the collapse of the Ottoman Empire.

The Ottoman Heritage in Palestine under British Mandate

The point of departure in this essay is the accumulative legal and administrative heritage of the *millet* system as consolidated since the nineteenth century and transferred to Palestine under the British Mandate. Practically speaking, the main components of this heritage are: judicial autonomy in matters of personal status in accordance with the community's religious law, administration of the communal property (*waqf*, church property), observance of religious worship, and a recognized status of the heads of the communities as their representatives towards the state.[10]

Following World War I, Palestine ceased to be part of a Muslim territory, which status had legal and political repercussions. At first blush, one would expect a complete redefinition of the status of the Muslims and the tolerated religious communities within the new political framework. With the collapse of the Ottoman Empire, however, its heritage of legal pluralism as anchored in the *millet* system did not change overnight. The policy of the British government—in line with its colonial legal policy at the time[11]—was to preserve the status quo[12] in matters pertaining to religion and law, subject to obligations undertaken under the Mandate and also subject to changes resulting from the turnover of the political rule. Britain's obligations under the Mandate entailed, inter alia, the safeguarding of the civil and religious rights, including the holy shrines, of all the inhabitants of Palestine, irrespective of race and religion; the guarantee to respect the personal status of all the people and communities and their religious interests; and the management of the administration of the religious endowments (*waqf*), in accordance with the religious law and the stipulations of their founders. Broadly speaking, the capitulary privileges, including the benefits of Consular jurisdiction and protection as formerly enjoyed by foreigners in the Ottoman Empire, were suspended.[13] The preservation of the status quo was required also to secure the continuity of the law in the transition period from the Ottoman to the Mandate rule. This policy is clearly reflected in the Palestine Order-in-Council, 1922–1947 (hereinafter POC), Article 46, which provides that the civil courts should exercise jurisdiction "in accordance with the Ottoman law in force in Palestine on November 1st, 1914, or otherwise declared to be in force by public notice."

The British policy of preserving the status quo regarding the autonomy of the recognized communities[14] is manifested in various domains. Formally, the Muslims were not included in the category of the recognized religious communities that had been granted judicial autonomy in matters of personal status,[15] though in actual fact they enjoyed judicial autonomy. The Muslims declined to be defined as a religious community (*ṭāʾifa*) within the same category as Jews and Christians. The British government was fully aware of this sensitivity, and the establishment in December 1921 of the Supreme Muslim Council (hereinafter SMC) seems to have been prompted by the desire to compensate the Muslims for the lack of a Muslim sovereign. At a Muslim conference held late in 1920, on the eve of the constitution of the SMC, the High Commissioner expressed the Government's desire

> to establish a body representing the country's Muslims in order both to assure them complete control over their religious endowments and that the Muslim community might feel that the *sharīʿa* courts were

being supervised by people of its choice. The Government does not want to take the place of the *sheikh ül-Islām*.[16]

After his election as president of the SMC, Ḥājj Amīn al-Ḥusaynī invested much energy in promoting the status of Jerusalem in the eyes of the Muslim world and enhancing the importance of the Temple Mount (*al-Ḥaram al-Sharīf*) with its mosques.[17] The president of the Council was empowered to nominate the qadis—a function traditionally vested in the Muslim ruler; the muftis—traditionally independent but nevertheless institutionalized in the Ottoman Empire; and the religious functionaries of the mosques, to manage the *waqf* properties, both *maḍbūṭ* and *mulḥaq*. Under the late Ottoman rule, the former were administered directly by the Ministry of Waqf while the latter were administered by the Shariʿa Courts subject to the Ministry's supervision.[18] The SMC was also in charge of the educational system. Indeed, well-informed observers defined the Muslim Council as "a state within a state."[19]

Various domains of the Shariʿa that had been codified, such as the Ottoman civil code of 1876, known as the Majalla, the Family Rights Law of 1917, as well as the Land Law of 1858 and the Procedure of the Shariʿa Court Law of 1917 (both of which rely heavily on the Shariʿa), survived in Palestine. Moreover, the Majalla, which is based almost exclusively on Hanafi doctrine, was applied in the civil courts with respect to all the residents of the country regardless of religion or community, as it was during the Ottoman period. Needless to say, domains of the Shariʿa that had not been codified, such as criminal law entailing fixed Qurʾanic punishments (*ḥudūd*), and homicide and bodily injury entailing retaliation (*qiṣāṣ*), which are within the area of private law, though remaining intact, were not applied in practice; this is due to the fact that the Shariʿa as a jurists' law is a personal rather than territorial law. Naturally, these sanctions could not be applied in a non-Muslim state.

Article 52 of the POC, the principal enactment defining the powers of the Shariʿa courts, granted them exclusive jurisdiction in all matters of personal status of Muslims, both nationals and foreigners (the latter on condition that under their own national law they were amenable to the jurisdiction of Muslim religious courts), as well as in cases of *waqf* constitution or internal administration (subject to the provisions of the 1921 Ordinance establishing the SMC pertaining to the *waqf*). The Shariʿa courts were bound to apply the Ottoman Sharʿi Law of Procedure of 1917.

The Rabbinical and Christian religious courts, on the other hand, had exclusive jurisdiction only in matters of marriage and divorce, alimony, and confirmation of wills (but concurrent jurisdiction, i.e., with the consent of the parties, in other matters of personal status) of nationals belonging to the Jewish and Christian communities, as well as the constitution or internal administration of *waqf*s founded before the Rabbinical and Christian courts, respectively, according to the respective religious law (Arts. 53 and 54). The difference regarding the scope of jurisdiction between the Muslim and non-Muslim judiciary is a clear heritage from the Ottoman *millet* system. Moreover, although the Shariʿa courts ceased to be state courts with residuary jurisdiction with respect to non-Muslims, they nevertheless retained remnants of this jurisdiction. Thus they had concurrent jurisdiction in matters pertaining to the establishment or validity of *waqfs* founded by Jews and Christians before a Shariʿa court prior to the promulgation of the Palestine Order-in-Council.[20] Such endowments were common practice during the Ottoman period and had continued to some extent into the Mandate period. In cases of blood money (*diya*), i.e., compensation or damages for homicide or bodily injury, the Shariʿa courts had exclusive jurisdiction where all parties were Muslims, and where the parties were non-Muslims, concurrent jurisdiction, that is, conditional on the parties' consent to litigate before the Shariʿa court.[21] This, too, is a heritage from the Ottoman period. According to the Shariʿa, blood money is part of the victim's estate and hence should be divided among the victim's relatives in accordance with Islamic rules of inheritance.

The autonomy pertaining to the legal system (the constitution of religious courts and nomination of judges), the administration of *waqf* and church property, and the appointment of clergy and other positions in Christian churches remained intact during the Mandate because the Patriarchs were located outside the territory of Palestine. Thus the Patriarchs could function regardless of political changes in the region. Out of ten recognized religious communities, nine were Christian: Orthodox and Catholics of various denominations as well as Latins. Each of these communities had an internal constitution. The constitution of the Greek Orthodox (the largest Christian community in Palestine) served, in its broad outlines, as a model for other communities. Each of these communities was headed by a Patriarch or Archbishop assisted by a synod or other central body.[22] The organization of the Jewish community, headed by the Sefaradi Ḥakhambashı, was based on Ottoman regulations of 1864. The Jewish Community Rules of 1928 resolved some uncertainties regarding membership in the community.[23] Other religious communities, such as the Druze, the Evangelical Episcopal, and other Protestant groups, were not recognized during the Mandate in the best Ottoman tradition, notwithstanding pressures exerted on the British Government to the contrary.

The Mandate's sporadic intervention in matters of personal status was carried out by means of criminal legislation intended to deter potential violators of the law without infringing upon the validity of the religious law. This was the case, for instance, with respect to the restrictions imposed on the age required for contracting marriage. Moreover, Muslims *qua* Muslims were exempted from the criminal sanction imposed on polygamy;

since polygamy is permitted under the Shariʿa, they had a "good defense" against this charge.[24]

Occasionally, even the declared policy of non-discrimination between inhabitants on grounds of religion, as anchored in the Mandate and statutory legislation with a view to adapting the legal norm to international obligations, failed to stand the test of implementation. Thus Article 15 of the Mandate, which guarantees complete freedom of conscience and free exercise of all forms of worship "subject only to the maintenance of public order and morals," could secure against execution on the charge of apostasy from Islam (*ridda*), but not the deprivation of a Protestant widow of a Muslim from his estate on grounds of difference in religion (*ikhtilāf fī l-dīn*). Nor did the Succession Ordinance of 1923, which prohibits the deprivation of a legal heir from the estate on grounds of difference in nationality or religion (with respect to the deceased), provide the widow with a remedy. The Supreme Court ruled that the decision handed down by the Shariʿa court was unassailable because Article 24(2) of the Succession Ordinance contradicted Article 52 of POC which grants the Shariʿa court exclusive jurisdiction in all matters of personal status pertaining to Muslims.[25]

Naturally, the subordination of the Muslims in Palestine to the British Mandate put them in a serious dilemma, to wit, the Shariʿa is not properly equipped to be applied in a non-Muslim territory.[26] In Muslim medieval legal discourse, to the extent that the jurists were ready to address this issue, they debated whether Muslims might reside in the Domain of War (*dār al-ḥarb*) and whether the observance of religious prescriptions outside the Domain of Islam (*dār al-islām*) was a valid fulfillment of religious duties from the point of view of the religious law.[27]

Another problem faced by Muslims in Palestine devolves upon the structure of authority in the state. Islam does not recognize the concept of separation of powers. In accordance with the Shariʿa, the executive and judicial powers (theoretically there is no legislative authority in Islam) are vested in the Muslim sovereign, who may delegate to his representatives any of these powers or the combination of both at one and the same time. In the late Ottoman period, qadis quite often were engaged in administrative functions in the provinces alongside their judicial function. Thus the qadi of Jerusalem served as the chief administrative officer in his district.[28] In spite of the introduction of the concept of separation of powers in Palestine, remnants of the traditional conception of authority still survived. The President of the SMC had the power to nominate the qadis, which is one of the symbols of sovereignty in a Muslim state. Moreover, as president of the Council and Mufti of Jerusalem, Ḥājj Amīn al-Ḥusaynī combined both temporal and religious-legal authorities in the best tradition of the Righteous Caliphs. Earlier, the British Military Governor designated the

Mufti of Jerusalem as the Grand Mufti (*al-muftī al-akbar*), a title that did not exist previously in Palestine, and in fact treated him as the "Representative of Islam in Palestine." The Muslims regarded the function of the Mufti of Jerusalem as equivalent to that of the "Shaykh al-Islām," i.e., "Mufti of Palestine." Broadly speaking, the British administration, too, considered the Mufti of Jerusalem as the "head of the Muslim community in Palestine.[29] Needless to say, both the SMC and the Shariʿa courts operated by virtue of secular statutes.

Article 51 of POC defines "matters of personal status" (marriage, divorce, etc.) in accordance with Western rather than Islamic legal conceptions. This in turn restricted the Shariʿa courts' jurisdiction. Thus, for instance, "legal capacity" is not defined as a matter of personal status, and hence it is not included in Article 51,[30] though in judicial practice it was presumed to "accompany" matters that were within the jurisdiction of the religious courts. Article 52 curtailed the personal jurisdiction of the Shariʿa courts with respect to non-Muslims. In the event that the parties to a dispute belonged to different religions or communities, the Chief Justice (in Israel, the President of the Supreme Court) would decide the competent tribunal to deal with the dispute.[31] In 1919 the British government adopted the Ottoman Family Rights Law of 1917, but excluded from its applicability non-Muslims. The original version of the law regulated the matters of personal status of all Ottoman subjects regardless of religion or community.

The British Mandate integrated the religious laws of all the communities in the general legal system and all the religious courts were brought under the control of the High Court of Justice. The jurisdiction vested in civil courts (alongside concurrent jurisdiction of the religious courts, i.e., with the consent of the parties, and incidental jurisdiction) in matters of personal status indirectly curtailed the scope of application of the religious law of the respective communities.

Under the Shariʿa, renouncing Islam (*ridda*) publicly is punishable by death for Muslims. According to the Hanafi doctrine, apostasy is not a crime entailing Qurʾanic punishment (*ḥadd*), but nevertheless male apostates are liable to the death penalty on the grounds that they have become potential enemies to Islam. It is recommended (not obligatory) to grant the apostate a delay of three days to repent, failing which he is put to death. Female apostates, on the other hand, must be imprisoned and beaten until they repent.[32] Clearly, the British government in Palestine could not reconcile the Islamic doctrine pertaining to conversion with its international obligations under the Mandate. It therefore circumvented the harsh sanctions under the Shariʿa by channeling the procedure of conversion from one religion to another to the technical secular procedure of transferring from one religious community to another. The Religious

Community (Change) Ordinance of 1927 enables a Muslim or a member of any other religious community to abandon his religious community and to join another; the change of community according to specified procedure was valid and effective under the general law without bearing any consequences on the validity of the religious law.[33]

The government made it possible to endow property for charitable purposes, education, and religion other than by means of the religious court and religious law and to convert religious endowments into secular endowments for charitable purposes. In the second half of the 1930s, in the midst of the Palestinian national revolt, the British government transferred the administration of Muslim *waqf* from the SMC to an appointed state committee in accordance with Defense (Muslim *Waqf*) Regulations of 1937.[34]

The Ottoman Legal Heritage in Israel

The Ottoman legal heritage as anchored and consolidated in Mandatory legislation passed into Israel by virtue of Section 11 of the Law and the Administration Ordinance of 1948, which provides that the law in force in Palestine on the day of the declaration of the establishment of the State of Israel shall remain in force so long as it is not repugnant to this Ordinance or to other laws which may be enacted in future legislation by the State.[35]

With the end of the British Mandate and the outbreak of war in 1948, the communal organization of the Muslims in Israel collapsed completely. The members of the SMC and the religious-legal elite (muftis, qadis, and ulama) left the country; the religious judicial system, the *waqf* administration, and communal educational and welfare institutions crumbled and ceased to exist. The government of Israel set about rehabilitating the organization of the Muslim community. The undefined status of the Muslims remained, however, intact: they were not recognized as a "religious community" within the meaning of the POC.

The Muslim judicial system was reconstituted within the general legal system. Until 2001, the Shariʿa courts enjoyed the widest jurisdiction in matters of personal status compared to any other religious community. Moreover, they still deal with conversion to Islam of Jewish and Christian women (mainly for marriage purposes) in much the same way they did during the Ottoman period. Occasionally, the Shariʿa courts conclude marriages of mixed parties, that is, a Muslim male with a non-Muslim female, and deal with disputes of such couples, although, as already noted, in the event that the spouses belong to different communities, it is up to the President of the Supreme Court to determine the court competent to deal with the matter. Some of the qadis have not internalized the fact that specified domains of the Shariʿa that had been codified, as in the case of the family law pertaining to marriage and divorce, ceased to be jurists' law applicable everywhere and became territorial law that bears no validity outside the boundaries of Israel.[36]

At the same time there is ample evidence to the effect that Israeli Muslims are losing their unique status dating back to the Ottoman Empire. The government has rejected all their attempts to run their communal affairs in total independence from the state, in contrast with the practice of some Christian communities. Muslim attempts to establish a religious or secular-temporal authority in charge of the Shariʿa judiciary outside of the general legal system, of the *waqf* administration, and of the religious services were frustrated by the government.[37] Moreover, while promulgating the Qadis Law of 1961, the Knesset, under the impact of the political events that transpired during the Mandate under the leadership of Ḥājj Amīn al-Ḥusaynī, the president of the SMC, abrogated the 1921 Ordinance pertaining to the constitution of the Council (Art. 25).

Until 2002 the Shariʿa courts were subject administratively to the Ministry for Religious Affairs and since then to the Ministry of Justice. The decisions of the Shariʿa courts are subject to judicial review by the Supreme Court in its capacity as a High Court of Justice (hereinafter HCJ) rather than an instance of appeals; in practice, however, the HCJ is seldom resorted to. Qadis are elected by an appointment committee (the majority of whose members are Muslims) chaired by the Minister of Justice, and appointed by the president of the State; and they are required to pledge allegiance to the State. Article 7 of the Qadis Law, however, does not require qadis to dispense justice in accordance with Israeli statutes. In daily practice the Shariʿa Court of Appeal ignores Israeli laws pertaining to personal status unless these have been explicitly addressed to religious courts.

With the establishment of the State of Israel, the Jews ceased to be a "religious community";[38] in some respects their status approximated that of Muslims in a Muslim state. Jewish law, however, does not apply in matters other than personal status. Christian communities enjoy the widest autonomy as far as the status of the heads of church, organization of the judiciary, and church property are concerned. The Catholic churches have a hierarchical structure with a supreme authority and their institutions engage in legislating, judiciating, executing penalties, and imposing social sanctions. They do not need the support of the state to run their internal affairs.[39]

In 1957, the government recognized the Druze as a religious community on the basis of the Religious Communities (Organisation) Ordinance of 1926, which regulates the establishment of communal institutions. In 1963 the Druze were again recognized as a religious community, this time within the meaning of the POC, for the purpose of establishing religious courts with jurisdiction similar to those of the Rabbinical courts. Earlier, in 1961, the Spiritual Leadership of the Druze community in its statutory capacity as "Religious Council," adopted the law of personal status of the Druze community in Lebanon of 1948 in order for it to be applied, with some important modifications, by the Druze religious courts in Israel.[40] Needless to say, the Druze, who had seceded completely from Islam, could not be tolerated and hence recognized as a religious community under any kind of Muslim rule. The Evangelical Episcopal Church in Israel and the members of the Bahai Faith were subsequently recognized in 1970 and 1971, respectively, as religious communities within the meaning of POC.

The Majalla, the Ottoman civil law, was abolished in 1984 as far as the civil courts are concerned, but it is still valid and applicable in the Shariʿa courts. The Ottoman Land Law of 1858 was replaced by the Land Law of 1969.[41]

The Knesset intervened intensively in matters of personal status and succession with a view to improving the legal status of women. Section 1 of the Women's Equal Rights Law of 1951, the keystone of legislation in these matters, provides: "A man and a woman shall have equal status with regard to any legal act; any provision of law discriminating, with regard to any legal act, against women as women shall be of no effect." The Knesset, for obvious reasons, could hardly adopt the legislative techniques, such as a ruler's administrative regulations (*siyāsa sharʿiyya*), public interest (*maṣlaḥa*), the eclectic expedient (*takhayyur, talfīq*), and reinterpretation of textual sources (neo-*ijtihād*), that were customary in Arab countries to give the reforms the character of an internal refurbishing of the Shariʿa.[42] However, out of regard for the legal systems of the various religious communities anchored in the Ottoman *millet* system, the Knesset abstained from interfering with any religious prohibition or permission as to marriage and divorce; in this sensitive domain procedural provisions and penal sanctions were adopted as deterrents in preference to substantive provisions which would have invalidated the relevant religious law. Another self-enforced restriction was in matters for which provisions superseding religious law were enacted, whereby the parties were usually given the option of litigating in accordance with religious law.

The following are the main reforms introduced by the Knesset, from the perspective of Islamic law:[43]

(1) The minimal age of marriage for women (which is not recognized in Islamic law) was raised from 15 years, as under Mandatory law, to 17 years, as under the Ottoman Family Rights Law of 1917, but at the same time the "good defenses" based on the Shariʿa (such as the guardian's consent to the marriage of a minor girl) against a charge of contravention of age-of-marriage legislation were abrogated, and the penal sanction was increased. A district court (but not a religious court) was empowered to permit the marriage of a girl of sixteen.

(2) Polygamy (which is permitted under Islam) was prohibited. The defense granted to Muslims qua Muslims by the Mandatory government against a charge of polygamy was abolished. Instead, Muslims have been granted two defenses against such a charge: prolonged absence or mental illness of the spouse.
(3) Divorcing one's wife against her will (which is permitted in Islam)—unless permission to do so has been given by the qadi—was forbidden by criminal legislation.
(4) The woman was acknowledged as a natural guardian of her children along with their father, but the Shariʿa court may decide otherwise if it deems it in the best interest of the child. Under the Shariʿa, only the father and after him agnates in a specified order are natural guardians. The terminal age of guardianship was raised to 18 for both sexes.
(5) The Ottoman Law of Succession of 1913, a replica of a German law which does not differentiate between males and females and between agnates and cognates, applied originally only to the category of *mīrī* property, the full ownership of which is vested in the state while possession and usufruct are vested in the individual. The British government adopted the law in 1923. Since 1951, the law was applied also to property in full private ownership (*mülk*) and movable unless all the parties, being adults, agreed to litigate in accordance with the religious law of inheritance. The Succession Law of 1965 provides for perfect equality between the sexes in all categories of property, either *mīrī* or *mülk*, and secures complete freedom of testamentary disposition. Unlike the religious *ultra vires* doctrine, the Israeli law permits the disposition of the entire estate by will and in favor of a legal heir. However, the law applies only in the civil court; in cases where the Shariʿa court is empowered by the parties to deal with the matter, it may apply the Shariʿa rules of inheritance to all categories of property.
(6) The Maintenance (Securing Payment) Law of 1972 transferred the burden of securing maintenance to the wife after being fixed by a Shariʿa court judgment, to the National Insurance Institute, and the latter is required to collect the debt from the husband.
(7) The Law of Property Relations between the Spouses of 1973 provides that upon the dissolution of a marriage, the value of the spouses' combined property, in the absence of agreement, should be equally divided between husband and wife. This is a far-reaching innovation from the point of view of the religious law, which does not recognize community property between the spouses; a divorced wife is entitled only to waiting-period maintenance and deferred dower (if stipulated in the marriage contract).

Needless to say, the Knesset's reforms undermine the patrilineal and patriarchal infrastructure of the traditional Muslim family.[44] The Ottomans started this process with the codification of the family law dealing with marriage and divorce, followed by some of the Arab countries which even expanded the domains of codification within the family law. Although these reforms were inspired to a very large extent by European norms and ideas regarding the status of women, the reforms were presented as an internal development within the Shariʿa. In Israel the reforms in the family law are the result of social and political pressures for liberation of women initiated by Jewish feminist organizations. The reforms have been imposed from above on Muslim society although significant parts of it are not yet ready to absorb them.

In 2001, following pressures exerted by Arab feminist organizations, the exclusive jurisdiction of the Shariʿa courts was downgraded significantly concurrently with the extension of the jurisdiction of the civil Family Courts to matters of personal status, other than marriage and divorce, pertaining to Muslims (and Christians).[45] In other words, the Family Courts now share jurisdiction on equal terms with the Shariʿa courts. Thus, in a matrimonial dispute between spouses in matters of personal status (to the exclusion of marriage and divorce), either of the spouses who precedes the other in filing a suit before any of the two tribunals, the Shariʿa court or the Family Court, determines the court before which the matter is to be heard. One would expect the spouses to choose the tribunal according to the nature of the issue being disputed, e.g., the wife would prefer the Family Court in a case of maintenance while the husband would prefer the Shariʿa court in a case of obedience.[46] Undoubtedly, the jurisdiction shared by the two tribunals will bring about far-reaching changes in the status of the Shariʿa in Israel since whenever an issue is brought before the Family Court, the Shariʿa will be applied in the light of the principles of Israeli law and in accordance with the civil rules of evidence and procedure.[47] In a meeting on June 14, 2006 with civil judges of the Family Court in Jerusalem, intended to brief them regarding the application of the Shariʿa in matters pertaining to maintenance, custody, and guardianship, the judges expressed concern about subject matters that have not undergone codification within the Ottoman Family Rights Law. Since most of the judges lack free access to Arabic legal literature, the present writer forwarded the suggestion to have the second legal circular (*marsūm qaḍāʾī*) issued by the Shariʿa Court of Appeal in 1995 translated into Hebrew. This circular provides criteria for assessing the rates of maintenance due to the wife in accordance with current requirements and transfers the discretion for fixing these rates from the informants (*mukhbirūn*) to the qadi.[48] A further suggestion was made for the compilation of a concise comparative manual of Islamic legal rules of the subject matter according to the different schools of law (*madhhabs*) in order to enable the civil judges to adopt the doctrine that yields the desirable judicial result according to the judge's discretion. In other words, the Family Court will not be bound by the Hanafi school, which since

Ottoman rule in this region has been the officially recognized one in the Shariʿa courts, regardless of the school affiliation of the parties involved. This suggestion is inspired by the judicial practice of the Shariʿa Court of Appeal presided over by Qadi Aḥmad Nāṭūr. Nāṭūr views the legal literature of the schools as a global reservoir out of which it is possible to derive elements in harmony with the conditions of modern times.[49] This technique is calculated to spare the civil judges the need to resort to English literature on Anglo-Muhammadan Law. Clearly, where the Knesset has intervened in matters of personal status or where the Supreme Court has handed down decisions pertaining to these matters that are deemed binding precedents, the civil judges are bound by the Israeli civil legal norms and are exempted from applying the Shariʿa.

In matters pertaining to succession, since 1965 the Shariʿa courts have concurrent jurisdiction, that is, depending on the consent of all the parties concerned, failing which the jurisdiction remains with the civil court.

In circumstances where the Shariʿa cannot offer solutions appropriate for a modern society, Muslims have recourse to civil courts. The Supreme Court does not hesitate to intervene in such circumstances by creating civil legal norms complementary to the Shariʿa as in the case of civil paternity based on biological relationship regardless of whether or not the child's parents are married to each other. The Supreme Court's decision is based on the Israeli legislation and the courts' judicial practice, on norms of the State of Israel as a Jewish democratic state, on Jewish law, and on American and English judicial practice. To clarify the position of Islamic law on the relevant issues, the Supreme Court, due to lack of access to Islamic legal literature, resorts to the Anglo-Muhammadan law.[50]

The Shariʿa Court is the main arena in which Muslims in Israel can exercise some measure of autonomy, especially with respect to application of those parts of the Shariʿa that have not been codified. Most of the qadis nominated in the first years after the emergence of the state were graduates of al-Azhar, and, broadly speaking, their judicial decisions reflect a traditional approach. Thus they rejected provisions in the Ottoman Family Rights Law that are not in harmony with Hanafi doctrine, but this did not deter them from applying without inhibition the Knesset's legislation in matters of personal status explicitly addressed to religious courts. The present generation of qadis comprises no graduates of al-Azhar (although there was a graduate of the University of Hebron, which in terms of its attitude to Islamic law is as traditional). Most of the qadis have degrees from faculties of humanities, social sciences, education, and law conferred by Israeli universities. They regard themselves as avant-garde in the movement for legal and social reform. However, they insist on carrying out reforms their own way without the intervention of the Knesset. Thus President Nāṭūr of the Shariʿa Court of Appeal recently turned down a suggestion to replace the Ottoman Family Rights Law by a new law of personal status which would absorb the reforms introduced in Middle Eastern and North African countries. A committee consisting of religious functionaries and experts on Islamic law was to prepare a bill of family law to be endorsed by the Knesset *en bloc*, i.e., without interference in its substance. The reason for the rejection of the legislative initiative was Qadi Nāṭūr's reluctance to allow the Knesset's involvement in the process of preparing such a law. In his view, statutory codification is appropriate for independent Muslim countries; in the absence of a Muslim sovereignty or Muslim legislative authority in Israel, the only option left is to introduce reforms by means of legal circulars and judicial practice of the Shariʿa Court of Appeal.[51]

Apparently for the same reason, the qadis of the Shariʿa Court of Appeal—under the strong effect of the Israeli Supreme Court—absorb and Islamize Israeli legal principles and institutions, such as the welfare of the child, natural justice, legal precedent, and the right of standing, by means of traditional Islamic legal mechanisms such as *maṣlaḥa* and *siyāsa sharʿiyya*.[52] Islamization of legal institutions from foreign cultures was characteristic of the Shariʿa in its formative period when it displayed an impressive assimilative power upon reaching close contact with the conquered cultures in the West and East.[53] Needless to say, the situation of Israeli Muslims as a tolerated community puts them on the defensive. Due to the disconnection of Israeli Muslims from high Islamic legal educational institutions in the Muslim world (Egypt is disinclined to admit Israeli Muslim students to al-Azhar), it is unlikely that Israeli qadis will come up with a new legal methodology, within the framework of orthodox Shariʿa, capable of carrying the burden of legal reform in family law. On the contrary, the impression is that the Shariʿa in Israel is being discomfited by Israeli principles of law on its own soil, that is, in the Shariʿa courts.[54]

The Supreme Court, on its part, imposes on the Islamic judiciary legal norms, which are occasionally not in harmony with the Shariʿa, in matters of personal status pertaining to basic civil rights in the light of the principles of the Basic Law: Human Dignity and Liberty (1992) and other basic laws promulgated in the early 1990s. Some observers do not rule out the possibility of the development of a dual legal system in matters of personal status according to the division of the judiciary: the Shariʿa courts will apply the Shariʿa (either in its codified or non-codified version), subject only to the changes introduced by the Knesset's legislation, and the civil courts will apply a pure civil law (though not in matters pertaining to marriage and divorce).[55]

The events following the 1947 United Nations resolution on the partition of Palestine and the war of 1948 and, in its wake, the migration of large sections of the Arab population from Israel to Arab countries or to areas in Palestine then held by Arab forces, created the problem of absentee property of which Muslim *waqf* is a part. The members of the *waqf* committee appointed by the British government to replace the *waqf* committee of the SMC in accordance with Defense (Muslim *Waqf*) Regulations of 1937, also left the country and hence the *waqf maḍbūṭ* property administered by that committee was declared absentee property. The *waqf mulḥaq* property was declared absentee property only to the extent that their private administrators (*mutawallī*), subject to the Shariʿa court supervision, were deemed absentee. Although Israeli law, jurisdiction, and administration were applied to East Jerusalem in 1967,[56] the Israeli government decided, out of political considerations, to exclude *waqf* property in East Jerusalem from the status of absentee property within the meaning of the law of 1950.[57]

In view of the requirements of the Muslim community, the Custodian of Absentees' Property transferred the management of holy places, such as mosques and cemeteries, and their non-religious appurtenances to the Director of the Division of Muslim and Druze Affairs of the Ministry of Religious Affairs as the Custodian's agent. Out of the income of the non-religious *waqf* property, the Custodian made allocations for Muslim religious purposes through Muslim advisory committees appointed by the Minister of Religious Affairs in towns in which Muslim communities existed. The Custodian spent the consideration (*amwāl al-badal*) received for *waqf* property acquired by the statutory Development Authority on the establishment of institutions in the fields of education, health, social welfare, religious services, and the like for the benefit of the Muslim community throughout the country.

This state of affairs did not satisfy the Muslims, who demanded a revival of the SMC and the transfer to it of the *waqf* property. The fact that the Custodian had released to the Greek Orthodox and Greek Catholic (Melkite) communities their *waqf* and other ecclesiastical assets that were likewise absentee property (these properties were registered in the names of the Patriarchate of Jerusalem and the Archbishop of Acre, Haifa, Nazareth, and the rest of Galilee, respectively), of course, aggravated the dissatisfaction among the Muslim community. The legality of the vesting of the Muslim *waqf* in the Custodian was challenged on the grounds that according to the dominant view in the Hanafi school, the bare ownership (*raqaba*) of the *waqf* property belongs to God, the entitlement (*istiḥqāq*) to the beneficiaries, and the management of the *waqf* to the administrator (*mutawallī*). Broadly speaking, the HCJ adopted this view and held that what had been vested in the Custodian was not the ownership of the *waqf* but rather the right of management for the absent *mutawallī*. On one occasion the HCJ decided that this right became void upon the appointment of a new *mutawallī* by the Shariʿa court. These decisions applied to *waqf mulḥaq*, and did not affect the status of *waqf maḍbūṭ*, this being outside the supervision of the Shariʿa court.

In 1965, far-reaching reforms—modeled on the Egyptian reforms in the *waqf* institution in the 1950s—were introduced in the Muslim *waqf* to the extent that it fell within the category of absentee property:

(1) The *waqf* property "free from any restriction, qualification or other similar limitation prescribed [...] by or under any law [i.e., the Shariʿa] or document relating to the endowment [i.e., the *waqfiyya*]" was vested in the Custodian retroactively since 1950. In other words, full ownership in the *waqf* property, in addition to the right of management and the right of entitlement, was vested in the Custodian provided the person having either possession or the right of management, or the beneficiary was absent. This reform was intended to remove doubts that had arisen following the aforementioned decisions of the HCJ regarding the substance of the right vested in the Custodian and to assert the original intention of the legislator.
(2) The Custodian is empowered to transfer the family *waqf* property to the beneficiaries in full ownership, free from any restrictions hitherto applying to the *waqf*, in accordance with their shares in the entitlement. In other words, the beneficiaries become owners of their shares in the released property and can dispose of it at will without any limitation.
(3) The Custodian is authorized to release public *waqf* property (*khayrī*) in full ownership in six towns in which Muslim communities exist. The released property is to be entrusted to Muslim boards of trustees to be appointed by the Government. The boards may dispose of the property (provided it does not include a mosque), use the income thereof for social and cultural purposes without being bound by the founder's stipulations, and invest the consideration of property sold in institutions established for the aforementioned purposes. The boards are subject to inspection by the State Comptroller.
(4) In places where no Muslim community exists and hence no board of trustees is to be appointed, the Custodian is instructed to allocate the proceeds of and consideration received for the *waqf* property for the same purposes as are prescribed for the boards of trustees.[58]

In the past the *waqf khayrī* institution played an important role in fostering charity, social welfare, religious services, and education in sovereign Muslim societies. Generally, in view of the limited involvement of the Islamic state in providing social services,[59] these functions were performed by the *waqf* institution—in the Ottoman Empire, rulers, governors, and senior officials assumed this function as individuals rather than in their capacities as servants of the state. Clearly, the importance of the role of the *waqf khayrī* increases in the absence of Muslim sovereignty.[60] During the Mandate period in Palestine, the administration and control of the *waqf* property by the SMC provided the funds for the maintenance and promotion of Muslim communal affairs.

In the past, the founder's desire to preserve the integrity of the agnatic patrimony seems to have been the main motive for establishing family *waqf* (*dhurrī, ahlī*). Since there is no full freedom of testamentary disposition in Islam, it being bound by the *ultra vires* doctrine of the Shariʿa, the family *waqf* was one of the main devices used to circumvent the Shariʿa rules of inheritance. The Ottoman Succession Law of 1913 prohibited the drawing up of a will on *mīrī*, or state-owned, property. The Israeli Succession Law of 1965, which does not distinguish between *mülk* and *mīrī* estates, permits full freedom of testamentary disposition and hence there is no longer any need to resort to the *waqf* mechanism in order to preserve the patrimony within the agnatic family. Indeed, the motive to establish family *waqf* in Israel has almost completely disappeared.

Conclusion

The Ottoman-Muslim concepts of *umma* and *millet* can be said to have virtually lost their original raison d'être in Israel. The transition from the Mandate to the State of Israel promoted the Jewish nature of the State at the expense of the Muslim legacy. The Knesset persistently strives to disconnect itself from the Ottoman-Muslim (and British) legal heritage[61] and to replace it by genuine Israeli legislation deriving its inspiration from Jewish law ("religious legislation")[62] and the so-called "Israeli heritage." The jurisprudence of the civil courts, which in recent years have enjoyed wide jurisdiction in matters of Muslim personal status (to the extent that they are not inhibited from resorting to these courts) and a fortiori the jurisprudence of the Supreme Court, which creates new civil legal norms (as in the case of civil paternity) alongside the Shariʿa or in its place, have left their mark on the judicial practice of the Shariʿa courts.

Nevertheless, parts of the Ottoman legacy based on the concept of the *umma* and *millet* system still survive. Although Muslims in Israel have ceased to be an *umma* in the original sense of the term and for all practical purposes have actually become a religious community, no formal positive expression of their new status is to be found in Israeli law: they are not recognized as a religious community within the meaning of POC or any Israeli statute (although the Shariʿa courts are recognized and integrated within the state legal system). The traditional concept of the *millet*, i.e., "religious community," as a functional and organizational framework ostensibly survived with respect to all religious communities (to the exclusion of the Jews) subject to one very significant difference: the communities are no longer connected to a Muslim state; rather they are connected to a Jewish state.

Legal pluralism is, in essence, another residual element of the Ottoman legal heritage in Israel: the division between religious and secular law or between religious and secular courts has survived in the country, although with some variations. Thus the individual has some leeway to maneuver between one judiciary or another, in accordance with court jurisdiction. Moreover, secular law and religious law coexist even within the same court—be it religious or secular. This represents the outcome of a situation whereby secular legislation is administered in religious courts and religious law in the civil courts with respect to specific matters in the realm of personal status. This coexistence of two profoundly different legal systems is historically based on the tolerance bestowed by the Muslim sovereign upon the tolerated religions within the framework of the *millet* system. In Israel, the survival of this spirit of tolerance towards religious communities will depend on several factors, such as the strength of the Jewish religious parties within the government, the international protection extended by European powers to various Christian communities since the eighteenth and nineteenth centuries,[63] and the forces of inertia, or status quo, dating back to the Ottoman Empire.[64] We are not dealing here with two independent legal systems, civil and religious, that coexist side by side; rather, we are dealing with autonomy exercised by the Shariʿa within the space reserved for it by Israeli law. With due reservations, the roles of *umma* and *millet* can be said to have been reversed: The Jews have replaced the Muslims as *umma*, and the Muslims the Jews as a *millet*.[65]

Of course, in domains outside the jurisdiction of religious courts, such as worship and religious prescriptions, the Shariʿa is still sovereign and unassailable, allowing for the circumstance that in a non-Muslim state it is impossible to impose their application on Muslims by means of the executive authority; at most, social sanctions may be used to this end.

Finally, due to the Israeli-Palestinian conflict, the concepts of *umma* and *millet* have acquired a national dimension par excellence. Both Muslims and Jews in Israel define themselves in religious and political terms. The loyalty to the religious framework, regardless of whether the religious community is the majority or the minority, has been translated into national political terms. This is, not surprisingly, not new; in the nineteenth century, the Greek and Armenian *millet*s in the Ottoman Empire emerged as national entities.[66]

NOTES

[1] This essay is based on a lecture held at Yad Izhak Ben-Zvi, Jerusalem, during a conference on "The Ottomans in Palestine and the Middle East" organized under the auspices of the Hebrew University, Ben-Gurion University, Haifa University, and Tel Aviv University on June 8–9, 2005 on the occasion of Prof. Amnon Cohen's retirement from the Hebrew University. Prof. Ruth Lapidoth (Faculty of Law, Hebrew University), Prof. Assaf Likhovski (Faculty of Law, Tel Aviv University), and Dr. Ido Shahar (Departmment of Sociology and Anthropology, Tel Aviv University) read an earlier draft of this essay and offered useful comments for which I am most grateful.

[2] Dupret, Berger and al-Zwaini, *Legal Pluralism in the Arab World*.
[3] Bosworth, "The Concept of *Dhimma* in Early Islam;" Lewis, *The Jews of Islam*, 20–40; Braude and Lewis, "Introduction," 5–10; Friedmann, *Tolerance and Coercion in Islam*, General Index, *dhimma, dhimmīs*.
[4] Cohen, "On the Realities of the *Millet* System," 8; cf. Braude and Lewis, "Introduction," 30.
[5] Karpat, "*Millets* and Nationality;" Lewis, *The Emergence of Modern Turkey*, 329; Ursinus, "Millet," 62b.
[6] Cahen, "Dhimma," 227a.
[7] Braude, "Foundation Myths of the *Millet* System," 69–70, 73–4 (the citation is from p. 74); Lewis, *The Jews of Islam*, 125–26.
[8] Braude and Lewis, "Introduction," 30–1.
[9] Ibid., 28–9, 32.
[10] Cf. Englard, *Religious Law in the Israeli Legal System*, 13.
[11] Likhovski, *Law and Identity in Mandate Palestine*, 55–8.
[12] On status quo in different contexts, see Lapidoth, *The Basic Law*, 16 n. 6.
[13] Vitta, *The Conflict of Laws*, 6–7.
[14] For details, see Englard, *Religious Law in the Israeli Legal System*, 13; Cohen, *Personal Introduction*, 230.
[15] See Annex to the Palestine-Order-in-Council, 1939 and First Schedule to Succession Ordinance, 1923, in Vitta, *The Conflict of Laws*, 284.
[16] Cited from Porath, *The Emergence of the Palestinian Arab National Movement*, 195–96.
[17] Ibid., 205–7. On other considerations that may have prompted the establishment of the SMC, see ibid., 199–200; Kupferschmidt, *The Supreme Muslim Council*, 24–8.
[18] Reiter, *Islamic Endowments in Jerusalem under British Mandate*, 6–16.
[19] Porath, *The Emergence of the Palestinian Arab National Movement*, 197.
[20] Layish, "The Muslim *Waqf* in Israel," 47.
[21] Art. 6 of the Civil and Religious Courts (Jurisdiction) Ordinance, 1925; Vitta, *The Conflict of Laws*, 146 n. 1.
[22] Vitta, *The Conflict of Laws*, 65, 113–14.
[23] Ibid., 65–7, 105, 125.
[24] Ibid., 54–5.
[25] Ibid., 9.
[26] Layish, "Adaptation of a Jurists' Law to Modern Times," 169–70.
[27] Abou El Fadl, "Islamic Law and Muslim Minorities."
[28] Porath, *The Emergence of the Palestinian Arab National Movement*, 186.
[29] Ibid., 188, 190, 194.
[30] Legal capacity is included in "matters of personal status" within the meaning of Art. 7 of the Ottoman Procedure of the Shariʿa Court Law of 1917.
[31] Vitta, *The Conflict of Laws*, 14–6.
[32] Peters, *Crime and Punishment in Islamic Law*, 64–5.
[33] For further detail on application of the Ordinance, see Vitta, *The Conflict of Laws*, 68–76.
[34] Layish, "The Muslim *Waqf* in Israel," 45–6, 57.
[35] Friedmann, "The Effects of Foreign Law on the Law of Israel," 194ff.

36 Layish, "Adaptation of a Jurists' Law to Modern Times," 170–1. On the repercussions of the codification of Jewish law by Western-oriented scholars, see Likhovski, "The Invention of 'Hebrew Law' in Mandatory Palestine," 351, 353.

37 Peled, *Debating Islam in the Jewish State*, 53–7, 141–48, 158; Dumper, *Islam and Israel*, 38; Abou Ramadan, "Judicial Activism," 292–96.

38 The voluntary registration in the Register of "Knesset Israel," the Jewish community in Palestine organized by statute under the Jewish Community Rules of 1928, was replaced, in 1949, by the obligatory registration of all the inhabitants of the State. Hence, the statutory "Jewish community" ceased to exist. Cohen, *Personal Introduction*, 230; Englard, *Religious Law in the Israeli Legal System*, 13; Vitta, *The Conflict of Laws*, 65–7, 105.

39 Englard, *Religious Law in the Israeli Legal System*, 13.

40 Layish, *Marriage, Divorce and Succession in the Druze Family*, 1–15.

41 Layish, *Women and Islamic Law in a Non-Muslim State*, 280–82.

42 Layish, "The Transformation of the *Sharīʿa* from Jurists' Law to Statutory Law," 92–5.

43 Layish, "The Status of the *Sharīʿa* in a Non-Muslim State," 174–76.

44 Cf. Layish, "Reformist Matrimonial Legislation and the Collapse of the Muslim Patrilineal Family."

45 Family Court Law (Amendment No. 5), 2001. *Sefer Haḥuqim*, 1810, 14.11.01; Abou Ramadan, "Judicial Activism," 293–94.

46 Shortly after the establishment of the state, the government considered the possibility of abolishing the religious judiciary of all communities and transferring their jurisdiction in matters of personal status to the civil courts. The Jewish religious parties in the coalition vehemently rejected the initiative. They joined forces to this end with the spokesmen of the Shariʿa courts. Cohen, *Personal Introduction*, 227.

47 Layish, "Adaptation of a Jurists' Law to Modern Times," 173–74.

48 Ibid., 184–88.

49 Ibid., 192–94.

50 Ibid., 180–82.

51 Ibid., 213–14.

52 Ibid., 198–207; cf. Likhovski, "The Invention of 'Hebrew Law' in Mandatory Palestine," 365.

53 Schacht, *An Introduction to Islamic Law*, 15–22.

54 Cf. Abou Ramadan, "The Transition from Tradition to Reform," 635.

55 Layish, "Adaptation of a Jurists' Law to Modern Times," 219–20 and the reference to I. Naveh's Ph.D. dissertation.

56 Lapidoth, *The Basic Law*, 22, 53.

57 Reiter, *Islamic Institutions in Jerusalem*, 42; Dumper, *Islam and Israel*, 101, 108–9.

58 Layish, "The Muslim *Waqf* in Israel." For analysis of the 1965 law and its implementation, see Dumper, *Islam and Israel*, 43–62, 126–27; Reiter, "An Assessment of the Reform in the Muslim *Waqf*;" Peled, *Debating Islam in the Jewish State*, 137–39.

59 Cf. Schacht, *An Introduction to Islamic Law*, 76–7, 206–7.

[60] Cf. Dumper, *Islam and Israel*, 126 (the *waqf* system as a "mediating institution" in a non-Muslim state).

[61] Friedmann, "The Effects of Foreign Law on the Law of Israel," 201–6.

[62] Elon, *Religious Legislation*.

[63] Lapidoth, *The Basic Law*, 15–6.

[64] The issue of status quo is still relevant today. See the Fundamental Agreement between the Holy See and the State of Israel of 1993; Lapidoth, *The Basic Law*, 36, 101.

[65] Hooker's distinction between a "dominant legal system" and a "servient legal system" (Hooker, *Legal Pluralism*, 7–8), though borrowed from a colonial situation, may be relevant in the Israeli context. I owe this observation to Ido Shahar.

[66] Karpat, "*Millet*s and Nationality;" Lewis, *The Emergence of Modern Turkey*, 329.

REFERENCES

Abou El Fadl, Khaled, "Islamic Law and Muslim Minorities: The Juristic Discourse on Muslim Minorities from the Second/Eighth to the Eleventh/Seventeenth Centuries," *Islamic Law and Society* 1 (1994), 141–87.

Abou Ramadan, Moussa, "Judicial Activism of the Shariʿah Appeals Court in Israel (1994–2001): Rise and Crisis," *Fordham International Journal* 27 (2003), 254–98.

——. "The Transition from Tradition to Reform: The Shariʿa Appeals Court Rulings on Child Custody (1992–2001)," *Fordham International Journal* 26 (2003), 594–655.

Bosworth, C. E., "The Concept of *Dhimma* in Early Islam," in B. Braude and B. Lewis (eds.), *Christians and Jews in the Ottoman Empire. The Functioning of a Plural Society*, vol. 1. *The Central Lands* (New York 1982), 37–51.

Braude, B., "Foundation Myths of the *Millet* System," in B. Braude and B. Lewis (eds.), *Christians and Jews in the Ottoman Empire. The Functioning of a Plural Society*, vol. 1. *The Central Lands* (New York 1982), 69–88.

Braude, B. and B. Lewis, "Introduction," in B. Braude and B. Lewis (eds.), *Christians and Jews in the Ottoman Empire. The Functioning of a Plural Society*, vol. 1. *The Central Lands* (New York 1982), 1–34.

Cahen, Cl., "D͟himma," *The Encyclopaedia of Islam*, New ed. (1991), 2:227–31.

Cohen, A., "On the Realities of the *Millet* System: Jerusalem in the Sixteenth Century," in B. Braude and B. Lewis (eds.), *Christians and Jews in the Ottoman Empire. The Functioning of a Plural Society*, vol. 2, *The Arabic-Speaking Lands* (New York 1982), 7–18.

Cohen, H., *Mavo' Ishi; Autobiographia* ["Personal Introduction. Autobiography"] (Or Yehuda 2005).

Dumper, M., *Islam and Israel. Muslim Religious Endowments and the Jewish State* (Washington, D.C. 1994).

Dupret, B., M. Berger, and Laila al-Zwaini (eds.), *Legal Pluralism in the Arab World* (The Hague 1999).

Elon, M., *Ḥaqiqa datit be-ḥuqei medinat Yisra'el uba-shephiṭa shel batei mishpaṭ u-batei din rabaniyim* ["Religious Legislation in the Laws of the State of Israel and in the Adjudication of the (Civil) Courts and the Rabbinical Courts"] (Tel Aviv 1968).

Englard, I., *Religious Law in the Israeli Legal System* (Jerusalem 1975).

Friedmann, D., "The Effect of Foreign Law on the Law of Israel: Remnants of the Ottoman Period," *Israel Law Review* 10 (1975), 192–206.

Friedmann, Y., *Tolerance and Coercion in Islam. Interfaith Relations in the Muslim Tradition* (Cambridge 2003).

Hooker, M. B., *Legal Pluralism: An Introduction to Colonial and New-Colonial Laws* (Oxford 1975).

Karpat, H. K., "*Millets* and Nationality: The Roots of the Incongruity of Nation and State," in B. Braude and B. Lewis (eds.), *Christians and Jews in the Ottoman Empire. The Functioning of a Plural Society*, vol. 1, *The Central Lands* (New York 1982), 141–69.

Kupferschmidt, U., *The Supreme Muslim Council. Islam under the British Mandate for Palestine* (Leiden 1987).

Lapidoth, Ruth, *Ḥoq-yesod: Yerushalayim birat yisra'el* ["The Basic Law: Jerusalem, Capital of Israel"] (Jerusalem 1999).

Layish, A., "Adaptation of a Jurists' Law to Modern Times in an Alien Environment: The *Shari'a* in Israel." *Die Welt des Islams* 46/2 (2006), 168–222.

——, "Reformist Matrimonial Legislation and the Collapse of the Muslim Patrilineal Family," *Awrāq* 21 (2000), 57–80.

——, *Marriage, Divorce and Succession in the Druze Family. A Study Based on Decisions of Druze Arbitrators and Religious Courts in Israel and the Golan Heights* (Leiden 1982).

——, "The Muslim *Waqf* in Israel." *Asian and African Studies* 2 (1966): 41–76.

——, "The Status of the *Sharī'a* in a Non-Muslim State: The Case of Israel," *Asian and African Studies* 27 (1993), 171–87.

——. "The Transformation of the *Shari'a* from Jurists' Law to Statutory Law in the Contemporary Muslim World," *Die Welt des Islams* 44 (2004), 85–112.

——. *Women and Islamic Law in a Non-Muslim State. A Study Based on the Decisions of the Shari'a Courts in Israel* (New York 1975).

Lewis, B., *The Emergence of Modern Turkey* (London 1961).

——. *The Jews of Islam* (Princeton, N.J. 1984).

Likhovski, A., "The Invention of 'Hebrew Law' in Mandatory Palestine." *The American Journal of Comparative Law* 46 (1998), 339–73.

——. *Law and Identity in Mandate Palestine* (Chapel Hill, N.C. 2006).

Peled, Alisa Rubin, *Debating Islam in the Jewish State. The Development of Policy Toward Islamic Institutions in Israel* (Albany, N.Y. 2001).

Peters, R., *Crime and Punishment in Islamic Law. Theory and Practice from the Sixteenth to the Twenty-first Century* (Cambridge 2005).

Porath, Y., *The Emergence of the Palestinian Arab National Movement, 1918–1929* (London 1974).

Reiter, Y., "Ha'arakhat ha-reforma be-mosad ha-heqdesh ha-muslemi be-yisra'el: Ha-*waqf* be-'Acco" ["An Assessment of the Reform in the Muslim *Waqf* in Israel: The *Waqf* in Acre"], *Hamizrah Hehadash* 32 (1989), 21–45.

——, *Islamic Endowments in Jerusalem under the British Mandate* (London 1996).

——. *Islamic Institutions in Jerusalem. Palestinian Muslim Organization under Jordanian and Israeli Rule* (The Hague 1997).

Schacht, J., *An Introduction to Islamic Law* (Oxford 1964).

Ursinus, M. O. H., "Millet," *The Encyclopaedia of Islam*, New ed. (1993), 7:61–4.

Vitta, E., *The Conflict of Laws in Matters of Personal Status in Palestine* (Tel Aviv 1947).

9

CLASS AND VIOLENCE IN NINETEENTH-CENTURY EGYPT

Amira El-Azhary Sonbol

In 1885, Egypt's Ministry of the Interior laid down regulations governing the activities of female prostitutes working in houses of prostitution, referred to as "Maisons de Tolérance" in the legal record.[1]

> Considered houses of prostitution are those houses where two or more women are together who make their living habitually through prostitution. It is the responsibility of the local administrative authority to decide whether a house should be classed among houses of prostitution; however, in the case where one of the associates is of foreign nationality, this classification cannot be made without the consent of the relevant consul. This classification, with the confirmed agreement of the consul, will be administratively notified to the tenants with intent to close the house or for regular registration, if that was to take place, within fifteen days.[2]

As Egypt's Shariʿa court records dating from the Ottoman period (1516–1882) demonstrate, prostitution was not new to Egypt; also not new were government efforts to control prostitution either in Egypt or the Ottoman Empire at large, as various Ottoman *firmān*s and Egypt's sultanic decrees (*Qānūn-nāme*) show. Even well before Ottoman times Mamluk chroniclers, such as Ibn Taghrībirdī, al-Suyūṭī, al-Maqrīzī and Ibn Iyās, spoke of legal recognition and control of prostitution. From their writings we get a glimpse of the place of prostitutes in Egyptian society, where they practiced, and how they were organized. The number of prostitutes seemed to be large, according to these sources, and even though prostitution was not formally legal and was considered a sinful profession, it existed, its practice regulated like other crafts, and its practitioners often taxed.

While general attitudes toward prostitution continued into the nineteenth century, the arrival of the modern state brought about the legalization of prostitution and the licensing of those who practiced it. This situation continued until 1949 when prostitution was made illegal and punishable by law. In other words, from the late nineteenth century until the middle of the twentieth, prostitution was made a legitimate profession through state licensing and regulations. Regulations included such things as the designation of particular town-quarters where houses of prostitution could be opened, the form of entry into these houses, how prostitutes were to comport themselves, and medical inspections required for practicing the profession. While echoes of these practices could be found in earlier ages of Egyptian history, a significant new development brought about by the modern ordinances was the involvement of foreign prostitutes or foreign owners of houses of prostitution. Because of capitulatory privileges and their extension into Egypt through the establishment of Mixed Courts, all affairs regarding foreigners were to be dealt with by the consulate of the individual country to which the foreigner belonged. Disputes involving more than one nationality were adjudicated before Mixed Courts where the laws applied were European as opposed to the Egyptian laws applied in the National Courts.[3] Both the National and Mixed Courts were creations of the modern state. The first, established in 1883, addressed the interests of Western-oriented Egyptian propertied classes and held jurisdiction over commercial, national, and criminal law which were earlier the domain of Shariʿa courts, leaving personal status, inheritance, and *waqf* issues as the purview of new Shariʿa courts established by the state as part of its legal reforms. Mixed Courts created in 1876 were an innovation allowing foreigners to enjoy extra-territorial rights inside Egypt even while Consular courts continued to be responsible for handling citizens of their particular country who commit crimes inside Egypt.[4]

The new legal system meant that prostitutes and houses of prostitution were differentiated according to whether the prostitute, the customer, or the owner of the prostitution establishment was an Egyptian or a foreigner. The capitulatory logic according to which the legal system benefited foreigners was thus extended to business practices that differentiated according to nationality and discriminated against Egyptian nationals. The same discriminatory logic was extended to Egyptian society itself, differences being made between rich and poor and between men and women.

State centralization and efforts at reform during the nineteenth century also witnessed the codification and standardization of law, which allowed the state to establish and extend its powers of order and organization. In the course of codification, particular codes were drafted through the work of government committees which selected and compiled laws that they considered appropriate, laws which were compiled from Shariʿa law, *ʿurf* (custom), and Western laws with a strong class and gendered outlook favoring the new patriarchal monarchical structure coming into being in Egypt at the time. The result of the legal reforms was the expansion of a legal system that was elitist and class oriented and at the same time gendered. This development left a wide chasm between Egypt's classes and between men and women as the country moved steadily toward independence from foreign and monarchical rule. Thus the reformed legal system introduced in nineteenth-century Egypt reflected deep connections between ethnicity, nationality, gender, and class. It is not that class was not a factor in earlier laws; fines paid to the state for committing particular crimes were certainly based in Ottoman *qānūns* on ability to pay, for example. But there did not seem to be the conscious construction of and differentiation by gender and class as was the case under the modernizing laws. As the nineteenth century started and Muḥammad ʿAlī Pasha began this centralizing of the state as a step toward independence from the Ottoman Empire, laws differentiating poor from rich and men from women pointed toward the patriarchal structure that evolved by the end of the nineteenth century and continued into the twentieth. While some of these laws and regulations were innovative, others extended rules that were long-standing traditions in Egypt but which were now introduced as part of systematic plans of the government's efforts to organize and categorize people.

The first part of this essay discusses the state's treatment of prostitution and other sexual offences by pre-modern courts. The essay will then move on to discuss the changes introduced during the nineteenth and early twentieth centuries. This will be followed by a focused analysis of sexual crimes and the handling of sexual crimes by modern laws and courts. More specifically, sex crimes will be used as specific case studies to illustrate the class and gendered approach to law that was introduced and established as the norm in modern Egypt.

Sex and Crime in Pre-Modern Egypt

The handling of prostitution by Shariʿa courts before the modernization and codification of law in nineteenth-century Egypt is surprising in many ways. The variety of cases seen by the courts that can be classified under sexual crimes opens doors for our understanding of the legal process and the handling of sexual crimes and prostitutes in the Ottoman Empire. The following discussion presents some tentative conclusions based on Ottoman laws and the case record from Egypt's Shariʿa courts; obviously much more research is needed.

> Before our lord Shaykh Naṣr al-Dīn ʿAlī al-Mināwī al-Ḥanafī came his honored equal and peer al-Nāṣirī Muḥammad b. Shuʿayb al-Dīn al-Sikandarī, the *tābiʿ* of the honored Janāb al-ʿAlī Maṣilī Katkhuda, the Prince leader (*amīr al-liwāʾ, al-qabiṭān*) of the port, may his greatness last. He reported that the afore-mentioned Katkhuda was informed that a strange woman was in the company of a strange man inside a warehouse located along the path between the two towers in the said port with the intention of committing sin (*faḥshāʾ*), so he sent him to the said warehouse to apprehend them. He asked permission from the judge (*ḥākim*) to do so and was given it. Inside the said hall located at the said spot, he found a male whose name was ʿĀmir b. Khafājī

al-Sarnābawī from Buḥayrat Banī ʿIssa, who resides in the said hall, together with a strange woman who said that her name was Faṭma bint Muḥammad al-Manṣūrī. There is no relationship or marriage between the two. The said ʿĀmir was her betrothed before that date but he did not marry her. That is what the investigation and witnesses produced. The witnesses went to the judge and informed him by way of the investigation as explained above. Each was found to deserve the proper discretionary punishment (*taʿzīr*) that is deserved by them and those like them in accordance with the Shariʿa. This was written down to keep a record to be referred to if necessary. Written on [...]. (Dumyat Shariʿa Court, 1016 [1607], 47:368–750)

While not a unique case, the completeness of its account makes it particularly important because cases in the archival record do not always include the decision of the court. Very often the case is discussed in summary and the decision is left to later judgment. In this case, perhaps because the drama took place away from the court, a complete record had to be kept for future reference, so we learn about some details of the legal process, the hierarchy of authority in regards to legal matters, and the treatment of sexual offences. For example, we learn that the political authority, here in the shape of the *katkhudā*, who held a position like that of a representative of the viceroy, could not take the law into his own hands and investigate a legal matter without prior permission of the court. Having investigated the crime, it was the court that decided the fate of those involved, and court witnesses, i.e., witnesses attached to and working for the court, were responsible for reporting back to the judge after investigating. A written record was kept in court "to be referred to if necessary," which indicates the importance of accountability in regards to actions taken and decisions arrived at. The punishment passed was discretionary (*taʿzīr*), which usually meant flogging. Since it was not a *zinā* case, which traditionally required the testimony of four male witnesses to an act of sexual intercouse between an unmarried couple, there was no sentence of stoning; in determining the punishment the question whether either the man or woman was married was not even investigated. Marriage was traditionally the differentiating factor between stoning or not, according to interpreters who insist that stoning is Islam's punishment for a married adulterer or adulteress.

This conclusion is substantiated by the "Ottoman Criminal Code" issued during the reign of Sultan Süleymān (1520–1566). As Nūr Faraḥāt states in his study of Ottoman law in Egypt,[5] codes issued by Sultans were valid only during their reign, yet they could become the basis for future action in regard to the handling of crimes and other aspects of the law. It is interesting to see how the state interpreted laws in writing *qānūns*. Was the Shariʿa the guiding principle, and if so, to what extent and according to whose interpretation? Comparing *qānūns* issued by the Ottoman central government with the application of the laws in the courts of provinces of the empire also provides a glimpse of how the legal system actually worked in the empire, how decisions were arrived at in court, what the role was of the central government and of social customs in determining which laws were applied in courts, and what legal traditions were followed.

These questions are important for another reason. Today we are hearing increasingly of attempts to implement the stoning penalty for *zinā* in certain countries. Fundamentalist groups and scholars seem to take it for granted that Islamic law demands the stoning of married persons involved in fornication, despite the absence of such a ruling in the Qurʾan, while, if unmarried, they are banished or whipped. Books, articles, and discussions on the Internet propagate these ideas with those opposing doing so on the basis of its inappropriateness to modern society.

The question of how *zinā* was handled by a great Islamic empire like the Ottoman is important to our discussion. Regarding *zinā*, Sultan Süleymān's Criminal Code, 1534–1545, reads as follows:

> 1. If a person commits fornication and [this] is proven against him: if the fornicator is married and is rich, possessing one thousand *akçe* or more, a fine of 300 *akçe* shall be collected [from him], provided he does not suffer the [death] penalty; if he is in average circumstances, his property amounting to six hundred *akçe*, a fine of 200 *akçe* shall be collected; if he is poor, his property amounting to four hundred *akçe*, a fine of 100 *akçe* shall be collected; and if he is [in even] worse [circumstances], a fine of 50 *akçe* or a fine of 40 *akçe* shall be collected.
> 2. If the fornicator is unmarried and is rich, his property amounting to one thousand or more, a fine of 100 *akçe* shall be collected; if he is in average circumstances, a fine of 50 *akçe* shall be collected and if he is poor, [a fine of] 30 *akçe* shall be collected.
> [...]
> 5. If a married Muslim woman commits fornication, she shall, if she is rich, pay the fine [imposed] on a rich man after [her offence] has been proved; if she is in average circumstances, she shall pay the fine [imposed] on a man in those circumstances.[6]

According to these rules, the penalty for adultery was payment of fines and *taʿzīr*. Stoning is given no mention; the circumstances of "provided he does not suffer the [death] penalty" are left unexplained. Perhaps that depended on the particulars of the case, which could have involved rape and assault. What is evident is that mention of a death penalty pertained only to men and was not mentioned as applying to women.

In the court litigation quoted above, the court of Dumyat seemed to follow the Ottoman edicts to a certain extent but not fully. While the two guilty parties were sentenced to *ta'zīr*, no fines were demanded from the perpetrators of the crime. Court practices seemed to follow the Qānūn-nāme of Egypt issued in 1528 by Ibrāhīm Pasha, Sultan Süleymān's viceroy in Egypt. While not a document establishing laws by which Egypt was to be ruled, the Qānūn-nāme took a realistic look at the situation in Egypt at the time, at the presence of Ottoman forces there, and at the best means by which to control the country, raise taxes, and insure the production of certain food staples like wheat and sugar.[7] The Qānūn-nāme therefore can be read as a document establishing principles to be followed by those left in charge of the administration and protection of Egypt. Continuity seemed to be central to this pragmatic approach reflected in Sultan Süleymān's calling for the laws established earlier by the Sultan al-Ashraf Qā'itbāy (1468–1495) to be upheld and to the Qānūn-nāme being used as a basis for the laws by which Egypt was to be ruled.

It seems that the Ottomans found a situation in Egypt which they considered "outside of Islamic morals" and the Qānūn-nāme gives some details about this. While the collection of taxes is central to the orders detailed in *Qānūn-nāmat Miṣr*, the law was directed at *muqāṭa'a* taxes which had been previously collected for *muḥarramāt* or forbidden practices. It stated that immoral practices should not be allowed because the Sultan's position demands that he "establish religious rules and follow the *sunna* of the lord of the Messengers (*sayyid al-mursalīn*) and therefore all *muqāṭa'a*s of that type had to be cancelled." Forbidden practices included "taverns (*ḥānāt*) located in towns first and villages and cities later." The explanation given for the prohibition of drinking was that it was due to the sinfulness and depravity that these practices encouraged "since they [taverns] are a refuge for the depraved and a location for public drinking of alcohol." The orders continue: "Also forbidden are locations for *ghubayrā'*[8] (or *būza*, a local drink made of fermented dates) where alcohol is drunk by groups under the pretext that it is [the less potent] *ghubayrā'*. Forbidden is sexual activity (*faḥshā'*) and whatever is against religion (*munkar*) that has become widespread and forbidden are *zinā* and other great sins (*kabā'ir*)."[9]

> There seems to be a repulsive tradition and appalling scandalous practice (*sunna*) existing since ancient times. On the wedding night the bride appears before the crowd seven times as they drink alcohol (*khamr*) and commit sin and depravity. Each time she appears in a new dress and appearance. When she arrives at the assembly she plays, sings, and dances. Those present then affix money to her feet. This is a custom against what is required by the holy Shari'a, and therefore said practice is absolutely prohibited.[10]

Given the profusion of cases having to do with drunkenness and prostitution, it seems that Ottoman laws did not effectively accomplish their purpose; the courts did, in their handling of both offences, comply with the laws in question, although according to what court records show, it seems to have been more in answer to complaints that the courts act against drunks or prostitutes. When such a complaint was brought to court and the correct procedures followed and the right witnesses produced, the court was generally firm against drunkards, and usually ordered *taʿzīr*, though not, it seems, a monetary penalty (Dumyat, *Ishhādāt*, 1022, 51old:4–11).

> [...] informed the court that eight years earlier he was married to a woman by the name of Ḥalīma [...] from whom he had a daughter [...] and then he divorced her irrevocably [three divorces] and the judge awarded her support (*nafaqa*) for the infant. After sometime, people witnessed (*shāhada*) that the ex-wife's mother was not sexually honorable [i.e., promiscuous], that strange men would go into her home, and that the judge (*ḥākim*) had her punished through *taʿzīr* time and again, and he feared that harm could befall his daughter [...] and asked that he be given custody of his daughter (Alexandria, *sijill* 1189, 95:367–521).

The judge accepted the man's plea and turned the daughter over to him rather than leaving her with the mother and thereby facilitating her being influenced by the grandmother. This case is interesting since the court accepted the allegations against the grandmother and applied a *taʿzīr* punishment, a discretionary punishment that she underwent several times by sentence of the court. This may indicate that the *taʿzīr* punishment was not all that serious, certainly not maiming. There was also no mention of a monetary fine as required by the Ottoman criminal code. Where the code seemed to have been followed especially closely, perhaps because it agreed with local tradition, was in the matter of expelling prostitutes—or women of ill-repute—from communities in which they lived at the demand of these communities. Here the relevant Ottoman criminal code is number 124 and reads as follows:

> Furthermore, if the community of his (or her) [town-quarter] or of his (or her) village complains that a person is a criminal or a harlot, and, saying, "He (or she) is not fit [to live with] us," rejects him (or her), and if that person has in fact a notoriously bad reputation among the people, he (or she) shall be banished, i.e., ejected from his (or her) quarter or village. (Heyd, 130)

The following court record illustrates a case in which women and men whose morals were wanting could be expelled from their town-quarters and villages on the demand of the inhabitants.

> Appearing before the Shariʿa court (*majlis al-sharʿ al-sharīf*) the revered pilgrim Yaḥyā, son of the deceased Ḥassan al-Hadinī, and his equal ʿAlī, son of the deceased Yūsuf Abū Sanab, and the revered pilgrim ʿAbd al-Wahhāb and his brother al-Zaynī Muṣṭafā, sons of the deceased pilgrim ʿAlī Falidut, and the revered pilgrim ʿAbd al-Rāziq, son of the deceased pilgrim Khayr ʿAlī and his paternal cousin al-Ḥājj Aḥmad Farghalī and the revered pilgrim ʿAlī, son of the deceased ʿAbdallāh al-Misdī and the venerable Aḥmad b. Ḥassān [...], all of whom are residents of the town-quarter al-Maghāriba (North African quarter) in the port [of Alexandria], their concern being in regards to the woman Fāṭuma, daughter of Aḥmad ʿAllām, who is known [by the name of] Bint al-Sitt, and the wife of her son Khalīl, who is absent from the port at present because of travel in *bilād al-rūm*, the woman Makiyya, daughter of Ibrāhīm al-Qiṭṭ, and the woman Khadīja, daughter of the pilgrim Ḥamīda al-Masidūnī. Accompanying the group was a group representing the *katkhudā* of the port, al-Sharīf Muḥammad. [They came] with a document (*ḥujja*) [delegated] by the people of the quarter [explaining] that most people have left their places closed and abandoned because of the immorality exhibited by the women and the thugs who visit them night and day and that the [people] are not comfortable with this and fear for themselves and the Muslims on account of the drawing of weapons and occurrence of [violence?] and murder. [They indicated] that her son Khalīl, mentioned earlier, absent [at present], had disowned these immoral women and the meeting of wicked people in his mother's house. When gossip spread of this, and the above-mentioned Khalīl was called to appear before the Shariʿa court to be questioned, he ran away to *bilad al-rūm* as mentioned. They asked that the aforementioned women be expelled from the said location and that the missing Khalīl not be allowed to live there after his return. [The qadi] granted them their demand and gave legally sanctioned orders for the expulsion of the said women from their quarter [?] and for the missing Khalīl not to be allowed to live there when he returned, until they show better morals [...], signed and written end of Muharram 1189. (Alexandria, 1189 [1775], 95:384, case 346)

From the above case we learn that, at least in Alexandria, houses of ill-repute existed within normal residential quarters, and that people moved against them only when they became a source of trouble for their neighbors and the activities that took place there became public knowledge and the subject of gossip. The case also shows that the elders of the quarter—all of whom are referred to by various honorary titles including *ḥājj* (pilgrim)—took it upon themselves to go to court as delegates of their community and that the court listened to them without the need for further witnesses to the allegations they brought forth. The fact that they were all highly placed and that most were members of the clergy undoubtedly played a role in the court's decision. Another interesting fact presented by this case is that the court was willing to consider restitution of the offenders to the quarter of the city in which they lived once they showed that the conduct that got them into trouble in the first place had ceased and that they had corrected their ways. One conclusion that can be reached from the story being told here is that the connection between law, the courts, and the community of Alexandria was quite strong and that the wishes of the people were directly linked to the decisions of the court, i.e., the principle of the public interest (*maṣlaḥa*) worked well in cases involving social disturbances and immorality. The handling of crime illustrates well the organic link between the legal system and the society in which the legal system functioned. Clearly recognized as a sinful occupation that was punishable by law, prostitution was nevertheless widely practiced in Egypt, yet there were limits to what the people accepted in regards to this practice. The Ottoman criminal code specified the illegality of the practice and the legal system as practiced in Egypt seemed to apply the spirit of what the code intended, but specifics were left to the courts, which always took the situation on the ground into consideration.

According to the Ottoman criminal code,

> Art. 57. If a person practices procuring, the *cadi* shall chastise [him or her] and expose [him or her to public scorn; in addition] a fine of one *akçe* shall be collected for each stroke.[11]
> Art. 75. A [woman][12] for whom (?) procuring is patently committed or [a person] who practices procuring shall have his [or her] forehead branded.

In the above case, the women were clearly chastised and so was the son, Khalīl, who may have exposed what was happening in his own home but who was held responsible together with his mother, wife, and the other women involved. He also ran away when things became threatening. The qadi's expelling the women from their homes was a severe chastisement and rebuke and could be said to have been an explicit application of the Ottoman code, although it stands to reason that banishment also occurred much earlier in Egypt. However, we do not see any branding of the forehead taking place in this case or in any other surveyed for this paper; no fine was paid either as required by Art. 57, and there was no corporal chastisement. Court decisions therefore differed according to the specifics of the situation, evidence, and witnesses presented, and the wishes of the community.

Class and Law in Nineteenth-Century Egypt

Law no. 49 for 1933 reads:

> Will be punished by a prison term no longer than two months each person sound of body, male or female, aged fifteen years or over, who is found begging on public roads or public places even if he claimed to be or pretended to be performing a duty for someone else or to be displaying or offering toys or any other item for sale.[13]

and goes on to specify that if the beggar is not "physically sound" he or she is to receive a prison sentence no longer than one month if caught in a "town or village where a shelter has been organized and his/her admission was possible."[14] Confinement of the unwanted in areas separating them from the rest of society was part of the modern state's effort to control and separate populations into manageable, observable groups. With the introduction of new land-tenure laws—specifically Saʿīd Pasha's law of 1858 establishing private ownership rights in Egypt, which brought about the dispossession of large number of peasants and their movement to Egypt's towns in search of a better life—the state became interested in returning peasants to their villages to cultivate fallow land, on the one hand, and to keep towns free of beggars and crime, increasingly in evidence as the nineteenth century grew older, on the other. Sending peasants "back home" was not new in itself, having been practiced much earlier in Egypt, if not for the same reasons: the Qānūn-nāme of Sultan Süleymān, for example, states that "if the inhabitants of a village run away and their lands remain fallow, the village chief and the *kashshāf* should ask their neighbors about them, try finding them, and pressure them to return and cultivate their land [...] so that not a single inch of the Sultan's land remains uncultivated."[15] The same orders are repeated during Muḥammad ʿAlī's reign, but in a more organized and aggressive form, in ordinances detailing the role expected of Egypt's peasantry who were to cultivate the soil and be forcibly returned to their towns for that purpose. In 1829 the first system of registration requiring all men to carry identity papers to present for passage to and from Cairo and other major cities was introduced. These identity papers contained information such as name, address, and other details, and all peasants were required to carry such a certificate.[16]

The laws passed during the last quarter of the nineteenth century promoted the same political philosophy of bringing about a new social order that would be controlled through mapping and surveillance. In *The History of Railway Thieves* Vinay Lal described how the British in India, though clearly ruling on the basis of "naked power," at the same time brought about a "conquest of knowledge [...] that gain[ed] them the acquiescence of their subjects and enable[d] their rule; the British put into place a set of epistemological imperatives [...] [by which they] sought to consolidate their gains in the realm of knowledge [...] introducing new methods of surveillance, and mapping sacred and profane territories."[17] Surveillance and mapping of populations become normal activities for Egypt during the nineteenth and early twentieth centuries. From the quarantine of boats and travelers, particularly those returning from the Pilgrimage,[18] in order to ensure control of infectious diseases, to the medical inspection of prostitutes and the creation of administrative positions for inspectors in all areas of government activities and service—most such superior supervisory positions were the purview of Englishmen.[19]

This new order superimposed on Egypt was meant to make it more efficient and "sanitize" it through better methods of health and cleanliness; it resulted in the creation of new patriarchal lines devising legal grids through which to define relations between an elite formed of men headed by foreigners, on the one hand, and the masses of Egypt's public and particularly its women, on the other, and between the sound of body or mind, on the one hand, and the unsound of body or mind, on the other. The philosophy behind the laws and grids differentiated little between categories of women and children and those unsound of mind or body—both were placed under the custody of guardians whether fathers, uncles, brothers, or the state, all men wielding patriarchal power supported by law.

> By personal status is meant the totality of what differentiates one human being from another in natural or family characteristics, according to which the law applied legal principles in regards to one's social life, such as whether the human being is male or female, a husband or a widower, a divorcé, a father, or legitimate son, or whether he is a full citizen or less due to his age or imbecility or insanity, or whether he is fully civilly competent, or is limited in his competency as per a legal reason.[20]

In other words, the legal system would define individual rights, including citizenship rights, according to gender and mental competency. Those who fit within the patriarchy were kept in; those outside the patriarchy, whether by not accepting it or by being impervious to it, were mapped out. Hence the appearance of lunatic asylums which separated people totally from society, similar to societies' treatment of lepers. At this same time orphanages began to be established as philanthropic organizations where abandoned children were housed and separated from the larger society. Where once abandoned children were supported by the state, which handed them over to families to raise,[21] these children were now to be looked at as unwanted products of sin. Their very placement into institutions removed from the larger society made them victims of the new state patriarchy. It is ironic that while earlier courts had customarily handed over foundlings to families so that they would be raised within the bounds of family life, and had used money from the Treasury (*bayt al-mal*) to help these families to raise the children, the new welfare state chose to consign foundlings into a grid of the unwanted and place them in institutions separating them from the rest of the community. They became a source of social pity and derision, as children of sin, unwanted and isolated.[22]

Vagrancy laws taxed police with the duty of watching out for vagrants, widely defined as anyone walking at night in towns and villages. Under the same term were included a wide range of possibilities such as narcotics dealers, known felons, gypsies, and soothsayers, and all those who had no specific residential address. Also included were prostitutes and procurers.[23] The laws were justified by security needs; they resulted, however, in limiting the freedoms of the general public and in establishing clear lines separating foreigner from local, rich and the connected from the poor and non-connected, and women from men. The laws of vagrancy, prostitution, and personal status, while having disparate purposes and domains, at the same time created unequal relations of subservience and assertion based on a patriarchy supported and enforced by the state, whether on the streets or in the home. A new moral regime accompanied and gave relevance to this mapping, which process as a whole was set off by a significant rise in violence in modern Egypt. Since various forms of violence were regularly recorded in pre-modern Shariʿa court records, it was hardly a new phenomenon; but the persistent increase in rate and types of violence reflected the social dislocation produced by the migration of populations from rural to urban centers in search of a better life. These migrating populations left behind a once secure way of life that had been torn out from under them with the introduction of new agricultural land property laws that alienated the once land-owning peasantry and turned them into labor, wanted or unwanted depending on the new, rich land-owners' needs and whims. A noticeably increased rate of suicides was also a reflection of the growing violence, unease, and restlessness facing Egypt's society. If suicide existed before the modern age, it was not a familiar phenomenon among Egyptians; it became a usual occurrence only with the turn of the century. Police records show almost daily suicides in large cities such as Cairo and Alexandria, whose populations were growing from year to year;[24] joblessness and gender violence,[25] including marital violence,[26] constituted the prominent cause of suicide. Crimes committed by and against children are a particularly interesting indicator of the rise and change in the crime scene. Seventy thousand criminal cases were brought to trial in Egypt in 1898; by 1908 the number had exceeded one hundred and fifty thousand.[27] Juveniles often appeared as defendants before the court, which dealt with them harshly. Cairo courts tried 1,836 cases involving juveniles in 1912, of whom 246 were acquitted, 47 sent to prison, 91 entrusted to family, 1,200 were whipped, and 151 were sent to reformatory, while 100 paid a fine.[28] Crimes against children were also an interesting phenomenon, particularly because they almost always involved the children of the poor and unprotected. Where it did involve the children of the rich, it was usually a case of kidnapping, although poor children constituted the majority of stolen[29] or abandoned children.[30] The fact that most crimes against children were either sexual crimes or involved some sort of accident suffered by children working in factories or playing in streets, tells of the class from which they originated.[31] Infanticide is the most revealing, given the almost daily reporting by the police of bodies of newborn babies found on street corners, near bridges, main thoroughfares, in mosques, train cars, and other public places.[32] The growth in numbers of foundlings as well as discarded bodies of newborn babies leads to the possible conclusion of increased gender violence including incest. While reports of incest were either lacking or not included in police reports, cases of rape were reported daily, including reports of rape against members and friends of the family.[33]

To sum up, significant differences began to appear during the nineteenth century which can be attributed to nation-state centralization and its need to control populations and the parallel codification of the law, which reflected the new class-driven, intellectual, and cultural realities of the modernizing westernizing elite pushing forth this process. A new organization of knowledge underlay the whole endeavor, one that took into account the presence of increasing number of citizens of western countries on Egyptian soil, and the need to ensure them extended privileges. Law was molded to ensure this approach in all its concerns, including inheritance.

> Egyptian law provides for the division of an estate in accordance with the inheritance laws obtaining in the deceased's home country. Property belonging to Egyptians of any religious denomination is inherited or bequeathed according to *sharīʿa* law, and that belonging to foreign nationals according to the laws of their own countries, which as a rule involve less fragmentation, and allow land to be bequeathed to a single heir.[34]

This approach of organizing the legal system around specifics other than principles of common rights and rules of law also benefited new status-aspiring national elite classes since class hierarchy gave them financial and social privileges over other citizens. The hegemony developing during that period was one that constructed and mapped out a class system differentiated according to linguistic ability, culture, and state-recognition through titles and jobs, and the accompanying financial privileges. This process which produced land-owning classes by the end of the century caused increasing peasant migration to urban centers. The joblessness and vagrancy ensuing from this may not have been new to Egypt, but it seems to have become a serious issue to the state in the nineteenth century, not only because of the increase in numbers but also because of the state's efforts to beautify and westernize Egypt's cities through parks, palaces, museums, and statues. Vagrants had no place in such a picture. Neither did prostitutes. The answer was a series of laws defining and controlling vagrancy, prostitution, and other shady practices. The approach was one of confinement and control with a distinctly elitist approach.

Class differences became part of modern Egypt's social fabric reflected in the urban environment contrasting between the older ("traditional") and newer ("modern") parts of towns. The differences were also reflected in public institutions and public space which was on the whole divided according to class, with the exception of mosques. Thus new railway cars introduced to transport passengers on Egypt's new railways in the second half of the nineteenth century were organized by class, as were tram cars and buses introduced later on. The same occurred in movie theatres, football stadiums, and even hospitals, which were divided into five sections serving people according to the class to which they belonged.[35] The first class was for foreigners and dignitaries, the second for senior government employees, the third for the middle class, and the lowest were for the general public with the last section free of charge for the poor. Even when it came to the Pilgrimage, an undertaking organized by the government to accompany the *maḥmal* (cover for the Kaʿba) during the first years of the twentieth century, the announced costs were gradated: LE 50, 25, 23, 20, and 14, depending on conditions of travel.[36] The same divisions would be reflected in the handling and practice of prostitution, as will be explained below.

Prostitution in Nineteenth-Century Egypt

The presence of British troops on Egyptian soil and the increased numbers of foreigners who came to work and live in Egypt following the British invasion in 1882 can be said to have had a direct impact on the state's approach to prostitution. Rules were passed to control prostitution and to regulate who practiced prostitution and where, and what clientele could be served by these licensed prostitutes; and health regulations were required of prostitutes and houses of prostitution before they were given licenses.[37]

It should be pointed out that the connection between health, prostitution, and armies was familiar to Egypt. According to one account, because of the spread of syphilis and gonorrhea among Napoleon's army in Egypt and the army's inability to control the access of prostitutes to French barracks, which were described as infected with diseases, General Dugua, then governor of Cairo, wrote to Bonaparte in 1799, "to keep them away, it would be necessary to drown those caught in the barracks." Stories differ as to what happened to the prostitutes; some indicate that Napoleon ordered 400 of them beheaded and thrown into the Nile, while others say that he ordered them sent to the hospital but that his orders were countermanded by the *āghā* who followed normal practice in regards to prostitutes.[38] There are stories from much earlier epochs about the drowning of prostitutes in the Nile by the authorities, recorded by chroniclers, such as Ibn Iyās, who tell of cases of humiliation, punishment, and public execution of evildoers—including prostitutes—during the years following the Ottoman invasion of Egypt.[39] But these seem to be rare stories that could have been generated by the instability and revolts against the Ottoman presence in Egypt during the early days of Ottoman rule, which necessitated severe reprisals and actions by the Ottoman authorities. The Qānūn-nāme of Egypt of 1528 was issued at a time when the Sultan's governors (*walī*) found themselves faced by revolts from all sides—by the *kāshif*s (supervisors, inspectors, provincial governors), contingents of the Ottoman forces, Mamluk *amīr*s, Arab tribesmen, and the population at large. Continued revolts forced the Ottomans to rethink their policy and treat the population in mellower ways, hence the Sultan's orders:

> Let the usual practice (*ʿāda*) and law that were dominant (*sāʾidin*) at the time of Qāʾitbāy in regards to *kushūfiyya* fees, be respected and put in force, and they should not be superseded to begin with.[40]

So even though the Qānūn-nāme of Egypt contained strong language about the condition of morals in Egypt and gave orders not to raise taxes levied on immoral activities (*fawāḥish*), such taxes continued to be levied on prostitutes and houses of prostitution, and lists for both were kept by the local police (*sūbāshi*). This changed with the nineteenth century when in 1834 the state first prohibited public dancing, following in 1837 by making prostitution illegal, a law that made prostitution punishable by fifty stripes up to "hard labor of one to two years."[41] Fighting venereal diseases was one of the duties of female doctors who were graduated from the Qasr al-ʿAyni School of Medicine, which opened in 1839. Venereal diseases were associated with the military and with prostitutes, so graduates of the medical school staffed Egypt's hospitals. The first responsibility of women doctors was to fight epidemics, which claimed thousands of victims every year, by traveling through the countryside, entering people's homes, and performing medical services and giving vaccinations. But they were also required to provide a badly needed service in fighting venereal diseases, particularly among the wives and followers of Muḥammad ʿAlī Pasha's army.[42]

The prohibition of prostitution in 1837, however, did not mean that the practice stopped. As attested by Zabtiyya records from the first half of nineteenth-century Egypt, this was far from true. There are cases that illustrate the existence of houses of prostitution; when clients of the prostitutes became drunk or caused disturbances, the police were called in. In one such case from 1865, the drunk man was dragged to court and was sentenced to prison. Even though a house of prostitution was indicated as the place where the arrest had taken place, no questions were raised by the qadi about the house or about the prostitutes in it.[43] Women acting immorally in public were also brought before the court without suffering the court's recrimination. The case of a woman who joined a group of men at night asking for a smoke and ended up being hurt by one of them brings the condemnation of the court against the man, who was sentenced to prison for one year.[44] As for the crime of *zinā*, it did not seem to play much of a role, as the case of a wife who left her husband for another man, whom she met at the local *mawlid* (saint's day celebration), shows. She later married him, thereby committing bigamy. After her first husband found her, he went to court to ask that his marriage to her be recognized because he wanted her to return to him.[45] When harm results from prostitution, however, the court did punish those who caused the harm, as in the case of two prostitutes who received one-year prison sentences because they had given a man venereal disease (*qurūḥ afrankiyya*).[46]

After the British invaded Egypt prostitution became legitimized; an ordinance dated November 11, 1882 required the registration and health inspection of prostitutes.[47] Health seemed to be the main reason for controlling sexual practices; regularized prostitution, as defined by the Ministry of the Interior's ordinance dating July 1, 1895, was primarily focused on the health of prostitutes. Articles 1 and 2 of the ordinance read:

> 1. Offices of morality for Cairo and Alexandria will be formed of a doctor aided by an assistant-doctor, a midwife, a clerk who knows Arabic and a European language, and a representative of the police assisted by a sufficient number of guards.
> 2. For the provinces and ports, the functions of the offices of morality will be undertaken by the doctor of the hospital assisted by a midwife.[48]

The regulating of prostitution was implemented first in Egypt's two major cities, Cairo and Alexandria, and was not intended for the country as a whole. The ordinances were later extended to port cities and major provincial towns frequented by foreigners or men of wealthier and professional classes, and it was not until much later that regulations were extended to major provincial towns that were not normally associated with the travel of foreigners or wealthier classes. As stated, the 1895 ordinance was particularly interested in ensuring the health of prostitutes who served in certified houses of prostitution. The certification of such establishments is in itself an indication of the level of the clientele that frequented them. The presence of non-native prostitutes serving in these houses is another indication.

> Any local or European woman who makes prostitution her trade, whether in a house of prostitution or in her own home, must be registered through the agency of the police at the office of morality, which will provide her with a yearly certificate containing a record of medical visits and observations made by [the office]. This certificate will have a registered number and will show the name, nationality, age, and address of the known girl, as well as other significant characteristics, and the name of the master or mistress heading the house.[49]

As for the medical tests themselves, all prostitutes were required to undergo a medical test at least once per week, showing up at designated locations in Cairo and Alexandria from 8:00 in the morning to 1:00 in the afternoon in summer and from 10:00 in the morning to 2:00 in the afternoon in winter, and at the local hospital in other towns covered by the ordinance.[50] When a prostitute was found to have a venereal disease, she was to be admitted to the hospital from which she was not to be dismissed until she received a medical certificate attesting to the cure of her disease. Dismissal from hospitals in Cairo and Alexandria had to be certified by the doctor-in-chief of the hospital after which new licensing and registration procedures had to be undertaken by the office of morality before she could return to practice her profession. In provincial areas with no office of morality, dismissal from the hospital with a clean bill of health testified to by the chief physician sufficed.[51] The same health controls applied to owners of houses of prostitution, who also had to submit to weekly health inspections. This law, however, applied only to women under the age of fifty,[52] this presumably being the age defining the end of a woman's attractiveness as a sexual partner. No such requirement was made for a male owner of a house of prostitution, nor of male prostitutes, even though the courts acknowledged the existence of male prostitutes.

As for who could open such a house and what was required of him or her, the process was relatively simple. Any Egyptian or European could open a house of prostitution by submitting a request attached to which was a fiscal stamp of 30 mills and a certificate of good conduct. The request had to include the location of the proposed establishment and the number of rooms it comprised. Each partner had to submit a separate request for the same establishment. Forbidden from opening such houses were minors and holders of criminal records for various offences, such as stealing, rape, and public immorality.[53] It took a three-month waiting period to receive authorization to open the house for service and owners were expected to keep officials informed regarding all changes in their establishments once official authorization was granted. Such information included the number of girls working at the house, their names, age, and nationality, as well as information regarding those who no longer worked there, those who were added, and those who had died while in the employment of the house. For the purpose of keeping records, the owners of houses of prostitution were required to "keep a special register, which was to be presented whenever they are required to do so by representatives of the office of morality."[54] The law also held the owner of the establishment responsible if any of the prostitutes did not undergo the required weekly medical examination; the fine for delinquency was set at one hundred piastres to be paid by the owner of the establishment. Frequent delinquency led to the closing of the establishment.

The law differentiated between locals and foreigners who practiced prostitution or who owned houses of prostitution. According to Article 1 of the ordinance of July 15, 1895, following article 351 of Egypt's penal code and article 340 of the mixed penal code, the local governing authorities were authorized to either keep a prostitution establishment in business or to close it for any reason. Local governing authorities, however, had no jurisdiction with regard to prostitutes or owners of houses of prostitution who were holders of foreign citizenship, against whom no action could be taken without the consent of the consul of the country concerned.[55] Thus laws regulating prostitution differentiated between locals and foreigners as they did between males and females. Distinctions were also made between cities where those frequenting such establishments mostly belonged to the wealthy and cities where prostitutes served the community at large. While the laws applied to all prostitutes, the details of the law really involved houses of prostitution rather than prostitutes working outside such houses. Furthermore, the particular interest that Mixed Courts took in this type of business illustrates its importance within the foreign community in Egypt. The same type of scrutiny did not seem to apply to prostitutes serving the general population. Even though all prostitutes were supposed to undergo a medical examination of some form, there was no real enforcement of the regulations even in situations where the police was involved. Houses of prostitution operated without licenses even though the law required them to have one—this was known and tolerated by the authorities although court records differed from one case to the other regarding this issue. A 1938 Court of Cassation (*naqḍ*) trying of a case in which the police entered a private home without permission and proceeded to take the owners of the home into custody after finding minor girls who were being forced into prostitution, concluded:

> It is to be concluded from the various articles in the ordinance regarding prostitution issued November 16, 1905 that the right of the police

> to enter houses of prostitution is limited to licensed establishments alone and does not include those that are run without licensing; therefore the Court's decision being contested on the basis of this ordinance in defense of the right of the police to enter the house of the litigant is wrong because the home that she set up in which secret prostitution was practiced was not licensed in accordance to the ordinance regarding prostitution.[56]

In an earlier case dating from 1927, the court published an opposing decision, making it clear that all houses of prostitution were required to be licensed.[57]

The state was thus not so much interested in controlling prostitution as it was in ensuring the conditions of houses of prostitution that served particular client groups. This is evidenced by the appearance in court of registered houses of prostitution while unregistered houses continued to practice. Formal and informal prostitution could be one way of looking at the situation. Both existed and were acknowledged by the authorities, but while the former was licensed, supervised, and controlled, the latter was left in the realm of customary practices and the police only interfered when other laws, such as gambling or forcing minors into prostitution, were broken. One factor the two had in common was that the whole profession was regarded as being outside the realm of the morally licit. Houses of prostitution, certified or not, were described as "secret houses" (*buyūt sirriyya*); this secrecy was part of a new Victorianism which made sin available but in the realm of the secret or the unseen. The state's handling of prostitution therefore meant that particular practices defined by the state were legalised but that the rules were largely intended to keep prostitutes outside of the mainstream and to put sexual activities outside of marriage into a dark area of secrecy. This seemed to fit well with the Victorian moral regime being introduced which had as goal making a nuclear family with the father as the legal head the basic unit of society. Ending slavery also brought an end to sexual rights to enslaved women within the homes; ironically, while the state increased efforts to record marriage and divorce by standardizing marriage contracts and laws pertaining to marriage and family, unofficial (*ʿurfī*) marriage became the resort for men to marry without registration and therefore without the need for public acknowledgement. The result was continued male access to sexual activity outside of the official marriage and the transference of this activity to illicit areas outside of the home. Regularized but kept in the realm of the shady and secret, prostitution served the same purpose.

The rules regarding the running of establishments of prostitution and their location ensured their insularity and secrecy. They had to be located in particular quarters designated by the governor's ordinance, there was to be no communication between the apartments housing such businesses and other apartments in the same building, and they had to have a separate entrance.[58] In addition, prostitutes were forbidden from allowing themselves to be seen through windows, presumably so as not to procure business off the street, but also to keep the nature of the business a secret.

Conclusion

It is curious that at the same time as prostitution was being legalized and regularized by the modern state, a strict moral code was becoming normative. This code is best exemplified by a court's decision about safeguarding public morality by requiring that "meetings between the two sexes must be kept secret and news of them be suppressed."[59] This higher court decision gave prosecutors permission to retry a case involving a seller of pornographic material who had been acquitted by a lower court whose judge had grounded his decision in the fact that the stories the books contained were mostly in the French language and were customary to European culture and therefore to Europeans living in Egypt, and that nakedness was not alien to Egypt's new environment since it was to be found in the theatre, in nightclubs, and on beaches. The Court of Appeals found that this reasoning did not take all aspects of the crime into consideration and that it was "not permitted for judges to relax the upholding of moral values (*faḍīla*) and enforcement of the law."[60] Curiously, in rendering this verdict, the judge referred to an 1819 French law about public morals and the upholding of good manners.[61] French laws and court decisions were used as precedent in Egyptian courts and employed by lawyers and judges as a basis for the arguments they presented.[62]

The nineteenth century witnessed a surge in morality which included placing prostitution and other sexual matters outside the realm of what was public. This does not mean that immorality was acceptable in Egypt—prostitution and other immoral practices were not acceptable to the population, as this study has shown, and courts were cognizant of these wishes and based their judgments on what communities considered best for themselves. This is one of the most important divergences that can be discerned upon the establishment of the modern nation-state under conditions in which foreign interests played a determinant role. Prostitution was but one aspect of the new moral and legal discourse that favored male interests and worked for the benefit of foreign and elite interests. The laws enacted to guide the practice of prostitution and the existence of houses of prostitution mirror aspects of the legal system that discriminated and differentiated according to gender and nationality. Laws benefited the men within the family, within the public sphere, and even in the undertaking of (im)moral practice, inequalities from which Egyptian society still suffers today.

NOTES

[1] Philippe Gelat, *Répertoire général annoté de la législation et de l'administration égyptiennes 1840–1900* (Alexandria 1906–11), 3:364: "Sont considérées comme maisons de tolérance, les maisons où il y a deux ou plusieurs filles réunies qui se livrent habituellement à la prostitution. Il appartient à l'autorité administrative locale de déclarer si une maison doit être classée parmi les maisons de tolérance; mais dans le cas une des associées serait de nationalité étrangère, cette déclaration ne pourra être faite que du consentement des consuls dont ils relèvent. Cette déclaration, avec l'avis conforme du consul, sera signifiée administrativement aux tenanciers avec sommation de fermer la maison ou de se faire inscrire régulièrement, s'il y a lieu, dans les quinze jours."

[2] Ibid., 364.

[3] *al-Kitāb al-dhahabī li l-maḥākim al-ahliyya, 1883–1933* (Bulaq: Maṭābiʿ al-Amīriyya, 1938), 118, 124, 128. Another court system that made its appearance toward the end of the nineteenth century was that of the Milla Court, which can be considered an extension of religious prerogatives of non-Muslim communities officially recognized by the Egyptian state. These courts oversaw personal status issues similar to Shariʿa courts for Muslims.

[4] Nathan J. Brown, *The Rule of Law in the Arab World: Courts in Egypt and the Gulf* (Cambridge: Cambridge University Press, 1997), gives a good discussion of changes in law and courts in modern Egypt.

[5] Muḥammad Nūr Faraḥāt, *al-Taʾrīkh al-ijtimāʿī li l-qānūn fī Miṣr al-ḥadītha* (Cairo: Dār Suʿād al-Ṣabbāḥ [Ibn Khaldūn Center publication], 1993), pp. 109–10.

[6] Heyd Uriel, *Studies in Old Ottoman Criminal Law*, ed. V. L. Menage (Oxford: Clarendon Press 1973), 95 (for a complete discussion, 95–131).

[7] *Qānūnnāmat Miṣr alladhī aṣdarahu al-Sulṭān al-Qānūnī li-ḥukm Miṣr*, trans. into Arabic by Ahmad Fuʾād Mutawallī (Cairo 1986), 32: "Let the traditions and laws in general practice during the time of Qāʾitbāy concerning supervisory lists be applied. It is not permitted to displace these laws to begin with."

[8] An intoxicating beverage made from millet, or a wine made from the fruit of the tree (the service-apple), according to Lane's *Arabic-English Lexicon.*

[9] Ibid., 74.

[10] Ibid.

[11] Heyd, 10.

[12] Ibid., 114.

[13] Muḥammad al-Gamal, *al-Tasawwul fī l-qānūn al-miṣrī wa l-qānūn al-muqāran* (Giza 1989), 7.

[14] Ibid.

[15] ʿAbd al-Raḥīm ʿAbd al-Raḥmān ʿAbd al-Raḥīm, *al-Rīf al-miṣrī fī l-qarn al-thāmin ʿashar* (Cairo: Maktabat Madbūlī, 1986), 155.

[16] Samīr ʿUmar Ibrāhīm, *al-Hayʾa al-ijtimāʿiyya fī madīnat al-Qāhira khilāl al-nisf al-awwal min al-qarn al-tāsiʿ ʿashar* (Cairo: al-Hayʾa al-Miṣriyya al-ʿĀmma li l-Kitāb, 1992), 181.

[17] Vinay Lal, "Criminality and Colonial Anthropology," http://www.sscnet.ucla.edu/southasia/History/British/Criminality.html. Originally published as introduction to the reprint edition (Gurgaon, Haryana: Vintage Press, 1995, pp. i–xxvii) of Rai Bahadur M. Pauparao Naidu, *The History of Railway Thieves, with Illustrations and Hints on Detection*, 4th ed. (Madras: Higginbothams Limited, 1915).

[18] *Recueil des documents officiels* (Cairo 1893), 590–609.

[19] For example, inspectors of primary and secondary schools (orders dating August 13, 1892 establishing inspectors for all schools in Cairo and the provinces). *Recueil des documents officiels* (Cairo 1893), 463–66.

[20] *al-Majmūʿa al-rasmiyya li l-maḥākim al-ahliyya* (Bulaq: Maṭbaʿa al-Amīriyya, 1937), 11.

[21] For a discussion of adoption before the modern period, see "Adoption in Islamic Society: A Historical Survey," in *Children of the Modern Arab World*, ed. Elizabeth J. Fernea (Austin: University of Texas Press, 1995).

[22] Ministry of Justice, The Judicial Adviser, *Report for the Year 1908* (Cairo: National Printing Department, 1909), 13–4.

[23] Ibid., 129, quoting *al-Waqāʾiʿ al-miṣriyya*, no. 68 for 1923.

[24] Cairo and Alexandria, *Taqārīr Amn* (Police Records), 1940, box 24, Sayyida Zaynab 11 May; Alexandria, *ḍabṭ*, box 24, May 1940; Miṣr al-Jadīda, March 3; 1927, box 40, sijill 3, October 15, 27.

[25] Alexandria, *Taqārīr Amn* (Police Records), sijill 3, 1927, file 40, October 10; Cairo and Alexandria, *ḥawādith*, box 24, May 1940; Qism al-Darb al-Aḥmar, March 10, 1940; Bāṭiniyya, May 4, 1940.

[26] *Taqārīr Amn* (Police records), Cairo and Alexandria, *ḥawādith*, box 24, 1940, Qism Shubra, March 11. *Taqārīr Amn* (Police records) Cairo, October 1927, case 877, 2288 shooting of wife, 1026 husband throws wife out of window; Cairo and Alexandria, *ḥawādith*, box 24, May 1940.

[27] Ministry of Justice, The Judicial Adviser, *Report for the Year 1908* (Cairo: National Printing Department, 1909), 4.

[28] Ibid., *Report for the Year 1912*, 9.

[29] Cairo and Alexandria, *Taqārīr Amn*, box 24, *ḥawādith*, 1940, Qism al-Sayyida, March 31; February 2, 1940, Rawḍ al-Faraj.

[30] Cairo, *Taqārīr Amn, jināyāt*, 1927 June, case 2055.

[31] Alexandria Shariʿa court, *daʿāwī*, 1285 [1867], 3:10; 1293, 92:95; Maʿiyya, *ṣādir, aqālīm wa-muḥāfaẓāt*, ʿArabī, 1272 [1856] part 4:1617, p. 29, case 38 from Qina, and p. 63, case 115 from Manfalut.

[32] *Taqārir Amn*, Cairo, 1927, October 20, case 2346; October 6, case 1368; Qism Miṣr al-Jadīda, box 24, 1940, police report 1378, May 11; and Alexandria, *ḥawādith*, box 24, 1940, Qism al-Khalīfa, May 22; Qism Shubra, *maḥḍar* 19, May 2; Cairo, Ḥārat al-Naṣārā, *Taqārir Amn*, Cairo, 1927, October 6, case 1368; Miṣr al-Qadīma, case 468, February 22, 1940; Cairo and Alexandria, *ḥawādith*, box 24, 1940, Qism al-Khalīfa, May 22; Qism Shubra, *maḥḍar* 19, May 2; Cairo, Ḥārat al-Naṣārā, *Taqārir Amn*, Cairo, 1927, October 6, case 1368; Miṣr al-Qadīma, case 468, February 22, 1940; *Taqārir Amn*, case 1498 *jināyāt*, March 3, 1940.

[33] *Taqārir Amn*, Cairo, October 1927, case 2143, rape of a sixteen-year-old boy.

[34] Gabriel Baer, *A History of Landownership in Modern Egypt, 1800–1950* (Oxford: Oxford University Press, 1962), 117.

[35] Amira Sonbol, *The Creation of a Medical Profession in Egypt, 1800–1922* (Syracuse: Syracuse University Press, 1990).

[36] Gelat, *Répertoire*, 6:118.

[37] E.g., "Regarding secret prostitution houses, military order no 237 will be enforced whether those frequenting [these houses] belong to the British army or

others." Decision of the High Military Court, 15–6–1942 (5/411) published in *al-Majmūʿa al-rasmiyya li l-maḥākim al-ahliyya* (1949), 24.

[38] J. Christopher Herold, *Bonaparte in Egypt* (New York: Harper and Row, 1962), 161.

[39] Michael Winter, *Egyptian Society under Ottoman Rule, 1517–1798* (London: Routledge, 1992), 230.

[40] *Qānūnnāmat Miṣr*, 22.

[41] Edward William Lane, *An Account of the Manners and Customs of the Modern Egyptians Written in Egypt during the Years 1833–1835* (London: East-West Publications, 1978), 372 n. 28

[42] Cairo, National Archives, Maʿiyya Turkī to Matush Bey, 11 Dhū l-Qaʿda 1248 [ ], 45:120.

[43] Asyut, Maʿiyya Saniyya, Ṣādir Awāmir, 1282 [1865], 1:1–19.

[44] Sharqiyya, Maʿiyya Saniyya, Ṣādir Awāmir, 1282 [1865], 1:22–5.

[45] Asyut, Maʿiyya Saniyya, Ṣādir Awāmir, 1282 [1865], 1:46–9.

[46] Asyut, 1:38–7.

[47] Edward Ghālī al-Dhahabī, *al-Jarāʾim al-jinsiyya* (Cairo: Maktabat Gharīb, 1988), 181.

[48] Gelat, *Répertoire*, 3:362.

[49] Ibid.

[50] Ibid., Art. 5.

[51] Ibid., Arts. 6–9.

[52] Ibid., Art. 12.

[53] Ibid., 364: Art. 6.

[54] Ibid., 363: Arts. 17–18.

[55] Ibid., 364, Art. 1.

[56] *al-Majmūʿa al-rasmiyya li l-maḥākim al-ahliyya* (1940) no. 9, 461–63.

[57] Azbakiyya, 22–1–1927 (5/112) published in *al-Majmūʿa al-rasmiyya li l-maḥākim al-ahliyya* (1941), 21.

[58] Gelat, *Répertoire*, 6:2.

[59] Naqḍ Court case published in *al-Majmūʿa al-rasmiyya li l-maḥākim al-ahliyya* (1932), 71.

[60] Ibid.

[61] Ibid., n. 4.

[62] Ibid., 72.

10

SHARIʿA ETHNOGRAPHY

Brinkley Messick

The United States often is described as a litigious society. Adjusting for many historical and institutional differences, the same may be said of Yemen, and in particular of Ibb, where I conducted ethnographic field research, starting in 1974. Well watered by summer rains and relatively wealthy, post-revolutionary Ibb was known at the national level as the "province of problems." Many people I knew in Ibb town were involved in some type of a "matter"—a *qaḍiyya* (also, more formally, a "case"), *sha'n*, or *mas'ala*—an unresolved and more or less preoccupying conflict, whether great or small, longstanding or just emergent. People with pressing matters also came to the town from the surrounding rural areas of the province. Such conflicts mainly concerned some form of property, but there could be intangibles such as perceived insults and honor questions, and physical violence might have been involved, or threatened. Carrying documents in their coat pockets or tucked behind their belted daggers, men pursuing their matters circulated in the morning streets. Women attending to theirs wrapped their documents in garment or veil cloth. Stopping by marketplace shops and frequenting government offices and the courts, these disputants encountered their friends, relatives, and associates and, occasionally, they had to confront their adversaries. They also were approached by men who, like some in the offices or at the courts, sought to involve themselves in their affairs. These included the town's advocates, mediators, and notaries, the local specialists in the word and the pen.

In my early work, the basic rationale for attention to such "matters" was that in the course of assertion and argument otherwise implicit features of social life often were made explicit. The aim, in short, was general social analysis. Over the years, however, I came, more and more, to concentrate on the law itself, and also on history. Instead of my initial focus (like most anthropologists) on the contemporaneous "present" of my research residence in Yemen, my current work concerns the Shariʿa as it existed in recent history, specifically, prior to the Revolution of 1962, in the last decades of the classically-styled Islamic state of the Zaydi imams. This research has concerned both Zaydi doctrine (Messick 2001, 2002) and period court cases (Messick 1995, 1998, 2005, n.d.). In this paper I discuss the role of ethnographic research in this study of the Shariʿa and also the development of what may be termed an archival anthropology. In Part I, I retrace some of my research steps, detailing a form of ethnographic inquiry that incorporates written textual materials. In Part II, I give two vignettes based on my early research in Ibb. These provide contextual views of the Shariʿa courts of their era, and they also permit me to raise some issues about the possibilities and the limitations of written sources, notably court records, for legal history, in this instance that of the former imamic state.

I

Conflicts may be instructive but they can be difficult to study. And this is aside from the fact that one is continually in pursuit of trouble and of conduct considered unbecoming. In 1975, in an attempt to get an overview of the formal dimension of conflict activity, I hired a local man to make case summaries from Shariʿa court records. As part of the difficulties I had in actually getting my hands on the records in question I learned that court secretaries often kept active registers at home. In 1980, during my second lengthy residence in Yemen, as I began to focus directly on legal processes, I collected similar summary material myself directly from four men, two judges, and two court secretaries, who read to me from their respective court registers. The information obtained from such registers was limited to Shariʿa court activity and, more specifically, to cases that had resulted in judgments. More schematic in nature, but representing a far broader spectrum of conflicts, were the data I gathered on written petitions presented by individuals to the local government. Petitioning of this sort had been known to states across the Middle East for many centuries, and in the Ottoman Empire records were kept of them. I also worked at a number of more specialized venues. One was the Police Administration, founded after the Revolution, where I overcame my initial avoidance to obtain permission to collect data on crime reports. At two other just-instituted judicial organs, the Prosecution Office (Messick 1983) and the Traffic Court, I was given a desk and permitted to take detailed notes on case folders.

To this type of case annotation I added small collections of written documents gathered from the Mufti of Ibb and from the local Chamber of Commerce, two further venues, and a larger corpus from the Ibb Shariʿa courts. Ordinary fatwas were written atop the same piece of paper as the question and were returned to the questioners, who then carried them away, leaving behind no archival record. I hired a man to sit in the afternoon reception room of Muḥammad al-Wahhābī, the Ibb Mufti, to make copies of the unrecorded papers that he issued there, which included both fatwas and a miscellany of other documents, such as the occasional wound evaluation (Messick 1993, Ch. 5). A decade later, I photocopied a large corpus of broadcast fatwas drafted in the capital by my friend, a former Ibb resident and local Endowments official, Muḥammad al-Ghurbānī (Messick 1996). The Ibb Chamber of Commerce, chartered in the years after the Revolution, specialized in the settlement of disputes among members of the merchant community. In the three larger highland cities (Sanʿaʾ, al-Hudayda and Taʿizz) there were new (and short-lived) Commercial Courts, which, among other innovations, introduced the first typing of court records. The Director of the local Chamber, al-Ghurbānī's son, wrote out transcripts for twenty cases he helped settle in 1976–80. Finally, I photographed a large corpus of Shariʿa case records obtained from a number of private individuals and from various contemporary court registers, including two from the special jurisdiction for Endowments cases. For these last, al-Ghurbānī's friend Yaḥyā al-ʿAnsī, the former judge of this special court, sent a note to his former secretary, who soon appeared at my door with the registers in a shawl over his shoulder.

I also frequented the morning sessions of the Ibb Shariʿa courts. Small but sometimes boisterous crowds milled about in the hallways and gathered in the courtrooms. Angry and anxious men and, occasionally, women shouted and jostled and leaned over the judge's table to get his attention. It was by no means always clear to me what was going on. From this type of work one got fleeting views of one or, much less frequently, both parties in what usually amounted to brief installments in wider and more extended processes. Both ordinary matters and formal cases also commonly stalled, or they jumped in and out of venues. From any one vantage point it was rare to see what happened from start to finish. In later years, however, after important procedural reforms and with a new generation installed in the judiciary and using the first specialized court facilities, it would be feasible to follow the far more orderly presentation of cases (see Würth 1995, 2000).

Judge Aḥmad b. Muḥammad al-Ḥaddād, who in 1975 signed himself as "Judge of Ibb," could be seen making his way through the stone-paved streets of old Ibb to and from the Shariʿa court. He wore his scholar's *ʿimāma* turban and used a cane and he wore a long formal coat during the cooler months. At the time, he resided on the alley that descends along the west wall of the Great Mosque, in a rented house just down from the stone archway of the old water-lift tower and not far from where the rear gate to the town had stood. Judge al-Ḥaddād's morning court sessions were held on the other side of the walled town, near the location of the former main gate. He had me sit next to him when I attended his morning court, which he convened with an ordinary table and a few chairs in what would otherwise have been a room in a new-style residential apartment. At his house in the afternoons, as his lounging soldier-retainers chewed qat and monitored the ground floor entrance, disputants and petitioners were received up a flight of stairs, in a semi-public sitting room furnished with rough mats and floor sitting cushions, and with ankle irons hanging from the pegs on the wall. On any given afternoon the judge would come and go, but his primary court secretary, who also was his son-in-law, regularly took an accustomed place at the head of the room to chew qat, copy out documents, and listen to people who came to see the judge. When the secretary worked on one of the long final judgment document rolls the court issued to litigants, coils of paper spilled out of his lap.

One afternoon in the spring of 1980, however, I arrived at his house to a surprise: the old judge had moved out. Like many others before them in recent years, the judge's family relocated from the walled town to a new house in one of the spacious outlying quarters, from which he now would be driven to court in the family Toyota. At his former house I encountered one of his soldier-retainers, a man with a rifle and crossed cartridge belts named Muṣṭafā, who enjoyed the light banter the Judge and I occasionally engaged in. As we talked we went upstairs and in the hallway across from the now empty sitting room I noticed that a door stood ajar to a small, windowless storeroom and that a rubbish pile of documents had been left behind. There were fragments of judgment rolls and various legal instruments, mostly faded copies made on the older type of wet-process photocopier, the remnants of a judicial archive. Among the discarded documents, however, was a damaged Shariʿa court register. Muṣṭafā held the register pages down with his fingers as I photographed the few entries it contained.

Regarding private archives, my colleague Martha Mundy (1979, 174), who also conducted legally-oriented ethnographic research in Yemen, noted the existence of "documentation of ownership and inheritance—stored in the trunks of most every home," and in his superbly synthetic book, *History of Modern Yemen*, anthropological historian Paul Dresch (2000, 65) remarks that the documentary source materials for the country's pre-revolutionary social history generally "remain in private hands." We know from Isaac Hollander's excellent social history of rural Jewish communities that they too kept all manner of personal legal documents (Hollander 2005). The first of my many contacts with private archives came at the home of another scholarly employee at the Endowments, a slight and elegant man named ʿAbd al-Karīm al-Akwaʿ. With landed property inherited from his mother, ʿAbd al-Karīm had led a life of refinement and leisure before the Revolution, although he also engaged in seasonal, harvest-related tax collection work for the provincial government. In those days he would chew qat regularly in the afternoon with other local literati and friends in his formal reception room on the fifth floor atop Dār al-Thajja, one of the massive named houses of old Ibb, where the assembled men looked out across the rooftops as the afternoon light changed on the surrounding mountainsides. By the time I arrived on the scene, what remained of Dār al-Thajja was a mound of rubble in a lot next to the Jalāliyya Mosque.

A couple of years earlier, following a series of loud warning creaks, the great house had collapsed. ʿAbd al-Karīm, who had sold much of his property over the years, now could be found every afternoon in the new house he built around the corner from Dār al-Thajja. There, in his small personal room, ʿAbd al-Karīm sat to chew qat everyday in a skull cap and herringbone vest over a full-length white gown. Hanging from the pegs above him on the wall were his suit jacket, shawl, and sheathed dagger in its embroidered belt, and his scholar's *ʿimāma*.

We had been talking about inheritance. To illustrate what he was saying, ʿAbd al-Karīm opened a simple white cloth bag in which he kept a bundle of rolled or folded documents, his personal archive. My document photo No. 1, in a numbered series that would extend into the thousands, is a contract of sale dated AH 1298 (1881) for fractional parts of certain rooms in an Ibb house purchased by ʿAbd al-Karīm's grandfather for the sum of five silver riyals. Nos. 2–3–4 concern an individual inheritance document, dated AH 1265 (1849), pertaining to a female ancestor, and No. 5 is an endowment instrument, by another al-Akwaʿ, that man's two sisters and their mother, concerning the old house, Dār al-Thajja, dated AH 1278 (1861), with an added note, dated AH 1311 (1893), by a judge prohibiting an attempted sale of the house. I shot the remainder of that initial roll of film at his place of work, the Ibb Endowments office, where I posed a large register on one of the deep windowsills, holding the pages down with the old-style, hand-forged key to my house. In my third roll, photos Nos. 35–42 were of ʿAbd al-Karīm's mother's quite lengthy document of inheritance from her father, dated AH 1328 (1910), listing properties that later became the principal source of his own wealth. I noticed that both of the inheritance documents were covered with small marginal notes next to many of the individual items listed, indicating that these properties had been sold.

Private archival holdings varied in their overall extent according to an individual's wealth or the family's former wealth, but there also was some variation by occupation. Former judges and secretaries, or their descendants, again, retained the still extant registers of Shariʿa court decisions. Any extant originals of such records and of other dispute documentation only could be obtained from the litigant parties themselves, or their descendants. Variation by occupation aside, the standard contents of personal archives consisted of basic property instruments plus any documentation generated by disputes or litigation. Typically, the latter referred to the former, that is, documented conflicts usually concerned property relations that also were the subject of one or more basic property instruments. Both the property instruments and the dispute and litigation records had distinct genres and sub-genres. Among the basic instruments, all of which were privately written, the major types were sale/purchase contracts, which served as the real estate property deeds of the era; building and agrarian leases; marriage contracts and divorce documents; inheritance papers and associated wills and endowment formation instruments, plus a variety of other specialized instruments of agency, transfer, exchange and debt, with an occasional receipt. Conflict documentation subdivided into in-court and out-of-court, and into judgments and settlements, and included a number of sub-genres, such as appeals and arbitration authority texts. Tied in bunches, such documents were placed together in one or more cloth bags to be securely stored in upper floor rooms, sometimes in locked cabinets or in chests. It was only in the years following the Revolution of 1962, with the advent of the nation state and constitutional citizenship, that the characteristic modern types of public documents began to be issued and archived in highland Yemen. These now included the many possible varieties of standardized, state-issued identity papers, licenses, certificates, and attestations, bearing equally newly established serial numbers and residential addresses and often accompanied by photographs. Involving mechanically produced printed forms and photo-reproduced copies, such distinctly modern documents were archived in newly constituted files and dossiers now held by both private individuals and the nation state.

Initial guidance regarding such private archival documents came from the people who provided them to me and consisted mainly of brief identifications. I sent my early rolls of film home to my father in Ohio, who sent me back 8" × 10" glossy prints, but this soon became impractical and I turned to local developing. With prints in hand, I sought the help of various local men. We began by reading short, simple instruments such as sale/purchase contracts and endowment documents. I did not start systematic readings of the lengthy and more complex court cases until years later, and then mostly on my own, and in tandem with my study of Shariʿa doctrine. These early readings in Ibb acquainted me with the basic terms and types of property relations in the former agrarian world, including patterns of formal naming, technical matters involving boundaries, weights, and measures, and the vocabularies of roles and relationships. My co-readers also identified correct and defective passages, pointed out words and clauses they deemed required or superfluous, and expounded generally on what was mentioned and what was not. I also watched how people handled documents, unrolling or unfolding as they read and rotating the paper when the writing turned a corner and continued in the margin upside down or at an angle. I noticed when a reader's attention gravitated at the outset to any added notes placed in the significant spaces left at the top or in the margin of a document. Stylistic markers of the past, such as the rhymed prose that frequently embellishes period instruments, were remarked upon, and certain well-known scripts that lacked signatures were identified. Our discussions touched also on the basic textual security devices. When forgeries were suspected, I asked that the material indications in features such as ink, paper, and handwriting be specified. I found that unpointed, difficult or careless hands often were a challenge for even expert local readers to decipher.

I took technical questions that emerged in my research to local scholars such as al-Ghurbānī, Judge al-Ḥaddād, al-Akwaʿ, and al-ʿAnsī. Al-Ghurbānī cautioned me when I first knew him in 1975 that one could not study the Shariʿa piecemeal as I appeared to be doing, but in 1980, during my second extended stay in Yemen, he led me through the main points of the standard doctrinal chapters on the "Judgeship" and on "Claims." Open in his lap as he instructed me was volume four of an authoritative commentary on the classic Zaydi school law book he had studied in his youth (in his northern plateau hometown of Yarīm), a late fourteenth-century work by Ibn al-Murtaḍā known as *The Book of Flowers*. Later, I would commence studying this doctrine on my own, reading the *Flowers* mainly through the last of some thirty commentaries, *The Gilded Crown*, which was written for print publication in the 1930s and 1940s, by Aḥmad b. Qāsim al-ʿAnsī (d. 1970). This was the same four-volume work that Martha Mundy had studied with a scholar in Wādī Ḍahr and that had formed part of the doctrinal basis for her work on inheritance law (Mundy 1979, cf. 1988) and for her important ethnographic monograph, *Domestic Government* (Mundy 1995).

By the 1990s, following the publication of my book, *The Calligraphic State* (Berkeley 1993), which is on the period spanning the late Ottoman to the Republic eras, my interests had narrowed and also intensified. My new focus was on the Shariʿa system, the doctrinal and litigation practices of the venerable Islamic state of twentieth-century Yemen. My early work of sitting with judges and secretaries to go through court records, collecting copies of case documentation, and sitting in the several types of venues had amounted to essential preliminary training in the local legal culture and its institutional landscape. From the perspective of this new project, such work represented part of the ethnographic basis for cautious retrospection. Pre- and post-revolution, there were important continuities of legal institutions as well as of many practitioners, including jurists such as Judge al-Ḥaddād. Together with the Shariʿa courts, which had had similar levels and jurisdictions, institutions such as the petition and the fatwa crossed over into the new era of the republic. But the discontinuities also were significant: Shariʿa principles were modified and repositioned in legislation, institutions were newly framed in a nation state polity, subjects became citizens.

The new project required further research and I returned to Yemen three times in the 1990s to look for additional judicial archives concerning the mid-century period. Experience told me that the most likely places to find such records would be at the homes of former judges and their secretaries, but I also inquired at the recently erected, modern-style Ibb

Province courthouse, the first such local building to be constructed as a dedicated judicial facility. An imposing curved bench in the main courtroom of the new structure now accommodated the panel of judges of the Ibb appeal court—the addition of a provincial level of appeals was one of the major innovations of the republican legal system. At the court complex I found a number of old acquaintances, such as Judge al-Ḥaddād's former retainer, Muṣṭafā, and also Muḥammad al-Ṣabāḥī, a proverb collector and jokester, who still worked as a court secretary. I also met Judge Muḥammad al-Wushalī, who had been appointed to a lower jurisdiction in 1980 and whom I remembered as the first Ibb judge to come to court carrying a briefcase. The modern court building now had a designated room for the judicial *arshif* (after the French), which was part of a much broader institutional initiative of those years that included the founding of the first national archive in the capital city. As I expected, the Ibb court had no case records from before 1962, but in a helpful gesture, using their now standard in-house technology, a photocopy was made for me of a current case that had an attached documentary record extending back before the Revolution.

Late one afternoon in the fall of 1995, I went to the residence of Judge Muḥammad b. Ḥasan al-Iryānī, whom I had known in the 1970s as the Judge of the 3rd Shariʿa Court and, later, as the Assistant in Judge al-Ḥaddād's 2nd Court. I now sought him out, however, as the son of one of the principal Ibb judges from the 1950s (on the father, see Messick 2006). I showed him my recently published book and described my new project. When asked about the whereabouts of his father's pre-revolutionary court records, he showed me to a shelf of registers in an adjoining storage area. With these registers were others that had been passed along to his father after the death of a colleague, the former Judge of Ibb Province, Ismāʿīl ʿAbd al-Raḥmān al-Manṣūr (Messick 2006). Seeing these carefully archived volumes caused me to recall the different fate of the damaged register of another prior Ibb judge that I had photographed years before at Judge al-Ḥaddād's house. Judge al-Iryānī permitted me to remove four registers of completed cases, two each for his father and for Judge al-Manṣūr, to be photocopied at a local studio.

On the same trip I also met an important pre-revolutionary judge, Muḥammad b. Yaḥyā Ibn al-Muṭahhar, who lived an hour to the south in Taʿizz, the major old city which had served as the capital of Imam Aḥmad during the 1950s. I contacted him through his son, a Sanʿaʾ University official who held a Ph.D. from the University of Michigan, where I then taught. Initially, Ibn al-Muṭahhar met me in Sanʿaʾ where he represented Taʿizz in the National Consultative Assembly. Ibn al-Muṭahhar also is the author of a two-volume comparative work on the modern, Shariʿa-derived law of "personal status" (Ibn al-Muṭahhar 1985, 1989). Yemeni historian Aḥmad Zabāra (see below) describes this book as "modern in style" and as "the first of its type by a Yemeni scholar." Ibn al-Muṭahhar characterized his own book to me just as al-Ghurbānī once had his own unpublished work on *ḥadīth*: as fundamentally new in that it was intended to be read and studied directly, "without a teacher." At our first meeting, Ibn al-Muṭahhar responded to questions I had about some of the pre-revolutionary court cases I had started to work on.

A few weeks later he received me at his home in Taʿizz. In the rear of his residential compound, with windows facing on the flower beds of an interior garden with crossing tiled pathways, stood the long, ground-floor sitting room Ibn al-Muṭahhar referred to as his "court" (*maḥkama*). His former "court" is silent now, but during my stay he invited some of his old cronies to chew qat, and, for my benefit, started the afternoon as in former times, with singing and a round of jokes. In the 1950s, Ibn al-Muṭahhar had worked as a quasi-independent judge who received cases transferred from the former ruler's circle or from one of the provincial governors. A small storeroom next to his garden courtroom housed his court registers, which contained the texts of his judicial acts and rulings, as recorded by his secretary. In addition to other cases, I read and photocopied some Ibb-area matters he had handled, including a case brought against the local Endowments Office and another, from the mountains to the east of town, over landed property. Cases concerning property often required travel to the districts in question to see the disputed land and to hear testimony, and in some of his case records Ibn al-Muṭahhar drew diagrams of the boundaries of contested terraces. In the records of his homicide convictions, he later added notes at the bottom to the effect that an execution subsequently had been ordered by the ruler and carried out. During my stay with him in Taʿizz, Ibn al-Muṭahhar also placed me in touch with the son of a secretary of the former high judicial review organ, the Shariʿa Panel, who brought over some of that institution's registers to show me.

Since I could not personally know most of the imamic-era judges whose judgments I was reading, an essential collateral source was the biographical dictionary, notably the posthumous *The Entertainment of the Gaze*, by Muḥammad Zabāra, published in 1979, on prominent Yemenis of the 14th hijri century. I went to see the author's son, Aḥmad b. Muḥammad, in search of supporting information on Ibb judges. When I met him at his house in Sanʿaʾ, Aḥmad Zabāra was the Mufti of the Republic, but in the 1950s he had served in Taʿizz as the Presiding Judge of the Shariʿa Panel, the final appellate authority before the Imam himself. After managing to survive the turbulent early years of the Revolution, when a number of men with his descendant of the Prophet identity and connection to the old regime were executed or exiled, he was named to the newly created post of Mufti of the Republic. Although his position had little more than a symbolic place in the new legal order of the nation state, Zabāra nevertheless carried out the occasional work of writing ordinary fatwas from his old city residence (Messick 1996). Small children carried written queries up from the street to his sitting room and his fatwa-answers later were retrieved from where he had them placed, in a slot in the stonework outside his front door. With my friend al-Ghurbānī, Zabāra also was one of three men who prepared answers for the "Fatwa Show" on the national radio broadcast service. About ninety years of age, tall, stout and vigorous at the time I knew him, Zabāra was the son of one of Yemen's most distinguished modern historians. After the Revolution, the Mufti also taught jurisprudence at the new College of Shariʿa and Law at Sanʿaʾ University, which had opened in 1965. He later presented me with the small book he wrote for use in this teaching—a photocopy of an unpublished manuscript written out in a notebook in his exceptionally clear handwriting.

After I asked him about several specific judges posted to Ibb in the imamic period, he rose from his accustomed corner seat next to the glass-windowed book cabinets in his spacious sitting room and, crossing the carpeted floor in stocking feet, he went out to the hallway and climbed the stone stairs to an upper floor. When he came back downstairs he was carrying some loose handwritten pages of biographical text on the individuals in question. He said they were from his father's last book, *The Entertainment of the Gaze*. I was confused: I knew his father's book as a printed volume which I had consulted from the Michigan library collection. Later, when I bought my own copy from the Center for Yemeni Studies, in Sanʿaʾ, I found that my purchased copy had been crudely censored. Entries on leading figures in the pre-revolutionary state had been physically cut out. The Mufti had been enraged at this censorship of his father's book, and his response was remarkable: he painstakingly returned the book from print to manuscript form, writing it out in his lucid script. Only a man of his generation and facility with the pen could have contemplated such an act. In the process, however, he had augmented the book with many additional biographies. It was the pages of this much expanded, now dual-authored, father-and-son work that he had brought down to provide answers to my questions about men in Ibb judgeships. Later, he showed me the complete work, consisting of four thick handwritten volumes. Although the manuscript retained the father's title, *The Entertainment of the Gaze*, its new title page stated that it was "written in the script of the author's son." He permitted me to take these four volumes of enhanced twentieth-century biographical history to be photocopied.

II

Some important ethnographic lessons for my historical inquiry emerged from chance encounters made possible by friendships and associations developed over many months of residence in Ibb, and it is to examples of these that I now turn. These materials both enable a further portrayal of the contemporary Shariʿa court of the republican era and also on occasion some specific observations about an archival anthropology focused on mid-century Shariʿa court records.

* * *

I went to visit my friend Hajj Aḥmad at his house in Ibb one day in July 1975, and happened upon a gathering of men in what at first appeared to be an ordinary afternoon qat-chew. The Hajj, who was literate but by no means a scholar, had started out as a local trader and then spent a lengthy period living as a migrant in Brooklyn where he worked in basic jobs in restaurants, a hospital, and a synagogue before serving as the "super" of an apartment building. Two passport photos, of a turbaned young man departing Aden in the 1950s and of a returning U.S. citizen in a dark suit, tie, and combed hair, offer bracketing images of this experience. With remittances sent back over the years, the Hajj had built a large stone house surrounded by a walled garden in one of the new quarters of Ibb. In the same years his eldest son, who in 1975 lived with his own family on the lower floor of the same house, completed a Sociology degree in Czechoslovakia.

The Hajj directed me to a place at the head of his sitting room. Furnished with a floor-level sitting ensemble of covered cushions and matching back and arm rests, the room had large recessed windows set nearly at floor-level and topped, as was the style, with decorative lunettes of colored glass in stucco tracery. The windows looked east and south, towards a terraced mountainside in the near-ground and across a cultivated valley to a blue range in the distance.

Immediately it became clear that there was more going on than the casual socializing of friends. From his place on one side of the room, Hajj Aḥmad slid a stack of money across the narrow rug to the young man sitting across from him. He said, "That's 1,500 riyals, count it." The young man had just finished counting and was putting the money down when a shuffling in the hallway outside the door to the room signaled an arrival. The young woman was not visible to any of the men in the room, except for one, a man who stood up and went to stand just inside the open door. He spoke to her so that all could hear. There was a pause, and the man put his hand to his throat, indicating she was unable to speak. But then she was heard to blurt out, "no, no, no," a delayed response to three questions he had posed to her. The man at the door then turned to the young man sitting in the room, expecting a response from him. The young man said, "That ends it." The man looked back at the woman in the hall and said, "Good-bye"; he then returned and sat down. A series of documents then was prepared and passed around to be read. After a couple of phrases were discussed the documents were signed and two were handed to the young man to keep. He placed them alongside the money he had received. When the documents were completed, the older man sitting across from the young man, who turned out to be the young woman's father, got up and left. The others stayed and we talked about other things until the gathering broke up. As I left, Hajj Aḥmad said I had been present at a settlement for a divorce.

Although I recognized the local man who went to the door, except for Hajj Aḥmad I did not know the other men present, and, after this fleeting encounter, never saw them again. I learned from the Hajj the next day that the marriage had involved male-line first cousins, so that the young woman's father was also the young man's paternal uncle. In this particular type of divorce instigated by the wife, the husband must agree to it and she has to compensate him. This compensation is understood to be for monies spent by the husband's side at the outset of the marriage, notably the significant sum paid outside the frame of the marriage contract (and thus distinct from the small sum that must be mentioned in the contract, the payment of which commonly was postponed). Beyond the marriage-money questions, there was another issue. Bad behavior by the husband (which the Hajj detailed to me) had caused his wife to want to end the marriage. To start this process she fled to her father's house, as wives with marital problems often did. Further, the husband also had attacked the older man who was both his uncle and father-in-law, who then went to have his wounds evaluated (perhaps at the courts, or at the Mufti's). The documents I had seen prepared, by the maternal uncle of the young woman, were: (1) a receipt for the 1,500 paid in cash, (2) a promissory note for an additional payment due in six months, the total representing partial compensation to the husband's side for the larger marriage payment (which had amounted to 3,500 riyals), and (3) a document canceling the wife's father's right to the amount stipulated in his injury evaluation (which had been set at 1,500 riyals). A fourth document, the divorce instrument itself, which I did not see, was to be written the following morning by the man who had gone to the door to pose the questions. Unlike the maternal uncle, this man was acting as a professional "writer," a *kātib*, or private notary (there was no state licensing), who earned a fee for this work. On the basis of having heard the binding statements from the wife and the husband, he would write the appropriate divorce document. Matching the wife's spoken responses would be clauses to the effect that she gave up three things: her rights to the man, to support money, and to the postponed payment stipulated in the marriage contract.

Part of the environment of any Shariʿa court is the out-of-court settlement. In Ibb, a difficult to track category of such settlements occurred privately, behind closed doors. As in this instance, out-of-court settings did not necessarily mean terms beyond the Shariʿa. Hajj Aḥmad had acted as an unpaid, friendly intermediary who virtuously sought to bring the two sides together. In the informal venue of his personal sitting room these parties reached a resolution to a compound conflict that would have been more drawn out and expensive to conclude at the Shariʿa court, and that also would have exposed both sides to harmful insults and damages to their reputations. In principle, everyone understood and valued the efficiency, lower costs, and privacy associated with such out-of-court settlements, but fighting matters out in court was by no means always avoided. In this instance, according to Hajj Aḥmad, the young man's side originally had gone to the court. He remarked that it was shameful for people of "families" to litigate in cases involving women. Most of an intermediary's efforts involved getting the sides to agree separately and in principle to settlement terms in advance of actually confronting one another and confirming the agreement, at which point little had to be said. I saw other such sessions where snags occurred. A flurry of notes would pass around the room and pairs of men would step out of the room to talk in the hall. Once disputing parties permitted an intermediary to become involved, his presence could add a certain level of guarantee to the process. Hajj Aḥmad's role continued inside the sitting room itself where he physically took money from one side and passed it across the rug to the other.

Compound matters were broken down into their component parts. Frequently this led to the production of multiple documents and sometimes involved legal stratagems. Multiple documentation and stratagems also figured in some uncontested undertakings. A land sale contract, for example, could be kept "clean," or unburdened, by the existence of a second document that specified the terms of an underpinning loan from the seller for part of the purchase price. From an archival perspective, the practice of breaking matters down into multiple documents meant that the relevant dimensions were treated separately, as if the several discrete acts had happened in isolation. Here, although the overall settlement had been predicated, in part, on the resolution of another issue, the attack and injury, the final divorce document would make no mention of it. Further, while this document would mention the wife's giving up her rights to any support payments and to the smaller marriage sum contracted for but postponed, following standard practice in the genre, it would not mention the main monetary compensation paid by the wife's side, although this sum was covered by a simple receipt.

What would the archival trace of such a session be? If the matter (or some part of it, typically an action seeking the "return" of the wife, if she had fled to her natal family) had been presented to the judge by the young man's side in the form of a petition, there would be no official record. Judges did not keep originals, copies or any other records of petitions. If a note in reply had been written by the judge on the returned petition paper, however, it might have been retained by the petitioner. If a formal court claim had been entered, the text of this would appear in a type of court register devoted to opening claims and to the minutes of any ensuing litigation. Many such entered claims were not followed up with litigation and instead were abandoned for various reasons, as in this instance. There would be no record of such a matter in another type of register for recording finished cases since these records concerned litigation that had been carried though to a judges' ruling (or to a judicial settlement). With the passage of time, of course, such active court registers became the enduring judicial archive.

How would the resulting documents be archived? Important legal instruments could be registered in court. For a small fee, copies of such documents could be entered in a third type of court register specially earmarked for "Transactions," but this mainly applied, although not as a requirement, to significant land transfer documents. Court recording of copies was optional and it was relatively rare to find records of marriage contracts or, especially, divorce instruments. In republican Yemen, other than at the Shariʿa courts, there were no public registries or archives for these or any other types of written legal acts, although there were plans to institute them. As with the originals of all legal instruments, from marriage to land sale contracts, settlement documents were held privately in personal collections. In this instance, the documents involved—the work of both a non-professional and a professional writer—would be divided into at least two separate holdings. The promissory note and the wound award cancellation would be retained by the young man's side while the receipt for the main payment and the divorce instrument would go to the young woman's side (perhaps with a copy of the latter for the other side). These two private caches also would be the repositories for the prior documentation, including the original marriage contract and the wound evaluation. A subsequent effort to reconstruct what had transpired at such an event on the basis of these written sources would depend on locating the relevant private archives and bringing the dispersed texts together.

* * *

Just inside the old town wall, in a south-side quarter where many of Ibb's Jewish families once lived, Hajj Aḥmad grew up and, a couple of decades later, I twice resided, some neighbors fell into conflict. The mostly modest stone houses in the neighborhood in question were attached to each other along both sides of an alley narrow enough for a cat to jump across. I will narrate from an after-the-fact account I heard upon my return to Yemen in 1980 from Muḥammad, a young man on one side in the matter, and from a series of documents he saved.

At the coming of the Revolution, Muḥammad's family had been poor. His father had intermittent work in the endowments-run water distribution system as a "conductor of the water," responsible for repairs to the channels that brought water from sources on the mountainside. The water finally crossed an arched aqueduct and entered the town wall near the rear gate, at which point channels branched to serve the town bath, two sets of mosques, and several public outlets. His mother used to go out to terraces outside the walls to gather grass for fodder, sorghum stalks for fuel, and harvest leavings for food. Their house had a small upstairs room in which burlap sacks served as the floor furnishing. Nobody in the family had shoes. Muḥammad's education consisted of some time spent as a child learning the Qurʾan and his handwriting remained weak. On the night of September 26, 1962, hearing the tumult in the streets, he leaned out the window and said, "What's going on?" The word from the alley below was, "It's the Revolution." Muḥammad remembers that he replied, "What's a 'revolution'?"

A decade later, father and son had learned the pipefitting trade, acquired a large professional wrench and, with the construction of the new water system, found more regular work and began to prosper a bit. In the summer of 1977, Muḥammad wanted to build a new room atop their house, but his father predicted there would be trouble. Two older women, half-sisters from the same mother who lived in the attached house up the alley, said the proposed addition would block air and light to the windows of their existing rooms. Arwā, who always appeared in the alley with her headcloth covering her bad eye, went everyday to assist the women of a wealthy family in a new quarter, and Bilqīs, a tall old woman with a beautiful smile, cooked for weddings and other occasions. "The Shariʿa says that if you leave 30 centimeters between you and your neighbor it is okay to build," Muḥammad explained. The expression was that one had to allow room enough "for a bird to pass."

Building stone was delivered in an open space at the end of the alley at the base of a section of the old town wall and the initial dressing work began. Soon, however, a son of one of the women who served in the local military detachment went to his commanding officer and got him to dispatch soldiers to stop the construction. On another occasion there was fighting in the alley between Muḥammad and a brother from the other side and Muḥammad's mother scuffled with Arwā. Muḥammad was bested but he managed to wrest the man's dagger away and went with it the next day to the police to lodge a complaint. But the other side already had entered a complaint and also had deposited a "guarantee" (*ʿaddal*) to engage a settlement. "We didn't have anything to give for a guarantee—no dagger, watch or money—so a jailing order was written out for me and my father." A prominent journalist from Ibb who happened to be present intervened, taking the documents in his hand and promising to arrange things. When the construction later continued, the sisters threw rocks at the workers and Muḥammad hired guards to protect them. By the end of 1978, after running out of money for a time and then getting a burst of new work, the room finally was finished. Muḥammad estimated the total cost at about 35,000 riyals, 13,000 for the construction itself and 22,000 for "Shariʿa," that is, for the expenses of the legal process, including both proper fees and bribes, the latter in many installments. "It is dirty stuff," he said, "you get up at night with such troubles." With better luck, or with such social resources as the concerned intervention of someone like Hajj Aḥmad, the matter might have ended quickly. "We could have settled for 5,000," Muḥammad ruefully admitted.

Monies paid are not mentioned in the associated documents, a fact that must temper some conclusions in reading an historical archive. From the perspective of these written texts there were several key moments in the conflict. According to a document dated July 17, 1977, which identifies Muḥammad's father as the "claimant," a building expert and another respected man, who were chosen by the two sides, were dispatched to the building site by a mediator. These men found that Muḥammad's father should leave a "Shariʿa space" on his rooftop and then should be permitted to "build above his property." The legal instrument Muḥammad showed me embodying this finding was signed by the two men and countersigned by the mediator, and it states that an equivalent document is "in the hand of the other party." A second document, dated three days later and restating this result, was addressed by the mediator to Judge al-Ḥaddād. It reports that Muḥammad's father "indicated that he will leave a space for light measuring approximately three cubits between what he will build above his property and the property of the two aforementioned free women on the south side of their house." It also states that even though he had the right to build a larger structure, "he did not want that now out of respect for the neighbors." According to a note placed at the top of this original document by the court secretary, a copy was "entered in the register of the Subdistrict Court of Ibb, on page 22, entry number 73, by Secretary Muḥammad al-Ṣabāḥī."

In the meantime, the other side had gone directly to court where they obtained the opposite outcome. This is contained in a third document, dated July 18, 1977. A man from the other side, said to be representing "his two sisters," is identified as the "claimant." This document is written and signed by the First Secretary of the Ibb Court, a man named Ishām, who had been appointed to look into the matter by the Assistant to the "Judge of Ibb." First Secretary Ishām found that if Muḥammad's father were to build, "it will be the cause of darkness [cast] upon the house of the two free women, this by the closing of the windows." He concludes, "Therefore, it is necessary to forbid him to build." He also cites the old legal maxim on the avoidance of harm: "No damage and no mutual infliction of damage." In two notes placed at the top of this document, the finding "below" is countersigned by the Assistant "on behalf of the Judge of Ibb" and court secretary Muḥammad al-Ṣabāḥī writes that the document itself was entered in the "Transactions" register of the Subdistrict Court of Ibb, on page 21, number 69—one page and a few entry numbers earlier than the entry for the document written to the judge by the mediator. Muḥammad and his father were provided a copy of the text.

This finding against them provoked Muḥammad's side, in the same month of Shaʿban [July–August 1977], to seek a countering fourth document, for which Muḥammad said they paid a professional legal expert a drafting fee of 1,000 riyals. Although he did not write it, Muḥammad's father's name appears at the bottom as the "presenter" and the document is described as "my appeal against what was written by the First Secretary. . . ." Although it is not an appeal in any formal sense, the document is addressed to the Presiding Judge of what had been the 1st Ibb Court and was now the Provincial Appeal Court, rather than to Judge al-Ḥaddād. It states that First Secretary Ishām's writing "runs counter to the order of the Shariʿa in numerous respects." Procedural irregularities are mentioned: that in the session before the Assistant to Judge al-Ḥaddād, an explicit claim should have been made and a response from Muḥammad's father heard; that a valid agency document should have been shown by "h[im] who said he was the representative for them" [viz., the two women]; and, reiterating and extending the first point, that "when the document of the First Secretary was received by the mentioned Assistant to the Judge, it was required [of him] that he summon me together with this claimant and open the register of the Shariʿa court and carry out the Shariʿa of God Almighty." Such a proceeding would include "each one presenting evidence and showing what is in his hand, the claimant showing the document of Ishām [the First Secretary] and me showing the document of the respected men and building experts." The writer concludes with a mini-procedural lesson: ideally, he states, this process should end with "the requirement of him who has further evidence [to present it] and, if the interchange between the two parties has ended, the conveyance of the minutes for signature [by the parties], and the review of them by the Assistant to the Judge for a ruling as to what is required in the Shariʿa."

Substantively, Muḥammad's father's "appeal" argues that the First Secretary disregarded the prior finding, embodied in the document "I showed to him." It is asserted that the First Secretary violated "Shariʿa principles" out of "favoritism," a standard assertion made against members of the judiciary, often as a euphemism for corruption. In this instance Muḥammad said that the two sisters went to the court "with tears and money." The appeal ends by stating that the presenter, Muḥammad's father, attaches a copy of the prior "ruling" of the experts and also states that he is prepared to have the Presiding Judge come to see the building site, or for him to form a committee of his choice to look into the matter together with knowledgeable building experts.

Some time elapsed before the Presiding Judge responded. His response took the form of a note, dated October 20, 1977, which joined the two earlier notes atop the finding by the First Secretary. The Presiding Judge's note reads, "There should be from the learned father, the Judge of Ibb [i.e., al-Ḥaddād], God's greetings to you, a decision as to what is required according to the Shariʿa, by a Shariʿa judgment." Muḥammad said that the Presiding Judge had looked at the accumulated documents, found them lacking, and ordered Judge al-Ḥaddād to give a ruling. He also said that soon thereafter Judge al-Ḥaddād, who lived just a couple of quarters away, came to the alley with his soldier-retainers and some building experts.

On 12 Dhu l-Qaʿda 1397 [October 25, 1977], a fifth document was created. This described a truncated court proceeding. Now the claimant is Arwā, representing herself and also her brother and Bilqīs, who is identified as the daughter of a different father. Their claim is that the defendant, Muḥammad's father, intended to cause "damage" in his construction project by the "closing" of their windows. She mentions that court officials [i.e., the First Secretary] had found that this damage would occur and she asks that the construction be halted. The formal response from Muḥammad's father follows. He argues that the construction he intends could not possibly cause them damage and he specifies that he will leave four cubits for light. Without any regular presentation of evidence, or any other litigation activity, the document abruptly turns to an order "from us," that is, from Judge al-Ḥaddād, to a building expert. That expert's report, dated October 24, then is quoted. This third and last expert's finding is that Muḥammad's father had left a proper "space," that there was no "damage" caused the claimants, and that they had no right to forbid him to build. Here the formal process abruptly ends, without a ruling. Instead, according to the next line, which is in the different script of one of the public petition writers, a settlement had resulted: "This, and, finally, satisfaction and mutual consent occurred concerning what was mentioned." Below this line is a countersigning of the unspecified settlement in the script and signature, and under this, the official court seal of Aḥmad Muḥammad al-Ḥaddād, 'Judge of Ibb,' with the date, November 3, 1977.

The matter did not end there. The last document in the series is a petition addressed to the Governor of the Province. It is written in the fluid script of a public writer on behalf of Muḥammad's father, whose name appears below as the "presenter." The complaint is that the two women, Arwā and Bilqīs, continue to attack the workers to keep them from building, this without any right and after a resolution in court. The petition asks for an order from the Governor to the Director of the Provincial Police to "restrain them and stop them, and to send a soldier to guard the work." The Ibb Governor's note in reply was placed in the upper left hand corner of the petition paper: "In the Name of God. [To] The Brother, Director of the Provincial Police, Greetings of God. For a reading of the petition, and if you are assured of its validity, undertake the necessary, and thank you. Governor of Ibb Province [signature], November 6, 1977." With this note the documentation ends. About a year later the construction would be completed.

* * *

When legal documentation is brought into such an account, the Shariʿa court comes more fully into view, but not, in this instance, as a unitary institution. Engagements occurred with different levels of judges and several court secretaries and there were various delegations, extensions, and assumptions of authority. Beyond the court, but interacting with it, were other legal specialists, including mediators, experts, respected men, legal advisors, and public writers. In the imamic-period court records I have read, all of which concern completed cases, neither such interactions among local courts and their personnel nor movements in and out of court figure prominently. The period cases instead commence with formal claims and responses, continue with extensive evidence presentation and litigation argumentation, and conclude with judgments by individual judges. In each case a single Shariʿa court had emerged as the unitary frame for the proceedings. The pasts of such cases had been culled, leaving only passing references to prior stages or strategies.

Privately-held documents provide the main vantage point for this neighborhood conflict. Whatever their variety in terms of authors, recipients and genres (expert finding, mediator's memo, "appeal," petition, settlement document, etc.), in a private archive all the relevant paperwork concerning a given matter was held together and could be consulted together. Two of the documents in Muḥammad's cache again illustrate the use of such writings as settlement tools. Many such arrangements did not hold, however, and when parallel strategies were pursued, each produced its own paper trail. Over time, even a simple matter could accumulate a considerable mass of documentation. What later might be seen as documentary dead ends were carefully archived by the parties, at least in the short-term. As opposed to the records of completed cases kept in "Judgments" registers, for histories of the false-starts and fragments of unsettled matters that had in some manner reached the courts but were not finally resolved there, one had to turn to the two other types of court registers, those for entries of "Claims" (and later litigation minutes) and those for copies of "Transactions."

What of the little notes added to some of the documents? As is demonstrated by this small corpus, such notes jotted atop some of the documents could be of various types (genres): countersignatures and affirmations; annotations that refer to a copy being placed in a court register; and a variety of responses, including orders and transfers. Consisting of dated installments in the judicial chronos, and including a signature or at least an identifiable hand, notes resulted from several types of authoritative later readings of the texts appearing below. These apparently modest additions above main texts amount to acts in their own right and, as such, represent important links in documentary chains. In recognition of their significance, copies placed in court registers routinely quoted any notes found on original documents. But further notes also could be added to originals at later dates. As the third note to be placed above the main text, the line from the Presiding Judge was written after a copy of the document had been entered into the court register so that his important order to Judge al-Ḥaddād appears only on the privately-held original version.

If, in narrating, I had simply stated that the Presiding Judge of the higher court ordered Judge al-Ḥaddād to give a ruling, an enactment of judicial hierarchy and a turning point in the conflict would be accounted for but a key feature of the local institutional specificity would be lost. In this particular bureaucratic regime, as in that before the Revolution, such concise notes were the means of formal communication among local judges and between them and other officials. No parallel institution of internal memoranda assured the communication of orders within the court system or between the courts and other offices. The necessary physical transfers relied entirely on the initiative of the parties themselves who, outside of state channels (which did not exist for such purposes), effected the deliveries to the authorities in question.

BIBLIOGRAPHY

al-ʿAnsī, Aḥmad b. Qāsim, *al-Tāj al-mudhhab li-aḥkām al-madhhab* (The Gilded Crown), 4 vols. (Sanʿaʾ: Dār al-Ḥikma al-Yamaniyya, 1993).

Dresch, Paul, *A History of Modern Yemen* (Cambridge: Cambridge University Press, 2000).

Hollander, Isaac, *Jews and Muslims in Lower Yemen. A Study in Protection and Restraint, 1918–1949* (Leiden: Brill, 2005).

Ibn al-Muṭahhar, Muḥammad b. Yaḥyā, *Aḥkām al-aḥwāl al-shakhṣiyya min fiqh al sharīʿa al-islāmiyya* (Cairo: Dār al-Kutub al-Islāmiyya, 1985, [2]1989).

Messick, Brinkley, "Prosecution in Yemen: The Introduction of the Niyāba," *International Journal of Middle East Studies* 15 (1983), 507–18.

——, *The Calligraphic State. Textual Domination and History in a Muslim Society* (Berkeley: University of California Press, 1993).

——, "Textual Properties: Writing and Wealth in a Shariʿa Case," *Anthropological Quarterly* 68/3 (1995), 157–70.

——, "Media Muftis: Radio Fatwas in Yemen," in M. K. Masud, B. Messick, and D. S. Powers, *Islamic Legal Interpretation: Muftis and their Fatwas* (Cambridge, Mass.: Harvard University Press, 1996), 310–20.

——, "L'Écriture en proces: Les recits d'un meurtre devant un tribunal *sharʿī*," *Droit et société* 39 (1998), 237–56.

——, "Indexing the Self: Wording and Intentionality in Legal Acts," *Islamic Law and Society* 8/2 (2001), 151–78.

——, "Evidence: From Memory to Archive," *Islamic Law and Society* 9/2 (2002), 1–40.
——, "Commercial Litigation in a Shariʿa Court," In *Dispensing Justice in Islam. Qadis and Their Judgments*, ed. M. K. Masud, R. Peters, and D. S. Powers (Leiden: Brill, 2005), 195–218.
——, "Provincial Judges: The Shariʿa Judiciary of Mid-Twentieth-Century Yemen," in *Law, Custom, and Statute in the Muslim World*, ed. Ron Shaham (Leiden: Brill, 2006), 149–71.
——, "Interpreting Tears: A Marriage Case from Imamic Yemen," *The Islamic Marriage Contract. Case Studies in Islamic Family Law* (Cambridge, Mass.: forthcoming 2008).
Mundy, Martha, "Women's Inheritance of Land in Highland Yemen," *Arabian Studies* 5 (1979), 161–187.
——, "The Family, Inheritance, and Islam: A Re-Examination of the Sociology of Farāʾid Law," in *Islamic Law: Social and Historical Contexts*, ed. Aziz al-Azmeh (London: Routledge, 1988), 1–123.
——, *Domestic Government: Kinship, Community and Polity in North Yemen* (London: I. B. Tauris, 1995).
Würth, Anna, "A Sanaa Court: The Family and the Ability to Negotiate," *Islamic Law and Society* 2/3 (1995), 320–40.
——, *Aš-Šarīʿa fī Bāb al-Yaman. Recht, Richter und Rechtspraxis an der familienrechtlichen Kammer des Gerichts Süd-Sanaa (Republik Jemen) 1983–1995* (Berlin: Duncker & Humblot, 2000).
Zabāra, Muḥammad, *Nuzhat al-naẓar fī rijāl al-qarn al-rābiʿ ʿashar* (The Entertainment of the Gaze) (Sanʿaʾ: al-Markaz, 1979).
—— (and Aḥmad b. Muḥammad Zabāra), *Nuzhat al-naẓar*, 4 vols. (handwritten).

11

CONSTITUTIONS FOR THE TWENTY-FIRST CENTURY
Emerging Patterns—The EU, Iraq, Afghanistan...[1]

Chibli Mallat

I. Introduction: Constitutionalism's International Drive

Among the furthest encompassing contemporary reflections on law stand the works of Paul Kahn. In a contribution to a New England seminar on law and violence in 2003, he had this to say about the EU:

> The political project of the EU, for example, is about displacing a sacrificial politics with a set of bureaucratic arrangements for the administration of markets and social-welfare. If the romantic element in Western politics has been in its attachment to sacrifice of the body, the EU project is just the opposite: it is politics as management of the well-being of the body. The bureaucrat in Brussels is the very opposite of the romantic politician. The longing to join the EU among the countries of Eastern Europe is not just about economics, but also about depoliticalization, i.e., about an emerging perception of sacrificial politics as a form of pathology. Indeed, the entire effort of the international human rights movement is rooted in this vision of well-being. No one, in this view, should die or suffer for politics.[2]

There are several strands in the Kahnian view that will appear elusive to those who have not followed his fertile search for the triangle love-law-religion, and the meanings relevant to the triangle for such issues as war and international relations, the body, or human rights. In a vision that tends to be overall bleak, the silver lining is a peculiar form of legal optimism, which is of significance to anyone interested in reform despite the less humane aspects of human beings.[3]

Here we need to bifurcate our train of thought. One bifurcation strand regards the EU and constitution-making, the other is Kantian, and regards constitutions and war.

Strong moments in constitution-making often result from traumas brought about by sacrificial politics, among which the archetype is Abraham's offer to sacrifice his son for God in order to save his people, religion, and nation. The case of the EU, which is universally considered as a triumph of Europe over its most tragic traumas in the twentieth century—two World Wars and a Cold War—is a living, acknowledged example, Afghanistan and Iraq another. Nothing defines trauma for Afghanis and Iraqis more than war, internal and international, for over a quarter of a century, and their most lasting response, if war is to be transcended, will be a working constitution. Here stands the contribution of Kahn at its best: twenty-first-century constitution-making conceived as a response to the failures of the twentieth century, and a new prism—the love-religion-law triangle—to go beyond comparing the trite and the insignificant, or the incomparable, or the hard to compare.

This chapter follows a similar quest. Rather than looking at these three perforce unique constitutions simply through black-letter law, I shall try to look beyond the arrangements of the respective constitutional texts for the emerging patterns of constitution-making.

Before I begin, a brief word off the Kantian bifurcation onto a path that is not totally unrelated to the argument of this chapter—that there is a core common thematic constitutional horizon across the planet. This aspect of the journey is the subject of a separate enquiry. As Kahn also says, "After Einstein, we are all Kantians,"[4] and no person has written a more meaningful treatise on war, constitutional treatises, and international law than Immanuel Kant. On the occasion of the bicentenary of Kant's death, the Goethe Institut was particularly inspired in its illustration of the 2004 *Zeitgeist* with a poster that puts, on the one side, the 300+ wars that have befallen mankind since 1804, on the other the text of his *Treatise for a Perpetual Peace*.[5] As said, this dimension belongs to a separate work, in progress, on Kant's *TPP*, but it cannot be totally shorn from our present reflection, so steeped in war are these societies working out their constitutional texts, and so menacing to both domestic and international peace if they fail their promise. Should Iraq, Afghanistan, and the EU continue to roll their constitutions back, much of the promise of peace will fall by the wayside.

In Europe, the new constitutional order was designed by Jean Monnet to prevent a repeat of World Wars I and II, both classic wars. A collapse of the Afghani and Iraqi theatres of violence into the so-called "war on terrorism", a sui generis development increasingly dubbed as the third or fourth world war, will have incalculable consequences for the peoples of Iraq and Afghanistan, but also for the rest of the planet.[6]

So while that part of the Kantian bifurcation would appear at first glance to stand outside the pale of the present study, constitution as antidote to war suffuses it throughout: already the inside-outside image of constitutions is ripping at the seams. Traditionally, constitutions are eminently sovereign texts, made by people to rule themselves by themselves. This is no longer the case. The fiction of a self-organized Iraqi constitution, or of a self-organized Afghani constitution, might be naturally peddled by the Iraqi and Afghani governments, but few believe their constitutional input and output is not international. As for the European Union, even a fiction encompassing the 15 Member-States, or indeed the additional ten delegations from the enlarged continent that attended the Constitutional Convention, renders the effort characteristically non-national. More importantly, the international drive of E.U. constitutionalism is now formally enshrined in the European Union's "proximity policy."

Proximity is not only about Turkey, the immediate next-door giant of the EU. Perhaps the most interesting article in the European Constitution in terms of emerging patterns—read here challenges—of the twenty-first century appears in Part One, Title viii of the text:

> Title viii, The Union and Its Neighbours
>
> Article I-57:
>
> The Union and Its Neighbours
> 1. The Union shall develop a special relationship with neighbouring States, aiming to establish an area of prosperity and good neighbourliness, founded on the values of the Union and characterised by close and peaceful relations based on cooperation.[7]

Much has been built on this seemingly innocuous article, on different levels. On the political plane, a full and daring proximity policy was announced and followed through, from a European perspective, by the then head of the Commission, Romano Prodi. This policy suggests the inclusion of any willing neighbouring state in the EU system, except for the institutions. Short of voting and being represented in Brussels, "everything else" could be common, European.[8] On the academic level, I have tried to develop this concept as a solution to the Arab-Israeli problem by way of a Hegelian-style *Aufhebung* resting on the freedom of circulation and establishment through the new immense territory constituted by the EU and its Mediterranean neighbourhood.[9] The EU as model-solution to the hundred-year conflict over Palestine is one striking illustration, following which the right to return for Palestinians would find its application in their freedom of movement over the new "EU" territory that includes Israel. For Israel, the fear of a destabilizing influx would be tempered by its opening up to a European space where part of its security would be naturally one shared with the EU.

This is a long shot, at least a generation away. Still, if emerging patterns for the twenty-first century are to be sought, one can see how the EU has now internalized, in the revolutionary text of Art. I-57, that pattern of constitutional internationalization. While it sounds excessive to think of it in such grandiloquent terms as the chance of a peaceful Mediterranean, and more specifically a solution to the Arab-Israeli conflict much in the manner that Europe has "solved" the Northern Ireland problem, one sees in Art. I-57 the promise of a century, not just of a few years. And if the Good Friday Agreement marks a real turning point in Irish history in its four-centuries long pattern of violence, it is undoubtedly the result of European integration. For it can hardly be conceived of outside the framework of the concept of regionalization—and the hankering for a realization of subsidiarity across Europe and within its regions, the well-established as well as the contentious ones.[10]

II. Simplifiers: Persistent Montesquieuian Issues

So much for constitutionalism's international drive. Let us take a step back, and indulge in a few simplifiers. By simplifiers I mean those trusted milestones that are the basics of constitution-making, and which any drafter needs to contemplate in accordance with a received vision which is essentially an eighteenth-century legacy of political science/constitutionalism, more specifically a Montesquieuian one. This is the concept of separation of powers, or the checks and balances in American lore, coupled with the concept of federalism to accommodate regional disparities. Such a vertical and horizontal division of powers is the stuff of any constitution-making, arguably since Plato and Aristotle,[11] and raises a number of classical questions from both sides of society.

Seen from the top, how solid and impermeable are the boundaries between powers in the state? This, reduced to its simplest expression, presents the need to make a choice between a presidential and a parliamentarian constitution, and a choice between a federal system and a centralized one. Is a Prime Minister who commands the largest bloc of parliamentary votes a better head for the executive branch than a president directly elected by universal suffrage? What are the powers of federated states, and if there are no federated states, how is power devolved and exercised by regional entities?

Seen from the bottom, what voting power does the citizen have, as an individual and as a member of a collectivity? What recourse does the individual have in the event of infringement on his or her rights as enshrined in the text?

Now even simplifiers can make life complicated when comparisons are exercised in dual terms, let alone when three nascent constitutions are being compared. National systems of law, the first-year law student learns quickly, are self-sufficient. In a fiction which is essential to understanding its realm, law operates outside history as well as outside geography. Legal history might explain much, but it works in a way that is irrelevant to the substance, or content, provided by any given law. Comparative law is an additional luxury: use of comparative law may be edifying, enlightening or enriching, even persuasive, but it is never decisive. Yet, there are increasing numbers of exceptions in global law.[12]

Legal history, as well as comparative law, remain luxuries. The law stands for what it disposes of *hic et nunc*, not for how it came about, or what country it compares with beyond the realm of the jurisdiction in which it holds sway. It therefore makes sense, from the vantage point of simplifiers, at the overall architectonics of our three constitutions, to consider each as a self-contained arrangement.

Afghanistan

I will start with the simplest, the Constitution of "the Islamic Republic of Afghanistan," as defined in Article 1. Simplest because it has now been adopted (January 24, 2004), while the other two remain transient, either being superseded by repeated amendments as in Iraq, or frozen, as for the EU, after the rejection of the agreed text by a majority of the French and Dutch citizens. Simplest because it is essentially a presidential constitution, with a person—Hamid Karzai—in mind drawing the constitution and implementing it. Simplest because there is no federalism in the text. Simplest because, despite the international convulsions in the modern history of Afghanistan, the non-Afghani input, unlike for Iraq and the EU, is limited. And simplest, finally, because there does not seem to have been too much traceable work behind it.[13] By contrast, the emergence of the Iranian Constitution in 1979 has left constitutional scholars a formidable trail of constituents' minutes.[14]

Composed of a preamble and one hundred and sixty articles, and divided into twelve neat chapters, the Afghani Constitution was written in Pashtu and Dari, two of the several languages recognized by Article 16.[15] Following a familiar and didactic terrain, the Constitution presents the main attributes of the State of Afghanistan in the Preamble and first chapter—flag, languages, religion, economic traits and state responsibility for citizens' welfare, education, place in the international order—followed by the citizens' fundamental rights (chapter 2). The organs of the state cover chapters 3 to 8: presidency, government, national assembly, Loya Jirga, judiciary, administrative divisions. "Special dispositions" are enshrined in the last four chapters, including the state of emergency and the amendment process. Most significant in terms of separation of powers is the establishment of Afghanistan as a centralized presidential republic, where the head of the executive is elected directly by popular suffrage if he or she gets over 50% of the vote. The two candidates with the highest vote in the first round, as in France, fight it out in a second round.[16] "No one can be elected as president for more than two terms."[17]

The president is extremely powerful under the Constitution, as he heads the Cabinet—there is no Prime Minister. The list of presidential prerogatives is long and wide-ranging, to which should be added the prerogatives of a cabinet which cannot be brought down by Parliament by a vote of confidence, with the exception of individual ministers. The president is even entitled to name some of the members of the Upper House (the Elders' House). Parliament under the Constitution is composed of two houses, to which should be added the Loya Jirga, originally a congregation of tribal leaders in which the Constitution vests some historical mantle of sovereignty.[18] The Loya Jirga under the new Constitution is no longer openly tribal. It consists of the members of parliament, the members of government, and the provincial and district council heads. While it is supposed to deal with the supreme interests of the country, it is again the president who is entitled to convene it. Presumably, it can in some cases meet of its own accord, since it is also entitled to pass judgment on the president in case he dramatically fails his duties, such as committing crimes against humanity.[19]

Loya Jirga and "crimes against humanity," a phrase that appears in several articles of the Afghan constitution, provide the comparative lawyer with the most original concepts in the text. The bottom line is about centralized presidential power, where the battle will be fought for the foreseeable future, for Afghanistan as well as for Iraq, and, to an extent we also need to dwell upon, in the European Union. The place of the president as chief executive rallying the country is the more important locus of constitutional attention since the Afghani and Iraqi experience, despite sharing common "international" input, underline the difficulty of agreeing on the place of the head of the executive branch under a Montesquieuian scheme of things. In Afghanistan, as the text stands, the president trumps the rest of the Constitutional arrangements, be they central or federal. This may be unwise, especially since the incumbent owes his position to "being the smallest common denominator" picked by the UN.[20] The battle for executive power will continue to define constitution-making in the twenty-first century, as it has from time immemorial. This is certain. Whether it is wise is a different matter.

Iraq

In Iraq, the battle for the presidency has taken another shape, despite a similar international input, including the same UN envoy. It played itself out differently, and the idiosyncrasies of history got the upper hand on planning.[21]

Unfortunate Iraqis, they have been trying to find some peace after thirty-five years of solid dictatorship, including the longest Middle East war in twentieth-century history, and two or three invasions—their invasion of others, and others invading them—plus a twelve-year sanctions regime followed by occupation, in the midst of which mayhem they put together a "wonderful new Constitution."[22] It is true that the Iraqis, who forged ahead with a Constitution against all odds, deserve a burst of enthusiastic kudos.[23] But one should perhaps remain reserved on such elusive matters for fear of ridicule—getting "mugged by reality" is a fashionable term.

In the midst of so much violence, how did they do it in Iraq? "They," here, are a hapless though talented Iraqi-"international" (chiefly American) duo. One must realize what constitution-writing means in Iraq 2004, and it means a lot of English, not only because a UN Security Resolution had consecrated a governor of Iraq who is solely American-English speaking, and so wields the ultimate signature upon any text Iraqis may want to turn into law, but more fundamentally because the legal and judicial body politic of Iraq is simply inexistent. It is, unfortunately, as tragic as it sounds: so destructive of any judicial independence has the rule of the former Iraqi dictator been that Iraqi jurists who remained in Iraq simply lost confidence in their job and themselves. Even polyglottism (here the knowledge of a western language) was a mark of treason for dark, fascist Arabism in the "heyday of the long Baathist night."[24] The systematic destruction of Iraqi legal culture, its lawyers, judges, and law schools, meant that constitution drafting was left to those coming from the outside. There simply are not so many people capable of drafting a constitution in English words which are also Arabic, and occasionally, Kurdish. Not that there is not enough talent, dedication or competence: chapters of judicial and legal resistance under the long dictatorship in Iraq are yet to be written.

So hail to the two drafters, and their advisors. Friendship being involved here on both the drafting side and the advising side, all shall remain nameless. The result is what matters for the purpose of the present chapter, and that result is a longish text, with a didactic effort (62 articles in nine parts). The Transitional Administrative Law (TAL) self-erased when the elections planned for January 2005 resulted in a Parliament that was tasked with writing the ultimate text and putting it to the vote. Meanwhile, some constitutional landmarks have been posted for Iraq. While buffeted by barbaric violence on a scale that knows few such precedents on the planet, the process moved decisively forward in textual terms.

Three matters draw the TAL reader's attention: the first is the place reserved for women, who were to constitute a quarter of Parliament; the second is the open reference to federalism; and the third is the care given to the protection of the individual's right. All three remained in the 2005 Constitution.

If Iraq wishes to remain at the forefront of Middle Eastern democracy—a position it will continue to pretend to have, despite its being rocked by violence, both in terms of the freedoms it carries and of the fact that those in power owe it neither to a dynasty nor to the Middle East-dominant self-extension of presidential mandate—then Iraqi society needs to protect those two achievements of women representation and federalism. This will not be easy. As for the judicial protection of the person's basic rights, it will come only after Iraqi society overcomes the violence that plagues it, and finds a way to stand on its own two feet without foreign armies dictating the terms of social peace.

Much of this commentary is arguably hypothetical, but the morass of Iraqi politics should not mask the forest for the trees. In Iraq, constitutionalism has forged ahead in the most delicate of all arrangements, which is the attempt of a constitution to be inclusive of two dominant and competing national identities—Kurdish and Arab—and two dominant and competing religious sects—Shiʿi and Sunni Islam. Even under the most elaborate constitutional schemes, which Donald Horowitz has dissected in many different approaches over three decades of scholarly attention to "discrete and insular minorities" across the world,[25] one would find it difficult to draw a model that accommodates the Iraqi socio-historical set-up. Nor have the Iraqi constituents succeeded yet in convincing their people, and the world at large, that they are out of the woods of overwhelming sectarianism in the individual politicians' political expression. By multiplying the top executive positions of president and prime minister with vice-presidents and vice-prime ministers, they have underlined the difficulty of regulating the executive branch among the three political-sociological components of the country, Shiʿis, Sunnis, and Kurds.

The European Union

The Constitution finally agreed upon by the European Council (of heads of states) meeting in Dublin in June 2004 stands outside any recognizable model in the field, this for obvious reasons owing to the history of European integration. But it also stands out for technical reasons obtaining from its fissiparous genesis: the Constitution makes no sense for the reader without the accumulation of texts, ever since six European states came together as the so-called Common Market in Rome in 1957. This accumulation of treaties, and of legislative, judicial, and administrative acts, is known as "acquis communautaire."

In any appreciation of constitution-making, it is not enough to mark progress. There also are setbacks. One certain failure in the EU text concerns its style. However hard the constituents tried to make the text of the Constitution palatable to the educated but non-specialist reader, this effort was a failure. Even Valéry Giscard d'Estaing, the head of the Convention that drafted the text, discourages the reader from dealing with Part III of the text, which is the longest and most detailed.[26] The *Economist* rightly ran a cover page when the European constitutional project was disclosed suggesting to "bin it."[27] Could it have been otherwise?

One distinguished former Minister of Justice in France did write in 2002 a model constitution which had the advantage of being short and more palatable, including actually most of the provisions which found their way to the text.[28] It *was* possible to do better. But there is no point in trying to rewrite history, and there are already a number of reader-friendly editions and short commentaries, of which the introductions of Giscard and a *Que Sais-Je* by Professor Christian Philip stand their ground in terms of clarity and comprehensiveness.[29] One problem is the type of "consolidator Treaty" which integrates previous texts as so many layers, and the mechanisms in the Convention which, so as to include the largest number of proposals, fail to pay attention to style, which could have brought the text together in the U.S.-concise manner of 1787. It is certainly true that the U.S. constitution is a unique text as far as the excellence of its constitutional style is concerned, hardly matched elsewhere on the planet. But even the U.S. Constitution has been faulted for its opaque style, and few Americans have read its 4,000 or so words. The prose of the *Federalist Papers* is of far more interest for the reader, but the American Constitution is at least brief.

The EU Constitution consists of four parts, and a number of protocols of which two are important. Starting with the end, a brief Fourth Part deals with amendments and transitional measures. A Third Part consolidates all previous treaties and is therefore the longest and most verbose. A Second Part integrates the bill of rights known as "The European Union Charter for Fundamental Rights," which had been approved in Nice four years earlier. The First Part is the most novel, and I shall mostly dwell on it to discern meaningful trends in twenty-first-century constitution-making.

Let me suggest, for the sake of argument, an extreme critical line that flows from the universally acknowledged "democratic deficit" in Europe. Management of the current 27 state-strong EU creates in and by itself problems which have been dealt with in the EU constitution as best it could, with the creation of enhanced cooperation. This concept allows a group of EU countries to go forward with integration without being hampered by slow or reluctant member states. The Euro initiative, which does not include Britain and Sweden, is the most successful application of this principle. Already the EU operates on a system of *géométrie variable*, and this is fine as long as it does not burst at the seams. Even bursting at the seams has already been envisaged, and happily dealt with, when Austria found itself in the throes of a government threatened by racist extremism. From that emerged a "freezing out" procedure, which has worked well to temper extremism within Austria, without the EU imploding altogether from the shock. Of course, should one country turn so undemocratic as to threaten not only being frozen out of the EU, but also engaging in military hostilities against it, the issue would be grave; but even a major country or two turning in this nasty way at the same time may not make the system unravel, and that scenario might even be a privileged way to consolidate it. More immediate is the risk that new countries bring in their weak democratic systems of deliberation, as in the case of Romania or the republics of former Yugoslavia. But the remarkable democratic strides of Turkey to bring its legal system up to EU standards, both in terms of its books and, more importantly, in the application of its laws, are testimony to the immense leverage at the disposal of the EU for smaller countries. Indeed, the annual reports that the Commission prepares on Turkish alignment with EU legal and economic standards may be one of the most innovative tools for the spread of democracy, human rights, and the rule of law across the world since the collapse of the Soviet Union.[30]

The problem of the EU democratic deficit does not lie in its expansion; in fact, one can argue the exact opposite, namely, that the world EU-fashion, and more specifically the Middle East EU-fashion, is a unique opportunity allowed by the emergence of a unified Europe.[31] The problem of the EU democratic deficit has been building up since the Treaty of Rome, and that problem is constitutional, more specifically one of separation of powers. In eighteen months of deliberation, the EU Constitutional Convention simply failed to address it successfully.

This problem is eminently Montesquieuian, and results from the vesting of legislative and executive powers in a strange EU mixture of a triangle Council-Commission-Parliament, in which the first two institutions are dominant. Those who are elected "Europeanly," that is, the EU MPs, represent at best a fifth wheel on the carriage, as the French expression has it. By eliminating most of the EU Parliament, the maximum loss would be a faint forum for deliberation, and an even fainter one in terms of legislation. While the legislative process has time and again been redrawn at the margins in order to enhance its powers, any person familiar with the institutional working of the EU knows that Parliament is a place for occasional protest, and for elaborate and meandering "comitology," but not a power that anyone seriously takes into account.

The Council, however, being composed of governments that are representative of their people, is indispensable. It is indispensable because it actually does represent the people within the member states, and thus brings into the federal European model the voice of the constituent peoples. The Council is also indispensable because even if it does not contribute a federal voice, one can hardly imagine how laws enacted by the Union could be binding within each country—in that ever wider field of European competence—if implementation were not carried out by the Council's governments at home.

Finally, the Commission has real power. *This is the problem*, since the Commission has no popular legitimacy, and its members are appointed by the Council to play a *European* role. To make matters worse, the Constitution has managed to establish a number of new high positions, including a would-be president for the Council who battles the president of the Commission for pre-eminence (much as the High Representative for the Common Foreign Policy and Security has already fought it out with the Commissioner in charge of foreign affairs, a sorry sight indeed). The result, inevitably, is more muddle, and with poor legitimacy at that, for the new bicephalous institutions. None of these positions will be filled by direct popular vote.

The only step needed to bring democracy to Europe would have been to scrap the Commission in its present form by transforming it into the excellent civil servants' administration which it really is, to create an executive elected by the people, and to give Parliament a real legislative role. One would still remain in the throes of the federal problem, but the democratic deficit would have been tackled head on, in a way that would have made it finally meaningful to vote for a European MP. It is now, alas, mostly a waste of time, and the electors are far savvier than the institutional cooks of Europe give them credit for. They simply do not bother to vote for Parliament, nor do they show the slightest interest in what it does.

To underline further the democratic deficit in the EU version of separation of powers, an "error" in the text is telling: no doubt attentive to the subdued role of Parliament, and to the absence of popular legitimacy for the Commission, the constituents entrusted EU MPs, as the text goes, with "electing" the president of the Commission.[32]

This is further detailed under Article I-27, on the President of the European Commission:

> 1. Taking into account the elections to the European Parliament, and after having held the appropriate consultations, the European Council, deciding by qualified majority, shall propose to the European Parliament a candidate for the President of the Commission. This candidate shall be elected by the European Parliament by a majority of its members. If he or she does not obtain the required majority, the European Council, acting by a qualified majority, shall within one month propose a new candidate who shall be elected by the European Parliament, following the same procedure.

An election without contest is a strange concept indeed. Behind the awkward wording stands a battle for legitimacy for the head of the executive: is it the president of the Council or the president of the Commission? One can imagine the confusion about the presidency, much in the way of the confusion over who is in charge of foreign policy: the Commissioner with the portfolio or the Council's High Representative? Or indeed the president of the Commission? Maybe the ruse of the constituents was deliberate, and some comments suggest that the bicephalous anomaly of two presidents (a president of the Council and a president of the Commission) was purposefully left open by the Convention to force a solution to their redundancy.[33] Nothing in the text bars such a possibility. The problem remains. Both positions result from a choice exercised by the Council, not by an election between competing candidates.

To return to the basics of the democratic deficit: the constituents were unable to see boldly enough into the strange system of separation of powers they were perpetuating since the Treaty of Rome. They tinkered with it by establishing a president of the Council, who would conceivably stay in position for five years instead of the current rotation of six months, which was made impossible by EU enlargement. They also tinkered with the presidency of the Commission by suggesting that the person in charge would be elected by Parliament, whereas the candidate—only one—is nominated by the Council, making a mockery of his or her trumpeted "election."

This leaves little democratic legitimacy in the choice of both executive and legislative powers in Europe, if indeed we mean by legitimacy the direct election of their EU leaders by the people of Europe. Both the presidents of the Council and of the Commission are nominated by the Council. In the case of the Council's president, the parliamentary representatives of European voters have no say. In the case of the Commission's president, parliamentary function is at best perfunctory, despite the constitutional language intimating his "election" by Parliament. And to top it all, Parliament does not legislate. The bottom line is that the EU has still not solved the problem of its executive branch, a characteristic problem that it shares with Afghanistan and Iraq.

III. Acid Tests and Emerging Patterns

In this search for emerging patterns in twenty-first-century constitutionalism, I would like to introduce another concept that has been of assistance in writing on family and gender issues: the acid test.[34] Acid is a metaphor which conjures up for different people and different cultures so many different images. One image, for Westerners of my generation, is that of a powerful mind distorter which clouds one's miserable life with a worldly vision induced by hallucinogenic drugs. For Iraqis emerging from 35 years of dictatorship, acid is a far more material reality as the most harrowing method of torture used by the former regime: it is said to have been a specialty of the elder Hussein son, consisting of lowering the victim on a pulley into a basin of acid, first the toes, and pulling back the pulley up and down repeatedly. One shudders at the image, and we should leave it at that. What the small *Oxford English Dictionary* says about "acid tests" is that they are "severe and conclusive." In the Iraqi context, one has no doubt they are conclusive. In all cases, acid tests are certainly severe, the more severe as they include faith-based, and for all intents and purposes, "irrational" convictions imbued with religion that have competed with each other at least since God became word. Let me pursue comparatively three such acid tests at the heart of twenty-first-century constitutionalism which bring people literally up in arms: religion, federalism—two areas that did not constitute such a contentious arena of constitutionalism in the twentieth century—and the perennial issue of who is to be master: the presidency.

Religion

Perhaps the most trying of all acid tests is the place of religion in the constitution. The "law and religion complex" operates as acid test not merely in an Eastern, Muslim context. It was, and continues to be, a central point of disagreement in European constitution-making. For those who have followed that particular aspect of the debate, suffice it to point out the discrepancy between the German and French texts in the translation of the Preamble to the Charter of Fundamental Rights in Nice in 2000, a discrepancy that is, in constitution-writing, unprecedented. While the French text acknowledges the "spiritual" tradition in Europe, the German version renders it "religious."

The European constituents eventually succeeded in preventing that acid test from blocking the whole process. Ironically thanks to the Irish, they finally produced a version that leaned towards the French disposition. Much to the dislike and vocal protests of the Vatican, they declared the *cultural* heritage of the peoples of Europe to be that which they had in common, skipping the mention of Christianity, religion, and spirituality altogether.

How does one deal with such a difficult test, the religion of the land in a constitution? Of tons of ink spilled on matters constitutional, one would venture that this is the issue of unique portent in the United States as well as in Europe and the Middle East, bringing religious affiliation in the domestic context to international "clashes of civilisations" defined religiously. The concern is not about to abate.

To make some progress in the shape of religion in twenty-first-century constitutionalism, it may help to make a literary detour into the quasi-universal law of individual psychology, much in the vein of Freud's Oedipus complex: it is acknowledged that adolescence generally, if not a later age, raises a form of religious libido in each and every individual on earth. Of that experience two literary expressions are particularly telling. The first is by Bertolt Brecht, whose alluring though not likeable character, Mr. K., was once asked whether there was a God:

> Herr K. sagte: "Ich rate dir, nachzudenken, ob dein Verhalten je nach der Antwort auf diese Frage sich ändern würde. Würde es sich nicht ändern, dann können wir die Frage fallenlassen. Würde es sich ändern, dann kann ich dir wenigstens noch soweit behilflich sein, dass ich dir sage, du hast dich schon entschieden: Du brauchst einen Gott."[35]

That adolescent part of the argument fits well with a rigid view of separation between church and state, and can be comforted with all kinds of citations, including from the most canonical sources, to wit, the words of Christ to render unto Caesar what is Caesar's,[36] or the lapidary injunction in the Qur'an to let there be "no compulsion in religion."[37] As one makes peace with God or religion on this basis, acknowledging in the process that there is more to it than Brechtian need or Qur'anic rejection of state force to deal with one's professed faith, another citation comes to mind, that of the Levantine poet admonishing his children about the penumbra of dignity that religion brings to the believers,

> *wa lā tataʿaṣṣabu abadan li-dīnin, fa-kullu taʿaṣṣubin yushqī wa-yurdī*
> *li-kullin dīnuhū wa li-kulli dīnin maṣūnu karāmatin taʾbā al-taʿaddī.*[38]

This is more subtle than Brecht, because of the consideration of one's religion as a shield, and not a sword, to borrow a distinction from English contract law.[39] The positive use of religion to shape the state is one thing, the defence of religion against aggression and other such humiliations is another. In our respective constitutions, this is generally the position adopted by the constituents: the state, or group of states in the EU, is not so much neutral about religion—the classical position of a rigid doctrine of separation between state and religion—as acknowledging a heritage, which in the case of Europe includes churches receiving constitutional recognition, and eventually tax relief and subsidies;[40] and in the case of Iraq and Afghanistan, includes a role for Islam which is not militant. Islam is to be perceived as shield, and not as sword.

The foundation of both the Iraqi and Afghani constitutions is alluring in this respect. As for the first, Art. 3 reads, "No amendment to this Law may be made to affect Islam." Article 7 of the Iraqi TAL is equally protective: "Islam is the official religion of the State and is to be considered a source of legislation. No law that contradicts the universally agreed tenets of Islam, the principles of democracy, or the rights cited in Chapter Two of this Law [i.e., the bill of rights] may be enacted during the transitional period. This Law respects the Islamic identity of the majority of the Iraqi people and guarantees the full religious rights of all individuals to freedom of religious belief and practice."

In Afghanistan, the more specific formulation of compatibility between Islam and law is similar: "No law can be contrary to the sacred religion of Islam and the values of this Constitution." In comparative Middle Eastern constitutionalism, where the acid test has generally taken the form of Islamic law being considered "the" in opposition to "a" source for the Constitution, this novel formulation upholds a conception of religion as shield in ways that shift the terrain of the debate onto areas that may relieve the test from some of its acid severity.

This is not the end of the matter, however, as the law and religion complex in modern constitutionalism must be perceived increasingly, in twenty-first-century constitutionalism, on a far more elusive register: namely, the absence of religion—as religious affiliation—in the constitution. The problem is no longer whether Islam is a "state" religion or not, but rather how collectivities that identify themselves on the basis of religious affiliation can be ignored by the constitutional setup. I have used several occasions over the past years to discuss this vexing issue in modern constitutionalism, so I will not pursue it further here, except to note that even the EU, secular as it may pretend to be, was unable to escape some form of recognition for established churches.[41]

Federalism

Directly related to the issue of collective identification with a given religious denomination is the problem of sectarianism, or communitarianism as Indian constitutionalists call it. This is an issue that conjures up an eminently *federal* mirror.

Federalism operates as a unique acid test in twenty-first-century constitutionalism; indeed, it acts as the proverbial elephant in the room. Of the three constitutions, only the Iraqi TAL mentions the word, and it may well be the most courageous. In the Afghani Constitution there is mention of peoples, tribes, and "men" in various articles.[42] In the EU context, Valéry Giscard d'Estaing explains how the word "communitarian" came to replace the word "federal" in Art. I.1 of the Constitution,[43] bringing an end to the heated debate between European federalists and European sovereignists among the constituents. A more "federalist" form of government than the European one is hard to conceive, and the refusal of the constituents to get drawn in by the word indicates areas of "irrationality" in the public discourse in ways typical of acid tests, as English and French national forms of the Anti-Federalist get pitted against mostly German and more recently Spanish adhesion to the concept as a perfectly acceptable one constitutionally.

Even a perfunctory approach to EU, Iraqi, and Afghani constitution-making shows that all these issues are very much alive. Indeed, the *f*-word is as much of a hot potato in Europe as it is in Afghanistan or Iraq, and federalism could indeed represent the topic that galvanizes the inchoate world of twenty-first-century constitutionalism. Much has been said about European federalism and that inspired by national politics is at least frank.[44] It might have proved expedient for the constituents to have ended up avoiding the word altogether in their would-be founding text, for they knew they were all practicing federalism like Molière's character speaking in prose without knowing it.

In Iraq, the battle for the inclusion of the word is far from over: I have often opined to Iraqi colleagues that constant resort to sui generis categories may not be useful (in this case the use of the concept of *wilāya* in Ottoman fashion to avoid using the Arabic *fidirālī*). This lobbying has even found its way to Security Council Resolution 1546.[45] The jury is still out on whether it is preferable to practice federalism à la Molière, or whether some greater courage would not be amiss for the enrichment of the debate and its integrity. Eventually the 2005 Constitution openly acknowledged Iraq as federal.

Presidency

Lest we lose our bearings, constitutions are about who is to be master. Put in less crude terms, twenty-first-century constitutionalism cannot escape the battle, ongoing since the dawn of history, about leadership and its democratic credentials. Here appears the most muddled pattern in the present comparative exercise: in Afghanistan, the tailoring of the constitutional text to fit a particular person is simply wrong, and the sacrifice of real checks and balances to presidential power—alas, predictable—is recipe for trouble to come. In Iraq, matters are still in a situation of flux, owing to the duality of President–Prime Minister in the Transitional Administrative Law (and in the 2005 Constitution), but also to the real test of federalism as it is wont to develop—or perhaps to get smothered by authoritarianism and/or chaos, both equally capable of marking the death of constitutionalism in the country for another generation. In the EU, the naked emptying of the concept of election with regard to the choice of the president of the Commission is indicative of a major problem yet to be solved.

What, then, does this tell us about that long-standing acid test of ultimate executive power? The president as leader voted in directly by the people underlies the central problem of constitutional theory, which is couched, perhaps even papered over since Montesquieu, in terms of a natural result of a doctrine of separation of powers. The Montesquieuian scheme has arguably always been in crisis, and its difficult birth remains with us, as troubling in the twenty-first century as it was in the second half of the eighteenth.[46] The separation of powers, in that description, is a way to say that society cannot vote in its parliament by universal suffrage, and vote in its president also by universal suffrage, without having to explain why there should be two bodies so elected. The solution was a functional one, based on the idea that the first body legislates, and the second executes. Power becomes therefore segmented functionally, but such segmentation is a human construct that divides up power in a disturbing and incoherent manner. What does it mean to issue a law as opposed to executing it?

Federal arrangements are more convincing, because they point to a horizontal division of powers based on a tangible division of territory and land. A horizontal devolution of power is more coherent than the functional division of powers between a parliament that enacts laws, a president or prime minister who applies them, and a judiciary that arbitrates conflicts arising from that application. A comparative reading of the three constitutions informing this essay suggests that federalism as a successful constitutional arrangement has many more credentials than the domestic functional division of powers extant in twenty-first-century constitutionalism. While the Montesquieuian scheme lags behind, there is not one decidedly convincing route out of the conundrum, as is illustrated in the three acid test questions by the absence of a convincing mechanism to resolve them.

Epilogue

The federal order, religion's proactive challenge to constitutionalism, and the confusion in the tripartite separation of powers underlying the role of the presidency and its legitimacy, are three problem areas that define the shape of things constitutional in the twenty-first century. Beyond the natural disparity in the respective traditions of the EU, Iraq, and Afghanistan, and the widely different conditions for the emergence of their three constitutions, it may be helpful to end with the special form of internationalism that seems to mark twenty-first-century constitutionalism.

On a planet that no longer recognizes the domain of internal affairs as a self-contained one, one needs to reflect on the mechanisms that will ensure that domestic problems do not spill over regionally and internationally. Even more positively, the question of constitutions as model can no longer be avoided: "the world modeled after Europe," in the fashion adumbrated by the so-called proximity policy of Art. I-57, is a case in point, and there is little doubt that success in Afghanistan and/or in Iraq will make constitutional standards affect an immense area, reaching into India through Pakistan and Kashmir, and across the Middle East, including Palestine and Israel.

There is no harm in fitting the matter into the first leg of the Kantian bifurcation scheme that began this chapter, with the contrasting vantage points drawn from Kant's *Treatise on Perpetual Peace*: its failure on the ground since 1795 and its continuous success in the battle of ideas in ways that compel us to rediscover the treatise again and again at key junctures in human history, e.g., the French-Atlantic Revolution, which saw its birth, the failed attempts in the Congress of Vienna to go beyond the Westphalian paradigm of sovereign nation-states, through the collapse of the Wilsonian vision in Versailles, and the shortcomings of the UN in the wake of World War II.

The three constitutions just examined constitute, through their birth and potential projections beyond their borders, an attempt to include Kant's cosmopolitan law into their frame. This is halting and timid, but the pattern is there for the discerning, whether in terms of federalism for Iraq, a unique novelty in the Middle East; crimes of war as a constitutional category in Afghanistan; or transnational projections of the EU, both federal and international.

I would like to conclude with this "world human rights' horizon," which conjures up, in converging ways two millennia apart, Aristotle and Paul Kahn. At its simplest, the issue is one of man—less so woman, and this in itself is telling—"as a political animal": "The entire effort of the international human rights movement is rooted in this vision of well-being. No one, in this view, should die or suffer for politics."[47] One can find this in the Preamble to the interim Iraqi constitution: the people of Iraq, it says, "reject violence and coercion in all their forms, and particularly when used as instruments of governance." One can also hear it plainly in a more relative, but potentially more "applicable" utterance interspersed, in a manner that seems novel in constitution-writing, in the repeated references throughout the Afghani text to the scourge of "crimes against humanity." Both Iraq and Afghanistan, societies that have been bled white through three decades of continuous horror, are showing the way to others, even to Europe, whose constituents remain behind in terms of the crucial task of preventing crimes against humanity from remaining unpunished.[48]

This points to the meta-conclusion of our emerging patterns, which is the next horizon of constitutionalism. How can human beings structure their domestic and international worlds to make politics redundant? Depoliticisation, I would like to conclude, is the ultimate horizon of comparative constitutionalism, that moment in history when it matters little what politics and politicians say because they have become by-and-large irrelevant to the happiness of the citizen. But perhaps this is better left to constitution-making in the twenty-second century.

NOTES

1 This is a lightly footnoted version of the Third Herbert L. Bernstein Annual Memorial Lecture in International and Comparative Law, read at Duke Law School on September 28, 2004. I have slightly updated the text considering the important changes in both the EU and Iraqi constitutional scenes, but the central argument has not changed.

2 Paul W. Kahn, "Sacred Violence," *SELA* (2003), 13. SELA, acronym of "Seminario en Latinoamérica de Teoría Constitucional y Democracia," brings together a group of leading academics mostly from Latin American and North American law schools, who meet usually once a year under the auspices of the Yale Law School. SELA is animated by Professor Owen Fiss. I read here Depoliticization instead of Depoliticalization.

3 We find Kahn bleak on the intersection of psychology and law (*Law and Love: The Trials of King Lear*, New Haven 2000) and international law ("Universal Jurisdiction and the Rule of Law," in John Borneman [ed.], *The Case of Ariel Sharon Case and the Fate of Universal Jurisdiction*, Princeton 2004, 131–45); more positive on

domestic law, *The Reign of Law: Marbury v. Madison and the Construction of America*, New Haven 1997; *Legitimacy and History: Self-Government in American Constitutional Theory*, New Haven 1992.

[4] Kahn, "Sacred Violence," 3.

[5] All the major wars are listed on a poster published on the anniversary of Kant's double centenary's death in 2004 by the Goethe Institut. Kant's famous treatise, *Zum Ewigen Frieden*, appeared first in 1795.

[6] James Woolsey, CIA director during the first Clinton Administration, is to my knowledge at the origins of the description of the post-September 11 era as the "fourth world war." For a robust legal debate on the contours of the new "war," see Bruce Ackerman, "The Emergency Constitution," *Yale Law Journal* 113 (2004), 1029, and the forum in the same issue devoted to the responses of David Cole, "The Priority of Morality: The Emergency Constitution's Blind Spot" (p. 1753), and of Laurence Tribe and Patrick Gudridge, "The Anti-Emergency Constitution" (p. 1801), together with the rejoinder of Ackerman, "This Is Not a War" (p. 1871).

[7] EU Constitution, final draft as agreed in the Dublin Council Summit, 18 June 2004 (hereinafter EU Constitution).

[8] Romano Prodi, "L'Europe et la Méditerranée: Venons en aux faits," speech given at Louvain-la-Neuve, November 26, 2002; Romano Prodi, "L'Europa più grande: una politica di vicinato come chiave di stabilità," address at ECSA conference, Brussels, December 5–6, 2002, COM (203) 104, Brussels March 11, 2003; Mallat, "Des relations privilégiées entre l'Union et les pays voisins," talk given at ECSA 2002, December 5, 2002, forthcoming as EU Commission publication.

[9] See Mallat, "George Weidenfeld's Bright Idea", *The Daily Star*, July 16, 2003; "L'UE entre déficit démocratique et Méditerranée en feu," *L'Orient-Le Jour*, June 21, 2004.

[10] For some of the extensive treatments in this vein of Northern Ireland and Palestine, see, e.g., the works of Gideon Gotlieb and Donald Horowitz. There is a large, albeit not decisive, literature on the Maastricht-introduced "principle of subsidiarity."

[11] Central reference is to Plato's *Republic*, ix, Aristotle's *Politics*, ch. 1, and Cicero's *De Republica*, chs. 1 and 2.

[12] While resistance is considerable, progress in comparative law can be read in the context of the death penalty in *Stanford v. Parker*, 266 F.3d 442 (6th Cir. 2001) cert. denied 71 USLW 3236 (S.Ct. 2002), decided on October 7, 2002 (execution of juvenile offenders), and in *Atkins v. Virginia*, 536 U.S. 304 (2002) (execution of mentally retarded defenders). The trend is adumbrated and developed in Kim Lane Scheppele, "Aspirational and Aversive Constitutionalism: The Case for Studying Cross-Constitutional Influence through Negative Models," *International Journal of Constitutional Law* 1 (2003), 296–324; Harold Koh, "Paying 'Decent Respect' to World Opinion on the Death Penalty," *U.C. Davis Law Review* 35, 1085–1131, at 1104; Judith Resnik, "Law's Migration: American Exceptionalism, Silent Dialogues, and Federalism's Multiple Ports of Entry," *Yale Law Journal* 115 (2006), 1564.

[13] The little that is available can be found in a report by the Secretariat of the Constitutional Commission of Afghanistan, "The Constitution-Making Process," March 10, 2003. Henceforth reference is to "Afghani Constitution," text available

in English, Pashtu, and Dari on the Internet, e.g., on http://www.loc.gov/law/guide/afghanistan.html. In western languages, there are few studies, despite some important conferences, notably in Heidelberg in 2004. Proceedings of a conference organized by the Rand Corporation in 2003 were published in a short booklet, Khaled Abou El Fadl et al., *Democracy and Islam in the New Constitution of Afghanistan*. See also an early assessment by an active Western participant, Barnett Rubin, "Crafting a Constitution for Afghanistan," *Journal of Democracy* 15 (2004).

[14] They can be found in two series of official documents, of three and four volumes respectively, entitled *Sūrat-e mashrūḥ-e muzākarāt-e shūrā-ye majles-e barrāsi-ye nihā'ī-ye qānūn-e asāsī-ye jumhūrī-ye islāmī-ye īrān* (Tehran 1985–89) and *Sūrat-e mashrūḥ-e muzākarāt-e shūrā-ye bāznegarī-ye qānūn-e asāsī-ye jumhūrī-ye islāmī-ye īrān* (Tehran 1990).

[15] Afghani Constitution, Art. 16: "Pashtu and Dari (which is a variation of Persian) are the official languages of the state."

[16] Afghani Constitution, Art. 61.

[17] Afghani Constitution, Art. 62.

[18] Afghani Constitution, Art. 110; for the Loya Jirga as historical "manifestation of the people of Afghanistan," see the classic work of the late Louis Dupree (d. 1989), *Afghanistan* (Princeton 1980).

[19] Afghani Constitution, Arts. 110 to 115.

[20] As explained by the UN mediator Lakhdar Brahimi, who supported Hamid Karzai's nomination on the basis that his name appeared on all the lists requested from the various leaders and warlords of Afghanistan.

[21] For some of these highly unusual circumstances, see Mallat, "Malgré tout, une leçon de démocratie à Bagdad," *L'Orient-le Jour*, June 2, 2004.

[22] The description of the Constitution as "wonderful" is owed to the editors of *The New York Times*, who propped up the comment I submitted with excessive enthusiasm, "East Meets West, at Least on Paper," *The New York Times*, March 11, 2004.

[23] Here I discuss what became know in English as the Transitional Administrative Law (TAL, *Qānūn idārat al-dawla*, literally the law for the governance of the country, agreed on March 1, 2004 by the Iraqi Governing Council, and published by the Coalition Provisional Authority on March 8 as "Law of Administration for the State of Iraq for the transitional period"). The TAL, which preceded the "final" Constitution of 2005, exhibits similar trends. The "final" Constitution of 2005 mentions that it needs to be completed, and so its finality is relative even on its own accord.

[24] Conversation with the late Hani Fukaiki, May 2002, in Kurdish Iraq, who, as a former active member of the Baath leadership, explained to me how knowledge of a Western language was suspicious and frowned upon as a sure mark of "treason."

[25] See e.g. Horowitz, *The Deadly Ethnic Riot*, Berkeley 2001.

[26] Valéry Giscard d'Estaing, "Introduction," in *La Constitution pour l'Europe* (Paris 2003), 75: "Je ne pense pas qu'il y ait lieu pour vous, lecteur, d'entreprendre la lecture en continu de cette troisième partie." (Hereinafter, Giscard, "Introduction")

[27] *The Economist*, June 19, 2003.

[28] Robert Badinter, *Une Constitution européenne*, Paris 2002.

[29] Giscard, "Introduction"; Christian Philip, *La Constitution européenne* (Paris 2004). The literature on the draft treaty known as the European Constitution is extensive. Most interesting are the minutes of the debates during the Convention, especially specialists' reports, available on the EU convention site.

[30] Commission reports on Turkey since 1999, available on the EU Commission's site.

[31] Original reflection in Robert Fossaert, ch. "Le Monde façon Europe," in his *Le Monde au 21ème siècle: Une théorie des systèmes mondiaux* (Paris 1991).

[32] EU Constitution, "Article I-20: The European Parliament: 1. The European Parliament (...) shall elect the President of the Commission."

[33] Philip, *La Constitution européenne,* 92–3.

[34] Chibli Mallat, "The Search for Equality in Middle Eastern Family Law," *al-Abḥāth* 48–49 (2000–2001), 7–63, which developed into chapter 10 of my *Introduction to Middle Eastern Law* (Oxford, 2007).

[35] "Die Frage, ob einen Gott gibt" ("On the Question Whether There is a God"), in Bertolt Brecht, *Ausgewählte Werke in sechs Bänden* (Frankfurt: Suhrkamp, 1997), vol. 5: *Kalendergeschichten, Geschichten vom Herrn Keuner*, 218—originally written ca 1929–30. (Mr K. answered: "I advise you to reflect first on whether your behaviour would change depending on the answer to that question. If it doesn't change, then we can leave the question behind. If it does, then I can at least be helpful by telling you that you have already decided: you need a God.")

[36] Matthew 22:21.

[37] Qur'an 2:256.

[38] Shiblī Mallāṭ ("Poet of the Cedars," d. 1961), *Dīwān* (Beirut, 1952), 2:521: "Never follow a religion fanatically, all fanaticism brings misery and death/ to each his religion, and to each religion a penumbra of dignity that dislikes being attacked" (a variation reads: *ta'bā al-taḥaddi*, "that dislikes being challenged").

[39] Lord Denning, in *Central London Property Trust Ltd. v. High Trees House Ltd. [1947]* K.B. 130.

[40] Article I-52 of the EU constitutional project: "Status of churches and non-confessional organizations. 1. The Union respects and does not prejudice the status under national law of churches and religious associations or communities in the Member States." The parallel is expressed in Art. 17 of the Afghani Constitution as the duty of the state to "organise and improve mosques, madrasas and religious centres," and in the debt of the Iraqi, in the Preamble of the Iraqi Constitution, to "religious leaders."

[41] Idem. See, e.g., my "Du fait religieux dans les institutions," in Chibli Mallat (ed.), *L'Union européenne et le Moyen-Orient: Etat des lieux* (Beirut 2004), 83–95.

[42] Afghani Constitution, Introduction, paragraph 5, "*aqvām va mardum*"; Art. 6, "*aqvām va qabā'el.*"

[43] Giscard, "Introduction," 34: "Aussi, dans le texte que j'ai préparé pour le Praesidium, ai-je substitué l'expression 'sur le mode fédéral' la formule 'sur le mode communautaire'."

[44] Most heated was the celebrated debate in 2001–2002 between German Foreign Minister Joschka Fischer (EU as federation), French President Jacques Chirac and his Foreign Minister Dominique de Villepin (EU as assembly or confederation of nations), and former President of the EU Commission Jacques Delors (EU as people's federation sui generis).

[45] For my intervention with Iraqi Foreign Minister Hoshyar Zibari for the inclusion of federalism in Security Council Resolution 1546 (June 8, 2004), see the account in "2004, le Moyen-Orient en quête de non-violence: Un parcours personnel," published in Chibli Mallat, *Presidential Papers* (Beirut 2005).

[46] This is developed in Chibli Mallat, "Droit comparé au 18ème siècle: Influences françaises sur la common law," *Revue Historique de Droit Français et Etranger* 3 (1994), 383–400 (arguing that Montesquieu and Lord Mansfield understood separation of powers in a manner profoundly different from the way it became operational).

[47] Supra, text at n. 2.

[48] Mallat, "Des relations privilégiées", supra n. 8, section discussing transnational justice.

12

LEGAL RECONSTRUCTION AND ISLAMIC LAW IN AFGHANISTAN

Martin Lau

Introduction

Assessments of Afghanistan's progress towards the rule of law are marked by pessimism.[1] Only when compared with Iraq's seemingly unstoppable descent into anarchy, and perhaps even disintegration, is it possible to discern positive developments. Five years after the collapse of the Taliban regime, national unity has been preserved and is not under any immediate threat; the U.N.-endorsed Bonn Agreement of December 2001 is adhered to, if at times in form only; and all steps envisaged under the Agreement to turn Afghanistan into a modern democracy have been taken, with a new Constitution replacing that of 1964 adopted by a Constitutional Loya Jirga in December 2003 and coming into force on January 4, 2004. In addition, presidential and parliamentary elections were held in the course of 2005 and at the end of that year Afghanistan's parliament assembled for the first time. Despite these considerable achievements, however, there are still serious problems which, if not addressed, will endanger Afghanistan's progress. Without doubt the most serious threat to Afghanistan's rocky road to recovery are the continuing concerns over security,[2] the inability of the central government to extend its writ outside Kabul, and the blossoming of a shadowy drug economy.[3]

The difficulties experienced in the reconstruction of Afghanistan's legal system reflect the considerable tensions in the social and political fabric of the country. The reconstruction efforts have exposed three principal areas of concern: the conceptual roots of the legal system, its political and societal setting, and the material foundations of its institutions. Numerous reports have addressed and examined the virtual absence of the rule of law outside Kabul.[4] Local commanders continue to exercise more or less effective political control outside the framework established by the Bonn Agreement and, more recently, the new Constitution.[5] The localisation of "justice" and all fora for the resolution of disputes is combined with general lawlessness and impunity: in many regions local commanders represent the law. Even within the official legal system serious tensions persist between the three permanent justice authorities, namely, the Supreme Court, the Ministry of Justice, and the Attorney General's Office. After almost a quarter of a century of civil war the remnants of the physical infrastructure of Afghanistan's legal system—its courts, statutes, prisons, and detention facilities—are in a depleted state. Legal uncertainty is compounded by a lack of legal expertise and law enforcement.

Afghanistan's government, with the assistance of the international community, has begun to address many of these problems. Courts are being rebuilt, a national army and police force are being established, and numerous international organisations, funded mainly by European and North American governments, are actively engaged in the training of Afghan jurists.[6] However, the current focus on what may be termed mainly practical issues has obscured the view of the conceptual tensions caused by the lack of agreement on the role of Islam in the legal system of Afghanistan. This tension came into sharp relief in 2006, when an Afghan convert to Christianity was charged with the crime of apostasy. His arrest on a charge for a crime rooted in Islamic law revealed the conceptual divergence between Islamic and Western sources of law within the legal system of Afghanistan. Human rights' groups condemned his arrest as a violation of international human rights' law, as well as the rights guaranteed under the 2004 Constitution, while the Afghan prosecutors maintained that it was an offence under Afghan law for a Muslim to convert to Christianity. The issue was never resolved since the accused was released on procedural grounds, but had it gone to trial, a court would have had to decide two questions: firstly, is there an offence of apostasy under Afghan law, and secondly, if the answer is in the affirmative, is such an offence in accordance with the provisions of the 2004 Constitution.

This article examines an integral part of the second issue, namely, the jurisdiction of the Supreme Court of Afghanistan to review laws on the basis of the 2004 Constitution. The focus of this examination will be on the jurisdiction of the Supreme Court to review laws on the basis of Islam. Never before in the legal history of Afghanistan has a court been empowered to review legislation on the basis of the provisions of a constitution, let alone on the basis of Islam. The potential impact of the exercise of this newly founded judicial power will be examined in a comparative perspective; while there is no Afghan case-law on this issue, courts in other jurisdictions have been grappling with the compatibility of statutory laws with Islam for some time. Most prominent amongst these jurisdictions is Pakistan, where the 1973 Constitution not only provides that all laws must be in accordance with Islamic law, but also empowers certain courts to strike down laws found to be in breach of this stipulation.

The 2004 Constitution of Afghanistan

While Islam features prominently in the 2004 Constitution, there is no single article that expressly empowers the Supreme Court to strike down laws deemed to be repugnant to Islam. Article 1 of the 2004 Constitution establishes Afghanistan as an Islamic republic, while Article 2 declares the "sacred religion of Islam" as the state's religion.[7] The proclamation of Afghanistan as an Islamic republic is accompanied by references to Islam in the symbolism of statehood. The Afghan flag depicts in "the upper-middle part [...] the sacred phrase of 'There is no God but Allah and Mohammad is his prophet, and Allāh is Great'"[8] and although no particular national anthem is identified, the Constitution provides that it "shall be in Pashtu and mention Allahu akbar."[9] The Islamic provisions assume more concrete features in relation to the constitutional provisions on the government. The President must take an oath in which he pledges, inter alia, to "obey and safeguard the provisions of the sacred religion of Islam."[10] In the area of education, the state is obliged to adopt measures for, inter alia, the development of religious education and "the organisation and improvement of the conditions of mosques, and the religious schools and centres,"[11] and the implementation of a unified curriculum "based on the principles of the sacred religion of Islam."[12] The right to form a political party is subject to the condition that the "program and articles of association of the party are not contrary to the principles of the sacred religion of Islam."[13]

The Islamic characteristics of the state extend to its legal system. Article 3 provides that: "In Afghanistan, no law may be contrary to the beliefs and provisions of the sacred religion of Islam." This is reinforced by Article 130, which provides, inter alia, that "When no provision exists in the Constitution or the law for a case under consideration, the court shall, by following the principles of the Hanafi school of law and within the limitations set forth in this constitution, render a decision that secures justice in the best possible way."[14]

Constitutional provisions mandating that all laws be in accordance with Islam have featured in all constitutions of Afghanistan.[15] However, more recent constitutions, such as those of 1964, 1987, and 1990, had tempered this provision somewhat, by stipulating in the same provision that all laws also had to be in accordance with both Islam and the values of the constitution. In contrast, the absolute character of Article 3 accords Islam predominance over all other sources of law. The dominant role accorded to Islam sits uneasily with those provisions of the Constitution that guarantee individual fundamental rights, such as a right to equality,[16] and may also impede the state in adhering to the obligation under Article 7: "The State shall respect the United Nations Charter, international treaties and conventions that Afghanistan has ratified, and the Universal Declaration of Human Rights." As has been pointed out by others, international human rights' standards are in potential conflict with Islamic law.[17] The clear precedence given by the Afghan Constitution to Islamic principles cannot be altered even by constitutional amendment. Article 149 provides: "The provisions of adherence to the principles of the sacred religion of

Islam and the system of the Islamic Republic cannot be amended." The protection of constitutionally guaranteed fundamental rights is weaker. The same article provides that they can be amended only "to make them more effective," which must at the very least mean that they cannot be removed altogether.

Previous Afghan constitutions were silent on how the constitutional mandate, that all laws should be in accordance with Islam, should be safeguarded. There were no mechanisms that would have allowed an authority of the state to invalidate laws found to be in conflict with the principles of Islam. The 1987 Constitution, for instance, provided for the establishment of a Constitutional Council, which was "authorised to evaluate the conformity of laws, decrees, and international treaties with the constitution and to advise the President on legal matters."[18] However, being advisory in nature, the Constitutional Council could not enforce its findings.

The 2004 Constitution has departed from these precedents, albeit that this revolutionary innovation is somewhat hidden from view because it has to be constructed with reference to several provisions. Article 121 ("The Supreme Court has the competence to review laws, legislative decrees, international treaties and conventions on their compliance with the Constitution and to interpret them, in accordance with the law, upon the request of the Government or the courts") empowers the Supreme Court to review laws on the basis of Islam, since Article 3 provides that no law can be contrary to Islam. The reading of Article 121 with Article 3 leaves no doubt that Supreme Court has jurisdiction to review legislation on the basis of the Constitution, including Islam.

The fate of laws found to be contrary to the Constitution is addressed in the very last article of the Constitution: Article 162 provides that upon its promulgation, all laws and decrees contrary to the provisions of the Constitution shall be null and void. Only the Supreme Court has the power to review the constitutionality of laws, and it follows from this, that it is the Supreme Court that can declare these laws null and void.[19]

A Comparative Perspective

From the perspective of Afghan legal history, the establishment of a Supreme Court jurisdiction to review the constitutionality of legislation is nothing but revolutionary. In comparative perspective, however, such judicial powers constitute the norm, rather than the exception. There is a clear global trend towards the creation of courts with a special constitutional jurisdiction sufficiently wide to declare actions of the executive as well as laws passed by the legislative branch of the state ultra vires, unconstitutional, and invalid. By now, the protection of human rights is generally regarded as a legal rather than a political phenomenon. Christopher McCrudden goes as far as to state that "the phenomenon of judicial enforcement of human rights often seems to be accepted as axiomatic, so apparently accepted as part of legal life has it now become, in the developed world at least."[20] Case-law emanating from these constitutional courts has taken on a global dimension, with courts referring to and quoting from each other, and with human rights being interpreted and applied on the basis of comparative legal research and analysis. Comparative constitutionalism is no longer the exclusive domain of academia but is being practiced by many constitutional courts in a truly global fashion. This trend towards a globalised jurisprudence on human rights is not without controversy. While some courts have embraced the jurisprudence coming from other constitutional courts, others have been more reluctant or indeed hostile.[21] The latter is perhaps best exemplified by a report of the ruling of a Hong Kong judge that "resort to foreign judgements should be eschewed," since "other domestic and international instruments are the product of very different circumstances and situations," and courts should "decline to be seduced by the complex foreign jurisprudence and the seemingly inexhaustible literature from the European Court of Human Rights."[22] However, while this attitude is shared by some other constitutional courts—for instance, Singapore—the vast majority of constitutional courts refer to foreign judgements in cases concerning the interpretation, application, and enforcement of human rights. There are now numerous textbooks on comparative constitutional law,[23] and despite occasional political backlash[24] even the U.S. Supreme Court openly asserts its right to refer to foreign judgements in its interpretation of constitutionally guaranteed rights.

In the interpretation and application of the constitutionally guaranteed fundamental rights, therefore, the Supreme Court of Afghanistan has access to a rapidly growing body of case-law. The same is, however, not true for the Islamic judicial review clause contained in the Afghan constitution. There are, in fact, not many countries with a Muslim majority population that allow statutes to be judicially reviewed on the basis of Islam. A recent report of the United States Commission on International Religious Freedom identified 22 countries that have declared themselves to be Islamic states or have declared Islam as the state religion.[25] The vast majority of these 22 states, viz. Bahrain, Egypt, Iran, Iraq, Jordan, Kuwait, Libya, Oman, Qatar, Saudi Arabia, Syria, U.A.E., Afghanistan, Maldives, Pakistan, Malaysia, Gambia, and Sudan, accords a role to Islam as a source of legislation. However, the report does not identify with any precision which of these 22 states has empowered courts to review the validity of legislation with reference to Islam. The report mentions Afghanistan, Iraq, Egypt, Iran, and Pakistan as countries that have incorporated "repugnancy clauses" based on Islam, but concludes that the "ramifications of establishing a constitutionally-mandated legislative role for Islam vary from country to country, though a full analysis is beyond the scope of this study."[26]

In Afghanistan prior to the enactment of the Constitution, there were concerns about the potential harm that could result from recognising Islam as a source of law and from enabling courts to review legislation on the basis of Islam. The published proceedings of the RAND conference "Democracy and Islam in the New Constitution of Afghanistan" reveal that there was growing concern that the drafters of the new Constitution were not aware of the dangers inherent in the creation of a strong constitutional court with the power to invalidate legislation not just on the basis of human rights but also on the ground that it contradicts Islamic law:

> Finally, it is important that the drafters be aware of how different sections of the constitution can interact in unforeseen ways. For instance, the status of Islamic law and the matter of judicial review are often discussed separately and addressed in different clauses. But providing for strong language in both areas might have the effect of empowering judges in vague and unanticipated ways to address matters of Islamic law as part of their oversight of the constitutionality of legislation.[27]

The participants of the RAND conference thought that a recognition of the "principles of Islam" as a source of legislation would prevent Islamic law from being used in order to impose radical visions of an Islamic state, as long as the clause "however phrased, does not imply that any of Afghanistan's current laws ought to be invalidated."[28] The report of the conference proceedings singles out Pakistan as an example of what can happen to a state that allows courts to invalidate on the basis of Islam: "In Pakistan, for example, judges struck down vast portions of the statutory law because it did not conform to their notion of Islam, wreaking havoc in the economy and society in general."[29] While claiming that other countries have had similarly negative experiences, the conference proceedings do not refer to any specific examples.

It appears that the voices of the RAND conference did not convince the drafters of the new Afghan constitution; as noted above, the Supreme Court of Afghanistan will be able to effectively invalidate legislation on the basis of Islam albeit that it cannot do so on a suo moto basis. But will this provision wreak havoc with Afghan's legal system or, given the current state of the legal system, impair its reconstruction and development? Unlike comparative constitutionalism and the enforcement of constitutionally guaranteed human rights, there is no systematic collection of comparative Islamic constitutionalism that would offer an informed perspective on the effect and impact of such "repugnancy clauses."[30] To date, of the countries that allow for a judicial review of legislation on the basis of Islam, only Iran, Egypt, and Pakistan have been studied.[31] Of these three examples, it is the jurisdiction of the Pakistani courts that resembles the

Afghan constitutional provisions on judicial review most closely: Pakistan's Federal Shariat Court has the power to review existing legislation on the basis of law, albeit that some laws have been exempted from its jurisdiction. Egypt's Supreme Constitutional Court has jurisdiction to review legislation on the basis of Islam, but this power can only be exercised with respect to new laws. Existing legislation is immune from being challenged on the basis of Islam. As a result, the vast majority of Egyptian law is outside the jurisdiction of the Supreme Constitutional Court. The Iranian approach to the Islamisation of laws locates the power to review laws on the basis of Islam not in the courts, but in the Council of Guardians, consisting of six Islamic jurists appointed by the Leader in consultation with the head of the judiciary.[32] No such mechanism or procedure is envisaged by the constitution of Afghanistan, which places the power to review laws on the basis of Islam firmly in the Supreme Court.

In a comparative perspective the example of Pakistan is therefore most relevant to Afghanistan, for both the Afghan and the Pakistani constitution enjoin the judiciary to ensure that the legal system is not contrary to Islam and empower courts to examine and to invalidate existing and new laws on the basis of Islam.

Islamic and Judicial Review

In Pakistan, the power of courts to strike legislation on the basis of Islam was introduced for the first time almost exactly 25 years ago.[33] The drafters of Pakistan's first constitution, enacted in 1956, had rejected the proposal to allow courts to review laws on the basis of Islam on the ground that

> This provision gives a power to the Supreme Court which may be misused and, in any case, which the directly elected representatives of the people could be expected to exercise without any extra-parliamentary checks.[34]

Following the creation of Pakistan in 1947, the first document to emanate from Pakistan's Constituent Assembly was entitled "The Objectives' Resolution." It contained a blueprint and guiding principles for the new constitution, declaring that "the Muslims of Pakistan shall be enabled individually and collectively to order their lives in accordance with the teachings and requirements of Islam as set out in the Holy Qur'an and Sunnah."[35] The 1956 Constitution, like all its successors, contained a clause that was to give effect to this principle, by providing in seemingly stringent terms that "no law shall be enacted which is repugnant to the injunctions of Islam as laid down in the Holy Qur'an and Sunnah, hereinafter referred to as the injunctions of Islam, and existing law shall be brought in conformity with such injunctions."[36] The legal effect of this provision was, however, purely declaratory, since the Constitution provided no mechanisms to enforce this article. The structure of non-justiciable constitutional provisions urging the state to bring all laws in conformity with Islam, accompanied by provisions for the setting up of an advisory Islamic council, was replicated in the Constitutions of 1962 and 1973. As a result, courts could not review the constitutional validity of laws on the basis of Islam. Any attempt by petitioners to have certain laws declared un-Islamic was firmly rejected by Pakistan's higher judiciary.[37]

In 1980, just three years after the imposition of martial law, General Zia ul Haq created the Federal Shariat Court. The jurisdiction of the Federal Shariat Court was twofold. Firstly, it acted as the exclusive court of appeal in cases involving the Hudood Ordinances,[38] and secondly, the Federal Shariat Court was given exclusive jurisdiction to review existing statutes on the basis of Islam. This jurisdiction was, however, circumscribed: the Constitution, procedural laws, Muslim personal law, and, for a limited period, all laws dealing with taxation and fiscal matters were excluded from its jurisdiction. There is by now a substantial body of case-law concerned with the effect of the Islamic repugnancy clause on the validity of legislation. The picture emerging from Pakistan is a complex one but it is possible to present certain trends,[39] which are that the vast majority of Pakistan's statutory laws emerged from the process of Islamic judicial review unscathed, despite the fact that these laws were in many instances the product of colonialism. All main areas of the legal system were occupied by statutes that had their origins in British India. Despite their un-Islamic provenance, the Federal Shariat Court held most of them to be in conformity with Islam. The areas of law most vulnerable to be struck down as un-Islamic were concerned with the charging of interest in financial transactions, limitations on the right to own property, and pre-emption, as well as distinct areas of criminal and family law. In addition, the Federal Shariat Court also developed an Islamic right to justice.

The Federal Shariat Court's jurisdiction, in line with the judicial review of laws on the basis of constitutionally guaranteed rights, is limited to laws and customs having the force of law. This has limited in very practical terms the range of issues that can be examined by the Federal Shariat Court. Issues often associated with the creation of an Islamic society, such as dress codes, moral conduct, relations between genders, and depiction of women in the media, were not covered by laws. With no law in existence to force women to wear a headscarf, for instance, there is nothing the Federal Shariat Court could do to make the government introduce such a law—its jurisdiction is limited to striking down existing laws. This limitation has by now become apparent to religious political parties which have attempted to pass legislation in the North-West Frontier Province, where they form the provincial government, in order to create an Islamic ombudsman charged with, inter alia, ensuring that all Muslims adhere to an Islamic way of life. As will be seen later, this law was struck down by

Pakistan's Supreme Court as unconstitutional, among other reasons because it sought to create a parallel system of criminal law.

Afghanistan's Supreme Court is even further constrained. Similar to the Federal Shariat Court, Afghanistan's apex court has the power to invalidate laws, and cannot demand the passing of new laws. However, in contrast to Pakistan's Federal Shariat Court, which has the power to examine laws on its own motion or on the petition of an individual, the Afghanistan Supreme Court can only review those laws that either have been referred to it by the government or have reached it by way of appeal against a lower court's decision. These restrictions prevent the Afghanistan Supreme Court from embarking on a wholesale review of Afghanistan's body of statutes. The legal nature of its powers of judicial review also disallow the Supreme Court from issuing rulings on matters that do not involve the conformity of a law with Islam. This restriction was not recognised by Afghanistan's previous Chief Justice, Mawlawi Fazl Hadi Shinwari. On 14 January 2004, just ten days after the new Constitution came into force, he issued a ruling to the effect that a planned televised performance of a female singer was un-Islamic and therefore illegal. However, there was no law governing the performance of female singers on TV, and thus nothing to be invalidated by way of judicial review, nor had the issue been referred to the Supreme Court by way of appeal or by the government. The ruling seems to have been ignored by the TV station and the government did not seek to prevent the transmission from taking place.[40]

In Pakistan many laws were struck down as un-Islamic on grounds that were in fact quite similar to the grounds available under constitutionally guaranteed rights. In a series of decisions the Federal Shariat Court ruled that a right to be heard, a right to equality, a right to movement, and indeed a right to justice were Islamic norms. A law violating any of these norms was liable to be struck down as repugnant to Islam. Thus, perhaps surprisingly, in many cases there was no clash between constitutional rights and Islamic law but an overlap. However, the judges of the Federal Shariat Court enjoyed wide discretionary power under these Islamic human rights' norms, since they were all founded on one principal building block: an Islamic right to justice. What falls under the term "justice" is for the court to decide. In the absence of any established case-law judges were able to fill this lacuna with their own views of what was just and what was not. To give an example: a provision in the Pakistani Passports Act 1874, which allowed the government to withdraw a passport for up to four months from its holder without giving any grounds, was challenged as being contrary to Islam. The Federal Shariat Court decided that the "right of free movement from one place to another to all human beings has been fully recognised in Islam" and invalidated the impugned provision.[41]

The confluence of secular human rights guaranteed by the constitution and human rights anchored in Islamic law is of particular relevance to

Afghanistan, where the Constitution incorporates not only Islamic law into domestic law, but also the international human rights' treaties to which Afghanistan is a party.[42] The decisions of the Federal Shariat Court illustrate that in many instances Islamic law and secular human rights reinforce each other. Conversely, the Pakistani experience also indicates that there are areas where Islamic law and human rights are not easily reconciled. In the case of Pakistan, the areas of such conflict concern mainly the rights of women and of religious minorities. Legally-sanctioned discrimination against women has never been successfully challenged as un-Islamic, nor were the members of the Ahmadiyya community successful in their claim that declaring them non-Muslims was in fact un-Islamic and should be struck down on that ground.[43]

Land Law

The Federal Shariat Court has invalidated a number of laws aimed at social and economic reform. In Pakistan laws restricting maximum holdings of landownership and laws giving tenants of agricultural land a right of preemption were all invalidated by the Federal Shariat Court. The ability to circumvent extensive constitutional provisions meant to protect these laws against judicial review, and to strike them down as un-Islamic, testifies to the considerable powers inherent in the judicial review of legislation on the basis of Islam.[44] The Pakistani decisions all coincided with a period of economic liberalisation, which began in the early 1990s. As such, there was not much political opposition to the invalidation of these laws. The case of Afghanistan is not dissimilar: the restrictions on the maximum size of land holdings, introduced in the 1970s and 1980s, have not been adopted by the current government. As such, it is unlikely that in the foreseeable future the Supreme Court will have to deal with social and economic reform legislation, which limits rights to own property or involves the confiscation of private property.[45] Nevertheless, the experience of Pakistan suggests that any attempt to restrict the right of an individual to own property is liable to be challenged as a violation of Islamic norms.

Family Law

Laws aimed at reforming Muslim family law so as to offer better protection to women especially in the area of divorce and polygamy are at risk of being struck down as un-Islamic. In Pakistan, the Constitution expressly prohibited the Federal Shariat Court from examining issues relating to Muslim personal law.[46] However, after many years of adherence to this prohibition, in 2000 the Federal Shariat Court overruled its own precedence and held that it did have jurisdiction to examine the Muslim Family Laws Ordinance, 1961. Several provisions were held to be contrary to Islam, including the procedural steps to be followed in order to make a divorce legally valid.[47] An appeal against this decision is still pending before the

Shariat Appellate Bench of the Supreme Court. In the case of Afghanistan, the attempts to reform Islamic family law have been quite modest and are for the most part concerned with weeding out customary practices that are regarded as violative of Islam. Thus, there are laws to prevent extravagant marriage ceremonies and child marriages, and to discourage the practice of paying *walwar* (bride price) and excessive dower.[48] More controversial might be any attempt to restrict polygamy or the husband's right to a unilateral divorce. However, the Civil Law of 1977 does not impose any meaningful restrictions in these areas of Islamic family law. The Pakistan experience suggests that any attempt to introduce significant reforms to Islamic family law in Afghanistan is likely to be challenged as un-Islamic before the Supreme Court of Afghanistan.

Criminal Law

Western-style criminal laws are liable to come under intense scrutiny in any judicial review based on Islam. Given that many areas of Islamic criminal law are very different in both formal legal terms and terms of substance, any Western-inspired penal code is at risk of being invalidated on the basis of Islam. The areas of laws most vulnerable in such a review are those dealing with murder and bodily harm, theft, sexual offences, intoxication, blasphemy, and apostasy.[49] In Pakistan, the Federal Shariat Court, in a series of decisions, forced the government to amend the Pakistan Penal Code, 1860, so as to make the offences of murder and bodily harm comply with the Islamic law of *qiṣāṣ* and *diya*, i.e., retaliation and bloodmoney.[50] The effect on Pakistan's criminal law has been dramatic, with as many as eight out of ten convicted murderers escaping punishment because they agreed to pay monetary compensation to the families of their victims.[51]

In Afghanistan the principal source of substantive criminal law is the Afghan Penal Code of 1976. A superficial glance at the Code might suggest that it is in fact a Western-inspired penal code, since none of its chapter headings refers to Islamic criminal law. A closer look, however, shows the Penal Code to be a unique attempt to combine both Western and Islamic penal law. Article 1 of the Code provides that the non-Qurʾanic *taʿzīr* crimes and penalties will be regulated by the code and that the Qurʾanic *ḥadd*, *qiṣāṣ*, and *diya* crimes shall be punished in accordance with Hanafi law. This division is maintained for the offences of murder, theft, adultery, rape, and robbery. They are governed by the punishments contained in the Penal Code, if the Islamic religious law "is dropped or affected by one of the disqualifying reasons or lack of sufficient conditions."[52] The Islamic character of Afghanistan's penal law would make any challenge by way of judicial review unlikely. It should, however, be noted that it would be difficult to remove these Islamic features from the Penal Code. Any amendment of the Penal Code would require amending legislation to be passed by Parliament. Such a law could also be reviewed on the basis of Islam, and could be invalidated by the Supreme Court if found to be repugnant to Islam. The issue of Islamic criminal law received much publicity in 2006, when the above-mentioned apostasy case against an Afghan convert to Christianity was raised.[53] The man was eventually freed on procedural grounds, but his arrest demonstrated that Afghanistan's substantive criminal law has retained Islamic characteristics, despite its Western appearance.[54]

Commercial Law

The Pakistani experience shows that it is not just criminal and family laws that may be challenged on the basis of Islam; so also may laws governing financial transactions, or, more generally, all laws that provide for the payment of interest (*ribā*).[55] This is not limited to loans or other means of financing, but may also affect insurance contracts, laws allowing for gambling, and contractually stipulated payments of interests. Unlike Pakistan, where the issue of *ribā* has remained controversial for decades, there has been complete silence on this issue in Afghanistan. A new banking law, decreed in 2003, expressly authorises banks to engage in interest-bearing financial transactions and to charge interest on loans; it contains no single reference to Islamic banking at all.[56] Nor is there mention of Islamic finance in guides on foreign investment in Afghanistan.[57] Despite this silence, there is little doubt that the constitutional requirement that all laws must be in accordance with Islam could pose a challenge to Article 33 of the Law of Banking. The likelihood of such a challenge ever reaching the Supreme Court is high, since the issue is usually raised by loan defaulters in order to seek the entire loan agreement unenforceable on the ground that it violates the Islamic prohibition on the charging of interest. Arguments of this nature have even reached the English courts.[58] The English Court of Appeal was able to avoid any ruling on the merits of the argument that a contractual stipulation for the payment of interest was unenforceable if the contract was governed by Islamic law. The court decided that a simple reference to Islamic law was too vague to be recognised as a valid choice of law. The Supreme Court of Afghanistan, however, would have to face this issue head on: a decision that laws providing for the payment of interest are un-Islamic would have potentially far-reaching consequences for its frail economy. The financing of development projects as well as the provision of capital for private investment projects would be severely hampered if interest-based lending were to be prohibited as a result of a ruling of the Supreme Court, without an alternative—Islamic—finance system having been developed. There has not been any published research on the issue of Islam and banking operations in Afghanistan, but historical sources indicate that at least in the nineteenth and early twentieth century, Muslims there did not engage in the lending of money on religious grounds. As a result, Hindus dominated the business of money-lending.[59] The issue of money-lending resurfaced briefly, and mysteriously, in the tumultuous events leading to the resignation of Afghanistan's modernising King Amanullah, when a petition drawn up by the ulama of Kandahar and Kabul contained among others the demand that "no restriction should be placed on the lending and borrowing of money."[60] Olesen terms this "a curious demand and it appears that the only justification could be to protect the money lenders (who then presumably were tribal leaders, mullahs and *hajjis*)." While Olesen's speculation that money-lending was conducted by tribal leaders and mullas cannot be verified, it is correct that with the founding of a state bank in 1924, the Bank-i Milli, the state took control over all banking operations. Ever since, only banks licensed by the state bank have been permitted to operate. It appears from the silence of the literature on this point that throughout the twentieth century banks were permitted to charge interest on loans, a practice continued expressly in the new Banking Law. Given the experiences of Pakistan, it is possible to speculate that this silence will be broken as soon as a loan defaulter faces his creditors in court. The Supreme Court would then have to decide whether section 30 of the Banking Law is compatible with the principles of Islamic law.

Impact of Judicial Review

A discussion of the effects of a judicial review on the basis of Islam would be incomplete without mentioning the potential impact of this jurisdiction on the courts. A strong and independent judiciary is widely regarded as a prerequisite for the existence of the rule of law and the protection of human rights against the state. In the vast majority of countries with constitutionally guaranteed human rights, judges perform an important role in enforcing these rights, albeit that the extent of enforcement and the exact demarcation of the scope of these rights vary from jurisdiction to jurisdiction. Judicial review on the basis of Islam is in theory no different. There is a judiciary charged with enforcing a certain body of norms against which legislation can be tested. The difference lies in the nature of these norms. Constitutionally guaranteed rights are contained in a law that was drafted and enforced in a constituent process. It can therefore be changed and most countries with written constitutions have experienced amendments and changes to the constitutionally guaranteed rights. Indeed, amendments have at times taken place in order to weaken constitutionally guaranteed rights so as to prevent certain laws from being reviewed. In India the right to own property was completely removed from the constitution by way of constitutional amendment. This was done in order to protect land reform legislation against judicial review and possible invalidation.

In theory at least, Islamic law is not amenable to amendment or change. Revealed to the Prophet Muḥammad it is believed to be the word of God and not a law made by man. To quote Khaled Abou El Fadl, one of the authors of the RAND Report on the new Afghan constitution, "There is no single code of law or particular set of positive commandments that represent the sharia." Modern constitutions struggle with the potential vagueness of "Islamic law" and attempt to demarcate with greater precision what is included in the term. Pakistan's constitution refers to Islamic law as laid down in the Qur'an and Sunna, Afghanistan's constitution refers to the Hanafi school of jurisprudence, and the Iraq constitution refers to the "universally agreed tenets of Islam." Nevertheless, all of these formulations leave ample room for judicial interpretation. Even more significantly, unlike constitutionally guaranteed rights, which at least in theory can be amended, expanded or even removed, no such power is available with respect to individual judicial rulings on what constitutes the correct interpretation of Islamic law.

In very practical terms, in seeking to restrict the potentially wide-ranging powers of a review of laws on the basis of Islam, the elected representatives of the people and the government have only two options. Firstly, these powers can be taken away or at least restricted. In practical terms, however, a constitutional amendment to remove the provisions for Islamic judicial review would in most countries be difficult both politically and legally. In Afghanistan such an amendment would be unconstitutional, while in Pakistan it is likely that such an amendment would be invalidated as being violative of the basic structure of its constitution. However, even more serious would be the political difficulties inherent in such an attempt since it could easily be interpreted as an attack on Islam or at least the Islamic foundations of the state. It must therefore be concluded that once introduced, provisions allowing for the judicial review of legislation on the basis of Islam are unlikely to be removed or restricted through political processes.

The second option is to control the judiciary itself. The RAND report states this succinctly: "The 'who' (who is interpreting the law) is as important as the 'what' (what law is being interpreted)." For the Afghan constitution RAND favoured a provision that would prohibit judges from taking up issues on their own motion, would impose educational requirements on judges, and would discontinue the practice of a self-selecting judicial body, recommending instead that judges be nominated by the executive, reviewed by a specialised commission, and, finally, confirmed by the legislature. While this process might ensure that candidates deemed too radical or too conservative would not become judges, there is nothing that could be done once a judge has been appointed to the Supreme Court. The contemporary international standards on the independence of the judiciary would not support the dismissal of a judge merely because his interpretations of Islamic law lead to wide-ranging changes of the law.

After all, he is only exercising a jurisdiction expressly conferred on him by the constitution.

In Pakistan at least, it has been the control of the judges of the Federal Shariat Court and the Shariat Appellate Bench of the Supreme Court that at times has reined in the broad rulings of activist judges. Both General Musharraf and General Zia ul Haq blatantly interfered with the independence of the judiciary, removing those judges who were regarded as problematic. This approach cannot be regarded as legally defensible. However, as could be seen above (text at n. 24), even in the U.S. there are calls to restrict the judicial review powers of judges and judicial appointments are under intense political scrutiny because judges are not only powerful but also difficult to remove once they sit on the bench.

Conclusion

The experience of Pakistan shows that the judicial review of legislation on the basis of Islam is beset with problems. The enormous power of judges to strike down legislation as un-Islamic is difficult to control within democratic institutions, and once introduced is also difficult to remove. While it is correct to summarise that in Pakistan the Islamisation of laws has been a primarily judge-led process, it is also correct that this in turn has made it tempting to interfere with the independence of the judiciary. Most worrying is probably the fact that many of Pakistan's criminal laws have come into existence as a result of rulings of the Federal Shariat Court that had invalidated their precursors. As a result, the power of the legislature to make laws is severely limited. Pakistan's experience also shows that the interaction and relationship between constitutionally guaranteed rights and Islamic law do not always lead to results consistent with international human rights' norms. This becomes most apparent in cases involving the legal status of women, the right to freedom of religion, and the prohibition of cruel and inhumane punishments.

The Islamic provenance of much of Afghanistan's body of statutory laws makes it likely that it will emerge largely intact from a judicial review on the basis of Islam. The charging of interest, however, might become Afghanistan's Achilles heel. In Pakistan, the matter remains unresolved after almost ten years of litigation. However, there is little doubt that most Islamic jurists and Muslim judges would regard an interest-free banking system to be an essential characteristic of an Islamic state, and of a legal system that is in accordance with Islam.

NOTES

1 For a recent evaluation of the efforts to rebuild governmental institutions, see International Crisis Group, "Afghanistan's Endangered Compact," Policy Briefing No. 59, 29 January 2007, which states (p. 1): "While the growing insurgency is attracting increasing attention, long-term efforts to build the solid governmental institutions a stable Afghanistan requires are faltering."

[2] "Slow Progress on Security and Rights," Human Rights Watch, Press Release, New York, January 30, 2007, finds that 4,400 Afghans died in conflict-related violence in 2006, twice as many as in 2005.

[3] "The Opium Situation in Afghanistan: 2006 Annual Opium Poppy Survey Summary of Findings," UN Office on Drugs and Crime, September 2, 2006.

[4] See, for instance, "Afghanistan: Spiralling Lawlessness Highlights Need for Promised International Aid," Amnesty International, AI Index: ASA 11/010/2004 (Public) News Service No. 156, June 17, 2004.

[5] There is evidence that the U.S. and its allies in Afghanistan continue to bolster the influence of local commanders outside Kabul; see Sonali Kolhatkar and James Ingalls, *Bleeding Afghanistan. Washington, Warlords, and the Propaganda of Silence* (New York: Seven Stories Press, 2006).

[6] For an overview of the ongoing activities to reform the justice sector in Afghanistan, see Charles Briefel, *Afghanistan Justice Sector Overview* (Kabul: UNAMA, December 2006).

[7] There is no official English translation of the 2004 Constitution, written in Dari and Pashtu. In this article all references to provisions of the 2004 Constitution are to an unofficial translation; see Nadjma Yassari (ed.), *The Shariʿa in the Constitutions of Afghanistan, Iran and Egypt: Implications for Private Law* (Tübingen: Mohr Siebeck, 2005), 269ff.

[8] Article 19 of the 2004 Constitution.

[9] Ibid., Article 20.

[10] Ibid., Article 63. All ministers have to swear, inter alia, "to observe the sacred religion of Islam," cf. Article 74 of the 2004 Constitution, while Supreme Court judges are obliged to swear that they will "support justice and righteousness in accordance with the sacred religion of Islam, this Constitution and the laws of Afghanistan," cf. Article 119, ibid.

[11] Ibid., Article 17.

[12] Ibid., Article 45.

[13] Ibid., Article 35.

[14] The obvious injustice in specifying Hanafi jurisprudence as the governing school of Islamic law in a country with a substantial Shiʿi minority is somewhat lessened by Article 131, which provides that "Courts shall apply Shia school of law in cases dealing with personal matters involving the followers of Shia Sect in accordance with the provisions of law. In other cases if no clarification by this constitution and other laws exist and both sides of the case are followers of the Shia Sect, courts will resolve the matter according to laws of this Sect." Nevertheless, the express reference to Hanafi jurisprudence limits the courts' ability to choose from among the schools of Islamic law those rules that are best suited to the requirements of modern Afghanistan.

[15] For an analysis of the Islamic provisions in the constitutions of 1923, 1931, 1964, 1978, 1980, 1987, 1990, 1992, and 2004, see Mohammad Hamid Saboory, "The Progress of Constitutionalism in Afghanistan," in Yassari (ed.), *The Shariʿa in the Constitutions of Afghanistan, Iran and Egypt*, 23–44.

[16] For an analysis of the impact of Islamic law and customs on women, see Mark Drumbl, "Rights, Culture, and Crime. The Role of the Rule of Law for the Women of Afghanistan," *Columbia Journal of Transnational Law* 42/2 (2004), 349–90.

[17] For a recent analysis, see Mashood Baderin, *International Human Rights and Islamic Law* (Oxford: Oxford University Press, 2003). Baderin argues that there are only very few conflicts between Islamic law and international human rights law, and that the likelihood of these instances ever manifesting themselves could be reduced by procedural and evidential safeguards. A more pessimistic assessment is offered by Ann Elizabeth Mayer, *Islam and Human Rights: Tradition and Politics* (Boulder, Colo.: Westview, [3]2007).

[18] Saboory, "The Progress of Constitutionalism in Afghanistan," 21.

[19] See also Rainer Grote, "Separation of Powers in the New Afghan Constitution," *Zeitschrift für ausländisches öffentliches Recht und Völkerrecht* 64 (2004), 912, who comes to the same conclusion.

[20] Christopher McCrudden, "A Common Law of Human Rights? Transnational Judicial Conversations on Constitutional Rights," *Oxford Journal of Legal Studies* 20/4 (2000), 506.

[21] Ibid.; see also William N. Eskridge, "Lawrence v. Texas and the Imperative of Comparative Constitutionalism," *International Journal of Constitutional Law* 2/3 (2004), 555–60.

[22] Quoted in Christopher McCrudden, "A Common Law of Human Rights?," 508.

[23] See for instance Norman Dorsen et al., *Comparative Constitutionalism: Cases and Materials* (St. Paul, Minn.: West, 2003).

[24] See for instance the statement of John Corney, a U.S. Senator from Texas: "I fear, however, that today some judges may be departing so far from American law, American principles, and American traditions, that the only way they can justify their rulings from the bench is to cite the law of foreign countries, foreign governments, and foreign cultures—because there is nothing in this country left for them to cite for support." John Corney, "Domestic, Not Foreign," *The National Review*, March 28, 2005.

[25] Tad Stahnke and Robert Blitt, *The Religion-State Relationship and the Right to Freedom of Religion or Belief. A Comparative Textual Analysis of the Constitutions of Predominantly Muslim Countries*, United States Commission on International Religious Freedom, March 2005. The declared Islamic states are Afghanistan, Bahrain, Brunei, Iran, Maldives, Mauritania, Oman, Pakistan, and Saudi Arabia, whereas Islam has been declared as state religion in Algeria, Bangladesh, Egypt, Iraq, Jordan, Kuwait, Libya, Malaysia, Qatar, Tunisia and the U.A.E.

[26] Ibid., 10.

[27] Cheryl Bernard and Nina Hachigian (eds.), *Democracy and Islam in the New Constitution of Afghanistan* (Santa Monica, Calif.: Rand, 2003), 1.

[28] Ibid., 4.

[29] Ibid., 5.

[30] See Nathan Brown, *Constitutions in a Nonconstitutional World. Arab Basic Laws and the Prospects for Accountable Government* (Albany: State University of New York Press, 2002), 180–93, for a comparison of Islamic constitutionalism in Iran and Egypt.

[31] On Egypt, see Frank E. Vogel, "Conformity with Islamic Shariʿa and Constitutionality under Article 2: Some Issues of Theory, Practice, and Comparison," in *Democracy: The Rule of Law and Islam*, ed. Eugene Cotran and Adel Omar Sherif (The Hague: Kluwer Law International, 1999), 525–44; Baber

Johansen, "The Relationship Between the Constitution, the Shariʿa and the Fiqh in the Adjudication of Egypt's Supreme Constitutional Court," *Zeitschrift für ausländisches öffentliches Recht und Völkerrecht* 64/4 (2004), 881–96; and Clark Lombardi, *State Law as Islamic Law in Modern Egypt: The Incorporation of the Shariʿa into Egyptian Constitutional Law* (Leiden: Brill, 2006); on Pakistan, see Martin Lau, *The Role of Islam in the Legal System of Pakistan* (Leiden: Brill, 2005); and on Iran, see Ashgar Schirazi, *The Constitution of Iran. Politics and the State in the Islamic Republic* (London: I. B. Tauris, 1997).

[32] Article 96 of the Constitution of the Islamic Republic of Iran, 1979.

[33] See Constitution (Amendment) Order, 1980, adding a new Chapter 3A to the Constitution of Pakistan, 1973. The new Article 203–C created the Federal Shariat Court, which was empowered to invalidate laws found to be contrary to Islam, as laid down in the Qurʾan and Sunna.

[34] Lau, *The Role of Islam in the Legal System of Pakistan*, 6.

[35] The Objectives Resolution 1949 served as a preamble to all of Pakistan's constitutions. In 1985 it was incorporated into the main body of the Constitution 1973 in the form of a new Article 2–A. See Dieter Conrad, "Conflicting Legitimacies in Pakistan: The Changing Role of the Objectives Resolution (1949) in the Constitution," in Subrata Mitra and Dietmar Rothermund, *Legitimacy and Conflict in South Asia* (New Delhi: Manohar, 1997), 122–55.

[36] See Article 25(1) of the 1956 Constitution.

[37] See for an early decision, Chaudhary Tanbir Ahmad Siddiky v. The Province of East Pakistan and others PLD 1968 SC 185, where: "Such a plea [to invalidate a statute as contrary to Islam] is, however, not justiciable in Courts under present Constitution. The responsibility has been laid to the Legislature to see that no law repugnant to the Islamic law is brought on the statute book. The grievance, if any, therefore should be ventilated in a different forum and not in this Court." (203–05)

[38] The term "Hudood Ordinances" refers to the Islamic criminal laws promulgated by Zia ul Haq in 1979 and 1980. They comprise the Offences against Property (Enforcement of Hudood) Ordinance 1979, the Offence of Zina (Enforcement of Hudood) Ordinance 1979, the Offence of Qazf (Enforcement of Hadd) Ordinance 1979, and the Prohibition (Enforcement of Hadd) Order 1979.

[39] See Lau, *The Role of Islam in the Legal System of Pakistan.*

[40] See Mohammad Hashim Kamali, "Islam and its Shariʿa in the Afghan Constitution 2004 with Special Reference to Personal Law," in Yassari (ed.), *The Shariʿa in the Constitutions of Afghanistan, Iran and Egypt*, 37.

[41] See Re: Passports Act 1974 PLD 1989 FSC 39, at 43.

[42] See Articles 7 and 121 of the Constitution of Afghanistan, 2004.

[43] See Mujeeb-ur-Rehman v. Federal Government of Pakistan PLD 1984 FSC 136.

[44] See Lau, *The Role of Islam in the Legal System of Pakistan*, 189ff., for a discussion of these cases.

[45] For a comprehensive analysis of the history and current state of land law in Afghanistan, see Conor Foley, *Guide to Property Law in Afghanistan* (Oslo: Norwegian Refugee Council, 2005).

[46] See Article 203-B of the Constitution of Pakistan, 1973.

[47] See Allah Rakha v. Federation of Pakistan PLD 2000 FSC 1.

[48] See Hashim Kamali, *Law in Afghanistan. A Study of the Constitutions, Matrimonial Law and the Judiciary* (Leiden: E. J. Brill, 1985), 83ff.

[49] See Ruud Peters, "The Enforcement of God's Law: The Shari'ah in the Present World of Islam," in Philip Ostien, Jamila M. Nasir, and Franz Kogelmann (eds.), *Comparative Perspectives on Shari'ah in Nigeria* (Ibadan, Nigeria: Spectrum Books, 2005), 11.

[50] The changes to the Pakistan Penal Code, 1860, were effected by the Criminal Law (Amendment) Act, 1997.

[51] See Tahir Wasti, "The Introduction and Application of Shariah in the Law of Culpable Homicide and Murder in Pakistan," Ph.D. thesis, London, 2005.

[52] See Article 396 of the Penal Code, 1976. The possibility of imposing *ta'zīr* punishments as the alternative to *ḥadd* punishments was already established in Afghanistan's first Penal Code, drawn up in 1924 during the reign of King Amanullah; see Vatan Gregorian, *The Emergence of Modern Afghanistan. Politics of Reform and Modernization, 1880–1946* (Stanford: Stanford University Press, 1969), 249. This Code was rescinded during the reign of Nadir Shah (1929–1933), and Afghanistan's criminal law remained based wholly on Islamic law until the passing of the Penal Code 1976. See Gregorian, 299.

[53] For an analysis of the crime of apostasy under Afghan law, see Mandana Knust Rassekh Afshar, "The Case of an Afghan Apostate. The Right to a Fair Trial between Islamic Law and Human Rights in the Afghan Constitution," in *Max Planck UNYB* 10 (2006), 593–605.

[54] The application of Islamic criminal law is particularly visible in the case of female prisoners, many of whom are convicted for moral crimes, which would not constitute an offence under any secular criminal law. See Anou Borrey, *Legal Aid Program, Facts and Figures* (Kabul: Medica Mondial, 2004), 26.

[55] For a concise account of the legal saga surrounding the abolition of interest from the Pakistani economy, see Parvez Hassan and Azim Azfar, *Moving Toward an Islamic Financial Regime in Pakistan*, Occasional Publication 2 (Cambridge, Mass.: Islamic Legal Studies Program, 2001).

[56] See Article 33, Banking Law of Afghanistan, 2003.

[57] See for instance "Doing Business in Afghanistan: A Country Commercial Guide for U.S. Companies" (U.S. and Foreign Commercial Service and U.S. Department of State, 2005).

[58] See Beximco v. Shamil Bank of Bahrain [2004] EWCA Civ 19.

[59] See Mountstuart Elphinstone, *An Account of the Kingdom of Caubul*, Book 1 (London: Longman et al., 1815), 332, for the early nineteenth century, and Frank A. Martin, *Under the Absolute Amir* (London: Harper, 1907), 251, for the early twentieth century.

[60] Quoted in Asta Olesen, *Islam and Politics in Afghanistan* (London: Curzon Press, 1995), 154.

13

THE QADI AND THE MUFTI IN AKHBARI SHIʿI JURISPRUDENCE

Robert Gleave

> It is hardly surprising that all the four schools, with the exception of the Ḥanafī, impose as a condition to qualification as judge the capacity of ijtihād, that is to say, that the appointee must be a mujtahid... Does the practice of ijtihād, if by a mujtahid, cut the knot of uncertainty by ritual effect, sealing the result with God's certainty? Does the mujtahid by a charismatic priestly office transmute uncertainty to certainty, and infuse the concrete with the transcendent? Neither of these. Ijtihād's claim to truth remains dependent on its objective arguments and proofs from knowledge conveyed in revelation; properly, no regard is paid to the person of the mujtahid beyond requiring a minimum of piety.
>
> Frank E. Vogel, "Islamic Law and Legal System"[1]

Frank Vogel's summation of the relationship between the judge (*qāḍī*, henceforth qadi) and the *mujtahid* (or more accurately, his summary of the reasons why a qadi needs to be a *mujtahid*) raises the recurrent theoretical problem of the authority of the qadi's judgement in Islamic law. If, as the four Sunni schools agree, the *mujtahid* produces (mere) personal opinion as to the law of God, then how can a qadi (who, for most, is a *mujtahid* and exercises his *ijtihād* when making his ruling) produce a ruling in a case that has the sufficient legal authority to justify implementation? What, logically speaking, distinguishes the judgement of a qadi from the fatwa of a mufti, when both are *mujtahids*?

The interlinked discussions of issuing decisions (*qaḍāʾ*) and issuing fatwas (*iftāʾ*) in Muslim works of legal theory and positive law (*uṣūl al-fiqh* and *furūʿ al-fiqh*, respectively), and the conflicting positions proposed by jurists of the various legal traditions of Islam, are testimony to the fact that this problem was never solved to everyone's satisfaction. The demand for the qadi to be a *mujtahid*, almost universally upheld by classical jurists, means that the qadi not only knows the law through his own (personal) investigation of the sources, but is also able to exercise his *ijtihād* in the assessment of the legally relevant facts of a case, and then to apply the law (as he understands it) to particular cases.

Ibn Qudāma (d. 620/1223) summarises the dispute as follows:

> The third qualification [for a qadi] is that he be one of the people of *ijtihād* (*min ahl al-ijtihād*). Mālik, al-Shāfiʿī and some Hanafis support this. Other [Hanafis] say that it is permitted for him to be a non-*mujtahid* (*ʿāmmī*) and give a ruling based on *taqlīd*. This is because the aim [of the judicial process] is to solve disputes, and if this can be done by *taqlīd*, then this is permitted... [Ibn Qudāma then cites two Qurʾanic verses and the famous *ḥadīth* of qadis being of three types, two of which are in hell]... The non-*mujtahid* who gives a judgement is, then, basing it on [his] ignorance.[2]

In line with Hanbali thinking generally, Ibn Qudāma considers it necessary that the qadi be a *mujtahid*. His argument is that being a qadi is more demanding than being a mufti. A mufti just gives legal opinion (*futyā*), but the qadi is involved in both giving a legal opinion and implementing it (*futyā* and *ilzām*). If a mufti is required to be a *mujtahid*, then, *a fortiori*, the qadi (whose task is more demanding) must also be a *mujtahid*. The reason, of course, for the lack of a requirement of *ijtihād* in a qadi in Hanafi literature is linked to their "high" view of *ijtihād*. A more demanding conception of the qualifications to be *mujtahid*s makes them thinner on the ground, which in turn makes it difficult to conceive of an effective judicial system. Note that the minimum level of a qadi's skills and learning may not vary between the different schools. Rather, it is the description of this level of attainment as *ijtihād* (and hence the naming of the qadi as a *mujtahid*) that is the primary topic of dispute. As Reinhart puts it:

> If some Hanafis, along with others, held high views of the significance of *ijtihād*, they held a correspondingly low view of the possibility of novel and independent *ijtihād* for all who lived after Islamic law's formative period.[3]

Whether this constitutes a closing of the door of *ijtihād* is another question,[4] but for Hanafis at least, it does seem to have been the case that at least some types of *ijtihād* ceased after the end of the formative period (the exact point in time is, naturally, the subject of dispute), and therefore one could no longer demand that qadis be *mujtahid*s.[5]

This paper examines how these stock juristic debates were played out within the Imami legal tradition, in particular how they influenced the presentation of ideal systems of judicial procedure by Akhbari jurists during the Safavid period and later. As is presented below, Akhbari conceptions of the scholar-judge diverge from Vogel's assessment described above. For some Akhbaris, the qadi is presented as having a quasi-sacred role, the intermediary between the Imams' words and the application of the law. His personal qualities (piety, moral probity, and level of learning) are crucial to the effective (that is, legally valid) operation of the Shariʿa during the absence of the Imam. The question of whether or not the divergence between Vogel's assessment and the evidence from the Imami tradition is due to uniquely problematic elements of Imami *fiqh* (including the possibility of legitimate government in the absence of the Imam) is discussed in the conclusion.

Imami Discussions of *Qaḍāʾ* and *Iftāʾ*

Whether or not a qadi must be a *mujtahid* depends, of course, on an acceptance of (at least the terminology) of *ijtihād*. As is well known, the early Imami jurists did not accept *ijtihād*, considering it epistemologically suspect (based on *ẓann*) and introduced by the Sunnis in order to overcome their lack of a sinless Imam. The Imamis, with their sinless Imam, had no need of it. Numerous statements of the Imams condemn *ijtihād*, and these were taken up in early works of Imami legal theory, written after the onset of the occultation (*ghayba*).[6] Without the Imam's presence, the rejection of *ijtihād* could not be maintained indefinitely. First, Imami writers of legal theory began to incorporate elements of Sunni *ijtihād* theory (though still maintaining a terminological polemic against it). Later, the inevitable legal indeterminacy brought on by the absence of the Imam was accepted and Imami works of legal theory began to incorporate chapters on *ijtihād*. Tracing the history of Imami discussion of whether a qadi should be a *mujtahid* is, then, complicated by the fact that early Imami jurists did not recognise the *mujtahid*'s position as legal authoritative. Various locutions were tried and tested before Imami jurists could securely say that a qadi must be a *mujtahid*.

Ibn Barrāj (d. 481/1088) states:

> [The judge] is not permitted to do *taqlīd* in any ruling; he is not permitted to consult with anyone else; he may not request a fatwa from another, and then rule according to that fatwa… [Legitimate] *qaḍāʾ* is only attached to a qadi when he is a member of the people of knowledge, moral probity, and competence (*ahl al-ʿilm wa l-ʿadāla wa l-kamāl*). He should know the Book, the Sunna, consensus, differences of opinion, and the Arabic language. As for analogical reasoning (*qiyās*), we do not include it because, in our opinion, the use of *qiyās* in the law is invalid.[7]

These conditions are, of course, famous in Sunni literature as being among the qualifications of a *mujtahid* (excepting *qiyās*),[8] though, of course, the qadi cannot be a *mujtahid* for Ibn Barrāj. Ibn Zuhrā al-Ḥalabī (d. 585/1189–90) states it more succinctly:

> He who judges by *taqlīd* is not certain of what God has revealed... he who judges on the basis of a fatwa [of another scholar] has judged out of ignorance.[9]

Once again, there is no mention of the qadi being a *mujtahid* here, but there is a requirement that he not be a *muqallid*.

Al-Muḥaqqiq (d. 676/1277) employs slightly different locutions in his two famous works of positive law. In the *Sharāʾiʿ al-Islām* he states:

> [*Qaḍāʾ*] cannot be legitimately attached to one who is not an *ʿālim* and able to give fatwas independently.[10]

In his *Muʿtabar*, he writes:

> [*Qaḍāʾ*] can only be legitimately attached to one who is qualified to give fatwas.[11]

In both, the level of learning required of a qadi is attached to the qualifications for issuing fatwas. However, the ability to give fatwas was not, formally or rhetorically, linked to *ijtihād*. Then again, *ijtihād* was not explicitly denied either.

Once *ijtihād* was fully legitimised in Imami legal theory (from the time of al-ʿAllāma al-Ḥillī onward), these locutions were reinterpreted by the commentators to refer to a *mujtahid*. Al-Shahīd al-Thānī (d. 966/1559), for example, commenting on the first of al-Muḥaqqiq's formulations, writes:

> [Al-Muḥaqqiq] means by *ʿālim* here a jurist who is a *mujtahid* in the rulings of the Shariʿa. There is a consensus of the *ʿulamāʾ* that this [i.e., being a *mujtahid*] is a condition of being a qadi... [al-Muḥaqqiq] means by the phrase "[the qadi] must know all that he is charged with" that he is an absolute *mujtahid* (*mujtahid muṭlaq*). [The qadi's] *ijtihād* in some areas of the law and not others, that is, "partial *ijtihād*," is not sufficient.[12]

This position on the essential qualities of a qadi took time to reach the mature expression we see here. Al-ʿAllāma (d. 726/1325), for example, who himself had incorporated *ijtihād* into his legal theory, was not yet able to break away from the reluctance to demand that the qadi be a *mujtahid*. For him, the qadi must "bring together all the qualities of a mufti" (*jāmiʿ li-sharāʾiṭ al-fatwā*), but these are not (at least in his *Irshād*) identified as identical with being the qualities of a *mujtahid*.[13]

Once it was established that the qadi must be a *mujtahid*, it became a canonical doctrine in Imami works of positive law,[14] and this was not challenged until the rise of the Akhbariyya in the eleventh/seventeenth century. The Akhbari movement rejected al-ʿAllāma's incorporation of *ijtihād* into Imami jurisprudence, claiming that the *mujtahid*'s opinion (*ẓann*) is both epistemologically unsound (it is after all, only his *opinion* as to the law) as well as in contradiction to the many reports from the Imams in which *ijtihād* is condemned. The *mujtahid*s had reinterpreted these reports as referring to the personal reasoning (*raʾy*) of the Sunni jurists, and not the process of *ijtihād* itself, but the Akhbaris, beginning with Muḥammad Amīn al-Astarābādī (d. 1036/1626–7) were unconvinced. It was, they claimed, possible to gain knowledge (and not mere opinion) of the duties an individual must perform through a consultation of the texts in which the Imams' words and deeds (the *akhbār*) were recorded. The *akhbār* should be the only guide for action (for some Akhbaris, the *akhbār* even took precedence over the Qurʾan and the Sunna of the Prophet).[15]

This has been considered by some to indicate some sort of "democratic" and anti-clerical element in the Akhbari movement,[16] which would reduce (or even eliminate) the authority (and practical role) of the qadi and the mufti.[17] I have argued that the Akhbari movement did not represent a rejection of clerical power as such, but a shift in the basis of that power. In the Usuli system, the scholar's authority is based squarely on his ability to perform *ijtihād*. In the Akhbari system, it is based on his ability to "read" (in both the simple sense and the more complicated hermeneutic idea of interpreting) the *akhbār* accurately. That is, the sub-section of the *ʿulamāʾ* who should occupy the roles of community leadership was not the *mujtahid*s, but the *muḥaddithūn* (*ḥadīth* transmitters) and the *akhbāriyyūn* (those who both transmit and rely upon the *akhbār* in their legal pronouncements). Al-Astarābādī himself had argued in this way in his *al-Fawāʾid al-madaniyya*, the work which set in motion the dispute between Akhbaris and Usulis. In *al-Fawāʾid*, al-Astarābādī lists all the *akhbār* of the Imams which relate to *qaḍāʾ* and *iftāʾ*, concluding that they all indicate that "those to whom one should refer for fatwas and legal judgements (*qaḍāʾ*) were the transmitters (*ruwāt*) of the [Imams'] reports and rulings."[18] The "moderns" (i.e., jurists after al-ʿAllāma) ignorantly claim that the Imams are referring to the *mujtahid*s in these reports. Their reason for making such a claim is based on their view that one cannot always be certain of the Imams' opinions on certain matters of law, because the *akhbār* are either weak or appear to be silent on certain legal issues. Therefore, the qadi needs to be a *mujtahid*. This, al-Astarābādī states, is incorrect. One can be certain of the Imams' words and deeds found within the *akhbār*, because (he argues) of the careful manner in which the *akhbār* were transmitted and eventually collected. The transmission process precludes any possibility of falsification. Furthermore, when the Imams appear to be silent upon a particular legal issue, they have left clear hermeneutic principles which, when applied, make legal judgements binding and certain. There is, then, no need for the fanciful hermeneutic techniques laid out by the *mujtahids* in their tracts on *ijtihād* and its necessity.

All this means that the qadi and the mufti, when they make a pronouncement, are passing on *ʿilm* to the people (rather than inferior *ẓann*). This *ʿilm*, in a largely illiterate society, is made available to the qadi and mufti through their scholarly status and training. In their activities of *iftāʾ* and *qaḍāʾ*, they have (perhaps) a heightened level of charisma and authority because they trade in knowledge (rather than opinion) of the law of God. This, then, was al-Astarābādī's position, and it was broadly followed by subsequent Akhbaris. The role they assign to the qadi and the mufti is, I would argue, (theoretically) more extensive than that proposed by the Usulis.

Al-Astarābādī's reformulation of the qualifications for the post of qadi received speedy rebuttals from the defenders of the Usuli hermeneutic hegemony. The Safavid jurist Muḥammad Bāqir al-Sabzawārī (d. 1090/1679), in his *Kifāyat al-aḥkām*, naturally argues that while the *akhbār* do not mention *ijtihād* as an essential quality of the qadi, it is clearly implied within the Imams' choice of words (specifically, their demand that the qadi "know the rulings of the Imams"). The key source for al-Sabzawārī, as it was for most Imami discussions of *qaḍāʾ* and *iftāʾ*, was the much-cited report, ʿUmar b. Ḥanẓala's *Maqbūla*. In this report, Imam Jaʿfar al-Ṣādiq is asked whether two Shiʿis in dispute are permitted to turn to the qadis of the reigning sultan (when this is not the Imam himself) for a resolution. The answer is direct: it is not permitted, even if the qadi in question rules in accordance with the Shariʿa. The point here is that the qadi does not only need to strive to rule correctly. He also needs to have a valid (i.e., religiously legitimate) appointment.[19] The appointment of the qadi by the Sultan of the day (who is not the Imam, and does not act with the Imam's permission or authority) is invalid, and this invalidity infects even a "correct" ruling. On al-Sabzawārī's interpretation of the *Maqbūla* (and this is an interpretation he shares with nearly all Imami jurists), the validity of a qadi's judgement rests not only on the ("objective") accuracy of the ruling he gives, but also, and crucially, on the qadi's right to judge (a characteristic that flows from the manner of his appointment). In fact, the only way to optimise the potential of the former is through the latter. I return to this issue below, but I have shown elsewhere[20] that the Akhbari-Usuli dispute does not appear to have had any significant bearing on the question of the legitimacy of either the ruling Sultan or the qadi he appoints. Here it is sufficient to note that al-Sabzawārī interprets the *Maqbūla* as commanding an informal system of dispute resolution which avoids involvement with the state apparatus (even if that state is avowedly Shiʿi).[21]

On the other hand, the qualifications of the qadi (need he be a *mujtahid* or not?) does appear to have been influenced by the Akhbari-Usuli dispute. Al-Sabzawārī, predictably, argues that he must be a *mujtahid*. After citing various *ḥadīth*, he states:

> The majority opinion is that he [the qadi] must be an absolute *mujtahid.* [Al-Shahīd al-Thānī] in the *Masālik* states that *ijtihād* in some areas and not others—that is, the claim to partial *ijtihād*—is not sufficient. No dispute is recorded on this, and this view is clearly agreeable. [However] the view that partial [*ijtihād*] is sufficient when there is no absolute *mujtahid* is not far-fetched…on the basis of the passage [in the *Maqbūla*] that one should show preference to the most learned.[22]

Al-Sabzawārī is arguing, then, that when no absolute *mujtahid* is available, a partial *mujtahid* can be a legitimate qadi. His reasoning is based on the requirement (found in the *Maqbūla*) that the individual should turn to the "most learned" (*aʿlam*) scholar for *qaḍāʾ*. If the most learned happens to be only partial in his *ijtihād*, then he should be used. By arguing in this way, al-Sabzawārī is attempting to maximise the possibility of valid, Shariʿa-based, juridical proceedings taking place by entertaining valid alternative judgeships to those of the absolute *mujtahid.*

Al-Sabzawārī denounces al-Astarābādī's claim that mere *ḥadīth* transmitters qualify as qadis:

> One recent scholar thinks that it is clear from the above-mentioned report of ʿUmar b. Ḥanẓala that the one who makes the decision (*ḥākim*) is the one who transmits the *ḥadīth* of the People of the House, considers what is forbidden and permitted [therein], and knows both, even if he is not a *mujtahid* in all matters.[23]

Now, this could be seen as a (possibly wilful) misrepresentation. Al-Astarābādī had argued in a stricter manner: a *mujtahid*, because he will rule according to his *ẓann*, is not qualified to be a judge. Al-Astarābādī's was a partisan expression of an intra-*ʿulamāʾ* dispute over who was qualified to judge: the *muḥaddithūn* (and the Akhbaris) had this privileged right over the *mujtahidūn* (and the Usulis).

Al-Sabzawārī's adjusted description of al-Astarābādī's view is probably part of a greater Usuli polemic, in which al-Astarābādī (and the Akhbaris) are portrayed as lowering the qualifications for entry to valid judgeship, or (in a modern legal context) lowering the bar (in both senses). Al-Astarābādī is, in fact, arguing for a different (but, he would probably claim, equally demanding) set of qualifications for the qadi. In any case, al-Sabzawārī considers al-Astarābādī's position to be in conflict with the *Maqbūla* itself. The Imam's stipulation that the judge "know our rulings" is, he argues, general in reference. It is not enough simply to know the *akhbār* and the rulings found therein. Being "knowledgeable of the Imams' rulings" requires knowledge of the Qurʾan, knowledge of the opinions of the Sunni and Shiʿi jurists, and skills in the various religious sciences. In short, it requires the same set of competences as those found in a *mujtahid.*

Hence by stating that the judge should "know the Imams' rulings," Imam Jaʿfar is actually implying that the qadi must be an absolute *mujtahid*. In his maximal interpretation of the above phrase, al-Sabzawārī is presenting a more demanding set of qualifications for judgeship. In these ways he portrays himself as the preserver of academic standards, and al-Astarābādī (and the Akhbaris) as petty vulgarisers.

Returning to Akhbari responses to these criticisms, al-Astarābādī left the task of a more precise description of the roles of qadis and the muftis to his followers. One would normally expect to find such discussions in a *fiqh* work, and al-Astarābādī, for doctrinal reasons, refused to write a work of *fiqh* (he considered the genre too closely tied to an individual scholar's *ijtihād*).[24] Other Akhbaris had fewer worries about the genre of *fiqh*, though they clearly attempted to compose *fiqh* works that did not contradict their commitment to Akhbari legal theory. An interesting Akhbari discussion of the respective roles and qualifications of the qadi and the mufti can be found in Muḥsin Fayḍ al-Kāshānī's work of *furūʿ* entitled *al-Nukhba*, and the commentary on it by ʿAbdallāh b. Nūr al-Dīn al-Jazāʾirī. Al-Kāshānī (d. 1091/1680) is well known as an Akhbari, and is described as such in the biographical literature. Though he differed from al-Astarābādī on a number of points of legal theory (most notably on the permissibility of direct interpretation of the Qurʾan),[25] his rejection of *ijtihād* was formed at an early stage in his scholarly career, most probably during his period of study in Shiraz with Mājid al-Baḥrānī, who received a license to transmit (*ijāza*) from al-Astarābādī. Al-Kāshānī's works of legal theory, entitled *Naqḍ al-uṣūl al-fiqhiyya*, *al-Uṣūl al-aṣīla*, *al-Ḥaqq al-mubīn*, and *Safīnat al-najāt* have been analysed elsewhere.[26] I have already described his theory of *qaḍāʾ* and the role of the qadi, as found in his famous work of substantive law *Mafātīḥ al-sharāʾiʿ*,[27] arguing that his commitment to Akhbari principles of jurisprudence did not result in a significantly different conception of the legitimacy of state *qaḍāʾ* as compared with that of his Usuli colleague (and friend) al-Sabzawārī. Neither did it prevent him from taking up judicial office in the Safavid state and maintaining close connections with the Shah. His *Nukhba* is an unusual work of *furūʿ al-fiqh* in that it blends certain Sufi-influenced themes into the usual structure of a work of *furūʿ* (in imitation of al-Ghazālī).[28] This aspect of the work, interesting as it is, is not the focus of my enquiry, since I am interested in the strictly legal question of his views on the qualities of a mufti and qadi. As is outlined below, these are presented in the *Nukhba* in a manner that refines the presentation in the *Mafātīḥ*. He completed the *Mafātīḥ* in 1042 AH, and the *Nukhba* in 1050 AH,[29] and although the two works are quite different, there are occasional similarities in the phrasing and presentation.

The *Nukhba*, in all or in part, elicited at least five separate commentaries,[30] including one by al-Kāshānī's son, Muḥammad b. Muḥsin (d. early 12th/18th century),[31] two by Nūr al-Dīn b. Niʿmat Allāh al-Jazāʾirī (d. 1158/

1745),[32] and one by Nūr al-Dīn's son ʿAbdallāh b. Nūr al-Dīn al-Jazāʾirī (d. 1173/1759–60).[33] It is the last of these commentaries, entitled *al-Tuḥfa al-saniyya fī sharḥ al-Nukhba al-muḥsiniyya*[34] and written over a century after the composition of the *Nukhba* (it was supposed to have been completed in 1163 AH), which is analysed below. All of these commentators either identify themselves as Akhbaris or are described as Akhbaris in the subsequent Imami biographical tradition.[35]

ʿAbdallāh al-Jazāʾirī comes from a family line of Akhbari scholars, beginning with his grandfather Niʿmat Allāh al-Jazāʾirī (d. 1112/1700) and his father Nūr al-Dīn. ʿAbdallāh is perhaps best known as the author of the *Tadhkira-ye Shushtar* (a biographical and historical work of the town of Shushtar in south-western Iran) and his *al-Ijāza al-kabīra*.[36] At the beginning of the *Tuḥfa* he proudly proclaims his Akhbari commitment in the following terms:

> One can see that contradictory fatwas are much fewer among our Akhbari colleagues than the Usulis. [This is] because we leave unclear whatever God has left unclear, and are silent when God is silent. We restrict ourselves to what is clear and certain, and leave everything else to God, his Prophet, and the Possessors of the Order [the Imams], for they know best.[37]

The contentment with the sufficiency of the revelatory material available to the community and the criticism of those who wish to go beyond the text and pronounce on issues about which God (and his emissaries) are silent, are a recurrent theme in Akhbari writings.

Since the Akhbaris denied the validity of *ijtihād*, the description of the relationships between *iftāʾ* and *qaḍāʾ* common in *fiqh* texts before al-Astarābādī required adjustment. However, deciding whether the relationship is substantially altered by the elimination of *ijtihād* as a common qualification of the qadi and mufti requires a more detailed analysis.

Al-Kāshānī's brief examinations of *iftāʾ* and *qaḍāʾ* in the *Nukhba* are linked, not least of all by their being positioned sequentially within a larger section on *ḥisba*,[38] which is divided into eight subsections (*abwāb*):[39]

jihad (war—in which there is an oblique reference by al-Kāshānī to the usual greater/lesser jihad distinction)
al-amr bi l-maʿrūf wa l-nahy ʿan al-munkar (commanding good and forbidding evil)
iqāmat al-ḥudūd (upholding, or implementing the punishments for specific crimes laid down in revelation)
futyā (giving fatwas)
qaḍāʾ (judging, including a sub-section on imprisonment)
shahāda (giving testimony)

akhdh al-laqīṭ (caring for the foundling)
ḥajr (restrictions on legal capacity)

No explicit rational is stated for the grouping of issues under this heading, though one can be easily reconstructed. Indeed, al-Jazāʾirī in his commentary states that these issues are grouped because the implementation of these elements of the Shariʿa benefits Muslims generally (*taʿummu maṣāliḥuhā*). Maintaining these duties within society ensures the stability and orderliness of the Muslim community (*yaqūmu bihā niẓām al-muslimīn*). For al-Jazāʾirī, the order of subsections here represents al-Kāshānī's assessment of the relative importance of each element in relation to the others (that is, jihad is the most important and *ḥajr* is the least).[40]

As one expects in an abridged work (*mukhtaṣar*), expression is compressed, composed in an almost intentionally referential style as a prompt for commentary. In the section on giving fatwas, al-Kāshānī explains that *futyā* is only permitted for the Imam himself, or one whom he has delegated. The delegation may be specific (that is, specific to the task of *futyā*), or it may be general (that is, a general delegation for a person, or perhaps a person with particular qualities, to perform the societal functions of the Imam generally). The nature and extent of this delegation (*niyāba*) was disputed within Shiʿi jurisprudence, though the general trend was for later Shiʿi scholars to include a greater range of the Imam's functions within the delegation, and to identify the recipients of the delegation more exclusively as the *ʿulamāʾ* (and even a specific stratum of the scholarly hierarchy). The culmination of this development was the delegation of nearly all of the Imam's political authority and power to the *ʿulamāʾ* (and more specifically, scholars with particular skills) during the occultation, a position most famously expounded by Rūḥ Allāh al-Khumaynī.

Treating the duty to perform *futyā* as resting on the Imam's delegation dispenses (to an extent) with the need to outline the qualifications of a mufti, at least during the Imam's presence. Al-Kāshānī explains that the one seeking the fatwa (*al-mustaftī*) must "seek out the one most suitable to give fatwas (*lahu ahliyyat al-iftāʾ*). He indicates that the *mustaftī* can only refer to a trustworthy transmitter of the Imam's words (*thiqa nāqil ʿan al-maʿṣūm*), thus characterising the role of the mufti in a decidedly Akhbari manner, echoing the position of al-Astarābādī himself. If such scholars are numerous, then the individual must choose the "most learned and most pious" (*al-aʿlam al-atqā*). If there are two scholars, one most learned and the other most pious, then the most learned should be followed. If one is unable to identify the most learned or most pious (i.e., if one does not know, or the transmitters all equally share these qualities), then one can choose freely. One should be prepared to travel (whatever distance—*wa-in baʿuda*) to study with and show respect to the most appropriate mufti.

These criteria, whereby the most appropriate mufti is brought into focus for the individual *mustaftī*, are derived from the famous "delegation" *ḥadīth* of ʿUmar b. Ḥanẓala (the *Maqbūla*), though interestingly the report is here applied not to qadis (the referent normally assumed), but to muftis. There is almost no explanation for the *mustaftī* as to how he is to judge whether a transmitter is *thiqa*, nor who is the most learned and pious. The decision appears to be left to the individual's personal conviction.

The apparently subjective assessments by the *mustaftī* of a scholar's suitability for *futyā* in al-Kāshānī's sketchy schema potentially undermines the hierarchic basis of *ʿulamāʾ* authority. Al-Jazāʾirī naturally sees his task to be the elaboration of this process in order to restrict the potential for popular sentiment deciding the most appropriate mufti to guide the community. In order to do this he draws on previous (non-Akhbari) delineations of how an individual is identified as a *mujtahid*, and more specifically, how the most learned *mujtahid* can be known when there is more than one candidate for an individual's *taqlīd*. Al-Jazāʾirī lists the possibilities:

> It is necessary for the *mustaftī* to seek out the one who is suitable for *iftāʾ*, such that he will attain knowledge of his suitability, or [at least] an overwhelming opinion. This can be
> (1) by techniques whereby one might come to know his status, providing [the *mustaftī*] himself has knowledge of these techniques;
> (2) by the testimony of two just witnesses;
> (3) by widespread knowledge that the person is to be described [as the most learned, etc.]; and
> (4) by submitting to a group of learned *ʿulamāʾ*.[41]

These means whereby, according to al-Jazāʾirī, the most learned might be known are not novel, but are adapted from al-Shahīd al-Thānī's exposition of how the individual *mukallaf* might become a *muqallid* through the selection of the most learned *mujtahid*.[42] The techniques perform the function of formalising the selection procedure, objectifying the results and making them less dependent upon an individual *muqallid*'s personal preference. Al-Kāshānī's abbreviated style left the possibility of "the suitability to give fatwas (*ahliyyat al-iftāʾ*)" being decided by popular whim. Al-Jazāʾirī's techniques enable the learned hierarchy to retain some control over the selection process (though this is not entire since (2) and (3) are potentially populist).[43] While these procedures enable the individual believer to choose his mufti through identifying the most appropriate person, they also determine whom has been delegated by the Imam with the responsibility of giving fatwas. The mufti is thereby given an almost sacerdotal role, making it possible for the individual to be a faithful servant of the Shariʿa. The one who rejects the mufti identified in this way is "like the one who rejects the Ahl al-Bayt, who is like the one who rejects God himself, and this is equivalent to [the sin of] association [of something non-divine with the divine—*shirk*]."[44]

Turning now to the qadi, we note that al-Kāshānī, in line with Shiʿi jurisprudence generally, makes an explicit link between *qaḍāʾ* and *iftāʾ*: "[*Qaḍāʾ*] is appropriate for the one who has *futyā* and no other." This, al-Jazāʾirī remarks in his commentary, means that it is a duty restricted to those who can be muftis (i.e., the Imam and those he delegates to the task).[45] While there is both danger and glory in being a mufti, these are amplified (*ajall minhā wa-ashaddu khaṭaran*) in the case of the qadi. As Imam ʿAlī said to Shurayḥ, the qadi is one who "sits in a place where no one other than the Prophet, the executor (*waṣī*) of the Prophet or the miscreant sits."[46] The themes of both the benefits and the risks of being a qadi, found regularly in Muslim juristic literature, are played out here also. Once again, the discourse is employed to serve the greater purpose of Akhbarism, when al-Kāshānī requires that the choice between two qadis should be decided on the basis of the "more just, the more learned in *fiqh*, the more reliable in *ḥadīth*, and the more pious." The inclusion of reliability in *ḥadīth* transmission as an element in the selection procedure is based on similar phrasing in the *Maqbūla* (here applied more explicitly to *qaḍāʾ*). The emphasis is intended to establish the privilege of Akhbari scholars over their opponents in the assumption of the duty of *qaḍāʾ*. One should note also that al-Kāshānī has added expertise in *fiqh* as one of the criteria. Al-Jazāʾirī's comment on this description of the qadi and his selection once again exemplify the fleshing out of the Akhbari themes latent in al-Kāshānī's passage:

> If you ask: Into which of the three categories [i.e., the Prophet, the *waṣī* of the Prophet or the miscreant] does the [above-mentioned] specific or general delegate fall?
>
> Then I say: Into the second [i.e., the *waṣī* of the Prophet] for the *ʿulamāʾ* are the inheritors of the Prophets. We have already mentioned his call to his successors (*khulafāʾihi*), and these are those who transmit his *ḥadīth*, and implement his Sunna.
>
> The third category are the judges of error—those who judge according to their own opinion, like the Sunni judges, or [those who judge] according to the fatwa of others out of *taqlīd*, like most judges today: ignorant ones who are not suitable for *taqlīd*, never mind *ijtihād*.[47]

Al-Jazāʾirī continues al-Astarābādī's original description of the role of qadis and muftis. Akhbarism did not entail a rejection of *iftāʾ* and *qaḍāʾ*. Rather, Akhbaris argued for a particular set of qualifications as to who (within the class of *ʿulamāʾ*) can adopt these community roles. Crucially, Akhbaris stipulated that the essential qualification for these roles was excellence in *ḥadīth* transmission (or possibly, upholding the *akhbār* as the primary source of legal knowledge, such was the ambiguity of the terms *muḥaddith* and *akhbārī*). These transmitters are also those who should "implement his Sunna" (i.e., act as qadis). The designation of both Sunni judges and those active today (Shiʿi judges who support *ijtihād*, but are not qualified to exercise *qaḍāʾ*) as "miscreants" is clearly a reflection of an Akhbari polemic against the *mujtahid* Usulis. The accusation is that *ijtihād* and its associated elements are not authentically Shiʿi, but derived from Sunni Islam.

Akhbari methodology also causes al-Kāshānī to express doubt about the manner in which certain elements of the Shariʿa during the occultation should be implemented. His short section on the implementation of the *ḥudūd* penalties precedes the section on *futyā* and begins:

> [Implementing the *ḥudūd*] is only obligatory for the Imam or his specifically appointed delegate (*nāʾibuhu al-khāṣṣ*).[48]

The term *al-nāʾib al-khāṣṣ*—mentioned above in relation to *qaḍāʾ* and *iftāʾ*—refers to the period of the Imam's presence. The Imam can delegate the task of implementing the *ḥudūd* to an individual, but this designation is specific to a particular person for a particular task (and is perhaps even restricted to the Imamate of the delegating Imam). Other tasks cannot be subsumed under this individual's charge. The term refers to a functionary of the current Imam only. Al-Kāshānī continues:

> The general [*nāʾib*] is the one who oversees the permitted and the forbidden, who knows the rulings [of the Shariʿa] and is able to derive the *furūʿ* from the *uṣūl*, having attained [the qualities of] faith, [sound] transmission [of *ḥadīth*] and moral probity, both outwardly and internally. He should act with caution whenever he inflicts the [*ḥudūd*] during the occultation.[49]

The *ḥudūd* can, then, be upheld during the occultation, but it is subject to a stream of limitations. The person charged with implementing them (i.e., the individual in receipt of a general delegation) must have certain scholarly and personal qualities (i.e., be able to derive *furūʿ* from *uṣūl*,[50] have sound faith, transmission, and moral probity,[51] etc.), and "exercise caution." Furthermore, the obligation only comes about when this individual (with all the qualities outlined in the above quote) is able to implement the *ḥudūd*, meaning that a lack of ability to perform the *ḥudūd* (due to the presence of a political system which prevents implementation) causes the obligation to lapse for that individual. Implicit in this is the point that the individual is not encouraged to attempt to change the political reality in order to bring about circumstances in which the *ḥudūd* might be implemented. Finally, the presence of an obligation on the individual only comes about when there is no danger of harm being inflicted on the individual himself or on any Muslim (outside, of course, of the bodily "harm" which will come about through the implementation of the *ḥudūd*).

Al-Jazāʾirī's comment on this passage demonstrates the manner in which he wishes to develop al-Kāshānī's minimal presentation. To the *ḥudūd* he adds judicial discretionary punishments (*taʿzīr*), thereby widening the scope in which the general delegate might work. He glosses this by stating that "implementing" (*iqāmat*) the *ḥudūd* and *taʿzīr* punishments cannot be merely recommended, discouraged or permitted. Rather, it is either forbidden or obligatory for an individual on account of his "suitability" (*ahliyya*). This, effectively, rebuts those who argue that the implementation of these punishments is a "general" duty, given by the Imam to the community as a whole. If the Imam's own appointment (*naṣb*) of the whole community as the recipients of the obligation brought about the duty, then after the appointment, the community would have no need of the Imam, whether he is present or absent. Al-Jazāʾirī is arguing, then, that the view that the community (rather than an individual) is responsible for the implementation of *ḥudūd* penalties effectively makes the Imam redundant. For this reason it cannot be a communal duty that, when performed by some community members, is lifted from the whole. Rather it must be an individual duty imposed upon the individual who fulfils the qualifications laid out by al-Kāshānī. In technical language, *iqāmat al-ḥudūd* is not a *farḍ kifāʾī*, but a *farḍ ʿaynī*.

The refusal to classify the implementation of *ḥudūd* as a communal duty, and the concomitant identification of individuals upon whom it is an obligation, is significant. First, and most obviously, it personalises the duty. In most areas of *fiqh*, the focus is personal. A jurist attempts to outline the duties an individual believer should perform in order to comply with the law of God. These duties are, to an extent, personalised: if one fulfils certain criteria, or if one has or attains certain characteristics, then a set of duties is activated in the law. If one owns a certain amount of property, then one has to pay the *zakāt* tax; if one has a capacity to perform the pilgrimage, then it becomes a duty. When one fails to fulfil these criteria, *zakāt* and the pilgrimage are not duties, and no transgression of the law is attached to a failure to perform them. By arguing in this way, al-Jazāʾirī is making al-Kāshānī's implication explicit; implementing the *ḥudūd* (and implementing the discretionary punishments also) is only a duty for those who fulfil certain criteria (adult, sane, able to derive substantive law from theory, etc.). This leads to the second significant element of his presentation. If there is no one who fulfils these criteria, then implementing the *ḥudūd* cannot be (legally) performed. It is a lapsed duty (*sāqiṭ*), awaiting some trigger (which might be either the appearance of a suitably qualified individual, or the return of the Imam). In this sense, implementing the *ḥudūd* and the discretionary punishments may, under certain circumstances, constitute disobedience to the Shariʿa. Kevin Reinhart has distinguished between "personalists" and "formalists," i.e., Muslim jurists who located the "charisma of the transcendent assessment" in the person of the mufti or qadi, and those who posited the process of *ijtihād* as "religiously significant."[52] Vogel, as we have seen, interprets the regulations in Sunni *fiqh* as de-personalising the status of the *mujtahid*, and thereby reducing his charisma. By opting for the former, al-Jazāʾirī avoids any hint whereby the process of *ijtihād* might be legitimised, and his position represents a specific application of the Akhbari rejection of *ijtihād* to the implementation of the *ḥudūd*. In this sense, Reinhart's characterisation of the qadi's quasi-sacred role more accurately reflects the conception of the judge depicted by these two Akhbari authors.[53]

State-Sponsored *Qaḍāʾ*

The debate within Shiʿi law concerning the legal validity of state-sponsored *qaḍāʾ* during the occultation of the Imam has been documented by others.[54] The debate emerges from the problematic nature of any state during the occultation, since there is a residual illegitimacy for any state that is not lead by the Imam himself. In a sense this problem is not limited to the occultation itself, since while the Imams were present, they rarely held political power. The issue is intensified by the disappearance of the Twelfth Imam and the promise of some future reappearance, since there is no immediately obvious prospect of the Imam taking power. Neither are there any means whereby the Imam might give judgement on whether working for a particular government not led by the Imam might be obligatory, permitted or forbidden. The occultation makes the legal problem more acute, but does not alter the basic nature of the issue. There is a large amount of secondary literature on the legitimacy or otherwise of states during the occultation, and little unanimity has emerged both among commentators within the Shiʿi tradition and outside of it.

Material related from the Imams themselves was ambiguous on this issue, though there was a raft of general prohibitions on taking community cases to the qadis of the "illegitimate" sultan (*al-sulṭān al-jāʾir*). However, opinion is divided on whether all states during the occultation are illegitimate, or whether it is possible for a sultan other than the Imam to be considered just (*ʿādil* and hence legitimate). Wilferd Madelung, for example, considers a treatise (*risāla*) from al-Sharīf al-Murtaḍā (d. 436/1044) to be evidence that a sultan other than the Imam could be legitimate, providing he acted justly, implemented the Shariʿa of the Imams during the occultation, and did not claim the Imamate for himself.[55] Norman Calder, on the other hand, considers all states to be technically (i.e., *de jure*) illegitimate during the occultation, though this is a legal category rather than a moral judgement on the quality of the sultan's rule.[56] A more general problem is related to whether Imami qadis who accepted work with the illegitimate sultan can be considered to be qadis of that sultan. While they might be outwardly working for the sultan, can it be said that they are actually working for the hidden Imam, using the mechanisms of government to implement the true justice of the Shariʿa? The legal discussions on these issues are complex, though there was certainly a tendency over time for jurists to consider working as qadis for an illegitimate sultan permissable, providing the jurist considers himself to be working for the true Imam. Some have linked this permission to perform *qaḍāʾ* to the scholarly prerogative promoted by the Usuli clerics during the early Safavid period.[57] One question to emerge, then, is whether Akhbari writers held significantly different views to their Usuli contemporaries.

Elsewhere I have made an examination of al-Kāshānī's views on the legality of taking up employment (specifically, taking up judicial appointments) with a state not lead by the Imam.[58] Another extensive discussion of the issue can be found in the 12th/18th-century Akhbari author Yūsuf al-Baḥrānī (d. 1186/1772). His position is similar to al-Kāshānī, though it is less circumspect in its advice to the scholar over taking up a government-sponsored judicial appointment. Al-Kāshānī expresses himself in careful phrases, qualifying particular permissions with provisos and demonstrating how a scholar can use finesse to express uncomfortable legal truths. Al-Baḥrānī on the other hand is more straightforward in his expression, though no less detailed and careful in justifying his position. The difference is most probably due to al-Kāshānī's association with the Safavid state and close relations with the Safavid shahs ʿAbbās II and Sulaymān. Al-Baḥrānī was a more self-subsistent, independent scholar with no need to ally himself with particular dynasties. Indeed, he needed to be, as he was living between the collapse of the Safavids and the rise of the Qajars, based in the ʿAtabat. Al-Baḥrānī had few of the sources of serious Shiʿi patronage that were available to al-Kāshānī.

Al-Baḥrānī's thoughts on this issue can be found in the chapter on trade (*tijāra*) of his influential and voluminous work of *fiqh* entitled *al-Ḥadāʾiq al-nāḍira fī aḥkām al-ʿitra al-ṭāhira*. This work generally is an experiment in the application of Akhbari legal methodology to the usual array of legal issues found in a work of *furūʿ*. It is, unfortunately, unfinished (though even in its unfinished state it runs to 25 printed volumes), and contains no chapter on implementing the *ḥudūd* or on *qaḍāʾ* (he mentions that he intentionally omitted a chapter on jihad since it was, in his view, of little use in the modern period).[59] There are, however, a number of places in *al-Ḥadāʾiq*, particularly in the chapter on legitimate trade activities, where taking employment generally (and employment as a judge specifically) with a sultan is discussed.

Whether it is permitted to work as a judge during the occultation is only one element of the discussion concerning working in any capacity for illegitimate (i.e., non-Imam-led) governments. Al-Baḥrānī describes the various Shiʿi views. The general view of Imami law is that one should not help the oppressors (*ẓālimīn*) in any way. Some have argued for a total ban on all involvement with the oppressors. Some have permitted helping them when the action is, in itself, not forbidden (such as "tailoring for them or building"). Yet others have permitted such actions, though recommended avoidance of them (*iḥtirāz*). Al-Baḥrānī lists nine *akhbār*, and summarizes what he considers to be their clear and undisputed meaning (*ẓāhir*): "The prohibition on helping the oppressors is general, including that which is forbidden and that which is not forbidden."[60] However, the term *ẓālim* (and its cognates) in these reports refers only to "those illegitimate sultans (*salāṭīn al-jawr*) who make a claim for the Imamate—the Umayyads, the ʿAbbasids and those like them... However, if one wishes to remain as a judge of illegitimate, believing and Shiʿi rulers (*ḥākim jawr min al-muʾminīn wa l-Shīʿa*), because of one's love for the believers [i.e., the Shiʿa], and to preserve the land of religion from [attack from] the enemies and the Sunnis,"[61] then this is not forbidden. There is, then, a difference between a sultan who is both illegitimate and oppressive (*jāʾir* and *ẓālim*) and one who is merely illegitimate.[62] It is, al-Baḥrānī argues, obligatory to enter into employment with Shiʿi, believing (but still illegitimate) sultans, providing that, first, one will not perform forbidden actions by doing so, and, second, one will be able to carry out "promoting the good and preventing evil."[63] However, one must not be involved for earthly gain (*ḥubb al-dunyā*) or personal aggrandisement. The qadi must take up employment "purely to do good" (*maḥḍ fiʿl al-khayrāt*). Fulfilling these criteria is difficult, but not impossible.[64] The *akhbār* make it clear that it is forbidden "to show affection for the leaders, to become essential for [their work], or to desire their continued existence."[65] One should not accept wages for such work (either on a piecework or salaried basis) because such work is an obligation upon the suitably qualified scholar, and one should not receive payment for the performance of obligatory duties.[66] In holding these positions, al-Baḥrānī's views are not particularly novel within the Imami tradition, and his presentation is not, therefore, evidence that Akhbaris held substantially different positions from Usulis on issues of state legitimacy.[67] On the other hand, al-Baḥrānī's mode of argumentation is distinctively Akhbari, for he presents his views as based solely on the *akhbār*, denying any substantial interpretive effort on his part, and refusing to employ any interpretive technique derived from reason.

Conclusion

Vogel presents the measure of a *mujtahid*'s ruling (whether in *iftāʾ* or *qaḍāʾ*) as based on an "external" assessment of the adequacy or otherwise of his argumentation. The *mujtahid*'s own qualities have little bearing on the assessment. This was certainly the perspective of a good proportion of classical Muslim jurists, as the judge and mufti appear as legal functionaries with little or no sacred aura. The Shiʿi legal tradition generally, and Akhbarism in particular, counterbalance this perspective. The transmission of the Imam's knowledge from the texts, through the scholar and on into the Shiʿi community, has a clear revelatory resonance. Furthermore, the rejection of *ijtihād* as an essential criterion of *qaḍāʾ* enabled Akhbaris such as al-Kāshānī, al-Jazāʾirī, and al-Baḥrānī to explore other (charismatic) elements of a scholar's qualification to become a judge. For Akhbaris, the scholar becomes "appointed" as qadi by the hidden Imam through attaining certain qualities. Through this appointment, the scholar shifts legal categories: he is now commanded to perform the role of the judge or mufti. Without him, elements of God's law (such as the *ḥudūd*) remain permanently inactive. The state during occultation, permanently illegitimate even when led by a good Shiʿi Muslim, is unable to render the Shariʿa legally valid; only the suitably qualified scholar can do this. Through the qadi's legal judgements, for example, individuals who commit the *ḥudūd* crimes become "purified" (*ṭāhir*) as they undergo punishment prescribed by God. When the qadi enters into state employment, he must do so with a pure heart, and with no hope of personal gain. *Qaḍāʾ* is a personal obligation, placed upon him and him alone by the Imam. In Shiʿi characterisations of the *ʿulamāʾ* generally, and in Akhbari portrayals of the judge and mufti, one can see the sacrality of the scholar's role being gradually brought to the fore. While such a portrayal is a legal consequence of the Imami adoption of the doctrine of the occultation, it was not inevitable. Some Imami scholars, particularly those who valorised *ijtihād* and measured a scholar purely by his intellectual capabilities, were less keen to portray the *ʿulamāʾ* in this quasi-sacerdotal role. Even for Usulis, however, the authority of a *mujtahid*'s fatwa was always unavoidably linked to the person of the *mujtahid*, rather than any dispassionate assessment of the validity of his arguments. These are the features that may account for the differences between Vogel's portrayal and the general tenor of Imami Shiʿi discussions of *iftāʾ* and *qaḍāʾ*.

NOTES

1 Frank E. Vogel, "Islamic Law and Legal System. Studies of Saudi Arabia" (Ph.D. dissertation, Harvard University 1993; rev. dissertation published with same title, Leiden: Brill, 2000), 144–45.

2 ʿAbdallāh Ibn Qudāma, *al-Mughnī*, 12 vols. (Beirut: Dār al-Kutub al-ʿArabī, n.d.), 11:382.

3 A. Kevin Reinhart, "Transcendence and Social Practice: Muftīs and Qāḍīs as Religious Interpreters," in *Annales Islamologiques* 27 (1993), 20. Generally speaking, Reinhart's view (from the perspective of the history of religion) conflicts with Vogel's description (more influenced by legal studies). Vogel states that "no regard is paid to the person of the mujtahid beyond requiring a minimum of piety" (see n. 1 above), considering the mujtahid's role (as qadi or mufti) in epistemological and non-sacerdotal terms. Contrast this with Reinhart's statement that "[t]he oft quoted dogma [that Islam does not have priests] has lead Islamicists to undervalue the sacral and even sacerdotal roles of the mufti and the qadi." ("Transcendence

and Social Practice", 24). The difference probably comes from the distinctive Hanbali view when compared with other Sunni schools.

[4] See W. B. Hallaq, "Was the Gate of *Ijtihād* Closed?," *International Journal of Middle East Studies* 16/1 (1984), 3–41, and alternatively Norman Calder, "Al-Nawawī's Typology of Muftīs and Its Significance for a General Theory of Islamic Law," *Islamic Law and Society* 3 (1996), 137–64.

[5] See Shams al-Dīn al-Sarakhsī, *al-Mabsūṭ*, 30 vols. (Beirut: Dār al-Maʿrifa, 1306/1986), 16:83–4 (where the qadi can be a *mujtahid*, but need not be).

[6] See Norman Calder, "Doubt and Prerogative: The Emergence of an Imāmī Shīʿī Theory of *Ijtihād*," *Studia Islamica* 70 (1989), 57–78.

[7] ʿAbd al-ʿAzīz Ibn Barrāj, *al-Muhadhdhab*, 2 vols. (Qum: Muʾassasat al-Nashr al-Islāmī, 1406 AH), 2:596–97.

[8] See Hallaq, "Was the Gate of *Ijtihād* Closed?", 4–7.

[9] Ibn Zuhrā al-Ḥalabī, *Ghunyat al-nuzūʿ* (Qum: Muʾassasat al-Imām al-Ṣādiq, 1417 AH), 436.

[10] Jaʿfar b. al-Ḥasan al-Ḥillī al-Muḥaqqiq, *Sharāʾiʿ al-Islām*, 4 vols. (Tehran: Intishārāt-e Istiqlāl, 1409 AH), 4:860.

[11] al-Muḥaqqiq, *al-Muʿtabar*, 2 vols. (Qum: Muʾassasat Sayyid al-Shuhadāʾ, 1364 sh), 2:271.

[12] Zayn al-Dīn al-ʿĀmilī al-Shahīd al-Thānī, *Masālik al-afhām ilā tanqīḥ Sharāʾiʿ al-Islām*, 15 vols. (Qum: Muʾassasat al-Maʿārif al-Islāmī, 1413 AH), 13:328.

[13] al-Ḥasan b. Yūsuf al-ʿAllāma al-Ḥillī, *Irshād al-adhhān ilā aḥkām al-īmān*, 2 vols. (Qum: Muʾassasat al-Nashr al-Islāmī, 1410 AH), 2:138–39.

[14] For example, Muḥammad b. Jamāl al-Dīn al-ʿĀmilī al-Shahīd al-Awwal, *al-Lumʿa al-Dimashqiyya* (Qum: Manshūrat Dār al-Fikr, 1411 AH), 94, states that the qadi should be *al-faqīh al-jāmiʿ li-sharāʾiṭ al-iftāʾ* (keeping to ʿAllāma's formulation), but his commentator, Shahīd II, expands this locution to include *al-ijtihād fī l-aḥkām al-sharʿiyya wa-uṣūlihā*, going on to list the various disciplines of which a *mujtahid* must have mastery (al-Shahīd al-Thānī, *al-Rawḍa al-bahiyya fī sharḥ al-Lumʿa al-Dimashqiyya*, 10 vols. (Najaf: Manshūrāt Jāmiʿa al-Najaf al-Dīniyya, 1398 AH), 3:52). Shaykh Bahāʾ al-Dīn al-ʿĀmilī, *Jāmiʿ-e ʿAbbāsī* (Tehran: Farahānī, n.d.), 350, states explicitly that the qadi must be a *mujtahid*.

[15] See generally, Gleave, *Scripturalist Islam: The History and Doctrines of the Akhbārī Shīʿī School* (Leiden: Brill, 2007). Studies of the Akhbari movement in the secondary literature include: Juan R. I. Cole, "Shiʿi Clerics in Iraq and Iran 1722–1780: The Akhbari-Usuli Controversy Reconsidered," *Iranian Studies* 18/1 (1985), 3–34; Abdoldjawad Falaturi, "Die Zwölfer-Schia aus der Sicht eines Schiiten: Probleme ihrer Untersuchung," in E. Graf (ed.), *Festschrift Werner Caskel: Zum siebzigsten Geburtstag 5. Marz 1966 gewidmet von Freunden und Schülern* (Leiden: Brill, 1968), 62–95; ʿAlī Ḥusayn al-Jabīrī, *al-Fikr al-salafī ʿinda l-shīʿa al-ithnāʿashariyya ʿalā wajh al-khuṣūṣ min al-manṭiq wa-falsafat al-yūnān* (Beirut: Manshūrāt ʿUwaydat, 1977); Etan Kohlberg, "Aspects of Akhbari Thought in the Seventeenth and Eighteenth Centuries," in N. Levtzion and J. O. Voll (eds.), *Eighteenth-Century Renewal and Reform in Islam* (Syracuse: Syracuse University Press, 1987), 133–55; Andrew J. Newman III, "The Development and Political Significance of the Rationalist (Uṣūlī) and Traditionalist (Akhbārī) Schools in Imāmī Shīʿī History from the Third/Ninth to the Tenth/Sixteenth Century" (unpublished Ph.D. thesis presented to the University of California at Los Angeles, 1986); Gianroberto Scarcia, "Intorno

alle controversie tra Akbārī e Uṣūlī presso gli imamiti di Persia," *Rivista degli Studi Orientali* 33 (1958), 211–50; Devin Stewart, *Islamic Legal Orthodoxy: Twelver Shiʿite Responses to the Sunni Legal System* (Salt Lake City: University of Utah Press, 1998), 175–208.

16 See Todd Lawson, "The Hidden Words of Fayḍ Kāshānī," in M. Szuppe (ed.), *Iran: Questions et connaissances* (Paris: Association pour l'avancement des études iraniennes, 2002), 433–34.

17 See Andrew Newman, "The Nature of the Akhbārī-Uṣūlī Dispute in Late Ṣafawid Iran. Part 2: The Conflict Re-Assessed," *Bulletin of the School of Oriental and African Studies* 55 (1992), 261. Newman is here referring to the "pure" Akhbari as one who opposed the extension of judicial authority (among other things) during the occultation.

18 Muḥammad Amīn al-Astarābādī, *al-Fawāʾid al-madaniyya* (Qum: Muʾassasat al-Nashr al-Islāmī, 1424 AH), 305.

19 This mirrors one of the Sunni solutions to the problem of the legal authority of the qadi's ruling, locating it within a system of legitimate state appointment.

20 Gleave, "Two Classical Shiʿi Theories of *qaḍāʾ*," in J. Mojaddedi, A. Samely, and G. Hawting (eds.), *Studies in Islamic and Middle Eastern Texts and Traditions in Memory of Norman Calder* (Oxford: Oxford University Press, 2001), 105–21.

21 Calder ("Legitimacy and Accommodation in Safavid Iran: The Juristic Theory of Muḥammad Bāqir al-Sabzavārī," *Iran* 25 [1987], 91–105) argues that al-Sabzawārī considered all sultans other than the Imam to be *de jure* illegitimate (even if they be good Shiʿi Muslims). This is supported by the following passage from al-Sabzawārī's chapter on judging in *Kifāyat al-aḥkām* (Isfahan: Mahdavī, n.d.), 262: "It is well attested in the report of ʿUmar b. Ḥanẓala [i.e., the *Maqbūla*] and the report of Abū Khadīja and others that it is not permitted to refer to the judges of illegitimate rulers (*quḍāt al-jawr*), whether they are believers (*muʾminīn*) [i.e., Shiʿis] or not." I adjust here my previous translation of this passage (see Gleave, "Two Classical Shiʿi Theories", 110), in that the use of *muʾminīn* here refers, I am sure, to Shiʿis rather than Muslims generally. The passage is ambiguous in that the subject of "whether they are believers..." could mean the judges, or the sultans, or both.

22 al-Sabzawārī, *Kifāyat al-aḥkām*, 261 (also adjusting my previous translation, Gleave, "Two Classical Shiʿi Theories," 114).

23 al-Sabzawārī, *Kifāyat al-aḥkām*, 261.

24 See al-Astarābādī, *al-Masāʾil al-ẓāhiriyya*, 569 (found as an appendix to *al-Fawāʾid al-madaniyya*).

25 See Gleave, *Scripturalist Islam*, 216–44.

26 See Kohlberg, "Aspects of Akhbari Thought," and Gleave, *Scripturalist Islam*, 216–35, 288–89, and 293–94.

27 Gleave, "Two Classical Shiʿi Theories."

28 See R. Gleave, "Scripturalist Sufism and Scripturalist Anti-Sufism: Theology and Mysticism amongst the Shiʿi Akhbariyya," in A. Shihadeh (ed.), *Sufism and Theology* (Edinburgh: Edinburgh University Press, 2007), 158–76.

29 See Āghā Buzurg al-Ṭihrānī, *al-Dharīʿa ilā taṣānīf al-shīʿa*, 29 vols. (Beirut: Dār al-Aḍwāʾ, 1983–1988), 21:303 no. 5188, 24:97 no. 501.

30 Modarressi, unfortunately, mentions only one, that of ʿAbdallāh al-Jazāʾirī, see *Introduction to Shiʿi Law: A Bibliographical Study* (London: Ithaca Press, 1984), 87.

[31] al-Ṭihrānī, *al-Dharīʿa*, 24:98.

[32] Ibid., 3:366 and 24:98 (see also 14:103).

[33] The final commentary known to me is that by ʿAbdallāh b. Muḥammad Kāẓim al-Tabrīzī (d. 1119 AH). Al-Ṭihrānī, *Ṭabaqāt aʿlām al-shīʿa*, 7 vols. (Qum: Muʾassasat Ismāʿīlīyān, n.d.), 6:455, considers him an Usuli jurist, claiming that this is obvious from his discussions on the issue of Friday prayer.

[34] The *Tuḥfa* is now available in a four-volume Beirut edition, though this was unavailable to me at the time of writing, as was the 1370/1950 lithograph edition. Hence, the references below are to the folios of the Āstān-e Quds manuscript no. 2269 (see T. Bīnish [ed.], *Fihrist-e alifbāʾī-ye nuskhahā-ye khaṭṭī-ye Kitābkhāna-ye Āstāna-ye Mashhad* [Tehran: Intishārāt-e Āstān-e Quds, 1351 sh/1972]).

[35] See Gleave, *Scripturalist Islam*, 140–76.

[36] al-Jazāʾirī (referred to as al-Shūshtarī), *Tadhkira-ye Shūshtar* (Calcutta: Asiatic Society of Bengal, 1924); al-Jazāʾirī, *al-Ijāza al-kabīra* (Qum: Maktabat Āyatallāh al-Marʿashī, 1409/1989).

[37] al-Jazāʾirī, *Tuḥfa*, f. 7.

[38] al-Kāshānī, *Nukhba*, 180–82.

[39] Ibid., 175–86.

[40] al-Jazāʾirī, *Tuḥfa*, f. 198.

[41] Ibid., f. 205.

[42] al-Shahīd al-Thānī, *Munyat al-murīd* (Qum: Maktabat al-Iʿlām al-Islāmī, 1409), 304.

[43] A modern instance of the various causes in which these criteria can be employed can be seen in the juristic theories of the modern Ayatollahs al-Sīstānī, al-Ḥāʾirī, and the late Muḥammad Bāqir al-Ḥākim. See R. Gleave, "Conceptions of Authority in Iraqi Shiʿism," *Theory, Culture and Society*, 24/2 (2007).

[44] al-Jazāʾirī, *Tuḥfa*, f. 205. While al-Kāshānī's text appears to place being more learned (*aʿlam*) above being more pious (*awraʿ*), al-Jazāʾirī entertains another scenario, namely, one in which two contenders are equally learned, but differ in piety. Here piety acts as a tiebreaker, indicating that he considered it possible that one will not, through these methods, find the most learned, and one might have to turn to other characteristics (such as piety) in one's search for the one delegated by the Imam (al-Jazāʾirī, *Tuḥfa*, ff. 205–06).

[45] Ibid., f. 207. "[*Qaḍāʾ*] is judging among the people, and it is only appropriate for the one who has *futyā*, being the Imam, or his specific or general delegate, and no other."

[46] al-Shaykh al-Ṣadūq Ibn Bābūyah, *Man lā yaḥḍuruhu al-faqīh*, 4 vols. (Qum: Muʾassasat al-Nashr al-Islāmī, n.d.), 3:5, no. 3223.

[47] al-Jazāʾirī, *Tuḥfa*, f. 207.

[48] al-Kāshānī, *Nukhba*, 179.

[49] Ibid.

[50] al-Jazāʾirī's gloss here makes al-Kāshānī's expression simultaneously more explicitly in line with Akhbari legitimacy and easier for an individual to attain. He notes, almost disdainfully, that the one who implements the *ḥudūd* is called "in the terminology of the later scholars (*ʿurf al-ākhirīn*) the *faqīh* and the *mujtahid*." He does not seem convinced by this, and sticks to calling this person *al-ḥākim*. The *ḥākim* need not be able to derive all of the *furūʿ* from the *uṣūl*, but merely "most of them" or even "a considerable portion" of them. Finally, the *ḥākim* may only use

al-uṣūl al-ṣaḥīḥa (sound *uṣūl*), most probably a reference not to abstract principles of hermeneutics, but to the sources of *ḥadīth* employed in Imami *fiqh*. Even if this is a reference to hermeneutic principles rather than *ḥadīth* collections (the context is unclear), then the descriptor "sound" is a reference to hermeneutic principles revealed by the Imams themselves, and not gained through the independent juristic reasoning of the Usulis (al-Jazāʾirī, *Tuḥfa*, f. 204).

51 al-Jazāʾirī does mention a disagreement between himself and al-Kāshānī over whether moral probity (*ʿadāla*) is an essential quality of the one charged with the implementation of *ḥudūd* (the *ḥākim*). Al-Kāshānī includes the attainment of moral probity (both internal and external) as an (essential) quality of the *ḥākim*. External moral probity (*al-ʿadāla ẓāhiran*) is assessable by the community generally. Internal moral probity (*bāṭinan*) would appear to be only assessable on a subjective basis (by the prospective *ḥākim* himself). This requirement further personalises the duty to implement *ḥudūd*, and takes it out of the realm of community assessment (and hence community duty). Al-Jazāʾirī argues that the inclusion of moral probity as an essential quality of the *ḥākim* is disputed. While al-Kāshānī argues that it is a condition of valid implementation of *ḥudūd*, al-Jazāʾirī considers it non-essential. Al-Kāshānī's position is based on his view that the qualities of the *ḥākim* delegated by the Imam when present (i.e., the *nāʾib khāṣṣ*) included (both internal and external) moral probity. Presumably the Imam had privileged access to the internal moral probity of a *ḥākim*, and this was part of his reason for selecting an individual as the recipient of his delegation. Al-Kāshānī considers there to be no indications (*adilla*) in the sources that the essential nature of this quality was restricted to the time of the Imam's presence (that is, it is not restricted to the *nāʾib khāṣṣ*). For al-Jazāʾirī, however, this attempt to force an analogy between the time of the Imam's presence and that of his absence (by arguing that the qualities of the *ḥākim* do not change) is forbidden by Shiʿi jurists, since analogy is itself forbidden. Hence, one can conclude (though it is not stated explicitly) that for al-Jazāʾirī, moral probity is not a condition of the *ḥākim*. The loss of this potential condition means that it is more likely, for al-Jazāʾirī, that a *ḥākim* will be present at any given time during the Imam's absence than it is for al-Kāshānī, making implementation (*iqāma*) of the *ḥudūd* more likely to be a duty that can be legitimately activated in the Imam's absence. See al-Jazāʾirī, *Tuḥfa*, f. 203.

52 Reinhart, "Transcendence and Social Practice," 18–19.

53 The sacred role of the qadi is further emphasised in al-Kāshānī's *Nukhba* when he places a section on *iqāmat al-ḥudūd* within the chapter on purity (*kitāb al-ṭahāra*), stating that the judge "purifies" the individual who has performed illegitimate sexual intercourse (*zinā*) by stoning him (al-Kāshānī, *Nukhba*, 52).

54 Norman Calder, "The Structure of Authority in Imāmī Shīʿī Jurisprudence" (unpubl. Ph.D. thesis presented to the School of Oriental and African Studies, University of London, 1980), 70–107; A. K. Moussavi, *Religious Authority in Shiʿite Islam* (Kuala Lumpur: International Institute of Islamic Thought and Civilization, 1996), 64–73; A. Sachedina, *The Just Ruler (al-sulṭān al-ʿādil) in Shīʿite Islam* (New York: Oxford University Press, 1988), 119–72.

55 Wilferd Madelung, "A Treatise of the Sharīf al-Murtaḍā on the Legality of Working for the Government," *Bulletin of the School or Oriental and African Studies* 43 (1980), 18–31.

[56] Calder, "The Structure of Authority," 90.

[57] See Newman, "The Nature of the Akhbārī-Uṣūlī Dispute," 258–61.

[58] Gleave, "Two Classical Shiʿi Theories."

[59] Yūsuf b. Aḥmad al-Baḥrānī, *Luʾluʾat al-Baḥrayn* (Najaf: Maṭbaʿat al-Nuʿmān, 1966), 446.

[60] Idem, *al-Ḥadāʾiq al-nāḍira fī aḥkām al-ʿitra al-ṭāhira*, 25 vols. (Qum: Muʾassasat al-Nashr al-Islāmī, n.d.), 18:119.

[61] Ibid., 18:122.

[62] The neatness of this categorisation schema is compromised somewhat by a passage elsewhere in *al-Ḥadāʾiq* (18:269), in which al-Baḥrānī argues that one can accept wages from the oppressor, but that it counts as *ḥalāl* mixed with *ḥarām*, and is therefore liable for *khums*.

[63] al-Baḥrānī, *al-Ḥadāʾiq*, 18:126. He rejects the opinion of "some Shiʿi jurists" that it is only recommended to work for the illegitimate sultan when these conditions are in place.

[64] "Like extracting pure cheese from blood and faeces" (al-Baḥrānī, *al-Ḥadāʾiq*, 18:133).

[65] Ibid., 18:131.

[66] Ibid., 18:216–18.

[67] Compare, for example, the views of other jurists summarised in Calder, "The Structure of Authority" and in Calder, "Legitimacy and Accommodation."

BIBLIOGRAPHY

al-Astarābādī, Muḥammad Amīn, *al-Fawāʾid al-madaniyya* (Qum: Muʾassasat al-Nashr al-Islāmī, 1424 AH).

al-Baḥrānī, Yūsuf b. Aḥmad, *al-Ḥadāʾiq al-nāḍira fī aḥkām al-ʿitra al-ṭāhira*, 25 vols. (Qum: Muʾassasat al-Nashr al-Islāmī, n.d.).

Calder, Norman, "The Structure of Authority in Imāmī Shīʿī Jurisprudence," (unpubl. Ph.D. thesis presented to the School of Oriental and African Studies, University of London, 1980).

——, "Legitimacy and Accommodation in Safavid Iran: The Juristic Theory of Muḥammad Bāqir al-Sabzavārī," *Iran* 25 (1987), 103–51.

——, "Doubt and Prerogative: The Emergence of an Imāmī Shīʿī Theory of *Ijtihād*," *Studia Islamica* 70 (1989), 57–78.

——, "Al-Nawawī's Typology of Muftīs and Its Significance for a General Theory of Islamic Law," *Islamic Law and Society* 3 (1996), 137–64.

Gleave, Robert, "Two Classical Shiʿite Theories of *qaḍāʾ*," in J. Mojaddedi, A. Samely, and G. Hawting (eds.), *Studies in Islamic and Middle Eastern Texts and Traditions in Memory of Norman Calder* (Oxford: Oxford University Press, 2001), 105–21.

——, *Scripturalist Islam: The History and Doctrine of the Akhbāri Shiʿi School* (Leiden: Brill, 2007).

al-Jazāʾirī, ʿAbdallāh b. Nūr al-Dīn, *al-Ṭuḥfa al-saniyya* (Astan-e Quds Library, Mashhad: MS no. 2269; also available in lithograph: 1370/1950) (Beirut: Muʾassasat al-Tārīkh al-ʿArabī, 2006).

al-Kāshānī, Muḥsin Fayḍ, *al-Nukhba fī l-ḥikma al-ʿilmiyya wa l-aḥkām al-sharʿiyya* (Qum: Sāzemān-e Tablīghāt-e Islāmī, 1418 AH).

Kohlberg, Etan, "Aspects of Akhbari Thought in the Seventeenth and Eighteenth Centuries," in N. Levtzion and J. O. Voll (eds.), *Eighteenth-Century Renewal and Reform in Islam* (Syracuse: Syracuse University Press, 1987), 133–55.
Reinhart, A. Kevin, "Transcendence and Social Practice: Muftīs and Qāḍīs as Religious Interpreters," *Annales Islamologiques* 27 (1993), 5–28.
al-Sabzawārī, Muhammad Baqir, *Kifāyat al-aḥkām* (Isfahan: Mahdavī, n.d.).
al-Sarakhsī, Shams al-Dīn, *al-Mabsūṭ*, 30 vols. (Beirut: Dār al-Maʿrifa, 1306/ 1986).
Vogel, Frank E., "Islamic Law and Legal System: Studies of Saudi Arabia" (Ph. D. dissertation, Harvard University 1993; rev. dissertation published with same title, Leiden: Brill, 2000).

14

A PERFECT LAW IN AN IMPERFECT SOCIETY

Ibn Taymiyya's Concept of "Governance in the Name of the Sacred Law"

Baber Johansen

I. Mamluk Rule: Its Political and Religious Legitimation

Mamluk rule (1250–1517) over Egypt and Syria was fraught with specific legitimation problems. The Mamluks created a political system run by military slaves captured or bought in the Kipchak steppes or among the Circassians of the northern Caucasus and sold into Egypt and Syria. Once acquired by their new owners, themselves Mamluks, they were converted to Islam, trained in the military arts, and finally emancipated by their master in order to join the military or the administration. The loyalty of these Kipchak or Tcherkessian slaves to the masters in whose household they grew up and to their fellow military slaves in those households, whom they considered as their "family," was a central element of Mamluk military and political ethics. The division of the Mamluk class into competing households and divided loyalties is, therefore, a structural phenomenon of Mamluk political culture.[1]

As emancipated slaves of foreign origin, the Mamluk rulers could neither base their rule on the authority of a famous Arab genealogy nor on a prominent role in Islamic history, factors that had given great Islamic prestige to the dynasties of the Umayyad (661–750) and Abbasid (750–1258) caliphs. Such a lack of a religious genealogy had been a problem for the Turkish and Daylamite dynasties in earlier centuries, but before the Abbasid dynasty vanished under the onslaught of the Mongols in 1258, the Abbasid caliph in Baghdad had been a source for the legitimacy of all Eastern dynasties whose rulers would recognize the caliph as their suzerain.[2] When, in 1258, Baghdad was sacked by the Mongols and the Abbasid dynasty disappeared, religious legitimacy through the caliph's recognition was no longer an option for new dynasties. The Mamluk's efforts to use a refugee Abbasid caliph of uncertain origins in order to bolster their political prestige remained largely meaningless.[3] In other words, their rulers could not base their claim to political and religious prestige and recognition on the history of their predecessors. They had to rely on success to prove their military and administrative capacity to rule. The defense of Syria and Egypt against the crusaders and the Mongols,[4] the centralized control of Egypt's agricultural resources,[5] the support for a thriving foreign trade,[6] the demographic growth of the population under their control,[7] the immigration into Cairo of learned families from all over the Muslim world that underlined Cairo's reputation as the cultural and religious center of the Sunni Muslim world,[8] the stability of their Empire's currency,[9] and the magnificent Mamluk architecture that still gives the city of Cairo its particular urbanism[10] all served as their title to fame. The militarization of the administration that took place from the end of the 1280s on[11] did not diminish its competence. The period of decline of the economy, demography, currency, and finances in Egypt and Syria that began in the second half of the fourteenth century and that, finally, undermined also the Mamluks' military strength, lies beyond the purview of this article.

The Mamluks' religious legitimation depended on their support for Sunni Islam, that is, for groups, institutions, and doctrines that claimed conformity with the normative tradition of the Prophet (*sunna*) and made this conformity the decisive criterion for the legality and legitimacy of all scholarly and religious activity. In 1265, Sultan Baybars decided to treat the four Sunni law schools on an equal footing and to create for each of them the post of a chief qadi in the major cities of his empire.[12] Mamluk Sultans and military leaders consequently founded charitable foundations to support Sunni law schools,[13] and appointed scholars to or dismissed them from the posts of judges, market inspectors (*muḥtasib*s), professors in institutions of higher—mostly legal—learning (*madāris*), administrators of charitable foundations, and treasury functionaries, thus on the one hand controlling access to the major offices of public life and on the other forming alliances and clientele relations with groups of scholars. The learned professions of religious scholars increasingly became stepping stones for administrative careers; religious scholars were increasingly brought into contact with the Mamluk elite.[14]

Religious scholars sought the support of Mamluk dignitaries in order to bolster the dominating position of their doctrines and institutions, whereas scholars who defended minority positions needed the protection of Mamluk authorities against the dominating groups. The Mamluk sultans and governors, on the other hand, sought the support of dominant Sunni groups in order to mobilize the urban elite. For the same reason they encouraged popular Sufi groups whose representatives often had close relations with Mamluk sultans. Religious scholars and mystics in the Mamluk period were addressing a growing public of laymen interested in playing an active part in the learned activities of religious life.[15] The institutional foundations for this growing interest in religious literature were created by the growing number of endowments for institutions of legal studies (*madāris*) that provided scholarships for their students and thus made religious texts accessible to a growing public.[16] This public—even if often ridiculed by elite scholars—entertained the ambition to participate in the manifestations of religious knowledge and pious practice and, consequently, took a vivid interest in the discussions and conflicts among religious scholars. It took sides and, as Stefan Leder underlines, "popular following and partisanship constituted a factor of considerable importance in the politics of religion and of public order."[17] The attitude of this educated social stratum to religious scholars and doctrines, therefore, always had a political dimension. Mamluk dignitaries were well aware of their importance. As they were among the main providers of endowments and enjoyed influence and respect within the institutions of public learning, they could use them as instruments to strengthen their religious reputation and support.[18] Unavoidably, religious scholars were increasingly implicated in the factional fights of the Mamluk leaders, and the Mamluk leaders, much as they tried, could not remain neutral in the conflicts between major Sunni factions.[19] In the last instance, the Mamluk commanders were the ones who provided protection to religious scholars and made as well as ended their careers.[20]

This fact is borne out by the trials and imprisonments of Taqiyy al-Dīn Aḥmad ibn Taymiyya, the scion of a well-known family of scholars adhering to the Hanbali school of law.[21] Aḥmad ibn Taymiyya was born in 1263 in Harran, from where his family fled during his early childhood to Damascus in order to avoid the onslaught of the Mongols. He died while imprisoned in the citadel of Damascus, in 1328.[22] Between 1305 and 1326, he was imprisoned five times as a result of his conflicts with Muslim mystics, jurists, and theologians, who were able to persuade the political authorities of the necessity to limit Ibn Taymiyya's range of action through political censorship and incarceration.[23] The reaction of the Mamluk authorities may seem surprising given the fact that Ibn Taymiyya attempted to give a religious legitimacy to Mamluk rule through the concept of "governance in the name of the sacred law" (*siyāsa sharʿiyya*)[24] and the principle of religious and political censorship that obliges all Muslims to "command the good and forbid the evil" (*ḥisba*). His efforts to that purpose were appreciated by leading Mamluk military dignitaries and also, for a short period, by at least one Mamluk Sultan who protected him against his scholarly adversaries. But Ibn Taymiyya's difficulties show that it was impossible for him to win enduring political support for the creed as well as for the system of religious and legal identity on which he wanted to base his concept of "governance in the name of the sacred law." One of the reasons for this failure were his conflicts with leading jurists and judges from the Shafiʿi and the Maliki schools of law over their theological and legal doctrines and with pantheist[25] mystics whose veneration and teaching he often attacked violently. In a number of instances, public demonstrations and disorder arose from these altercations. The other reason for his loss of favor with the political authorities may have been a reaction to his growing influence on major Mamluk dignitaries that made others fear the formation of a new religious and political group that could enhance the factionalism among the Mamluks.[26]

II. Mamluk Dignitaries and Religious Scholars: The Case of Ibn Taymiyya

The Shafiʿi school of law was the dominant intellectual and institutional embodiment of Sunni reasoning in the Mamluk empire.[27] This school traces its history back to Muḥammad ibn Idrīs al-Shāfiʿī, the school's founder (d. 820). Under the Ayyubids (1170–1250), the Shafiʿis held the post of the chief qadi. The attribution, in 1265, by the Mamluk Sultan of one post of chief qadi for each Sunni school of law was seen by the Shafiʿis as a loss of their control over the judiciary.[28] Many among them were fervent adherents of the Ashʿari theology that by the thirteenth century had become the leading school of Sunni theology[29] and which makes it a religious duty for Muslims to search for rational proofs for God's existence and the principal tenets of Islam. The Ashʿaris find these rational proofs in a theory of the adventitiousness of substances. They hold that substances cannot exist without accidents, that all accidents are adventitious and have no duration in time, and that, therefore, a contingent world of substances that are dependent on adventitious accidents cannot be eternal. It is in need of a non-contingent creator of accidents and substances.[30]

As a law school, the Damascene Shafiʿis were engaged in continuous, sometimes violent conflicts with the Hanbali school of law.[31] The conflicts between Ibn Taymiyya, the Shafiʿis[32] (and Malikis), and the mystics in Damascus and Cairo concern questions of cult, theology, and law: Ibn Taymiyya is accused of anthropomorphism because of his creeds in 1298 and 1306,[33] and in 1318–20 his legal expertise on the conditional oath of repudiation is declared unacceptable and he is forbidden to reiterate it in public. When he insists, he is imprisoned in the citadel of Damascus.[34] His polemics against the cult of the Sufis is one of the motives for the investigation against him in 1305–06 and for his imprisonment in 1307 as well as in 1326.[35]

Against the Ashʿaris (among them many of the leading Shafiʿis), Ibn Taymiyya held that there is no rational proof for God's existence unless this proof is recognized by the Qurʾan. It is through God's revelation that one understands His existence and the way in which one can talk about Him. God's acts and attributes can only be described in the words revealed by God himself.[36] Belief in God's revelation is the condition for the understanding of His existence and His attributes. The rational proof for God's existence presented by Ashʿari theologians, i.e., the doctrine on the relation of accidents and substances, is consistently rejected by Ibn Taymiyya.[37] The Prophet, according to Ibn Taymiyya, has given a complete exposition of the principles and rules of Islam, therefore, all rules of law and ethics can be derived from the texts of Qurʾan, the normative praxis of the Prophet, the Sunna, and the consensus of the learned, *ijmāʿ*.[38] The Qurʾan, according to Ibn Taymiyya, contains the spirit and the letter of all religious knowledge[39] and from God's revelation not only all major principles of the law but also all rules of detail can be deduced.[40] In the light of this premise he criticizes the doctrines of the various schools of law, in particular those of the Shafiʿis.

Ibn Taymiyya claimed that his doctrine mirrors the life praxis and the teaching of the first three generations of Muslims, the historical consensus of the community that is based on the Qurʾan and the Prophetic Sunna. It should, therefore, be acceptable to all Muslim jurists and, as it is founded on God's word and the Prophet's normative praxis, Sunni scholars and political authorities should subscribe to it because it embodies everything that is essential in the theological and legal heritage of Islam. He appealed to scholars from the dominant schools of Sunni law to adhere to this creed and legal system while, at the same time, using this creed and his approach to legal questions as the basis for an unrelenting and polemical critique against the theology and the legal constructions of those to whom he appealed.[41]

Much like his Shafiʿi (and Maliki)[42] opponents, Ibn Taymiyya tried to forge alliances with members of the Mamluk elite in order to find political backing for his religious doctrine. His opponents in turn denounced his political influence on major Mamluk dignitaries as posing a danger for the Sultan's control of his empire.[43] Ibn Taymiyya was for some time a legal advisor to Sultan Muḥammad ibn Qalāwūn,[44] had close relations to the commander Sayf al-Dīn Arghūn, a man in the Sultan's entourage,[45] and was protected by the Governor of Damascus, the commander al-Afram, during his first legal encounters with his Shafiʿi accusers in 1305.[46] In these procedures his adversaries, who accused him of anthropomorphism, had offered him a way out: they suggested that his creed was nothing else than the belief system of the Hanbali school of law and that he should admit this fact. As the Hanbalis are a recognized school of Sunni law, such an acknowledgement would have legitimized his creed as that of a scholar who interprets and defends the traditions of his own school of Sunni law. It would thus have exonerated Ibn Taymiyya from the accusation of heretical doctrines, but it would also have deprived his doctrine of its claim to universal, Islamic validity that, according to Ibn Taymiyya, made it obligatory for all religious scholars to adhere to it. He refused to accept this offer and insisted in turn that those who attacked him avowed by this very fact that they did not adhere to the creed of the entire early Muslim community.[47]

The three Damascene hearings of religious councils, organized by the political authorities in 1306 to examine the accusations against Ibn

Taymiyya, found him innocent of any heretical position. It was only in a fourth procedure, organized by the Sultan in Cairo and led, in April 1306, by the chief judges of the four Sunni law schools in combination with high representatives of the Mamluk state, that he was found guilty. Ibn Taymiyya was imprisoned until September 1307 at which moment two influential commanders obtained his release.[48] Not long after his release in 1307 he was sent back to prison as a result of Sufi complaints about his polemics against their doctrines.[49] He was released in 1309, and stayed for three years in Cairo where—according to Laoust—he exerted a certain influence on the Sultan. In 1311 he persuaded the Sultan to grant the commander al-Afram, the protector of Ibn Taymiyya in 1306, the position of governor of Tripoli. In the same year he obtained from the Sultan the imprisonment of the governor of Damascus, Sayf al-Dīn Karay.[50] According to Laoust, some of the fiscal rescripts of the Sultan, dated between 1311 and 1314, have their origin in Ibn Taymiyya's counsel.[51] In 1312 he returned to Damascus where, for six years, he led an active life as teacher and scholar. In 1318 he issued an expert opinion on the conditional oath of repudiation that was considered unacceptable by his scholarly adversaries and the political authorities. The authorities forbade him to give further legal opinions on this problem and, when he continually disobeyed, put him in prison from 1320 to 1321.[52] Finally, in 1326, his polemics against the Sufis' veneration of the saints' tombs caused the Sufis to intervene with the political authorities and to demand his punishment. Again, Ibn Taymiyya was imprisoned and, in 1328, died in the Citadel of Damascus.[53] The history of the trials, imprisonments, and releases of Ibn Taymiyya shows how his success in winning over important Mamluks to his normative positions was, on the one hand, a necessary element of survival in the quarrels, trials, and intrigues among scholars, and created, on the other, fears of the possible political consequences of his teachings.

III. Three Meanings of "Sacred Law"

Ibn Taymiyya's treatise on *Governance According to the Sacred Law*[54] was written, according to Laoust, in the period between 1309–12. In 1309, Ibn Taymiyya had been released from prison by Sultan al-Nāṣir Muḥammad b. Qalāwūn who had just started his third reign (1309–40) and the scholar had begun to exert a certain influence over the Sultan.[55] The text on *Governance* (*siyāsa*) reflects Ibn Taymiyya's concept of the Sultan's role in conflicts between factions of religious scholars. In 1298, when a Shafiʿi judge had summoned him to defend an early creed of his, the *Ḥamawiyya*, Ibn Taymiyya had refused to obey, stating that "the Sultan had appointed [the qadi] to judge between people, not to discuss dogma."[56] But to judge from his treatise on *Governance*, he did not consider it to be illegitimate for the Sultan and those who represented the political authorities to require explanations and information about the dogma or the law as expounded by religious scholars. Ibn Taymiyya himself often appealed to Sultans and commanders to fight, punish or kill heretics.[57] In his legal opinions, he required that the Sultan obligate all participants in debates about doctrinal questions to adhere strictly to the standards propounded by Qurʾan, Sunna, and the consensus of the early community. If no consensus could be reached about these standards, it is, according to Ibn Taymiyya, the Sultan's task to guarantee the religious scholars freedom to follow the tenets of their own schools and their own approach (*madhhab*). Should the authorities be reluctant to intervene, given the complexity of the subject matter, the religious scholars should take the initiative and establish the truth of the matter "so that punishment follows on proof, because it would be illegal to punish before the proof is established."[58] But, Ibn Taymiyya insists, if "the [heretical] innovation is clear (...) the Sultan has to fight the falsifications spread by these sects in the same way in which he has to fight all other forms of scandalous misbehavior."[59]

How Ibn Taymiyya conceived of the norms that the Sultan must apply in debates about religious dogma is evident from a letter that he sent to his brother, Sharaf al-Dīn, and in which he comments about the Cairo trial of April 1306 in which he was condemned as an anthropomorphist. He writes:

> The term "sacred law" is used in three meanings in the customary parlance of people: "The revealed law" (*al-sharʿ al-munazzal*) and that is what the Prophet [...] brought, one has to follow it and whoever disobeys it has to be punished.
>
> The second [meaning] is "the interpreted law" (*al-sharʿ al-muʾawwal*). These are the legal opinions of qualified jurists who bring them about through their individual legal reasoning (*ārāʾ al-ʿulamāʾ al-mujtahidīn fīhā*), such as the method of Mālik and similar (scholars). It is justifiable to follow this law, but it is neither obligatory nor forbidden. Nobody is entitled to impose it on all people nor should all people be forbidden [to follow] it.
>
> The third [meaning] is "the perverted law" (*al-sharʿ al-mubaddal*). It [consists of] lies against God and His Prophet, or against people through false testimony and other things, and of clear injustice. Whoever pretends that this [law] belongs to God's law has indisputably fallen into disbelief. He is like someone saying: [to ingest] blood and carrion is licit—even if he said: this is my school of law and similar things.[60]

We will show below that Ibn Taymiyya claims for his own construction of legal norms that it is entirely derived from the "revealed law." The "interpreted law" is legitimate and respectable but no scholar can be obligated to follow it. Ibn Taymiyya, therefore, is entitled to question the correctness and validity of the normative suggestions of other scholars if his arguments are better than theirs. The "perverted law," finally, has been applied to him by the judge who condemned him in Cairo. The one law that is obligatory for each and every Muslim is the "revealed law" and in the debates among scholars they have to prove that their doctrine corresponds to the revealed law. Otherwise their normative suggestions are in no way binding on other scholars. What is evident in this argument is that even the perfect law, if it falls into the hands of dishonest and unjust people, can be altered into a perverted praxis.

After Ibn Taymiyya's death in the citadel of Damascus, his most intimate and most famous student, Ibn Qayyim al-Jawziyya (d. 1350), quoted his statement on the three forms of law, adding significant changes that clearly reveal the political implications of the conception. He wrote:

> Our teacher said: Some rulers have neglected [the real significance of the law] and others have violated it. This has rendered obligatory the ignorance of the truth and the injustice against mankind. The term "sacred law" no longer corresponds to its original meaning, rather the term "sacred law" is divided in these times into three parts: [first] "the revealed law" (*al-sharʿ al-munazzal*), that is, Qurʾan and Sunna. Adherence to this [revealed] law is obligatory and those who break it have to be fought. This law comprises the foundations and the rules of religion, the leadership competencies of the military commanders and of those in charge of finances (*wulāt al-māl*), the decisions of the magistrate and those who control the markets (*mashyakhāt al-shuyūkh*), the market inspectors (*wulāt al-ḥisba*), and others. All of these have to judge by the revealed sacred law and are not allowed to disagree with it.
>
> The second [form of the] sacred law consists of free interpretation (*taʾawwul*), and this is the realm of conflict and individual legal reasoning. Those who find a solution [to a problem] that can be licitly solved by individual legal reasoning (*ijtihād*) are confirmed in it. All people do not have to consent to [this norm] except [if it is supported] by an indisputable proof from God's book or from the normative praxis of His Prophet.
>
> The third [form of the] sacred law is the "perverted law," such as is established by false testimony. In this law one judges by ignorance and injustice or one imposes in it a void confession so as to cause the loss of valid right, such as the instruction given to a mortally ill person to acknowledge a debt vis-à-vis one of his heirs to which, in fact, the heir is not entitled, so as to void the claims of the other heirs. To order [such a thing] is forbidden. To witness it is forbidden.

> And if the qadi knows the hidden aspect of the matter and that its [visible aspect] does not correspond to the truth, and if he still judges [according to the false aspect], he acts as an oppressor and a sinner. If he does not know the inner aspect of the matter, he does not sin.[61]

In other words, the military and administrative elite, the judges, and those who control the markets have to apply the norms established by Qurʾan and Sunna and those rules that are derived from them in a correct and licit procedure. The reference to the foundations and rules of religion as well as to the practices of governance under the category of the "revealed law" provides an extremely broad standard for the application of "revealed law." The legal doctrines of famous jurists are respectable products of qualified human reasoning but as such they cannot command general obedience and do not, therefore, qualify as the law that should be applied by the political authorities. On the third level, the "perversion of the law" takes place through ignorance of its rules, the injustice in their application,[62] and the use of their form for illegal ends. This category clearly opens the disquieting perspective that a perfect law when applied by unjust and unqualified people may alter its character and become an unjust praxis. This thought has continuously preoccupied Ibn Taymiyya.

IV. How Should Governance Relate to the Sacred Law?

It is obvious that the tripartite concept of the "sacred law" (*sharʿ*) suggested by Ibn Taymiyya and Ibn Qayyim al-Jawziyya requires the establishment of a close link between governance and the sacred law. It seems obvious that neither Ibn Taymiyya nor Ibn Qayyim al-Jawziyya look for such a link in the judiciary as constituted by qadis who are learned specialists of the sacred law. It may, in fact, have been the close link between the schools of law and the judiciary that rendered them skeptical as to the capacity of the qadis to guarantee the application of the revealed law in all matters of governance. Whether a judgeship is given to a religious scholar or to a military commander does not, according to Ibn Taymiyya, constitute a difference of principle. I quote from his treatise on *ḥisba*:

> The general and the particular characteristics of the public functions and competencies that are conveyed to persons who exercise the office depend on the expressions used, the circumstances, and the political practice (*ʿurf*). *The sacred law defines none of this* (italics mine, BJ). At some times and in some places, the qadiship comprises competencies that at other times and in other places fall under the authority of the military, and vice versa. The same holds true for the *ḥisba* and for the revenue administration.[63]

All public offices serve to command the good and forbid the evil and thus are religious offices (*manāṣib dīniyya*).[64] "One has to know," writes Ibn Taymiyya, "that the exercise of a public office forms part of the loftiest religious duties. In fact, the religion could not exist without it."[65] The political apparatus of the religious community is religious in character. Those who are best qualified to shoulder the responsibilities that come with them should be given the job:

> According to the political practice in our time, in the regions of Syria and Egypt it is the military authority that carries out the prescribed punishments for the violation of God's claims (*ḥudūd*) that involve destruction, such as the amputation of a thief's hand or the punishment of the highway robber and similar things. It may also happen that the military authority imposes a punishment that does not involve destruction such as, for example, the flogging of a thief. It is competent also in violent conflicts, brawls, and "trials of suspicion" (*daʿāwī al-tuhma*)[66] in which there are neither written documents nor witnesses.
>
> The office of the qadi is competent in these matters if there are written documents and witnesses. The qadi has to establish the legal claims [of individuals] and to judge in this matter. He has to check the status of those who inspect pious foundations and administer the property of orphans and other well-known things. In other countries, such as the Maghrib, the military authority has no judicial competence at all. It serves merely to execute the orders of the qadi. This practice corresponds to the old Sunna. For this there are reasons based in doctrines and customs that are mentioned elsewhere.[67]

In this context, Ibn Taymiyya sums up his opinion as follows "All social offices in Islam serve the same aim: to command the good and to forbid the evil."[68] He underlines that there is no reason to preserve certain competencies for the military and others for the specialists of the legal norms of the sacred law. The term "qadi," he says,

> is a name that applies to each and every one who issues a decision in a conflict between two parties or who arbitrates between them, no matter whether he is a caliph, a sultan, a deputy, or a governor, or whether he was appointed in order to judge according to the sacred law; or as the deputy of such a judge deciding in a conflict between parties, even if he judges nothing more than the quality of the handwriting among children who turned to him for this purpose.[69]

In a very similar vein, the Maliki jurist Shihāb al-Dīn al-Qarāfī, who flourished in Cairo at the beginning of the Mamluk period (1228–85), subsumes under the term "judge" (*ḥākim*) not only the qadi, the judge who decides cases in the light of norms developed by Muslim law schools, but also many representatives of the political authorities such as the caliph, the vizier, the local rulers, the army's leading officers, the overseer of the market, the arbiters, the tax collectors, and the tax assessors.[70] It seems evident that at least some Muslim jurists of the Mamluk period consider as judges (*ḥākim* or *qāḍī*) any major administrative and political officials who impose sanctions or obligations on persons subject to their authority. The organization and functioning of the judiciary is neither conceived of as dependent on the separation of powers nor as dependent on a clear division of labor requiring a highly specialized legal expert. The judge is rather seen as a representative of the political power that serves "to command the good and forbid the evil" and thus helps to guarantee the survival of religion.

Such judges have to apply the "revealed law." The system of "governance in accordance with the sacred law" is dominated, according to Ibn Taymiyya, by the concern for the preservation of power as the main guarantee for the survival of religion. The reference by those in power to the law that justifies their decisions does not necessarily refer to individual norms. Rather it is often defined by the broad general principles referred to, since the twelfth century, as "the aims of the sacred law" (*maqāṣid al-sharīʿa*), and by the practices necessary for their realization. Such a perspective has been developed in many different ways in Islamic law since the eleventh century. Al-Ghazālī's theory of the "aims of the sacred law" was a very limited and disciplined Shafiʿi form of legal reasoning.[71] In the Hanbali school much more ambitious projects were voiced at the same period. In the course of a discussion with a Shafiʿi scholar, who held "that there is no valid government except that which agrees with the revealed law," Ibn ʿAqīl (1039–1119), the senior Hanbali scholar of Baghdad at the end of the eleventh and the beginning of the twelfth century,[72] defines the relation between "governance"[73] and the "sacred law" as follows:

> Government is that activity whereby people are enabled to tend toward good and away from evil, even if the Apostle [Muḥammad] had not instituted it, or if it had not been the object of a revealed law. Now if by your statement "except that which agrees with the revealed law," you mean an administration that does not contradict the revealed law, then that would be right; but if you mean that there is no valid administration except that which is stated explicitly in the revealed law, that would be wrong. Moreover, it would put the Prophet's Companions in the wrong; for the executions and exemplary punishments ordered by the Rightly Guided Caliphs [...] are such as not to be denied by anyone who knows the Traditions, even if this

> involved only the burning of the copies of the Qurʾan—a judgment they based on the welfare of the Community—and the burning of the heretics in the trenches by Caliph ʿAlī […], who said: "When I witness something reprehensible, I light a fire [to burn the heretic] and call for a celebration."[74]

The same quotation is approvingly cited by Ibn Taymiyya's most prominent student, Ibn Qayyim al-Jawziyya, who supplements it with reports on torture in the early Muslim community.[75] As seen above, Ibn Qayyim al-Jawziyya provides an extremely broad standard for his definition of "the revealed law" and leaves a wide margin of action for those who apply it. It is evident that such a broad definition of the norms to be applied diminishes the dominating position of the doctrines developed by the law schools of Sunni Islam. Whereas the systems of norms developed by the Sunni law schools consist of general rules for specific human acts, the broad standard of politics and governance developed by Ibn ʿAqīl, Ibn Taymiyya, and Ibn Qayyim al-Jawziyya is rather a reference to inexhaustible sources of norms-generation that render superfluous all references to sources and methods that are external to Qurʾan and Sunna. It is to these sources that the political and religious elites have to turn for guidance. The debate on the limits of licit government between Ibn ʿAqīl and his Shafiʿi opponent shows that the introduction of this broad standard is conceived of as a way to produce larger visions of political decision-making, an attempt to make sure that the rules of the Sunni law schools should not be considered as being identical with the sacred law, an identification that was clearly seen as limiting the margin of action of the political and religious elite.

V. The Sacred Law as a Perfect and Independent System

Ibn Taymiyya starts from the assumption that the Prophet in his normative praxis, his Sunna, has determined the principles and the details of the Islamic religion.[76] In the Prophet's normative praxis, the authority of revelation goes hand in hand with the exposition of the rational proofs for the truth of Islam that are offered by the Qurʾan. Through these rational proofs and based on the authority of the revelation, the Prophet has explained how God's sovereignty, his attributes, and the life in the hereafter ought to be understood.[77] Therefore, there is no need for extra-Qurʾanic rational proofs to establish the truth of Islam and the existence of God. According to Ibn Taymiyya, the Qurʾan contains the spirit and the letter of all religious knowledge.[78] The Qurʾan and the normative praxis of the Prophet provide the believers with the signs, the proofs, and the arguments that enable them to understand their religion.[79] The Prophet has also explained the individual rules of the sacred law.[80] All new cases and problems are, in principle, already decided in God's word and in the Prophet's Sunna, because God has revealed the general principles to which all individual cases can be reduced.[81] Every correct analogy, therefore, corresponds to a Qurʾanic text.[82]

In Ibn Taymiyya's conception, the consensus as a source of law is restricted to the consensus of the four Rightly Guided caliphs who reigned after the Prophet's death from 632–61, as well as to that of the other Companions of the Prophet and the two generations of Muslims who followed them.[83] The Companions of the Prophet and the second and third generation of Muslims knew the Qurʾan and the Sunna better than those who followed later. The reports on the Prophet or the Rightly Guided caliphs that are transmitted by the Prophet's Companions are more reliable than those that were transmitted by others. Muslim scholars of later generations often chose to refer to consensus as the source of a rule because they did not have the same knowledge of Qurʾan and Sunna as their predecessors.[84] The Companions of the Prophet very rarely resorted to their own consensus as a source of law because they knew the details of Qurʾan and Sunna. In fact, every consensus is always based on texts from the Qurʾan and the Sunna. The consensus, therefore, is not an independent source of the law but it confirms independently what is contained in the Qurʾan and the Sunna.[85] As not all qualified jurists know all the texts of the Sunna, it is licit and legitimate to arrive via consensus or analogy to the same rules that the Qurʾan and the Sunna already established.[86]

In submitting these three sources of the law to the process of analogical reasoning, the qualified jurist, through his own personal effort of legal reasoning, arrives at the rule of the sacred law that applies to a given case.[87] The analogical conclusion constitutes truth if it is based on a correct understanding of the revealed rule from which the analogy is drawn and on the precise understanding of the object to which the analogy applies:[88] "God and His Prophet apprise [men] of the identity of similar things and the distinction between different things and that is also the function of analogical conclusion."[89] The correct performance of analogical reasoning reproduces in the conclusion the *ratio legis* of the premise, the original case on whose analogy the solution of the second case is built. The analogical reasoning is incorrect if the second case is so distinct from the first one that it is impossible to give them the same legal status.[90]

In other words, Ibn Taymiyya treats the revealed sources of the law and the way in which rules can be derived from them as a complete and self-sustaining system. He uses his thesis of the Qurʾan's rational proofs in order to show that the Muslims do not need philosophers in order to perform the rational demonstration of the truth of creation and revelation, nor theologians who do not even understand the rational character of the Qurʾanic proofs or, if they do, still try to base their concepts of creation and revelation on their own extra-Qurʾanic rational proofs such as the relation of accidents and substances. The Philosophers and the Ashʿaris (closely allied to the Shafiʿi school of law) are therefore dismissed, the first as conscious heretics[91] and the second as heretics against their own will.[92] Christians and Jews are dismissed as unbelievers because they do not believe in Muḥammad as a Prophet. As all Prophets shared one religion, Islam, those who believe in one prophet have to believe in all the others. If they refuse to do so, they prove to be unbelievers in their own religion, in their own prophet, and in God.[93] They follow not the true religion brought to them by their Prophets but a "perverted (or altered) religion" (*dīn mubaddal*) in which falsehoods replace truth.[94] Polytheism is in its entirety an "altered religion."[95] According to Ibn Taymiyya, the radical communities of Shiʿi Islam—such as those constituted by the Qarmatians and the Ismaʿilis—neither follow the true message of the Prophet nor obey the obligatory prescriptions of the Qurʾan and, therefore, do not belong to the Muslim community.

To defend the practice and doctrine of "governance according to the sacred law" as a self-sufficient and revealed politico-religious system, independent of philosophy, theology, and other religious beliefs, Ibn Taymiyya had to reconstruct the notion of the Sunna and to redefine the concept of analogy. He defined the Sunna as a system of rules without any internal contradiction.[96] He quotes the eponym of the Hanbali school of law, Aḥmad ibn Ḥanbal (d. 855 in Baghdad), as holding the opinion that "[t]here is no question or, at least, no genus of questions, which the Companions of the Prophet neglected to discuss." And Ibn Taymiyya draws from this the conclusion that all practical and theoretical questions raised during the period of the Muslim conquests of the seventh century CE were solved by the Prophet's Companions through recourse to the Qurʾan and the Sunna. Only a small minority, he says, did not derive their arguments from these two sources.[97]

The Prophet's Sunna, according to Ibn Taymiyya, is a rich source of normative thought and practice because it does more than only refer to his acts and words, his silence in the face of events, and his attitude towards practices. It also refers to all the crafts and contracts that existed before and during the Prophet's lifetime and which he did not forbid. "The Sunna consists of the Prophet's propositions, acts and confirmations [of institutions and practices]," says Ibn Taymiyya. As examples of such practices, Ibn Taymiyya quotes the commenda contract (*muḍāraba*) but also "agriculture and other crafts such as tailoring and cobbling."[98] In other words, crafts and contracts that existed at the time of the Prophet and that he did not disallow, become part of his normative practice and, in this way, normative models of Muslim societies after him. It is evident that a normative praxis that is conceived of in such a broad sense would cover a wide field of technologies, crafts, exchange contracts, and other institutions. Laoust underlines that in Ibn Taymiyya's reasoning also the Sunna of the Rightly Guided caliphs is annexed to the Sunna of the Prophet and that it "constitutes in fact a sort of transition from the Sunna of the Prophet to the consensus of his Companions."[99] On the basis of his definition of consensus, Ibn Taymiyya concludes that the Sunna cannot be separated from the consensus, because the consensus is only a confirmation of the Sunna.[100] In the last instance, all sources of the law are related directly to the Prophet and his Companions.

Ibn Taymiyya construes the sacred law as a complete and closed system that guarantees the foundational identity of all its parts through their dependence on Qur'an and Sunna. His concept of analogy is of decisive importance for the demonstration of this point. Analogy, in his system, is the derivation of new rules from reasons contained in the revealed sources and in consensus. It is a tool that he uses powerfully in the field of contract law to justify forms of contracts more adequate to the social and economic practices of his society than those transmitted in the doctrine of the different Sunni law schools.

Ibn Taymiyya sets out to prove that analogies from Qur'an and Sunna, and from legal institutions based on their texts, serve to solve all practical requirements of the law. He criticizes the assumption, shared by most Muslim jurists, that fundamental legal institutions, such as the contract of tenancy or the sharecropping contract, cannot be based on analogies to revealed texts.[101] Such an assumption puts into question the role of the *fiqh* as a complete system of sacred law, independent of external influences. For Ibn Taymiyya, the reasoning of jurists who argue that a legal institution contradicts the analogy to revealed texts is specious. "In reality, there is no legal rule that contradicts a correct analogy," he holds.[102] Most of the pretended contradictions between legal institutions and analogy are based on wrong interpretations of the Qur'an and Sunna. A correct interpretation of the revealed texts, in Ibn Taymiyya's view, shows that the incriminated legal institutions are in perfect harmony with them. The jurists have to understand that analogies ought to be based on the nature of the compared objects and treat equal things as equal and different things as different. To identify things of a different nature and to treat them as equal creates specious analogies.[103] The influence of Aristotle on this formula can hardly be overlooked. It seems obvious that Ibn Taymiyya uses his intimate knowledge of Greek logic[104] in order to construe analogy as an instrument that enables him to present the sacred law of Islam as a coherent system of norms, independent of all external factors and influences. He insists that once differences are taken seriously and unequal things are not treated as analogous, it becomes obvious that, to give just one example, the tenancy contract is not analogous to the sale contract, because the things exchanged against pecuniary value are not the same in the two types of contract. In the sale contracts physically existing goods, existing bodies, are exchanged; in the contract of tenancy, the object of the contract is the right to use a rented object. The commodities sold do materially exist before the sale contract; the use of the rented property comes only into existence after the contract's conclusion. The objects of the two contracts are unequal and cannot be identified as analogous. The analogy between the contract of sale and the contract of tenancy is specious. The correct analogy is the one between synallagmatic contracts in general and the tenancy contract.[105] The contract of tenancy, therefore, is analogous to other legal institutions based on Qur'an and Sunna; it is not based on analogy to the sale contract.

In pursuing this methodological approach, Ibn Taymiyya establishes the principle of an unchangeable harmony between the revealed texts and the *fiqh*'s correctly established institutions and doctrines.[106] He uses his concept of a legal system that is entirely based on Qur'an, Sunna, and consensus and on analogies drawn from them to prove that an important number of customary contracts can be integrated in such a concept of the sacred law.[107] Much like other jurists of the Mamluk period, Ibn Taymiyya thus opens the way for a growing influence of social and economic practices of non-jurists on the content of the sacred law. He surpasses them in the large space that he opens for the principle of the freedom of contracts.

VI. The Functions of the Religious State

Political power is a necessary and indispensable premise for the functioning of such a legal and religious order. Human beings, Ibn Taymiyya asserts, using a well-known formula of classical antiquity, are "political (*madanī*) by nature," bound to live in society in order to survive. To do so they have to institute hierarchies and to obey those among them who are normative authorities.[108] But hierarchization creates a problem: all men belong to the same humankind and are, therefore, equal. Their hierarchical organization creates inequality and domination and is, therefore, unjust. Only the religious character of the political and social hierarchies, the fact that the two highest normative authorities, God and His Prophet, have made them part of religion, makes them acceptable and just.[109] They serve, as Ibn Taymiyya says, "to improve the religious condition of human beings (*dīn al-khalq*)" and "to improve the material conditions which are indispensable for the triumph of religion." These last are divided into the "the just distribution of goods (*qasm al-amwāl*) and the application of the prescribed penalties of the law (*iqāmat al-ḥudūd*).[110] The improvement of the material conditions is a fundamental requirement because "human beings do not accept justice if it does not help them to satisfy their needs. The satisfaction of their need has thus to be regarded as part of the service and the obedience that one owes to God."[111]

In a state that serves to realize the aims of religion, the rulers and the ruled are united in the obedience of God's Word. The oath of allegiance to the ruler that the subjects take is their recognition of this common obligation, and not an election.[112] In such a state the authorities (*ulū l-amr*)

(Q 4:59) to whom the subjects owe obedience and respect are the military commanders and the religious scholars. These are the two groups on whose sound understanding of their tasks the whole society depends. The Sultan rules in cooperation with the religious scholars in the framework set by the Qurʾan and the Sunna. He has to follow the counsel of the religious scholar who "shows him the way outlined by the Holy Book, the Prophet's Sunna, and the consensus. He must not obey anybody outside of this way, be it the most respectable religious scholar or political dignitary."[113] One may assume that with this formulation Ibn Taymiyya speaks about his own relation to the Sultan, but the concept is not restricted to his personal expectations. It shows how Ibn Taymiyya defines the relation between the ruler and religious authority in an Islamic state: in all questions concerning governance in the name of the sacred law, the Sultan uses his power in following the counsel of the scholar who bases his advice on a concept of religion, law, and politics that is entirely based on the concept of "revealed law" as a complete and independent normative system that contains solutions to all problems.

Collectively also, the religious scholars play an indispensable role for the religious state. Ibn Taymiyya underlines this fact when he sets forth the priorities of public expenditure: after the soldiers and the governors follow the judges, the legal scholars, the imams and muezzins, and the tax collectors as those on whom public money should be spent.[114] The public offices of a religious state, be they military, religious or fiscal, perform religious functions.[115] They help to command the good and forbid the evil.[116] They are "powers conferred by the sacred law" (*wilāyāt sharʿiyya*) and "religious functions" (*manāṣib dīniyya*).[117] "One has to consider," writes Ibn Taymiyya, "the exercise of a [public] power as one of the loftiest duties of religion, or rather as one without which the religion [of Islam] could not exist." It is "one of the forms of religion, one of the acts through which the human being approaches God."[118] To fund these public offices is one of the most important priorities of the ruler. But public funds should also be used to soften the opposition or even the armed violence of enemies. If one cannot beat them, one has to buy them. Public money, contrary to the dangerous doctrines of those who parade their pietism, should be spent on the rich and the powerful if that helps to guarantee the Sultan's political power.[119] Religion depends on power, and the separation of power and religion corrupts both.[120] Ibn Taymiyya's doctrine on governance in the name of the sacred law (*siyāsa sharʿiyya*) is thus based on the premise that power has a religious and religion a political dimension. The institutional form in which this power is exerted is less important than the religious functions exerted by those in power. The individual political or judicial act has to be evaluated in its function for the political and social order of the Muslims.

VII. The Sultan's Control over Cult, War, Production, and Distribution

Contrary to the classical doctrine of the Muslim *fiqh*, Ibn Taymiyya does not consider the caliphate as the obligatory form of Muslim rule. Instead he states that there is no prescribed legal form for political rule in Islam.[121] He thus provides religious legitimacy for localized, non-universal forms of political rule, insisting that a strong political power is the condition of all religious order and that the exercise of power should be conceived of as a religious duty.[122]

The preservation and control of the cult, war against and punishment of the enemies of the political and social order of the Muslims, and the guarantee for the supply of food and other goods necessary for the survival of the population constitute the measures that the political authorities must perform in order to keep the politico-religious system of "governance in the name of the sacred law" alive. The rulers have to engage their power in order to guarantee the survival of a religious order. Ibn Taymiyya gives special weight to three forms of such engagement. Prayer and war, according to Ibn Taymiyya, are the two supreme political forms of religion.[123] War is conceived of as a form of punishment for the adversaries and, therefore, may be led against foreign and domestic enemies. The third major state function is to watch over production, trade, and pricing of all goods that are necessary for the survival of the population for which the ruler is responsible. All three forms of governance under the revealed law entail the punishment of those who oppose them. Punishment, therefore, is an always present dimension of such governance and is itself defined as serving the aim "to command the good and forbid the evil."

The political authorities must carefully control their subjects' performance of their cult obligations.[124] Those who neglect to pray should be flogged until they agree to pray. Those who refuse to pray but also those who continually neglect their five obligatory daily prayers should be put to death.[125] The political authorities should watch over the defense of the correct religious doctrine. The heretic who publicly propounds his dangerous doctrines should be punished by the Sultan, if need be by capital punishment.[126] The authorities should lead war against the heretic and rebellious groups and punish those who do not respect their religious and political obligations.[127]

The legal war (*jihād*) should be directed against non-Muslim powers. Ibn Taymiyya conceives of it as a punishment inflicted on them because they did not respond to the Prophet's appeal to embrace Islam.[128] But he also insists that the war against the Sultan's rebellious subjects, much as the war against non-Muslim powers, can be either offensive or defensive and often remains the only means to uphold security and public order within the Sultan's realm. Jihad against rebellious groups of heretical minorities is a duty for the ruler.[129] If bandits engage in highway robbery, thus challenging the political authorities, war against them is more legitimate and urgent than the war against those Muslim groups who refuse to fulfill all their fundamental legal obligations. The bandits in this case can be killed until the last man, but war against them remains a war against Muslims. Their crime does not make them unbelievers.[130] Here Ibn Taymiyya is not entirely consistent. On the one hand, he says that this war cannot be assimilated to the legal war against non-Muslims and heretics and that a Muslim bandit does not cease to be a Muslim. On the other hand, he holds that if Muslim bandits enter into an alliance with a kingdom that departs from the sacred law of Islam, war against them has the same status as the war against heretic rebels.[131] In another context he does not shrink from calling it a jihad, a legally obligatory war for the sake of Islam that should be led by the regular army and paid from the public treasury.[132] If, on the other hand, the bandits turn out to be too strong for the government, Ibn Taymiyya suggests that the Sultan ought to reconcile them through paying, from the treasury, a certain amount of money to some of their chiefs so as either to bring them over to his side or to persuade them to refrain from robbery.[133] To sum up, Ibn Taymiyya distinguishes between three types of war: the legally obligatory war against foreign non-Muslim powers, the war against heretical rebels, and the war against bandits and robbers. The robbery discussion provides Ibn Taymiyya with an occasion to name the "usual suspects": Bedouins, Turkmens, Kurds, peasants, urban gangs, and plebeian city dwellers are singled out as suspects who, routinely engaged in robbery and law-breaking, ought to serve as objects of the rulers' punishing power.[134] Ibn Taymiyya, on the other hand, does not have a clear opinion of what Muslims ought to do if two Muslim Sultans lead war against each other and the army of one enters the territory of the other. Should the subjects of the second Sultan defend themselves (and their Sultan) in taking up arms or must they abstain from all action? Ibn Taymiyya answers: "The two doctrines are upheld in the Hanbali school and in other [Sunni] schools of law."[135] He does not hint at what his own recommendation in such a case would be. In other words, he sees the loyalty of the Sultan's subjects as a loyalty to Islam and not to the political representative of a specific local community. As long as a Sultan represents the political dimension of Islam, his subjects must be obedient and loyal to him. If two Muslim Sultans fight against each other, their subjects should remain passive and neutral in the armed conflict. The subjects are only called to arms to defend a Muslim government if it is attacked by non-Muslims. If the attack is led by a Muslim ruler, the subjects are not concerned and should let the outcome of the war decide the new government. In other words, the subjects play no role in establishing the rulers nor do they have a stake in defending them against other Muslim powers. Ibn Taymiyya clearly thinks in terms of subjects and not of citizens.

Ibn Taymiyya legitimizes the intervention of political authorities in production, trade, and markets. Justice and the fulfillment of the Muslim's obligations towards God, he insists, can only be realized if and when human needs are satisfied.[136] In principle, he pleads—as most Muslim jurists would—for the protection of private property. He considers it unjust to impose tariffs on the merchants as long as they fulfill their obligations towards their fellow Muslims.[137] He explains that under normal conditions a rise in prices that can be explained in terms of population growth or a scarcity of goods does not justify government intervention in the market exchange.[138] The Prophet himself, according to a famous transmission of his words, refused to interfere in the merchants' pricing and declared such interference as an arbitrary act that is not justified by any religious principle.[139]

But all these arguments, according to Ibn Taymiyya, are valid only if the merchants and the market community respect their duties towards the buyers and consumers. Problems arise when merchants, peasants or craftsmen use their economic power to impose excessively high prices on the buyers of goods or services. Ibn Taymiyya discusses four cases of such illicit exploitation of economic power. The first one is the stocking of foodstuffs by merchants in times of need in expectation of raising the price level. If people are in need of these nutriments, the political authorities should force the merchants to sell for the "average value" (*qīmat al-mithl*) of these goods, i.e., the value that is attributed to them in normal times, when no particular need or scarcity pushes the price up. The needy population, he explains, can also appropriate these goods against the will of the merchants as long as they pay the average price. The political and social "fixing of the price" (*tasʿīr*) in this case consists of imposing an "average price" and an "average value" to the goods stocked by the merchants.[140]

The second example discussed—and justified—by Ibn Taymiyya are the trade monopolies on certain goods imposed by the political authorities. Certain goods, he says, can only be sold to carefully chosen persons and only these persons are entitled to resell them. All other persons are excluded from this trade. This exclusion may constitute an injustice when it is brought about by unjust fiscal means. Even then it may serve the good and justifiable purpose to avoid the chaos (*fasād*) that might arise from a free trade in these goods. Here a political pricing (*tasʿīr*) imposes itself that obligates these monopolists to buy and sell according to the "just value" of the goods concerned. If, says Ibn Taymiyya, these people are given trade monopolies, it would be doubly oppressive to grant them the right to buy and to sell at a free price: it would constitute oppression of those from whom they buy and of those to whom they sell. They must buy and sell at the average price for such goods (it being understood that this price is fixed by the political authorities).[141] The third example provided by Ibn Taymiyya concerns agreements between groups of buyers or sellers to raise or lower the price because such an agreement puts into jeopardy the principle of the "average price."[142]

Ibn Taymiyya also discusses the *corvée* of peasants and craftsmen as a problem of political pricing (*tas'īr*). If certain goods such as food, cloth, and housing are needed by all members of the society, the government must make sure that they are sold according to their market value (*qīmat al-mithl*) or the average price (*thaman al-mithl*) that can be obtained for the species, kind, and quality of the good in question. If peasants and craftsmen do not respect this basic principle, the political authorities have not only to fix these prices but also to force the peasants and craftsmen to perform the tasks to which they are called. This holds true for peasants who have to work the lands of military officers, for weavers and masons, as well as for craftsmen who are obliged to serve the production of military goods. The political authorities in all these cases will fix the just price for the services they require.[143] According to Ibn Taymiyya, the peasants and craftsmen produce goods and services that are vitally necessary for the whole population. The production of such goods is a collective duty of the community. If the community does not fulfill this duty, the political authorities are entitled to act in the community's place specifying the individuals or groups who must perform these tasks.[144]

The system presented by Ibn Taymiyya clearly grants primacy to the supply of consumer goods for the local population. It attributes to the political authorities the right to obligate a sizeable group of peasants and craftsmen to produce goods and services and it gives the authorities the right to fix the compensation for their labor or the price for their products. A system that assigns a monopoly over certain goods to a politically authorized group of merchants fixes at the same time the prices at which they can market the products the producers have to sell to them. In other words, the political authorities exercise a strong influence on production, marketing, and pricing. Their control over the economy gives them not only a powerful hold over the everyday life of the population, it also strengthens their political and religious authority. The political authorities appear as the guarantors of the survival of the population.

VIII. The Subjects' Duties

Justice, according to Ibn Taymiyya, is the supreme principle that governs the relation between the political authorities and their subjects. Following an established tradition of Islamic political thought, Ibn Taymiyya holds that a perfect religion and a sacred law cannot necessarily guarantee practical justice. If the Muslim political authorities cannot guarantee justice in the application of the "revealed law," they risk rendering an Islamic legal and religious order impossible. States run by non-Muslims may be more just than those led by Muslims, because the just application of an imperfect and faulty law is better than the unjust application of a perfect law. According to Ibn Taymiyya, God will preserve the just political organization of unbelievers for a longer time than the political organization of unjust Muslims:

> In this world the affairs of men are kept in better order with a justice stained by all kinds of sin than with an unjust exercise of law even if this law is not touched by any sin. Therefore it has been said that God preserves the just state even if it is unbelieving and does not preserve the oppressive state even if it is Muslim. It is said that the world persists with justice and unbelief and does not persist with oppression and Islam.

In the same context Ibn Taymiyya continues:

> The fact is that justice gives order to everything. If the matters of this world are put into order by justice, they will remain in order even if the one responsible for its state does not have any share in the hereafter. If the world is not put into order by justice it will not remain, even if its master has a belief for which he will be rewarded in the hereafter.[145]

The concept of justice thus helps to protect a certain autonomy of the political vis-à-vis the religious sphere.

Ibn Taymiyya discusses the concept of political justice in his discourse on the duties of subjects vis-à-vis their government. As human beings in society need hierarchies in order to survive, subjects are obliged to obey those in power. Therefore, subjects are not entitled to refuse to pay taxes imposed on them by the unjust ruler.[146] Ibn Taymiyya admits that ruler and subjects have a tendency to behave unjustly towards each other, the first in demanding from their subjects more than they are entitled to, the latter in refusing to pay what they owe their political authorities.[147] He accuses the political authorities of searching for easy compromises with those who break the law and of imposing fines on them instead of capital punishment or mutilation, thus selling justice and crime and behaving no better than the chiefs of bandits. He calls the graft that the agents of the authorities receive as price for their leniency the salary of prostitution.[148] He describes military commanders, notables, and the army under disloyal chiefs as potential political risks for the Sultan. But the even less controllable social groups among the Bedouins and farmers, the Turkmens, the Kurds, the peasants, and the mountaineers, as well as plebs and gangs of the big cities, are the more dangerous troublemakers.[149]

Against the corrupt and disloyal agents of the ruler and the uncontrollable social groups, the full punishing power of the political apparatus is required. Torture—or as one would say today, in a new style of political correctness, hard interrogation methods—is already recommended by the Prophet against those who hide the treasures that they acquired through their crimes.[150] The war against crime is a duty of the rulers because "punishments are instituted in order to constrain men to do the good and to avoid the evil."[151] Even the unjust ruler is therefore fully entitled to execute them.[152] The law, to be certain, knows of other means to attain the same goals and these means should not be neglected, but harsh punishment is a necessity for the preservation of a viable religious and social order. It is an essential part of Ibn Taymiyya's *siyāsa sharʿiyya.* To replace capital punishment and mutilation with fines is a form of corruption that destroys the state's authority in the eyes of its rebellious subjects.[153] The religious state in an imperfect society is a punishing state.

IX. The Principles of Governance and the Limits of the Law

Ibn Taymiyya construes the sacred law as a closed system that contains answers to all questions. He justifies the political authorities' control over the performance of the cultic obligations and war in pointing out that cult and war are the two highest forms of religion. He legitimizes the political control over the production and the marketing of basic goods through the interest of the community. He underlines the importance of political authorities for the stability of the social and religious order. He justifies the licit use of torture and other coercive measures as means of investigation by the authorities when they look into cases against individuals or groups, so that they can preserve the political and legal framework of the religious community. His position on these matters clearly contradicts the classical teaching of Islamic law until the thirteenth century, that—at least in the Hanafi, Shafiʿi, and Hanbali schools—forbade torture as an instrument of interrogation because it was considered to destroy the truth value of any statement or testimony and thus put into jeopardy the whole law of procedure on which classical Islam rests.[154] One could, therefore, be tempted to paint him as a scholar who derives his political concepts and strategies from religious convictions and requires their realization, without regard for the consequences of such a policy in the political and judiciary practice as well as in the doctrine of the sacred law.

Ibn Taymiyya, though, is well aware of the risks implied in the imposition of a perfect law on an imperfect society by an imperfect class of rulers. He is extremely critical of those who hold that politics can be reduced to the application of religious rules and maxims without concern for the practical consequences of such application. He distinguishes three groups of people dangerous to the religious community and its political institutions. The first group are those who take the law lightly and shy away from fulfilling their religious and legal duties. The second group consists of

> those who want to give commands and to impose prohibitions in an absolute way either by action (*bi-yadihi*) or by speech (*bi-lisānihi*) without understanding (*fiqh*), self-constraint (*ḥilm*) or patience and without looking into which [of these measures] is apt [to produce the desired effects] and which one they can perform and which one not.[155]

These people, according to Ibn Taymiyya, believe that they follow the Prophet's order to command the good and forbid the evil. But they forget that the Prophet himself has drawn limits to this order: when people do not listen to good counsel and rather follow their own mundane interests, it is better, according to the Prophet, to take care of oneself and to leave those who go astray to themselves. But the people whom Ibn Taymiyya criticizes:

> go on to command and to forbid believing that doing so they obey God and His Prophet, but in fact they are transgressing the limits. Many of the adherents to blameworthy innovations and uncontrolled sectarian passions such as the Kharijites, the Muʿtazila, the Rāfiḍa, and others follow this pattern (*intaṣaba*). On this basis they have erred in their commands and prohibitions and in religious war. The evil they caused was much more momentous than the benefit [they produced].

Ibn Taymiyya concludes that for this reason the Prophet ordered the Muslims to obey unjust Imams.[156] But extremist political-religious activists are not the only danger for the religious community. Those who are afraid to commit illicit acts in pursuit of their religious duties form a third group that is equally dangerous:

> This is the case of many would-be religious people who, for fear of being tempted to follow their [illicit] desires, leave their duty to command and to forbid and to perform religious war efforts [. . .]. [But in doing so] they have already fallen [victim] to a temptation that is much bigger than the one they pretend to flee from. They are obligated to fulfill their duty and to avoid what is forbidden. The two are inseparable. And they leave [that obligation] because they can only persuade themselves to perform them together or to leave them together. That happens often to those who love leadership and wealth and the passions of transgression. It is in fact unavoidable that if they perform their duty to command and forbid and to lead religious war and military command and similar things, they also commit forbidden things. It is [then] incumbent upon them to look at which of these two things outweighs the other. If [to follow] the command brings greater reward than to refrain from the prohibited

> [action], they should not refrain from performing it for fear of an evil that is of lesser importance [than the evil that would result from abstaining from action]. If the reward for abstaining from performing a forbidden act is greater, they should not risk losing this reward, hoping to acquire a recompense for the fulfillment of a duty that is of lesser value [than the abstention from the prohibited act]. This holds true for all things that have at the same time good and bad consequences. This is so and a detailed discussion would take too much time.[157]

In other words, positive action may oblige the Muslim and in particular the political leaders to commit prohibited acts. It is their duty to weigh the evil and the good consequences of their action and then to decide in favor of the greater good. Ibn Taymiyya here comes close to an ethics of responsibility (*Verantwortungsethik, ethicsethics ethic*) such as developed by Max Weber in his famous lecture on "Politik als Beruf" (Politics as a Calling) (1919). The decision whether to perform an action or to refrain from it depends on the outcome to be expected. For Ibn Taymiyya, neither religious extremism that draws radical conclusions from recognized religious principles, nor a religious quietism that renders its adherents unable to act in the interest of the religious community, is acceptable. Both attitudes follow religious convictions without taking into consideration the results of their own activism or passivity. Ibn Taymiyya suggests that everyone who is engaged in governance must, by necessity, commit forbidden acts in the course of his political action. These forbidden acts can only be justified if they bring about a greater good connected with the duty that the actors have to fulfill.

While each Muslim, and in particular each religious scholar or public dignitary, is obliged "to command the good and forbid the evil," this obligation should always be weighed against its consequences. It should only be performed if, for the Muslim community, its positive results are more important than its negative consequences. Ibn Taymiyya summarizes this approach to the *ḥisba*-principle in the following words:

> One can subsume all this under a general rule (*qāʿida*): If a contradiction arises between the advantages and the harm [caused], between the good and the bad results [of applying the *ḥisba*-principle], or if many such conflicts [are implied in its application] one should consider as preponderant [the aspect] that outweighs [the other] [...]. Even if the duty to command [the good] and forbid [the evil] aims at procuring advantages and at fending off harm, one has to look into the obstacles that stand in the way of [the performance] of this duty. If the loss of advantages and the harm ensuing [from its performance] are more important [than the advantages assured and

the harm avoided], it is no longer a legal order, rather its [performance] is prohibited if the harm that follows from it is clearly more important than the advantages.

But the consideration of the extent of advantages and harm [has to be controlled] on the scales of the sacred law. If human beings can follow its [revealed] texts, they should not deviate from them. If not, they should exert their individual power of personal reasoning (*ijtihād al-ra'y*) in order to evaluate the similar and analogous cases. But it is rare that those who are experienced in the [interpretation] of revealed texts and know how to indicate legal rules lack the texts.

If, therefore, an individual or a group [finds itself in a situation] that comprises the elements of the good and the evil [in such a way] that they cannot be disentangled and one either has to accept them both or leave them both, it is not permissible to command all good and forbid all evil. One has, rather, to study the case and command the good if it is more important—even if some lesser evil cannot be separated from it. One does not forbid the evil if that would lead to the loss of a more important good [inseparable from the evil]. Such a prohibition would be equivalent to barring God's way, to striving for disobedience to God and His Prophet, and to doing away with the performance of good actions.[158]

X. The Principles of Governance and the Autonomy of Political Power

To what extent are we justified in treating Ibn Taymiyya's books on "political decision-making" (*siyāsa*), the principle of "commanding the good and forbidding the evil" (*ḥisba*), and his writings on analogy and methodology as texts on governance? Is the modern term appropriate to these fourteenth-century texts?

Ibn Taymiyya seeks the support of the political authorities for a creed and a law that define Islam as a complete and perfect system of belief and law, of ethical and legal norms and of proofs that provide rational and revealed knowledge. Islam, defined in this way, is independent as a religious, legal, and political system from all external sources, be they Greek logic, legal institutions that are not derived from the revealed law, or social needs that cannot be integrated into analogies from the revealed sources. It has no internal contradictions, is entirely consistent, does not need to be open to foreign influences, and combines all the rational and revealed reasons for its knowledge and its norms. It is the basis for the identity of the Muslim community and it constitutes the fundamental legitimacy of the political order of that community.

In order to find the political support for such an understanding of Islam, Ibn Taymiyya has to define the margin of action that the political authorities have vis-à-vis the perfect system of Islamic law. Ibn Taymiyya focuses his attention, as befits a doctrine on governance, on political decision-making. His system is efficiency oriented: political power is a necessary condition for the survival of religion and law and, for that reason, one has to assign to the political authorities the means and competencies to use that power in a way that yields results and realizes goals pursued by the authorities.

Ibn Taymiyya holds that political power in the service of religion must be restricted to rather narrow groups of stakeholders. Mamluk dignitaries and religious scholars should cooperate: the scholars in controlling the religious legitimacy of the political means and suggesting goals for its use, the administrative and military elite in using these means effectively. All other social groups are excluded from the process of licit political decision-making. Ibn Taymiyya does note that these other groups can be political actors. Dozens of recurrent references in his work underline the illegal character of the activities not only of bandits, but also of tribes, ethnic groups, peasant organizations, urban gangs, and heretical communities. Ibn Taymiyya leaves no doubt that these activities exert an important influence on the political decision-making process and the social and political order. But he does not envisage the inclusion of even some of these groups into the political decision-making process.[159] He suggests that actors like these, if they are too powerful to be fought, should be paid so as to renounce their criminal activities. But apart from such a distribution of tax money on powerful law-breakers, Ibn Taymiyya does not envisage their integration in the process of licit political decision-making.

Ibn Taymiyya gives a large margin of action to the political authorities in their persecution of heretics and non-Muslim minorities, in their control of the cult and religious doctrine, in war against foreign and domestic enemies, and—last but not least—in the control and direction of the production, distribution, and pricing of basic goods. It is obvious that in attributing to the government such a strong position in so many domains, he suggests a policy of conflict with those groups that he does not admit into the rank of licit political actors. His doctrine on political decision-making is more conflict than consensus oriented: the perspective is more that of the imposition of a perfect law on a very imperfect and often unruly society through political authorities about whose injustice he leaves no doubt, than the reconciliation of different groups through their integration into the rank of licit political actors.

Does this mean—as has been suggested by eminent scholars—that Ibn Taymiyya's doctrine on "governance in the name of the sacred law" establishes the rule of law as an essential part of political decision-making? The answer has to be in the affirmative if one looks at the degree to which the whole process of political decision-making should, according to Ibn Taymiyya, be directed and oriented by revealed law. If, on the other hand, one understands the rule of law as a guarantee for the protection of individuals and groups in their legitimate conflicts with political authorities and the judiciary, its presence in Ibn Taymiyya's concept of governance is much less certain. The procedural protection of individual defendants in judiciary procedures which has played such an important role in classical Islamic law is certainly not among the preoccupations of Ibn Taymiyya and his followers in the fourteenth century.[160]

If we compare Ibn Taymiyya's writings on "governance in the name of the sacred law" with the definition of good governance as provided by the United Nations Economic and Social Commission for Asia and the Pacific,[161] striking differences are apparent. The Commission stresses consensus orientation, encouragement of participation, rule of law, transparency, responsiveness, equity, and inclusiveness, as well as the orientation towards effective and efficient solutions. Ibn Taymiyya's system of governance does not encourage consensus (except through imposition of the sacred law), participation or inclusiveness, and it establishes the rule of law only within the limits pointed out above.

But it should be kept in mind that the Commission adds a small note to its text, saying: "From the above discussion it should be clear that good governance is an ideal which is difficult to achieve in its totality. Very few countries and societies have come close to achieving good governance in its totality." This note throws into relief the difficulty entailed in developing doctrines of governance that come to terms with the different dimensions of the society to which they apply. In this light, Ibn Taymiyya's system of governance is clearly not the only one that creates its own blind spots.

One may, in fact, be entitled to ask whether Ibn Taymiyya's concept of the imposition, through coercive power used by imperfect rulers, of a perfect law on an imperfect and unruly society did not contribute to his own political failure. By limiting the process of licit political decision-making exclusively to military and administrative dignitaries on the one hand, and to religious scholars on the other, he excluded from the sphere of governance an urban public ready to play its part in religious life while at the same time subordinating rural interest entirely to that of the urban elites. He insisted on political power as an important dimension of religious life and a condition for its survival, on the necessity to grant a large margin of action to the licit political actors, and on the justification of the negative consequences of positive acts as long as these produce a greater good than the evil that is their consequence. He has thus legitimized the political evaluation of the positive and negative consequences of political decisions on religious doctrines and acts. The Mamluk authorities pursued a consensus-oriented policy and relied on their alliance with the dominant Sunni law schools and with the mystics instead of engaging in a policy of religious conflict with these forces in the name of a creed and a law that claims universal Islamic validity. In their hands, what Ibn Taymiyya conceived of as perfect and "revealed law" was altered in what he must have lived as a "perverted law." His relation to the political authorities of his time raises the question of where, in the system projected by Ibn Taymiyya, individuals could find the means to protect themselves in their conflicts with the political authorities. The classical doctrines of Islamic law had solidly anchored the procedural protection of the defendant into the norms of the law but Ibn Taymiyya's concept of governance (*siyāsa shar'iyya*) abandoned them because he thought that they belonged to the system of "perverted law" that protected the evildoer and deprived the victims of their rights. In his quest for justice he created a system that delivered the suspect and the accused to the appreciation and evaluation of those in power. When he himself fell victim to this mechanism, there was little in his own concept of governance, with regard to the legitimate political actors or to the law of proof and procedure, that he could have invoked for his political or legal defense.

NOTES

[1] For the political history of the Mamluks, see Ulrich Haarmann, "Der arabische Osten im späten Mittelalter 1250–1517," in Ulrich Haarmann (ed.), *Geschichte der arabischen Welt* (München: C. H. Beck, 1987); Thomas Philipp and Ulrich Haarmann (eds.), *The Mamluks in Egyptian Politics and Society* (Cambridge and New York: Cambridge University Press, 1998); Michael Winter and Amalia Levanoni (eds.), *The Mamluks in Egyptian and Syrian Politics and Society* (Leiden: Brill, 2004); Stephan Conermann and Anja Pistor-Hatam (eds.), *Die Mamluken: Studien zu ihrer Geschichte und Kultur. Zum Gedenken an Ulrich Haarmann, 1942–1999* (Hamburg: EB-Verlag, 2003). For the loyalty of the Mamluks to the masters who emancipated them, see David Ayalon, "L'Esclavage du Mamelouk," in David Ayalon, *The Mamluk Military Society* (London: Variorum Reprints, 1979), 1:27–37, 54–64.

[2] Hugh Kennedy, *The Prophet and the Age of the Caliphates. The Islamic Near East from the Sixth to the Eleventh Century* (London and New York: Longman, 1986), 203–04.

[3] Stefan Heidemann, *Das Aleppiner Kalifat (A.D. 1261): Vom Ende des Kalifats in Bagdad über Aleppo zu den Restaurationen in Kairo* (Leiden: E. J. Brill, 1994).

[4] Haarmann, "Der arabische Osten im späten Mittelalter 1250–1517," 217–18, 221, 239–40.

[5] Ibid., 235–36, 243.

[6] Ibid., 249; E. Ashtor, *A Social and Economic History of the Near East in the Middle Ages* (London: Collins, 1976), 297–301, 321.

[7] André Raymond, *Le Caire* (n.p. [Paris]: Fayard, 1993), 122; Ashtor, *A Social and Economic History of the Near East in the Middle Ages*, 288–90, 303.

[8] Carl F. Petry, *The Civilian Elite of Cairo in the Later Middle Ages* (Princeton: Princeton University Press, 1981), 38–81.

[9] Ashtor, *A Social and Economic History of the Near East in the Middle Ages*, 292–92.

[10] Raymond, *Le Caire*, ch. 5, 122–42.

[11] Haarmann, "Der arabische Osten im späten Mittelalter 1250–1517," 231–33, 238, 254; P. M. Holt, s.v. "Mamluks," *The Encyclopaedia of Islam, New Edition* (Leiden: E. J. Brill, 1991), 6:326–27 (hereinafter *EI*²); Ira Marvin Lapidus, *Muslim Cities in*

the later Middle Ages (Cambridge, Mass.: Harvard University Press, 1967), 48–53, 255; Petry, *The Civilian Elite of Cairo in the Later Middle Ages*, 23.

[12] Henri Laoust, *Les Schismes dans l'Islam. Introduction à une étude de la religion musulmane* (Paris: Payot, 1965), 251–52 (hereinafter *Schismes*); idem, *Essai sur les doctrines sociales et politiques de Takī-d-Dīn Aḥmad b. Taimīya canoniste ḥanbalite né à Harran en 661/1262, mort à Damas en 728/1328* (hereinafter *Essai*) (Cairo: Imprimerie de l'Institut Français d'Archéologie Orientale, 1939), 33; Mohamed Menasri, *Kitab Tuhfat al-Turk: Oeuvre de combat hanafite au XIVe siècle* (Damascus: Institut Français de Damas, 1997), 32–3.

[13] For an important systematic discussion, see Michael Chamberlain, *Knowledge and Social Practice in Medieval Damascus, 1190–1350* (Cambridge: Cambridge University Press, 1994), 51–90; see also Menasri, *Kitab Tuhfat al-Turk*, 26–7, 31–2, 35, 37. Daniella Talmon-Heller, "Fidelity, Cohesion, and Conformity within Madhhabs in Zangid and Ayyubid Syria," in Peri Bearman, Rudolph Peters, and Frank E. Vogel (eds.), *The Islamic School of Law. Evolution, Devolution, and Progress* (Cambridge, Mass.: ILSP/Harvard University Press, 2005), 101. The importance of madrasas and mosque constructions for the urbanism of Cairo is underlined in Raymond, *Le Caire*, 140–41, 182.

[14] For the kind of offices that the commanders and Sultans tried to control, see Chamberlain, *Knowledge and Social Practice in Medieval Damascus, 1190–1350*, 50, 94–9. Chamberlain interprets Baybars' introduction of one chief qadiship for each of the four Sunni schools of law as part of this policy of controlling the notables' offices. For scholars beginning their careers in religious offices and continuing them in high administrative positions, see Petry, *The Civilian Elite of Cairo in the Later Middle Ages*, 206–9, 230. Both Chamberlain and Petry show how the control over the filling of religious or judiciary positions implicates the *ʿulamāʾ* into the factional strife of the Mamluks and vice versa: Petry, 24–5 and Chamberlain, 94–6.

[15] Stefan Leder, "Postklassisch und vormodern: Beobachtungen zum Kulturwandel in der Mamlukenzeit," in Conermann and Pistor-Hatem (eds.), *Die Mamluken: Studien zu ihrer Geschichte und Kultur*, 289, 293, 295–300. The best example for their participation in the city's religious life are the popular *ḥadīth* recitations that were often ridiculed by elite scholars, but showed a spreading ambition to participate in activities that brought religious prestige (ibid., 297–300).

[16] See ibid., 295: "Ibn Ǧubayr, der sich 1184 in der Stadt [Damascus] aufhielt, berichtet bereits von dem gewaltigen Ausmass des Stiftungsguts, das fast alles umfasse, was an bebaubarem Land und gewerblich genutzten Gebaeuden vorhanden war [...]." See also p. 296 for a statistic of madrasas in the Ayyubid and the Mamluk periods.

[17] Ibid., 293.

[18] Ibid., 296–97.

[19] Donald P. Little, "The Historical and Historiographical Significance of the Detention of Ibn Taymiyya," in idem, *History and Historiography of the Mamlūks* (London: Variorum Reprints, 1986), 322–27.

[20] Ibid., 309.

[21] Henri Laoust, *Essai*, 7–11. The Hanbali school owes its name to that of its eponym, Aḥmad ibn Ḥanbal (d. 855 in Baghdad).

[22] Ibid., 143–50.

[23] Little, "The Historical and Historiographical Significance of the Detention of Ibn Taymiyya," 312–13; Laoust, *Essai*, 110–17 (for the episode of 1298), 125–37 (for the period 1305–9), 144–45 (for 1318, 1321) and 145–50 (for 1326–28).

[24] On this topic, Frank Vogel has written extensively; see among his other publications on this subject, his article on *siyāsa* in *EI*², 9:694–96. See Ibn Taymiyya's *al-Siyāsa al-sharʿiyya fī iṣlāḥ al-rāʿī wa l-raʿiyya* (Beirut: Dār al-Āfāq al-Jadīda, 1988). I quote this text from the translation by Henri Laoust, *Le Traité de droit public d'Ibn Taymiyya. Traduction annotée de la Siyāsa sharʿiyya* (Beirut: Institut Français de Damas, 1948) (hereinafter Laoust's "Introduction" is quoted in this article as *Traité*, followed by Latin numbers, while the translation of Ibn Taymiyya's text is quoted as Ibn Taymiyya, *Traité*, followed by Arabic numbers).

[25] Ibn Taymiyya accuses the followers of Ibn al-ʿArabī of not respecting the fundamental difference between the Creator and His creatures. In other words, he accuses them of pantheism. Ibn al-ʿArabī's followers and defenders refused to accept this attribute and defined their system as "the unity of existence" or "the unity of being."

[26] Little, "The Historical and Historiographical Significance of the Detention of Ibn Taymiyya," 321–24.

[27] Laoust, *Essai*, 33–5.

[28] Ibid., xl–xli; Menasri, *Kitab Tuḥfat al-Turk*, 22–6; Little, "The Historical and Historiographical Significance of the Detention of Ibn Taymiyya," 323–24; Talmon-Heller, "Fidelity, Cohesion, and Conformity within Madhhabs in Zangid and Ayyubid Syria," 102–3, 111–12.

[29] Talmon-Heller, "Fidelity, Cohesion, and Conformity within Madhhabs in Zangid and Ayyubid Syria," 108–9; Sherman Jackson, *Islamic Law and the State: The Constitutional Jurisprudence of Shihāb al-Dīn al-Qarāfī* (Leiden: E. J. Brill, 1996), 12–13, 52–6, 64–8; Menasri, *Kitab Tuḥfat al-Turk*, 21–6. On Shafiʿis who reject Ashʿari theology, see Little, "Did Ibn Taymiyya Have a Screw Loose?," in idem, *History and Historiography of the Mamlūks*, 102, 104. For the Malikis who rejected Ashʿari theology, see Talmon-Heller, "Fidelity, Cohesion, and Conformity within Madhhabs in Zangid and Ayyubid Syria," 109, 115.

[30] Daniel Gimaret, *La Doctrine d'al-Ashʿarī* (Paris: Editions du CERF, 1990), 235–45.

[31] Little, "The Historical and Historiographical Significance of the Detention of Ibn Taymiyya," 323–24; Laoust, *Essai*, 33–5; Talmon-Heller, "Fidelity, Cohesion, and Conformity within Madhhabs in Zangid and Ayyubid Syria," 108–9. See also Chamberlain, *Knowledge and Social Practice in Medieval Damascus, 1190–1350*, 169.

[32] The first investigation into Ibn Taymiyya's creed, in 1298, was led by a Shafiʿi and not—as is often asserted—by a Hanafi qadi; see Laoust, *Essai*, 113–14 and 113 n. 2.

[33] Laoust, *Essai*, 111–17, 125–31.

[34] Ibid., 144–45.

[35] Ibid., 125–31, 136–39, 145–47.

[36] Ibid., 21–22; Henri Laoust, *La Profession de foi d'Ibn Taymiyya. Texte, traduction et commentaire de la Wāsiṭiyya* (Paris: Geuthner, 1986), 38–40, 61 [hereinafter *Wāsiṭiyya* ("Introduction") when it refers to Laoust's introduction (pp. 9–35) and as Ibn Taymiyya, *Wāsiṭiyya* (pp. 37–87) when it refers to the translation of Ibn Taymiyya's text]. Henri Laoust, *Contribution à une étude de la méthodologie canonique*

de Taḳi-d-Dīn Aḥmad b. Taimīya. Traduction annotée du Maʿariǧ al-wuṣūl ilā maʿrifat anna uṣūl ad-dīn wa-furūʿahu ḳad bayyanahā ar-rasūl et d'al-Qiyās fī sh-sharʿ al-Islāmī (Cairo: Imprimerie de l'Institut Français d'Archéologie Orientale, 1939), 61–5. References to this book refer to three texts: (a) Laoust's "Introduction," pp. 3–51; (b) the translation of Ibn Taymiyya's text *Maʿārij al-wuṣūl ilā maʿrifat anna uṣūl al-dīn wa-furūʿahu qad bayyanahā al-rasūl* under the title *Principes généraux de méthodologie canonique*, pp. 55–112; and (c) the translation of Ibn Taymiyya's text *al-Qiyās fī l-sharʿ al-Islāmī* under the title *Le Raisonnement analogique en droit musulman*, pp. 113–216. For the long history of conflicts between the defenders of Ashʿari dogmatic theology and those of the traditionalist creed of the Hanbalis, see Laoust, *Schismes*, 129–30, 200–12, and idem, *Essai*, 21–2.

[37] Laoust, *Contribution,* 60, 61, 65, 95 (*Méthodologie canonique*); see also Wael B. Hallaq, *Ibn Taymiyya against the Greek Logicians* (Oxford: Clarendon Press, 1993), xvii–xx.

[38] Laoust, *Contribution*, 72, 76, 78–80, 99.

[39] Ibid., 12 ("Introduction"), 72 (*Méthodologie canonique*).

[40] Ibid., 81 (*Méthodologie canonique*).

[41] Ibid., 21, 23–5, 32 ("Introduction") for examples of the critique of the legal doctrine of other schools. For the trials of Ibn Taymiyya and their background in his conflicts with the Shafiʿis, see Little, "The Historical and Historiographical Significance of the Detention of Ibn Taymiyya," 322–23, 325.

[42] Little, "The Historical and Historiographical Significance of the Detention of Ibn Taymiyya," 322, 324; Laoust, *Essai*, 128, 133.

[43] Little, "The Historical and Historiographical Significance of the Detention of Ibn Taymiyya," 322–23.

[44] Laoust, *Traité*, xxvii, xxix; for the relation between the Sultan's norm-creating power and the precepts of Qurʾan and Sunna, see ibid., xxxvii.

[45] Ibid., xxviii.

[46] Ibid., xxviii. For Ibn Taymiyya's influence on other military dignitaries, see Little, "The Historical and Historiographical Significance of the Detention of Ibn Taymiyya," 322–23.

[47] *Majmūʿ Fatāwā Shaykh al-Islām Aḥmad Ibn Taymiyya*, ed. ʿAbd al-Raḥmān ibn Qāsim al-ʿĀṣimī (Maṭābiʿ al-Riyāḍ, 1381 h.), 260–68; Laoust, *Wāsiṭiyya* ("Introduction"), 21, 23–25, 32.

[48] Laoust, *Wāsiṭiyya* ("Introduction") 31–32; idem, *Essai*, 131–33.

[49] Laoust, *Essai*, 136–39.

[50] Laoust, *Traité*, xxviii.

[51] Ibid., xxviii–xxix.

[52] Ibid., 144–45.

[53] Ibid., 145–47.

[54] *al-Siyāsa al-sharʿiyya fī iṣlāḥ al-rāʿī wa l-rāʿiyya* (in this article quoted as *Traité* from the French translation by Henri Laoust, see n. 22) clearly refers to a way of governing rather than to a form of government. For the date of its composition, see Laoust, *Traité*, xxvii.

[55] *Traité* ("Introduction"), xxvii–xxix.

[56] Laoust, *Wāsiṭiyya* ("Introduction), 13. Laoust, *Essai*, 113 n. 2 shows that, contrary to a widely-held opinion, the qadi who summons Ibn Taymiyya in 1298 is not a Hanafi, but a Shafiʿi qadi.

[57] Haarmann, "Der arabische Osten im späten Mittelalter 1250–1517," 237–38, 241, 245; Laoust, *Traité*, xxv–xxvi; Ibn Taymiyya, *Traité*, 73–4, 76, 122, 129–35; *Wāsiṭiyya*, 27–8.

[58] *Wāsiṭiyya* ("Introduction"), 27.

[59] Ibid., 27–8.

[60] *Majmūʿ Fatāwā*, 3:268; cf. *Wāsiṭiyya* ("Introduction"), 29–30, see also 29 n. 131.

[61] Ibn Qayyim al-Jawziyya, *al-Ṭuruq al-ḥukmiyya fī l-siyāsa al-sharʿiyya aw al-firāsa al-marḍiyya fī aḥkām al-siyāsa al-sharʿiyya*, ed. Muḥammad Ḥāmid al-Faqī (Beirut: Dār al-Kutub al-ʿIlmiyya, n.d.), 100–01.

[62] Ibn Taymiyya, *al-Ḥisba fī l-islām—Traité sur la hisba*, trans. Henri Laoust (Paris: Geuthner, 1994), 85, see also 82–3.

[63] Ibn Taymiyya, *Ḥisba*, 31. The translation of *wilāyāt* by "social functions" is certainly misleading. The term refers in *ḥisba* and *siyāsa sharʿiyya* to public offices.

[64] Ibn Taymiyya, *Ḥisba*, 31.

[65] Ibn Taymiyya, *Traité*, 172.

[66] For the special trials called *daʿāwī al-tuhma*, see my article "Signs as Evidence: The Doctrine of Ibn Taymiyya (1263–1328) and Ibn Qayyim al-Jawziyya (d.1351) on Proof," *Islamic Law and Society* 9/2 (2002), 168–93, in particular 190–92.

[67] Ibn Taymiyya, *Ḥisba*, 30–1.

[68] Ibid., 29.

[69] Ibn Taymiyya, *Traité*, 12.

[70] Shihāb al-Dīn Abū l-ʿAbbās Aḥmad ibn Idrīs al-Qarāfī, *al-Ihkām fī tamyīz al-fatāwā ʿan al-aḥkām wa-taṣarrufāt al-qāḍī wa l-imām*, ed. ʿAbd al-Fattāḥ Abū Ghudda (Aleppo: Maktabat al-Maṭbūʿāt al-Islāmiyya, 1967), 157–71.

[71] Abū Ḥāmid Muḥammad al-Ghazālī, *al-Mustaṣfā min ʿilm al-uṣūl* (Cairo: al-Maktaba al-Tijāriyya al-Kubrā 1937), part 1, 139–44.

[72] According to George Makdisi, *Ibn ʿAqīl. Religion and Culture in Classical Islam* (Edinburgh: Edinburgh University Press, 1997), 43, Ibn ʿAqīl became, in the second half of his life (1077–1119), "head of the Hanbali guild" of Baghdad.

[73] Makdisi, *Ibn ʿAqīl*, 160, translates the Arabic term *siyāsa* once by "government" and the second time by "administration."

[74] Ibid., 160.

[75] Ibn Qayyim al-Jawziyya, *Iʿlām al-muwaqqiʿīn ʿan rabbi l-ʿālamīn*, ed. Muḥammad ʿAbd al-Salām Ibrāhīm (Beirut: Dār al-Kutub al-ʿIlmiyya), 2nd ed., 2/4:283–84, 287.

[76] Laoust, *Contribution*, 9 ("Introduction"), 55 (*Méthodologie canonique*).

[77] Ibid., 60–9, 80, 110 (*Méthodologie canonique*).

[78] Ibid., 12 ("Introduction"), 72 (*Méthodologie canonique*).

[79] Ibid., 61, 80–1, 99, see also 72, 76, 78 (*Méthodologie canonique*).

[80] Ibid., 78 (*Méthodologie canonique*).

[81] Ibid., 80–1, 110–11 (*Méthodologie canonique*).

[82] Ibid., 80–1 (*Méthodologie canonique*), see also 12 ("Introduction"), 141 (*Raisonnement analogique*).

[83] Ibid., 13, 14 ("Introduction"), 82, 84, 99–100, 102–03, 105, 110–11 (*Méthodologie canonoique*), 215–16 (*Raisonnement analogique*).

[84] Ibid., 103, 105, 111–12 (*Méthodologie canonique*).

[85] Ibid., 102–3, 105, 110 (*Méthodologie canonique*).

[86] Ibid., 103, 105, 110 (*Méthodologie canonique*).

[87] Ibid., 81 (*Méthodologie canonique*), 179 (*Raisonnement analogique*).

[88] Ibid., 80–1 (*Méthodologie canononique*).

[89] Ibid., 81 (*Méthodologie canonique*): the influence of Greek logic on such statements of identity is obvious, but not admitted by Ibn Taymiyya. Laoust translates *qiyās* as syllogism and Hallaq, *Ibn Taymiyya Against Greek Logicians*, 35–9, analyses the functional identity that Ibn Taymiyya attributes to both forms of conclusions. I would still shy away from following Laoust in translating *qiyās* as syllogism, mainly because Ibn Taymiyya's use of the term clearly refers also to the classical doctrine on the sources of the law which defines *qiyās* as analogy. Ibn Taymiyya upholds the ambiguity of the term.

[90] Ibid., 137, 139, 141–42, 151–52, 157–58, 160–61, 179 (*Raisonnement analogique*).

[91] Ibid., 55–9, 61, 65, 92–3 (*Méthodologie canonique*).

[92] Ibid., 61–5 (*Méthodologie canonique*).

[93] Ibid., 85–6, 91 (*Méthodologie canonique*): all prophets adhere to the same religion, Islam; 91, 93, 96 (*Méthodologie canonique*): not to believe in one of these prophets means to believe in no religion, no prophet, and no God.

[94] Ibid., 86–8 (*Méthodologie canonique*); for the notion of *tabdīl* in a context of revelation, see Q 14:28, 50:29, 2:211, 48:15, 40:26, 10:64, 33:62, 30:30; 6:34, 115, 18:27.

[95] *Contribution*, 87–8 (*Méthodologie canonique*).

[96] Ibid., 141 (*Raisonnement analogique*).

[97] Ibid., 110–11 (*Methodologie canonique*).

[98] Ibid., 104 (*Methodologie canonique*).

[99] Ibid., 13 ("Introduction").

[100] Ibid., 102–05 (*Méthodologie canonique*).

[101] Ibid., 115–57, 165–79 (*Raisonnement analogique*).

[102] Ibid., 179 (*Raisonnement analogique*).

[103] Ibid., 152, 157–58, 160–61, 163–64, 174–75, 179 (*Raisonnement analogique*).

[104] Ibn Taymiyya has written a detailed "Refutation of the Logicians" (*al-Radd ʿalā l-manṭiqiyyīn*). A shortened version of the text, established by Jalāl al-Dīn al-Suyūṭī (d. 1505), has been introduced and translated by Wael B. Hallaq [see above, n. 34]. See also Laoust, *Essai*, 84–9.

[105] Laoust, *Contribution*, 153, 157 (*Raisonnement analogique*); see also 34, 38, 40–1 ("Introduction"), cf. Baber Johansen, *Islamic Law on Land Tax and Rent* (London: Croon Helm, 1988), 28–32, where the arguments on which the classical *fiqh* schools base their denial of an analogy between the sales contract and the contract of tenancy are treated.

[106] Benjamin Jokisch, *Islamisches Recht in Theorie und Praxis. Analyse einiger kaufrechtlicher Fatwas von Taqī d-dīn Aḥmad b. Taymiyya* (Berlin: Klaus Schwarz Verlag, 1996), 177.

[107] *Contribution*, 115, 120–21, 125–26, 148–51, 160–61, 163–65 (*Raisonnement analogique*); for a concrete example, see Jokisch, *Islamisches Recht in Theorie und Praxis*, 54–64, 192, 205 on the *ḍamān* contract. See, in particular, the way in which Ibn Taymiyya links the concept of *maṣlaḥa* to the concept of analogy, ibid., 183, 193, 245–46, 248 and his treatment of customary law, ibid., 187, 200, 228–29, 239. The example of the *ḍamān* contract shows how Ibn Taymiyya uses analogy in

order to legalize customary contracts, see ibid., 243–48, and to invalidate general prohibitions as far as specific contracts are concerned, see ibid., 260–61.

[108] Ibn Taymiyya, *Ḥisba*, 26–7; idem, *Traité*, 172–73.

[109] Ibn Taymiyya, *Traité*, 176–77.

[110] Ibid., 20.

[111] Ibid., 143.

[112] Ibid. ("Introduction"), xxxv–xxxvi.

[113] Ibid., 169–70.

[114] Ibid., 47.

[115] Ibid., 172–74.

[116] Ibn Taymiyya, *Ḥisba*, 29, 39–40.

[117] Ibid., 31. On the Mamluks' control of the *manāṣib*, "the semi-autonomous offices" held by the notables of social and religious life, see Chamberlain, *Knowledge and Social Practice in Medieval Damascus, 1190–1350*, 50ff, 91ff.

[118] Ibn Taymiyya, *Traité*, 172, 173–74.

[119] Ibid., 49–53.

[120] Ibid., 177–78.

[121] Ibid., 2–3; see also ibid., "Introduction," xxxiii.

[122] Ibid., xxvi, xxxix, xlii ("Introduction"), 172–74.

[123] Laoust, *Essai*, 360–61.

[124] Ibn Taymiyya, *Traité*, 19, 73, 135; idem, *Ḥisba*, 32–3.

[125] Ibn Taymiyya, *Traité*, 72–3, 134–35.

[126] Ibid., 118–19.

[127] Ibid., 73, 132–36.

[128] Ibid., 122, 128–30.

[129] Ibid., 122, 130–34; Laoust, *Essai*, 365–69.

[130] Ibn Taymiyya, *Traité*, 84–6.

[131] Ibid., 85, 86.

[132] Ibid., 90.

[133] Ibid., 90–1.

[134] Ibid., 67–8, 74, 78–9, 82.

[135] Ibid., 88.

[136] Ibid., 143–44.

[137] Ibn Taymiyya, *Ḥisba*, 36.

[138] Ibid., 37.

[139] Ibid., 37, 48–9.

[140] Ibid., 37, 38.

[141] Ibid., 37.

[142] Ibid., 38.

[143] Ibid., 39, 41, 44, 46.

[144] Ibid., 40–1.

[145] Ibid., 85.

[146] Ibn Taymiyya, *Traité*, 26.

[147] Ibid., 39.

[148] Ibid., 67, 69–70.

[149] Ibid., 67–8, 74, 78–9, 81, 82.

[150] Ibid., 40.

[151] Ibid., 146.

[152] Ibid., 59.

[153] Ibid., 67.

[154] See n. 65; see also Baber Johansen, "Vérité et torture: *Ius commune* et droit musulman entre le Xe et le XIIIe siècle," in Françoise Héritier (ed.), *De la violence* (Paris: Odile Jacob, 1996), 123–68; idem, "La Découverte des choses qui parlent. La Légalisation de la torture judiciaire en droit musulman (XIIIe–XIVe siècle)," *Enquêtes* 7 (1998), 175–202; idem, "Vom Wort- zum Indizienbeweis: Die Anerkennung der richterlichen Folter in islamischen Rechtsdoktrinen des 13. und 14. Jahrhunderts," *Ius Commune. Zeitschrift für Europäische Rechtsgeschichte* 28 (2001), 1–46.

[155] Ibn Taymiyya, *Ḥisba*, 72.

[156] Ibid., 73.

[157] Ibid., 100–1; see also 56, 131–32.

[158] Ibid., 73–4.

[159] This is all the more surprising as Bedouin tribal chiefs, for example, did play a role in the Mamluk army and some of them had effectively intervened in Ibn Taymiyya's favor.

[160] See my article on "Signs as Evidence," cited in n. 65.

[161] United Nations, *Economic and Social Commission for Asia and the Pacific: What is Good Governance*? http://www.unescap.org/pdd/prs/projectactivities/ongoing/gg/governance.asp, last seen on May 28, 2007, 6:09 pm.

15

TALKING IN CODE

Legal Islamisation in Indonesia and the MMI Shari'a Criminal Code

Tim Lindsey and Jeremy Kingsley

In 2002, the *Majelis Mujahidin Indonesia* (MMI, Indonesian Mujahidin Council) released its "Proposal for a Criminal Code for the Republic of Indonesia Adjusted to Accord with Islamic Shari'a." It contains an introduction or preamble and five chapters divided into 69 Arts:[1] "General Provisions" (Arts. 1–3); "Criminal Offences and Criminal Responsibility" (Arts. 4–42); "Punishment and Conviction" (Arts. 43–52); "Trial" (Arts. 53–68), and "Closing Provisions" (Art. 69).

The MMI Code is controversial because it proposes the application of an extreme interpretation of Shari'a through the application by the state of strict Qur'anic punishments (*ḥudūd*), something unknown in modern Indonesia. The Code is, however, titled a "Proposal" and it remains just that. It has not been passed into law by any Indonesian government, local or national, nor is there any proposal to do so at present. The question thus arises as to why a document that was drafted by a fringe group and which is not applicable law anywhere deserves scholarly attention. The answer lies in the influence exercised by MMI and those around it. The Code provides a window into the thinking of this small but influential group whose objective is to turn Indonesia into a state governed by their ultra-conservative interpretation of Islamic law.

Over the last decade and, in particular, since the fall of Suharto in 1998, there has been a significant shift in public discourse on the role, practice, and interpretation of Islam in Indonesia. For example, twenty years ago laws requiring women to wear a head covering (the *kerudung*, or *jilbab* in Indonesia) would have been inconceivable but it is now a vigorously enforced legal requirement in many parts of Indonesia, including the autonomous province of Aceh.[2] PerDA[3] (local regulations) that seek to codify Shari'a and "Islamic morality" in private and public life by making ritual and moral behaviour—including, in many cases, the wearing of *jilbab*—enforceable criminally, have been introduced piecemeal by municipal councils across Indonesia, at least 48 of them at last count.[4] This shift in attitudes is visible also in attempts to pass similar legislation at the national level in the form of a so-called "Anti-Pornography Law" that is still being debated in the national legislature, the People's Representative Council (DPR[5]) at the time of writing.

As will be seen, the MMI and its fellow travelers have supported these attempts to "Islamise" laws in Indonesia at the local and national levels. They have also acted as a conduit for the entry of a reinvigorated ultra-conservative Islamic discourse into the long-running debate in Indonesia regarding the relationship between state and Shariʿa. This has its origins outside Indonesia and, ultimately, in the Middle East; and it is hostile to, first, the religious pluralism guaranteed by Indonesia's existing state ideology *Pancasila*;[6] second, the democratic rights and freedoms introduced by post-Suharto reforms; and, third, often the very existence of a secular state.

Accordingly, while the MMI Code is not law, it is a codified statement of the thinking and political and legal ambitions of a group of loosely-linked movements that are helping push public debate about the role of Islam and Shariʿa within formal Indonesian state structures in a radically conservative direction.

MMI, Abu Bakar Baʾasyir, and Islamic Codes

MMI was founded in August 2000 in Yogyakarta, in central Java, and its founding president or *amir* and leader is Abu Bakar Baʾasyir, the radical Islamic leader[7] who is also alleged to be the spiritual leader of terrorist organization Jemaah Islamiyah (JI).[8]

JI is a terrorist network spanning Southeast Asia that is widely believed to be behind the Bali bombings of 2002 and 2005, the bombing of the Marriott Hotel in Jakarta, and the attack on the Australian Embassy in the same city on September 10, 2004.[9] Baʾasyir has been widely accused of inspiring these attacks, although in December 2006 he was acquitted on appeal by Indonesia's Supreme Court of involvement in a conspiracy to carry out the first Bali bombing.[10] Although a close connection between JI and the MMI is often asserted,[11] they do not constitute the same organisation.[12] Membership in one group does not automatically indicate membership in the other, although the International Crisis Group (2002b) believes it does provide a good indicator.

Baʾasyir has consistently promoted total reliance on Shariʿa to resolve the troubles of Indonesia.[13] In an Internet article written with his close collaborator Abdullah Sungkar,[14] for example, he called upon Indonesians to "have belief that corruption, crime, nepotism and various other misdeeds will only be removed totally by the laws of Islam."[15] This view is inoffensive in itself (if somewhat naive and not in accord with the often contrary experiences of contemporary societies that have introduced "Islamic laws"). It does, however, raise the question of exactly how the "laws of Islam" in a form of which Baʾasyir would approve might be introduced to Indonesia, a secular state that since independence in 1945 has strongly and consistently resisted attempts to make Shari'a norms enforceable beyond the narrow field of restricted private law (marriage, divorce, guardianship, *zakāt, wakf*, etc.) inherited from the Dutch colonial system.[16]

This is a question that has long been debated in Indonesia[17] and it is sometimes argued that the respective responses to this question constitute a critical point of difference between the MMI and JI. On this view, MMI is usually seen as publicly advocating a "political approach," rather than the use of direct violent action, for example, through terrorist attacks.[18] This distinction is not, however, always clear-cut. In his speech at the establishment of MMI in 2000, for example, Ba'asyir seemed uncompromising in his support for armed struggle as the principal obligation for Muslims:

> (...) we must nurture both comprehension of, and zeal for, *jihad*, so that love for it, and for martyrdom, grow in the soul of the *mujahidin*: this is the most important task of Muslim social organizations in guiding and developing their members. I am convinced that the firm establishment of *din al-Islam* [the Religion of Islam] can never be achieved without practicing *jihad* on the path of Allah (...) [and] providing instruction in the tactics and strategy of war and training and fighting and the use of weapons. Among the Prophet's Companions there wasn't a single man who couldn't handle weapons (...). It is desirable for Islamic organisations to have their own, special camps specifically for developing [and implementing] the laws of *jihad* and the laws of war.[19]

In any case, whatever the detail of their relationships with JI and their views about violent jihad, it is clear that MMI and Ba'asyir have been high-profile and influential in supporting proposals at different levels of Indonesian government to introduce regulations that embody norms derived from their highly-conservative readings of Shari'a. Two examples will suffice to demonstrate this.

The Sulawesi Shari'a Code

The first example relates to Ba'asyir's involvement with a South Sulawesi Islamic group known as the Preparatory Committee for the Implementation of Islamic Shari'a (KPPSI).[20]

In December 2001, KPPSI held a three-day meeting, "Congress II of the Islamic Ummat [community] of South Sulawesi," in Makassar from which they produced a document titled "Draft Special Autonomy Law to Implement Islamic Shari'a for the South Sulawesi Province." This Draft Law purports to offer a framework for the grant to South Sulawesi of a form of special autonomy, similar to that granted to Aceh in 1999, in order to facilitate the Islamisation of the Province through the formal introduction of "laws for Muslims." These are claimed to be based on norms derived from the Qur'an and Sunna and, as in Aceh, are described as "Qanun." The Draft Law was presented to the national legislature by a delegation from Sulawesi but has largely been ignored by Jakarta.

The KPPSI's initiative needs to be read in the context of Indonesian history and, in particular, that of South Sulawesi, where, like Aceh, Islam has firmly established itself as part of the perceived identity of local communities and continues to have significant impact as a political and cultural symbol. This can be seen from a succession of militant movements that led rebellions in Java and South Sulawesi in the first two decades of Indonesian independence, all supporting the creation of an Islamic state. During the 1950s, Darul Islam's west Java pseudo-state, Negara Islam Indonesia (NII), with its rudimentary bureaucracy and nominally Shari'a-based legal system, had built links with militant counterparts in Aceh, South Kalimantan, and South Sulawesi, although these uprisings met with far less success than in west Java.[21]

Darul Islam was suppressed in Java in the early 1960s through military operations that led to the death of its leader, S. M. Kartoswiryo, in 1962. In 1965, however, Abdul Qahhar Mudzakkar staged another attempt at armed struggle, this time in support of South Sulawesi's secession from the Republic. As with Darul Islam, this rebellion was, again, justified in terms of aspirations for an Islamic polity and the broad implementation of the Shari'a law, and it likewise met with failure. These rebellions and, in particular, Mudzakkar himself as folk hero, continue to have considerable resonance in the South Sulawesi area, where proposals for secession, usually cast in terms of Islamic identity and application of Shari'a, are part of political discourse. As in Aceh, the result has been a linking in local popular culture of the idea of independence with a highly romanticized image of the region's history and utopian ideas about Shari'a as the key to a revival of a golden age outside the secular Republic ruled from Jakarta.

This history and the ideas underpinning these events directly informed the creation of the KPPSI Draft Law in South Sulawesi. They should now be understood as part of an idealistic and radical contemporary agenda tied to broader historical aspirations for the application of Islamic law in Indonesia. This is acknowledged in the Draft Law itself:

> The aspirations of society of South Sulawesi are very strong and need to be well-received by government (...) if not, the voices or aspirations seeking secession will get bigger and bigger, like a snow ball and will be increasingly difficult to overcome (...). The aim of granting Special Autonomy for the implementation of Islamic Syari'at is [thus] to improve the provision of social services and public welfare, develop democracy, justice and equality.[22]

It is also suggested, however, by the fact that among those attending the Congress in 2001 were both Mudzakkar's son and Ba'asyir, who has, himself, often been linked to Darul Islam and has been, of course, a strong proponent of legislating for Shariʿa in Indonesia.[23]

The Art. 29 Amendment Proposal

The second example that shows the influence of MMI and Ba'asyir in Indonesia's legal Islamisation trend is his role in campaigning in 2001–2002 for the effective creation of an Islamic state in Indonesia, through amendment of the 1945 Constitution to impose an obligation upon Muslims to obey Shariʿa.[24] Again, some history is required to understand the politically highly-loaded, even volatile, context of this campaign.

Indonesia's Constitution does not refer to religion except in vague terms, and in standard formulae asserting freedom of religious expression. But this does not mean that Islam or, more specifically, Shariʿa, has been totally distanced from the Constitution. On the contrary, Islam was an important issue—perhaps the most important—in the debates surrounding the drafting of the Constitution when Indonesia was established in 1945.

Before turning to those events, however, it should be understood that the question of the relationship between Islam and the then-putative Indonesian state did not spring into being, fully formed, in the tumultuous months before the Japanese surrender. Rather, it was the product of decades of dispute, typified by the celebrated debate between the secularist nationalist leader (and later first President) Sukarno and the Islamic politician, Mohammed Natsir, from 1938 to the early 1940s. Their public correspondence showed the high degree of mutual incomprehension,[25] or even refusal to see another point of view that marked the way the parties dealt with the question of Islam or a secular ideology as the "basis of the state" (*dasar negara*) in 1945 and, indeed, how their successors continue to navigate this issue in political debate today.

In 1945, all sides of politics agreed on a Preamble to the Constitution that was an uneasy compromise between the contesting ideologies and beliefs represented among the nationalist leaders, cobbled together by the future first President, Sukarno. The Preamble declared five fundamental and uncontroversial slogans (*Pancasila* or "Five Principles") to be the "basis of the state." These are "Belief in One Supreme God," "Just Humanitarianism," "Unity of Indonesia," "Democracy Guided by Consultation," and "Social Justice." There was, however, and remains, serious and seemingly insoluble disagreement as to the first *sila* (principle)—the "Belief in One Supreme God."

In 1945, Muslim politicians had succeeded in adding the words "with obligation to carry out [implement] Shariʿa for adherents of Islam" to the obligation of belief in God. Comprising seven words in Indonesian, the phrase was, however, omitted from the final draft of the Constitution when it was finally promulgated in August that year. The "Seven Words" had been dropped at Sukarno's insistence as the Constitution was finalised.[26] The original draft of the Constitution with these words is usually referred to as the Jakarta Charter, or *Piagam Jakarta*.[27]

"Belief in one Supreme God" has therefore been, and still is, the official formulation of the first *sila* and, so far as the state is concerned, it still marks the outer limits of religious obligation for Indonesians, whether Muslim, Christian, Hindu, Buddhist or other faith groups. Despite this official position, however, the seven words of the *Piagam Jakarta* have never disappeared from the debate on the relationship between the state of Indonesia and Islam, the religion to which the vast majority (over 80% at least) of the population adhere. The seven words are so central, in fact, that some Muslim groups have persistently called since 1945 for the reinclusion of the seven words in the Constitution. It has even been argued that insofar as the words were only removed by informal agreement, they were never validly erased and are, as it were, therefore still there.

On 29 August 2002 the issue of the seven words was reopened in the Indonesian legislature, this time as a formal proposal to amend Art. 29 of the 1945 Constitution in order to make the practice of Shariʿa an obligation for adherents of Islam, in other words, to reinstate the seven words in the Constitution, albeit not in the Preamble. By overwhelming majority, however, the People's Deliberative Assembly (MPR),[28] the second truly democratically-elected assembly in Indonesian history,[29] vindicated Sukarno's position 57 years earlier by formally rejecting the proposal. They did this despite initial support for the amendment from the Vice President, Hamzah Haz, his party PPP,[30] and several smaller Islamic parties.[31] Other Muslim parties, including PKB[32] and PAN,[33] both influential parties, opposed the amendment. This demonstrated, once again, that while secular nationalist leaders and non-Muslim religious groups oppose the *Piagam Jakarta*, there are also deep divisions within Muslim society on the issue. There are different reasons for this split.

In 1945, the *Piagam Jakarta* was dropped at President Sukarno's insistence, in part because of fears that Christians in Eastern Indonesia would abandon the new Republic to support returning Dutch colonial forces; and in part because of secular nationalist objection.[34] Certainly, fears of dividing largely Christian Eastern Indonesia from the overwhelming Muslim majority in central and western Indonesia, thus provoking secession and possible collapse of the state, still played a role in the thinking of Muslim politicians in 2002.

There were, however, other, probably more influential, reasons for rejecting the reinstatement of the *Piagam Jakarta*. First, it is by no means clear what Shariʿa means. As in most countries with a significant Muslim population, there are many different interpretations of Islamic doctrine in Indonesia. Islamic opinion has thus always been peculiarly fragmented there and consensus is never easily reached on issues of Islamic law in particular, especially on controversial issues. Accordingly, if Shariʿa became a constitutional obligation for Indonesian Muslims, the question would immediately arise: whose version of Shariʿa?[35] Resolving this issue would inevitably lead to great social conflict.

Likewise, the two leading popular Islamic movements in Indonesia, Nahdlatul Ulama and Muhammadiyah, are moderates on the issue of "basis of the state." Together they claim a membership of around 70 million but they have long feared the *Piagam Jakarta* on the grounds that it could hand a political weapon to their smaller, more radical competitors. Both PKB (created by Nahdlatul Ulama) and PAN (which has links to Muhammadiyah) therefore opposed the amendments and this was probably fatal.[36] This is despite Ba'asyir and his colleagues campaigning hard and despite their well-developed links with Hamzah Haz, a relationship that has since soured.[37]

Substance of the MMI Code

Within a year of the KPPSI Congress, with the Art. 29 debate still current, the MMI Code was released. We will turn shortly to an examination of the substance of the Code itself, but before we do so, one further contextual point needs first to be made, namely, that the Code is one of a large number of attempts at legal Islamisation in Indonesia that have been influenced, albeit in different ways, and to differing extents, by the Shariʿa Criminal Codes passed in Kelantan and Terengganu in 1993 and 2002, respectively, by the PAS (All-Malaysia Islamic Party)[38] governments of those two Malaysian states. As will be seen below, neither of these Codes has ever been enforced, due to Constitutional barriers,[39] and both are marked by careless drafting, impracticality, and an obsession with sexuality, morality, and harsh physical punishments, including crucifixion, stoning, and amputation. Indeed, M. B. Hooker has gone so far as to say that the Kelantan document "leaves much to be desired (...) and the draftsman must be ashamed of himself for having put forward such a sloppy piece of work."[40]

In Indonesia, the PAS Codes inspired two groups of "Islamising" laws. The first group comprises the far more ambitious, far more moderate, and far better-drafted Qanuns of Aceh, some 15 or so Regional Regulations (PerDa) passed pursuant to powers granted to the elected Provincial government of Aceh, as part of a series of autonomy packages negotiated with Jakarta since 1999. The Qanuns were directly inspired by the Malaysian Codes, according to Dr. Al Yasaʾ Abu Bakar, the head of the Syariah Office[41] of Aceh that drafted the Qanuns, but they are a very significant improvement on them. We have considered the Qanuns in detail elsewhere,[42] showing that they aim to create a complete system of governance for Aceh, extending beyond crime and sexuality into governance, dispute resolution, and public health, for example, and that they have achieved some success in doing so.

The other group of "Islamising" laws inspired by the Malaysian Codes—in which we would include the MMI Code and many local-level PerDa in Indonesia—echo the technical and substantive weaknesses and impracticality of the originals, as well as their sense of disconnection from contemporary Southeast Asian societies they seek to reform. They are, if anything, even less impressive than the PAS legislation.

The MMI Code, for example, is underpinned by the utopian ambition specified in the Code's "Introduction." In paragraph two of the "Introduction" it asserts that the application of the MMI Code will result in a removal of "the criminality, disharmony of life, moral decadence, and the decay of human values" flourishing under the current (secular) Criminal Code. It goes on to say that the Code will likewise return "equilibrium to social interactions within Indonesian society" and it concludes with the claim to "bring about justice and prosperity for all people." This repeats earlier comments posted on the Internet by Ba'asyir and Sungkar who said that "... a fair and peaceful prosperity can only be materialised by the practice of Islamic *Syari'ah* in this nation."[43] These are broad and lofty aspirations for any statute and depend on a naive acceptance that a "divine" force for change will be activated simply by promulgating the Code. The Code thus implicitly makes the proposal that communal redemption rests not on personal piety, scholarly learning or ritual devotion, but on legal instrumentalism.[44]

This attitude so saturates the text of the MMI Code that little attention is paid to specificities and practicalities, presumably because these are matters that will take care of themselves once God's law is in force. This, of course, makes the Code less a legal instrument and more a statement of religious belief: liturgy, not law.

Legal Language

These problems are seen, for example, in the language used in the MMI Code, which is often emotive or inflammatory or, more often, vague and ambiguous, to an extent unusual even in Indonesia, where poorly-drafted legislation is common. This is especially true of the Code where sexuality is involved.

A broad range of criminal offences and specific punishments are detailed, including property offences (Arts. 10–14); immoral sexual practices (Arts. 15–26); the prohibition on consumption of alcoholic drinks (Art. 27); blasphemy (Art. 28); and violent acts leading to death or bodily injury (Arts. 30–42), but throughout all the provisions, sex and violence are the major themes. Thus, a plethora of sexual acts are prohibited: anal sex, sex between a human and an animal, sex between a human and a corpse, and sexual activities between women (Arts. 15–26), providing an emphasis equal only to the specificity and extent of prohibitions and punishments for violent crimes. By contrast, only one Art. deals with another point of "social control," the prohibition of the consumption of alcohol (Art. 27), while gambling seems to have been entirely forgotten in the rush to deal with sexuality. Banning gambling is often a strong concern of Muslim reformers, including in Southeast Asia, and has, for example, been at the forefront of Aceh's criminal law reforms. We can only speculate that its absence is a consequence of the drafter's preoccupation with sexuality and violence.

The overwhelming attention given to sex and violence in the Code is highly inflammatory and this is reflected in the language chosen. In Art. 21, for example, the act of anal sex (targeting homosexuals, although not exclusively) is prohibited by reference to a graphic anatomical description involving the anus (*dubur*),[45] raising the question of why the drafter did not use the well-understood legal term *sodomi* (sodomy)? The provision reads more like an exercise in moral didactism intended to shock than a formal prohibition.

Paradoxically, this explicit and emotive approach can sometimes make the intended prohibition less effective. Art. 24(1), for example, provides that "*Musahaqa* is a *ta'zir* crime consisting of an act of satisfying sexual desire between a woman and another woman by means of rubbing their *farji* together. . . ." *Farji* is defined in Art. 1(22) to mean literally "private parts." As this is the only provision of the Code that deals with lesbianism, the drafter seems implicitly, if doubtless unintentionally, to be permitting a range of other lesbian sexual practices, such as oral sex, penetration, and mutual masturbation. Why not simply prohibit "sexual relations between women"? The choice of words again seems intended to shock but this time also suggests either ignorance of what the drafter was seeking to prohibit or perhaps simplistic and limited (male) fantasies about female sexuality.

There are other significant ambiguities in the language used in the MMI Code. Another example is Art. 28, which deals with the significant offence of *riddah* (apostasy), for which the penalty is execution, unless the offender repents. Art. 28 provides that *riddah* occurs not when a person expressly renounces Islam but simply where a comment "denigrates or conflicts with the *aqidah* [the fundamental beliefs] of Islam" (Art. 28(1)). Obviously, the issue here is exactly what is caught by the term *aqidah* and who decides that? Lawyers, and those who become entangled with a criminal justice system, need certainty, or at least clear parameters, within which to work, especially where a capital offence is involved. There is much serious scholarship about what *riddah* entails,[46] however, this is ignored, with the Code offering no guidance as to what is intended to be prohibited under Art. 28. This leaves this provision so broad that it could easily be used as a means of repression—or even extermination—of any group with a different theological position than that of the elite controlling the apparatus of state.[47] This problem was noted in the very different context of Iran by Ayatollah Maḥmūd Ṭāliqānī[48] who warned of "the harm that might be done when religious functionaries are given near-total control of the state apparatus."[49]

The reader is left wondering whether the vagueness of Art. 28 is, in fact, carelessness in a document that even the drafter expects will never become law, or, more disturbingly, an intentional feature of the drafting, designed to confer sweeping power on the religious elite in the MMI's putative Indonesian Shariʿa state.

Procedure and Administration

Another serious problem with the Code relates to deficiencies in the provisions dealing with procedures and court administration. This is particularly apparent in relation to appeals and, indeed, it remains unclear as to whether appeals are possible at all. There is reference to a "Deliberative Institution" beyond the level of trial, but it is not clearly defined. Art. 61 asserts that the "Deliberative Institutions are those that have the authority to give deliberations before validating every decision of a Court Institution that relates to *ḥudūd* punishments and punishments of death...."

This definition raises technical questions. For instance, does this mean that the Deliberative Institution is a court of appeal or merely some form of bureaucratic verification for judicial decisions involving physical punishment? The interpretation of this provision does not become clearer if guidance is sought from traditional applications of Shariʿa, where appeals often did not exist.[50] And even if it the Deliberative Institution were found to be an appellate court, on what basis and by what process would appeals lie? Would the Institution, for example, provide for merits review or would appeals be allowed only upon points of law? By contrast, even the Kelantan Code specifically provides for an appellate jurisdiction,[51] while the far more sophisticated Aceh Qanuns offer clear procedures delineating appellate processes, first to the High Shariʿa Court in Aceh and then to the Indonesian Supreme Court in Jakarta.[52]

In general, provisions relating to procedural and administrative matters are minimal in the MMI Code. It does provide guidelines as to the qualification of Shariʿa judges and their salary, and guarantees their independence (Arts. 61–68), while basic evidential rules appear in Arts. 52–61. No details are provided, however, as to the mechanisms for court administration, such as the appointment of Clerks of Court and other staff or the management of cases, such as the listing of matters for hearing or the places of court sessions, as are dealt with in detail in Aceh Qanun No. 7 of 2000.

The MMI may perhaps not have intended this Code to be a comprehensive document dealing with all institutional and procedural matters.

However, it has not drafted any supplementary Codes or regulations to support or complement the original Code since its release over four years ago, nor is there any indication that it intends to do so. Consequently, the Code must be read as a complete guide to the MMI's intended criminal justice system, and as such, it is flawed and incomplete.

Again, this suggests that the Code does not represent a genuine attempt at law reform but is, rather, a political platform from which the MMI can propagate its vision of Islam—that is, the drafter's aspirations are political and rhetorical, rather than legal. In this light the highly discriminatory nature of the Code is of particular significance, particularly as regards religious minorities and women.

Discrimination Against Non-Muslims

Traditionally, the position and role of religious minorities under Shariʿa is that they have a protected status,[53] as the celebrated *ḥadīth* has it: "One who hurts a *dhimmī*, hurts me; and one who hurts me, hurts God." The clear principle here is that Muslim rulers are to provide "protection from all internal tyranny and persecution" for the *dhimmī*.[54] This issue is complicated, because the traditional laws relating to the *dhimmī* [non-Muslim] minorities referred to the "people of the book," that is, Jews and Christians, but many scholars have highlighted the importance of protecting any religious minority in the midst of Muslim majority populations, such as Abdur Rahman Doi (p. 427), who asserted that a state guided by Shariʿa cannot "annihilate the non-Islamic elements within its fold."

With this protection in mind, Art. 3(2) creates a central problem for any application of the MMI Code: it would bind non-Muslim minorities. It provides that the "criminal provisions in the Syari'ah criminal legislation are to apply to every citizen within the territory of the Republic of Indonesia." This is, of course, contrary to the traditional *dhimmī* system, which allowed non-Muslims to apply non-Muslim laws within their communities. For a country such as Indonesia, with a non-Muslim population of approximately 40 million out of 245 million people, most of them Christian and thus indisputably *dhimmī* on any reading of that term, the application of Art. 3(2) would inevitably lead to significant social unrest and, ultimately, conflict.

The difficulty is compounded by the fact that in addition to imposing a religious value system that is not the minorities' own, the Code would also place them in a vulnerable position of weakness in any legal proceeding. This is because all offences under the MMI Code must be proven either by testimony or by confession of the perpetrator (Art. 53). Oral evidence would thus have a central role in any trial run under the Code, but it excludes non-Muslims from being witnesses. Under Art. 55, a "witness" is defined as "one Muslim man or two Muslim women who are *mukallaf* [legally responsible] and are a just person." Beyond the gendered nature of this provision (considered further below), it clearly disenfranchises non-Muslims from participation in the provision of testimony, and consequently, the justice system as a whole. The result is that non-Muslims are bound by a Code, while simultaneously being unable to participate in its legal processes—except, of course, as defendants and convicts.

Upon even the most cursory observation, this is clearly contrary to the teachings of the Qur'an, *ḥadīth*, and *fiqh* with regards to the *dhimmī*, which focus upon providing them with "a protective covenant."[55] Christians and Jews are considered to have their own divine law (Q 5:48), but the only way they could properly participate in a justice system administered under the MMI Code would be to convert to Islam. Therefore, even putting aside notions of human rights protection for minorities, the MMI Code directly infringes divine revelation and conventional Islamic thinking about the rights of non-Muslim minorities.[56]

Discrimination Against Women

As mentioned, women are the other major target of discrimination in the MMI Code, not just because their testimony is not considered to be of the same value as that of men but, in particular, by reason of their vulnerability to sexual aggression. The scheme of the Code is such that women victims of a sexual assault can be charged as a result with a *zinā*[57] [illicit sexual relations] offence, as Art. 15 makes clear:

> 1. *Zina* is a crime that consists of sexual intercourse between a man and a woman who are not husband and wife and that sexual intercourse does not fall under the definition of *wati syubhah* as stated in sub-section (3).
>
> (...)
>
> 3. *Wati syubhah* is sexual intercourse committed by a man with a woman who is not his wife and that sexual intercourse is committed:
>   (a) in doubtful circumstances where he believes that the woman with whom he is having sexual intercourse is his wife, whereas the women is not his wife; or
>   (b) in doubtful circumstances where he believes that the marriage with the woman is valid according to Shari'a law, whereas the truth is that the marriage is not valid according to Shari'a law.

This provision makes *any* form of sexual intercourse between unmarried men and women—thus including rape—a criminal offence, as *zinā*. The sole defence of mistake as to the marital status of the couple who have sexual intercourse (Art. 15(3)) is only made available to the man. In the words of one observer commenting on similar provisions in Pakistan, Sudan, and Iran: "One cannot escape the conclusion that these women were actually victimised twice: first by the men who assaulted them, and then by the legal authorities who treated each of them as the guilty party."[58] It is little wonder then that the recent official Report reviewing Pakistan's Hudood Ordinance for the government (considered in more detail below) recommends the repeal of such provisions, arguing that "[i]n the name of an Islamic law, such flagrant injustice is totally unacceptable."[59]

Quite apart from the unfairness of these provisions, it is also significant that these attitudes to women are entirely at odds with prevailing legal cultures regarding women among Southeast Asian Muslims. In Indonesia, for example, women prosecutors, defence lawyers, and judges are common: a current Deputy Chief Justice of the Supreme Court, for example, is a woman, as was the former Chief Judge of the Aceh Shariʿa Court. Women are well represented throughout the judiciary—Shariʿa and secular—and enjoy identical rights to men, while Indonesia's current Criminal Code is largely expressed in gender-neutral language and has a range of provisions specifically designed to protect women from sexual assault (see the Indonesian Criminal Code,[60] Arts. 285–288).[61]

Similarly, when comparable provisions were introduced in Kelantan and Terengganu, Malaysian women rallied successfully against the implementation of the Codes. The influential NGO Sisters in Islam[62] (1997) described them as "barbaric" and submitted a detailed "Memorandum on the Provisions in the Syari'ah Criminal Offences Act" to the then Malaysian Prime Minister, Dr. Mahathir Mohamad, which contained a detailed attack on the application of *zinā*. Their criticisms represent a Southeast Asian Muslim perspective and, given the links between the Malaysian Code and the MMI text, they would likely apply with equal weight to the MMI Code and its discriminatory approach to women.

This all reflects the fact that the MMI's objectives are often on a collision course with expectations of law and religion common among many Southeast Asian Muslims. This becomes even more apparent still when the Code's provisions on *ḥudūd* punishments are considered.

Punishments

Ḥudūd punishments are defined in Art. 1(29) of the MMI Code as severe penalties "for a particular crime other than murder or wounding that has a particular penalty imposed on it that is determined by the Qurʾan or Ḥadīth." No discretion is given to courts to interpret these penalties or their application (Art. 43).

For example, Art. 14 provides for a cascading series of *ḥudūd* penalties for causing a *hirabah* (civil disturbance) offence. For situations where the victim is killed and his or her property taken, the punishment is "execution and then crucifixion" (Art. 14(a)).[63] Where the victim is killed, but no property taken, then the punishment is only execution (Art. 14(b)). If property has been taken, but no injury or death caused to the victim, then the punishment is the amputation of the right hand and left foot, as well as payment to the family of *diyat* (a fine) (Art. 14(c)). The final level of punishment upon this cascading scale applies only if threats were made without any property taken or injury caused: exile[64] for a period decided upon by the qadi, to allow for repentance to God (Art. 14(d)).

Ḥudūd punishments are considered by many to be harsh and controversial, and heated debate about their appropriateness has taken place in Indonesia, Malaysia, and, more recently in Pakistan (see below). Even advocates of *ḥudūd* such as Abdul Hadi Awang, formerly Chief Minister of Terengganu, recognises these concerns: "Although our penalties are harsh and terrifying, we must realise that these offences and sins (...) are truly evil and despicable." More progressive Muslims have suggested outright that these punishments are simply not consistent with modern societies, such as in Malaysia and Indonesia[65] and, indeed, in Aceh *ḥudūd* were specifically omitted from the Qanuns on the grounds that they were not considered socially acceptable.[66]

M. B. Hooker has argued that *ḥudūd* punishments and their application should be implemented only conditionally and with an emphasis on the punishment not being prescriptively applied. He asserts that the "[d]ivine imperative and punishment for non-compliance rests on the assumption that there is a general social acceptance that punishment is, in fact, appropriate."[67] Appropriateness needs to be designated according to the circumstances of time and place, lest punishments be excessive and improperly applied. This position is supported by Pakistani scholar Muhammad Khalid Masud, who notes that social appropriateness has traditionally been an important element connected with the practice of the *ḥudūd*.[68]

Problems relating to the interpretation and application of Qurʾanic punishments are an area of controversy among Muslims generally, but it is clear that the MMI Code is in this regard out of step with the generally accepted practices and understandings of Indonesian and Malaysian Muslims.[69] The MMI Code does not provide any direct guidance as to whether the drafter considered that punishments should, in fact, be socially acceptable or reflect local Islamic practices, but we think it would be safe to assume that the drafter took for granted that the rules and punishments provided for in the Code would become socially acceptable once it was implemented and Indonesian society found the "equilibrium" and "harmony" predicted in the Introduction to the Code. The drafter must have felt assured that negative social implications would be outweighed by the benefits the Code itself would bring.

> In an effort to bring about supremacy of law and bring order to the community and social life of the people of Indonesia (...) there is no law whatsoever in this world that is capable of fulfilling this matter, except if a man submits to the law of Allah and His Prophet totally and comprehensively.

In other words, no justification or discussion is necessary about the appropriateness of penalties, because once the Code is implemented, Indonesian society would transform itself and those subject to its application would naturally conform to its rules.

Debate over the formal place of Islam and, in particular, Shariʿa in Indonesian law and the life of the state is not new and there have long been conservative voices in Indonesian Islam, albeit not usually in the mainstream, urging a move to a more conservative "Arabian" form of Islam. Despite this, the MMI Code is unusual, even dissonant, in an Indonesian setting. This, then, makes one ask from where the inspiration for this Code has come if it is, in fact, not indigenous?

The Malaysian Lineage

It seems clear from the discussion above that the Code reflects ideas about Islamic law that originate from beyond Indonesia's shores, many of which have found their way to Indonesia through Malaysia, in part at least. The personal journey of MMI's *amir*, Baʾasyir, gives some indication how this linkage likely developed.

After fleeing a prison sentence for subversion in Indonesia while awaiting appeal, Baʾasyir and Sungkar found refuge in self-exile in Malaysia from 1985 until 1998.[70] During this time PAS began to enjoy local electoral success[71] and it seems probable that Baʾasyir, Sungkar, and their supporters were influenced by the introduction and attempted enforcement of strict Shariʿa Criminal Codes in Kelantan (and, later, Terengganu).[72] We suggest that one of the consequences of this personal and intellectual contact is the MMI Code and, indeed, as we have indicated above, echoes of the Kelantan Code can be heard in the MMI Code's use of language, structure, and the substantive law applied.

The sources of inspiration for the Kelantan and Terengganu Codes are therefore significant in trying to understand the objectives and intellectual and political contexts of the MMI Code and it is our supposition that the PAS Codes probably have their intellectual foundations to the west of Malaysia—particularly in approaches to Islamic criminal regulation in Pakistan and Saudi Arabia. These foreign influences thus also require exploration, albeit briefly for reasons of space.

Pakistani Influence

In 1979, two significant "Islamic" Codes were promulgated through Presidential Decree by Pakistan's then President, General Zia ul-Haq, in part to shore up political support from Muslim groups:[73] The Offence of Zina (Enforcement of Hudood) Ordinance (1979) (Pakistan) and The Prohibition (Enforcement of Hadd) Order (1979) (Pakistan).

The implementation of these laws in Pakistan started a trend across the Muslim world—spilling into Iran, Sudan, and Malaysia—where *ḥudūd* punishments were increasingly incorporated into criminal laws.[74] This dramatic form of punishment became important to many Muslim political leaders who felt that rigid application of doctrine was a key ingredient in the process to "re-Islamise" their societies.[75] This was, of course, exactly what PAS was doing within their "Islamic laboratory" of Kelantan and, later, Terengganu.[76]

From the early 1980s, a prominent Malaysian legal scholar, Ahmed Ibrahim, published a series of influential articles exhorting the application of codified Shariʿa, advocating the application of Shariʿa and eventually endorsing the Kelantan approach.[77] He stated that "[T]he recent trend towards the Islamisation in Malaysia is only the attempt to restore to Muslims the right to profess and practise their religion, from which they have for long been deprived."[78] More pertinently, Ibrahim saw the Pakistan Ordinances as an example of the benign effects of *ḥudūd* punishments, in which deterrence was all that was necessary. Yet the fact of the matter is that women in particular faced severe consequences arising from these laws, such as penalties from public whipping to stoning for *zinā* offences, pursuant to Section 5 of the Enforcement of Hudood Ordinance, with the result that by 1991 over 2000 women were languishing in prison for these offences.[79]

The draconian effect of the Ordinances has increasingly fuelled proposals for their repeal and in a recently released Government report, prepared by Masud on behalf of Pakistan's influential Council of Islamic Scholars, there is a powerful call for significant amendments to these "experimental" laws. Specifically, Masud suggests that the Ordinances do not comply with the Qurʾan and Sunna, arguing that these sources had been questionably interpreted and their application in the Ordinances do not comply with the thinking of important Islamic jurists.[80] Another important finding of Masud's report is that enforcing the *ḥudūd* does not bring about, in and of itself, positive social changes as imagined by proponents such as MMI and which, indeed, underpin much of the MMI Code. In fact, crime rates have slowly increased during the period the Ordinances have been in force.[81]

Masud's Report has been accepted by the government of Pakistan and reforms to these Ordinances are reportedly currently underway.[82]

Saudi Arabian Influence

A second important, if less direct, influence on the radical Codes that are the subject of this chapter comes from Saudi Arabia. Both PAS and MMI have been directly and indirectly influenced by Saudi Arabian interpretations of Islam.[83] This can be seen, for example, in statements such as that of PAS President Abdul Hadi Awang in which he gave a ringing endorsement of the Saudi Arabian model of criminal justice, which he stated, allows for "peace and security."[84]

Saudi influence is not, however, restricted to doctrine and ideology. The NGO Sisters in Islam has disapprovingly acknowledged Saudi Arabian influence in Malaysia, noting their provision of generous financial support to Islamic organizations sympathetic to Saudi values, allowing those organizations to earn influence that is often difficult to resist. PAS, in particular, has benefited from this.[85] The religious "leadership" emanating from Saudi Arabia gains its impetus from an informal "transnational Salafi *daʿwa* movement" fuelled by oil revenues and gives Saudis the ability to "influence cultural and religious activities throughout the Muslim world."[86]

Middle Eastern traditional influences have been influential in providing religious training to Indonesian ulama (religious leaders) since the sixteenth century.[87] Studying at Cairo's al-Azhar University has been, and is still for many, a desirable course of action, parallel to Western students wanting to attend Oxford, Cambridge or Ivy League universities. The Indonesian ulama who are alumni from Middle Eastern institutions have traditionally formed a component of Indonesian Islamic scholarship that emphasised "scriptural orthodoxy."[88] However, the increase in Saudi religious training for Indonesians during the twentieth century has added new ideological elements to this Middle Eastern heritage. In particular, Saudi Wahhabi influences have strengthened radical conservative approaches to apostasy, jihad, and Qurʾanic interpretation in Malaysia and Indonesia.[89] The MMI Code represents this particular intellectual and theological position and the criminal justice system of Saudi Arabia embodies many of the values and ideas espoused in the MMI Code, especially as regards *ḥudūd*.

This is disturbing because, as Frank Vogel has said, the Saudi Arabian legal system is a mystery to most people inside the Kingdom, let alone those outside it[90] and this opaqueness and ambiguity allows for broad legal discretion. When this is combined with the Wahhabi emphasis upon "strict adherence to classical principle of obedience to the ruler,"[91] there are fertile circumstances for human rights violations and, indeed, state-sanctioned human rights abuses have been widely alleged.[92] In the Amnesty International Report "Saudi Arabia: A Secret State of Suffering", it was claimed, for example, that "... torture is endemic. Executions, flogging, and amputations are imposed and carried out with disregard for the most basic international fair trial standards."[93]

Whether, and to what extent, Shariʿa should or should not be applied in Indonesia is a matter for debate among Indonesian Muslims, but whatever position they adopt, it is clear that the Saudi Arabian justice system—one of the inspirations for the MMI Code—lacks a local context in Indonesia where a Dutch version of French civil law long ago replaced Islamic or traditional jurisprudence in criminal matters, where recent popular democratic reforms have introduced a "bill of rights" into the Constitution that is modeled on the Universal Declaration of Human Rights, and where a "rule of law" system is developing with surprising rapidity in the post-Suharto period.[94]

Conclusion

There is little prospect that the MMI Code will ever become law in Indonesia. MMI does not have any representatives or even obvious proxy representatives in Indonesia's national assembly and it is not clear that it even seeks a seat. In any case, secular parties have dominated Indonesian politics since Independence in 1945.[95] Islamist parties are not today a significant force in the current democratically elected Indonesian legislature, controlling, at best, marginally over 30% of the assembly; most of these parties, in any case, predominantly promote only moderate ideological positions.[96] The political position of MMI is marginal and has little (if any) influence in the formal political process.

Even if MMI did somehow win representation, the fate of PAS in Malaysia also does not bode well for the political prospects of any regional party running on a conservative Shariʿa agenda. The 2004 elections saw PAS lose power in Terengganu and their position significantly weakened in Kelantan, while the number of their seats in the national parliament fell from 27 to seven.[97]

In the unlikely event that the MMI Code ever did become law in Indonesia, there would be solid grounds for challenging its validity before the Indonesian Constitutional Court.[98] Even a cursory reading of the Code would suggest prima facie contravention of the following Constitutional provisions:

> Art. 28D
> Each person has the right to the recognition, the security, the protection and the certainty of just laws and equal treatment before the law.
> Art. 29
> The State guarantees all persons the freedom of worship, each according to his/her own belief.

In the end then, the MMI Code is not a serious or practical alternative to Indonesian criminal law, for all the flaws and weaknesses of the latter;

nor, we suspect, was it ever really intended to be. It is a poorly drafted, technically clumsy, and at times rhetorical text that is more political dream than technical legal document.[99]

In this sense the MMI text is not a Code so much as a coded political message: a call to support a conservative vision of Indonesia rooted in a Middle Eastern past, not the Indonesian present. And in this respect, as part of the argument for imposing ultra-conservative morality by regulation being put forward by MMI and similar hard-line groups, the ideas it embodies are finding some success, even if the Code itself has not. Across Indonesia, mini-MMI Codes are appearing at the municipal level, and are passed as by-laws, picking up the sort of themes embodied in the Code. None of these imposes *ḥudūd* and most are more moderate than the MMI Code, but many are as severe in their treatment of women and religious minorities as the Code. The national legislature, too, is now considering a Bill on criminal law inspired by the same values as the MMI Code and equally focused on sexuality and women's morality that, if passed, would require a radical reinvention in Indonesia's traditionally relatively permissive societies.

The question is now how the secularist government will respond to these growing challenges to its *Pancasila* republic. It has the power to strike down the by-laws and could muster legislators against the Anti-Pornography Bill. So far it has done neither of these things and the question must be, why?

NOTES

[1] Any reference to Articles where no Code or Statute is specified should be read as a reference the MMI Code.

[2] Lindsey, Hooker, Kingsley and Clarke 2007.

[3] *Peraturan Daerah.*

[4] Candraningrum 2006.

[5] *Dewan Perwakilan Rakyat.*

[6] The *Pancasila* is Indonesia's secular state ideology. It is discussed in detail below.

[7] Baʾasyir (and Behrend) 2003, 1.

[8] International Crisis Group (hereinafter ICG) 2002b.

[9] ICG 2002a, 2002b, 2003, 2005; Fealy and Hooker 2006, 442; Council on Foreign Relations 2006.

[10] Hermawan 2006.

[11] Hill 2002.

[12] ICG 2002b.

[13] Behrend 2003.

[14] Sungkar and Baʾasyir jointly founded the Al-Mukmin *pesantren* or Islamic boarding school in Ngruki, central Java, and the two worked closely together in Indonesia and Malaysia until Sungkar's death in 1999. Sungkar is also said to have been a leader of JI: ICG 2002a.

[15] Sungkar and Baʾasyir 1998.

[16] Hooker 1999, 98–100; Lindsey, Hooker, Kingsley and Clarke 2007. Although note that recent amendments made by Law No. 3/2006 to Law No. 7/1989 on the Religious Courts has now granted those courts jurisdiction over "Syariah Economy," by which is presumably meant financial institutions offering Islamic banking products.

[17] Pranowo 1990; Hooker 1999; Hefner 2000; Feener 2001; Azra 2001; Fealy and Hooker 2006.

[18] Jamhari 2003, 14; Behrend 2003.

[19] Ba'asyir (and Behrend) 2003, 9.

[20] *Komite Persiapan Penegakan Syari'at Islam.*

[21] Jackson 1980; ICG 2005.

[22] KPPSI Draft Law, paras f. and h., Elucidation.

[23] ICG 2005; Neighbour 2004.

[24] The following discussion of the proposed amendment to Art. 29 draws on Hooker and Lindsey 2002.

[25] Passages are reproduced in Noer 1973, 273.

[26] Yamin 1959–1960, 145.

[27] Feener 2001, 86.

[28] *Majelis Permusyawaratan Rakyat.*

[29] Lindsey 2002.

[30] *Partai Persatuan Pembangunan*, United Development Party.

[31] These included PBB (*Partai Bulan Bintang*, Crescent Star Party) and PDU (*Partai Daulat Ummah*, Sovereignty of the Community of Islam).

[32] PKB (*Partai Kebangkitan Bangsa*, National Awakening Party).

[33] PAN (*Partai Amanat Nasional*, National Mandate Party).

[34] Ricklefs 1993, 258, 262.

[35] Pranowo 1990.

[36] Indrayana 2005.

[37] This highly-publicised liaison began to become a political liability for the PPP following Ba'asyir's prosecutions, and Haz, no longer so prominent a figure, has subsequently distanced himself from Ba'asyir and his followers. The political damage caused by the relationship with Ba'asyir may, however, have been considerable, although this is, of course, impossible to measure with certainty. In any case, for whatever reason, Haz's United Development Party found its representation in the MPR quite significantly reduced after the April 2004 elections (see Fealy 2001; Jakarta Post 2004).

[38] *Partai Islam Se-Malaysia.*

[39] Art. 74 of the Malaysian Constitution outlines that legislative power is divided between the State and Federal authorities in Schedule 9. The Federal authorities have sole legislative authority over criminal law and procedure. Therefore, the Kelantan Codes were *ultra vires* (see Imam 1997).

[40] Hooker 2003, 93.

[41] *Dinas Syariah*, a Department of the Provinicial Governor's Office.

[42] Lindsey, Hooker, Kingsley and Clarke 2007.

[43] Sungkar and Ba'asyir 1998.

[44] While there is undoubtedly widespread support among Muslim Indonesians for Shari'a, there is little consensus about what the term actually means or whether it should be enforced as positive law. One interview about the possible implemen-

tation of Shariʿa in Indonesia with the Chair of the Executive Committee of the MMI, Irfan Awwas, reflected this ambivalence. He suggested that Indonesians wanted it to be applied. When pressed by the interviewer about evidence of this, he claimed that although there was no clear data or anecdotal evidence to suggest Indonesians wanted its application, nevertheless, if they were educated about "true" Islam they would want it (Subkan 2004, 5).

In the "Introduction" to the MMI Code there is a clear assumption that a legislative form of Shariʿa is appropriate. It asserts very simply that the secular law is failing, that religious law needs to be applied, and that codification of Shariʿa is the appropriate way of fixing the problems with Indonesian law. There is, however, no discussion at all about whether legislating Shariʿa is appropriate or not, either from a historical or jurisprudential perspective. There is also no mention of any *madhhab* or of any anti-madhhabic position.

[45] Stevens and Schmidgall-Tellings 2004.

[46] See Saeed and Saeed 2002.

[47] Abou El Fadl 2004, 15.

[48] Ayatollah Maḥmūd Ṭāliqānī was a "spiritual and intellectual leader" of the 1979 Iranian revolution, see Noor 2004, 738.

[49] Ibid.

[50] Glenn 2004.

[51] Section 67, Kelantan, Syariah Criminal Code (II) Bill (1993).

[52] Regional Qanun of the Special Autonomous Province of Nanggroe Aceh Darussalam, Number 7 of 2000: The Islamic Syariah Judicature.

[53] Santos 2001, 105.

[54] Doi 1984, 429.

[55] Doi 1984, 435.

[56] For more detailed analysis of the protection afforded to the *dhimmī* under Shariʿa, see Doi 1984, 426–35.

[57] *Zinā* is sexual intercourse between a man and a woman who are not husband and wife: Art. 1(72).

[58] Sidahmed 2001, 198.

[59] Masud 2006, 87.

[60] *Kitab Undang-undang Hukum Pidana*.

[61] Art. 285: Anyone who with violence or the threat of violence forces a woman who is not his wife to have sex may be punished for rape with imprisonment of up to 12 years. Art. 286: Anyone who has sex with a woman who is not his wife, knowing that she is unconscious or enfeebled, may be punished with imprisonment of up to 9 years. Art. 287: (1) Anyone who has sex with a woman who is not his wife, knowing, or [in circumstances where he] should have known, that her age was less than 15 years, [or], where her age is not clear, that the woman was not yet marriageable, may be punished with imprisonment of up to 9 years. (2) An indictment can only be made [pursuant to paragraph (1)] if there is a complaint, unless the woman is aged less than 12 years or if there exists one of the matters provided for in Sections 291 and 294. Art. 288: (1) Anyone who has sex with his wife, knowing, or [in circumstances where he] should have known, that she was not yet of marriageable age may be punished with imprisonment of up to 4 years, if the act resulted in injury to the woman's body. (2) If the said act results in the woman being seriously injured, received imprisonment will be for up to 8 years.

(3) If the said act results in the death of the woman, he will receive imprisonment for up to 12 years. Art. 289: Anyone who with violence or the threat of violence forces a person to do to another, or to perform upon him or herself, an obscene act may be punished for indecency with imprisonment of up to 9 years. Art. 290: Seven years punishment for: (1) Anyone who performs an obscene act with a person, knowing that the person is unconscious or enfeebled. (2) Anyone who performs an obscene act with a person, knowing, or [in circumstances where he] should have known, that the person's age was less than 15 years, [or], where the age is not clear, that the person was not yet marriageable. (3) Anyone who seduces a person, knowing, or [in circumstances where he] should have known, that the person's age was less than 15 years, [or], where the age is not clear, that the person was not yet marriageable, or performs or allows to be performed on him or herself an obscene act, or has sex with a person outside marriage.

Art. 291: (1) If an offence under section 286, 287 or 290 results in the person being seriously injured, imprisonment will be for up to 12 years. (2) If an offence under section 285, 286, 287 or 290 results in the death of the person, he will receive imprisonment for up to 15 years.

Art. 292: An adult who commits an obscene act with a person who is not yet an adult and of the same sex, knowing or [in circumstances where he] should have known, that the person was not yet an adult, will be punished with imprisonment of up to 15 years. [Translation from Indonesian by the authors].

[62] "Sisters in Islam" describes itself as "an independent non-governmental organisation which believes in an Islam that upholds the principles of equality, justice, freedom and dignity." It is one of the most prominent voices of moderate Islam in Malaysia. See Sisters in Islam 2006.

[63] As in pre-modern times, the public display of the corpse is considered an extra deterrent.

[64] This Article provides another example of ambiguity as it does not define what "exile" means—exile from Indonesia, exile from a region or, merely exile from a local village, town or city?

[65] Sisters in Islam 1993.

[66] Elucidation and Arts. 20–23, Regional Qanun of the Special Autonomous Province of Nanggroe Aceh Darussalam, No. 11 of 2002.

[67] Hooker 2003, 86.

[68] Masud 2006, 109–10.

[69] Amal and Panggabean 2006.

[70] Behrend 2003.

[71] Imam 1997.

[72] ICG 2002a; Behrend 2003.

[73] Ismail 2002, 23.

[74] Sidahmed 2001, 188–99.

[75] Ibid., 188.

[76] Noor 2004, 497.

[77] Ibrahim 1981; 1985; 1993.

[78] Ibrahim, 1993, 52.

[79] Ismail 2002, 23.

[80] Masud 2006, 85.

[81] Ibid., 4.

[82] Hasan 2006.
[83] Fealy and Hooker 2006, 258.
[84] "The Pas View." 2002; Siang 2002; Fealy and Hooker 2006, 258.
[85] Noor 2004.
[86] Hasan 2005, 84.
[87] Azra 2005, 8.
[88] Ibid.
[89] Ali 2002.
[90] Vogel 2000, xi.
[91] Ibid., 209.
[92] See Amnesty International 2000; 2003; Human Rights Watch 2003.
[93] It is not just international bodies that have been highly critical of Saudi Criminal Justice, but Saudi dissident groups, such as the Committee for the Defence of Human Rights on the Arabian Peninsula (CDHRAP), have also criticised the Saudi Arabian justice system on similar grounds; see CDHRAP 2006.
[94] Lindsey 2002.
[95] Hooker and Lindsey 2002.
[96] Nakamura 2005.
[97] *The Age* 2004.
[98] Hari 2003; Harijanti and Lindsey 2006.
[99] Art. 1, for instance, speaks not of the Indonesian currency (the rupiah) but of payments and fines made in dinars, dirhams, and camels.

BIBLIOGRAPHY

Abou El Fadl, Khaled, 2003. "Islam and the Challenge of Democracy," *Boston Review* (Boston).

Ali, Tariq, 2002. *The Clash of Fundamentalisms. Crusades, Jihads and Modernity* (London: Verso).

Amal, Taufik Adnan and Samsu Rizal Panggabean, 2006. "A Contextual Approach to the Qur'an," in Abdullah Saeed (ed.), *Approaches to the Qur'an in Contemporary Indonesia* (Oxford: Oxford University Press).

Amnesty International, 2000. "Saudi Arabia: A Secret State of Suffering," www.amnesty.org.

——, 2003. "Saudi Arabia: An Urgent Reform of the Criminal Justice System is Needed," www.amnesty.org.

al-Azhar, 2006. Webpage, www.alazhar.org.

Azra, Azyumardi, 2001. "Islamic Perspective on the Nation State," *al-Jami'ah* 39, 292.

——, 2005. "Islam in Southeast Asia: Tolerance and Radicalism," Islamic Briefing Paper, Centre for the Study of Contemporary Islam, the University of Melbourne.

Ba'asyir, Abu Bakar, 2003. "A System of Caderisation of Mujahidin in Creating an Islamic Society" (trans. and comments by Tim Behrend) (address delivered at the first Indonesian Congress of Mujahidin, August 5–7, 2000, Yogyakarta, Indonesia), www.arts.auckland.ac.nz.

Behrend, Tim, 2003. "Reading Past the Myth: Public Teachings of Abu Bakar Ba'asyir," www.arts.auckland.ac.nz.

Candraningrum, Dewi, 2006. "Perda Sharia and the Indonesian Women's Critical Perspectives," www.asienhaus.de/public/archiv/PaperPERDASHARIA.pdf.

CDHRAP (Committee for the Defence of Human Rights on the Arabian Peninsula), 2006. www.cdhrap.net.

Council on Foreign Relations, 2006. "Jemaah Islamiyah," www.cfr.org.

Doi, Abdur Rahman, 1984. *Shari'ah: The Islamic Law* (London: Ta-Ha Publishers).

Fealy, Greg, 2001. "Parties and Parliament: Serving Whose Interests?" in Grayson Lloyd and Shannon Smith (eds.), *Indonesia Today. Challenges of History* (Singapore: Institute of Southeast Asian Studies).

Fealy, Greg and Virginia Hooker, 2006. *Voices of Islam in Southeast Asia: A Contemporary Sourcebook* (Singapore: Institute of Southeast Asian Studies).

Feener, Michael, 2001. "Indonesian Movements for the Creation of a 'National Madhhab'," *Islamic Law and Society* 9 (2002), 84.

Glenn, H. Patrick, 2004. *Legal Traditions of the World* (Oxford and Melbourne: Oxford University Press).

Haria, Kurniawan, 2003. "Constitutional Court Makes First Hearing," www.thejakartapost.com.

Harijanti, Susi and Tim Lindsey, 2006. "Indonesia: General Elections Test the Amended Constitution and the New Constitutional Court," *International Journal of Constitutional Law* 4 (2006), 138.

Hasan, Syed Shoaib, 2006. "Strong Feelings over Pakistan Rape Laws," www.bbc.co.uk.

Hefner, Robert, 2000. *Civil Islam: Muslims and Democratization in Indonesia* (Princeton: Princeton University Press).

Hermawan, Ary, 2006. "Supreme Court Clears Ba'asyir of Bali Bombing Role," www.thejakartapost.com.

Hill, Robert, 2002. "Future Strategic Challenges in the Region" (address delivered at the Australian National University's Strategic Studies Program Dinner, 23 October 2002).

Hooker, M. B., 1999. "The State and Syariah in Indonesia 1945–1995," in Tim Lindsey (ed.), *Indonesia Law and Society* (Sydney: Federation Press).

——, 2003. "Submission to Allah? The Kelantan Syari'ah Criminal Code II, 1993," in Virginia Hooker and Norani Othman (eds.), *Malaysia: Islam, Society and Politics* (Singapore: Institute of Southeast Asian Studies).

Hooker, M. B. and Tim Lindsey, 2002. "Public Faces of Syariʿah in Contemporary Indonesia: Towards a National Mazhab?" *Australian Journal of Asian Law* 4:259.

Human Rights Watch, 2003. "The Criminal Justice System in the Kingdom of Saudi Arabia. Recommendations for Basic Human Rights Protections," www.hrw.org.

Ibrahim, Ahmad, 1981. "Islamic Law in Malaysia," *Jernal Undang-Undang* (Journal of Malaysian and Comparative Law) 8:21.

——, 1985. "Towards an Islamic Law for Muslims in Malaysia," *Jernal Undang-Undang* (Journal of Malaysian and Comparative Law) 12:37.

——, 1993. "The Future of the Shariah and the Shariah Courts in Malaysia," *Jernel Undang-Undang* (Journal of Malaysian and Comparative Law) 20:41.

Imam, Mohammed, 1997. "Islamic Criminal Law in Malaysia: Federal/State Jurisdictional Conflict," CLJ Network, www.cljlaw.com.

Indrayana, Denny, 2005. "Indonesian Constitutional Reform 1999–2002: An Evaluation of Constitution Making in Transition," Ph.D. dissertation, The University of Melbourne.

International Crisis Group, 2002a. "Al-Qaeda in Southeast Asia: The Case of the "Ngruki Network" in Indonesia," Asia Briefing No. 20.

——. 2002b. "How the Jemaah Islamiyah Terrorist Network Operates," Asia Report No. 43.

——. 2003. "Jemaah Islamiyah in South East Asia: Damaged but Still Dangerous," Asia Report No. 63.

——. 2005. "Recycling Militants in Indonesia: Darul Islam and the Australian Embassy Bombing," Asia Report No. 92.

Ismail, Rose. 2002. "The Practice of Hudud in Other Countries," in *Hudud in Malaysia: The Issues at Stake*, ed. Sisters in Islam (Kuala Lumpure: Ilmiah Publishers).

Jackson, Karl, 1980. *Traditional Authority, Islam and Rebellion: A Study of Indonesian Political Behavior* (Berkeley: University of California Press).

Jakarta Post, 2004. "Legislative Elections Final Results," www.thejakartapost.com.

Jamhari, 2003. "Mapping Radical Islam in Indonesia," *Studia Islamika* 10:5.

Lindsey, Tim, 2002. "Indonesian Constitutional Reform: Muddling Towards Democracy," *Singapore Journal of International Law* 6:244.

Lindsey, Tim and M. B. Hooker, with Jeremy Kingsley and Ross Clarke, 2007. "Shari'a Revival in Aceh," in Mark Cammack and Michael Feener (eds.), *Islamic Law in Contemporary Indonesia. Ideas and Institutions* (Cambridge, Mass.: ILSP/Harvard University Press).

Masud, Muhammad Khalid, 2006. "Hudood Ordinance 1979 (Pakistan): An Interim Brief Report," The Pakistan Government.

Nakamura, Mitsuo, 2005. "Islam and Democracy in Indonesia: Observations on the 2004 General and Presidential Elections," Occasional Publications 6 (Islamic Legal Studies Program, Harvard Law School), www.law.harvard.edu.

Neighbour, Sally, 2004. *In the Shadow of Swords: On the Trail of Terrorism from Afghanistan to Australia* (Sydney: HarperCollins).

Noer, Deliar, 1973. *The Modernist Muslim Movement in Indonesia, 1900–1942* (Kuala Lumpur: Oxford University Press).

Noor, Farish, 2004. "Islam Embedded: The Historical Development of the Pan-Malaysian Islamic Party, 1951–2003," vol. 2 (Kuala Lumpur Malaysian Sociological Research Institute).

Pranowo, Bambang, 1990. "Which Islam and Which Pancasila," in Arief Budiman, ed., *State and Civil Society in Indonesia* (Melbourne: Monash University, Centre of Southeast Asian Studies).

Saeed, Abdullah and Hassan Saeed, 2002. *Freedom of Religion, Apostasy and Islam* (Burlington: Ashgate Publishing).

Santos, Soliman, 2001. *The Moro Islamic Challenge: Constitutional Rethinking for the Mindanao Peace Process* (Quezon City: University of the Philippine Press, Diliman).

Siang, L. K. 2002. "Malaysians Who Accept or Do Not Oppose Saudi Arabia as a Model for an Islamic State Based on Syariʿah Have Lost the Right to Speak on Human Rights or Condemn the ISA as the Saudi Arabia Justice System is a Hundred Times Worse than ISA," www.malaysia.new.dap/lks1726.htm.

Sidahmed, Abdel Salam, 2001. "Problems in Contemporary Applications of Islamic Criminal Sanctions: The Penalty for Adultery in Relation to Women," *British Journal of Middle Eastern Studies* 28:187.

Sisters in Islam, 1993. "Memorandum on the Syariʿah Criminal Code (II) 1993 State of Kelantan," http://talk.to/sistersinislam/.

——, 1997. "Memorandum on the Provisions in the Syariʿah Criminal Act," http://talk.to/sistersinislam/.

——, 2006. Webpage, http://www.sistersinislam.org.my.

Subkhan, Imam, 2004. "Islam and Democracy Cannot Meet Inside Indonesia," http://www.insideindonesia.org/.

Sungkar, Abdullah and Abu Bakar Baʾasyir, 1998. "The Latest Indonesian Crisis: Causes and Solutions," www.islam.org.au.

The Age, 2004. "Islamists Routed in Malaysia Vote," www.theage.com.au.

"The PAS View," 2002. In *Hudud in Malaysia: The Issues at Stake*, ed. Sisters in Islam (Kuala Lumpur: Ilmiah Publishers).

Vogel, Frank, 2000. *Islamic Law and Legal System. Studies of Saudi Arabia* (Leiden: Brill).

Yamin, Muhammad, 1959–1960. *Naskah Persiapan Undang-undang Dasur 1945* (Jakarta: Yayasan Prapanca).

16

SHARIʿA IN THE SECULAR STATE

A Paradox of Separation and Conflation

Abdullahi Ahmed An-Naʿim

Introduction

Whereas scholarship about Shariʿa tends to focus on its history, I am more concerned with the future of this religious normative system.[1] Accordingly, I will examine the nature of Shariʿa and its relationship to modern legal systems in order to consider how it might continue to operate in the context of the modern secular state under which all Muslims live today. This essay draws on a forthcoming book: *Islam and the Secular State: Negotiating the Future of Shariʿa.*[2] I will briefly summarize the theoretical framework I am proposing for the future of Shariʿa in that work in the last section of this essay.

To begin by noting what specialists in the field may take for granted, the study of Shariʿa should not be approached in the expectation of finding a comprehensive or systematic code or codes that present definitive answers to precise legal issues of the day. But the inaccessibility of such legal formulations does not mean that such principles do not exist, or are necessarily inappropriate for modern application. As demonstrated by Frank Vogel and other scholars in the field, Islamic jurisprudence includes many outstanding examples of legal precision and sophistication in comparison to the most recent or advanced doctrine and analysis. Shariʿa principles of property, contracts, and commercial law have been incorporated in the civil codes of several countries, such as Egypt, Kuwait, and the United Arab Emirates, through the skillful synthesis techniques pioneered by the Egyptian jurist ʿAbd al-Razzāq al-Sanhūrī in the mid-twentieth century, as will be explained later. The difficulty in appreciating the high jurisprudential quality of the "lawyer's law" aspects of Shariʿa may be due to assumptions about the nature of law as a social and political institution. For comparative law purposes, the challenge is to understand the role of Shariʿa on its own terms, rather than "law" in the American or European sense of the term. As I will argue here, however, our understanding of Shariʿa and its role must take into account the drastic transformation of the economies, political regimes, social institutions, and legal systems of present Islamic societies.

From this perspective, I am concerned here with the relationship between Shariʿa as a religious normative system and the legal system of the modern "territorial" state, which is necessarily secular. To be clear on this point, I am not disputing that Shariʿa is very influential among Muslims, regardless of its formal legal status in the country. This is true not only on a personal and socio-political level, but also because it is an important source of state law and administration of justice in many parts of the Muslim world. It is also clear to me, however, that Shariʿa as such is not the legal system in any country, including those that claim to be Islamic states, such as Iran and Saudi Arabia. As I will explain below, the notion of an Islamic state is conceptually incoherent and historically false, and any Shariʿa principle that is enforced through the coercive authority of the state ceases to be part of the normative system of Islam and becomes an expression of the political will of the state. In other words, the state and its law are always secular, regardless of claims to the contrary. This does not mean that Shariʿa principles cannot be a source of state law, but the outcome of the enactment and enforcement of its principles by state institutions is always a matter of secular law and not of Shariʿa as the religious normative system of Islam.

Moreover, any understanding of the relationship between Shariʿa and state law must be founded on a clear appreciation of the extreme diversity of Muslims, including their interpretations and practice of Shariʿa. The early and enduring schism between Sunni and Shiʿi Muslims is now widely known, and remains politically and legally significant. There is also significant cultural and political as well as theologico-legal diversity among Sunni Muslims. Shiʿi Muslims generally share the belief that the ultimate leader of the Community (*imām*) should be a descendant of ʿAlī and Fāṭima, the Prophet's daughter. But they disagree on the exact historical line of descent for the Imams they accept, which has theological and political implications among various Shiʿi communities. Subject to these differences, the foundational doctrine of the Imamate for all Shiʿi Muslims has far-reaching theologico-legal and political consequences when the supreme role of the Imam is realized in this world; it is unfortunately not possible to discuss this here. At present, the largest Shiʿi sect is that of the Twelvers or Imamis, followed by the Ismaʿilis and Zaydis, but the demographic distribution of Sunni and Shiʿi communities and among the Shiʿa has shifted significantly throughout Islamic history.

For instance, Iran was predominantly Sunni until the end of the fifteenth century, and only gradually converted to Shiʿism, mainly Twelver Shiʿism, during Safavid rule (1501–1722). They now constitute the overwhelming majority in Iran, a slim majority in Iraq (both Arabs and Kurds tend to identify themselves as Sunni) and Bahrain, and smaller minorities in Lebanon, Syria, Kuwait, Eastern Saudi Arabia, Afghanistan, Pakistan, Azerbaijan, and among Muslims of India. Zaydis are now found only in Yemen, while Ismaʿilis are mainly in India, with smaller communities in Pakistan, Tajikistan, and Yemen, and diaspora communities in Africa, Europe, and North America. But the influence of the Shiʿa is far from limited to their own communities, at least in political terms, especially since the Iranian Revolution.

Muslims in general believe Shariʿa to be directly derived from the Qurʾan and Sunna through a specific methodology (*uṣūl al-fiqh*) that was developed by Muslim scholars in the eighth and ninth centuries. Paradoxically, that belief also underlies the ambiguous status of Shariʿa in relation to state law. On the one hand, the common perception of Shariʿa makes it "more than state law" because of its comprehensive scope, from doctrinal matters of belief and religious rituals, ethical and social norms of behavior, to apparently legal principles and rules. This comprehensive scope itself, on the other hand, means that Shariʿa is also "less than law," in the sense that its enforcement as law requires the intervention of legislative, judicial, and administrative organs of the state. Yet, this sort of state action is necessarily a product of mundane, human politics, and not divine command as such. In other words, the corpus of Shariʿa is commonly believed to include aspects that are supposed to be voluntarily observed by Muslims independently of state institutions, such as the performance of the five daily prayers or of the pilgrimage, and other aspects that require state intervention to enact and enforce them in practice, such as criminal punishment and remedies for breach of legal obligations. In practice, decisions whether an issue falls within the first or second category and what should be done about it are made by state officials or political leaders.

Another factor to emphasize is that the need for an active role for the state has drastically increased in the post-colonial context of present Islamic societies. The role of Shariʿa in the administration of justice probably worked well under the imperial states of the pre-colonial era, which had minimal involvement in the daily governance and administration of justice among local communities. But the situation has significantly changed with the introduction of the European model of the state and conceptions of law as a result of colonialism. All Muslims today live under the exclusive jurisdiction of territorial states, which exercise increasingly extensive powers in governing every aspect of the economic and social life of persons and communities. As noted above and to be explained and illustrated later, to enact Shariʿa into state law or to enforce it through state administration requires state institutions to choose among competing interpretations of Shariʿa. The paradoxical consequence is that the more precise and definite such selectivity becomes, the less truly Shariʿa-based the legal system will be, while allowing judges and administrators the degree of discretion assumed by the historical nature of Shariʿa makes the whole system arbitrary and unstable.

In light of these remarks, it seems that the distinctive issue in the comparative study of Shariʿa in relation to modern state law is the tension between perceptions of the "divinity" of Shariʿa and realities of secular experiences of present Islamic societies. Familiar themes in the comparative law field—the structure of courts and their jurisdiction, the legal profession, and the relationship of legislation to judicial practice—are coherent when understood in the context of specific countries, like Egypt, Indonesia, Iran or Pakistan. From this perspective, such legal systems may be broadly identified as part of civil law or common law traditions. It is also true that there is an "Islamic dimension" that defies a clear classification as either civil or common law systems. Yet, the present status of Shariʿa is ambiguous, even when it is claimed to be the actual legal system of a country. This unavoidable ambiguity, I suggest, is rooted in the nature and development of Shariʿa when viewed from the perspective of modern legal systems, as I will now try to clarify in the following review.

Nature and Development of Shariʿa

The primary sources of Shariʿa are the Qurʾan and Sunna, understood in the context of early Muslim communities, initially in Medina, the town in western Arabia where the Prophet established a state in 622 CE, and subsequently throughout the region known now as the Middle East.[3] Other sources, subject to slight variations among Sunni and Shiʿi Muslims, include consensus (*ijmāʿ*), reasoning by analogy (*qiyās*), and relatively independent juridical reasoning (*ijtihād*) when there is no applicable text of Qurʾan or Sunna.[4] But these were more juridical methodologies for developing principles of Shariʿa, rather than substantive sources as such. The early generations of Muslims are believed to have applied these techniques to interpret and supplement the original sources (Qurʾan and Sunna) in order to extrapolate rules for Muslims to observe. Some general principles began to emerge through the growing influence of the leading scholars at that stage which constituted early models of the schools of Islamic jurisprudence (*madhāhib*, sing. *madhhab*) that matured during subsequent stages of Islamic legal history.

Thus, it seems clear that the systemic development of Shariʿa as a coherent system began during the early Abbasid era (after 750 CE), as demonstrated by the emergence of the major schools of jurisprudence, the systematic collection of Sunna as the second and more detailed source of Shariʿa, and the development of legal methodology, which came to be known as the science of the foundations or principles of human understanding of divine sources (*uṣūl al-fiqh*). These developments took place about 150 to 250 years after the Prophet's death, which means that the first generations of Muslims did not know and apply Shariʿa in the sense in which this concept came to be accepted by the majority of Muslims for the last one thousand years. The early Abbasid era witnessed the emergence of the main schools of Islamic jurisprudence, including the main schools which survive to the present day that are attributed to Abū Ḥanīfa (d. 767); Mālik (d. 795); al-Shāfiʿī (d. 820); Ibn Ḥanbal (d. 855), and Jaʿfar al-Ṣādiq (d. 765, the founder of the main school of Shiʿi jurisprudence). That period also witnessed the emergence of authoritative compilations of Sunna (also known as *Ḥadīth*). Among Sunni Muslims, the most authoritative compilations are those by al-Bukhārī (d. 870); Muslim (d. 875); al-Tirmidhī (d. 892); Ibn Māja (d. 886); Abū Dāwūd (d. 888); and al-Nasāʾī (d. 915). For the Shiʿa the most authoritative compilations also emerged during that general timeframe, namely, those by al-Kulaynī (d. 941); Ibn Bābawayh (d. 991); and al-Shaykh al-Ṭūsī (d. 1067).

What came to be known among Muslims as Shariʿa was therefore the product of a very slow, gradual, and spontaneous process of interpretation of the Qurʾan, and collection, verification, and interpretation of Sunna during the first three centuries of Islam (the seventh to the ninth centuries).[5] That process took place among scholars and jurists who developed their own methodology for the classification of sources, derivation of specific rules from general principles, and so forth. Modern scholars debate whether, or to what degree, the early formative process was based on and responded to the concrete needs of daily practice in the communities or whether it was a product of more speculative development of theoretical principles leading to their logical conclusions.[6] For our purposes here, it is enough to confirm that the framework and main principles of Shariʿa were developed as an ideal normative system by scholars who were clearly independent of the state and its institutions. The fact that the founding jurists were not employed by the state or subject to its control, which is beyond dispute, may partly explain their drive to elaborate the normative system of Islam as they believed it ought to be, regardless of pragmatic factors that may diminish its practical application. Shariʿa evolved as a "jurist's law" in the sense that the founding jurists proclaimed the norms and institutions of Shariʿa as they believed them to be stipulated by the Qurʾan and Sunna, and not as judicial precedents in actual cases as happened some four to five centuries later in the development of English common law.

As to be expected, there was much disagreement and disputation among those early scholars about the meaning and significance of different aspects of the sources with which they were working. Moreover, although those founding scholars are generally accepted to have been acting independently from the political authorities of the time, their work could not have been in isolation from the prevailing conditions of their communities, in local as well as in broader regional contexts. Those factors must have also contributed to disagreements among the jurists, and sometimes to differences in the views expressed by the same jurist from one time to another, as is reported of the changes in the juridical opinions of al-Shāfiʿī when he moved from Iraq to Egypt. Even after those disagreements eventually evolved into separate schools of thought (*madhhabs*), differences of opinion persisted among scholars of the same schools, as well as between different schools.

The systematic development of the methodology and Shariʿa principles of the various schools of Islamic jurisprudence was done by the students of the master scholar whose name was adopted to identify the school, like Hanafi of Abū Ḥanīfa, Maliki of Mālik, among the majority Sunni schools, or Jaʿfari and Zaydi among Shiʿi schools. However, the subsequent development and spread of these schools have been influenced by a variety of political, social, and demographic factors. These factors sometimes resulted in shifting the influence of some schools from one region to another, confining them to certain parts, as is the case with Shiʿi schools at present, or even in the total extinction of some schools like those of al-Thawrī and al-Ṭabarī in the Sunni tradition. For example, having originated in Iraq, the center of the Abbasid dynasty in the eighth and ninth centuries, the Hanafi school enjoyed the important advantage of official support of the state, and was subsequently brought to Afghanistan and later to the Indian subcontinent, where immigrants from India brought it to East Africa. The Hanafi school continued to receive state support in the Middle East region up to the Ottoman Empire and into the modern era.[7] The Maliki school enjoyed similar status in North and West Africa, while the Shafiʿi school prevailed in Southeast Asia.

An aspect of the way in which Shariʿa evolved that is relevant for our purposes here is that the founding jurists followed an integrated approach to their subject as a total normative system that included matters of doctrine or dogma, ritual practices, and ethical norms as well as legal issues. The original manuscripts compiled by the early jurists from the oral tradition of their master scholars would normally begin with issues of confession of the faith, various ritual practices, rules of jihad and conduct of war, treatment of heretics and apostates, justice and fairness in social and commercial dealings, and so forth. While that approach and method of organizing original manuscripts and subsequent commentaries and elaborations were consistent with the essentially religious nature of Shariʿa, they make those foundational sources inaccessible to modern lawyers who have to go through the whole text to discover relevant legal principles and rules. Since those manuscripts and manuals were written by hand more than a thousand years ago, it is not surprising that they do not include a table of contents or subject index that would be helpful for modern readers.

But the approach and organization of these manuscripts were familiar and logical for the early scholars and jurists, as well as for judges and practitioners of subsequent generations who were trained in the specialized colleges (*madrasas*).[8] As the imperial states become more established, they also began employing judges and administrators who had enjoyed that specialized education in the various schools. When an individual Muslim sought an expert arbiter, or the ruler appointed a judge or official who specialized in a particular school, they were seeking legal opinions or judgments associated with that specific juridical tradition.[9] It was therefore possible for rulers to favor some schools over others through the appointment of judges trained in the chosen school and specification of their geographical and subject-matter jurisdiction. But that was not done by legislation or codification of Shariʿa principles until the middle of the nineteenth century under the late Ottoman Empire, as will be explained below.

The timing of the emergence and the early dynamics of each school also seem to have influenced the content and orientation of their views on Shariʿa. For instance, the Hanafi and Maliki schools drew more on pre-existing customary practices than the Shafiʿi and Hanbali schools, which insisted that juridical elaborations must have more direct textual basis in the Qurʾan or Sunna. These differences reflect the influence of the timeframe and intellectual context in which each school emerged and developed, which partly explains the similarities in the views of the latter two schools, in contrast to the stronger influence of reasoning and of social and economic experience in the Hanafi and Maliki schools. However, the principle of consensus (*ijmāʿ*) apparently acted as a unifying force that tended to draw the substantive content of all these four Sunni schools together through the use of juristic reasoning (*ijtihād*). Moreover, the consensus of all the main schools has always been that if there are two or more differing opinions on an issue, they should all be accepted as equally legitimate attempts to express the particular rule.[10] This consensus permitted believers free choice among competing views of Shariʿa on any specific issue, which is good for freedom of religion, but problematic if any of the schools is imposed as the legal system of any state, as in Iran and Saudi Arabia today.

A negative consequence of the strong emphasis on consensus was the drastic decline in the practice of *ijtihād* by the tenth century, probably on the assumption that Shariʿa had already been fully and exhaustively elaborated by that time. This rigidity was probably necessary for maintaining the stability of the system during the decline, sometimes breakdown, of the social and political institutions of Islamic societies. Some historians question this commonly held view that *ijtihād* ended by the tenth century,[11] but the point is, of course, relative. It is true that there were some subsequent development and adaptations of Shariʿa through legal opinions and judicial developments after the tenth century. But it is also clear that this took place firmly within the already established framework and methodology of *uṣūl al-fiqh*, rather than through significant innovation outside that framework and methodology. In other words, there has not been any change in the basic structure and methodology of Shariʿa since the tenth century, although practical adaptations continued in limited scope and locations.

While appreciation of the ways in which Shariʿa worked in practice at different stages of its history continues to grow,[12] it is clear that the traditional nature and core content of the system still reflect the social, political, and economic conditions of the eighth to tenth centuries, thereby growing increasingly out of touch with subsequent developments and realities of society and state, especially in the modern context. This conceptual and methodological deficit has been mitigated in the pre-colonial context by the ability of judges and legal practitioners to maintain nominal allegiance to the classical theory of Shariʿa, with minimal observance of that in their daily practice. But such expedient strategies have increasingly become untenable, especially in the present globally interdependent context of Islamic societies. The requirements of sustainable economic development, international investment, and trade with other countries, as well as political stability and democratic governance at home demand much greater predictability and consistency of legal practice throughout predetermined territorial jurisdictions.

The essentially religious nature of Shariʿa and its focus on regulating the relationship between God and human beings was probably one of the main reasons for the persistence and growth of secular courts to adjudicate a wide range of practical matters in the administration of justice and government in general. The distinction between the jurisdiction of the various state and Shariʿa courts under different imperial states came very close to the philosophy of a division between secular and religious courts.[13] That early acceptance of a "division of labor" between different kinds of courts has probably contributed to the eventual confinement of Shariʿa jurisdiction to family law matters in the modern era. Another aspect of the legal history of Islamic societies that is associated with the religious nature of Shariʿa is the development of private legal consultation (*iftāʾ*). Scholars who were independent of the state were issuing legal opinions (*fatwās*) at the request of provincial governors and state judges, in addition to providing advice for individual persons, from the very beginning of Islam.[14] This type of private advice has persisted through subsequent stages of Islamic history, and became institutionalized since the period of the Ottoman Empire,[15] but there is a significant difference between this sort of moral and social influence of independent scholars, and the enforcement of Shariʿa by the state as such.

The above-noted tension in the combination of religious and legal qualities of Shariʿa raises the following question: How can a legal ruling (*ḥukm*) derived by jurists from an empirical evaluation and research of facts and texts have divine authority? The obvious answer seems to be in the negative, because such a ruling would be human and not divine. Yet, such Shariʿa rulings are believed by Muslims to be binding from a religious perspective, regardless of whether or not it is supported by the coercive authority of the state. In an attempt to resolve this apparent contradiction, some scholars tend to emphasize a distinction between Shariʿa and *fiqh*. "*Shariʿa* Law is the product of legislation (*Shariʿah*), of which God is the ultimate subject (*shārīʿ*). *Fiqh* law consists of legal understanding, of which the human being is the subject (*fāqih*)."[16] This distinction can be useful in a technical sense of indicating that some principles or rules, as compared to others, are more based on speculative thinking than textual support from the Qurʾan and/or Sunna. But this does not mean that those which are taken to be Shariʿa rather than *fiqh* are the direct product of revelation because the Qurʾan and Sunna can neither be understood nor have any influence on human behavior except through the effort of fallible human beings. "Although the law is of divine provenance, the actual construction of the law is a human activity, and its results represent the law of God *as humanly understood*. Since the law does not descend from heaven ready-made, it is the human understanding of the law—the human *fiqh* [literally meaning understanding]—that must be normative for society."[17]

As noted earlier, the founding jurists and scholars of Shariʿa accepted diversity of interpretations and resisted imposing their views which could be wrong, while seeking to enhance consensus among themselves and their communities.[18] That position may have in fact provided valuable flexibility in local legal practices under highly decentralized imperial states. For present legal systems, however, the obvious question is how and by whom can reasonable and legitimate difference of opinion among schools and scholars be settled in order to determine what is the law to be applied by state courts and other authorities? The basic dilemma here can be explained as follows: On the one hand, there is the paramount importance of a minimum degree of certainty in the determination and enforcement of positive law for any society. The nature and role of positive law in the modern state also require the interaction of a multitude of actors and complex factors which cannot possibly be contained by an Islamic religious rationale. On the other hand, a religious rationale is key for the binding force of Shariʿa norms for Muslims. Yet, given the diversity of opinions among Muslim jurists, whatever the state elects to enforce as positive law is bound to be deemed an invalid interpretation of Islamic sources by some of the Muslim citizens of that state. The imperatives of certainty and uniformity in national legislation are now stronger than they used to be. This is not only due to the growing complexity of the role of the state at the domestic or national level, but also because of the global interdependence of all peoples and their states.

Reform and Adaptation

It is not possible or necessary here to examine the variety of mechanisms of negotiating the relationship between Shariʿa and secular administration of justice during earlier parts of Islamic history. Instead, this section will focus on recent developments in the period immediately preceding

European colonialism and its drastic impact on the legal systems of present Islamic societies. As openly secular state courts applying those codes began to take over civil and criminal matters during the colonial era and since independence in the vast majority of Islamic countries, the domain of Shariʿa became progressively limited to the family law field.[19] Even in this field, the state continues to regulate the relevance of Shariʿa as part of broader legal and political systems of government and social organization.[20] An earlier related development during the Ottoman Empire was the patronage of the Hanafi legal school that eventually resulted in the codification of that school's doctrine by the mid-nineteenth century.[21] That was the first ever codification of Shariʿa principles, which marked a significant shift to European models of the state and administration of justice, and away from traditional approaches to the role of Shariʿa in these fields. The symbolic significance of the Ottoman "capitulations" to European powers that culminated in the abolition of the caliphate by 1924 marked the irreversible shift to European models of the state and its legal system that came to prevail throughout the Muslim world.

Dominance and hegemony by military or other means have always been an integral part of the history of all human societies, including the expansion of Islam itself as well as struggles among Muslims through military and peaceful means for centuries. The rise of European colonialism since the sixteenth century can also be seen as the most recent expression of that ancient common human experience. However, European colonialism has been spectacularly successful not only in its scale and scope, but in transforming the global economic and trade system, as well as the political and legal institutions of the colonized societies. While it is difficult to document the timing and manner of the transformative colonial experiences of various Islamic societies and communities, the ultimate outcome has been the establishment of territorial "nation" states all the way from North and West Africa to South and Southeast Asia, and their incorporation into global economic, political, and security systems.[22] The point for our purposes here is the impact these new realities have had on the relevance and application of Shariʿa among Muslims.

This issue is not entirely new or peculiar to the post-colonial era, except in its scale and the more far-reaching consequences. During the rule of imperial states of the past, there was tension inherent in the needs of the daily administration of justice to be legitimized in terms of Shariʿa principles, which paradoxically required the state to respect the autonomy of scholars and jurists because that was necessary for their legitimizing role for the authority of the state. Rulers were supposed to safeguard and promote Shariʿa without claiming or appearing to create or control it.[23] That traditional tension has continued into the modern era, in which Shariʿa remains the religious law of the community of believers, independently of the authority of the state, while the state seeks to enlist the legitimizing power of Shariʿa in support of its political authority. This ambivalence persists as Muslims are neither able to repudiate the religious authority of Shariʿa, nor willing to give it complete control over their lives because it does not provide for all the substantive and procedural requirements of a comprehensive and practicable modern legal system.[24] These qualities came to be more effectively provided for by European colonial administrations throughout the Muslim world by the late nineteenth century.

While this process unfolded in different ways among Islamic societies, the experience of the late Ottoman Empire has probably had the most far-reaching consequences. The concessions made by the Ottoman Empire to European powers during the nineteenth century set the model for the adoption of Western codes and systems of administration of justice. Ottoman imperial edicts justified the changes not only in the name of strengthening the state and preserving Islam, but also emphasized the need to ensure equality among Ottoman subjects, thereby laying the foundation for the adoption of the European model of the state and its legal system. Those reforms introduced into Ottoman law a Commercial Code of 1850, a Penal Code of 1858, a Commercial Procedure of 1879, a Code of Civil Procedure of 1880, and a Code of Maritime Commerce, following the European civil law model of attempting a comprehensive enactment of all relevant rules. Although Shariʿa jurisdiction was significantly displaced in these fields, an attempt was still made to retain some elements of it. The Ottoman Majalla, which came to be known as the Civil Code of 1876, though it was not devised as such, was promulgated over a ten-year period (1867–1877), to codify the rules of contract and tort according to the Hanafi school, combining European form with Shariʿa content. This major codification of Shariʿa principles simplified a huge part of the relevant principles and made them more easily accessible to litigants and jurists.

The Majalla acquired a position of supreme authority soon after its enactment, partly because it represented the earliest and most politically authoritative example of an official promulgation of large parts of Shariʿa by the authority of a modern state, thereby transforming Shariʿa into positive law in the modern sense of the term.[25] Moreover, that legislation was immediately applied in a wide range of Islamic societies throughout the Ottoman Empire, and continued to apply in some parts into the second half of the twentieth century. The success of the Majalla was also due to the fact that it included some provisions drawn from other sources than the Hanafi school, thereby expanding possibilities of "acceptable" selectivity from within the Islamic tradition. The principle of selectivity (*takhayyur*) among equally legitimate doctrines of Shariʿa was already acceptable in theory, as noted earlier, but not done in practice. By applying it through the institutions of the state, the Majalla opened the door for more wide-reaching subsequent reforms, despite its initially limited purpose.[26]

This trend toward increased eclecticism in the selection of sources and the synthesis of Islamic and Western legal concepts and institutions not only became irreversible, but was also carried further, especially through the work of the Egyptian jurist ʿAbd al-Razzāq al-Sanhūrī (d. 1971). The pragmatic approach of al-Sanhūrī was premised on the view that Shariʿa could not be reintroduced in its totality, or applied without strong adaptation to the needs of modern Islamic societies. He used this approach in drafting the Egyptian Civil Code of 1948, the Iraqi Code of 1951, the Libyan Code of 1953, and the Kuwaiti Code and Commercial Law of 1960/1. In all cases, al-Sanhūrī was brought in by an autocratic government to draft a comprehensive code that was "enacted" into law without public debate. In other words, such reforms would probably not have been possible at all if those countries were democratic at the time, as public opinion would not have permitted the formal and conclusive displacement of Shariʿa by what was believed to be secular Western principles of law.

Those reforms had the paradoxical outcome of making the entire corpus of Shariʿa principles more available and accessible to judges and policy makers in the process of transforming their nature and role through formal selectivity and adaptation for their incorporation into modern legislation. On the one hand, Shariʿa principles began to be drafted and enacted into statutes that were premised on European legal structures and concepts. This was also done by often mixing some general or partial principles or views from one school of Islamic jurisprudence with those derived from other schools, without due regard to the methodological basis or conceptual coherence of any of the schools whose authority was being invoked. Another aspect of the paradox is that the emerging synthesis of the Islamic and European legal traditions also exposed the impossibility of the direct and systematic application of traditional Shariʿa principles in the modern context. The main reason for that is the complexity and diversity of Shariʿa itself, as it has evolved through the centuries. In addition to strong disagreement among and within Sunni and Shiʿi communities that sometimes coexists within the same country, as in Iraq, Lebanon, Saudi Arabia, Syria, and Pakistan, different schools or scholarly opinions may be followed by the Muslim community within the same country, though not formally applied by the courts. In addition, judicial practice may not necessarily be in accordance with the school followed by the majority of the Muslim population in the country, as in North African countries that inherited official Ottoman preference for the Hanafi school, while popular practice continues to be according to the Maliki school.

The legal and political consequences of these recent developments were intensified by the significant impact of European colonialism and global Western influence in the fields of general education and professional training of state officials, business leaders, and other influential social and economic actors. Changes in educational institutions not only dislodged traditional Islamic education, but also introduced a range of secular subjects that tend to create a different worldview and expertise among young generations of Muslims. Moreover, the monopoly of Islamic scholars of intellectual leadership in societies which had extremely low literacy levels has been drastically eroded by the fast growth of mass literacy and growing higher education in secular sciences and arts. Thus, Shariʿa scholars not only lost their historical monopoly on knowledge of the "sacred" sources of Shariʿa, but traditional interpretations of those sources are no longer viewed as sacred or unquestionable by ordinary "lay" Muslims. Regarding legal education in particular, the first generations of lawyers and jurists took advanced training in European and North American universities and returned to teach subsequent generations or hold senior judicial office.

More generally, the establishment of European model states for all Islamic societies, as part of a global system based on the same model, has radically transformed political, economic, and social relations throughout the region. By retaining these models at home and participating in them abroad after independence, Islamic societies have become bound by the national and international obligations of membership in a world community of states. While there are clear differences in the level of their social development and political stability, all Islamic societies today live under national constitutional regimes (including countries that do not have written constitutions, such as Saudi Arabia and the Gulf states) and legal systems that require respect for certain minimum rights of equality and non-discrimination for all their citizens. Even where national constitutions and legal systems fail to expressly acknowledge and effectively provide for these obligations, a minimum degree of practical compliance is ensured by the present realities of international relations. These transformations also affect the situation of Muslim minorities living in other countries, including Western Europe and North America, probably to a larger extent than those living as majorities. It is clear now that these changes are simply irreversible, though their full implications are not sufficiently developed or integrated in practice. It is also clear that such problems are not peculiar to Islamic countries, as they are also experienced by many other post-colonial states in Africa, Asia, and Latin America, where few Muslims live. But the question for this essay is whether it is possible to develop a coherent theory for the future of Shariʿa in a secular state, whether Muslims constitute the majority or the minority of the population.

A Theory for the Future of Shariʿa

As noted at the beginning of this essay, I am concerned here with the future relationship between Shariʿa and state law, rather than the history of Shariʿa in general. The theoretical framework I am proposing for this forward-looking perspective is premised on the need to ensure the institutional separation of Islam and the state, despite the organic and unavoidable connection between Islam and politics. In other words, the challenge is to maintain the neutrality of the state regarding all religious doctrine, although the political behavior of believers will continue to be influenced by their religion. The first part of this proposition sounds like "secularism" as commonly understood today, but the second part indicates the opposite. The relationship among Islam, state, and society is always the product of a constant and deeply contextual negotiation, rather than the subject of a fixed formula of either total separation or complete fusion of religion and the state.

At the risk of stating the obvious but to avoid confusion or misunderstanding of what I am proposing, various understandings of Shariʿa will remain, of course, in the realm of individual and collective practice as a matter of freedom of religion and belief, yet will also be subject to established constitutional safeguards to protect the rights of others. What is problematic is for Shariʿa principles to be enforced as state law or policy on that basis alone, because once a principle or norm is officially identified as "decreed by God," it will be extremely difficult to resist or change its application in practice. At the same time, the integrity of Islam as a religion will decline in the eyes of believers and non-believers alike when state officials and institutions fail to deliver the promise of individual freedom and social justice. Since Islamic ethical principles and social values are indeed necessary for the proper functioning of Islamic societies in general, the implementation of such principles and values would be consistent with, indeed required by, the right of Muslims to self-determination. This right, however, can only be realized within the framework of constitutional and democratic governance at home and international law abroad because these are the legal and political bases of this right in the first place. In other words, the right to self-determination presupposes a constitutional basis that is derived from the collective will of the totality of the population, and can be asserted against other countries because it is accepted as a fundamental principle of international law.

The paradox of separation of Islam and the state (religious neutrality of the state) and connection of Islam and politics can only be mediated through practice over time, rather than completely resolved by theoretical analysis or stipulation. The challenge is therefore how to create the most conducive conditions for this mediation to continue in a constructive fashion, rather than hope to resolve it once and for all. The two poles of this necessary mediation can be clarified as follows. First, the modern territorial state should neither seek to enforce Shariʿa as positive law and public policy, nor claim to interpret its doctrine and general principles for Muslim citizens. Second, Shariʿa principles can and should be a source of public policy and legislation, subject to the constitutional and human rights of all citizens, men and women, Muslims and non-Muslims equally and without discrimination. In other words, Shariʿa principles are neither privileged or enforced as such nor necessarily rejected as a source of state law and policy simply because they are derived from Shariʿa. The belief of even the vast majority of citizens that these principles are binding as a matter of Islamic religious obligation should remain the basis of individual and collective observance among believers, but is not accepted as sufficient reason for their enforcement by the state as such. I will now briefly explain how these two main elements of the proposed theory can work together in promoting individual freedom and social justice in Islamic societies.

Since effective governance requires the adoption of specific policies and enactment of precise laws, the administrative and legislative organs of the state must select among competing views within the massive and complex corpus of Shariʿa principles, as noted earlier. That selection will necessarily be made by the ruling elite. When the policy or law is presented as mandated by the "divine will of God" it is difficult for the general population to oppose or resist it. For example, there is a well-established principle of Shariʿa, known as *khulʿ*, whereby a wife can pay her husband an agreed amount (or forfeit her financial entitlement) to induce him to accept the termination of their marriage. Yet, this choice was not available in Egypt until the government decided to enact this Shariʿa principle into law in 2000. The fact that this principle was part of Shariʿa did not make it applicable in Egypt until the state decided to enforce it. Moreover, this legislation certainly gave Egyptian women a way out of a bad marriage, but the condition that this was possible only at a significant financial cost for the wife could not be contested because the legislation was made in terms of "enacting" Shariʿa, rather than simply a matter of good social policy. Since the legislation was framed in terms of binding Islamic principles, the possibility and requirements of the legal termination of marriage remains limited to general principles of Shariʿa as formulated by Islamic scholars a thousand years ago.[27] The broader point for my purposes here is that the inherent subjectivity and diversity of Shariʿa principles mean that whatever is enacted and enforced by the state is the political will of the ruling elite, not the normative system of Islam as such. Yet, such policies and legislation would be difficult to resist or even debate when presented as the will of God.

To avoid such difficulties, I am proposing that the rationale of all public policy and legislation always be based on what might be called "public reason," whereby Muslims and other believers should be able to propose policy and legislative initiatives emanating from their religious beliefs, *provided* they can support them in a public, free and open debate with reasons that are accessible and convincing to the generality of citizens, regardless of their religion or other beliefs. But since such decisions will in practice be made by majority vote in accordance with democratic principles, all state action must also conform to basic constitutional and human rights safeguards against the tyranny of the majority. Thus, the majority would not be able to override objections to any policy or legislation that violates the fundamental requirements of equality and non-discrimination. These propositions are already supposed to be the basis of legitimate government in the vast majority of present Islamic societies. Yet they are unlikely to be taken seriously by most Muslims unless they are perceived to at least be consistent with their understanding of Islam. This is the reason for my attempt to substantiate this theory from an Islamic perspective, including calling for reinterpretations of certain aspects of Shariʿa.

Part of the need for that Islamic argument, in my view, is that secularism as simply the separation of religion and the state is not sufficient for addressing any objections or reservations believers may have about specific constitutional norms and human rights standards. For example, since discrimination against women is often justified on religious grounds in Islamic societies, this source of systematic and gross violation of human rights cannot be eliminated without addressing their commonly perceived religious rationale. This must be done without violating freedom of religion or belief for Muslims, which is also a fundamental human right. While a secular discourse in terms of separation alone can be respectful of religion in general, as can be seen in West European and North American societies today in contrast to the present practice of Islamic societies, it is unlikely to succeed in rebutting religious justifications of discrimination without invoking a counter-religious argument. In contrast, the principle of secularism, as I am defining it here to include a public role for religion, can encourage and facilitate internal debate and dissent within religious traditions that can overcome such religiously-based objections. When a society ensures that the state is neutral in regard to religion, the coercive power of the state cannot be used to suppress debate and dissent. But that safe space still needs to be actively used by citizens to promote religious views that support equality for women and other human rights. In fact, such views are needed for promoting the religious legitimacy of the doctrine of separation of religion and the state itself, as well as other general principles of constitutionalism and human rights.

Allowing Shariʿa principles to play a positive role in public life without permitting them to be implemented as such through law and policy is a delicate balance that each society must strive to maintain for itself over time. For example, such matters as dress style and religious education will normally remain in the realm of free choice, but can also be the subject of public debate, even constitutional litigation, to balance competing claims. This can happen, for instance, regarding dress requirements for safety in the work place or the need for comparative and critical religious education in state schools to enhance religious tolerance and secularism. I am not suggesting that the context and conditions of free choice of dress or religious education will not be controversial. In fact, such matters are likely to be very complex at a personal and societal level. Rather, my concern is with ensuring, as far as humanly possible, fair, open and inclusive social, political, and legal conditions for the negotiation of public policy in such matters. Those conditions, for instance, are to be secured through the entrenchment of such fundamental rights of the persons and communities as the right to education and freedom of religion and expression, on the one hand, and due consideration for legitimate public interests or concerns, on the other. There is no simple or categorical formula to be prescribed for automatic application in every case, although general principles and broader frameworks for the mediation of such issues will emerge and continue to evolve within each society.

To reiterate, my call for recognizing and regulating the political role of Islam is untenable without significant Islamic reform. I believe that it is critically important for Islamic societies today to invest in the rule of law and protection of human rights in their domestic politics and international relations. This is unlikely to happen if traditional interpretations of Shariʿa that support principles like male guardianship of women (*qiwāma*), sovereignty of Muslims over non-Muslims (*dhimma*), and violently aggressive jihad are maintained. Significant reform of such views is necessary because of their powerful influence on social relations and political behavior of Muslims, even when Shariʿa principles are not directly enforced by the state.[28] One premise of my whole approach is that Muslims are unlikely to actively support human rights principles and effectively engage in the process of constitutional democratic governance if they continue to maintain such views to be part of their understanding of Shariʿa. The imperative need for reconciliation can also be illustrated by recalling earlier comments on the nature of the modern territorial state and its citizens.

Whatever possibilities of change or development can be proposed must begin with the reality that European colonialism and its aftermath have drastically transformed the basis and nature of political and social organization within and among territorial states where all Muslims live today. This transformation is so profound and deeply entrenched that a return to pre-colonial ideas and systems is simply not an option. Any change and adaptation of the present system can only be sought or realized through the concepts and institutions of this local and global post-colonial reality. Yet many Muslims, probably the majority in many countries, have not accepted some aspects of this transformation and its consequences. This discrepancy seems to underlie the apparent acceptance by many Muslims of the possibility of an Islamic state that can enforce Shariʿa principles as positive law and underlies widespread ambivalence about politically motivated violence in the name of jihad. Significant Islamic reform is necessary to reformulate such problematic aspects of Shariʿa, but should not and cannot mean the wholesale and uncritical adoption of dominant Western theory and practice in these fields. To illustrate the sort of internal Islamic transformation I am proposing, I will briefly review here how the traditional Shariʿa notions of *dhimma* should evolve into a coherent and humane principle of citizenship. Such evolution should take into account the following considerations.

First, human beings tend to seek and experience multiple and overlapping types and forms of membership in different groups on such grounds as ethnic, religious or cultural identity, political, social or professional affiliation, economic interests, and so forth. Second, the meaning and implications of each type or form of membership should be determined by the rationale or purpose of belonging to the group in question, without precluding or undermining other forms of membership. That is, multiple and overlapping memberships should not be mutually exclusive, as they tend to serve different purposes for persons and communities. Third, the term "citizenship" is used here to refer to a particular form of membership in the political community of a territorial state in its global context, and should therefore be related to this specific rationale or purpose without precluding other possibilities of membership of other communities for different purposes. Proposing this threefold premise is not to suggest that people are always consciously aware of the reality of their multiple memberships, or appreciate that they are mutually inclusive, with each being appropriate or necessary for its different purpose or rationale. On the contrary, it seems that there is a tendency to collapse different forms of membership, as when ethnic or religious identity is equated with political or social affiliation. This is true about the coincidence of nationality and citizenship in Western political theory that was transmitted to Muslims through European colonialism and its aftermath.

Thus, official or ideological discourse regarding the basis of citizenship as membership in the political community of a territorial state did not necessarily coincide with a subjective feeling of belonging or an independent assessment of actual conditions on the ground. Such tensions existed in all major civilizations in the past and continue to be experienced in various ways by different societies today. For our purposes here in particular, the development of the notion of citizenship in the European model of the territorial "nation" state since the Peace Treaty of Westphalia (1648) tended to equate citizenship with nationality. This model defined citizenship in terms of a contrived and often coercive membership in a "nation" on the basis of shared ethnic and religious identity and political allegiance that was both required by and assumed to follow from residence within a particular territory. In other words, the coincidence of citizenship and nationality was not only the product of a peculiarly European and relatively recent process, but was often exaggerated in that region itself at the expense of other forms of membership, especially of ethnic or religious minorities. This is the reason why I prefer to use the term "territorial" state to identify citizenship with territory, instead of nation state as that can be misleading, if not oppressive of minorities.

The term citizenship is used here to denote an affirmative and proactive belonging to an inclusive pluralistic political community that affirms and regulates possibilities of various forms of "difference" among persons and communities to ensure equal rights for all, without distinction on such grounds as religion, sex, ethnicity or political opinion. This term is intended to signify a shared cultural understanding of equal human dignity and effective political participation for all. In other words, citizenship is defined here in terms of the principle of the universality of human rights as "a common standard of achievement for all people and nations," according to the Preamble of the 1948 United Nations' Universal Declaration of Human Rights.

In my view, the desirability of this understanding of citizenship is supported by the Islamic principle of reciprocity (*muʿāwaḍa*), also known as the Golden Rule, and emphasized by the legal and political realities of self-determination. Persons and communities everywhere have to affirm this conception of citizenship in order to be able to claim it for themselves under international law as well as domestic constitutional law and politics. That is, acceptance of this understanding of citizenship is the prerequisite moral, legal, and political basis of its enjoyment. Muslims should strive toward this pragmatic ideal from an Islamic point of view, and regardless of what other peoples do or fail to do in this regard.

Moreover, there is a dialectical relationship between domestic and international conceptions of citizenship, whereby the agency of subjects at each level seeks to ensure human dignity and social justice everywhere in the world, at home and abroad. The same human rights principles underlie the proposed definition of citizenship in domestic politics as well as international relations, whether expressed in terms of fundamental constitutional rights or universal human rights. Citizens acting politically at home participate in the setting and implementation of universal human rights which, in turn, contribute to defining and protecting the rights of citizens at the domestic level. The relationship between citizenship and human rights is therefore inherent to both paradigms which are mutually supportive.

These reflections clearly emphasize the importance of creative Islamic reform that balances the competing demands of religious legitimacy and principled political and social practice which are simply inconsistent with the notion of an Islamic state. But this notion is so appealing to Muslims in the present domestic and global context that other possible justifications must also be confronted. For example, it is sometimes suggested that it is better to allow the idea of an Islamic state to stand as an ideal while seeking to control or manage its practice. This view is dangerous because as long as this notion stands as an ideal, some Muslims will attempt to implement it according to their own understanding of what it means, with disastrous consequences for their societies and beyond. It is impossible to control or manage the practice of this ideal without challenging its core claims of religious sanctity for human views of Islam. Once the possibility of an Islamic state is conceded, it becomes extremely difficult to resist the next logical step of seeking to implement it in practice because that would be regarded as a heretical or "un-Islamic" position.

Maintaining this ideal is also counterproductive because it will preclude debate about more viable and appropriate political theories, legal systems, and development policies. Even if one overcomes the psychological difficulty of arguing against what is presented as the divine will of God, charges of heresy can result in severe social stigma, if not prosecution by the state or direct violence by extremist groups. As long as the idea of an Islamic state is allowed to stand, societies will remain locked in stale debates about such issues as whether constitutionalism or democracy are "Islamic," and whether interest banking is to be allowed or not, instead of getting on with securing constitutional democratic governance and pursuing economic development. Such fruitless debates have kept the vast majority of present Islamic societies locked in a constant state of political instability and economic and social underdevelopment since independence. Instead, Muslims need to accept that constitutionalism and democracy are the ultimate foundation of the state itself and to engage in the process of securing them in practice.

It is not appropriate to offer here some concluding remarks because the ideas I outlined above are drawn from the large manuscript mentioned earlier, which itself is really a "work-in-progress." My purpose here is to simply present this essay in honor of our colleague and friend, Professor Frank Vogel, in recognition of his efforts to clarify the underlying issues and contribute to this vitally important debate.

NOTES

[1] I will use the term Shariʿa throughout this chapter and not Islamic law, which is a misleading translation for the reasons discussed below.

[2] Harvard University Press (March 2008).

[3] Fazlur Rahman, *Islam* (Chicago: University of Chicago Press, [2]1979), 11–29.

[4] Wael B. Hallaq, *A History of Islamic Legal Theories: An Introduction to Sunnī Uṣūl al-Fiqh* (Cambridge: Cambridge University Press, 1997), 1–35.

[5] Noel Coulson, *A History of Islamic Law* (Edinburgh: Edinburgh University Press, 1964).

[6] Ibid., 82–4; Joseph Schacht, *An Introduction to Islamic Law* (Oxford: Clarendon Press, 1964), 23–7, 76.

[7] Bernard G. Weiss and Arnold H. Green, *A Survey of Arab History* (Cairo: American University in Cairo Press, 1987), 155.

[8] George Makdisi, *The Rise of Colleges: Institutions of Learning in Islam and the West* (Edinburgh: Edinburgh University Press, 1981); Daphna Ephrat, *A Learned Society in a Period of Transition: The Sunni 'Ulama' of Eleventh Century Baghdad* (Albany: State University of New York Press, 2000).

[9] Noel Coulson, *Conflicts and Tensions in Islamic Jurisprudence* (Chicago: University of Chicago Press, 1969), 34–6.

[10] David Pearl and Werner Menski, *Muslim Family Law* (London: Sweet & Maxwell, [3]1998), 14–17.

[11] Haim Gerber, *Islamic Law and Culture, 1600–1840* (Leiden: Brill, 1999); Wael B. Hallaq, *Law and Legal Theory in Classical and Medieval Islam* (Aldershot: Variorum, 1994), 3.

[12] See, e.g., Aziz al-Azmeh, "Islamic Legal Theory and the Appropriation of Reality," in Aziz al-Azmeh (ed.), *Islamic Law: Social and Historical Contexts* (New York: Routledge, 1988), 250–61; Hallaq, *A History of Islamic Legal Theories.*

[13] Coulson, *A History of Islamic Law*, 122.

[14] Muhammad Khalid Masud, Brinkley Messick, and David Powers, "Muftis, Fatwas, and Islamic Legal Interpretation," in Muhammad Khalid Masud, Brinkley Messick, and David Powers (eds.), *Islamic Legal Interpretation: Muftis and their Fatwas* (Cambridge, Mass.: Harvard University Press, 1996), 3, 8–9.

[15] Hallaq, *A History of Islamic Legal Theories*, 123, 143.

[16] Bernard G. Weiss, *The Spirit of Islamic Law* (Athens: University of Georgia Press, 1998), 120.

[17] Ibid., 116, emphasis in original.

[18] Ibid., 120–22.

[19] Coulson, *A History of Islamic Law*, 149.

[20] Ibid., 218–25.

[21] Ibid., 151.

[22] See generally, for example, James P. Piscatori, *Islam in a World of Nation-States* (Cambridge: Cambridge University Press, 1986).

[23] Colin Imber, *Ebu's-Suʿud: The Islamic Legal Tradition* (Edinburgh: Edinburgh University Press, 1997), 25.

[24] Gerber, *Islamic Law and Culture*, 29.

[25] Brinkley Messick, *The Calligraphic State: Textual Domination and History in a Muslim Society* (Berkeley: University of California Press, 1993), 57.

[26] Pearl and Menski, *Muslim Family Law*, 14–17.

[27] Essam Fawzy, "Law No. 1 of 2000: A New Personal Status Law and a Limited Step on the Path to Reform," in Lynn Welchman (ed.), *Women's Rights and Islamic Family Law: Perspectives on Reform* (London: Zed Books, 2004), 58–86.

[28] On the approach I find most promising in achieving the necessary degree of reform, see Abdullahi Ahmed An-Naʿim, *Toward an Islamic Reformation: Civil Liberties, Human Rights and International Law* (Syracuse: Syracuse University Press, 1990).

17

THE EMERGENCE OF A NEW QUR'ANIC HERMENEUTIC

The Role and Impact of Universities in West and East

*Bernard K. Freamon**

> When one performs a valid sacrifice with a certain instrument, no account is taken, in deciding the validity of the sacrifice, of whether the instrument belongs to one who shares our religion or to one who does not, so long as it fulfills the conditions of validity.
>
> Ibn Rushd, in *Kitāb Faṣl al-Maqāl*[1]

Islam has a marvelous and deep-rooted tradition of vital and influential scholarship. This scholarly tradition is of critical and fundamental importance to both the Sunni and Shiʿi approaches to the Islamic project.[2] The oldest and most important branch of this tradition is the discipline concerned with the interpretation of the Qurʾan. There is perhaps no more important scholarly effort in Islamic studies that one can undertake, given the tremendous stresses and anxieties that afflict today's believing Muslims, than one seeking to translate the message of the Qurʾan into practical guidance for daily life. This is also the case for those seeking the Qurʾan's counsel in juridical and jurisprudential matters involving important affairs of state, political and civic life, family relations, pedagogy, commercial disputes, war and diplomacy, and the other more weighty pursuits of modern existence.

This essay will suggest that, in spite of its pedigreed and influential legacy, the traditional interpretive scholarship on the Qurʾan is losing its relevance in the lives of many believers. I will argue that a new Qurʾanic hermeneutic is replacing the traditional interpretive scholarship on the Qurʾan. This is a positive and constructive development in the history of the Islamic project, although it may not appear to be so at first blush. I will propose that universities in the West and the Far East are uniquely suited to play an important role in this rapidly evolving development and that there is a potential for a new discourse on the Qurʾan and its meaning, a discourse that could help reduce the size of the abyss between the Islamic world and the West that now exists. Before exploring these ideas, it will be helpful to define the meaning of "traditional" interpretive scholarship on the Qurʾan.

The traditional interpretive scholarship on the Qurʾan is best described as part of the hermeneutic discourse that emerged from "the Great Synthesis," to use Wael Hallaq's terminology, occurring during and after the resolution of the dispute between the "rationalists" (*ahl al-raʾy*) and the "traditionalists" (*ahl al-ḥadīth*) in tenth-century Iraq.[3] The dispute pitted those emphasizing independent reason in theology and jurisprudence against those who emphasized primary reliance on the commands of the revelatory texts—the Qurʾan and the Sunna. The "Synthesis" or compromise uniting these two streams of thought bestowed a primacy on the "traditionalist" mode of thinking and gave us many other things, among them the various methodologies used in the Islamic science of legal methodology (*uṣūl al-fiqh*) as well as the foundation for the doctrinal development of the body of legal scholarship that became known as *fiqh*. It also gave us the "traditional" hermeneutical approaches to the Qurʾan. These "traditional" approaches are one of the backbones of *fiqh* and rapidly became canonical. Although the "Great Synthesis" involved discourse among Sunni Muslims, the Shiʿa also accepted much of the doctrine advanced by the traditional interpretive scholarship, particularly the Sunni understandings of the Prophetic reports (*ḥadīth*), even though these interpretations were transmitted to the Shiʿi masses and scholars through the infallible interpretive authority of the Shiʿi imamate rather than through the vehicle of ulamaic or scholarly consensus.[4] This traditional interpretive scholarship has thus dominated Sunni and Shiʿi efforts to understand and interpret the meaning of the Qurʾan for almost the entire millennium since the deaths of the major protagonists in the original dispute.

The danger that now threatens the continued relevance of this traditional Qurʾanic hermeneutic is traceable to a number of contemporary factors, not the least being the legacy of colonialism, the intellectual hegemony and alleged supremacy of post-Enlightenment modes of thought, as well as the great political, social, and economic upheavals that currently affect Muslims in many parts of the post-colonial world. The impact of these factors is fueled by the traditional scholarship's inaccessibility and somewhat anachronistic content in many important areas of thought and belief. The cultural, linguistic, and demographic identity of the Muslim world has changed dramatically since scholars like al-Ṭabarī, al-Zamakhsharī, Ibn Kathīr, and al-Ṭūsī penned their monumental commentaries on the Qurʾan during the classical and medieval ages of Islam. Most of the contemporary Muslim world does not speak or read Arabic and a significant number of Muslims live in pluralist and secular societies in the West, the Indian sub-continent, and the Far East. These societies, while in most instances tolerant, open, and discourse-friendly, are dominated by largely secular non-Muslim majorities. Even communities in the Middle East are becoming increasingly religiously and culturally diverse and more influenced by secular concerns. The traditional scholars of the Qurʾan in both the Sunni and Shiʿi worlds are increasingly out of touch with the believers. These circumstances have created a new milieu for Muslims struggling to craft a new identity and a revitalized understanding of their sacred texts.

The new milieu has begun to generate a new form of interpretive scholarship on the Qurʾan, one that speaks to the contemporary situations and circumstances of Muslims in ways that the traditional interpretive scholarship on the Qurʾan never could. The emergence of this new Qurʾanic hermeneutic is profoundly important in terms of the future of scholarship on Islam. It is reminiscent of the interpretive breakthroughs accomplished by Ibn Rushd (Averroes) and the scholars who translated, studied, and taught from his writings in the thirteenth and fourteenth centuries, near the end of the medieval era. Recall that European universities and scholars seized on this knowledge at that time to advance new understandings of Aristotelian thought. These understandings are said to have ultimately become part of the foundation for the Enlightenment.[5]

Ibn Rushd did more than just preserve and comment on the works of Plato and Aristotle. He also crafted an innovative and original approach to interpretation of the Qurʾan, recognizing, perhaps for the first time, that the interpretive enterprise must take account of the practical and socio-religious circumstances of the interpreter.[6] His approach sought to harmonize claimed universal philosophical truths with the self-evident universal truths of revelation.[7] Ibn Rushd's controversial doctrine of "double truth," holding that "philosophical truth can appear to be inconsistent with but does not actually contradict revelation, which therefore need not be interpreted in a restricted fashion,"[8] was profoundly influential for Western philosophy and caused a number of pre-Enlightenment thinkers to reassess their view of the relationship between philosophy and religion. As is well known, Ibn Rushd's innovative ideas on interpretation of the Qurʾan had little impact on the development of traditional Qurʾanic hermeneutics in the Islamic world of his time.[9] On the other hand, his work "liberated philosophy in a sense from its dogmatic theological grip" and established a way whereby the Qurʾan could be read with a freedom that did not offend the time-honored traditions and methods of the Islamic religion.[10]

We may again be on the cusp of a similarly momentous irruption, generated by the new Qurʾanic hermeneutic that I have described. One of the main engines driving this new hermeneutic is the influential presence of scholars of Islam in universities in the West and Far East.[11] The fact of their presence in significant numbers distinguishes the current situation from that which existed at the time of Ibn Rushd. The new hermeneutic is also supported by a fresh, creative, resourceful, and broadly integrative approach to scholarship on Islam.[12] The development of interdisciplinary approaches to the philosophy of religion, as well as the sociology and anthropology of religion, including the use of ethnography and critical history, and the influence of philosophical hermeneutics, have greatly expanded the potential for a deeper comprehension and appreciation of the Qur'an. Western and Far Eastern universities are supporting this new scholarship in a number of important ways, particularly through the award of professorships, research grants, and sponsorship of fellowships, conferences, and symposia.[13] The systematic study of Islam and Islamic law now occupies a significant and valuable place in university life in many of the great universities of the world.[14]

In spite of these exciting developments, there is still today very little discourse between the proponents of the new Qur'anic hermeneutic and the traditional scholars of the Qur'an in the Arab world. These circumstances present a dual set of challenges and opportunities for Western and Far Eastern universities. On the one hand, the presence in these universities of jurists, social scientists, and theologians who are competent to translate and interpret the original religious texts gives them the ability and the resources to make the traditional scholarship on the Qur'an once again accessible to Muslims in the West and Far East. Concomitantly, these universities also now have the resources, and perhaps the credibility in the Arab world, to initiate and foster a meaningful discourse between the proponents of the new Qur'anic hermeneutic and the traditional scholars of the Qur'an. The opportunity for such a discourse has the potential to be of great practical service to Muslims and scholars of Islam all over the world, in addition to increasing the understanding of the Qur'an and closing the divide between the Islamic world and the West. The discourse can also help policymakers and academics in the West to better understand themselves and their role in history. It is an opportunity that should not be missed. The main purpose of this essay, therefore, is to offer a proposal on how this discourse might be initiated. Before exploring the contours of the proposal, it will be helpful to explore the background to the development of the new Quranic hermeneutic.

The intellectual effort involved in discovering and understanding the meaning of the Qur'an is as old as Islam itself. It has been described in a number of ways, in Arabic and in a number of other Western European languages. Westerners often describe such effort as a species of exegesis, the endeavor typically concerned with the interpretation of scripture and other religious texts.[15] The exegete comments on and explains the text, conveying its meaning through the use of descriptive narrative and other widely recognized forms of expository expression. The exegetical process is part and parcel of the discipline of hermeneutics. Unlike the concept of exegesis, it is not easy to arrive at a satisfactory definition of hermeneutics. One contemporary scholar of Islam has suggested that a definition of the term "may not be possible."[16] Nonetheless, it appears that the discipline of hermeneutics includes exegetical approaches within it but is, at the same time, a greater and more transcendent enterprise. It involves "both the understanding of the rules of exegesis and the epistemology of understanding—the study of the construction of meaning in the past and their relationship to the construction of meanings in the present."[17] Hans-Georg Gadamer, the leading Western theoretician of hermeneutics in the last century, described hermeneutics as "the classical discipline concerned with the art of understanding texts."[18] He further observed that the discipline is not just concerned with the meaning of texts but rather with the whole human endeavor associated with achieving an understanding of experience. Thus, the interpreter develops a "hermeneutical consciousness" which recognizes that "understanding must be conceived as a part of the event in which meaning occurs, the event in which the meaning of all statements—those of art and all other kinds of tradition—is formed and actualized."[19] He asserted that hermeneutics is "the basis of all the human sciences" and that

> It wholly transcended its original pragmatic purpose of making it possible, or easier, to understand written texts. It is not only the written tradition that is estranged and in need of new and more vital assimilation; everything that is no longer immediately situated in a world—that is, all tradition, whether art or the other spiritual creations of the past: law, religion, philosophy, and so forth—is estranged from its original meaning and depends on the unlocking and mediating spirit that we, like the Greeks, name after Hermes: the messenger of the gods.[20]

Gadamer's redefinition of the hermeneutic enterprise has had a significant impact on philosophical, theological, and jurisprudential approaches to interpretation of texts in the West.[21] His approach contemplates something much greater than simple exegesis.[22] As I shall show, the discipline of Qurʾanic interpretation is also viewed as something greater than simple exegesis, and further, this view comports with Gadamer's twentieth-century redefinition of the hermeneutical enterprise.

Thus we see that in Islamic religious discourse the interpretive enterprise is also generally described in at least two ways.[23] The first, and older, Islamic terminology describes the enterprise as *taʾwīl*, a word that connotes the intellectual task of ascertaining the hidden meaning of the language in texts.[24] The science of *taʾwīl* can be concerned with any text, although it is most often used as a description of the science of the interpretation of the Qurʾan, the preeminent text in the Arabic language. In spite of this usage, like Gadamer's view of hermeneutics, *taʾwīl* can also be applied to poetry, literature, and perhaps even art or music. The second, and somewhat newer, Islamic terminology describes the interpretive enterprise as *tafsīr*.[25] This term is widely employed in everyday parlance and it is commonly used and understood by scholars and ordinary believers to generally describe the hermeneutical tradition in Islam. The *tafsīr* literature is much more akin to the western exegetical literature in that it forms the doctrinal basis for liturgical and juridical decision-making by a broad variety of Muslim actors in all sectors of society, including community leaders, imams, teachers, military commanders, soldiers, parents, and ordinary believers.

Historically, there has been and continues to be great debate as to whether the enterprise of interpretation of the Qurʾan is properly described and understood as *taʾwīl* (focusing on hidden and esoteric meanings) or *tafsīr* (focusing on explanations and commentary on the text and offering practical and realistic exegesis).[26] To the extent that there are differences in the Sunni and Shiʿi approaches to the interpretation of the Qurʾan, those differences find their origin in the *taʾwīl-tafsīr* debate. Shiʿi jurists and theologians are much more concerned with esoteric interpretations of the Qurʾan and rely much less upon notions of scholarly consensus in arriving at determinations of meaning. These esoteric meanings are derived from the opinions of the divinely-inspired Shiʿi Imams and they tend to place much more emphasis on allegorical visions of particular verses of the text. Thus Shiʿis believe in differences between the "inner" and "outer" meanings of the Qurʾan and they will use these differences in meaning to justify particular theological or religio-political views.[27] Shiʿism has been described as characterized by a religious mood that stresses "messianic hopes and chiliastic expectations,"[28] as well as a "kerygmatic" piety.[29] This is to be contrasted with the textualism that characterizes Sunni juristic thought. Interestingly, even though there is a decided Shiʿi emphasis on allegorical interpretations, the Shiʿi jurists are more accepting of the role of reason in the interpretation of the text, following Muʿtazila influences, although this notion is also contested.[30] *Taʾwīl* then, in the view of most scholars, is based upon reason and personal opinion (*raʾy*), whereas *tafsīr* (or *tanzīl* in the parlance of the Shiʿa) is "based upon material transmitted from the Prophet himself or his Companions or the Successors in the form of *ḥadīth* (or *athar*)."[31]

Reflecting these tensions, it is said that there are indeed two "great streams" of exegetical or *tafsīr* literature in Islam, one emphasizing tradition (*tafsīr bi l-maʾthūr* or "interpretation by tradition") and the other emphasizing individual reason (*tafsīr bi l-raʾy* or "interpretation by opinion"). Andrew Rippin argues that the division of the literary genre and the scholarship into these two divisions is superficial, obscuring the wealth of interpretive opinion to be found in the vast corpus of literature comprising the *tafsīr* on the Qurʾan.[32] While this is undoubtedly true, my purposes in this essay are satisfied by noting that the two poles of "tradition" and "independent reasoning" always form the far horizons on a circle which encompasses all of the various aspects of the genre. Further, in Sunni Islam, the *tafsīr* literature emphasizing tradition "is considered the most authoritative form of *tafsīr* because it is based on one of the most important sources of religious authority: the Prophet and his companions who were able to elaborate on the meaning of the Qur'an based on the Prophet's instructions (*ḥadīth*)."[33] The Shiʿa, on the other hand, tend to focus in their *tafsīr* on the "unclear" or "ambiguous" (*mutashābihāt*) verses mentioned in the much discussed passage at Qur'an 3:7, which by some accounts, removed discovery of the meanings of these verses from all except God and "those who are firmly grounded in knowledge." In the classical Shiʿi view, the Imams, descended from ʿAlī ibn Abī Ṭālib, are the only ones who possessed that knowledge.

These tensions also tended to be mirrored in the great tenth-century theological dispute I referred to earlier, having its genesis in the celebrated quarrel between the Ashʿarite and Muʿtazilite theologians. We know that the Ashʿarite approach to the text eventually triumphed among the Sunnis. This triumph is reflected in expression of the Sunni *tafsīr* and is particularly evident in the way that Abdullah Saeed describes it:

> Key characteristics of Sunni *tafsīr* are emphasis on literal interpretation of the Qur'an whenever possible, strongly justified by linguistic evidence; reliance on tradition (*ḥadīth/athar*) in explaining the text; use of reason (*ra'y*) within limits; rejection of the idea of esoteric meanings as unjustified speculation; respect for the companions of the Prophet collectively as the most important source of religious authority after the Prophet; acceptance of a set of theological positions on God's attributes, eschatology, prophecy and revelation, the definition of a believer (*mu'min*), and sources of authority in law; and rejection of positions held by rationalist theologians known as Muʿtazilah.[34]

The Shiʿa are without doubt then the inheritors of the Muʿtazilite "rationalist" position. Yet, in spite of its supposed rationalism, contemporary Shiʿism, like Sunnism, is also plagued with the ossification that comes with rigid sectarian approaches to textual interpretation. There are now a number of Shiʿi sects, each professing a somewhat different approach to interpretation, and each claiming to represent the true guidance, both as against the other Shiʿi sects and as against the sectarian views of Sunni Islam. Lois and Isma'il R. al Faruqi, in commenting on this stifling sectarianism, made the following observation:

> Rational exegesis is, above all, critical and open. It accepts evidence wherever it may come from and wherever it may lead. It never prejudges. It cannot therefore have any loyalty to any school, except to the anonymous school of reason and truth. The value of [the exegetical works of the Muʿtazilah, the Shiʿa, the Sufis, and the modernists] lies therefore not in their consistent presentation or defense of their sectarian views but in their demonstration of the wealth of facets

of meaning which the verses of the Qur'an often carry, those which escape ordinary observation.[35]

It is important to note that each of the approaches to interpretation of the Qur'an that I have described, whether esoteric or exoteric, "traditionalist" or "rationalist," are all "traditional" in the classical hermeneutical sense. Each of these spheres has taken on the dogmatic and rigid trappings of orthodoxy. They are no longer concerned with the "what" of the enterprise but rather only with the "how." The Faruqi observation thus hints at another approach. It is the same approach championed by Ibn Rushd and by the new Qur'anic hermeneutic that I will describe momentarily. This new approach seeks to separate the domain of truth from the prison of methodology in the same way that Gadamer argues that the hidebound nature of method (relying on an overstimulated historical consciousness and a slavish devotion to tradition) often obscures the true meaning of texts and other forms of human experience and cognition.[36] This new Qur'anic hermeneutic, perhaps influenced by Gadamerian approaches to interpretation, does not reject historical consciousness as a source of understanding but instead seeks a new relationship with history and tradition, a relationship that is critical and much more self-conscious. The new hermeneutic involves the interpreter in the enterprise. In that way the understanding of the text can be made more relevant to the interpreter's contemporary circumstances. There is no doubt that the meaning of the Qur'an, as expressed in its inimitable language, is timeless and transcendent. The way in which the interpreter discovers that meaning however, is not, and can never be, timeless and transcendent. The new hermeneutic recognizes this fact and challenges the interpreter to be critical about herself and her circumstances in translating the meaning into practical and spiritual guides for action.

Perhaps the best example of the utility of this new hermeneutic is in the example of slavery. The Qur'an, like the other Abrahamic revelations before it, accepted slavery as a juridical and socio-economic fact of life and, viewing the text literally, it only sought to ameliorate the harshness of slavery and to exhort the believers to manumit their slaves as an act of piety or to expiate sin, crime, or some other moral transgression. There is no warrant to conclude, given this textual analysis, that the Qur'an sought the complete and unequivocal abolition of all chattel slavery. Yet, we now know that chattel slavery, at least in its classical medieval and early modern manifestations, has in fact been abolished by all nation-states, including those nation-states that purport to govern their populations in accordance with the Shari'a. What, then, is the believer to make of the verses in the Qur'an that appear to permit slavery? The traditional *tafsīr*, both Sunni and Shi'i, does not provide satisfactory answers. Some have argued that these verses ought to be ignored and considered to be "obsolete" or "anachronisms."[37] The modernists offered arguments intimating that the Qur'an contemplated, through its ameliorative provisions, the eventual disappearance of slavery and it is just an accident of history and the unfortunate result of greed and avarice that slavery persisted for some thirteen hundred years after the revelation.[38] While the modernist argument is somewhat comforting, it does not satisfactorily confront the textualist position which would, given the use of the traditional interpretive tools available to the interpreter, lead one to the conclusion that slavery might be revived under an Islamic regime. This position is untenable and everyone, even the textualist, knows that. Why do we conclude that it is untenable? It is because we must read the revelation, in whatever language it is presented in, with a critical understanding of our current history, including the post-Enlightenment history that tends to impact how we read texts today. The interpretation of the text must take into account the circumstances, foreknowledge, and perspective of the interpreter. An African-American descendant of slaves may very well bring a different perspective to the reading of the text than one who has no experience or understanding of the events that make up the aftermath of the history of chattel slavery, in the West or in the Islamic world. The same arguments might also be made by women who must interpret the text in the light of their current circumstances. This is what is meant by a "living" Qur'an.

The traditional discourse generating the *tafsīr* and *ta'wīl* literature found in libraries and book stores in the Arab world, whether Sunni or Shiʿi, tends to suffer from a lack of exposure to these new ways of thinking about the Qur'anic hermeneutic enterprise. This is actually quite understandable since the literature on the interpretation of the Qur'an tends to cluster itself either in Western European languages (including English), Arabic, or in the Iranian/South Asian languages of Farsi and Urdu. One rarely finds *tafsīr* or *ta'wīl* literature that is accessible in all three language groups.[39] The writers in each language group are rarely, if ever, in discourse with those in the other groups. Much of the *tafsīr* literature in Arabic, even the more recent, remains untranslated.[40]

This is unfortunate because in the West and the Far East a new hermeneutic approach to the Qur'an is increasingly capturing the attention of scholars and students. This new approach builds on the interpretive work of the early modernists but it seems to be striking out in a different direction. There are a number of widely cited examples of this new approach. One of the best known examples can be found in the writing of the Pakistani scholar Fazlur Rahman. Rahman's life is a paradigm illustrating the development of the new hermeneutic and the role of Western universities in its promotion. After obtaining his Bachelor's and Master's degrees in Arabic language from Punjab University in Lahore, Rahman took his Ph.D. from Oxford, writing his dissertation on Ibn Sīnā's philosophy.[41] He taught Islamic philosophy for eight years in the

U.K. and, after moving to Canada, he taught at McGill University for another three years.[42] He then returned to Pakistan, where he directed the Islamic Research Institute.[43] He left the institute in 1968 to take up the position of Professor of Islamic Thought at the University of Chicago.[44] He taught there for twenty years, until his death in 1988, training legions of students who later took up academic positions around the world, particularly in Turkey and Indonesia.[45] Rahman's impact on Islamic studies and scholarship on the Qur'an is in many ways incalculable. In addition to the training of students, he published a number of groundbreaking works that have resonated with intellectuals in a variety of academic settings. His books, including *Major Themes of the Qur'an* (1980), *Islamic Methodology in History* (1965), and *Islam and Modernity: Transformation of an Intellectual Tradition* (1982) posit an approach to the Qur'an that seeks to integrate history and tradition with a critical and sound understanding of the purposes of the revelation. He advocated a cautious use of *ḥadīth* in the interpretive process and, while he was extremely critical of Gadamer's "subjectivist" approach to texts, he accepted the premise, suggested by Ibn Rushd before him, of a dynamic relationship between the text and the interpreter. He agreed that a literalist approach to the text will obscure this relationship, retarding the interpreter's ability to discover the truth. In the best of both the philosophical and theological traditions of Islam, he called for a "double movement" from the interpreter's present situation back to the time of the revelation and then forward again, with a mind toward the socio-historical changes that have occurred since the time of the revelation.[46] He is thus mindful of the "effective history," to use Gadamer's phrase, given to us by the examples of Augustine, Aquinas, and Luther and he challenges students of Islam to craft a similar "effective history" of al-Ashʿarī, al-Ghazālī, and Ibn Taymiyya.[47] He builds on the notion of "effective history" to argue that the true hermeneutic in Islam is one that is self-aware and conscious of its role in Islamic history.

Fazlur Rahman's work was just the beginning of the new trend in Qur'anic hermeneutics. A number of his students as well as scholars influenced by him, including Nurcholish Majid (Indonesia), Amina Wadud (United States), and Alparslan Açıkgenç (Turkey), have continued to build on his ideas.[48] Majid (d. 2006) was the director of Universitas Paramedina in Indonesia. Wadud is Associate Professor of Islamic Studies at Virginia Commonwealth University. Açıkgenç is the Dean of the Faculty of Arts and Sciences at Fatih University in Istanbul. There are others in the Western and Far Eastern academies who are also advancing new approaches toward the Qur'an. Perhaps the most prominent is Muhammad Arkoun, Emeritus Professor at the Sorbonne and sometime Professor of Islamic Law at New York University School of Law. Arkoun's works, including *Lectures du Coran* (2nd ed., 1991), *Critique de la raison islamique* (1984), *L'Islam, morale et politique* (1986, 1992), *Rethinking Islam: Common Questions, Uncommon Answers* (1994), and *L'Islam: Approche critique* (1997), argue for a rereading of the Qur'an in radical and imaginative ways.[49] His position is also reminiscent of the hermeneutics of Ibn Rushd. In the United States, at least seven other university scholars deserve mention. Sherman A. Jackson, Professor of Arabic and Islamic Studies at the University of Michigan, while probably a traditionalist in his basic orientation, has been doing pioneering work in exploring the relationship between traditional Islamic theological teachings and the problems of identity that Muslim minorities face in the United States.[50] He is also in great demand as a speaker at Middle Eastern and Far Eastern university conferences and symposia. Khalid Abou El Fadl, Professor of Law and the Omar and Azmeralda Alfi Distinguished Fellow in Islamic Law at UCLA in California, while similarly traditionally trained, advocates an unabashedly rationalist and critical approach to the Qur'an in much of his work.[51] Significant contributions are also being advanced by Bernard Weiss, Professor of Languages and Literature at the University of Utah, Azizah al-Hibri, Professor of Law at the University of Richmond, Abdullahi Ahmed An-Na'im, Professor of Law at Emory University in Atlanta, and Asma Barlas, Professor at Ithaca College in New York and author of the groundbreaking book, *'Believing Women' in Islam: Unreading Patriarchical Interpretations of the Qur'an* (2002). Although these scholars, with the exception of Barlas, do not concentrate exclusively in their work on interpretation of the Qur'an, each contributes a rare and razor-sharp scholarship that enriches the current discourse on the Qur'an.

There are many other scholars in the prestigious group I have identified above, too numerous to mention here. The Islamic Legal Studies Program at Harvard Law School has been a beacon in attracting many of these scholars to its program of symposia and conferences, visiting fellowships, and occasional visiting professorships. This work and its great progress in advancing the knowledge of Islam and Islamic law would not have been possible without the steadfast and selfless leadership of Frank Vogel, to whom this volume is dedicated. I suggest that other universities in the West and the Far East should begin to emulate the Islamic Legal Studies Program at Harvard. Their work would not involve just hosting conferences and symposia, as many universities do on an occasional and ad hoc basis, but rather to form a consortium that would have as its aim three primary purposes: (1) to undertake the translation of the traditional Islamic *tafsīr* and *ta'wīl* literature on the Qur'an in order that this literature would be more readily accessible to both scholars and ordinary believers in the West; (2) to sponsor a series of conferences, in the Arab world and in the West and Far East, on the interpretation of the Qur'an and its relevance to modern day life in all of those settings. The first, and perhaps the second of these conferences would be held at major universities in the Arab world (such as Cairo University in Egypt) and strive to bring the major traditional interpreters of the Qurʾan to the same table as those who are the proponents of the new hermeneutic, in an effort to see whether a new "Great Synthesis" might be forged. Programs like the Islamic Legal Studies Program at Harvard, the Department of Near Eastern Studies at Princeton, and the Islamic Studies program at Michigan, together with the Shariʿa departments at Cairo University, Al Azhar University, and the International Islamic University Malaysia, acting through the consortium, would play a major role in organizing and hosting the conference; and (3) to initiate and operate a series of faculty (and perhaps student) exchanges between the consortium's university members, particularly in the area of Qurʾanic hermeneutics. These exchanges would grow out of the conferences and enable the universities involved to continue to expand the fund of knowledge on the Qurʾan.

The madrasa was the primary educational institution in the classical Islamic world.[52] Many scholars suggest that the medieval Islamic madrasas in Cairo, Damascus, and Baghdad, deriving their authority and sustenance from charitable deeds of religious trust endowing them with significant wealth and prestige, were the prototypes for the twelfth- and thirteenth-century establishment of the great European universities.[53] Much of the knowledge forming the intellectual base for the scientific investigation that eventually became the hallmark of the Oxford, Cambridge, Sorbonne, Bologna, and Heidelberg universities was transmitted to Europe through the Arab scholars of Spain.[54] These scholars, in turn, built their proofs, methods, and conceptions of theological, legal, and epistemological reality from the doctrines taught and foundations laid down in the classical madrasas. Ibn Rushd's contribution to this process is well known. Unfortunately, he was scorned in the lands that ultimately could have benefited the most from his erudition. It appears to me that Western and Far Eastern universities can return the great favor bestowed on them by the classical madrasas by again engaging Islamic scholars and Middle Eastern universities on an ambitious scale. In spite of the difficulties we are now experiencing as a result of the enmity and distrust bred by the Iraq war and the continued conflict between the State of Israel and its Arab and Muslim neighbors, there is a great hunger for knowledge in the Muslim world, knowledge that would be instrumental in solving problems and bringing comfort to people in their daily lives. Knowledge of the Qurʾan and its messages is one of the best ways to satisfy this hunger.

> Islam identified itself with knowledge. It made knowledge its condition as well as its goal. It equated the pursuit of knowledge with *ʿibādah* (worship) and poured its most lavish praise on those who committed themselves to its cultivation, making them the saints and friends of God, and raising their ink above the blood of martyrs in value.[55]

The interpreters of the Qur'an, whether traditional in the broad sense that I have used the term here, or those advocating new and innovative approaches toward the enterprise, some of whom I have also identified, are certainly deserving of the appellation "friends of God." The universities, in the Middle East, and in the West and Far East, have a great opportunity to bring together many of the important "friends of God" for the benefit of the Islamic world and all of humankind.

NOTES

* Thanks to Michael P. Ambrosio for his insightful comments and suggestions. Thanks also to Abed Awad for reading and commenting on an earlier draft. All errors are mine.

[1] Oliver Leaman, *Averroes and his Philosophy* (Oxford: Clarendon Press, rev. ed. 1998), 146. The translation is taken by Leaman from Averroes, *On the Harmony of Religion and Philosophy*, trans. G. Hourani (Luzac: London, 1961; repr. 1967, 1976).

[2] Many inquirers, particularly non-Muslims, are increasingly concerned with achieving an accurate understanding of the differences between the Sunni and Shi'i approaches to Islam. Such understandings are made more urgent by the Sunni-Shi'i violence that is currently lacerating Iraq in the aftermath of the fall of the government of Saddam Hussein and the failure of the American invasion. This violence has taken on a tribal character that tends to obscure the theological, jurisprudential, and political differences between the two factions. The question is difficult but, as I expect to show here, the perceived differences, while important, become less relevant if one takes a critical, universalist, and "integrative" view of Islamic scholarship, particularly scholarship on interpretation of the Qur'an.

[3] Wael B. Hallaq, *The Origins and Evolution of Islamic Law* (Cambridge: Cambridge University Press, 2005), 122–28.

[4] Andrew Rippin, "Tafsir," in *Encyclopedia of Religion*, ed. Lindsay Jones (Detroit: Macmillan Reference USA, 2005), 13:8954.

[5] John Marenbon, "Medieval Christian and Jewish Europe," in *History of Islamic Philosophy*, ed. Seyyid Hossein Nasr and Oliver Leaman (London: Routledge, 2001), 1004 (stating that Ibn Rushd's (Averroes') writings began to be used in the Faculty of Arts of the University of Paris in about 1220 C.E. and that from about 1250 C.E. onward Averroes' detailed commentaries proved "invaluable aids" to the masters in Oxford, Paris, and other European universities and that they continued to play this role through to the time of the Renaissance); see also Paul Kurtz, "Intellectual Freedom, Rationality, and Enlightenment: The Contributions of Averroes," in *Averroës and the Enlightenment: The First Humanist-Muslim Dialogue*, ed. Mourad Wahba and Mona Abousenna (Amherst: Prometheus Books, 1996), 29, and Ibrahim Y. Najjar, "Ibn Rushd's Theory of Rationality," *Alif: Journal of Comparative Poetics* 16 (1996), 192–93 (suggesting that Averroes' views on philosophy and religion, together with his interpretations of Aristotle, led to Thomism, scholasticism, and eventually to Cartesianism, "the cornerstone of Modern Western Philosophy"). For a well-articulated view asserting there is no relationship between Ibn Rushd's ideas and the Enlightenment, see Charles Butterworth, "Averroes, Precursor of the Enlightenment?" *Alif: Journal of Comparative Poetics* 16 (1996), 6.

[6] Oliver Leaman, *Averroes and his Philosophy*, 187–88. See also Mona Abousenna, "Ibn Rushd, Founder of Hermeneutics," in *Averroës and the Enlightenment*, 105.

[7] R. Arnaldez, "Ibn Rushd," in EI^2, 3:912.

[8] Catherine Wilson, "Modern Western Philosophy," in *History of Islamic Philosophy*, 1016.

[9] R. Arnaldez, "Ibn Rushd," in EI^2, 3:919.

[10] The quote is from Paul Kurtz, "Free Inquiry and Islamic Philosophy: The Significance of George Hourani," in *Averroës and the Enlightenment*, 235.

[11] See, e.g., *Modern Muslim Intellectuals and the Qur'an*, ed. Suha Taji-Farouki (Oxford: Oxford University Press, 2004) (collecting essays on the leading post-World War II interpreters of the Qur'an).

[12] The writings of Mohammed Hashim Kamali, although sometimes still shackled to traditional hermeneutical doctrine and often straining to harmonize modern jurisprudential conceptions with traditional Islamic approaches, are nonetheless an important pillar in this new scholarship. See, e.g., Mohammed Hashim Kamali, *Freedom of Expression in Islam* (Cambridge: Islamic Texts Society, 1997); Mohammed Hashim Kamali, *The Dignity of Man: An Islamic Perspective* (Cambridge: Islamic Texts Society, 2002); Mohammed Hashim Kamali, *Freedom, Equality, and Justice in Islam* (Cambridge: Islamic Texts Society, 2002). A number of other scholars, working both within a jurisprudential framework and within other disciplines, have made similarly important contributions to this new approach. See, e.g., Tariq Ramadan, *Les musulmans dans la laïcité: responsabilités et droits des musulmans dans les sociétés occidentales* (Lyon: Tawhid, 1998); Tariq Ramadan, *To Be a European Muslim: A Study of Islamic Sources in the European Context* (Leicester: Islamic Foundation, 1999); Tariq Ramadan (ed.), *Aux sources du renouveau musulman: d'al-Afghānī à Ḥassan al-Bannā, un siècle de réformisme islamique* (Paris: Bayard Éditions, 1999); Tariq Ramadan, *De l'islam* (Lyon: Tawhid, 2002); Tariq Ramadan, *Jihād, violence, guerre et paix en islam* (Lyon: Tawhid, 2002); Tariq Ramadan, *Western Muslims and the Future of Islam* (Oxford: Oxford University Press, 2004); Tariq Ramadan, *Arabes et musulmans face à la mondialisation: le défi du pluralisme* (Lyon: Tawhid, 2004); Mohammed Arkoun, *Essais sur la pensée islamique* (Paris: G.-P. Maisonneuve et Larose, 1973); Mohammed Arkoun, *Lectures du Coran* (Paris: G.-P. Maisonneuve et Larose, 1982); Mohammed Arkoun, *L'Islam, morale et politique* (Paris: Desclée de Brouwer, 1986); Mohammed Arkoun, *Rethinking Islam: Common Questions, Uncommon Answers*, trans. and ed. Robert D. Lee (Boulder: Westview Press, 1994); Mohammed Arkoun, *Humanisme et islam: combats et propositions* (Paris: Vrin, 2005); Sherman A. Jackson, *Islam and the Blackamerican: Looking Toward the Third Resurrection* (Oxford: Oxford University Press, 2005); Bernard G. Weiss, *The Spirit of Islamic Law* (Athens: University of Georgia Press, 1998); Khaled Abou El Fadl, *Speaking in God's Name: Islamic law, Authority and Women* (Oxford: Oneworld, 2001); Khaled Abou El Fadl, *Conference of the Books: The Search for Beauty in Islam* (Lanham, MD: University Press of America, 2001); Khaled Abou El Fadl, "The Place of Tolerance in Islam," in *Boston Review* (April/May 2003); Khaled Abou El Fadl, *Islam and the Challenge of Democracy*, ed. Joshua Cohen and Deborah Chasman (Princeton: Princeton University Press, 2004); Asma Barlas, *'Believing Women' in Islam. Unreading Patriarchal Interpretations of the Qur'an* (Austin: University of Texas Press, 2002); Abdullah Saeed, *Interpreting the Qur'an: Towards a Contemporary Approach* (London: Routledge, 2006).

[13] The most recent example is the 2005 appointment of the philosopher Tariq Ramadan as research fellow in St. Antony's College of Oxford University. See "Islamic Scholar Gets Oxford Job," available at http://news.bbc.co.uk/1/hi/egnland/oxfordshire/4190804.stm (last visited January 12, 2007). Khalid Abou El Fadl, a classically trained jurist, has held a chair in Islamic law at the University of California at Los Angeles (UCLA) since 2003.

[14] For example, The Oxford Centre for Islamic Studies, established in 1985 at Oxford University, publishes the well-respected *Journal of Islamic Studies*, offers a variety of visiting fellowships for scholars of Islam, and sponsors at least three research projects, including a project seeking the development of an atlas of Muslim social and intellectual history, a Bodleian Library manuscript project, and a study of Muslims in Europe. The University of Melbourne's Asia Institute (Faculty of Arts) and its Faculty of Law jointly sponsor a Centre for the Study of Contemporary Islam which is home for several faculty with significant expertise in contemporary Islamic studies, including interpretation of the Qur'an. McGill University's Institute of Islamic Studies, founded in 1952, boasts a full-time faculty of fourteen with a wide range of specialties, including Islamic law and Qur'anic studies. The International Islamic University Malaysia operates a very ambitious Institute of Islamic Thought and Civilization (ISTAC) in Kuala Lampur. It hosts a faculty of thirteen in a wide range of specialties. It recently sponsored a conference on the thought and work of Ibn Khaldūn. The University of Bergen in Norway sponsors a Centre for Middle Eastern and Islamic Studies that similarly hosts several faculty members with significant expertise and its visiting scholars program has attracted a number of important scholars to Norway for research and collaboration. American universities, including American law schools, have begun to follow suit. Four such important programs are located at New York University, Princeton University, the University of Michigan, and UCLA. The Islamic Legal Studies Program at Harvard Law School has been in the forefront in American law schools in developing scholarly resources and a research base in Islamic law. It currently sponsors several visiting fellowships and hosts a variety of symposia and conferences. In recent years it has sponsored conferences and symposia on such topics as Islamic trusts and violence. It also has a close relationship with other Harvard centers and programs on Islam, including the Center for Middle Eastern Studies, the Program on Islam in the West, and the Arabic and Islamic Studies Program of the Department of Near Eastern Languages and Civilizations. Harvard Law School was one of the first American universities to offer Islamic law in its curriculum and now over 60 other American law schools offer courses on Islamic law. See John Makdisi, "A Survey of AALS Law Schools Teaching Islamic Law," *J. Legal Educ.* 55 (2005), 583.

[15] The Oxford English Dictionary defines "exegesis" as an "explanation, exposition (of a sentence, word, etc.); esp. the interpretation of Scripture or a Scriptural passage" or "an explanatory note, a gloss" or "[a]n expository discourse." "Exegesis" in *The Compact Edition of the Oxford English Dictionary* (1971). The word is derived from a similar word having a similar meaning in the Greek language. Literally, it meant to "lead out" or "draw out" something from something else. In Greek culture and folklore the exegete was a character who inhabited the temple and explained divine events to visitors. Most of the other Western European languages use a similar word derived from the Greek "exegesis." German is

apparently the exception. Although *Exegese* is used, the word "exegesis" translates into German as *Auslegung*, a word derived from the German verb *auslegen* which also means "to lay out." Thus, *Auslegung* carries substantially the same meaning in the German language as "exegesis" does in the other Western European languages.

[16] Khalid Abou El Fadl, *Speaking in God's Name*, 118.

[17] Ibid., citing Duncan S. Ferguson, *Biblical Hermeneutics: An Introduction* (Atlanta: John Knox Press, 1986).

[18] Hans-Georg Gadamer, *Truth and Method*, 2nd rev. ed., trans. rev. Joel Weinsheimer and Donald G. Marshall (London: Continuum, 2004), 164.

[19] Ibid., 164–65.

[20] Ibid., 165.

[21] See, e.g., William Eskridge, "Gadamer/Statutory Interpretation," *Columbia Law Rev.* 90 (1990), 609 (applying a Gadmerian approach to problems of statutory interpretation); Donald G. Marshall, "Truth, Tradition, and Understanding," *Diacritics* 7/4 (Winter 1977), 70–7 (discussing Gadamer's impact on the philosophical foundations of contemporary interpretive methods); *Hermeneutik und Ideologiekritik* (Frankfurt: Suhrkamp, 1971) (reprinting particulars of the famous debate between Jürgen Habermas and Gadamer and collecting essays on the debate by Apel, Bormann, Bubner, and Giegel); Paul Ricoeur, "Ethics and Culture: Gadamer and Habermas in Dialogue," *Philosophy Today* (Summer 1973); William Schweiker, "Sacrifice, Interpretation and the Sacred: The Import of Gadamer and Girard for Religious Studies," *Journal of the American Academy of Religion* 55/4 (Winter 1987), 791 (assessing Gadamer's impact on the study of religion); Steven D. Kepnes, "Buber as Hermeneut: Relations to Dilthey and Gadamer," *Harvard Theological Review* 81/2 (April 1988), 193 (Gadamer's hermeneutics and Martin Buber).

[22] Alan Chan, "Philosophical Hermeneutics and the Analects: The Paradigm of 'Tradition'," *Philosophy East and West* 34/4 (October 1984), 421 n. 4 (observing that the *Shorter Oxford Dictionary* defines hermeneutics as "the art or science of interpretation, esp. of scripture" and that it is commonly distinguished from exegesis, which is "practical exposition" and further observing that the term "hermeneutics" in theological discourse is frequently spelled as "hermeneutic," without the final "s" and describes the "how" of interpretation and not the "what" of interpretation.) Gadamer made it clear that he was concerned with the "what" and not the "how." Ibid. (citing Gadamer's letter to the Italian legal historian Emilio Betti, found in *Truth and Method*, at Supplement I, p. 512).

[23] Andrew Rippin points out that historically the enterprise of interpretation was described in at least four ways in Arabic. Rippin, "Tafsir," 13:8950. In addition to the words *ta'wīl* and *tafsīr*, which eventually dominated the terminology, works interpreting texts were also described as *ma'ānī*, literally "meanings," or *sharḥ* "commentary."

[24] Mohammed Hashim Kamali, *Principles of Islamic Jurisprudence*, 3rd rev. and enl. ed. (Cambridge: Islamic Texts Society, 2003), 119. The word is derived from the Arabic root word *awwal*, which connotes the "first," "foremost," "most important," or "principal," and the secondary root word *awwaliyya*, which means, inter alia, "fundamental truth," "axiom," "constituent," or "essential component." Rippin asserts the word is "literally related to the notion of 'returning to the beginning'...." Rippin, "Tafsir," 13:8950. Poonawala agrees with this characterization.

See I. Poonawala, "Ta'wīl," in *EI*[2] (describing the word as "literally related to the notion of 'returning to its origin or source'").

[25] See generally Rippin, "Tafsir." See also Andrew Rippin, "Tafsīr" in *EI*[2]. The word is a verbal noun derived from the verb *fassara* "to explain, expound, explicate, elucidate, interpret," or "comment [on]." Wehr, 4th ed., 835. A "commentary" on the Qur'an is therefore usually described as a *tafsīr*.

[26] See Rippin, "Tafsir" in *Encyclopedia of Religion*, and Rippin, "Tafsīr" in *EI*[2].

[27] Abdullah Saeed, "Qur'an: Tradition of Scholarship and Interpretation," in *Encyclopedia of Religion*, 11:7566.

[28] Ira M. Lapidus, *A History of Islamic Societies* (Cambridge: Cambridge University Press, 1988), 119.

[29] G. Marshall Hodgson, *The Venture of Islam: Conscience and History in a World Civilization* (Chicago: University of Chicago Press, 1974), 1:373.

[30] See Bernard G. Weiss, *The Spirit of Islamic Law*, 39–40 (asserting that Shi'i juristic thought on Qur'anic interpretation is similarly bound up in textualism just as is Sunni juristic thought).

[31] See I. Poonawala, "Ta'wīl," in *EI*[2], 10:391.

[32] Rippin, "Tafsīr" in *EI*[2], 10:84.

[33] Abdullah Saeed, "Qur'an: Tradition of Scholarship and Interpretation," 11:7564.

[34] Ibid., 7565.

[35] Isma'il R. al Faruqi and Lois Lamya al Faruqi, *The Cultural Atlas of Islam* (New York: Macmillan, 1986), 246.

[36] Hans-Georg Gadamer, *Truth and Method*, xxiv.

[37] Nuh Ha Mim Keller's treatment of slavery in his translation of Aḥmad b. al-Naqīb's *Reliance of the Traveller* (Evanston: Sunna Books, 1991), a Shafi'i *fiqh* manual, is a good example of this approach.

[38] Rashīd Riḍā asserted this position in his early twentieth-century book on the purposes of the Qur'an. See Rashīd Riḍā, *The Muhammadan Revelation*, trans. Yusuf DeLorenzo (Alexandria, VA: Al-Saadawi Publications, 1996), 117. In his view, the abolition of slavery was one of the original purposes of the Qur'anic revelation.

[39] There are some notable exceptions. Much of Sayyid Quṭb's thirty-volume commentary, *Fī ẓilāl al-Qur'ān* (In the Shade of the Qur'an), has been translated into English, Farsi, Urdu, and other languages. See, e.g., Sayyid Quṭb, *In the Shade of the Qur'ān (= Fī ẓilāl al-Qur'ān)*, trans. and ed. M. A. Salahi and A. A. Shamis (Leicester: Islamic Foundation, 1999–). Similarly, Mawdūdī's commentary has also been translated into many languages. See, e.g., Abul A'lā Maudūdī, *The Meaning of the Qur'ān* (Lahore: Islamic Publications, 1967), 11 vols. There are now two English translations of the first volume of Muḥammad Bāqir al-Ṣadr's seminal work on Islamic jurisprudence. Although it is not a *tafsīr* in the classical sense, its publication offers an important window in English on the Shi'i approaches to interpretation of the Qur'an. See the translations by Roy Parviz Mottahedeh (Oxford: Oneworld, 2003) and by Arif Abdul Hussain (London: ICIS Press, 2003).

[40] An informal survey of bibliographical material in major libraries in the United States reveals that the Qur'anic commentaries of many important authors, including those of Ibn al-'Arabī, al-Ḥallāj, Fakhr al-Dīn al-Rāzī, al-Bayḍāwī, al-Ṭūsī, Ibn Taymiyya, al-Suyūṭī, Muḥammad 'Abduh, al-Shawkānī, Ibn Qayyim al Jawziyya, al-Juwaynī, al-Māturīdī, and Muḥammad Mutawallī al-Sha'rāwī all

remain untranslated into any Western European language. The Āl al-Bayt Institute for Islamic Thought, based in Amman, Jordan, has undertaken to translate a number of Qur'anic commentaries into English but progress has been very slow. It has posted English translations of the *tafsīr* of Ibn 'Abbās and the *Tafsīr al-Jalālayn* (The Tafsīr of "the two Jalāls," Jalāl al-Dīn al-Maḥallī and Jalāl al-Dīn al-Suyūṭī). See http://www.altafsir.com (last visited Sept. 17, 2007).

[41] Abdullah Saeed, "Fazlur Rahman: A Framework for Interpreting the Ethico-Legal Content of the Qur'an," in *Modern Muslim Intellectuals and the Qur'an*, 37 (citing Fazlur Rahman, *Revival and Reform in Islam: A Study of Islamic Fundamentalism*, ed. Ebrahim Moosa [Oxford: Oneworld, 2000], 1–2).

[42] Abdullah Saeed, "Fazlur Rahman: A Framework for Interpreting the Ethico-Legal Content of the Qur'an," 37–8.

[43] Ibid., 38.

[44] Ibid., 39.

[45] Ibid.

[46] Fazlur Rahman, *Islam and Modernity: Transformation of an Intellectual Tradition* (Chicago: University of Chicago Press, 1982), 5–11.

[47] Ibid., 10.

[48] See, e.g., Anthony H. Johns and Abdullah Saeed, "Nurcholish Madjid and the Interpretation of the Qur'an: Religious Pluralism and Tolerance," in *Modern Muslim Intellectuals and the Qur'an*, 67; Asma Barlas, "Amina Wadud's Hermeneutics of the Qur'an: Women Rereading Sacred Texts," in ibid., 97; Alparslan Açıkgenç, "Ibn Rushd, Kant, and Transcendent Rationality: A Critical Synthesis," *Alif: Journal of Comparative Poetics* 16 (1996), 164.

[49] For a concise summary, see Ursala Gunther, "Mohammed Arkoun: Towards a Radical Rethinking of Islamic Thought," in *Modern Muslim Intellectuals and the Qur'an*, 125.

[50] See, e.g., Sherman A. Jackson, *Islam and the Blackamerican: Looking Toward the Third Ressurection*.

[51] See, e.g., Khalid Abou El Fadl's *Speaking in God's Name: Islamic Law, Authority and Women* and "The Place of Tolerance in Islam"; and idem, *And God Knows the Soldiers: The Authoritative and the Authoritarian in Islamic Discourses* (Lanham, Md: University Press of America, 2001).

[52] Said Amir Arjomand, "The Law, Agency, and Policy in Medieval Islamic Society: Development of the Institutions of Learning from the Tenth to the Fifteenth Century," *Comparative Studies in Society and History* 41/2 (April 1999), 263; see also Syed Ali Ashraf, "Universities," in *The Oxford Encyclopedia of the Modern Islamic World*, 4:284.

[53] George Makdisi, *The Rise of Colleges: Institutions of Higher Learning in Islam and the West* (Edinburgh: Edinburgh University Press, 1981), 224–30; George Makdisi, *The Rise of Humanism in Classical Islam and the Christian West: With Special Reference to Scholasticism* (Edinburgh: Edinburgh University Press, 1990), 311–17, both cited in Arjomand, "Law, Agency, and Policy," 263; see also Charles M. Stanton, *Higher Learning in Islam: The Classical Period, A.D. 700 to 1300* (Savage, Md: Rowman and Littlefield, 1990).

[54] Ashraf, "Universities," in *The Oxford Encyclopedia of the Modern Islamic World*, 4:284.

[55] Isma'il R. and Lois L. al Faruqi, *The Cultural Atlas of Islam*, 230.

18

LAW AND HISTORIOGRAPHY
Legal Typology of Lands and the Arab Conquests*

Nimrod Hurvitz

History in Law

In the last three decades modern scholars of Islamic law have placed a strong emphasis on the notion that legal doctrine is in a state of constant flux and development. The premium placed on the historical development of doctrine has generated new ways of thinking about law and its place in Islamic societies.[1] One of them concentrated on the manner that historical circumstances shaped the law. This methodology has been used by historians of Islamic law throughout the twentieth century, but recent decades have witnessed the strengthening of this trend. Another angle of investigation was the study of "law in practice."[2] Focusing on legal institutions, such as courts of law, the police, or the public morals office (*ḥisba*), it asked how laws and regulations were implemented in real life situations.

There is a third perspective from which we can approach the relationship between history and legal texts. History, according to this way of thinking, is not merely the actual events and forces that shape society and its laws, but also the way in which events have been documented in texts. In other words it is historiography, the stories and anecdotes that have been recorded in books of history or integrated into other genres. In Islamic legal doctrine there were numerous instances in which historical materials were introduced into legal texts (as in literature about the Prophet, and in administrative and public law), whether explicitly or implicitly.[3] This study will focus on the way historiography was inserted into legal texts and the repercussions of this phenomenon.

The inquiry into the relationship between law and historiography follows a trajectory of research that was set out by Robert Cover in his renowned article "Nomos and Narrative."[4] The concept of "nomos" ("a normative universe") speaks of the interconnectedness of legal concepts and a wider moral outlook that is expressed in several ways, among them narratives about the past.[5] Cover writes: "Once understood in the context of the narratives that give it meaning, law becomes not merely a system of rules to be observed, but a world in which we live."[6] These narratives, which may be either fiction or the documentation of events, are laden with values that assign meaning to legal texts. In setting legal texts within "the context of narratives" and inquiring how law is influenced by them, Cover places legal doctrine within an intellectual context. However, since historiography is an expression of the thoughts and ideas about past social events, the historiographic-legal amalgam creates an interesting interplay between social reality and legal writing.

This study will inquire how historiography interacts with the law when it is written into an Islamic legal text. Before we deal with this issue directly, we need to note how Islamic legal texts and doctrine evolve. Since these texts are composed of several layers of writings and interpretations and often provoke debates, the historiographic materials that are included in them undergo a similar treatment. However, the explication of an event that appears in a legal text differs from the interpretation of other parts of that text. Jurists who inquire about the meaning and implications of historical data do not treat it in the same way as they treat statements that are perceived as divine or logical inferences. Rather, they begin by asking of it what a positivist historian asks of his materials: Did it really happen? Only after clarifying the veracity of an event (which often they fail to do), will they move on to its legal implications.

Historiography was grafted onto Islamic legal discourse in two ways. The first and most influential are the Prophetic traditions (*ḥadīth*)—accounts of what the Prophet said or did. Yet in the eyes of a Muslim believer, these are not mere descriptions of human conduct. Rather, these are acts performed by a Prophet that were guided by God and are therefore the manifestation of divine will. As a consequence, they are also binding legal precedents. However, even though the stories are assumed to describe acts of divine origin, story-telling is an earthly, human activity which often led to attempts at fabrication, or other deviations from the truth. As a reaction to the circulation of false prophetic traditions, Islamic scholars devised a method that enabled them to assess the soundness of each story. The corpus of Prophetic traditions that were deemed sound came to be the foundation of numerous fields of Islamic law.

Although Prophetic traditions were a crucial element in some areas of doctrine, they were barely present in other areas, such as administrative and public law. In these areas of the law jurists relied heavily on historical narratives. This was the second source from which jurists introduced historiography into legal discourse. In some cases references to history were explicit. In others, historical data were slipped in by way of summaries of past administrative and political patterns that were in tune with the moral and political vision of the writers. This essay will concentrate on one case study in which historical anecdotes were incorporated into legal texts: the classification of lands. The legal typology of lands shaped the Islamic discourse of tax and determined the amounts that could be levied as well as the rulers' ability to maneuver within the constraints of the law. The historical moment and events from which jurists drew the data that determined the legal status of the lands were the Arab conquests of the Near East which occurred during the first decades of Islam (early to mid-seventh century). The conceptual tools that they took from these events were the terms *ṣulḥ* ([a peace agreement resulting from] peaceful submission of the conquered, hereafter "peaceful submission") and *ʿanwa* (forcible conquest). At some point in time these terms were inserted into legal texts and became a basic premise from which the perceptions of land classification and taxation stemmed.

The first part of this essay will reveal the turbid nature of the terms and concepts of the Islamic doctrine of taxation, in which the concepts of *ʿanwa* and *ṣulḥ* were implanted. The second part will examine how these terms were applied to the lands of the Sawad—the heart of Iraq and one of the richest agricultural areas in the early Islamic empires. By tracing the jurists' references to *ṣulḥ* and *ʿanwa* in their discussions of the taxation of the Sawad, we will be able to detect the transmutations in the historical narratives and assess their legal implications. The third part will examine conflicting evaluations made by Islamic jurists about the use of history in two concrete cases and the measure by which they can assist in the process of legal reasoning. The conclusion will highlight some characteristics of the interaction between law and historiography.

The Tax System and Its Enigmas

Taxation and the legal classification of lands is an extremely complicated area of Islamic law whose labyrinthian details and opaque terminology have been pointed out by several modern historians.[7] Therefore, if we would like to understand how historical narratives merge with Islamic legal thinking in the area of taxation, we need to start with an examination of the inchoate state of the doctrine of taxation.

The medieval Islamic tax system was a mosaic of local practices. When the Arab conquerors took over vast areas of land, they often adopted the long-standing tax policies of the pre-Islamic empires. This has already been observed by Claude Cahen who described the Arab tax system as "...leaving to the indigenous authorities the task of raising the taxation according to their own traditions,.... Because of this continuity, the Islamic fiscal system varied from region to region...."[8] Thus, in the early stages of Arab control of Sassanian and Byzantine lands, the new rulers relied on the old local elites to gather the taxes and these officials tended to use the existing system. The following report is included in Yaḥyā ibn Ādam's (d. 203/818) *Kitāb al-Kharāj*: "But this our Sawad, we heard, was in the hands of the *Nabaṭ* who had been subjugated by the Persians to whom they paid property tax (*kharāj*). The Muslims, when they defeated the Persians, left Sawad and the Nabat and Dihqans who had not fought the Muslims, in the same position;...."[9] According to this description, *kharāj* was a form of taxation that was introduced by the Persians after they conquered the area from the *Nabaṭ*. The Muslims, according to this account, simply continued this administrative tradition. According to Dennett, the tax system in Syria was also the outcome of pre-existing, local traditions: "The tax administration of Syria, like that of the Sawad, can be understood only in terms of the events of the conquest and of the existing Byzantine fiscal machinery."[10]

A second factor that shaped tax policies was the dynamic in which booty was transformed into taxation. Initially, when the Arab warriors began their raids, their main purpose was to return home with as much plunder as possible.[11] Gradually, after a number of victories, their leaders decided to settle the areas they raided. As a result of this shift in outlook and policy, it was necessary to stop the looting and replace it with a tax system.[12] This step was taken by the caliphs and local rulers. One of the best known instances of such a change in course was ʿUmar b. al-Khaṭṭāb's (d. 23/644) decision regarding the Sawad. Once the Arab warriors won several victories most of the Sawad was deserted by the Persian ruling elite. It seems that this vacuum drew the Arabs in and they began to establish settlements and set up an administrative system. The warriors of the Arab army expected to be the main beneficiaries of the new political situation. After sending to Mecca the portion (a fifth) that was set aside for the rulers, these warriors asked that the land be divided among them.[13] In the beginning ʿUmar thought of going along with this arrangement, however, after some time he realized that it would not serve the interests of the Islamic community.[14] Instead of dividing the conquered areas among the warriors who fought for them, he decided to leave the land in the possession of the Islamic state.[15] At that point he imposed the *kharāj* on the local residents and used the income to advance the interests of the Islamic community. This alteration in the caliphal approach, from catering to the interests of the fighters to guarding the needs of the whole community, is the shift that led to putting in place a tax system. However, it should be kept in mind that the implementation of a tax system was fragmented since it was not always the caliphs who established the land tax, but their governors. As a result, different rates and assessments were implemented in the different regions.[16]

The most abstruse part of the Islamic tax system was its terminology. For example, when writing about different types of land and their revenues, Qudāma ibn Jaʿfar (d. 320/932) distinguished between the revenues of *fayʾ* and *kharāj*, specifying that *fayʾ* were lands that were conquered "by combat (*qitāl*)" whereas *kharāj* were lands that the Muslims came to control through peaceful submission (*ṣulḥ*).[17] Qudāma repeats this distinction in the following anecdote: "Yaḥyā b. Ādam said: I heard Sharīk say: *Kharāj* land is that which was taken under a peace treaty, on condition that the people pay *kharāj* to the Muslims. So I asked Sharīk: What is the position of al-Sawad? And he said: It was taken forcibly, and is *fayʾ*, but the inhabitants were left there and a certain payment was imposed upon them."[18] Clearly then, according to this outlook *fay'* is associated with combat whereas *kharāj* is associated with peaceful submission.

In contrast to Qudāma's distinction between *fay'* and *kharāj*, al-Māwardī combined the two. In his taxonomy of lands, if areas were taken over by peaceful submission, "*fay'* and *kharāj* will be imposed on it."[19] Whereas Qudāma and Sharīk considered *fay'* and *kharāj* as two separate categories that evolve out of distinctive historical circumstances, al-Māwardī viewed *kharāj* as a tax imposed on *fay'* land.

The terminological quagmire is even more perplexing when we examine Abū Yūsuf's (d. 182/798–99) use of the term *kharāj*. Whereas both al-Māwardī and Qudāma associate *kharāj* with peaceful submission, Abū Yūsuf defines *kharāj* land as areas that were conquered by force (*ʿanwa*).[20] However, in another part of the *Kitāb al-Kharāj* Abū Yūsuf links *kharāj* with peaceful submission.[21]

The multiplicity of meanings of tax-related terms is brought into relief in a comprehensive study of *kharāj* by Hossein Modarressi, who touches on the different usages of the term *kharāj* and writes "...it was used in a variety of related but different senses...."[22] He continues and specifies that it appears to describe revenue, crop from the land, imposts, different sorts of tribute, and land tax.[23] In his discussion of the term *fay'*, Modarressi states that "[T]here is some ambiguity about the meaning of this legal term due to difference in its usage in Islamic literature."[24] The situation of the basic terms used in the doctrine of taxation having multiple meanings was aggravated by the fact that they were also used in different regions with distinct tax arrangements whereby the terms were understood differently.

It was into these multilayered and fragmented systems of taxation that jurists introduced the crucial historical distinction between *ʿanwa*-lands, which were taken over by force, and *ṣulḥ*-lands, which passed into the hands of the Muslims by peaceful submission. Theoretically, the lands were classified in accordance with the historical events that led to their capture by the Muslims. In the words of Hossein Modarressi, it was "the general position of a community towards the Muslim army" that determined whether an area would be classified as having been taken by *ʿanwa* or *ṣulḥ*.[25] However, the sources indicate that Muslim jurists could not agree on the legal implication of the indigenous population's behavior. As a consequence we find them disagreeing if it was *ṣulḥ* or *ʿanwa* that led to *fay'*. As Frede Løkkegaard has noted, "[I]t is generally accepted by the Shafiʿites that *fay'* results from a *ṣulḥ*. Abū Ḥanīfa, too, professes the same view. But the opposite theory, namely, that it depends on a *ʿanwatan*-surrender is maintained by other scholars."[26] This observation demonstrates how difficult it was to combine historical events with terms that depict the legal status of lands.

Having noted that the inclusion of historiographic parameters only complicated the process by which jurists arrive at the appropriate legal category, it is important to identify the legal consequences of being labeled *ʿanwa* or *ṣulḥ*. The most important of them was that in the case of *ʿanwa*, the ruler had the right to alter the conditions of the agreement with the local inhabitants. Most Islamic jurists subscribed to the view that if an agreement was reached with the inhabitants after they fought against the Muslims, the ruler did not have to abide to it.[27] By contrast, when an agreement was signed without prior acts of hostilities between the two sides, as in the case of *ṣulḥ*, theoretically the ruler was not allowed to raise taxes. In his presentation of the differences between *ṣulḥ* and *ʿanwa* lands, Qudāma ibn Jaʿfar writes that although both pay *kharāj*, there exists "the right to take more than what was agreed upon from *kharāj*-paying *ʿanwa* lands, whereas there is no difference of opinion as to the prohibition of taking more than what was agreed upon from *ṣulḥ*-land."[28] This generalization is supported by a story that appears in Yaḥyā ibn Ādam's *Kitāb al-Kharāj* in which a person informed ʿUmar that "certain lands could bear more *kharāj* than was imposed on them. ʿUmar decided: Nothing can be done, for this was agreed upon in the peace treaty."[29] The two anecdotes suggest that once an area is labeled as *ṣulḥ*-land, the rulers' abilities to change and adjust the agreement's conditions are minimal. By contrast, in the case of *ʿanwa*-land, the rulers have the right to alter and adapt its rates of taxation.

The case of *ʿanwa* and *ṣulḥ* is an illustration of how historical conduct was grafted onto legal discourse and transformed into a parameter for determining the legal status of the land. As such, it became an important element in the legal doctrine of taxation. Yet implanting historical events into a legal discussion that is not based on well-defined, circumscribed terms and concepts does not lead to a clarification of the legal doctrine. In fact, it actually adds a factual enigma to the terminological confusion. Hence, alongside the issue of muddled legal definitions appears another insoluble riddle: How do the jurists know which lands were conquered by force (*ʿanwatan*) and which by peaceful submission (*ṣulḥan*). The next paragraphs will illustrate some of the problems faced by jurists that entered into the field of historical interpretation.

The Limits of Historiography

The dependence of land classification on events of the past meant that jurists were obliged to investigate the details of the conquests. This proved to be an insurmountable task and, as will be shown, the jurists were acutely aware of its difficulties.

In a study of doctrinal disagreements, the renowned jurist and historian, Abū Jaʿfar Muḥammad b. Jarīr al-Ṭabarī (d. 310/923) cites al-Shāfiʿī (d. 204/819–20), one of the greatest theoreticians of Islamic law:

> I do not know what to say about the land of the Sawad other than an educated guess [lit. opinion that is combined with knowledge]. I came to realize that the most reliable reports that the Kufans circulate among themselves about the Sawad do not constitute clearcut evidence. We found that some of their reports contradicted others. Some of them state that the Sawad was taken over by peaceful submission and others that state that it was taken by force. [In other reports] they claim that parts of the Sawad were taken over by peaceful submission and parts by force.[30]

According to al-Ṭabarī, al-Shāfiʿī makes no bones about admitting his bafflement regarding the legal status of the lands of the Sawad. It is also interesting to note that his candid admission of ignorance already appears in his *Kitāb al-Umm*, and al-Ṭabarī's reference simply adds to its circulation.[31] The most relevant aspect of this remark, to this study, is the connection that al-Shāfiʿī makes between his inability to reach a clearcut legal position and the historical reports coming out of Kufa. By stating that some Kufans reported that the Sawad was conquered by force while other Kufans reported that it was taken by peaceful means, and still other Kufans reported that it was a combination of the two, al-Shāfiʿī depicts historic discourse as incapable of supplying the kind of certain knowledge that jurists require if they are to reach a clearcut position on the matter. In other words, al-Shāfiʿī's comment is not simply an admission that he is incapable of arriving at an assured opinion regarding the Sawad, but it is also a commentary about the internal contradictions of historical reports and therefore, the hazard of depending on historical sources.

Another early source that indicates that Muslim scholars were not sure about the manner in which the Sawad was conquered appears in Yaḥyā ibn Ādam's *Kitāb al-Kharāj*, who cites Ibn Sīrīn: "We do not know who, of the people of the Sawad, has a treaty and who has not."[32] Judging by these two texts, Muslim scholars in the second/eighth century were quite forthright about their ignorance regarding the conquest of the Sawad. Most importantly, they were not sure about the legal consequences of the confrontations between the local population and the Arab conquerors.

Whereas al-Shāfiʿī's statement is reiterated and circulated by al-Ṭabarī, it seems to annoy the fifth/eleventh-century Hanafi jurist al-Sarakhsī, who writes about it: "But such a statement is contradictory and a sign of ignorance on the part of the person who made it.... The conquest of Sawad by force is too well known to be a secret to anyone."[33] The disagreement between al-Sarakhsī and al-Shāfiʿī is not simply about the historical fact whether the Sawad was conquered by force or not, rather it was about the ability to know for sure what happened in the past. Al-Sarakhsī seems somewhat flustered by al-Shāfiʿī's professed ignorance.

While al-Sarakhsī reacts to al-Shāfiʿī's confessed doubts with criticism, al-Māwardī, a fellow fifth/eleventh-century Shafiʿi jurist, simply ignored al-Shāfiʿī's stated uncertainty. He writes in the *Aḥkām*: "Jurists are in disagreement about the circumstances of its [Sawad's] conquest and rule. Iraqis argue that it was conquered by force [...] Al-Shāfiʿī's approach, may God approve of him, indicates that the Sawad was conquered by force."[34] Why al-Māwardī ignores al-Shāfiʿī's *Kitāb al-Umm* and al-Ṭabarī's repetition of al-Shāfiʿī's doubts is not clear, but he does. It may be that al-Sarakhsī's nonplussed remark reflects the general attitude towards this question and that by the fifth/eleventh century scholars came to be certain of the conquest of the Sawad, but that al-Māwardī's respect for the eponymous founder of his school of law (*madhhab*) obliges him to disregard his explicit doubts.

Be that as it may, Muslim scholars of that era and later knew about the disagreements regarding the conquest of the Sawad. In another, somewhat angry remark made by the eighth/fourteenth-century Hanbali scholar, Ibn Rajab (d. 795/1392–3), we read: "A group [of scholars] argued that ʿUmar, God's blessing upon him, did not divide the land between the warriors because they did not seize it by force."[35] Ibn Rajab continues with a caustic criticism of this opinion, resembling al-Sarakhsī's aggressive reaction to al-Shāfiʿī. Nevertheless, the harsh remarks reveal that he, too, is aware of the opinion that circulated among scholars that the Muslims did not conquer the Sawad by force.

The shift from the second/eighth-century scholars' admitted uncertainty regarding the events that took place during the conquest of the Sawad, to the fifth/eleventh-century jurists' unflinching self-confidence, reveals a fascinating process of reinterpretation of the historical events with far-reaching legal consequences. Before we discuss the implications of this transformation, it is worthwhile to examine some remarks made by Islamic scholars about the nature of historical sources and their place in legal discourse.

Ibn Rajab and al-Subkī (d. 756/1355) on History and Law

Although all jurists relied on historical data in their legal discussions, we find two contradicting approaches as to their reliability. The optimistic view, which perceived historical sources as reliable, was espoused by Ibn Rajab. In the comment cited above, Ibn Rajab argues against the opinion that ʿUmar did not divide the land because it was not seized by force. Angrily he states that there is no need to talk to anyone who adopts such an opinion. This remark is followed by the observation that "anyone who studies history books, conquest literature, and other sources attentively becomes aware of the complete falseness of this [opinion]."[36] It is not

ʿUmar's position regarding the Sawad that interests us in this study, but rather Ibn Rajab's reliance on historical literature. This is a rare moment in which a jurist refers explicitly to historical sources and expresses the view that they will help solve a legal question. However, we do need to keep in mind that Ibn Rajab's optimism was limited to a specific historical question. It does not reveal if he thought that historical sources can supply answers to many or any other factual questions.

The contradicting view of historical data, one that sees it as elusive and therefore unyielding of an exact reconstruction of the past, is found in al-Subkī's *Fatāwā*. He writes:

> Regarding Damascus, historians and jurists disagree among themselves whether it was conquered by force or by peaceful submission. The majority of our colleagues say that it was through peaceful submission, but the *shaykh* Abū Ḥamīd says it was by force. The reason that the jurists disagree [among themselves] is that the historians disagree [among themselves].[37]

There is nothing exceptional about al-Subkī's remark regarding the disagreements between jurists since differences of opinions are often mentioned openly by Islamic scholars and have elicited numerous books and countless comparisons. It is less common, though certainly not unheard of, that a jurist would examine the reasons behind the disagreements. However, it is quite rare that a jurist would admit that the cause of the jurists' inability to arrive at an agreed-upon doctrine is a non-legal factor. Al-Subkī's remark is a rare admission that in certain matters, such as the legal status of land, jurists look to historians for answers.

Al-Subkī continues this observation with a penetrating insight regarding the reliability of historical knowledge. He comments that even those who were present during the actual conquest of Damascus were not sure what happened in the course of its conquest, "and they maintained cautiously that it was through peaceful submission, [but] they were not sure about it."[38] In other words, even eyewitnesses do not always know precisely what happened. In this case the uncertainty is not the result of a Rashomon-like subjectivity or an ideological bias that distorts the information, rather it is the result of a technical problem, not being able to see the full picture at any given moment. In al-Subkī's words:

> Verily, Yazīd b. Abī Sufyān laid siege to the Small Gate while Khālid laid siege to the Eastern Gate [...] Yazīd seized an opportunity and forcibly entered through the Small Gate. Meanwhile, a Damascene monk went to Khālid, tricked him, and they signed a peace agreement. When [Khālid] entered, Yazīd was already inside, but Khālid did not know this until they met at the Oil Market.[39]

According to al-Subkī's description, the historiographic confusion was the outcome of accurate but contrasting information. The simple fact that two separate units entered the city more or less at the same time, one by force and the other by agreement with the local inhabitants, creates an historiographic conundrum. What al-Subkī implies in this account is that even if the story reaches the text through reliable and unbiased transmitters, we can never be sure that we have the full picture. One or several witnesses may report an event accurately, and still create a misleading impression regarding the full picture simply because the event that they saw was an exception. In the case of the above-mentioned report of the entry into Damascus, it is obvious that al-Subkī is trying to create the impression that it took place by force, since he depicts Yazīd's forcible entry as being the first of the two and the monk's peaceful and belated initiative as an act of deception. But it is also evident from the way that the story is told that al-Subkī does not have clearcut evidence to substantiate that impression. There is no witness to state that Khālid actually entered before Yazīd since no one was present at both gates and it seems that the entries were not coordinated. Furthermore, as al-Subkī mentions, the witnesses were not sure themselves and stated tentatively that it was a peaceful entry.

For the most part, jurists were well aware of the unreliability of the historical record. On the other hand, many jurists like Ibn Rajab, and even al-Subkī, relied upon historical data. Why did jurists turn to a source that was widely perceived as unreliable?

Concluding Remarks

The primary purpose of this essay is to explore the way that historiography was integrated into legal thinking and their mutual influence, through the case study of Islamic tax law. The insertion of the terms *ʿanwa* and *ṣulḥ* to describe an historical event into a legal discussion created a terminological and conceptual link between historical events and legal categories. However, the textual amalgam that was made up of historical narratives and tax law did not create a cohesive picture of the state of affairs nor did it bring about a consistent set of rules of taxation. Quite the contrary, it added another level of uncertainty since it raised the insoluble question: What happened during the conquests?

Even though the Islamic historical experience did not furnish a comprehensive and consistent set of principles that would guide the tax system, its infusion into legal texts offers important insights about the interaction between law and historiography. One important aspect that it reveals is related to the nature of the two genres. Islamic historiography is characteristically open-ended. It often describes a single event by evoking several, at times contradictory, anecdotes. Scholars who write chronicles often leave an episode with two or more possible explanations. Thus, there was nothing out of the ordinary when Ibn Sīrīn, al-Shāfiʿī, and al-Ṭabarī discussed the contradicting descriptions of the conquest of the Sawad. As a matter of fact, debating events is probably the most common way for Muslim scholars to discuss their past. By contrast, legal discussions are in need of single, authoritative descriptions of events. Be it in a court of law or for the articulation of doctrine, judges and jurists need certitude. Multiple descriptions of an event are an obstacle in the path of legal decision-making. This contradiction in the basic characteristics of the two disciplines makes for a very difficult assemblage.

However, despite their incongruence, Islamic legal discourse absorbs and utilizes a lot of historical materials. This is made possible due to the "softness" of historical materials. It is precisely because historical events are not considered as authoritative legal sources (notwithstanding Prophetic traditions) that they are pliable and easily adjusted to the needs and pressures of different interest groups. Historical data and interpretation are easily discarded and it seems that scholars do not expect one single narrative about a single event, such as the conquest of a city or region. Muslim scholars take a realistic stand regarding historiography: they seem to expect that there will always be several descriptions of a single event. As a consequence, historical information is easily rewritten and reinterpreted. This being the case, when historical narratives are included in legal texts, their innate flexibility adds to the malleability of legal doctrine and therefore enhances its responsiveness to social circumstances.

The shifts in the way that events were written into the doctrine of taxation are an example of this dynamic. The historiographic modifications that can be found when we compare second/eighth-century jurists with those from the fifth/eleventh century go hand in hand with an historical tendency that has been noted by Frede Løkkegaard, namely, "*ṣulḥ* conditions are disappearing during the Abbasid times."[40] In other words, *ṣulḥ* lands, whose legal standing made it more difficult for rulers to raise taxes imposed on them, were reduced in scope over time, so as to accommodate the needs of the ʿAbbasid rulers. In a candid and revealing remark, al-Subkī writes: "When we are not certain whether a city was conquered by force or by submission, [...] the rules of forcible conquest ought to be imposed on it."[41] As mentioned above, it was not known whether large areas of valuable land were conquered by force or by submission. By reinterpreting past events, jurists succeeded in obliterating their doubts and transforming an inchoate legal doctrine into a doctrine that is well-defined and cohesive. Hence, in the case of the Sawad, due to the tolerance of scholars and jurists towards reinterpretations of historical materials, they were able to articulate a widely-held position regarding its conquest, and in so doing, put forth a narrative that served the needs of the rulers.

In the case of Islamic law and historiography, historiography integrated social reality with legal discourse via two channels. The first is mediation. Historiography is a prism through which social reality and events of the past are viewed and interpreted. When such writings are included in legal texts, they weave into the legal discussion descriptions of economic, social, and political events and patterns. Although these are merely representations of the events, they influence the formulation of doctrine from within the text. In this fashion historiography serves as a mediating vehicle which links historical and legal discourses. The second is pliability. Since the historical record is not considered as an authoritative legal source, it is also not very rigid. In contrast to a Prophetic tradition whose authoritative status is very difficult to change once scholars agree that it is a sound tradition, the perceived veracity and authority of variant historical anecdotes can change over time. Thus, we find that in areas of the law in which historiography constitutes a large and pivotal part of the text, the suppleness of historical texts adds to the flexibility of the legal doctrine and serves as a means through which context molds the text.

NOTES

* This study began during my stay at the Islamic Legal Studies Program at Harvard Law School. Conversations with Peri Bearman and Aron Zysow have led me to this project. Frank Vogel's writings and remarks have helped me shape its main argument. I would like to thank all three for the stimulating period I spent with them. I would also like to thank Morton Horwitz, whose conversations and articles touching on this topic have helped shape the ideas that appear in this study. My debt and gratitude to Dina Hurvitz and Haggai Hurvitz, who read several drafts of this essay and offered penetrating criticism that helped me reshape this study, is immense.

[1] For a brief comment on this growing tendency and a list of historians who ascribe to the historicist methodology, see Vogel, *Islamic Law and Legal System*, xi–xii. On the debate over historicism in Anglo-American law, see Horwitz, "Why is Anglo-American Jurisprudence Unhistorical?"

[2] For an example of a thorough study whose central agenda is "law in practice," see Vogel, *Islamic Law and Legal System*.

[3] Two texts that synthesize massive amounts of historical accounts are ʿAlī b. Muḥammad b. Ḥabīb al-Māwardī, *al-Aḥkām al-sulṭāniyya* (Eng. trans. Wafaa H. Wahba, *The Ordinances of Government*), and Abū Yaʿlā, Muḥammad b. al-Ḥusayn al-Farrāʾ, *al-Aḥkām al-sulṭāniyya*. A study of these two works and the use their authors make of historical materials is available at http://www.law.harvard.edu/programs/ilsp/publications/occasional.php.

[4] Robert Cover, "Nomos and Narrative."

[5] Ibid., 95.

[6] Ibid., 96. A very similar observation about the law appears in Vogel, xii: "Legal literature is written within a larger universe in which it is to be understood and applied."

[7] For a study of the changes in terminology, see A. N. Poliak, "Classification of Lands in the Islamic Law and Its Technical Terms," *The American Journal of Semitic Languages and Literatures* 57 (1940); *EI*[2], "Kharādj" (Claude Cahen), 4:1030; Dennett, *Conversion and the Poll Tax in Early Islam*. For another thorough study of terms related to taxation, see Modarressi, *Kharāj in Islamic Law*.

[8] "Kharādj," loc. cit. A similar assessment appears in Dennett, 15–16. In fact, one of the aims of Dennett's study is to illustrate the local nature of taxation. See also Modarressi, 27–30. For a more complex presentation of this issue, see Michael G. Morony, *Iraq After the Muslim Conquest* (Princeton: Princeton University Press, 1984), 100, which argues that modern scholarship tends to view the Muslim taxation system as continuing the Sassanian system. He challenges this sweeping generalization and elaborates on three areas in which the two systems differed.

[9] Yaḥyā ibn Ādam, *Kitāb al-Kharāj*, trans. A. Ben Shemesh, 26–7. This anecdote is also quoted by ʿAbd al-Raḥmān b. Aḥmad Ibn Rajab, *al-Istikhrāj li-aḥkām al-kharāj* (Beirut: Dār al-Kutub al-ʿIlmiyya, 1985/1405), 15. A similar remark in al-Māwardī, 188, 221, Eng. trans. 164, 192.

[10] Dennett, 49.

[11] See, for example, Dennett, 16.

[12] Ibid., 19.

[13] Ibid., 19–20.

[14] Ibid., 21.

[15] Ibid., 20–1.

[16] Morony, 101.

[17] Qudāma ibn Jaʿfar, *al-Kharāj wa-ṣināʿat al-kitāba*, 204.

[18] Qudāma ibn Jaʿfar, *Kitāb al-Kharāj*, trans. A. Ben Shemesh (as *Taxation in Islam*, vol. II) (Leiden: E. J. Brill, 1965), 28. Qudāma, *al-Kharāj*, 209. A very similar anecdote appears in Yaḥyā ibn Ādam, 25. In this version Sharīk emphasizes that payment made by the inhabitants of the Sawad was not *kharāj*.

[19] al-Māwardī, 217.

[20] Abū Yūsuf, *Kitāb al-Kharāj*, 59–60.

[21] Ibid., 69.

[22] Modarressi, 2.

[23] Ibid., 2–3.

[24] Ibid., 11.

[25] Ibid., 107.

[26] Løkkegaard, *Islamic Taxation in the Classic Period*, 45.

[27] Dennett, 47.

[28] Qudāma (Ben Shemesh), 29; Qudāma, *al-Kharāj*, 210.

[29] Yaḥyā ibn Ādam, 47.

[30] Abū Jaʿfar, Muḥammad b. Jarīr al-Ṭabarī, *Kitāb al-Jihād wa-kitāb al-jizya wa-aḥkām al-muḥāribīn min kitāb ikhtilāf al-fuqahā'*, 220.

[31] Muḥammad b. Idrīs al-Shāfiʿī, *Kitāb al-Umm*, 4:279.

[32] Yaḥyā ibn Ādam, 47. Another series of remarks, on p. 45, suggest that the inhabitants of the Sawad did not have a treaty with the Muslims, but that once "*kharāj* was accepted from them, this became a treaty for them."

[33] Translated in Nicholas P. Aghnides, *Mohammedan Theories of Finance* (AMS Press, Inc., 1969), 365.

[34] al-Māwardī, 190–91.

[35] Ibn Rajab, 42.

[36] Ibid.

[37] ʿAlī b. ʿAbd al-Kāfī al-Subkī, *Fatāwā al-Subkī*, 2:394.

[38] Ibid.

[39] Ibid. In Muḥammad b. Aḥmad al-Dhahabī, *Siyar aʿlām al-nubalāʾ* (Beirut: Muʾassasat al-Risāla, 1413 AH), 1:21–2, there is an account of the conquest of Damascus in which Khālid enters through the Eastern Gate forcibly.
[40] Løkkegaard, 86.
[41] al-Subkī, 2:396.

BIBLIOGRAPHY

Abū Yaʿlā, Muḥammad b. al-Ḥusayn al-Farrāʾ, *al-Aḥkām al-sulṭāniyya* (Miṣr: Muṣṭafā al-Bābī al-Ḥalabī, 1966).

Abū Yūsuf, Yaʿqūb b. Ibrāhīm, *Kitāb al-Kharāj* (Cairo: al-Maṭbaʿa al-Salafiyya, 1352 AH).

Cover, Robert, "Nomos and Narrative," in Martha Minow, Michael Ryan, and Austin Sarat (eds.), *Narrative, Violence and the Law* (Ann Arbor: University of Michigan Press, 1993).

Dennett, Daniel C., *Conversion and the Poll Tax in Early Islam* (Cambridge, Mass.: Harvard University Press, 1950).

Horwitz, Morton J., "Why is Anglo-American Jurisprudence Unhistorical?," *Oxford Journal of Legal Studies* 17 (1997).

Ibn Rajab, ʿAbd al-Raḥmān b. Aḥmad, *al-Istikhrāj li-aḥkām al-kharāj* (Beirut: Dār al-Kutub al-ʿIlmiyya, 1985/1405).

Løkkegaard, Frede, *Islamic Taxation in the Classic Period* (Copenhagen: Branner and Korch, 1950).

al-Māwardī, ʿAlī b. Muḥammad b. Ḥabīb, *al-Aḥkām al-sulṭāniyya* (Beirut: Dār al-Kutub al-ʿIlmiyya, 1985/1405); Eng. trans., Wafaa H. Wahba, *The Ordinances of Government* (Garnet Publishing Limited, 1996).

Modarressi, Hossein Tabātabāʾī, *Kharāj in Islamic Law* (London: Anchor Press Ltd., 1983).

Qudāma ibn Jaʿfar, *al-Kharāj wa-ṣināʿat al-kitāba* (Beirut: Dār al-Rashīd li l-Nashr, 1981).

al-Shāfiʿī, Muḥammad b. Idrīs, *Kitāb al-Umm* (Damascus: Dār al-Maʿārifa, ^{2}1393 AH).

al-Subkī, ʿAlī b. ʿAbd al-Kāfī, *Fatāwā* (Cairo: Maktabat al-Quds, 1355 AH).

al-Ṭabarī, Abū Jaʿfar, Muḥammad b. Jarīr, *Kitāb al-Jihād wa-kitāb al-jizya wa-aḥkām al-muḥāribīn min kitāb ikhtilāf al-fuqahāʾ* (Leiden: E. J. Brill, 1933).

Vogel, Frank E., *Islamic Law and Legal System. Studies of Saudi Arabia* (Leiden: Brill, 2000).

Yaḥyā ibn Ādam, *Kitāb al-Kharāj*, trans. A. Ben Shemesh (Leiden: E. J. Brill, 1967).

19

TEXT AND APPLICATION

Hermeneutical Reflections on Islamic Legal Interpretation

Bernard G. Weiss

The last several years have witnessed a growing interest among legal scholars in this country in the work of Hans-Georg Gadamer. A good example of this interest is an edited volume that is scheduled to appear in June 2007 under the title *Gadamer and the Law* (Dartmouth Publishing) and containing essays by a roster of outstanding legal theorists and philosophers.[1] For many who share this interest, Gadamer's "philosophical hermeneutics" represents a refreshing alternative in legal thought to deconstructionist and radically realist approaches that see the law as nothing but a play of conflicting social forces. Francis J. Mootz III has provided a lucid account of the philosophical climate of continental Europe within which Gadamer lived and worked. In an article entitled "Responding to Nietzsche: The Constructive Power of *Destruktion*," he portrays Nietzsche as the herald of a radical reductionism that considered law to be institutionalized injustice and the rule of law to be nothing more than a "modernist fable that conceals the play of power."[2]

Bernard Freamon, in his contribution to this volume,[3] calls attention to the importance of hermeneutics in present-day Muslim discourse, noting especially the "new Qur'anic hermeneutic" that is currently in the making, a development in which the ideas of Gadamer are bound to play an important role. Traditional approaches connected with the two main modalities of interpretation—*tafsīr* and *ta'wīl*—are no longer adequate to meet current needs of Muslims living under post-colonial conditions; both approaches have taken on "the dogmatic and rigid trappings of orthodoxy." The new approach "seeks to separate the domain of truth from the imprisonment of methodology." Freamon finds a precedent for the new hermeneutic in the thought of Ibn Rushd, but whereas Ibn Rushd's ideas never were widely accepted, today's new hermeneutic is flourishing in certain areas of the Muslim world, especially among Muslims living in Southeast Asia and the West.

I believe that the notion of a new Islamic hermeneutic merits our investigation not only as it relates to the Qur'an but also as it relates to the entire enterprise of Islamic law, in which the Qur'an, of course, has a central role. And I am inclined to believe that just as the new Qur'anic hermeneutic is taking its boldest steps forward among Muslim intellectuals most open to "dialogic conversation" (Gadamer's famous term) so the same may be said of what can be called "a new Islamic legal hermeneutic." And if indeed, as Freamon suggests, the ideas of Hans-Georg Gadamer are proving to be useful in discussions of the new Qur'anic hermeneutic, so also they should prove useful in discussions of new approaches to the hermeneutics of Islamic law. Gadamer's ideas can, I think, be seen as offering a safe haven for Muslims and non-Muslims alike from the radically subjectivist and relativist post-modernist ways of thinking that have swept across so much of the landscape of contemporary thought.

Gadamer had quite a lot to say about the law and legal hermeneutics. He was especially interested in what he considered to be the "exemplary significance" of the law. For him legal hermeneutics exemplified with particular clarity what all hermeneutics—at least within the humanities—was about. Legal hermeneutics thus never stood alone. It was part of something much greater—the part that illuminated the whole in a particular manner while never constituting the whole.

It is my intention in the following pages to provide first an overview of Gadamer's philosophical hermeneutics[4] and then to explore its implications for Islamic legal thought and what these implications might mean for the project of development of a new Islamic legal hermeneutic.

I

Although the term "hermeneutics" originally referred to a body of methodological principles that governed biblical interpretation, it has within the last century or so gone through several transformations of meaning. In Gadamer's philosophical hermeneutics, we encounter a deliberate shift away from hermeneutics as method to hermeneutics as ontology, that is to say, hermeneutics as having to do with the human experience of being in the world. "Being in the world" means being interpreters of the world. Interpretation is not something we choose to do, a mere activity among activities. We interpret the world because the necessity of our doing so is woven into the very fabric of our being. The world is always the world as we interpret it; there is no such thing as a pre-interpretive world, a world given to us as a starting point from which to launch our particular projects of interpretation. Closely related to the concept of interpretation is the concept of disclosure. Interpretation is not so much an extraction of meaning from an object as it is an opening up of ourselves to disclosures of meanings in the world around us.

We are well accustomed to thinking of law as interpretation. This needs no justification. Gadamer's concern is rather to place legal interpretation within a broad framework that embraces all human interpretation and that grounds it in our "being in the world." Legal interpretation, in consequence, cannot be isolated from other "kinds" of interpretation; it is not sui generis, not *just* legal interpretation. Rather it is part of the broader spectrum of interpretation that makes up the "hermeneutic situation" that all humans find themselves in. That there could be no law without interpretation is but an instantiation of the broader principle according to which there could be no human reality without interpretation.

Gadamer wants us to understand that all human interpretation, be it legal, literary, theological, or historiographical, has the same grounding in our very being as interpreters of the world. All the considerations that arise in our thinking about human interpretation in general—considerations of prejudice, tradition, language, texts, understanding, truth, and practical application—arise also by way of instantiation in our thinking about legal interpretation in particular. And just as interpretation is an opening of ourselves to the disclosures of things in the world, so legal interpretation is an opening of ourselves to the disclosures of things that make up what we call law. And just as nothing in the world that we interpret comes to us in an uninterpreted state that can serve as a starting point for our individual interpretation, so the law never comes to us uninterpreted. All law is always law interpreted, whether the interpretation be ours or another's.

The world we interpret is a world mediated to us *through language*. Our being in the world is thus being in a linguistically mediated world, and interpretation is possible only within the limits that language imposes on us. Gadamer calls the state of being linguistically mediated "linguisticality"; it is a state that radiates throughout our experience of the world. He also calls language the "midworld" (*Zwischenwelt*) between thought and the world. In our thinking we cannot go outside the world that language mediates to us. It is language that defines our limits and our finitude. We are all born into language and live and think within language. And yet so transparent is language that its presence is sometimes not adequately taken into account, especially among those who work in the natural sciences and give priority to logic and mathematics, to "pure thought." "Insofar as it [i.e., language] once again comes into view as such, it demonstrates against [mathematics] [...] the primary mediatedness of all access to the world, and, more than this, it demonstrates the inviolability of the linguistic schema of the world." Language is "the schematization of our access to the world."[5]

Again, what is true of the world as a whole is true of that part of the world we call law. The law we interpret is a law linguistically mediated to us. There is no such thing as a language-free view of the law. The "midworld" of language is present in every phase of legal practice and the legal process. The linguisticality of law—of proceedings in a courtroom, a jurors' room, a law firm—is very apparent, since there is a plethora of language at every stage of the legal process. How much of the language is technical and how much ordinary does not matter; both contribute equally to the process.

In spite of the misunderstanding that often occurs between speakers of a given language, the natural tendency of language is in the direction of understanding. Every speaker normally speaks in order to be understood. Language is by its very nature outwardly directed—directed toward others, not allowing us to become insular beings. In the history of the human species, language has always served primarily to enable people to live together and to cooperate in joint activities necessary for survival. It is easy to think of law as an exception, since so much of the language heard in the legal process is the language of conflict. The courtroom is a place where lively, intense language occurs in great abundance. Nonetheless, the reality is that even in the courtroom, language is serving the cause of resolution of conflict and ultimate harmony.

Among the many sorts of things that make up the world and may be objects of interpretation, texts, especially written or printed texts, hold pride of place in most hermeneutical discourse because of their durability, fixity, and constant availability, making it possible to return again and again to the same text. Yet every text has its original moment of coming into being when it spoke its original message. As generations come and go, the task of those who want the text to stay alive is to enable it to speak meaningfully at all times; but in the long term it is not what the author originally said that is passed along but "what he would have said had I been his original interlocutor." This is not to say that a text is ever deliberately cut off from its original moment of communication. If that were the case, we would have to revise our usual notion of what writing is about quite drastically. The text is originally written with great care to communicate effectively, which is to say that it presents itself as something to be referred to again and again. Yet it is always the present context, not the original one, that will be ultimately determinative.

It is in regard to this very point that the exemplary role of legal hermeneutics begins to become apparent. In a more urgent way than obtains for interpreters of literature, historical narrative, theology, and so on, the interpreter of law—judge or attorney or even average citizen—is under an imperative to interpret something from a past long since gone in its relevance to the present moment, even if that relevance arises from the creative work of the interpreter and necessitates having to disregard the meaning it had in the original moment of its existence. The "freedom of speech" clause in the First Amendment is a good example of this in that it must in our day be somehow made to cover issues undreamed of in the days of its original framing.

Gadamer considered all interpretation as taking place within a setting of conversation among interpreters and as aimed at maximizing agreement. Participants in the conversation share with each other their readings of the text, always from the vantage point of the present situation. Thus they are simultaneously exploring the text itself and each other's views concerning the text. In exploring each other's views, participants in the conversation establish a dialogic relationship with each other. They also, according to Gadamer, establish a dialogic relationship with the text. The text is in a real sense a participant in the conversation. Just as individuals in the conversation ask questions of each other, so they ask questions of the text.

An important key to success in this enterprise is good-will along with a charitable spirit. Participants in effective conversation willingly open up to each other in an I-Thou encounter that treats one's fellows, not as objects, but as subjects. This entails what Gadamer calls "dialogic" risk, since by exposing one's thought to one's fellows one might discover that one's own view is invalid and that one will be constrained, as a result, to change a viewpoint that one had steadfastly held. However, the end result, which is agreement, makes the risk worth taking, for it is through agreement that truth is secured. Through conversation, participants with opposite points of view are able to shed their differences and discover common ground.

Such conversation does not necessarily entail face-to-face verbal interactions. If our mental image of conversation is that of a circle of people talking directly to each other, then we are bound to have difficulty making sense out of Gadamer's notion of conversation. Again, the law points the way. According to Mootz, law is, for Gadamer, conversational *in structure*, meaning "structured as a playful movement of questioning and answering. [...] Law is structured conversationally even if it is clearly not just a conversation."[6] One can imagine people sitting together and talking but not having conversation. More problematic, as far as the law is concerned, than the meaning of conversation is the crucial role that good-will plays in the kind of conversation Gadamer has in mind. One may at first blush be tempted to ask: Is not his notion of people of good-will engaged in dialogue over a text of the law in a charitable spirit that manifests itself in their opening up to each other's scrutiny even at the risk of being found mistaken on some point and having to give up a cherished conviction, all for the purpose of promoting communitarian values—isn't this all rather visionary and idealistic? Isn't the cynical acid of a Holmes, with his classic notion of the law as the offender's prediction of what the court will decide—or the acid of a Derrida, of a Critical Legal Studies movement, even, ultimately, of a Nietzsche—more conducive to clear thinking about the law, more efficient, cleaner? Against any charges of excessive idealism that might be made against him Gadamer had a ready reply. His hermeneutics, he could always say, was not about ivory tower ideals but about practical applications. Every thing had to pass the test of *praxis*. This means that it had to be concretized. We will be returning to this point shortly.

The common ground reached through conversation forms the basis of Gadamer's hermeneutical optimism. He describes it as a "fusing of horizons." By "horizon" he means

> the range of vision that includes everything that can be seen from a particular vantage point. Applying this to the thinking mind, we speak of [...] the opening up of new horizons [...].[7]

The human range of vision never does and never will encompass all that is. Human finitude makes this impossible. What we can or cannot embrace within our range of vision depends upon our situatedness. A bald eagle flying at an incredible height can take into its view an enormous segment of the earth's surface, but this view is still limited. On the other hand, our range of vision is constantly changing, and when we are able to fuse our horizons with the horizons of another person, we reach the high point of all inquiry. Here is where truth is to be found at its purest, waiting for its moment of disclosure, the moment when a multiplicity of minds are agreed on what they see.

Agreement is the fruit of charitable minds that have forsworn all attachment to self-centered subjectivist concerns and have freely transposed themselves into the point of view of "the Other."

> Into this other situation we must bring, precisely, ourselves. Only this is the full meaning of "transposing ourselves." If we put ourselves in someone else's shoes, for example, then we will understand him—i.e., become aware of the otherness, the indissoluble individuality of the other person—by putting *ourselves* in his position. Transposing ourselves consists neither in the empathy of one individual for another nor in subordinating another person to our own standards; rather, it always involves rising to a higher universality that overcomes not only our own particularity but also that of the other. The concept of "horizon" suggests itself because it expresses the superior breadth of vision that the person who is trying to understand must have.[8]

It is thus in this fusing of horizons—this harmonious coming together of minds—that Gadamer takes refuge from the subjectivism and relativism and heroic celebration of conflict that have weighed so heavily upon the Western mind ever since Nietzsche formulated his conflict-of-wills philosophy. In Gadamer's community of understanding, the presumption is that harmony is more fundamental than strife, that communitarianism is more endemic than individualism, that objectivity is closer at hand than subjectivity. It is within such a community that truth finds its home.

Gadamer does not, however, subscribe to the notion of absolute truth. While rejecting the subjectivism and individualism of his philosophical detractors, he does not swing in the opposite direction as far as the pendulum would take him. Instead, he finds his place somewhere in the middle ground and there locates the truth. It is not an absolute, unchanging, static truth. But neither is it a truth so loosely rooted in its soil that the slightest gust of wind will blow it completely away. It is a truth capable of change, but not susceptible to any whim of the moment. When change does come, it comes only because the members of the community of understanding have gone back to the drawing boards of interpretation and have charted a new course leading to a new truth, and once again new wine will cause the old wineskins to burst.

Truth and method are at odds with each other in Gadamer's thinking. Gadamer considers it wrong to suppose that simply by adopting and following a certain method we will be sure to arrive at truth. This is not to say that method can never be useful. Gadamer's point is that method is subordinate to truth, not truth to method. We can never count on a method to deliver the truth automatically once certain procedures are correctly performed. If we could, there would be no vital need for conversation or dialogue. Individuals, using the appropriate method, would be able to arrive at truth on their own. It would be assumed that other individuals, applying the same method, would come up with the same result. Conversation as such would contribute nothing, would not be determinative of anything. What would come out of conversation would be sheer concurrence, nothing more. The role of consensus would be strictly disseminative, not determinative.

Truth cannot be chained to a post. It cannot be put in the freezer of eternality. One generation's truth is not necessarily the next generation's truth. Each generation has to live truth afresh, has to open itself to new disclosures and understandings, even if this sometimes means reinventing the wheel. On the other hand, the flow of truth down through generations cannot be willy-nilly. Given the good-will of those involved in the dialogic search for truth, all understandings of truth will move only in those directions that are good for the community. Even when the forces of change are not at work, truth will never appear sterile or static; when those forces do prevail, the truth will, of course, adapt and renew itself.

Method puts the one using it in control of the process and the results, whereas in conversation no one is in control and the outcome is entirely unpredictable. This accounts for the fact that when minds reach agreement and when horizons are fused the result is experienced as a transcendent truth even though it is not transcendent in the traditional philosophical sense associated with metaphysics. Truth is not bound up with certainty. Descartes' method of searching for truth was ill conceived from the beginning, according to Gadamer.

Gadamer distances himself from the notion of truth as correctness and prefers to speak of truth as "unhiddenness,"[9] following Heidegger's lead.

Wahrheit ist Unverborgenheit ("Truth is unhiddenness"), he says simply in the German original of *Truth and Method*. Truth comes into being as something wrested from the domain of hiddenness and brought into the domain of the unhidden. This happens in the context of dialogic conversation. Hiddenness and unhiddenness are conceptual correlates. One cannot unhide what is not first hidden, unveil what is not first veiled. On the other hand, nothing is ever unhidden completely. With every unhiding there is a holding back in hiddenness. All unhiding is partial. Hence, truth is never authoritatively declared with finality, never reaches a last word. Rather, it arises continuously and freely as partners in the conversation explore areas of agreement and understanding. In principle this conversation can never end or be in process of moving toward an end. It is not empowered by a vision of light at the end of the tunnel. All light is the light of disclosure in the present moment.

Law again is an exemplar. The scholar of law or judge, in search of legal truth, which is always truth as it bears on a particular case, faces the task of drawing it out of its hiddenness and bringing it into view of the parties or clients or jurors. The unhiding of the law may entail a search for the relevant text or even the search for a relevant meaning once a text has been located. The language of the text can itself be a domain of hiddenness, given its frequent ambiguity and irrelevance.

The fact that practitioners of law are continually debating need not be seen as obstructing the unhiding of legal truth. The purpose of the law, after all, is communal harmony through fair and equitable settlement of disputes. In fact, in no other field of human endeavor is the good-will of participants in dialogue more imperative than in law, good-will implying dedication to communal harmony.

It is important from a Gadamerian perspective to understand that humans are historical beings and that all human interpretation is therefore conditioned by past experience. Interpretation itself is oriented to the present; the interpreter constructs the meaning of texts or artifacts in a manner that addresses a present situation. But the texts and artifacts themselves belong to the past, often a remote past. Interpretation must bridge the gap between a present situation and a situation in the past that gave rise to the text/artifact. The interpreter thus brings the past into the present, making it contemporaneous with the present. Tradition is what they bring to the interpretive task collectively—their inherited ways of doing or seeing things. Tradition is largely textual: it may be a literary canon, a religious scripture, a body of ritual—many things come under this heading. Tradition may also, of course, include art, artifacts, edifices, music, and so on, although the primacy remains with texts. Prejudice is more an individual thing. Although it has negative connotations, prejudice in its literal meaning of "pre-judgment" is not necessarily bad. It can, in fact, benefit the dialogic process and facilitate the progress toward agreement.

In any case, prejudice is unavoidable and total objectivity is unattainable. Rather than attempting to eliminate prejudice, the interpreter must become aware of it insofar as possible in order to monitor it so that the undesirable can be eliminated and only what is conducive to the communal good be retained. As historical beings, humans are unable to divest themselves of the influences of their past. These influences are bound to affect profoundly how they understand the present. There is no *tabula rasa*. We all are situated somewhere in the historical stream. The importance of this "situatedness" in Gadamer's thought cannot be overemphasized.

The law illustrates with particular clarity the weight that the past brings to bear upon present deliberation. It is in the interests of society as a whole that practitioners of the law maintain consistency and constancy of the law to the greatest extent possible. The law is therefore essentially conservative, seeking to perpetuate itself as a time-honored tradition rather than as a fragile, loose congeries of uncontrolled rules. It is not fortuitous that the vocabulary used even today in both the common law of the British Isles and the civil law of the Continent is heavily laden with Latin vocabulary. This external symbolism of the West's indebtedness to Roman law is matched as well by substantive inroads of Roman law into Western law. In addition, we have ingredients of ancient common and Germanic law that go back centuries.

We come now to the most important reason why, according to Gadamer, the law may be said to have "exemplary importance" for philosophical hermeneutics. Law, more than any other field of human endeavor, is fundamentally concerned with the practical aspect of interpretation. All interpretation rightly so called entails this concern, but in the case of law it stands out in bold relief. Like all texts the texts of the law are never in and of themselves entirely self-sufficient as bearers of meaning. They always leave empty spaces that the interpreter must fill. This is because interpretation must always address the present situation. It must do what the text alone cannot do, because the text has already addressed a previous situation in very concrete terms; it cannot be made to address the present situation in the same degree of concreteness. But concreteness is what every situation requires. Therefore, the interpreter must supplement the text with judgments of his or her own in order to provide the necessary concreteness. The text is most useful if interpreted in general terms which may then be concretized so as to fit the present situation. This means setting aside any manifestations, in the text, of concreteness that is rooted in an earlier time.

II

Turning now to the implications of this summation for Islamic thinking about law and legal hermeneutics, we begin, as might be expected, with the framing ontology: the notion of human experience as an experience of being in the world together with the closely related notion of the linguisticality of human experience. It would, of course, be asking too much of Islamic philosophy, notwithstanding its incredible richness, depth, and variability, to expect it to deliver a set of philosophical ideas identical or even close to identical with the Gadamerian philosophical outlook. Gadamer's ideas were shaped by a particular stream of influences going back to Nietzsche, Schleiermacher, Husserl, Dilthey, and others, the most proximate being Heidegger. But if we are looking for compatibility rather than identity or close similarity, we must at least allow that several major facets of the Gadamerian philosophy can be made to resonate with Islam. A good example is the notion of the linguisticality of human experience. Muslim philosophers down through the centuries have defined the human as the "articulate, i.e., speaking, animal." Elaborate commentaries have been written—many of them from a philosophical viewpoint—on the account in the second sura of the Qur'an of God's endowing man with language, thus completing, as it were, man's creation as the crowning phase of the creation of the world, making man worthy in a brief moment of divine accommodation to be worshipped by angels, making man worthy also to be called the deputy of God Himself upon the earth (Qur'an 2:30–36).

It would not be an affront to anything in Islamic belief to speak of language as the medium through which the world "unhides" itself, of the outer, physical word (*ẓāhir*) as the revealer of the inner "hidden" (*bāṭin*) meaning. The mystical notion of the world of secrets (*asrār*) waiting to become manifest certainly blends with reasonable harmony with the Gadamerian notion of a world without language as veiled, as nonexistent until through the medium of language made, as it were, to exist. Adam and his descendants are able, through their acquisition of language, to know what other creatures do not know, even if that knowledge pales in significance compared with God's. Adam and his descendants are always interpreting, finding meaning, opening themselves up to the disclosures that language makes possible—doing all of this because it is in their nature to do so. Here is much that can be integrated into a Gadamerian view of the world.

And let us not forget the God who speaks, who discloses his intentions through language, who makes a Book—or rather a replica of a portion of a Heavenly Book (*umm al-kitāb*)—the point of contact with his human creature. There in the words of that heavenly message, the Qur'an, is the interface between this world and the world beyond, an interface experienced by humans as a recitation in the Arabic language. The words of the Qur'an are the frame that gives meaning to the cosmos. It is for humans to be fitting receptacles of its meaning through their constant readiness to interpret, to open themselves to, that meaning.

That meaning is a product of the coming together of believing minds engaged in dialogic conversation with one another in a spirit of good-will. There is no other way to meaning, to truth, than this. And here we come to the quintessential function of the language with which humans are divinely endowed. As was stated earlier and now may be restated in the context of Islamic thought, language by its very nature brings minds together, fosters understanding, facilitates that social cooperation that is the absolute condition of human survival. The fact that humans often misunderstand each other and use language to set themselves apart from each other is no fault of language as such but rather is the result of an imperfect use—or even misuse—of language, a disabling of language that is not devoid of malevolent intention. The would-be interpreter who seeks but does not find meaning in what is said to him or her has not, in Gadamerian thinking, opened himself or herself to the disclosures that language is capable of bringing.

The interpreter who is a person of good-will hears the message: Seek and ye shall find; knock and it shall be opened unto you. By opening one's mind to the truth as one contemplates an object of interpretation—a text in most cases—one assures one's self that the truth will break forth. This is not to say that all truly sincere seekers of truth always find themselves in agreement. Disagreement is eminently possible, notwithstanding the sincerity of the interpreters and notwithstanding the efficaciousness of the language in use. But disagreement is not known except when interpreters talk to each other. A lone interpreter knows nothing in the way of agreement or disagreement, but if he is true to his calling he will seek the company of other interpreters, since he knows they are around and is able to locate them. (Only the denizen of an island living in solitude is not in such a position.) When two or more interpreters commence a dialogic conversation with each other, they begin to recognize domains of agreement and domains of disagreement, and when this happens and if the interpreters are people of good-will, the impulse to agree will prevail and through careful exploration of each other's minds a merging of horizons will take place. In other words, truth will be found.

Gadamer would not—nor could not—deny that there may be differences, not just between individuals, but also between groups of individuals, each group agreeing within itself but disagreeing with the other group. Does this mean that truth has not been found, or that there may be multiple conflicting truths? The first thing we must keep in mind in response to this question is that Gadamer rejects the notion of absolute truth. He refuses to equate truth with correctness or with certainty. Only with agreement can truth be identified. There is no realm in which agreement can be found other than the realm of multiple minds in dialogue. Dialogue along with good-will are the crucial factors. It is quite possible, as history shows, for human groups, in fact whole nations, to be swept up into the frenzy of diabolical ideologies and dogmatism, religious or nonreligious. But agreement of this sort is not what Gadamer has in mind; it entails no genuine meeting of minds. The second thing to keep in mind is that people of good-will, even when encountering each other as groups, will always manifest a desire to achieve agreement and will therefore view disagreement as something to be overcome by the attainment of mutual understanding. Mutual understanding is always possible, given the universal character of basic human problems and dilemmas.

A methodology can never be the guarantor of truth. If it could, one would in principle never need agreement as a guarantor of truth. One might hope for agreement or expect agreement as an outcome, but with methodology as the guarantor of truth one must allow for the possibility of the truth being in the possession of one person. Where methodology is determinative of truth, agreement is incidental. Where agreement is determinative, methodology is incidental. In this latter case, it matters not by what avenue of reasoning each individual who is party to an agreement reaches a particular conclusion. The agreement stands on its own feet as constitutive of truth. This is not to say that methodology can have no role. When individual interpreters are seeking truth by exploring each other's minds, they will usually be persuaded by the argument of the other. But even though argument brought the minds together, no argument is the sine qua non of the attainment of truth. There can be many roads to Rome.

Is this way of thinking compatible with Islam? Is it capable of being integrated into an Islamic worldview? Does Gadamer's notion of dialogic conversation have any parallel in Islamic jurisprudence? The usual Arabic terms for conversation, such as *muḥāwara* (or *ḥiwār*) and *muḥādatha*, are not found in classical legal texts with the meanings that serve Gadamer's purposes. One finds references in judicial etiquette (*adab al-qāḍī*) books to *mushāwara* ("consultation"),[10] but this refers to a judge's consultation with muftis or other kinds of experts for advice on particular issues or cases. It does not have the back-and-forth movement of thoughts and ideas that we expect to find in conversation. Is, then, "conversation" in Gadamer's sense of the term something foreign to Islamic legal thought? It seems that the answer to this question, if we mean by "conversation" precisely what Gadamer meant, must be yes. Instead of conversation, one had *munāẓara* to deal with, a term that ordinarily has the sense of disputation, debate, intellectual contest. Gadamer's conversation is all about coming together *for the purpose of* reaching agreement. The individual who isolates himself is deprived of the insights he might gain if he were actively involved with others. In Muslim scholarly encounters there is a much stronger will to prevail over one's opponent. One gives no thought to the risk one takes in entering the debate. One plunges into the fray gladly, eager to win. Makdisi tells of debates that ended in blows, the most spectacular example being a story told of the great al-Shāfiʿī. Al-Shāfiʿī, it is said, died of blows administered to him by students of a rival teacher in revenge for blows which al-Shāfiʿī's students had administered to them.[11] This sort of thing was surely the exception rather than the rule; but there is no doubt that the disputational encounters could be filled with tension. Sayf al-Dīn al-Āmidī (d. 1233) exemplifies the intensity of the scholarly climate engendered by public disputational contests. As a consistently unvanquished debater, he aroused the enmity of his peers wherever he resided, compelling him to move frequently during the course of his career. His frequent changes of residence typically had this scholarly ill-will as their cause.[12]

But would, one may wonder, consensus (*ijmāʿ*), traditionally regarded as one of the "sources" (*uṣūl*) of Islamic law, be a counterpart to Gadamer's agreement-through-conversation? It seems not. The *ijmāʿ* is not about people exploring each other's thinking and working together on a horizontal plane toward agreement. The *ijmāʿ* is categorically different from Gadamer's *mitsein.* It is agreement in the sense of sheer *coincidence* of like opinions arrived at independently by scholars each engaged in his own individual interpretive effort. It is not agreement of the kind envisioned by Gadamer: consciously arrived at through a cooperative mutual exploring of the "other." It just happens. It is not the natural product of a give and take conversation with a dynamic leading progressively toward agreement. Its validity has nothing to do with content. If some scholars hold opinion A and others hold opinion B, both remain at the level of opinion, but if all scholars hold opinion A, it is raised to the level of infallible doctrine. It is sheer happenstance, not active agreement, that brings this about.

For a Muslim legal practitioner deliberating on a case, the *ijmāʿ* has no immediate relevance. There is no way to bring about a fresh *ijmāʿ* on the spur of the moment to provide an urgently needed solution. The *ijmāʿ* is an instrument of doctrinal consolidation and fortification. The legal practitioner might utilize a text that is *ijmāʿ*-based, but he will never be able to come up with an *ijmāʿ* specific to a case at hand. And whether the text that the practitioner utilizes is endorsed by an *ijmāʿ* makes no difference. A decision or ruling in a case is always based on a careful weighing of opposing considerations on a scale. Whichever way the scale tips is the way the practitioner will go. The fact that differences might occur within the realm of opinion but not in the realm of *ijmāʿ* makes no practical difference.

In contrast to Gadamer's steadfast commitment to agreement and understanding as the ultimate desiderata and to the elimination of difference, the Muslim jurists are committed to difference as a positive good. So long as disagreement does not spill over the boundaries of Muḥammad's community, it can be put to profitable use, in the Muslim view. The Prophet's famous saying, "Disagreement in my community is a mercy (*raḥma*) from God," in combination with the oft-repeated phrase *allāhu aʿlam* (in effect meaning "God's knowledge surpasses ours") pinpoints a fundamental difference between Gadamer's philosophical hermeneutics and Islam. If disagreement concerning the details of how we should live our lives and conduct our affairs is sanctioned by God, then that must mean that on any issue on which there is disagreement there is no single valid way to go. One has choices to make within the bounds of acceptability. No choice can be invalidated provided it is based on sincere and competent interpretive effort.

What of the *uṣūl al-fiqh,* we may ask at this point? Is it not all about the methodology of legal interpretation? Is not this methodology a tool that we should expect a legal practitioner to be using to arrive at a decision? And should not use of this tool reduce disagreement among legal practitioners? My own sense of how to respond to such questions is to suggest that the real purpose of the whole discipline of *uṣūl al-fiqh* and its literature is not to expound a particular normative methodology but rather to provide instruction on how to debate methodological issues entailed in the enterprise of creating *fiqh.* On most of these issues—many of them extremely important issues—the scholars of the law are divided. The contents of the *uṣūl al-fiqh* books are, it is true, organized around the famous "four sources," but this does not mean that a fully-fledged methodology is waiting to leap out from its pages. The discipline is in reality extremely open-ended and flexible, and by studying its literature one becomes aware of the dynamism of classical Muslim jurisprudence. One finds discussions therein of argument-broadening concepts such as juristic preference (*istiḥsān*), human welfare (*maṣlaḥa*), custom (*ʿurf*), extra-revelational human interests (*maṣāliḥ mursala*), and the great ends of the law (*maqāṣid al-sharīʿa*).

Traditionally what mastery of the techniques of legal argument laid out in the *uṣūl* literature was thought to produce was, of course, *fiqh,* knowledge of legal doctrine, of rules. These days it is widely recognized that *fiqh* and the methods of formulating it are in the modern context often not helpful and may in fact under certain circumstances be harmful. Proponents of legal realism look to socio-economic, political, and cultural factors as the determinants of the law rather than abstract rules.

We come finally to what Gadamer considered to be the feature of law that was most illustrative of what hermeneutics was about, and that was the inseparability of interpretation from application. This feature was especially evident in the deliberations of the judge, for even though other legal practitioners were concerned with application, the judge was at the cutting edge of application. Interpretation without application is not authentic interpretation. Judicial interpretation without application is utterly inconceivable. Interpretation for the judge is entirely and exclusively case-related.

Its setting is the court, not the hall of learning. Academicians of the law compile rules in books; others study those books as part of their training to give legal advice; but only judges applied the law with finality. What Gadamer meant in saying that the judge best demonstrated the exemplary character of the law can be best stated in his own words. The following statement is to be found in a section of his *Truth and Method* entitled "The exemplary significance of legal hermeneutics." Gadamer argues against the contention that because of its preoccupation with adjudication rather than with the meaning of texts as such, legal hermeneutics is marginal to hermeneutics in general. To the contrary, argues Gadamer,

> legal hermeneutics serves to remind us what the real procedure of the human sciences is. Here we have the model for the relationship between past and present that we are seeking. The judge who adapts the transmitted law to the needs of the present is undoubtedly seeking to perform a practical task, but his interpretation of the law is by no means for that reason an arbitrary revision. Here again, to understand and to interpret mean to discover and recognize a valid meaning. [...] Does this not mean that it [i.e., the law] always needs to be restated? And does not this restatement take place through its being related to the present? [...] *In reality then, legal hermeneutics is no special case but is, on the contrary, capable of restoring the hermeneutical problem to its full breadth and so re-establishing the former unity of hermeneutics, in which the jurist and theologian meet the philologist* [emphasis Gadamer's]. [...] The work of interpretation is *to concretize* the law in each specific case—i.e. it is a work of *application.* The creative supplementing of the law that is involved is a task reserved to the judge, but he is subject to the law in the same way as every other member of the community. It is part of the idea of the rule of law that the judge's judgment does not proceed from an arbitrary and unpredictable decision.[13]

As this passage suggests, Gadamer contends that legal hermeneutics illustrates the following points with exemplary clarity. All of these points have to do with the role of the judge, from whom we learn that:

1. *Interpretation is inseparable from practical application; the two are not separate processes but are two aspects of a single process.* The judge does not simply take over the result of previously completed interpretation and apply it wholesale to the case at hand. Interpretation and application are not two separate steps: one does not first interpret, and then move on from there to application. The interpretation that a judge engages in is relevant from start to finish to the case at hand.

Gadamer frequently speaks of judicial interpretation as a process of relating the past to the present, which is to say that the judge "adapts the *transmitted* law to the needs of the present [emphasis mine]," thus performing "a practical task." He "restates" the law so as to give it relevance to the present. The law "always needs to be restated."[14] The purpose of the judge's restatement of the law is to "concretize" the law so as to make it applicable to the case at hand. Concretization and application are interchangeable concepts. Without application—without relevance to the present moment—no interpretation is complete.

2. *Texts are in themselves insufficient as a basis for practical application and therefore require judicial interpretation to establish their relevance to the case under consideration.* Gadamer refers to this interpretive activity of the judge as a "creative supplement." It is a supplement in the sense that it provides something the text by itself lacks, and it is creative in the sense that it is something the judge, and he (or she) alone, does with respect to a novel case, something unique and original that has a bearing upon a particular set of specific facts. "Legal texts do not require interpretation only when they are vague, as a prelude to their application [...] instead, understanding is possible at all only in an interpretive application of the law to a case at hand."[15] On the other hand, it is not as though the text comes to the judge without any meaning at all. The text is not an empty void to be filled in as the judge pleases. The text cannot be made to say anything a judge wants it to say. "The interpretive activity considers itself wholly bound by the meaning of the text. [...] [The jurist does not regard] the work of application as making free with the text." The text in its transmitted form does have meaning but it is a meaning that in every case requires concretization, and this is what judicial interpretation seeks to do. The judge's interpretation shapes, directs, and augments the meaning carried by the text:

> Legal hermeneutics always involves the interpretation *of binding texts* [emphasis mine], texts that make a claim on the interpreter. [...] the rule of law requires that the law is obeyed and that the interpreter does not freely twist the law to his subjective designs. An interpreter who objectifies and contorts a text for his own purposes. [...] remains within the grip of a subject-centered orientation that precludes genuine interpretive activity.[16]

3. *Although the judge alone renders the final decision in a case, his connectedness with the community and involvement in dialogic conversation with others prevent him from applying the law in a self-serving and idiosyncratic manner.* Any judge is conscious of being subject to the rule of law along with all other members of the community. His interpretation of texts will be informed by his participation in dialogic conversation in which individuals open their minds to the interpretive views of their fellows. Thanks to a fusion of horizons—a harmonious coming together of minds—judicial interpretation can be spared the insular subjectivism and relativism that Gadamer's philosophical hermeneutics is designed to counter. In Gadamer's community of understanding, the presumption is that harmony is more fundamental than strife, that community-mindedness is more endemic than individual-

ism, that objectivity is closer at hand than subjectivity. It is within such a community that truth finds its home.

All three of these points, it seems to me, may be applied to Islamic law.

1. Judicial interpretation is a requisite in every system of law if for no other reason than simply that the texts always fall short of the specificity required for application. They are not application-ready *qua* texts and can be applied, therefore, only through the interpretive offices of a judge, whose role it is to supplement the text as needed in order to apply to the case at hand. The judge's interpretation takes place within what Gadamer calls "free space," which is the space left to him by the limitation of the text. It is important that we understand that textual insufficiency does not mean that the text carries no relevant meaning whatsoever. The problem (which is often referred to by Gadamer as the "hermeneutical problem") is that the meaning carried by the text is not sufficient for application—it is necessary, we may say, but not sufficient. "The meaning to be understood is concretized and fully realized only in [the judge's] interpretation, but the interpretive activity considers itself wholly bound by the meaning of the text."[17]

No Muslim judge would regard the work of application as permitting him to take unrestrained liberty with the text. He knows that the words of the text cannot mean anything he wants them to mean. He must work from within a framework of given meaning that, however insufficient it may be for application purposes, forms a necessary starting point for developing a meaning that will fit the case at hand. Gadamer uses the term dialogue to characterize the interpreter's relationship to a legal text. Just how much weight will be given to the text as it comes to him and how much to his supplemental interpretation will vary from case to case.

Judicial decision-making without an explicit basis in a written *naṣṣ*[18] or *fiqh* text is by no means uncommon throughout the history of Islam. The accumulated experience of judges across generations taught that insistence upon strict adherence to the traditional written texts did not always produce the desired conclusion, that sometimes it was necessary to set aside the usual textual argument in favor of a consideration of best interests (*maṣāliḥ*). Lawrence Rosen has emphasized the importance of conflict resolution as a judicial aim and the crucial role of the judge in facilitating negotiation between the parties.[19] One can readily appreciate why a judge would regard reconciliation of difference between parties and the consequent promotion of social harmony as a more successful outcome of his judicial endeavors than strict application of a textual norm that might exacerbate conflict. Favoring domestic peace over blind allegiance to *naṣṣ* and *fiqh* texts was not without textual justification. One could cite, for example, the Prophet's saying, "Whatever Muslims deem good is good with God" (*mā ra'āhu al-muslimūn ḥasanan fa-huwa 'inda allāh ḥasan*)[20] or Imam Mālik's saying, "*Istiḥsān* is nine-tenths of knowledge [of the law]."[21]

One of the most famous narratives cited in support of judicial discretion is that which tells of the Prophet's appointment of Mu'ādh to a judgeship in the Yemen. According to the story, the Prophet asks Mu'ādh, "By what will you judge?" Mu'ādh responds, "By the Book of God." The Prophet then asks, "And if you do not find what you need in the Book of God, what then?" To which Mu'ādh replies, "I shall decide on the basis of the Sunna of the Messenger of God." Asks the Prophet, "And if you do not find what you need in the Sunna?" "Then," says Mu'ādh, "I shall exercise discretion." Immediately, the Prophet approves this procedure.[22] Like all such narratives, this one can be—and his been—interpreted in a variety of ways, and the responsible interpreter is likely to insist that there is no "single right interpretation." It is, I think, not far-fetched to understand this story as reinforcing the notion that texts—here identified as the Qur'an and Sunna—are in and of themselves insufficient as sole basis for application of the law to concrete situations but at the same time are necessary and indispensable as a framework or starting point of judicial deliberation that leads to judgment. One does not blindly plunge into the exercise of discretion. One gets to that point by way of serious consideration of what can be found in the *naṣṣ* texts. Discretion (*ra'y*) never stands alone. Legitimacy of the judge's final decision must come from the texts—be they the direct words of God or the Prophet as contained in Qur'an and Sunna or words in which are enshrined long-established and well-proven practices of daily life among Muslims wherever they may be found living in communities—but only as supplemented in crucial ways by the sagacity of the judge himself.

3. Text—interpretation—case: these then are the three basic constituents of the judicial process. The text represents what is already there, having come from an origin in the past—a transmitted given. Interpretation finds its space in the interstices of the text, its ambiguities and generalities. Gadamer calls this the judge's "free space." It is not always easy to determine where text ends and interpretation begins. We are all heirs to Stanley Fish's reflections on the question: "Is there a text in this class?"[23] That is a matter on which there is always difference of opinion. And yet, if we are not prepared to resign ourselves to a completely open-ended text, something intuition tells us just cannot be, we must suppose that such a line is there waiting to be drawn even if we think we shall never know precisely where to draw it. The human mind still has not fathomed the mysteries of a text. It is such a fluid thing, yet it cannot be all fluidity. The best methods of textual criticism have never captured it entirely, nor have the best methods of interpretation captured its meaning. Many regard a singular text and a singular meaning as too much to be hoped for,

if indeed it is something one would want to hope for in the first place. A text is something like a sponge: it absorbs the meanings we come up with, but with a squeeze and release is ready to take on different meaning. Yet it is not as though text does not itself include meaning. Even the firmest squeeze of a sponge leaves some moisture in its recesses.

The judge, we have noted, occupies free interpretive space, according to Gadamer. Yet it is free, not in the sense that the judge will carry on his work as he pleases, in a self-serving way, but in the sense that any constraints upon his work will come, not from external sources, but entirely from within himself. This is the point where Frank Vogel's notion of microcosmic law takes on its full significance.[24] In the moment of final decision-making, the moment when the law becomes known, the moment that constitutes the law's cutting edge, the judge is in his own private world, a world entirely of his own making, with nothing to guide him ultimately except his conscience. Vogel calls microcosmic law a "model [...] in which law is epitomized, not in a system of objective, formal, general, public, compulsory rules but in the unique decision of an individual conscience [...] applied to an evaluation of a concrete act."[25] The words "objective, formal, general, public, compulsory" describe its opposite, macrocosmic law. Macrocosmic law is the law of the insufficient text, as Gadamer would have it. Strictly speaking, it is not law at all. What goes by the name of law at the macrocosmic level must be united with the particularities of a concrete case and an exercise of conscience on the part of the judge. Only then does binding law emerge. We have echoes here of Gadamer's triad of (insufficient) text, case at hand, and judicial interpretation considered as creative supplement to the text. By itself, the formal, general rules, the transmitted text, float in a kind of limbo, without binding anyone until applied to the concrete case. General rules come "under a considerable cloud. Not being fortified by a state monopoly of legislation, prey to contradiction and divergent application by a myriad of law-makers and -appliers, and considered binding only when brought to bear on a particular concrete context, general rules scarcely deserve the name of law."[26]

Binding law therefore has its only locale in that free and private space where the conscience of a judge does its work. It exists only in the moment of application and only for the parties to which it is applied. Vogel calls it "instance-law" and contrasts it with the "rules-law" that makes up the realm of the macrocosmic. What we find in the public sphere in the way of formal, general rules has a staying power that instance-law does not have. On the other hand, instance-law has a binding quality lacking in general rules. In the almost ritualistic moment of application, the judge's conscience reigns supreme. His is, in that moment, an authority not enjoyed by the most erudite of tomes containing rule-law. His also is a responsibility for which there is no parallel, whence the dictum that two of every three judges have their final abode in hell, one has his in paradise.

The most potent restraint on the interpretive endeavors of the Muslim judge, insuring that he will judge responsibly, consistently, and not arbitrarily, is thus religious in nature. Like the Deuteronomic judge of old (Deut. 16:18–19; 17:8–9), the Muslim judge is under a divine mandate to ponder, not abstract rules contained in written scriptures, but the demands of elemental justice and wisdom as they become manifest to him case by case. He must not pervert justice by taking bribes—in other words, use his position to serve his own ends. For Gadamer, assurance of responsible, consistent, and predictable judging comes from the judge's participation in dialogic conversation. To the extent that the judge cultivates the habit of *mitsein*, of being-with-others, of experiencing with others a fusion of horizons, he can be counted upon to rise above self-centeredness and to open his mind to the kind of interpretation that will produce a "valid meaning."[27]

III

To return in closing to our original question: Do we find in philosophical hermeneutics of Hans-Georg Gadamer the makings of a new Islamic legal hermeneutic? Let us remember, first of all, that Gadamer remained to the end of his days a child of post-modernism, despite his best efforts to counter the subjectivity, relativism, and tendency to politicize associated with post-modernist thinking. He wanted to build a hermeneutics that promoted the values of community, social harmony, understanding, and truth without lapsing into the dogmatism of traditional epistemologies and rational systems that had reigned over human thought since the time of Plato and Aristotle and had taken its leave with the passing of the Enlightenment. In this respect Gadamer was a true heir of Nietzsche, who had said: "To speak seriously, there are good grounds for hoping that all dogmatizing in philosophy, the solemn air of finality it has given itself notwithstanding, may none the less have been no more than a noble childishness and tyronism."[28] To this vision of an end to dogmatism and all that goes with it Gadamer was determined to remain faithful, even while holding fast to values that were not typically Nietzschean.

It was, of course, Nietzsche's attack on the Enlightenment and his project of the dismantlement of philosophy that launched the post-modern world: on this all are pretty much agreed, both Gadamer and his critics. But with this huge commonality came huge differences, and among these were differences having to do with law. Many were cynical about the law. Gadamer was not. He was convinced that law could serve constructive purposes if made and applied by people of good-will who conversed with one another in a deliberate attempt to explore areas of agreement, fusions of horizons. It is on account of this conviction that Gadamer holds so much interest for scholars of the law today. The opening contribution to this book, in which Donahue shows how the law could be an instrument of social change for the better in twelfth- and sixteenth-century Europe, is a good example of what might be called a Gadamerian view of the utility of the law.

Does interest in Gadamer's hermeneutics among Western practitioners and academicians of the law necessarily mean that the same interest will be found in the halls of legal study and learning in the Muslim world? In attempting to answer this question we should first of all note that the Muslim world no longer can be imagined as geographically set apart from the West, given the millions of Muslims who live in the West, are educated in the West, and think like their non-Muslim counterparts in the West. Many Muslims have entered the legal profession and are as deeply concerned with law-related philosophical issues as are non-Muslims. They too feel the weight of post-modernism upon their intellectual shoulders and might just as conceivably be drawn to Gadamer's ideas as any others.

Contemporaneous with the movement of *people* from the Muslim world into the intellectual circles of the so-called West has been the complementary movement of *ideas* in the opposite direction: from the West into the intellectual circles of the Muslim world. This adds another dimension to the breakdown of geographical boundaries separating Islam from the West. Therefore we cannot say that the philosophical line of development that runs from Nietzsche to Gadamer is of no concern to Muslims. Among those shaped by this heritage are many Muslim thinkers.

"Rethinking Islam" is a phrase one frequently encounters these days, or phrases similar to it. Although there are many possible influences, Islamic and Western, that could have a part in the rethinking project, it is hard to deny that Gadamerian hermeneutics lends itself especially well to the task. It can have a powerful role in inviting people concerned with the law to come together in dialogic conversation, to have faith that the dialogic process can, if carried on by people of good-will, be trusted to yield what can most authentically and reliably be called the truth of the law, and to accept the priority of truth over method. The deeply traditionalist factions in the Muslim world today, of course, will say no. The world, they will tell us, has nothing to learn from the West. But we have only to reflect on the many external influences that were involved in the shaping of Muslim intellectual traditions in the first place to realize how wrong this claim is. Consider in closing what Fred Dallmayr has to say about Gadamer:

> Gadamerian hermeneutics is not just a parochial ingredient of Continental thought but an important building stone in the emerging global city and in a dialogically construed cultural relativism. [...] In a world rent by the competing pulls of Western-style universalism and bellicose modes of ethnocentrism, accent on cross-cultural engagement opens a vista pointing beyond the dystopias of melting pot synthesis and radical fragmentation.[29]

NOTES

[1] The publisher's note has this to say: "Hans-Georg Gadamer's philosophical hermeneutics is especially relevant for law, which is grounded in the interpretation of authoritarian texts from the past to resolve present-day disputes. [...] Part I considers the relevance of Gadamer's philosophy to longstanding disputes in legal theory such as the debate over originalism, the rule of law, and proper modes of statutory and constitutional exegesis. Part II demonstrates Gadamer's significance for legal theory by comparing his approach to the work of Nietzsche, Habermas and Dworkin."

[2] Francis J. Mootz, "Responding to Nietzsche: the Constructive Power of *Destruktion*," *Law, Culture, and the Humanities* 3 (2007), 127–54. Hereafter referred to as "Mootz."

[3] See Chapter 17 above.

[4] This overview is based on readings in a variety of sources and would be considered general knowledge in Gadamerian studies. I do rely most heavily on Gadamer's writings, especially his *Truth and Method*, 2nd revised edition (New York: Crossroad, 1990), and his essay "Text and Interpretation," in *Dialogue and Deconstruction: The Gadamer-Derrida Encounter*, ed. D. Michelfelder and R. Palmer (Albany: SUNY Press, 1989). These will be referred to here as TM and TI.

[5] TI, 28–9.

[6] Mootz, 146.

[7] TM, 302.

[8] TM, 305.

[9] I prefer "unhiddenness" to the more common rendering of the German as "unconcealment" or "uncovering." "Unhiddenness" suggests the notion of a *state* of being hidden, implicit in the German *-heit* as opposed to an *act* of hiding.

[10] Abū Bakr Aḥmad b. ʿAmr al-Khaṣṣāf, *Kitāb Adab al-qāḍī*, tr. Farhat J. Ziadeh (Cairo: American University in Cairo Press, 1978), 105.

[11] George Makdisi, *The Rise of Colleges* (Edinburgh: Edinburgh University Press, 1981), 136 (Makdisi cites Yāqūt as his source).

[12] For a brief biographical note on al-Āmidī, see B. Weiss, *The Search for God's Law* (Salt Lake City: University of Utah Press, 1990), 28–9.

[13] TM, 327–29.

[14] TM, 328.

[15] Mootz, 142–43.

[16] TM, 332.

[17] Ibid.

[18] The term *naṣṣ* refers to the foundational texts of Islamic law, that is, the Qurʾan and Sunna.

[19] See Lawrence Rosen, *The Anthropology of Justice* (Cambridge: Cambridge University Press, 1989).

[20] A highly ubiquitous and widely quoted saying attributed to the Prophet.

[21] The sources for this saying may be found in B. Weiss (ed.), *Studies in Islamic Legal Theory* (Leiden: Brill, 2002), 164 n. 9.

[22] al-Khaṣṣāf, op. cit., 44.

[23] Stanley Fish, *Is There a Text in this Class? The Authority of Interpretive Communities* (Cambridge, Mass.: Harvard University Press, 1980).

[24] Frank E. Vogel, *Islamic Law and Legal System: Studies of Saudi Arabia* (Leiden: Brill, 2000), 23–28.

[25] Idem, 23.

[26] Idem, 21.

[27] TM, 328.

[28] Friedrich Nietzsche, "Beyond Good and Evil," tr. R. Hollingdale, in *Great Books of the Western World* (Chicago: Encyclopaedia Britannica, Inc., 1990), 43:463.

[29] Quoted in Francis J. Mootz III, *Rhetorical Knowledge in Legal Practice and Critical Legal Theory* (Tuscaloosa: University of Alabama Press, 2006), xi–xii.

20

TWO THEORIES OF THE OBLIGATION TO OBEY GOD'S COMMANDS

Aron Zysow

The Two Theories Introduced

Islamic law grew out of God's commands and prohibitions as conveyed by the Prophet Muḥammad. It is perhaps out of place to ask why one should obey these commands and prohibitions. But the Qurʾan itself with noteworthy frequency sees fit to enjoin obedience to God and His messenger.[1] Is one therefore bound to obey God's commands and prohibitions because God has commanded that He be obeyed? But why obey this command to obey? A regress obviously looms. Recognizing this problem, modern Twelver Shiʿi legal theory distinguishes between God's authoritative commands (*amr mawlawī*) and His advisory commands (*amr irshādī*), of which the Qurʾanic commands to obey God are a paradigm instance. These commands, according to the Shiʿi theorists, do not impose independent obligations but serve rather to advise one of one's rational obligations.[2] Whether or not the question of why obey God was appropriate in the first place, it was one that Muslims thinkers did, in fact, ask. A variety of answers were proposed, answers that are in general terms akin to the answers that Western theologians have given to the same question and that Western political theorists have given to the analogous question: Why obey the laws of the state?

Broadly speaking, the leading answers to the question of why obey God are of two sorts, prudential and moral.[3] Probably the response to this question best known to students of Islamic thought is that grounded in prudence. This answer is associated with the theological school of Ashʿarism, espoused by so many distinguished Muslim thinkers. The Ashʿaris must ground the obligation to obey God in prudence because for them there is no moral order independent of revelation. The commands of God are what bring obligations into existence, and the concept of obligation as a technical legal term is rooted in the threat of punishment in the Hereafter.[4] The everyday sense of obligation apart from revelation is similarly prudential, for someone who does not believe in revelation might well say that it is obligatory for someone in extreme hunger, on the brink of dying of starvation, to eat any bread he comes across.[5] To what extent Ashʿari teaching on this matter was "internalized" by the many Muslims who over the centuries called themselves Ashʿaris, and to what extent Ashʿari theological doctrine is consistent with Islamic legal theory, in particular the theory of analogy (*qiyās*), are both important questions that cannot be addressed here.

A moral, as opposed to a prudential, answer to the question of why one should obey God's commands assumes the existence of a moral order apart from revelation. Recognition of obligations grounded in reason without revelation is commonly associated with the Muʿtazili theological tradition, but this notion was far from being found only among Muʿtazilis and those, such as Twelver and Zaydi Shiʿis, influenced by Muʿtazili thought.[6] Nonetheless it cannot be denied that Muʿtazilism, more than any other theological movement to which we have access, was engaged in elaborating the many implications of such recognition, including the question of the ground of obedience to God's commands. It was thus among Muʿtazilis that two leading moral justifications of the obligation to obey God came to be hotly debated.[7]

The older theory was that the obligation to obey God was grounded in the rational obligation of gratitude to a benefactor (*shukr al-munʿim*).[8] This was the theory espoused by the Baghdadi wing of the Muʿtazila, and is particularly associated with Abū l-Qāsim al-Kaʿbī (d. 319/931), who came to enjoy great prominence as the leading figure in this branch of the school. The theory of gratitude was also popular among prominent Twelver Shiʿi and Zaydi theologians and enjoyed notable support among the anti-Muʿtazili Central Asian Hanafis, whose outstanding theologian was al-Māturīdī (d. 333/944).[9] It also appears to have been the position of several prominent Shafiʿi jurists, who in espousing moral obligations founded in reason were later regarded as having fallen prey to Muʿtazili influence. Adoption of the theory of gratitude was not limited to Muslims but extended to Jews, most prominently Saadia Gaon (d. 942). The widespread popularity of the theory of gratitude and its at least initially intuitive appeal make it clear that it was the original moral justification in Islamic thought for the obedience due God.[10] The focus here will be chiefly on the Muʿtazili version of the theory of gratitude as defended by al-Kaʿbī and his followers.

For a time the Baghdadi theory of gratitude was in competition with the newer theory associated with the Basran Muʿtazilis and championed above all by Abū Hāshim al-Jubbāʾī (d. 321/933).[11] This is the theory of *lutf*, divine grace or assistance.[12] According to this theory, the acts and omissions made obligatory by the revealed law have an instrumental function, in that compliance with them brings one closer to compliance with one's rational obligations. Obedience to the law does so by strengthening one's motivation to do what is right. Although this theory can find some support in the Qur'an itself (e.g. 29:45), it clearly constitutes a far less obvious explanation of the obligation to obey God than the theory of gratitude.[13] Nonetheless, it was the *luṭf* theory that triumphed both among the Muʿtazila and among those Shiʿis—Twelvers and Zaydis—and Jews most influenced by developments in Muʿtazili thought. It was chiefly among the Yemeni Zaydis that the older doctrine of gratitude survived alongside the *luṭf* theory before being given new life by the powerful Yemeni Zaydi imam al-Manṣūr bi-llāh al-Qāsim b. Muḥammad (d. 1029/1620).

The Theory of Gratitude

Although very little survives of the writings of Abū l-Qāsim al-Kaʿbī and the Baghdadi school in general, the main outlines of al-Kaʿbī's position are fairly clear. According to him, God's limitless bounties made God the unparalleled benefactor of His creation and thus the primary object of the rational obligation of gratitude. Without revelation, however, mankind would be unable to discharge this obligation for lack of knowledge as to what it entailed in the case of God, who is beyond all needs and human favors. Revelation was required to give substance to the underlying rational obligation of gratitude. Human obedience to the law of God merited no divine reward in itself, since such obedience was simply a means of fulfilling the duty of gratitude already incurred to God. In this sense, in obeying God human beings were occupied in meeting an obligation they could never even come close to discharging, even as they continued to enjoy God's favors in the very expression of their gratitude. Al-Kaʿbī thus held that any reward God bestowed on those who obeyed His commands was in the nature of an act of generosity on God's part. By contrast, the Basran Muʿtazilis regarded reward for obedience to God as merited by the hardship (*mashaqqa*) of compliance given the opposing impulses with which God has endowed His subjects.[14] According to them, God was under an obligation to reward those who had obeyed Him.[15]

In itself the notion that God's commands simply spell out the content of the gratitude owed God does not directly address the content of these commands. Given that God is above all needs (*ghanī*), God has nothing to gain for Himself by what He commands. Might His commands simply be ways of testing the gratitude of those whom He has benefited? This is a possible position and would represent what might be termed a pure theory of gratitude as the ground of obedience to God. On this account the content of the revealed law would not necessarily be such as to provide any independent ground for compliance beyond the gratitude already due God for past benefits.[16] A theory of this sort is suggested by a passage in *al-Radd ʿalā l-mulḥid* attributed to the Medinese Zaydi imam al-Qāsim b. Ibrāhīm al-Rassī (d. 246/ 860).[17] In this work al-Qāsim explains that ritual acts such as prayer and fasting have no other ground in reason than obeying (*iʾtimār*) God's command. These obligations represent a test (*imtiḥān*) of obedience imposed by God. In fact, all of the revealed laws (*sharāʾiʿ*) share this ground. Al-Qāsim suggests an analogy with the similar unquestioning obedience owed the slave-master (*sayyid*) by his slave.[18]

In fact, however, this pure theory of gratitude was far less popular than another version of the theory of gratitude, according to which the obligations of the revealed law were themselves benefits bestowed by God upon his subjects.[19] This version accords with the characteristic Baghdadi Muʿtazili teaching that God always acts to achieve what is optimific (*al-aṣlaḥ*) for his creation in both worldly (*al-dunyā*) and religious matters (*al-dīn*). The Basran Muʿtazilis accepted this notion only with respect to religious matters, that is, entirely in terms of their concept of *lutf*. For them *maslaḥa* (utility) and *lutf* are treated as synonyms.[20] For the Baghdadi Muʿtazilis God is the ultimate utilitarian agent. Since the utility that God is ever maximizing is that of His creation, the essential relation between God and creature is that of gratitude. It was even argued that rationality (*ḥikma*) requires that God, the perfectly rational agent, exhibit His benefits, in order that He may be the object of gratitude.[21] On this account, God has to create the world and impose a system of moral and legal responsibility (*taklīf*). It would be irrational (*ʿabath*) for God to fail to do so.[22]

Like all other dimensions of God's activity, His legislation is necessarily utilitarian. The Baghdadis insisted that each obligation of the revealed law was imposed for the benefit of its human subjects. A fairly elaborate exposition of this version of the theory of gratitude is found in the recently published theological work *Ḥaqāʾiq al-maʿrifa* of the Yemeni Zaydi imam al-Mutawakkil ʿalā llāh Aḥmad b. Sulaymān (d. 566/1170).[23]

This version of the theory of gratitude sometimes looks to the obligation of gratitude toward parents as its human analogue. Loving parents will impose those obligations that they regard as in the best interests of their children, and their children will owe them obedience from gratitude for previous benefits.[24] Because God is above all need, the obligations He imposes will necessarily be free of any taint of self-interest.

The Muʿtazili Debate

It is important to keep in mind that both sides of the gratitude versus *lutf* debate, along with many others, recognized a rational obligation of gratitude to a benefactor.[25] This explains both the widespread early appeal of the gratitude theory as well as the rather scanty positive argumentation in its support that survives. The *lutf* theorists, committed as they were to the recognition of a rational obligation of gratitude to a benefactor, were compelled to construe this obligation in such a way as to preclude its use by the gratitude theorists. They also made a specific target of the nexus of Baghdadi utilitarianism and gratitude.

For the supporters of the theory of gratitude, gratitude was essentially expressed as obedience (*ṭāʿa*) and could take the most varied forms.[26] By contrast the proponents of the theory of *luṭf* understood gratitude in a far more attenuated sense. For them gratitude was defined in terms of acknowledgment (*iʿtirāf*) coupled with respect (*taʿẓīm*).[27] The acknowledgement of the benefit bestowed was essentially mental and verbal, as was the respect due the benefactor.

The Muʿtazili Ibn Mattawayh (d. 469/1076), a student of Qāḍī ʿAbd al-Jabbār (d. 415/1025), rejects completely the notion that the obligation of gratitude for benefits received could sustain such burdensome obligations as jihad and fasting. This claim was not supported by reason. God could only impose such burdensome obligations by attaching compensating rewards to their performance.[28] Equally misplaced was an appeal to an analogy with the obligations of gratitude due parents, which typically went beyond simple mental and verbal acknowledgement to include burdensome services. If there was a rational obligation of service to parents, it was grounded not in gratitude but rather in self-interest, in that in serving one's parents one was sparing oneself the unpleasant feelings (*ghamm*) that would attend contravening their wishes. Insofar as the revealed law introduced obligations of burdensome service to parents, these would have to be grounded in *luṭf*.[29] To the extent that the [Basran] Muʿtazili masters could be found basing the ritual acts of the revealed law on gratitude to God, what they meant was that such acts had to be performed with due respect and self-abasement (*khuḍūʿ*) as was the case with gratitude toward a benefactor. They did not mean that such acts were grounded on gratitude in the strict sense (*taḥqīq*).[30]

A further argument against grounding the obligation of obeying God's law in gratitude is that there is no apparent correspondence between the distribution of God's benefits and the burdens of His law as one might expect. In fact, one finds individuals varying widely in the benefits that God has bestowed upon them subject to the very same legal obligations.[31]

The nexus between the Baghdadi theories of utilitarianism and gratitude was the specific object of criticism by the Basran Muʿtazilis. Their criticism was one element in a broader Basran attack on the utilitarian theory of God's action that includes objections familiar from modern critiques of utilitarianism, e.g., it makes excessive demands, it fails to recognize the distinction between obligation and supererogation.[32] The Basran Muʿtazilis argued that since God is obligated to act for the maximal benefit of His creatures, they owe Him no gratitude. The obligation of gratitude only arises when the benefactor acts without being under an obligation.[33] An agent who performs an obligatory act may merit praise (*madḥ*) but definitely not gratitude. Thus the Baghdadi theory of God as the ultimate utilitarian cuts the ground from under the gratitude theory of obedience to God's law.[34]

Although the Baghdadis spoke of God's obligation to do what is most to the benefit of His creation, they did seek to mitigate this bold assertion by interpreting the obligation in question in such a way as to respond to the Basran argument. They thus claimed that the term "obligatory" might correctly be used for what was not required in the strict sense but was preferable (*awlā*).[35] Failure to comply with an obligation in this sense did not entail blame of the agent.[36] They sought to associate the obligation they had in mind with generosity (*jūd*). If God did not do what was most beneficial, He would not be generous (*jawād*), and if not generous, then He was miserly (*bakhīl*).[37] The Basran response to the Baghdadi defense of their utilitarianism came to be built around the analysis of an array of terms that called for careful preliminary scrutiny.[38]

Against the Basran argument that gratitude was not incumbent for the performance of an obligation, the Baghdadis counterattacked by pointing out that the Basrans themselves were of the view that gratitude was due God for His reward (*thawāb*), for the compensation (*aʿwāḍ*) He provided His creatures for their suffering, and for the various forms of *luṭf*, all of which they regarded as obligatory for God. The Basrans replied that although God's reward, compensation, and assistance were indeed obligatory, they only became so in consequence of God's supererogatory acts, whether the act of creation itself or the act of imposing moral responsibility (*taklīf*). The gratitude due God in all the cases cited by the Baghdadis was thus ultimately grounded not in acts that were obligatory for God but in acts of supererogation (*tafaḍḍul*).[39] It was, however, argued on behalf of the utilitarians that they too could trace the obligation of gratitude back to supererogatory acts on God's part.[40]

The Fate of the Two Theories

The general trend among Muʿtazilis and the Twelver and Zaydi Shiʿi theologians who wrote within a Muʿtazili framework was for gratitude to give way to *luṭf*. While the Baghdadi doctrine of optimificity (*al-aṣlaḥ*) enjoyed some continued support in the less ambitious version proposed by the influential Basran theorist Abū l-Ḥusayn al-Baṣrī (d. 436/1044), the theory of gratitude itself increasingly fell by the wayside.[41]

Evidence for the dating of the abandonment of the theory of gratitude for *luṭf* among Twelver Shiʿis comes from Muḥammad b. ʿAlī al-Karājikī (d. 449/1057), a student of al-Shaykh al-Mufīd (d. 413/1022). Al-Karājikī in general faithfully upholds his teacher's predominantly Baghdadi positions, even when they were given up for Basran views by al-Sharīf al-Murtaḍā (d. 426/1044) and Abū Jaʿfar al-Ṭūsī (d. 459/1067), fellow students of al-Mufīd. But whereas al-Mufīd appears to have fully endorsed the theory of gratitude, al-Karājikī suggests that *luṭf*, at least in some instances, may be a ground for revelation in addition to gratitude.[42] Although the contemporary political theorist A. John Simmons has argued that there is no virtue in positing a single ground for political obligation (what he terms singularity), he fails to note that different grounds may have incompatible implications.[43] We have already had occasion to note the vulnerability to Basran criticism of the Baghdadi combination of gratitude and utilitarianism. Singularity is by no means the rule in the Islamic context, but where we do encounter it in the classical and later periods, it appears to be linked to heightened efforts toward increased theoretical rigor. In any case, al-Karājikī illustrates the weakening hold of the theory of gratitude on those circles that had been most committed to it.

Outside of Yemen, after the 5th/11th century both Muʿtazili and Twelver Shiʿi theological works in enumerating the possible justifications for revelation (*ḥusn al-baʿtha*) cite the Basran theory of *luṭf* along with other theories but commonly omit any reference to gratitude.[44] The theory of gratitude survived longer in connection with another theological problem, that of the ground of the obligation of reasoning (*naẓar*) to God's existence and nature.[45] Here, too, the rival moral theories of gratitude and *luṭf* were invoked, with *luṭf* once again emerging as predominant.[46]

The same course of development is also in evidence among Jewish theorists. The theory of gratitude appears in a form familiar from Baghdadi Muʿtazilism in the Jewish rabbi and philosopher Saadia Gaon (d. 942).[47] According to Saadia, reason dictates that every benefactor be requited with a good deed (*iḥsān*) if he is in need of such, otherwise with gratitude. Because this is a universal rational obligation (*min wājibāt al-ʿaql al-kulliyyāt*), the Creator cannot fail to implement it with respect to Himself but must command His creatures to do service to Him and to show gratitude (*bi l-taʿabbud lahū wa-shukrihī*). Reason also dictates, according to Saadia, that God not permit Himself to be reviled and treated with contempt. The revealed law specifically related to gratitude is the law of prayer. The law was revealed through God's prophets not only to convey obligations independent of reason, but to indicate the manner of compliance with rational obligations. While reason recognizes the obligation of gratitude, it is not in a position to delimit this obligation. Such delimitation in terms of utterance, time, and manner (*min qawl wa-min waqt wa-min hay'a*) requires prophets, who have in fact so delimited gratitude in the form they have termed prayer (*fa-ḥaddathu wa-sammathu ṣalāt*).[48] Gratitude for Saadia is thus the ground for the obligation of some portion of the revealed law.[49]

In Jewish *kalām* the *luṭf* theory also came to supplant the theory of gratitude.[50] It was the theory propounded by the leading Jewish theologians, both Rabbinite and Karaite, during the highpoint of Muʿtazili influence on Jewish theology. Samuel ben Ḥofni Gaon (d. 1013) may be mentioned among the former, his contemporary Yūsuf al-Baṣīr (fl. first half 11th century) among the latter.[51]

In the period following Aḥmad b. Sulaymān, Yemeni Zaydi thinkers came increasingly under the influence of the Basran version of

Muʿtazilism, a development that led to the displacement of gratitude by *luṭf* as the accepted ground of the obligation to obey God.[52] The change from gratitude to *luṭf* did not pass without resistance. In Yemen the Zaydi ʿAbd Allāh b. Zayd al-ʿAnsī (d. 667/1269) rejected the doctrine of *al-aṣlaḥ*, but continued vigorously to defend the theory of gratitude in opposition to *luṭf*.[53] An attempt to mediate between the competing theories is attributed to ʿAbd Allāh b. Muḥammad al-Najrī (d. 877/1473), who, however, presented his own legal thought in terms of the *luṭf* theory.[54] A significant reassertion of the theory of gratitude among the Yemeni Zaydis did not, however, take place until centuries later with the imam al-Manṣūr bi-llāh al-Qāsim b. Muḥammad (d. 1029/1620), who championed this theory as the authentic teaching of the family of the Prophet against the theory of *luṭf*, which he sought to discredit. The theory of gratitude had already been supported by one of his predecessors, the imam al-Mutawakkil ʿalā llāh Yaḥyā Sharaf al-Dīn (d. 965/1558), as al-Qāsim himself acknowledged.[55] The popularity in Yemen of al-Qāsim's summary of theology, *Kitāb al-Asās li-ʿaqāʾid al-akyās*, ensured that the theory of gratitude would once again be regarded among the Yemeni Zaydis and those raised in the Zaydi tradition as a serious rival to the theory of *luṭf*.[56]

Al-Qāsim b. Muḥammad reasserted gratitude as the exclusive ground for both reasoning to God's existence and for the obligation of obedience to God's law.[57] At the same time, he argued that proponents of *luṭf* had no basis for their claim that the *luṭf* they located in both cases was obligatory for God. Al-Qāsim's defense of gratitude enjoyed notable success, to the point that an earlier Zaydi credo, the popular *Miṣbāḥ al-ʿulūm fī maʿrifat al-ḥayy al-qayyūm*, of Aḥmad b. al-Ḥasan al-Raṣṣāṣ (d. 656/1258), a proponent of the *luṭf* theory, came to be expounded in terms of the theory of gratitude.[58]

As popular as the theory of gratitude still appears to be among contemporary Zaydis, it has its critics, among them Ḥasan b. Ḥusayn al-Ḥūthī (d. 1388/1968–9), who propounds an innovative theory of obligation.[59] According to al-Ḥūthī, the obligation of reasoning to God's existence is not grounded on the rational obligation of gratitude to a benefactor, for al-Ḥūthī endorses the Basran argument that we can only know that we are the beneficiaries of God's bounty after knowing the moral nature of God. The rational obligation to reason to the existence and nature of God only arises with the proclamation of the prophetic mission by a person of known good character. Gratitude thus has no role to play in the obligation of reasoning, and in any case could not play such a role because there is according to al-Ḥūthī no general rational obligation of gratitude to a benefactor.[60] Reason can discern that requiting a benefactor is right (*ḥasan*), but not that it is an obligation.[61] There is, however, a rational prohibition of offending (*isāʾa*) a benefactor in the sense that reason recognizes such conduct to be wrong (*qabīḥ*). Ordinarily one infringes no principle of rational morality in failing to requite a benefactor, provided that one equally refrains from offending him. In the case of God, however, once it is established by reason that He is our creator, failure to obey God's commands as conveyed by the prophets amounts to offending our greatest benefactor. The rational ground of the obligation to obey God is thus not the rational obligation of gratitude but the rational prohibition of offending a benefactor that would inevitably be involved in employing our members, which belong to God as creator, in infringing God's commands, each of which is accompanied by an explicit or implicit prohibition of disabling ourselves from God's service.[62]

Among the Central Asian anti-Muʿtazili Hanafis the theory of gratitude left a lasting mark but is commonly invoked alongside other notions of the ground of obligation.[63] We find al-Māturīdī, the leading theologian to emerge from among these Hanafis, making repeated appeals to gratitude. In his *Kitāb al-Tawḥīd*, al-Māturīdī cites with approval the view of the theologian al-Ḥusayn al-Najjār (d. 3rd/9th century) that gratitude toward God is among the grounds for God's commands and prohibitions, in that these enabled His creatures to render the gratitude they owed Him.[64] Al-Māturīdī further argues that the rational necessity of prophecy can be founded on the consideration that God alone knows the appropriate measure of gratitude due for His all-encompassing bounties and conveys this through His messengers.[65] While al-Māturīdī does clearly recognize gratitude as a ground for the revealed law, he is equally clearly prepared to acknowledge other grounds as well. The tendency away from singularity on this issue is typical of the Central Asian Hanafis. In *Kitāb al-Tamhīd fī bayān al-tawḥīd* of Abū Shakūr al-Sālimī (dates uncertain), the author gives no fewer than eight possible grounds for prophecy, of which two have some relation to gratitude, one being the by now familiar notion that revelation conveys the due measure of gratitude and worship (*ḥadd al-shukr wa l-ʿubūdiyya*).[66]

In expounding the necessity of revelation in terms of gratitude, al-Māturīdī appeals to the notion that inasmuch as God's bounties touch every single sense organ, every organ must be used in expressing gratitude. Because reason cannot determine the measure of gratitude due from each organ, prophecy is required to communicate this.[67] This explanation survives in the well-known legal treatise *Badāʾiʿ al-ṣanāʾiʿ fī tartīb al-sharāʾiʿ* of the Central Asian Hanafi jurist al-Kāsānī (d. 587/1191), who throughout his exposition of the *ʿibādāt* makes reference to their rational ground.[68] For al-Kāsānī the rational ground in each case is typically a specific expression of gratitude related to the ritual obligation in question. Thus al-Kāsānī explains the complete ablution (*ghusl*) required to regain purity after sexual intercourse as expressive of gratitude for the pleasure experienced by the entire body.[69]

For al-Kāsānī gratitude for God's favors is, however, not the only possible justification in every case. He offers three rational grounds for the obligation of paying *zakāt*: assisting the poor in performing their obligations, purifying oneself from the vice of greed, and expressing gratitude to God for the blessing of wealth.[70] He similarly provides three rational grounds for the obligation of fasting: deprivation from food, drink, and sex brings one to recognition of and gratitude for these favors of God, abstinence breeds fear of God (*taqwā*), and fasting breaks the hold of nature (*ṭabʿ*) and appetite (*shahwa*).[71] The pilgrimage he explains as expressive of servitude (*ʿubūdiyya*) and gratitude, each of which is rationally required (*lāzim fi l-maʿqūl*).[72]

The theory of the moral obligation of gratitude as the ground of the obligation to obey God's law enjoyed, it seems, sufficient popularity to threaten the anti-rationalists. Some of the latter were apparently not content with attacking the notion of rational obligations in general, including any alleged rational obligation of gratitude. They also insisted, along the lines of the Basran Muʿtazilis, that gratitude was not a matter of actions. Ibn Taymiyya (d. 728/1328) found himself called upon to refute the claim made by an Ashʿari contemporary in the name of *ahl al-sunna* that gratitude is confined to words.[73] He would, in any case, have been familiar with the view of the Hanbali Abū Yaʿlā b. al-Farrāʾ (d. 458/1066) that there was no rational obligation of gratitude and that the gratitude prescribed by Islamic law itself was confined to the tongue and mind.[74]

Universalist Implications of the Theory of Gratitude

The theory of gratitude, insofar as it was seriously maintained, naturally supported a universalistic conception of the revealed law in two senses. In the first place, for committed gratitude theorists the revealed law had to be contemporaneous with the moral responsibility that followed from the possession of reason by humans. The revealed law was thus universal in the temporal sense. In a second sense, the revealed law was universal in that all morally responsible humans were necessarily subject to the valid revealed law of their day to the extent that they had knowledge of this law. Each of these points merits some elaboration.

Because the theory of gratitude regarded the rational obligation of gratitude, in this case gratitude to God, as empty without the information on how to exhibit gratitude that God provided by revelation, the relation between reason and revelation is quite different for the two theories of obligation. For the theory of gratitude, there is no gap between a state of being subject to the obligations of reason (*taklīf ʿaqlī*) and being subject to the obligations of the revealed law (*taklīf samʿī*).[75] The Twelver Shiʿi al-Shaykh al-Mufīd (d. 413/1022) notes that on this question the Baghdadi Muʿtazilis are in agreement with the Imami Shiʿis against the other

Muʿtazilis, Kharijites, and Zaydis. He points out that Imamis support their position with arguments additional to those employed by the Baghdadis.[76] For the Imamis their doctrine of the *imāma* was understood to require this constant conjunction of rational and legal obligation, whereas for the Baghdadis the conjunction rested upon the necessity of giving content to the rational obligation of gratitude, a position that al-Mufīd as a proponent of the gratitude theory could also endorse.

A forceful statement of this position comes from the grandson of al-Qāsim b. Ibrāhīm, the Zaydi imam al-Hādī Yaḥyā b. al-Ḥusayn (d. 298/911), the founder of the Yemeni Zaydi state. Al-Hādī explains that because we cannot know how to obey, and in this way express our gratitude, without information (*khabar*) from the Benefactor (*al-munʿim*) telling us how He wants us to obey, and there can be no direct information from God face to face, "one knows that the information on obedience is only possible through a messenger from the Benefactor, who differs from other humans in his marks and actions. It is thus incumbent on one who has reached physical and intellectual majority (*al-bāligh al-mudrik*) to know without the benefit of transmitted report that God does provide a messenger."[77] According to al-Hādī, reason alone is sufficient to establish the necessity of prophecy as a corollary of the rational obligation of gratitude.

The necessary conjunction between the states of rational and legal obligation that follows from the theory of gratitude was not accepted by the *lutf* theorists. For them it is conceivable that there be cases where individuals will comply with their rational obligations without the necessity for the assistance provided by the revealed law, that is, without *lutf* in the form of revelation. In such cases, there is no necessity for a Prophet to be sent.[78]

The universality of the revealed law in a second sense follows from the gratitude theory. All humans with moral responsibility are subject to the revealed law, the essential function of which is to give content to their universal moral obligation of gratitude to their common benefactor God; that is, to the extent that there is a revealed law, it obligates the very same humans who owe gratitude to God to the extent that they are in a position to have knowledge of the revealed law. The gratitude theorists are committed by their theory to a positive answer to the well-known question of whether unbelievers are subject to the revealed law, in the sense that they are punishable for infractions of this law.[79] The fact that the Central Asian Hanafis, as opposed to the Iraqi Hanafis, tended to give a negative answer to this question is a clear indication that their commitment to the gratitude theory was less than complete.[80] On their anti-Muʿtazili interpretation of rationalist ethics as ultimately imposed by God, not reason, the link between the rational obligation of gratitude and the revealed law should, if anything, be even tighter than for the Muʿtazili gratitude theorists. On this point, however, the Murjiʾism of these Hanafis seems to have proved dominant, in that they insisted on a sharp distinction between salvational belief and action.

On the *lutf* theory of obligation, it is less obvious what the answer to this question should be. The mainstream of Basran Muʿtazilis maintained the view that unbelievers were bound by the provisions of the revealed law.[81] Apart from appeal to Qurʾanic verses, this position could be defended in terms of the *lutf* theory.[82] But the dispute on this point among medieval Jewish theorists, also working with the *lutf* theory, shows that this conclusion was by no means inevitable.[83] Whereas the theory of gratitude looks to the objective role of the revealed law as instituted by God as an expression of the appropriate gratitude to which He is entitled, the *lutf* theory puts emphasis on the subjective operation of the revealed law on the motivation of each agent. It is correspondingly more accommodating of individual peculiarities and is to that extent compatible with the notion that the motivational efficacy of the law might depend on prior belief.[84] Both Baghdadi and Basran Muʿtazili ethics have deontological and consequentialist elements, but in their accounts of the justification of obedience to God the Baghdadis focus on the deontological, the Basrans on the consequentialist, which in their case happens to take a distinctly agent-relative form.

Further Implications of the Theory of Gratitude

Two further possible implications of the debate between gratitude and *lutf* theorists over the ground of legal obligation remain to be considered. The first is the relation between the two theories and the epistemic evaluation of independent reasoning (*ijtihād*), that is, the question of whether every *mujtahid* is correct or not. On this question the Basran Muʿtazilis from early on embraced infallibilism (*taṣwīb*), the view that every *mujthahid* is correct within the scope of his *ijtihād*. The Basran view was adopted by many Zaydis in connection with their growing adherence to Basran Muʿtazilism.[85] The Baghdadi Muʿtazilis, by contrast, for a long time rejected *ijtihād* altogether in its technical sense of probabilistic legal reasoning and insisted that all of the law could be the object of knowledge. They held a strong form of fallibilism (*takhṭiʾa*), the view that there was only one correct answer to every legal question. Although al-Kaʿbī was the central figure in the shift on the part of the Baghdadis toward acceptance of *ijtihād*, he continued to maintain fallibilism in a mitigated form: there was one correct answer but it might not be knowable.[86]

The possible conceptual link between the theory of gratitude and fallibilism once again lies in the objective quality of the law as an expression of gratitude ordained by God, as opposed to the law as a form of *lutf* operating on each psyche, such that the *mujtahid*'s subjective sense of probability might determine the effect on him of compliance with the law. It is significant that along with his championing of the theory of gratitude, the

Zaydi imam al-Qāsim b. Muḥammad endorsed fallibilism as the teaching of the majority of Zaydi imams and other jurists.[87]

The apparent early widespread appeal of the theory of gratitude to a variety of thinkers merits further study in relation to the development of legal reasoning. It is not unlikely that important early Shafiʿi jurists, who are reported to have upheld a rational obligation of gratitude, were in fact at the same time offering a rational ground for the obligation to obey the law.[88] If this is so, these same jurists are likely to have held the theory of gratitude in its impure form, that is, to have looked beyond simple obedience to the variety of benefits that God bestowed by revealing the law. The significance of this for legal history may then lie in the use made by these same jurists of analogy (*qiyās*).

If the revealed law is seen as a system imposed for the benefit of those subject to it, then each element of the revealed law will have to be scrutinized to discern the benefit it may be intended to achieve, and any extension of the revealed law by analogy will need to ensure that the aimed-at benefits are preserved in the process. We thus end up with an overtly utilitarian approach to the law. Just such an approach was taken by the leading early Transoxanian Shafiʿi al-Qaffāl al-Shāshī (d. 365/976), whose unedited *Maḥāsin al-sharīʿa* expounds the entire corpus of Shafiʿi law in terms of *maṣlaḥa* in the wide sense invoked by the proponents of the doctrine of *al-aṣlaḥ*.[89] Al-Shāshī understood the provisions of the revealed law as designed to create a just and stable social order.[90] Like some other leading early Shafiʿi jurists al-Qaffāl was regarded by later Ashʿari Shafiʿis as having adhered to Muʿtazilism at least for a time.[91]

There is no necessary relation between endorsement of either theory of legal obligation and the practice of legal analogy, and Twelver Shiʿi jurists held both theories of obligation while continuing to reject *qiyās*. Nonetheless for those jurists who did accept analogy, the adoption of the *lutf* theory in place of the theory of gratitude might be expected to bring with it a corresponding shift to a more narrowly individualistic view of the revealed law, as attention turned to the underlying relationship, a psychological one, that fitted the law to the rational morality it served, the so-called *munāsaba* between the two, and away from its social role.[92] In the absence of extensive information on the law of the leading Baghdadi and Basran Muʿtazilis, Zaydi law, too long neglected by Western scholarship in any case, would appear to be the most obvious place to look for such a change.

Summary

Two important theories of the moral ground for obedience to God's commands held by Muslim theorists were the theory of gratitude (*shukr*) and the theory of grace (*lutf*). The theory of gratitude was widely popular in early Islamic thought and even later among those who recognized some form of rational ethics. The theory of grace was that of the Basran Muʿtazila and those, including Shiʿis and Jews, who came under their influence. In the wake of extensive debate within Muʿtazili circles between proponents of the two competing theories, the theory of grace emerged dominant. The theory of gratitude did, however, enjoy a renewed life among Yemeni Zaydis after it was championed by the imam al-Manṣūr bi-llāh Muḥammad b. al-Qāsim (d. 1029/1620). The theory of gratitude points in the direction of a more universalist notion of revealed law in that it makes the revealed law necessarily contemporaneous with morality and binding on all humans. The theory of gratitude also appears to favor the doctrine of the fallibility of *ijtihād* (*takhṭiʾa*) and a broadly utilitarian approach to the practice of analogy (*qiyās*).

NOTES

[1] On obedience to God, see "Obedience" (Khalid Yahya Blankinship), in *Encyclopaedia of the Qurʾān* (Leiden 2001–6), 3:366–69; and "Ṭāʿa" (D. Gimaret), in *EI*[2], 10:1–2.

[2] On this terminology, see, for example, Muḥammad Ḥusayn Mukhtārī Māzandarānī, *Farhang-i iṣṭilāḥāt-i uṣūlī* (Tehran 1377 s), 78; Muḥammad Ṣanqūr ʿAlī, *al-Muʿjam al-uṣūlī* (Qum 1380 s/2001), 264–65, 275. Both authors adduce the Qurʾanic command to obey God, as does ʿĪsā Wilāyī, *Farhang-i tashrīḥī-i iṣṭilāḥāt-i uṣūl* (Tehran 1374s), 125–26, who notes that the classification of a specific command is a matter of reason. Thus the general classification of the command to obey God as *irshādī* leaves open the possibility of specific contextual considerations that point to other functions in certain Qurʾanic verses, as may be gathered from discussions throughout Muḥammad Ḥusayn al-Ṭabāṭabāʾī, *al-Mīzān fī tafsīr al-Qurʾān* (Beirut n.d.).

[3] This classification, of course, assumes that prudence is not itself a moral category, a point that is far from obvious. Furthermore, not all answers to the question readily fit either category. One can also go on to ask why one should obey the demands of morality, on which question see the well-known discussion in John Hospers, *Human Conduct: An Introduction to the Problems of Ethics* (New York 1961), 174–95. On this question a prudential answer came to dominate Muʿtazili thought: it is rational to avoid harm; see, for example, the Twelver Shiʿi Abū l-Ṣalāḥ Taqī al-Dīn al-Ḥalabī, *Taqrīb al-maʿārif*, ed. Fāris Tabrīziyān al-Ḥassūn (n.p., 1417 AH), 65–6, on the obligation of reasoning (*naẓar*) as to the existence of God.

[4] The focus here is on obligation. Needless to say, Ashʿaris might prefer to regard their obedience to God as growing out of love, and the ties between Ashʿarism and Sufism are well known. Al-Ghazālī, in the chapter *al-maḥabba* of his *Iḥyāʾ ʿulūm al-dīn* (Aleppo 1419/1998), 5:4, speaks of obedience as derivative of love and its fruit.

[5] al-Ghazālī, *al-Iqtiṣād fī l-iʿtiqād*, ed. İbrahim Agah Çubukçu and Hüseyin Atay (Ankara 1962), 171–72.

[6] George Makdisi, "Ethics in Islamic Traditionalist Doctrine," in Richard G. Hovannisian, *Ethics in Islam: Ninth Giorgio Levi Della Vida Biennial Conference* (Malibu 1985), 47–63, especially the citation from Ibn Taymiyya's *Minhāj al-sunna*, on

p. 60, which adduces support for rationalist ethics among Karramis, Malikis, Shafiʿis, and Hanbalis. For an Ismaʿili reference to the rational obligation of gratitude, see Jaʿfar b. Manṣūr al-Yaman, *The Master and the Disciple: An Early Islamic Spiritual Dialogue*, ed. and trans. James Morris (London 2001), Arabic 46, trans. 116.

⁷ I address here the obligation of obedience to God, sometimes put as obedience to His messengers. I do not take up the question of obedience to rulers except insofar as this follows directly from God's commands.

⁸ The two-part article "Shukr" (Alma Giese and A. K. Reinhart) in *EI²*, 9:496–98, provides essential information on the Islamic discussions of the topic of gratitude in general. Several papers on gratitude in Islamic thought, including Reinhart's "Thanking a Benefactor," may be found in John B. Carman and Frederick J. Streng (eds.), *Spoken and Unspoken Thanks: Some Comparative Soundings* (Dallas 1989). To some extent, research on the topic in Islamic texts is made more difficult by the fairly consistent failure of editors to include the term *shukr* in their indices.

⁹ For the Ismaʿilis, see n. 6 above.

¹⁰ On the Qurʾanic source for the notion and its development in early Islamic thought, see the brief but valuable discussion in Reinhart, "Thanking the Benefactor," 120–25, 127 n. 26, and the parallel but shorter treatment in his *Before Revelation: The Boundaries of Muslim Moral Thought* (Albany 1995), 110–13.

¹¹ Abū Hāshim in particular identified the prophetic function as exclusively legislative (Ibn Mattawayh, *Kitāb al-Majmūʿ fī l-muḥīṭ bi l-taklīf*, vol. 3, ed. Jan Peters [Beirut 1999], 438), although some of his followers are reported to have relaxed this requirement to a certain extent (al-Sharīf al-Murtaḍā, *al-Dhakhīra fī ʿilm al-kalām*, ed. Aḥmad al-Ḥusaynī [Qum 1411], 325).

¹² On the theory of *luṭf*, see Binyamin Abrahamov, "ʿAbd al-Jabbār's Theory of Divine Assistance (*Luṭf*)," *Jerusalem Studies in Arabic and Islam* 16 (1993), 41–58, which includes an annotated translation of the relevant section of Mānkdīm's *Sharḥ al-uṣūl al-khamsa*; and David E. Sklare, *Samuel Ben Ḥofni Gaon and His Cultural World: Texts and Studies* (Leiden 1996), 150–52. The topic, which goes well beyond the revealed law, deserves far more extensive treatment than it has so far received. Because Abrahamov, like some others, is concerned lest translation of the term *luṭf* by "grace" introduce misleading Christian connotations (47 n. 16), it is worth noting that Louis Gardet, a Roman Catholic priest, felt free to adopt the translation "grace divine" in his *Dieu et la destinée de l'homme* (Paris 1967), 101–7 (with comparative remarks). In any case, the final word has not been said on possible Christian influence.

¹³ The accessibility of the notion of an obligation of gratitude to God perhaps goes some way in explaining the prominent role it sometimes continues to play in the popular writing of theologians who are committed to the theory of *luṭf*, for example, al-Ḥakim al-Jishumī (d. 493/1101), *Taḥkīm al-ʿuqūl fī tashīḥ al-uṣūl*, ed. ʿAbd al-Salām b. ʿAbbās al-Wajīh (Amman 1421/2001), 31–2, cf. 197–98.

¹⁴ According to al-Kaʿbī, the hardship involved in obeying God's laws was fully justified by God's pre-existing benefits (Mānkdīm, *Sharḥ al-uṣūl al-khamsa*, ed. ʿAbd al-Karīm ʿUthmān [Cairo 1384/1965], 217–18; also attributed to al-Kaʿbī and the Baghdadis in al-Ṭabrisī, *Majmaʿ al-bayān*, on Q 57:21, cited in *Tafsīr Abī l-Qāsim al-Kaʿbī al-Balkhī*, ed. Khiḍr Muḥammad Nabhā [Beirut 1428/2007], 294)

(this is a modern collection of citations from al-Kaʿbī's lost commentary, one of a series of such works on Muʿtazili *tafsīr*). But this cannot be a complete answer, since it addresses only the question of the justice (*ʿadl*) of demanding obedience, but not the utilitarian aspect of imposing such hardship that al-Kaʿbī's adherence to *al-aṣlaḥ*, discussed below, would require. This was sometimes explained by the Baghdadis in psychological terms: the previously experienced hardship enhanced the enjoyment of God's reward (Ibn Mattawayh, *Kitāb al-Majmūʿ*, 3:147).

[15] The far-reaching Basran critique of the ethics of the Baghdadis focused on their recognition as grounds of obligation what were not so and their failure to recognize what were in fact grounds (al-Qāḍī ʿAbd al-Jabbār, *al-Mughnī fī abwāb al-tawḥīd wa l-ʿadl*, vol. 14, ed. Muṣṭafā al-Saqqā [Cairo 1385/1965], 23).

[16] On the importance of identifying an independent argument from gratitude, see A. D. M. Walker, "Political Obligation and the Argument from Gratitude," *Philosophy and Public Affairs* 17/3 (Summer 1988), 203. The criterion of independence, as Walker terms it, need, however, apply to only a part of one's obligations. Mark C. Murphy, *An Essay on Divine Authority* (Ithaca 2002), 115–18, presents arguments for a gratitude theory of obedience to God that does not claim such independence and thus supports, as he readily acknowledges, a very thin notion of divine authority.

[17] On the character of this work, see Wilferd Madelung, *Der Imam al-Qāsim ibn Ibrāhīm und die Glaubenslehre der Zaiditen* (Berlin 1965), 100.

[18] *Kitāb al-Radd ʿalā l-mulḥid*, ed. Muḥammad Yaḥyā Sālim ʿIzzān (Sanʿaʾ 1412/1992), 52–3; also published with his *al-Dalīl al-kabīr*, ed. Imām Ḥanafī ʿAbd Allāh (Cairo 1420/2000), 102–3, and included under the title *Munāẓara maʿa l-mulḥid*, in *Majmūʿ kutub wa-rasāʾil al-Imām al-Qāsim b. Ibrāhīm*, ed. ʿAbd al-Karīm Aḥmad Jadabān (Sanʿaʾ 1422/2001), 1:313–14. Cf. *Tafsīr Abī l-Qāsim al-Kaʿbī al-Balkhī*, 156 on Q 3:186. Al-Qāsim argues that reason cannot itself arrive at the various legal obligations but can recognize them as right when they are imposed as tests, compliance with which will be rewarded. To the extent that the rationality of compliance depends on the supposition that a reward will be given for obedience, the theory of gratitude here is only relatively pure. Saadia Gaon offers a similar account (*Kitāb al-Mukhtār min al-amānāt wa l-iʿtiqādāt*, ed. and trans. Yosef Kāfiḥ [Jerusalem 1970], 118–19), but goes on to observe that there must exist some, albeit modest, rational ground in terms of benefit for the obligations. In inquiring into the content of the obligations, Saadia goes beyond the relatively pure theory of gratitude that justifies the obligations imposed by the benefactor solely as means for the beneficiary to gain a reward. For the pure and relatively pure theories of gratitude, the rationality of performing the obligatory acts is extrinsic to their nature: they function either as merely arbitrarily chosen expressions of gratitude or as such expressions joined with the promise of reward for performance. On the rationality of God's imposing obligations for the sole purpose of rewarding their performance (as defended by Saadia, for example, op. cit., 117: *wa l-ʿaql yujawwiz ayḍan an yastaʿmila al-ḥakīm ʿāmilan fī shayʾ mā wa-yuʿṭiyahū ʿalayhī ujratahū li-wajh taʿrīḍihī ilā al-nafʿ khāṣṣatan*), see the critical discussion in Ibn Mattawayh, *Kitāb al-Majmūʿ*, 3:434–35, where the widespread appeal to the notion in earlier Muʿtazili writing is mentioned.

[19] The pure theory of gratitude, like any other Islamic theory of obligation, has to face the question of variations in God's law, that is, the question of why

God's tests, if that is what His laws are, vary, whether across individuals, across revelations, and even within the single revelation to Muḥammad. Inasmuch as God is understood to be unchanging, the explanation, unless it is to be an appeal to the mystery of the divine will (cf. Ibn Fūrak, *Mujarrad Maqālāt al-Shaykh Abī l-Ḥasan al-Ashʿarī*, ed. Daniel Gimaret [Beirut 1987], 199–200 on abrogation), would have to be in terms of differences in His creatures; thus the development away from the pure theory.

[20] Sklare, *Samuel ben Ḥofni*, 150. On the meaning that the Basrans attached to the term *al-aṣlaḥ*, see ʿAbd al-Jabbār, *al-Mughnī*, 14:37. See further the comprehensive article of Robert Brunschvig, "Muʿtazilisme et optimum (*al-aṣlaḥ*)," *Studia Islamica* 39 (1974), 5–23.

[21] Naṣīr al-Dīn al-Ṭūsī (d. 672/1274) argues that if obedience were due God for His benefits, then God, not his creature, would be in the position of the one rewarded (*muthāb*) (*Talkhīṣ al-Muḥaṣṣal*, ed. ʿAbd Allāh Nūrānī [Tehran 1359 s], 343). The philosopher Terrance McConnell is of the view that a benefactor who acts for the purpose of putting his beneficiary in his debt is not entitled to gratitude (*Gratitude* [Philadelphia 1993], 22–5).

[22] Ibn Mattawayh, *Kitāb al-Majmūʿ*, 3:170–71.

[23] Ed. Ḥasan b. Yaḥyā al-Yūsufī (Sanʿaʾ 1424/2003), 247–309.

[24] On parents as one's primary human benefactors, see the gratitude theorists al-Karājikī, *al-Taʿrīf bi-wujūb ḥaqq al-wālidayn*, ed. Muḥammad Bāqir al-Nāṣirī (Baghdad 1398/1978), 25, and al-Qāsim b. Muḥammad, *Majmūʿ kutub wa-rasāʾil al-Imām al-Manṣūr bi llāh al-Qāsim b. Muḥammad*, vol. 1, ed. Muḥammad Qāsim Muḥammad al-Mutawakkil (Sanʿaʾ 1424/2003), 207–20. The Basran view of the relation between children and parents was cynical to the extent that their analysis was in terms of prudence. Both parents and children in their dealings with one another were motivated above all by avoidance of harm to their own interests. According to ʿAbd al-Jabbār, *al-Mughnī*, 14:27, parents are under no independent moral obligation to benefit their children. Since God is above all harm, He is bound neither by prudence nor morality to act to the benefit of anyone. Cf. the Jewish gratitude theorist Baḥyā ibn Paqūda, *Kitāb al-Hidāya ilā farāʾiḍ al-qulūb*, ed. and trans. Yosef Kāfiḥ (Jerusalem 1973), 128, who acknowledges that a father's benefits to a son are self-interested, "for the son is part of the father" (*al-walad qiṭʿa min al-wālid*).

For a rejection of gratitude as the basis for obedience to either parents or God, see Joseph L. Lombardi, "Filial Gratitude and the God's Right to Command," *Journal of Religious Ethics* 19 (1991), 93–118. On the analogy sometimes made between gratitude owed to parents and to the state, see A. John Simmons, *Moral Principles and Political Obligations* (Princeton 1979), 161, 183.

[25] For representative opinions by Western philosophers on the rational obligation of gratitude, see "Gratitude" (Mary A. McCloskey), in Lawrence C. and Charlotte B. Becker (eds.), *Encyclopedia of Ethics*, 2nd ed. (New York 2001), 1:629–31. Two book-length philosophical studies of gratitude are Terrance C. McConnell, *Gratitude*, already cited, and the more historical Antonio Poliseno, *La gratitudine: tra obligazione morale et debito legale* (Rome 2005). Two collections of papers on the topic are Josef Seifert (ed.), *Danken und Dankbarkeit* (Heidelberg 1992), which includes a contribution from the Islamic (largely Sufi) perspective by Hadi Sharifi, 197–210; and Giuseppi Galli, *Interpretazione e gratitudine*

(Macertoa 1994). Both volumes include papers on the obligation of gratitude in Roman law.

[26] On *ṭāʿa* as the appropriate form of gratitude to a superior, see al-Karājikī, *Maʿādin al-jawāhir wa-riyāḍat al-khawāṭir*, ed. ʿAlī Riḍā Hazār (Qum, 1422), 87. Note also the definition of *ṭāʿa* in Baḥya ibn Paqūda, *Kitāb al-Hidāya*, 136 as *khuḍūʿ al-munʿam ʿalayhī li l-munʿim bi l-niʿma wa-mukāfaʾatihī alā niʿamihī ḥasab ṭāqatihī*.

[27] See the definitions of gratitude collected in *Sharḥ al-muṣṭalaḥāt al-kalāmiyya* (Mashhad 1414 AH), 177–78, and Abū Hilāl al-ʿAskarī, *al-Furūq al-lughawiyya*, ed. Muḥammad Bāsil ʿUyūn al-Sūd (Beirut 1421/2000), 162, according to whom gratitude is exclusively verbal, to which add ʿAbd Allāh Ibn Ḥamza, *Sharḥ al-Risāla al-nāṣiḥa bi l-adilla al-wāḍiḥa*, ed. Ibrāhīm Yaḥyā al-Darsī al-Ḥamzī and Hādī b. Ḥasan b. Hādī al-Ḥamzī (Saʿda 1423/2002), 49. The Zaydī imam al-Hādī ilā l-Ḥaqq Yaḥyā b. al-Ḥusayn (d. 298/911), a gratitude theorist, already insists that gratitude includes actions not only words (*Kitāb al-Aḥkām fī l-ḥalāl wa l-ḥarām* [n.p. 1410/1990], 1:535). The Shafiʿi Ashʿari Ibn Barhān (d. 518/1124) in his *al-Wuṣūl ilā l-uṣūl*, ed. ʿAbd al-Ḥamīd ʿAlī Abū Zunayd (Riyad 1403/1983), 1:67, incorrectly states that for the Muʿtazilis, compliance with the rational obligation of gratitude consists in refraining from actions condemned by reason and performing actions approved of by reason. He argues that they have to locate gratitude in action because reason dictates no specific form of words to express gratitude, nor can gratitude consist in knowledge of God, for that must precede gratitude. This account corresponds to neither Baghdadi nor Basran teachings. As far as the Basrans are concerned, a verbal expression of gratitude, however articulated, is rationally obligatory only under specific circumstances (ʿAbd al-Jabbār, *al-Mughnī*, 14:167; Mānkdīm, *Sharḥ al-uṣūl al-khamsa*, 83). Cf. another Ashʿari Shafiʿi, Abū l-Muẓaffar al-Isfarāyīnī, who also presents the rational obligation of gratitude for the Muʿtazilis as operating outside of the Shariʿa (*al-Tabṣīr fī l-dīn*, ed. Muḥammad Zāhid al-Kawtharī [Baghdad 1374/1955], 62–3.

[28] Ibn Mattawayh, *Kitāb al-Majmūʿ*, 3:147.

[29] Ibid. According to the Basrans, gratitude, whether to God or to those legally entitled to it, merits reward from God insofar as it is burdensome (Mānkdīm, *Sharḥ al-uṣūl al-khamsa*, 82–3).

[30] Ibn Mattawayh, *Kitāb al-Majmūʿ*, 3:148. The same point is made in ʿAbd al-Jabbār, *al-Mughnī*, 14:168. This explanation should be contrasted with the exposition of the relation between gratitude and physical action (in the form of the *ʿibādāt*) found in Mānkdīm, *Sharḥ al-uṣūl al-khamsa*, 82, and al-Sharīf al-Murtaḍā, *Sharḥ jumal al-ʿilm wa l-ʿamal*, ed. Yaʿqūb al-Jaʿfarī al-Marāghī (Tehran 1419 AH), 133, and alluded to in passing in *al-Mughnī*, 14:166, l. 19 reading *bi-niʿamihī*. Al-Sharīf al-Murtaḍā, *al-Dhakhīra*, 207, speaks of *ʿibāda* as a *kayfiyya fī l-shukr* but otherwise makes it clear that gratitude is primarily a verbal act (277–78), as he also does in his *al-Ḥudūd wa l-ḥaqāʾiq*, ed. Muḥammad Taqī Dānishpazhūh, in *Chahār farhangnāmah-i kalāmī* (n.p. n.d.), 164–65. Elsewhere he states: *lā shukr awfā min al-ʿibāda* (*Majmūʿa fī funūn min ʿilm al-kalām*, in *Nafāʾis al-makhṭūṭāt, al-majmūʿa al-khāmisa*, ed. Muḥammad Ḥusayn Āl Yāsīn [Baghdad 1375/1955]). His explanation in *al-Dhakhīra* is followed by Abū Jaʿfar al-Ṭūsī's commentary on *Jumal al-ʿilm wa l-ʿamal*, *Kitāb Tamhīd al-uṣūl fī ʿilm al-kalām*, ed. ʿAbd al-Muḥsin Mishkāt al-Dīnī (Tehran 1362 s), 250. It appears that older forms of speaking reflecting the gratitude theory of obligation

were only gradually brought into line with the singularity of the *lutf* theory. In this respect Ibn Mattawayh is particularly consistent.

[31] Ibn Mattawayh, *Kitāb al-Majmū'*, 3:148. The compressed argument in 'Abd al-Jabbār, *al-Mughnī*, 14:168, appears to make the quite different point that the variability of legal obligations makes sense on the theory of *lutf* but not on the theory of gratitude, since all are subject to the same rational obligation of gratitude vis-à-vis God, having all received the same basic benefits (*uṣūl al-ni'am*), including life itself. These basic benefits already create a limitless and unceasing obligation of mental gratitude. Presumably the Baghdadis would respond to Ibn Mattawayh along these lines, but include action as integral to their notion of gratitude.

[32] These two criticisms are prominent in the convenient summary of Sterling Harwood, "Eleven Objections to Utilitarianism," in Louis P. Pojman (ed.), *Moral Philosophy: A Reader* (Indianapolis 1993), 142–44. The argument that the Baghdadi teaching is overly demanding was particularly relied upon by Abū 'Alī al-Jubbā'ī according to *al-Mughnī*, 14:56. *Al-Mughnī*, 14:70, attributes the argument from the elimination of supererogation (*tafaḍḍul*) to his son Abū Hāshim.

[33] The question whether obligatory benefits can ground a duty of gratitude continues to be debated (see McConnell, *Gratitude*, 14–6). Cf. the polite contemporary expression used to decline thanks, *lā shukr 'alā wājib*.

[34] Ibn Mattawayh, *Kitāb al-Majmū'*, 3:149. This anti-utilitarian argument appears in *al-Mughnī*, 14:67, where it is attributed to *shuyūkhinā*.

[35] Ibn Mattawayh, *Kitāb al-Majmū'*, 3:156.

[36] 'Abd al-Jabbār, *al-Mughnī*, 14:12.

[37] Op. cit., 14:47.

[38] Ibn Mattawayh, *Kitāb al-Majmū'*, 3:156.

[39] 'Abd al-Jabbār, *al-Mughnī*, 14:67–8. This text mentions God's *alṭāf*, as does the Karaite Yūsuf al-Baṣīr, in Georges Vajda, *al-Kitāb al-Muḥtawī de Yūsuf al-Baṣīr*, ed. David R. Blumenthal (Leiden 1985), Judaeo-Arabic 752, trans. 513–14. Elsewhere only reward and compensation are adduced: e.g., al-Sharīf al-Murtaḍā, *al-Dhakhīra fī 'ilm al-kalām*, 207. *Al-Yāqūt* by the Twelver Shi'i Abū Isḥāq b. Nawbakht (dates uncertain) in Ḥasan b. Yūsuf b. al-Muṭahhar al-Ḥillī, *Anwār al-malakūt fī sharḥ al-Yāqūt*, ed. Muḥammad Najmī Zanjānī (Tehran 1338 s), 156, introduces the *alṭāf* as an additional point, which suggests that the original form of this anti-utilitarian argument goes back to a pre-*lutf* stage.

[40] Al-Ḥillī, *Anwār al-malakūt*, 156. 'Abd al-Jabbār, *al-Mughnī*, 14:68, insists that this reply is not open to the utilitarians.

[41] For al-Baṣrī's position on *al-aṣlaḥ*, see al-'Allāma al-Ḥillī, *Kashf al-murād fī sharḥ Tajrīd al-i'tiqād (qism al-ilāhiyāt)*, ed. Ja'far al-Subḥānī (Qum 1375 s), 147–48. Sadīd al-Dīn al-Ḥimaṣṣī al-Rāzī (d. after 600/1204) speaks of al-Baṣrī mediating between the two camps (*al-Munqidh min al-taqlīd* [Qum 1412 AH], 1:300).

[42] *Kanz al-fawā'id*, ed. 'Abd Allāh Ni'ma (Beirut 1405/1985), 1:225. Al-Mufīd's position is noted below.

[43] *Moral Principles and Political Obligations*, 35.

[44] For example, al-Ḥimaṣṣī al-Rāzī, *al-Munqidh*, 1:373–74, al-Ḥillī, *Kashf al-murād*, 151–4; al-Ḥillī, *Manāhij al-yaqīn fī uṣūl al-dīn*, ed. Muḥammad Riḍā al-Anṣārī al-Qummī (Qum 1416 AH), 264–65; al-Miqdād al-Suyūrī (d. 826/1423), *Kitāb al-Lawāmi' al-ilāhiyya*, ed. Muḥammad 'Alī al-Ṭabāṭabā'ī (Tabriz 1397 AH), 166,

gives seven grounds in justification of prophecy, of which the third is the modality of gratitude *and* legal provisions not attainable by reason. Ibn Mattawayh already accords gratitude only the briefest mention in his discussion of the grounds for prophecy (*Kitāb al-Majmūʿ*, 3:435, referring the reader to the treatment of the topic in *al-aṣlaḥ*). On the topic of the justification of prophecy, see Sabine Schmidtke, *The Theology of al-ʿAllāma al-Ḥillī (d. 726/1325)* (Berlin 1991), 136–41. The Twelver Shiʿi al-Shahīd al-Awwal, Muḥammad b. Makkī al-ʿĀmilī (d. 786/1384), does take the trouble to expound what he takes to be al-Kaʿbī's teaching on gratitude as the ground of obligation, but then makes the fanciful suggestion that al-Kaʿbī may not have meant that the obligations of the revealed law constitute forms of gratitude, but that their performance would strengthen one's motives to discharge the rational obligation of gratitude (*al-Maqāla al-taklīfiyya*, in *Rasāʾil al-Shahīd al-Awwal* [Qum 1385 s], 95; also in *Arbaʿ rasāʾil kalāmiyya* [Qum 1423 AH], 51, with the commentary of ʿAlī b. Muḥammad al-Bayāḍī [d. 877/1472], *al-Risāla al-Yūnusiyya*, 166). This suggestion amounts to treating the theory of gratitude as a special limited form (*shuʿba*) of the *luṭf* theory.

45 Abū l-Ṣalāḥ al-Ḥalabī, *Taqrīb al-maʿārif*, 65–6 (reasoning grounded in *luṭf* or gratitude), 152 (prophecy grounded in *luṭf*); Anonymous, *Khulāṣat al-naẓar*, ed. Sabine Schmidtke and Hasan Ansari (Tehran 2006), 22 (reasoning grounded in gratitude), 130 (prophecy justified in terms of *luṭf*) (this Twelver Shiʿi text is dated by the editors to the late 6th/12th or early 7th/13th century); al-Miqdād al-Suyūrī (d. 826/1423), *Kitāb al-Lawāmiʿ al-ilāhiyya*, 9–11; al-Suyūrī, *al-Nāfiʿ yawm al-ḥashr fī sharḥ al-Bāb al-ḥadī ʿashar*, ed. Mahdī Muḥaqqiq (Tehran 1365 s), 3, published with Abū l-Fatḥ b. Makhdūm al-Ḥusaynī (d. 976/1568), *Miftāḥ al-Bāb*, 74.

46 To the extent that they were not construed as simply alternative versions of the argument from prudence (see n. 3 above). It may be surmised that a number of later theologians found the attenuated Basran notion of gratitude sufficient to support the mental obligation of reasoning about the existence and nature of God. They apparently were unconvinced by the Basran argument that the moral obligation of gratitude was not a suitable basis for the obligation of reasoning since it could not be known that one was the recipient of God's benefits until one had come to know something of the moral nature of God, for there can be no benefit without the intention to do good (Mānkdīm, *Sharḥ al-uṣūl al-khamsa*, 70–1). Ibn Mattawayh, *al-Majmūʿ fī l-muḥīṭ bi l-taklīf*, vol. 1, ed. J. J. Houben (Beirut 1965), 19–20, published as *al-Muḥīt bi l-taklīf*, ed. ʿUmar al-Sayyid ʿAzmī (Cairo, 28–9), rejects the notion that one can render conditional gratitude when unsure that one has been the recipient of benefits. This line of argument appears to represent a step toward the singularity of *luṭf* and away from any recognition at all of gratitude in the obligation of reasoning. The Zaydī Aḥmad b. Muḥammad al-Sharafī (d. 1055/1646), *Sharḥ al-Asās al-kabīr*, ed. Aḥmad ʿAṭā Allāh ʿĀrif (Sanʿaʾ 1411/1991), 1:195, has the anti-gratitude theorists urging that a vague form of gratitude (*shukr al-munʿim ʿalā l-jumla*) or conditional gratitude (*al-shukr al-mashrūṭ*) is sufficient to discharge one's rational obligation of gratitude but at the same time insufficient to initiate the necessary further reasoning to arrive at God's existence, precisely the argument found in al-Ḥimaṣṣī al-Rāzī, *al-Munqidh*, 1:268. Presumably, one response available to the gratitude theorists would be to accept a vague or conditional form of gratitude as merely the initial stage of theological reasoning. Such a response is suggested by al-Zamakhsharī's comment on Q 4:147,

which has vague gratitude (*shukr mubham*) coming to be followed by knowledge of God and obedience (*al-Kashshāf ʿan ḥaqāʾiq al-tanzīl* [Beirut n.d.], 1:582). Ibn Mattawayh may have sought to block this response. *Khulāṣat al-naẓar*, 22, responds that conditional gratitude is inappropriate when knowledge of the benefactor is possible, as in the case of God, while al-Sharafī rejects the notion of conditional gratitude as irrational. A further consideration in explanation of the survival of the argument from gratitude for theological reasoning is that such reasoning is a one-time affair, unlike the continuing obligation of obedience. Precisely what initiates such reasoning is thus less critical than that it be accomplished and come to serve as the foundation for the revealed law. A particularly striking example of eclecticism here comes from the Twelver Shiʿi Abū l-Ṣalāḥ Taqī al-Dīn al-Ḥalabī (d. 447/1055) (cf. n. 3 above), a student of al-Sharīf al-Murtaḍā, who gives all four of what he takes to be the possible solutions: if the primary obligation is knowledge of God (the Baghdadi view), this may be based on either gratitude or *luṭf*, but if the primary obligation is reasoning (*naẓar*), that too may be based on either gratitude or *luṭf (al-Kāfī fī l-fiqh*, ed. Riḍa Ustādī [Isfahan 1403], 38–9).

[47] That Saadia wrote on revealed law under Baghdadi as opposed to Basran Muʿtazili influence was noted by Moshe Zucker, *Saadya's Commentary on Genesis* (in Hebr.) (New York 1984), 306 n. 20, but the evidence he cites for this is not entirely cogent in light of what Ibn Mattawayh tells us (n. 18 above). Saadia as a proponent of a gratitude theory of obedience to God's commands is discussed by the philosophers Avi Sagi and Daniel Statman in their book on divine command ethics, *Religion and Morality*, trans. from Hebr. by Batya Stein (Amsterdam 1995), 74–8.

[48] In what survives of the introduction to his prayer book, Saadia states that while the obligation of gratitude in known by reason, terming it prayer (*ṣalāt*) is based on revelation (*Siddur R. Saadja Gaon*, ed. I. Davidson et al. [Jerusalem 2000], 3).

[49] *Kitāb al-Mukhtār*, 116–23. Addressing the challenge that it would be *aṣlaḥ* for his creatures if God were to freely grant them eternal bliss, Saadia, like the Baghdadi Muʿtazilis, explains that compensation for the hardship of obedience to God's law will come in the form of their enhanced enjoyment of what has been achieved by their own efforts rather than simply given (116). Cf. al-Shaykh al-Mufīd, *Awāʾil al-maqālāt*, in *Muṣannafāt al-Shaykh al-Mufīd* (Qum 1413 AH), 4:60, translated in Martin J. McDermott, *The Theology of al-Shaikh al-Mufīd (d. 413/1022)* (Beirut 1978), 76; al-Karājikī, *Kanz al-fawāʾid*, 2:70–2. Both al-Mufīd (*Awāʾil al-maqālāt*, 4:59–60, translation and discussion in McDermott, 71–6) and al-Karājikī (*Kanz al-fawāʾid*, 1:126–31), defended the theory of *al-aṣlaḥ*.

[50] In Spain Baḥyā ibn Paqūda (ca. 1080) in his *Kitāb al-Hidāya ilā farāʾiḍ al-qulūb*, 127–84, presents a highly developed theory of gratitude, undoubtedly influenced by Saadia's work but taken well beyond known *kalām* models. My thanks to Professor Moshe Berger for reminding me to look at the works of Saadia and Baḥyā.

[51] On Samuel ben Ḥofni, see the work already cited of David E. Sklare. On Yūsuf al-Baṣīr, see in addition to the posthumously published edition and translation of his *al-Muḥtawī* by Georges Vajda, referenced above, the introduction and bibliography of the first part of his shorter *Kiṭāb al-Tamyīz*, published as *Das Buch der Unterscheidung*, ed. and trans. Wolfgang von Abel (Freiburg 2005). *Luṭf* was rendered as *leʾūṭ* in the Hebrew of the Byzantine Karaites (Eliezer Ben-

Yehuda, *Thesaurus totius hebraitatis* [in Hebr.] [Jerusalem 1948–59], 5:2583, cf. Simon Hopkins, "Arabic Elements in the Hebrew of the Byzantine Karaites," in Joshua Blau and Stefan C. Reif [eds.], *Genizah Research after Ninety Years: The Case of Judaeo-Arabic* [Cambridge 1992], 93–9).

[52] On the massive introduction of Muʿtazili literature into Yemen under Aḥmad b. Sulaymān, see Ayman Fuʾād Sayyid, *Taʾrīkh al-madhāhib al-dīniyya fī bilād al-yaman ḥattā nihāyat al-qarn al-sādis al-hijrī* (Cairo 1408/1988), 254–59, largely relied upon in the account of Richard C. Martin and Mark R. Woodward (with Dwi S. Atmaja), *Defenders of Reason in Islam* (Oxford 1997). Leading Caspian Zaydi imams had already adopted the Basran Muʿtazili *luṭf* theory (see, for example, al-Muʾayyad bi-llāh Aḥmad b. al-Ḥusayn, *al-Tabṣira*, ed. ʿAbd al-Karīm b. Aḥmad Jadabān [Saʿda 1423/2002], 30, on the obligation of reasoning as based on *luṭf*).

[53] Quoted from an otherwise apparently no longer extant section of his *al-Maḥajja al-bayḍāʾ* in al-Sharafī, *Sharḥ al-Asās al-kabīr*, 2:276–79; cf. Madelung, *al-Imam al-Qāsim*, 222. On al-ʿAnsī, see ʿAbd al-Salām b. ʿAbbās al-Wajīh, *Aʿlām al-muʾallifīn al-zaydiyya* (Amman 1420/1999), 589–91.

[54] The two theories are said to be close by Aḥmad b. ʿAbd Allāh al-Ṣanʿānī (d. 1080/1669), who ascribes the same view to al-Najrī's *Kitāb al-Munāsabāt (al-Ghuṣūn al-mayyāsa)*, ed. Ayman ʿAbd al-Jābir al-Buḥayrī (Cairo 1421/2001), 29. Al-Najrī's work, still unpublished, is, however, formulated according to the *luṭf* theory as is clear from the reproduction of part of its preface in al-Najrī, *Shāfī al-ʿalīl*, ed. Aḥmad ʿAlī Aḥmad al-Shāmī, vol. 1 (Sanʿaʾ 1406/1986), 47.

[55] *Majmūʿ kutub wa-rasāʾil*, 1:206.

[56] There are now two editions of *Kitāb al-Asās*, that of Albert Nader (Beirut 1980) and that of Muḥammad Qāsim ʿAbd Allāh al-Hāshimī (Saʿda 1415/1994). Gratitude and *luṭf* as the two standard rival theories of the obligation of obedience appear in al-Ḥasan b. Aḥmad al-Jalāl (d. 1084/1673), *al-ʿIṣma ʿan al-ḍalāl*, ed. by Ḥusayn b. ʿAbd Allāh al-ʿAmrī, in *al-ʿAllāma al-mujtahid al-muṭlaq al-Ḥasan b. al-Jalāl* (Beirut 1421/2000), 110, and al-Ḥusayn b. Nāṣir al-Sharaf (d. 1111/1699), *Maṭmaʿ al-āmāl*, ed. ʿAbd Allāh b. ʿAbd Allāh al-Ḥūthī (Sanʿaʾ 1422/2002), 400.

[57] *Kitāb al-Asās*, ed. Nader, 55, 135–6, ed. al-Hāshimī, 18, 120. Al-Qāsim adduced the usage of the term *kāfir niʿma* by the early imams for one who had committed a single major sin as evidence for their acceptance of the gratitude theory (ed. Nader, 188–89, ed. al-Hāshimī, 184). The gratitude theory espoused by al-Qāsim and by al-ʿAnsī before him is generally speaking Baghdadi, although both insist that God is under no obligations.

[58] Al-Raṣṣāṣ's short text, also known as *al-Thalāthūna masʾala*, has been edited by Muḥammad Kafāfī (Beirut 1971). Two of its commentaries expounding the gratitude theory are those of Aḥmad b. Yaḥyā b. Ḥābis, *Kitāb al-Īḍāḥ*, ed. Ḥasan b. Yūsuf b. Yaḥyā al-Yūsufī (Sanʿaʾ 1420/2000), 48–51 and al-Nāṣir li-Dīn Allāh Ibrāhīm b. Muḥammad, *al-Iṣbāḥ*, ed. ʿAbd al-Raḥmān b. Ḥusayn Shāyim (Sanʿaʾ 1422/2002), 23 (in the section added by the contemporary editor). Al-Raṣṣāṣ's adherence to the theory of *luṭf* is clear from his recently published *al-Khulāṣa al-nāfiʿa*, ed. Imām Ḥanafī Sayyid ʿAbd Allāh (Cairo 1422/2002), 42, 48.

[59] Al-Ḥūthī's *tanbīh* on the subject, dated 1381/1961, is included as a footnote to the edition of Muḥammad b. Ṣalāḥ al-Sharafī's *ʿUddat al-akyās fī sharḥ maʿānī al-Asās* (Sanʿaʾ 1415/1995), 1:63–8. On al-Ḥūthī, see al-Wajīh, *Aʿlām al-zaydiyya*, 316–17.

[60] Al-Ḥūthī suggests that the gratitude theory came to be adopted in light of the legal obligation of gratitude coupled with gratitude being morally right (1:64).

[61] The Twelver Shiʿi Ibn Shahrāshūb (d. 588/1192) makes reference to instances of gratitude that are supererogatory (*taṭawwuʿ*) but gives no examples (*Mutashābih al-Qurʾān* [Tehran 1328 AH], 1:124). He may have been thinking of a verbal expression of gratitude where such is not made obligatory by special circumstances (see n. 27 above).

[62] Al-Ḥūthī's theory of obligation bears a strong resemblance to that of Abū ʿAlī al-Jubbāʾī (*Sharḥ al-uṣūl al-khamsa*, 43). It is interesting to note that Walker, "Political Obligation and the Argument from Gratitude," 202, also favors a version of the argument from gratitude that rests on the obligation of not acting in ways incompatible with the goodwill due a benefactor.

[63] A Hanafi version of a rational morality, including the obligation of gratitude to a benefactor, was attributed to Abū Ḥanīfa. It holds that God, not reason, is the *mūjib* (Muḥammad b. ʿAbd al-Ḥamīd al-Usmandī [d. 552/1157], *Lubāb al-kalām*, ed. M. Sait Özervarlı, 30). My thanks to Professor Özervarlı for providing me with a copy of a preliminary edition of this text cited here. I have not seen the edition he published in *Alaeddin el-Üsmendi ve Lübabü'l-Kelam adlı eseri* (Istanbul 2005). On this Hanafi position on rational ethics, see Reinhart, *Before Revelation*, 52–6.

[64] Ed. Bekir Topaloğlu and Muhammad Aruçi (Ankara 2003), 156; cf. 274 (God's bestowing His benefits entails His making Himself known so as to enable His creatures appropriately to direct their gratitude).

[65] Op. cit., 278.

[66] Ed. Ömür Türkmen, Haran University Ph.D. dissertation, 100. My thanks to Professor Özervarlı for providing me with a copy of this edition. Strictly speaking, some of the grounds offered to support the necessity of prophecy do not go to the issue of obedience to the law, since they address possible functions of prophecy other than legislation. In the case of al-Sālimī's list, however, we find that one of the possible grounds for prophecy is conveying the obligation of gratitude, a ground quite incompatible with that of conveying the due measure of an existing rational obligation of gratitude.

[67] *Kitāb al-Tamhīd*, 278.

[68] Al-Kāsānī's father-in-law and teacher, ʿAlāʾ al-Dīn al-Samarqandī (d. 539/1144), it is worth noting, was a devoted exponent of al-Māturīdī's teachings. Al-Kāsānī's student Jamāl al-Dīn al-Ghaznawī (d. 593/1196–97) continues to regard the exposition of the details of gratitude as one of the two grounds for the rational necessity of prophecy (*Kitāb Uṣūl al-dīn*, ed. ʿUmar Wafīq al-Dāʿūq [Beirut 1419/1998], 120).

[69] Ed. ʿAlī Muḥammad Muʿawwaḍ and ʿĀdil Aḥmad ʿAbd al-Mawjūd (Beirut 1418/1997), 1:274. Further such explanations can be found at 1:458–59 (*ṣalāt*), 2:373 (*zakāt*), 2:550 (*ṣawm*), 3:41 (*ḥajj*).

[70] Op. cit., 2:373.

[71] Op. cit., 2:550.

[72] Op. cit., 3:41.

[73] Ibn ʿAbd al-Hādī, *Kitāb al-Intiṣār*, ed. Jalaynad (Cairo 1423/2003), 159–73. The contemporary was the Shafiʿi jurist Ibn al-Wakīl (d. 716/1317).

[74] *Kitāb al-Muʿtamad fī uṣūl al-dīn*, ed. Wadi Z. Haddad (Beirut 1974), 103.

[75] Saadia appears to express this notion when he states it is not possible for God to neglect (*lā yuhmiluhū*) to communicate to His creatures how to thank Him and (earlier) that reason requires that God provide legislation and not neglect us (*ihmālunā*) (*Kitāb al-Mukhtār*, 117). The same notion that humans would be neglected (*muhmalīn*) should God have failed to make them subject to the obligation to know and thank Him is found in al-Kaʿbī (*Tafsīr Abī l-Qāsim al-Kaʿbī al-Balkhī*, 113–4, on Q 2:35, cf. 236, on Q 10:4). Presumably Saadia also held Jewish law to be binding on gentiles, on which see n. 83 below.

[76] *Awāʾil al-maqālāt*, 4:44–5, translated in McDermott, *The Theology of al-Shaikh al-Mufīd*, 60, whose discussion of the Baghdadi position (61–2), however, fails to grasp the issue. Cf. al-Mufīd, *Taṣḥīḥ al-iʿtiqād*, in *Muṣannafāt al-Shaykh al-Mufīd*, 5:104–5 on the limitless debt of gratitude owed God.

[77] *Kitāb al-Bāligh al-mudrik*, in *Majmūʿ rasāʾil al-Imām al-Hādī*, ed. ʿAbd Allāh b. Muḥammad al-Shādhilī (Amman 1421/2001), 42 and n. 5 of the editor, whose interpretation coincides with that of the imam al-Qāsim b. Muḥammad, *al-Asās*, ed. Nader, 135, ed. al-Hāshimī, 119–20. The commentator al-Sharafī identifies the view attributed in *al-Asās* to al-Hādī as reflecting the teaching of *al-Bāligh al-mudrik* (*ʿUddat al-akyās*, 2:8). The passage is differently construed by the Caspian Zaydi imam al-Nāṭiq bi l-Ḥaqq Abū Ṭālib Yaḥyā b. al-Ḥusayn, *Sharḥ al-Bāligh al-mudrik*, ed. Muḥammad Yaḥyā Sālim ʿIzzān (Sanʿaʾ 1997/1417), 69, as meaning that reports are not sufficient to establish a claim to prophecy. Al-Hādī, it is worth pointing out, was a proponent of *al-aṣlaḥ (Kitāb al-Manzila bayn al-manzilatayn*, in *Majmūʿ rasāʾil*, 168–69).

[78] Ibn Mattawayh, *Kitāb al-Majmūʿ*, 3:425–26. There is equally no necessity for revelation where non-compliance with rational obligations is inevitable. It is significant that in explaining why some regard prophecy as necessary Ibn Mattawayh omits to mention the subject of gratitude.

[79] On how this question should properly be formulated, see Ibn Barhān, *al-Wuṣūl ilā l-uṣūl*, 1:91–2. For Ashʿaris like Ibn Barhān, the positive answer, once admitted to be rationally possible, must almost entirely be based on revealed texts, since obviously they have no general theory of legal obligation to which to appeal. Assuming a positive answer, there is the further question of how al-Ashʿarī would justify the legal obligation of unbelievers to be grateful to God if, as he held, God bestows no benefits at all on unbelievers, only apparent benefits that will in the end prove to be their ruin. The question is all the more acute in that al-Ashʿarī, like the Basran Muʿtazilis, tied the obligation of gratitude to freely bestowed benefits (Ibn Fūrak, *Mujarrad*, 35–6). According to Ibn Fūrak's explanation, the gratitude the unbelievers owe to God is for the benefits bestowed on the believers (ibid., 34). Al-Bāqillānī, however, held the position that the unbelievers are benefited by God (ʿAlī al-Qārī, *Sharḥ al-Fiqh al-akbar* [Cairo 1375/1955], 126–7, the dispute is verbal). Aḥmad b. Sulaymān, noting the parallel with Ashʿari doctrine, argues that the heretical Mutarrifi sect does not recognize God's favors to unbelievers or even to believers and so can provide no ground for an obligation of gratitude or *ʿibāda*: *al-Hāshima li-anf al-dullāl min madhāhib al-muṭarrifiyya al-juhhāl*, in *al-Ṣirāʿ al-fikrī fī l-yaman bayna al-zaydiyya wa l-muṭarrifiyya*, ed. ʿAbd al-Ghanī Maḥmūd ʿAbd al-ʿĀṭī (al-Ḥaram 2002), 111.

[80] See, for example, Ibn al-ʿAynī, on the margin of Ibn al-Malak, *Sharḥ al-Manār* (Istanbul 1308), 65–6.

[81] Abū l-Ḥusayn al-Baṣrī, *Kitāb al-Muʿtamad fī uṣūl al-fiqh*, ed. Muḥammad Ḥamīd Allāh et al. (Damascus 1384/1964), 1:294.

[82] Ibid., 1:295–96.

[83] See the helpful summary in Sklare, *Samuel ben Ḥofni*, 153–54. He has treated this subject further in "Yūsuf al-Baṣīr: Theological Aspects of His Halakhic Works," in Daniel Frank (ed.), *The Jews of Medieval Islam: Community, Society, and Identity* (Leiden 1995), 264–69, and most fully in "Are the Gentiles Obligated to Observe the Torah? The Discussion Concerning the Universality of the Torah in the East in the Tenth and Eleventh Centuries," in Jay M. Harris (ed.), *Be'erot Yitzhak: Studies in Memory of Isadore Twersky* (Cambridge, Mass. 2005), 311–46, especially 324–26 on the role of *lutf* in the debate. The position of Saadia is discussed on p. 320. The dispute is also addressed by Haggai Ben-Shammai, "Some Genizah Fragments on the Duty of the Nations to Keep the Mosaic Law," in Joshua Blau and Stefan C. Reif (eds.), *Genizah Research*, 22–30. Both Sklare ("Yūsuf al-Baṣīr," 268–9; "Are the Gentiles," 336) and Ben-Shammai, 28–9, misconstrue the position of ʿAbd al-Jabbār. According to ʿAbd al-Jabbār, unbelievers are obligated by the provisions of Islamic law (Ibn al-Murtaḍā, *Minhāj al-wuṣūl ilā Miʿyar al-ʿuqūl fī ʿilm al-uṣūl*, ed. Aḥmad ʿAlī Muṭahhar al-Mākhadhī [Sanʿa' 1412/1992], 257), as one would expect of a Basran Muʿtazili (see n. 81 above). In the passages from *al-Mughnī*, vol. 16, cited by Sklare and Ben-Shammai, ʿAbd al-Jabbār argues that a condition of the unbelievers being obligated is that they be in a position to know of the revelation to Muḥammad, not that they accept this revelation. He rejects the notion that they might mingle with Muslims and yet not come to know of Islam, that is, of Muḥammad's claims to be a prophet.

[84] This is the problem that Abū l-Ḥusayn al-Baṣrī specifically addresses in *Kitāb al-Muʿtamad*, 1:297–98, and he admits the force of the counterargument on 1:298, ll. 7–9.

[85] A representative list of Muʿtazili and Zaydi infallibilists can be found in Ibn Muẓaffar, *Kitab al-Bayān al-Shāfī al-muntazaʿ min al-Burhān al-kāfī* (Sanʿa' 1984), 1:18.

[86] Ibid.

[87] *Kitāb al-Asās*, ed. Nader, 152–56, ed. al-Hāshimī, 141–45.

[88] Some material on these jurists is provided by Reinhart, *Before Revelation*, 15–21, 121–23. Among later Shafiʿis who held that there is a rational obligation of gratitude is al-Rāghib al-Isfahānī, *Kitāb al-Dharīʿa ilā makārim al-sharīʿa*, ed. Abū l-Yazīd al-ʿAjamī (Cairo 1405/1985), 279. His classification of gratitude as of the heart, tongue, and limbs was widely cited by later authors (*Mufradāt alfāẓ al-Qur'ān*, ed. Ṣafwān ʿAdnān Dāwūdī [Damascus 1412/1998], 461).

[89] My thanks to Ahmed El-Shamsy for lending me his microfilm of the Istanbul copy of this work (Ahmed III 1317).

[90] Quoted in Fakhr al-Dīn al-Rāzī, *al-Tafsīr al-kabīr* (Tehran 1371–80/1992–2001), 2:66 on Qur'an 2:11.

[91] See Reinhart, *Before Revelation*, 20–1.

[92] Ibn Mattawayh, *Kitāb al-Majmūʿ*, 3:434. Of course, the social circumstances created by the law might have a role to play at the psychological level, but the individualism of the *lutf* theory, as opposed to the popular utilitarian version of the gratitude theory, is quite marked.

LIST OF CONTRIBUTORS

William Alford is Henry L. Stimson Professor of Law, Vice Dean for the Graduate Program and International Legal Studies, and Director of the East Asian Legal Studies Program at Harvard Law School. He has published *To Steal a Book is an Elegant Offense: Intellectual Property Law in Chinese Civilization* (Stanford University Press 1995), *Raising the Bar: The Emerging Legal Profession in East Asia* (Cambridge, Mass. 2006), and scores of articles. His teaching principally concerns Chinese law and legal history, and international trade. He was a principal founder (in the early 1980s) and executive director of the first academic program in American law established in the People's Republic of China and has been named an Honorary Professor of Renmin University, Zhejiang University, and the Chinese National School of Administration.

Abdullahi Ahmed An-Naʿim, Ph.D., is Charles Howard Candler Professor of Law, Emory University School of Law, formerly of the Faculty of Law, University of Khartoum, Sudan. He is the author of *Toward an Islamic Reformation: Civil Liberties, Human Rights and International Law* (Syracuse University Press, 1990); and *African Constitutionalism and the Role of Islam* (University of Pennsylvania Press, 2006). His research interests include human rights, comparative constitutionalism, and secularism from an Islamic perspective.

Peri Bearman is Associate Director of the Islamic Legal Studies Program at Harvard Law School. She founded the journal *Islamic Law and Society* and is an editor and member of the Executive Committee of the *Encyclopaedia of Islam*, New Edition, and co-editor, with Rudolph Peters and Frank E. Vogel, of *The Islamic School of Law: Evolution, Devolution, and Progress* (Cambridge, Mass. 2005). An article by her hand on Islamic law is forthcoming in Oxford's *Encyclopedia of the Modern World* (Oxford University Press, Spring 2008).

Mark E. Cammack is Professor of Law at Southwestern Law School. His articles and chapters on Islamic law in Indonesia and the Indonesian legal system have appeared in, among other places, *The International and Comparative Law Quarterly*, *The American Journal of Comparative Law*, and *Indonesia*. He is co-editor with Michael Feener of *Islamic Law in Contemporary Indonesia: Ideas and Institutions* (Cambridge, Mass. 2007).

Charles Donahue is Paul A. Freund Professor of Law at Harvard Law School. He teaches Roman law, English legal history, and Continental legal history, and undertakes research now almost exclusively in these fields, with particular emphasis on the legal history of the later Middle Ages and early modern periods. He was the general editor of and contributor to the two-volume series *The Reports of the Church Courts Records Working Group*, a survey of the surviving records of the medieval church courts in England and on the Continent, and also served as editor of three volumes of medieval English Year Book reports and of a volume entitled *Lex mercatoria: A Thirteenth Century Treatise and Its Afterlife*.

R. Michael Feener is Associate Professor of History at the National University of Singapore, and the Asia Research Institute. He has written on issues related to jurisprudence, Orientalism, mysticism, hagiography, diaspora studies, and Qur'anic interpretation. His publications include a monograph entitled *Muslim Legal Thought in Modern Indonesia* (Cambridge University Press, 2007) and an edited volume with Mark Cammack entitled *Islamic Law in Contemporary Indonesia: Ideas and Institutions* (Cambridge, Mass. 2007).

Bernard K. Freamon, currently the Slavery, Resistance, and Abolition Postdoctoral Fellow in the Gilder Lehrman Center for the Study of Slavery, Resistance, and Abolition at Yale University, is Professor of Law and Director of the Program for the Study of Law in the Middle East at Seton Hall Law School. The Program that he directs is based in Cairo, Egypt and is the only American Bar Association-approved study abroad program in the Arabic-speaking world. He has published several articles on Islamic jurisprudence, including "Slavery, Freedom and the Doctrine of Consensus in Islamic Jurisprudence," *Harvard Human Rights Journal* 11 (1998) and "Martyrdom, Suicide, and the Islamic Law of War: A Short Legal History," *Fordham International Law Journal* 27 (2003).

Robert Gleave is Professor of Arabic Studies at the University of Exeter, U.K. He is author of *Inevitable Doubt: Two Shiʿi Theories of Jurisprudence* (Leiden 2000) and *Scripturalist Islam: The History and Doctrines of the Akhbari School of Imami Shiʿism* (Leiden 2007).

Louise Halper is Professor of Law and Law Alumni Fellow in Teaching Excellence at Washington and Lee University School of Law. Her area of scholarship is gender law in the Middle East, with a particular focus on Turkey and Iran. She has been a Fulbright Scholar in Turkey and visited Iran recently. Her two most recent papers are "Law and Women's Agency in Post-Revolutionary Iran," *Harvard Journal of Law and Gender* 28 (2005) and "Law, Authority and Gender in Post-Revolutionary Iran," *Buffalo Law Review* 54 (2006).

Wolfhart Heinrichs is the James Richard Jewett Professor of Arabic at Harvard University (since 1996). He joined Harvard's Department of Near Eastern Languages and Civilizations in 1978 as Professor of Arabic. Between 1967 and 1978 he held various teaching positions in Islamic Studies and Semitic Languages at the University of Giessen, Germany. He received his doctorate in 1967 with a thesis in the field of Classical Arabic literary theory. His research interests are Classical Arabic literary theory, Islamic legal theory (in which field he published "*Qawāʿid* as a Genre of Legal Literature," in Bernard Weiss [ed.], *Studies in Islamic Legal Theory*, Leiden 2002), and—as a sideline—Neo-Aramaic. He is co-editor of the *Encyclopaedia of Islam*, New Edition.

Nimrod Hurvitz is the chairperson of the Department of Middle East Studies at Ben Gurion University. His publications include *The Formation of Hanbalism. Piety into Power* (RoutledgeCurzon) and "From Scholarly Circles to Mass Movements: The Formation of Legal Communities in Islamic Societies," *The American Historical Review* 108/4 (2003).

Baber Johansen is Professor of Islamic Studies at Harvard Divinity School, and Affiliated Professor and Acting Director of the Islamic Legal Studies Program at Harvard Law School. His research and teaching focus on the relationship between religion and law in the classical and the modern Muslim world. He is the author of a.o. *Islamic Law on Land Tax and Rent* (London 1988) and *Contingency in a Sacred Law: Legal and Ethical Norms in the Muslim Fiqh* (Leiden 1999). He is an executive editor of the journal *Islamic Law and Society*.

Jeremy Kingsley is a Ph.D. candidate in the Faculty of Law, a Research Fellow in the Centre for the Study of Contemporary Islam, and Principal Research Assistant in the Asian Law Centre, all at the University of Melbourne. His research is supported by an Endeavour Australia Cheung Kong Award and an ARC Federation Fellowship doctoral scholarship. He recently published "Legal Transplantation: Is This What the Doctor Ordered and Are the Blood Types Compatible?" in the *Arizona Journal of International and Comparative Law*.

Martin Lau is a Barrister and a Reader in Law at the Law Department of the School of Oriental and African Studies, University of London, where he teaches courses on South Asian law, constitutional law, and comparative environmental law. His research interests include Islam and constitutionalism, most recently explored in the context of Pakistan and Afghanistan, access to environmental justice for rural communities in South Asia, and the Islamisation of Pakistan's criminal laws. He is the author of *The Role of Islam in the Legal System of Pakistan* (Leiden 2006) and edits, with Eugene Cotran, the *Yearbook of Islamic and Middle Eastern Law*.

Aharon Layish, Ph.D. (1973), Emeritus Professor (2002), Hebrew University of Jerusalem, has published extensively on Islamic, customary, and Druze law and institutions, including *The Reinstatement of Islamic Law in Sudan under Numayri* (Leiden 2002, with G. R. Warburg) and *Shariʿa and Custom in Libyan Tribal Society* (Leiden 2005). He is an executive editor of the journal *Islamic Law and Society*.

Tim Lindsey is Professor of Asian Law and Director of the Asian Law Centre in the Faculty of Law at the University of Melbourne. He is Foundation Deputy Director of the Centre for the Study of Contemporary Islam and ARC Federation Fellow. Tim is also a founding editor of the *Australian Journal of Asian Law* and his publications include "Indonesia: Law and Society" and "Law Reform in Developing and Transitional Countries."

John Makdisi, S.J.D. Harvard Law School, is Professor of Law at St. Thomas University School of Law in Miami, Florida, where he served as Dean from 1999–2003. He has written extensively on American and Islamic property law. His most recent books include *Florida Property Law: I. Possession, Estates, and Tenancy* (Carolina Academic Press, 2006); *Florida Property Law: II. Conveyancing and Governmental Controls* (Carolina Academic Press, 2007); and *Islamic Property Law: Cases and Materials for Comparative Analysis with the Common Law* (Carolina Academic Press, 2005). His article "The Islamic Origins of the Common Law," *N. Car. L. Rev.* 77 (1999), offers a startling new theory for connections between Islam and the West.

Chibli Mallat is Professor of Law and Politics at the S.J. Quinney College of Law, University of Utah, and EU Jean Monnet Chair in European Law at Université Saint-Joseph, Beirut. He has held teaching and research positions at several institutions, including Yale Law School, Princeton University, the University of Lyon, and Virginia Law School, and is the author of numerous publications, most recently *An Introduction to Middle Eastern Law* (Oxford University Press, 2007). He received a Ph.D. in Islamic law (1990) from the School of Oriental and Asian Studies, London, and an LL.B. and LL.M. from Université Saint-Joseph and Georgetown University Law Center, respectively. He is the principal counsel at Mallat Law Offices in Beirut, and campaigned for the presidency of Lebanon between 2005 and 2007.

Muhammad Khalid Masud, Ph.D. (1973) Islamic Studies, McGill University, is presently Chairman, Council of Islamic Ideology, Islamabad. His recent edited publications include *Islamic Laws and Women in the Modern World* (Islamabad 1996), *Islamic Legal Interpretation. Muftis and Their Fatwas* (with B. Messick and D. S. Powers; Harvard University Press, 1996), *Travelers in Faith. Studies on Tablighi Jama'at* (Leiden 2000), and *Dispensing Justice in Islam. Qadis and Their Judgments* (with R. Peters and D. S. Powers; Leiden 2006).

Brinkley Messick, Professor and Chair of Anthropology at Columbia University, is the author of *The Calligraphic State. Textual Domination and History in a Muslim Society* (University of California Press, 1993) and a co-editor of *Islamic Legal Interpretation. Muftis and Their Fatwas* (Harvard University Press, 1996). His current research concerns the doctrine and application of Islamic law in mid-twentieth century highland Yemen.

Rudolph Peters teaches Arabic and Islamic Studies at the University of Amsterdam. His main interest is Islamic law. His recent publications include *Jihad in Classical and Modern Islam* (2nd updated ed., Markus Wiener, 2005) and *Crime and Punishment in Islamic Law. Theory and Practice from the 16th to the 21st Century* (Cambridge University Press, 2005).

Amira Sonbol specializes in the history of modern Egypt, Islamic history and law, women, gender and Islam and is the author of several books including *The New Mamluks: Egyptian Society and Modern Feudalism*; *Women, the Family and Divorce Laws in Islamic History*; *The Creation of a Medical Profession in Egypt: 1800–1922; The Memoirs of Abbas Hilmi II: Sovereign of Egypt; Women of the Jordan: Islam, Labor and Law; Beyond the Exotic: Muslim Women's Histories.* Professor Sonbol is Editor-in-Chief of *HAWWA: The Journal of Women of the Middle East and the Islamic World* and co-editor of *Islam and Christian-Muslim Relations*, a quarterly journal co-published with Selly Oak Colleges (UK). She teaches at Georgetown University on the History of Modern Egypt, Women and Law, and Islamic Civilization.

Kristen Stilt, Associate Professor, Northwestern University School of Law, is the author of "Recognizing the Individual: The *Muḥtasib*s of Early Mamluk Cairo and Fustat," *Harvard Middle East and Islamic Review* 7 (2006) and "Islamic Law and the Making and Remaking of the Iraqi Legal System," *Geo. Wash. Int'l L. Rev.* 36 (2004). She is currently preparing a book manuscript, *Constitutional Structure and Legal Practice in Medieval Cairo*, based on her Ph.D. dissertation.

Bernard Weiss is Professor of Arabic and Islamic Studies at the University of Utah. He has also taught at the American University in Cairo, McGill University, and the University of Toronto. He is the author of *The Search for God's Law: Islamic Jurisprudence in the Writings of Sayf al-Din al Amidi; The Spirit of Islamic Law*; and numerous articles on a variety of topics related to Islamic law. He was for thirteen years co-editor with Rudolph Peters of the multivolume monograph series "Studies in Islamic Law and Society."

Aron Zysow, currently Visiting Associate Professor in the Department of Near Eastern Studies, Princeton University, was for some years associated in various capacities with the Islamic Legal Studies Program, Harvard Law School. Previously he taught Arabic and Islamic Studies at the University of Washington, Seattle, WA, and Washington University in St. Louis. He holds degrees from Harvard College (A.B.), Harvard University (Ph.D.) and Harvard Law School (J.D.). His research focuses on Islamic law, particularly Islamic legal theory, and Islamic theology.

INDEX